ANDREW JACKSON

VOLUME ONE

THE COURSE OF AMERICAN EMPIRE, 1767–1821

ANDREW JACKSON

VOLUME ONE

THE COURSE OF AMERICAN EMPIRE, 1767–1821

Robert V. Remini

THE JOHNS HOPKINS UNIVERSITY PRESS
Baltimore and London

Originally published in 1977 as *Andrew Jackson and the Course of American Empire,
1767–1821,* by Harper & Row, Publishers, Inc.
Johns Hopkins Paperbacks edition, 1998
9 8 7 6 5 4 3 2

The Johns Hopkins University Press
2715 North Charles Street
Baltimore, Maryland 21218-4363
www.press.jhu.edu

Library of Congress Catalog Card Number 97-75802

A catalog record for this book is available from the British Library.

ISBN 0-8018-5911-5 (pbk.)

For Harriet C. Owsley and Sam B. Smith,
True Jacksonians in their friendship and loyalty

Brought up under the tyrany of Britain—altho young embarked in the struggle for our liberties, in which I lost every thing that was dear to me . . . — for which I have been amply repaid by living under the mild administration of a republican government. To maintain this, and the independent rights of our nation is a duty I have ever owed to my country to myself and to posterity, and when I do all I can to it support, I have only done my duty.

—Andrew Jackson to Willie Blount,
January 4, 1813

Contents

A section of photographs follows page 200

Maps

Preface, 1998

It has been fifteen years since I completed my three-volume biography of Andrew Jackson, and it strikes me as interesting that it took approximately the same amount of time to write the three volumes. I began researching the Jacksonian era in 1947, when I undertook a study of Martin Van Buren's early career for my doctorate at Columbia University; however, I did not turn my attention solely to Jackson's life until 1970.

Upon deciding to write the biography, I first approached Hugh Van Dusen, an editor at Harper & Row, now HarperCollins, and asked if he would consider such a work for publication. I had edited two books on the Jacksonian age for his company. Furthermore, we were old friends, having spent much time together at history conventions discussing opera and books and enjoying good food at fine restaurants. We were both devotees of Wagner and Mozart, a strange combination perhaps, and I frequently related to him (bragged is more like it) the many performances of Wagner I had seen as a youth at the Metropolitan Opera in New York City, sung by those two incomparable artists Kirsten Flagstad and Lauritz Melchior. Van Dusen liked my idea about a biography, and on January 28 (my eldest child's birthday and a good omen, I thought), 1970, we signed a contract for a one-volume Life.

And that's how it all began. Several years earlier, during a period in which I was working on several other books (*Martin Van Buren and the Making of the Democratic Party; The Election of Andrew Jackson; Andrew Jackson and Bank War;* and a brief two-hundred-page biography entitled *Andrew Jackson*—all happily still in print), I had acquired microfilm copies of the

22,500 items of the Jackson manuscript collection housed in the Library of Congress, thanks to the funds provided by the research board of the University of Illinois at Chicago, where I had been teaching. From the same depository I had also obtained microfilms of the Van Buren, Calhoun, Clay, and Webster papers. In the early 1960s I had also researched the Tennessee State Library and Archives in Nashville, ten miles or so from Jackson's home at the Hermitage, maintained by the Ladies Hermitage Association (LHA).

At the Tennessee State Library I met Mrs. Harriet C. Owsley, widow of Frank L. Owsley, a distinguished southern historian. She was the head of the manuscript division of the library and a very knowledgeable and well-trained (by her husband) historian, and we hit it off very well. She remembers that when I asked to see the Jackson papers in the library she said, "Which ones?" "All of them," I responded, not realizing they numbered 1,500. In time we became close friends, and whenever I visited Nashville she insisted that I stay at her large and comfortable house. Naturally we talked about Jackson a great deal and about how wonderful it would be if a project for the publication of Jackson's important papers could be initiated, such as those begun at various educational institutions with the papers of George Washington, Thomas Jefferson, Alexander Hamilton, and several other prominent American figures. Vanderbilt University would have been an obvious choice for Jackson. But Vanderbilt had already determined to begin collecting and publishing the correspondence of James K. Polk. So Harriet decided to ask the Ladies Hermitage Association if they might be interested, and she invited me to help. I was more than happy to do so.

Weeks passed, and then one day Harriet called to ask if I could come to Nashville and meet at her home with the regent of the LHA and several members of the board of directors and explain to them why a Jackson project would be in the interest of the association and in accordance with their mission as defined by the Tennessee legislature. It turned out to be quite a meeting; I should really say it was historic. The regent, Mrs. Kay Russell (the wife of the well-known sportswriter Fred Russell), pretty much directed the discussion.

Seated in Harriet's living room among these ladies I described the different projects that already existed, how they had originated, and what they involved in terms of equipment and personnel. I was quizzed at length, especially about the probable cost. I really had no idea how much would be involved but said I would investigate. I know it was a very difficult question for these women. They were charged with maintaining the Jackson properties, particularly his mansion, the Hermitage. But did that include sponsoring such a project as I proposed? I tried to reassure them by arguing how much Jackson's reputation and importance could be advanced with the publication of his papers, but questions remained, and I have often wondered whether the regent and her board consulted the Tennessee attorney general.

Thanks principally to Kay Russell and one or two very persuasive women on the board, the LHA in 1971 agreed to sponsor the Jackson Papers Project.* I was asked to participate in establishing the project as a salaried member. To get things started, the LHA built an extension to their administration building to house the staff of the project, and provided bookshelves, furniture, microfilm readers, typewriters, and the salaries for three researchers. Harriet Owsley retired from the Tennessee State Library and Archives to become the editor of the project, and I turned over my Jackson microfilms to the project from which the initial Jackson documentary library was begun. Furthermore, I agreed to help locate additional material, and over the years I traveled in search of Jackson documents to virtually every major repository in the country. I had whatever I found copied and sent to the Hermitage.

By 1972 it had been decided to involve the University of Tennessee at Nashville (now the Tennessee State University) in the project, and although Harriet remained as an editor, Dr. Sam B. Smith, former librarian of the Tennessee State Library and Archives, was appointed director of the project and coeditor. The operation remained at the Hermitage for a number of years. Later it was moved to the University of Tennessee at Knoxville, where it is presently located under the direction of Dr. Harold D. Moser. The LHA, of course, continued and is continuing their financial support. My contract with the university called for me to "perform such advisory and collection services, including but not limited to the search for certain documents, authentication of same, and similar work related to the Andrew Jackson Papers Project."

The process of collecting all these documents certainly enhanced my research into Jackson's life, and I was fortunate to be able to both write my biography and pursue the search for written material. But there was one piece of evidence we particularly sought and could not seem to find, namely, any evidence that Jackson and Rachel had in fact married in Natchez as claimed by the Nashville Central Committee during the 1828 presidential election. Actually, Rachel was still married to her first husband, Lewis Robards, although she thought a divorce had been granted. Laboring under that misunderstanding, Jackson and Rachel married sometime

*Two decades later, when the LHA decided to restore the Hermitage to its original condition when Jackson returned from Washington after his presidency, they were able to match exactly wallpaper, paint, and other decorations, thanks to the project, which provided invoices, receipts, and other documentary evidence of the original purchases.

in "the winter or spring of 1791," according to the Central Committee. But not until September 27, 1793, was the divorce finally granted by a Kentucky court. When the couple, who had been living together for two years, learned the awful truth, they were "remarried" on January 17, 1794, by Justice of the Peace Robert Hays, Rachel's brother-in-law. Nevertheless, substantial evidence of the original marriage was lacking, and we searched without success in Washington, Atlanta, New Orleans, Natchez, and all the other leading depositories in the country. I did discover the marriage certificate of the second marriage in the Houghton Library at Harvard University, but nothing more.

It then occurred to me that since Natchez (where the first marriage had allegedly been performed) was under Spanish rule in 1791, documentation might be found in Spain, in particular in the Archivo General de Indias in Seville, where most of the documentation for New Spain could be found. So I went to the LHA and asked them to support a search of the archive for that purpose. Again, the regent and her board readily and willingly consented.

In preparing for this trip I contacted friends in the profession who had researched the libraries in Spain, and as I recall it was John D. L. Holmes, a specialist in Spanish-American history, who suggested that I contact a graduate student by the name of G. Douglas Inglis, who was working at the time in the Seville archive doing a demographic study of colonial Cuba. That information proved a most fortunate breakthrough in terms of my research. I contacted Inglis immediately upon my arrival in Seville, and it helped that we were both staying at the same Escuelo, an excellent dormitory for graduate students and research professors.

Inglis guided me into what I regard as the seemingly bottomless pit that is the Archivo General de Indias. There were literally thousands of bundles (*legajos*) of documents in the depository, many of which had never been opened, and all uncataloged. The Papeles Procedentes de Cuba, for example, is made up of 2,375 legajos, each of which contains anywhere from a few to 2,000 documents. Inglis suggested that I start with the Cuba bundles, and with great determination and enthusiasm I began my search. Talk about hunting for a needle in a haystack! Within days it seemed to me to be a hopeless task. Inglis gave me a few Cuba legajos numbers to try, but I seemed to get nowhere.

On July 4, Independence Day, the Americans working in the Archivo decided to take the day off to celebrate, and we presented ourselves at the home of the American consul in Seville, expecting to find an outdoor party of some sort. Unfortunately, we were told by the housekeeper that the entire staff of the consulate had gone to Malaga for the celebration and that nothing had been planned in Seville. Dejected, we decided to return to the Archivo, since there was nothing else going on during that hot summer day. Then I remembered that a neighbor where I live in Wilmette, Illinois, Mrs. Betty Nesbitt, who always had a backyard party for the entire block on July 4, had given me a small American flag to remember them by, since I could not be with them that year. So I went back to the Escuelo, fetched the flag, returned to the Archivo, and propped the flag up on my desk. Seeing the flag, one of the porters who brought us the legajos from the stacks seized it and starting marching up and down the room, waving it and singing something in Spanish. Soon the other members of the staff joined the parade. The researchers stopped their work and laughingly marched around the large room with the others. I was mortified. When the "celebration" finally ended, one of the American researchers came up to me and said, "Andrew Jackson would have been proud."

After that bit of levity I went back to work, ordering another Cuba bundle. As I now recall it was something like legajos number 1754. But what the porter brought was Cuba 1745. I pointed out the mistake to him but he shrugged and said, "It will take another half an hour to get the correct bundle. Why don't you read this?" What could I do? He obviously wasn't going to get me what I asked for, so I reluctantly untied the string holding this huge package.

As I turned back the cardboard cover, the handwriting jumped out at me. It was Jackson's. No doubt about it. I could scarcely believe it. Not only was the first document written by Jackson but the next twenty documents were written by him also. I was ecstatic. I could hardly believe my good fortune. What made it so exciting was that here was a sizeable collection of letters written to and from Jackson and the Spanish governor in Florida at the time of Jackson's seizure of Florida in 1818, and they included correspondence from one Spanish official to another about the American invasion of their colony. I was fascinated as I learned the history of my country as seen through the eyes of aliens, and enemy aliens at that. And to my surprise and horror, I found that they did not think Americans were heroic, generous, kind, trustworthy, or any of those noble characteristics Americans believed about themselves in the 1970s. Quite the opposite. They saw them as thieving, murderous cut-throats, out to steal their empire. I remember muttering to myself, as if responding to the accusations, "You've got it all wrong; we're the good guys."

The Spanish had a name for Jackson, "the Napoleon of the woods," a man they predicted would drive them from the continent if given half a chance. Suddenly my understanding of the Spanish attitude and their concern for their colonies completely changed the overall interpretation of my book. I came to realize that Jackson was intent on acquiring, as he said in a letter dated 1806, "all Spanish North America." It meant that his early

fighting career did not consist merely of a series of military engagements
with the British, Spanish, and Native Americans but involved a larger quest
for Spanish territory. In an instant I had a thesis for this period of his life:
more than any other man of the nineteenth century, he determined the
course of American expansion.

It then struck me that I could never encompass his military exploits
together with his two terms as president of the United States in a single
volume. I needed at least two. But I had contracted for a single volume, and
I was not at all certain that Hugh would agree to a change. For months after
my return home I debated with myself about asking him to allow an
additional volume. I finally decided to wait until I saw him again at a history
convention to spring it on him. Then one day he phoned and said he was
coming to Chicago on business and wondered if I might be free for dinner.
It so happened that the Lyric Opera of Chicago was performing Mozart's
Marriage of Figaro on the day of his arrival. So we agreed to have dinner and
then go to the opera. Meanwhile, I made reservations at one of the best
French restaurants in Chicago (now gone), and I bought the best seats
available at the opera house.

The night Hugh arrived we went to the restaurant and had a splendid
meal. After cocktails and a glass or two of wine, I sprang my idea on him.
Throughout the course of the evening I kept badgering him about how I
had come across all this great new evidence in Spain and how I needed two
volumes to do justice to Jackson's life. But however hard I argued, it got me
nowhere. He was adamant about holding me to our original agreement.
He insisted that two volumes could not make the biography financially
profitable. Finally and regretfully, I gave up. We caught a taxi and arrived at
the opera house just in time for the start of the overture. And then it
happened. Good old Mozart somehow worked his magic once again. In the
middle of the second act, Hugh turned to me and said, "You can do two
volumes."

So the biography ballooned. The first volume, which took Jackson to
1821, was published in 1977. I never did find any evidence for the first
marriage and had to offer what I thought was a reasonable explanation of
what had taken place. Then I received quite a jolt. A story was published on
the front page of the *Nashville Tennessean* concerning what volume one said
about the marriage, and I received several phone calls from friends
throughout the state and at the University of Tennessee who told me that it
had created quite an uproar. I confess that I panicked. I was terribly afraid
that the members of the LHA would think I had repaid their generosity
and kindness with betrayal. But quite the reverse. That book's publication
became a defining moment for the LHA; at least I think so. What it did was
separate those who felt that the truth about Andrew Jackson was something

the association could and should face openly and honestly from those that did not. They understood what historical scholarship was all about and gave it their full support. Those in the LHA who wanted to hear nothing except what would glorify Jackson's name and reputation now seemed to recede from an active role in the organization. Educated women with a deep interest in the history of their country and the important role Jackson played in its development took over the leadership and have been heading the association ever since.

Shortly thereafter I began to work on volume two, and within a short time it became obvious to me that I could never properly encompass Jackson's senatorial career in the 1820s, his election to the presidency, his two terms as president, and the closing nine years of his life in a single book. After another great meal at a wonderful restaurant in Chicago and a performance of Wagner's *Tristan und Isolde* at the Lyric, Hugh agreed to three volumes, although I rather think the History Book of the Month Club's taking volume one as its main selection and its indication that it would take succeeding volumes had much to do with his decision. Moreover I was pleased when volume two later received the George Washington Medal of Honor from the Freedom Foundation.

I frankly must admit that I did think about a fourth volume—my "Ring" cycle, I laughingly suggested to Hugh, but that approach got me nowhere. So, I stopped at three, but it will be readily seen that the concluding volume is almost twice as long as volumes one and two.

When volume three won the National Book Award for 1984 I felt that the many years of research and fifteen years of writing had paid off handsomely. Standing in the main vestibule of the New York Public Library on 42nd Street while the names of the nominees for the award were read before the name of the winner was announced, I could barely understand what was being said, so awful were the acoustics in that cavernous space. The winner's name was finally pronounced, but I couldn't make out who it was. Then I saw my wife weeping, and I knew it was me.

Since the publication of my biography, one important piece of new information about Jackson has come to light; it needs to be included in this work, if only in this preface. Doug Inglis, who loved Spain and married one of the archivists at the Archivo, settled down in Seville and obtained a position at Siemens Nixdorf Company. But his interest in the history of New Spain never flagged, and he began a project on his own time which consisted of identifying the extant documentation relative to both the British and Spanish occupations of Natchez and entering the data into what he called the Colonial Natchez Database Project. One large part of this database consisted of documents of oaths of allegiance to the King of Spain taken by anyone who entered Spanish territory.

To conduct business and own property in the so-called Spanish borderlands, every male immigrant was obliged to take this oath of loyalty. Shortly after his arrival in Tennessee, that is, early in 1789, Jackson began traveling from Nashville to Natchez to offer his services to the inhabitants of Natchez, both as a lawyer and a trader. He purchased property and also practiced law in the town. Fully aware of his obligation to swear an oath of allegiance, he did not hesitate to do so. On July 15, 1789, at the age of twenty-two and in the presence of Governor Manuel Gayoso de Lemos and Josef Vidal, the governor's secretary, Jackson placed his hand on the "Holy Bible," swore by "God our Lord," and pledged his "word of honor . . . not [to] offend directly nor indirectly nor conspire against the Spanish nation[;] to the contrary [he promised to] defend it and help it with all [his] might, will, and power, especially obliging [him] to take up Arms against any Enemy that attempt to attack this Province; obligating [himself] to inform the Government of any conspiracy[,] declaring the Individuals that comprise the leaders, subjecting [himself] to all and for all the Spanish Laws, maintaining faithful and inviolably the orders, proclamations, edicts of the Kingdom and of this Government, obeying in all the same exactness and loyalty as the rest of the Vassals of H[is] C[atholic] M[ajesty] in whose class and standing from now [he is] included."*

While preparing the oaths of allegiance for entry into the Colonial Natchez Database, Inglis discovered this pledge. The document was signed by Jackson and seventeen others, and there can be no mistaking the signature.

Inglis immediately contacted me and sent photostats and transparencies of the three-page document. After examining it, I agreed with him totally that Jackson had indeed signed it. I confess I was shocked when I studied the document. I couldn't believe that Jackson had signed it, that he would do such a thing. It seemed so totally alien to his character. He had later said he "hated the Dons" and would "die in the last Ditch" before yielding a foot of American soil to the Spanish king. Here was an American citizen and future president of the United States swearing loyalty to a foreign power. No other president ever took such an oath. And Andrew Jackson, of all unlikely people!

I urged Inglis to prepare an article as soon as possible and describe his find and its significance. But he refused. He asked me to write it instead. So I wrote it up and the resulting article, which was published in the *Tennessee*

---

*Juramento de Fidelidad [Oath of Allegiance], Natchez, July 15, 1789, before Manuel Gayoso de Lemos and Josef Vidal, Archivo General de Indias, Papeles Procedentes de Cuba 2361, Seville, Spain.

Historical Quarterly,* won the John Trotwood and Mary Daniel Moore Memorial Award for best article to appear in the journal for 1995.

After I calmed down I realized that taking the oath was the only thing Jackson could have done. If he wanted to conduct business in Natchez, he had to take the oath. He probably took it without giving it a second thought, just as a great number of Americans had done before and after him. He did what necessity dictated. And Andrew Jackson was a very pragmatic man all his life.

In the years to come other facts about this very complex, sometimes exasperating, but always fascinating man will undoubtedly emerge. His biography will be written many more times. Each generation seems to feel a need to get a fix on him. But he can be very elusive and cunning and contradictory.

Had I known in the beginning that it would take me approximately fifteen years to complete the writing of this biography, I don't believe I would have undertaken it. I am now very happy I did not know. Andrew Jackson has been very good to me. He's taken me around the world to give lectures on his presidency and on Jacksonian Democracy. He made it possible for me to speak on his life and works in the East Room of the White House before President and Mrs. George Bush and a distinguished audience. And recently, the Ladies Hermitage Association asked me to join their National Advisory Committee to assist the organization in carrying out its mission to preserve Jackson's house and property and educate present and future generations about his legacy. Andrew Jackson has truly enriched my life, and I am profoundly grateful.

*For complete details of this incident, see Robert V. Remini, "Andrew Jackson Takes an Oath of Allegiance to Spain," in *Tennessee Historical Quarterly* 54, no. 1 (spring, 1995), 2–15.

Preface

Nearly fifty years have transpired since the publication of the last major scholarly life of Andrew Jackson. Marquis James's two-volume, Pulitzer-prize-winning biography, *Andrew Jackson, The Border Captain* (1933) and *Portrait of a President* (1937), successfully captured all the color and excitement of one of the most dynamic and important figures in American history. Each page of this biography shimmers with narrative power. Unfortunately, despite impressive research, a one-dimensional Jackson emerged from the book: a man heroic, larger than life, intensely nationalistic. Little of the complexity, the deep ambiguities, and the dark unease within Old Hickory surfaced in the book. Nor is the work particularly instructive about the era in which Jackson lived, his influence in shaping that era, or the meaning of what historians have come to call Jacksonian Democracy.

That interpretative "revolution" came a decade later in 1946 with the publication of another Pulitzer-prize-winning study, *The Age of Jackson*, by Arthur M. Schlesinger, Jr. This book, which is not a biography but a magisterial sweep across the first half of the nineteenth century, had a stunning impact on the historical profession; it excited an army of scholars to reexamine the meaning and significance of the Jacksonian era. Over the next thirty years some 227 books and 353 articles (and an even more appalling number of doctoral dissertations) tumbled from the minds and pens of scholars. Yet with all the words expended, few questions were answered and fewer problems solved. Historians have gone round and round with the issues raised by Schlesinger, and although some particulars of his thesis have been modified, this brilliant book remains an important and valid interpretation of the pre-Civil War period.

Not only has controversy raged around Andrew Jackson for the past generation but an enormous amount of new documentary material has been collected. Since the publication of *The Correspondence of Andrew Jackson* (1926–1934) in six volumes, edited by John Spencer Bassett, a sizable number of letters and papers have been added to the principal Jackson collection in the Library of Congress. In 1971 the Ladies Hermitage Association, the Tennessee Historical Commission, the University of Tennessee, and the National Historical Publications Commission joined to sponsor a project to collect all Jackson materials and to edit and publish the most important of them. Documents were collected throughout the United States and parts of western Europe; it soon became obvious that the Bassett edition of Jackson correspondence amounted to hardly a tenth of the material currently available. As a consulting editor for the Jackson Papers Project, I had the privilege and opportunity of assisting in the collecting process, and I can report that as of 1976 over 26,000 letters written to or by Jackson, and some 15,000 other materials directly related to his life, have been assembled by the project at the Hermitage.

Thus I felt a new big book on Andrew Jackson himself was long overdue, a book that would take advantage of the many insights revealed by recent historians as well as the tremendous collection of Jackson materials available at the Hermitage. Initially I planned to halt the first volume with Jackson's election to the presidency in 1828; it seemed that this would permit sufficient consideration of his early legal, political, and military careers before carrying him forward in the second volume to the more important presidential years. But something unexpected and exciting happened in Spain. While researching the archives in Seville, I began to see Andrew Jackson in a wholly different light. Quite frankly I learned to appreciate the Spanish point of view of American history during the early nineteenth century. I acquired a greater respect for Spanish colonial rule, particularly that of the borderlands; my notions about the role of Americans in the southwest and their expansionist ambitions had also changed. Then, sitting in a long reading room on a hot July day in Seville, it suddenly occurred to me that Andrew Jackson, more than any other man of the nineteenth century, had determined the course of American expansion.

A review of other research notes, including those taken earlier in the Public Record Office in London, reinforced this thesis. So it seemed more appropriate to halt this first volume with the discussion of Jackson's actions directly affecting the territorial expansion of the United States.

His tenure as governor of Florida, following the First Seminole War and the ratification of the Adams-Onís treaty, provided a fitting climax to his long efforts to resume the nation's territorial growth and expel the Spanish presence from the southwest.

There is considerable use of the term "southwest" in this book. It is used in its early nineteenth century meaning, which referred to Alabama, Mississippi, and Louisiana (not Texas, New Mexico, and Arizona). Also, the Indians are sometimes called "savages" in an effort to keep to the spirit of the documents and the sentiments of western frontiersmen whose attitudes are paraphrased. I trust the use of this pejorative word will not be misunderstood or misinterpreted. Finally, a number of documents cited in this book are published in several places. I have not always mentioned all of these publications in the notes because relevant sections of individual letters are sometimes omitted or my reading of the documents differed slightly from the printed text.

More people than I can possibly list individually aided in the research and writing of this book, from the guardians of the bottomless pit that is the Archivo General de Indias in Seville to the archivists at the Presbyterian Seminary in northern California. But I would be remiss if I did not acknowledge a special debt to a half dozen people who materially aided my work over the past several years. Sam B. Smith and Harriet C. Owsley, editor and associate editor of the Jackson Papers Project, have been my friends and colleagues since I first traveled to Tennessee in the early 1960s to research the life and times of Andrew Jackson. Harriet Owsley, who conceived and inaugurated the Jackson Papers Project, invited me to share the labor of working in the old man's vineyard. Trained by her husband, the distinguished Southern historian, Frank L. Owsley, she is a superb scholar and archivist, and she has shared with me her extensive knowledge of early Tennessee history and genealogy. Sam Smith, once he became editor of the project, extended every support possible to assist my research. I am free to say that as long as there are men like Sam Smith around, the term "Southern gentleman" has genuine meaning. Both these scholars read an early draft of this manuscript and gave me the benefit of their criticism. They did not always agree with what I wrote but they never urged me to change any part of it. I cannot possibly begin to thank them adequately for their unflagging support and encouragement, and in dedicating this volume to them I trust it will convey a small measure of my appreciation.

G. Douglas Inglis, a graduate student working in the archives in Seville, generously put aside his own work to assist my research and instruct me in the mysteries of the Spanish archival system. Even after I left Spain he continued to answer all my requests for information and copies of documents. Because of his own work in the demography of the southwest in the late eighteenth century he provided me with many leads in tracing Jackson's movements after his arrival in Tennessee. I am also grateful to the University of Illinois, Chicago Circle, for a grant that permitted me to research the libraries and archives of England and France. But I owe a special debt to the Ladies Hermitage Association— in particular Mrs. Cawthon A. Bowen, Jr., the present regent; Mrs. Fred Russell, the former regent; and Mrs. Harry A. J. Joyce, research coordinator and member of the board of directors. Under the leadership of these officers, the Association has moved beyond its charge of maintaining the Hermitage properties and accepted a role in support of Jacksonian scholarship. I am the direct beneficiary of their generosity and confidence, and I am profoundly grateful. Lastly, I wish to thank my friend and editor at Harper & Row, Hugh Van Dusen, who allowed me every extravagance in writing this biography of Andrew Jackson, including its Wagnerian length.

October 1976   ROBERT V. REMINI
Wilmette, Illinois

Chronology of Jackson's Life, 1767–1821

1767, March 15	Born, Waxhaw settlement, South Carolina
1775–1780	Attends schools conducted by Dr. William Humphries and James White Stephenson
1780–1781	Serves in American Revolution; captured and wounded by British officer; imprisoned in Camden and later released in a prisoner exchange
1781	Death of mother, Elizabeth Hutchinson Jackson
1781	Lives briefly at the homes of Thomas Crawford and Joseph White; assists in saddler's trade
1782	Attends school conducted by Robert McCulloch
1783–1784	Teaches school in Waxhaw
1784–1786	Moves to Salisbury, North Carolina, and reads law with Spruce McCay
1786–1787	Reads law with John Stokes
1787, September 26	Licensed an attorney in North Carolina; practices law and tends store in Martinsville, North Carolina
1788	Appointed public prosecutor for Western District of North Carolina and migrates west
1788	Arrives in Jonesborough and obtains license to practice law

1788, August 12	Fights first duel with Waightstill Avery
1788, October 26	Arrives in Nashville
1790/1791	"Marries" Rachel Donelson Robards
1791, February 15	Appointed attorney general for the Mero District
1792, September 10	Appointed judge advocate for the Davidson County militia
1794, January 18	Marries Rachel Donelson Robards
1794	Takes up residence at Poplar Grove; elected trustee of Davidson Academy in Nashville
1794, May 12	Forms partnership with John Overton for land speculation
1795	Forms partnership with Samuel Donelson; sells land to David Allison; Allison defaults
1795, December 19	Elected delegate to Tennessee Constitutional Convention
1796, January 11–February 6	Participates in Tennessee Constitutional Convention
1796	Purchases Hunter's Hill property; elected to U.S. House of Representatives
1796, November	Defeated in election for major general of Tennessee militia
1797	Elected to U.S. Senate; reveals Glasgow land fraud
1798	Resigns Senate seat
1798	Elected judge of Superior Court of Tennessee
1801, September 5	Organizes first Masonic Lodge in Nashville
1802, February 16	Forms business partnership with Thomas Watson and John Hutchings
1802	Elected major general of Tennessee militia; sells Hunter's Hill property
1803	Quarrels with John Sevier
1803, August 6	Dissolves partnership with Watson

1804, April	Forms business partnership with John Coffee and John Hutchings
1804, July 24	Resigns as judge
1804, August 4	Purchases Hermitage property
1805–1807	Participates in Burr conspiracy
1806, May 30	Kills Charles Dickinson
1809	Adopts son of Elizabeth and Severn Donelson
1812–1815	Leads troops against Indians and British
1813, January 7	Leads troops to Natchez
1813, March	Returns with troops to Nashville; nicknamed Old Hickory
1813, September 4	Gunfight with Jesse and Thomas Hart Benton
1813, October 7	Leads troops against Creeks
1813, November 3	Victory at Tallushatchee; "adopts" Lyncoya
1813, November 9	Victory at Talladega
1813–1814, November–January	Faces mass desertion of troops
1814, January 22	Emuckfaw engagement
1814, January 24	Enotachopco engagement
1814, March 14	Executes John Woods
1814, March 27	Defeats Creek Indians at Horseshoe Bend (Tohopeka)
1814, April	William Weatherford surrenders
1814, May 28	Commissioned major general in U.S. Army
1814, August 9	Imposes Treaty of Fort Jackson on Creek Nation
1814, August	Nicknamed Sharp Knife and Pointed Arrow by Indians
1814, August 22	Occupies Mobile and garrisons Fort Bowyer
1814, September 15	Repulses British attack at Mobile
1814, October 25	Begins invasion of Florida
1814, November 7	Captures Pensacola
1814, November 9	Evacuates Pensacola and returns to Mobile
1814, November 22	Departs Mobile for New Orleans

1814, December 1	Arrives in New Orleans
1814, December 16	Imposes martial law on New Orleans
1814, December 23	Halts British invasion with night attack
1814, December 28	Repulses British advance toward New Orleans
1815, January 1	Directs artillery duel
1815, January 8	Defeats British and forces their withdrawal
1815, March 5	Arrests Judge Hall
1815, March 31	Convicted of contempt of court and fined $1,000
1816, September 14	Signs treaty with Cherokees
1816, September 20	Signs treaty with Chickasaws
1817, April 22	Quarrels with War Department and General Winfield Scott
1817, July 8	Signs treaty with Cherokees
1817, December	Assumes command of Seminole War
1818, March 15	Invades Spanish Florida
1818, April 6	Captures St. Marks
1818, April 16	Attacks Bowlegs's Town
1818, April 29	Executes Alexander Arbuthnot and Robert Ambrister
1818, May 24	Captures Pensacola
1818, June 2	Declares Seminole War ended and returns to Tennessee
1818, October 19	Signs treaty with Chickasaws
1819, February 8	Congressional censure of Jackson for seizure of Florida rejected
1819	Builds Hermitage mansion
1819	Tours west with President Monroe
1820, October 18	Signs treaty with Choctaws
1821	Appointed and confirmed governor of Florida Territory
1821, June 1	Resigns army commission
1821, July 17	Receives Florida from Spanish
1821, November 13	Resigns as governor and returns to Tennessee

GENEALOGIES OF
THE DONELSON, BUTLER, JACKSON,
AND HUTCHINSON FAMILIES

DONELSON FAMILY

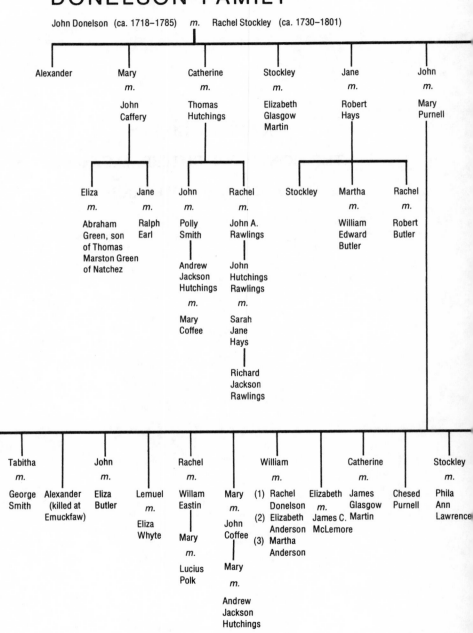

John Donelson (ca. 1718–1785) *m.* Rachel Stockley (ca. 1730–1801)

Alexander

Mary
m.
John
Caffery

Catherine
m.
Thomas
Hutchings

Stockley
m.
Elizabeth
Glasgow
Martin

Jane
m.
Robert
Hays

John
m.
Mary
Purnell

Eliza
m.
Abraham
Green, son
of Thomas
Marston Green
of Natchez

Jane
m.
Ralph
Earl

John
m.
Polly
Smith

Andrew
Jackson
Hutchings
m.
Mary
Coffee

Rachel
m.
John A.
Rawlings

John
Hutchings
Rawlings
m.
Sarah
Jane
Hays

Richard
Jackson
Rawlings

Stockley

Martha
m.
William
Edward
Butler

Rachel
m.
Robert
Butler

Chesed

Tabitha
m.
George
Smith

Alexander
(killed at
Emuckfaw)

John
m.
Eliza
Butler

Lemuel
m.
Eliza
Whyte

Rachel
m.
Willam
Eastin
|
Mary
m.
Lucius
Polk

Mary
m.
John
Coffee
|
Mary
m.
Andrew
Jackson
Hutchings

William
m.
(1) Rachel
Donelson
(2) Elizabeth
Anderson
(3) Martha
Anderson

Elizabeth
m.
James C.
McLemore

Catherine
m.
James
Glasgow
Martin

Chesed
Purnell

Stockley
m.
Phila
Ann
Lawrence

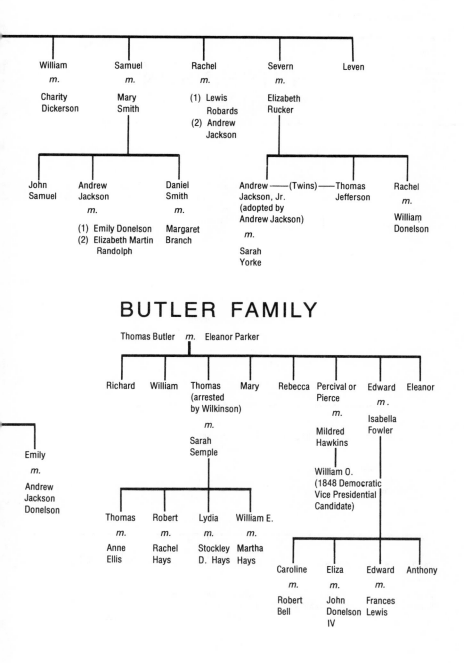

William	Samuel	Rachel	Severn	Leven
m.	m.	m.	m.	
Charity Dickerson	Mary Smith	(1) Lewis Robards	Elizabeth Rucker	
		(2) Andrew Jackson		

John Samuel

Andrew Jackson
m.
(1) Emily Donelson
(2) Elizabeth Martin Randolph

Daniel Smith
m.
Margaret Branch

Andrew ——(Twins)—— Thomas
Jackson, Jr.   Jefferson
(adopted by
Andrew Jackson)
m.
Sarah
Yorke

Rachel
m.
William Donelson

BUTLER FAMILY

Thomas Butler m. Eleanor Parker

Richard	William	Thomas (arrested by Wilkinson)	Mary	Rebecca	Percival or Pierce	Edward	Eleanor
		m.			m.	m.	
		Sarah Semple			Mildred Hawkins	Isabella Fowler	

William O.
(1848 Democratic
Vice Presidential
Candidate)

Emily
m.
Andrew Jackson Donelson

Thomas	Robert	Lydia	William E.
m.	m.	m.	m.
Anne Ellis	Rachel Hays	Stockley D. Hays	Martha Hays

Caroline	Eliza	Edward	Anthony
m.	m.	m.	
Robert Bell	John Donelson IV	Frances Lewis	

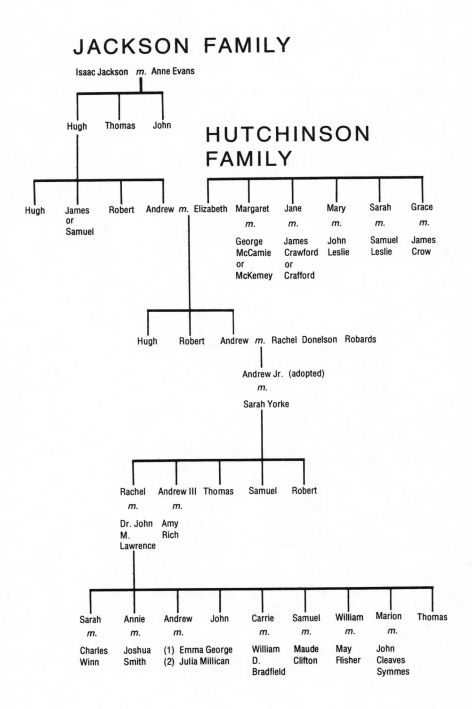

JACKSON FAMILY

Isaac Jackson *m.* Anne Evans

Hugh   Thomas   John

HUTCHINSON FAMILY

Hugh   James or Samuel   Robert   Andrew *m.* Elizabeth

Margaret
m.
George McCamie or McKemey

Jane
m.
James Crawford or Crafford

Mary
m.
John Leslie

Sarah
m.
Samuel Leslie

Grace
m.
James Crow

Hugh   Robert   Andrew *m.* Rachel Donelson Robards

Andrew Jr. (adopted)
m.
Sarah Yorke

Rachel
m.
Dr. John M. Lawrence

Andrew III
m.
Amy Rich

Thomas   Samuel   Robert

Sarah
m.
Charles Winn

Annie
m.
Joshua Smith

Andrew
m.
(1) Emma George
(2) Julia Millican

John

Carrie
m.
William D. Bradfield

Samuel
m.
Maude Clifton

William
m.
May Flisher

Marion
m.
John Cleaves Symmes

Thomas

ANDREW JACKSON

VOLUME ONE

THE COURSE OF AMERICAN EMPIRE, 1767–1821

CHAPTER 1

Beginnings

AT ONE TIME IN THE HISTORY of the United States, General Andrew Jackson of Tennessee was honored above all other living men. And most dead ones, too. The American people reserved to him their total love and devotion. Nothing within their sovereign power did they deny him. Nothing satisfied the need to acknowledge his greatness or the enormous debt they owed him. As a mark of that devotion and confidence—if not the mark of madness—some men continued to vote for him for President of the United States nearly fifteen years after his death. As the nation stumbled toward the crisis of Civil War these votes desperately sought to summon him from his tomb to rescue once again his beloved country.

No American ever had so powerful an impact on the minds and spirit of his contemporaries as did Andrew Jackson. No other man ever dominated an age spanning so many decades. No one, not Washington, Jefferson, or Franklin, ever held the American people in such near-total submission.

An early and reliable biographer of this impossible Hero tried to convey to his readers the strength and longevity of the bond forged between Jackson and the American electorate. Hard pressed to find the appropriate words, he finally summed it up this way: "Columbus had sailed; Raleigh and the Puritans had planted; Franklin had lived; Washington fought; Jefferson written; fifty years of democratic government had passed; free schools, a free press, a voluntary church had done what they could to instruct the people; the population of the country had been quadrupled and its resources increased ten fold; and the result of all was,

1

that the people of the United States had arrived at the capacity of honoring Andrew Jackson before all other living men."[1]*

And justly so. For the story of Andrew Jackson's life is one of the most important and significant chapters in the history of the United States. As both military commander and political leader, he reshaped and redirected the course of American expansion and democracy. That a man of such towering influence in his country's growth and development should have been born into relative obscurity and poverty added to his achievement and popularity. To many Americans his life scored the final proof that their new nation was an unparalleled success.

The story of Andrew Jackson and his immediate family begins in Northern Ireland in 1765. There were four brothers, the sons of Hugh Jackson, a well-to-do linen weaver. Each of the brothers occupied a "large Farm" and paid the usual rents to the "Lord of the Soil."[2] Each was known for his "hospitality" and "strict adherence and attachment to the faith as professed by the Kirk of Scotland." They were Scotch-Irish, their ancestors having crossed from Scotland to Northern Ireland after the army of William III defeated James II at the Battle of the Boyne in 1690. Though they had been born in Northern Ireland it was reported that the Jackson brothers preserved "a great portion of Scottish phraseology and Dialect."[3] If this was true (some historians have doubted the source of this information[4]) it would seem to indicate that these Scotch-Irish were a tightly knit, insulated group.

The youngest brother, Andrew, father of the future President, lived near Castlereagh, a hundred and twenty-five miles from Carrickfergus, on the eastern coast of Northern Ireland. He had married Elizabeth Hutchinson, by whom he had two sons, Hugh and Robert. In 1765, when his sons were aged two years and six months respectively, Andrew decided to improve his station by pulling up stakes, selling his property, and sailing to America. Andrew was probably encouraged in this adventure by his wife's sisters, all of them intent on moving to America and all but one apparently unmarried at the time of their crossing. Andrew and family sailed from Carrickfergus in 1765 accompanied by his neighbors, James, Robert, and Joseph Crawford (or Crafford). James Crawford's wife was Elizabeth Jackson's sister. It was now two years since the signing of the peace treaty ending the European Seven Years' War, called the French and Indian War in America; it was also the year American colonists met together in congress to protest the Stamp Act that Parliament had enacted to increase taxes to help pay the costs of an expanded empire.

*Notes begin on p. 425.

The Scotch-Irish were arriving in America in ever-increasing numbers in the mid-eighteenth century. Attracted by the promise of a new life, impelled by the disappointments of the old, and encouraged by the sheer numbers of emigrants leaving Ireland to seek another start, they swarmed across the ocean, landed at every conceivable port along the American coastline, and quickly fanned out into the upland interior. The early history of the Jackson family as it relocated in the colonies is extremely difficult to trace because of the sparseness of documentary evidence, but it is probable that Andrew, Elizabeth, and their two boys landed in Pennsylvania and slowly moved southward, following the route taken by several of Elizabeth's sisters.[5] In time they settled in the Waxhaw region, which straddled North and South Carolina and was watered by Waxhaw Creek, a branch of the Catawba River where the Catawba Indians once roamed. Because of the creek the region was a fertile island in a wasteland of pine woods, and it had a slight reputation for the quality of its grapes. A meeting house had been erected to provide community life. And, of course, there was a church which was Presbyterian in its denomination.

Despite the generally unpromising location of the region it attracted a substantial number of people from the north country of Ireland. One Scotch-Irish family followed another into the Waxhaw, trailing down from Pennsylvania and huddling together for protection and comfort. The Jacksons and Crawfords headed for it because they could expect to find family already established in the Waxhaw who would assist them in settling in a new and frightening world.

They were not disappointed. Waiting to greet them was the George McCamie family, Mrs. McCamie—a recent bride—being the sister of Mrs. Jackson and Mrs. Crawford. Several other sisters lived in the Waxhaw, two of whom were now married to brothers by the name of Leslie. So when the Jacksons and Crawfords finally reached this pine country there was a sort of family reunion. The moment of arrival for the two families, who had crossed a fierce ocean and tramped through a wilderness to reach the Waxhaw, must have occasioned great joy.

It was a good beginning. The several families linked by a common female tie sustained each other during the terrible struggle for survival that lay ahead. For the Jacksons it was particularly difficult; unlike the Crawfords, who had a little money and thus bought land on the more fertile side of the Creek, the Jacksons scraped along at near subsistence level and were forced to settle on new land around Twelve Mile Creek, another branch of the Catawba. Whether Jackson was a squatter or not is uncertain, and some early biographers of President Jackson have taken the position that his father "never *owned* in America one acre of land."[6] Certainly the elder Jackson claimed he owned the land on which he settled. Unfortunately, one Thomas Ewing also claimed it. After the death of her husband, and with the assistance of her brother-in-law, James Crawford, Elizabeth Jackson received an indenture in the name of her children for the land in question from Ewing on payment of fourteen pounds "Currant Money of North Carolina."[7] According to this deed the extent of the property began at a white oak on the south side of Twelve Mile Creek "by a small Branch & Runs thence N 10 E 180 poles to a Red Oak by a Small branch Thence N 80 W 180 poles to a R. O. thence S 10 W 180 poles to a Red Oak thence to the Beginning."[8] In all, the property encompassed approximately 200 acres of land.

For two long, difficult years Andrew Jackson sweated over this sour land to make it yield. For his wife it was a continuation of the hardship she had always known, one that extended back to her early life in Ireland. Her family had been weavers of linen, and the women had sometimes toiled half the night to earn extra money while the men worked the farms they did not own but paid high rents to occupy. At least now, in America, they worked for themselves.

The area around Twelve Mile Creek later became part of Union County, North Carolina. It got that name in tribute to President Jackson and as a rebuke to its neighboring "nullifiers" in South Carolina. At one time there had been a plan to call the county Jackson County, but it was finally decided that Union County was a worthier compliment, particularly since the county arrogantly poked itself partway into South Carolina.

The short time that the elder Jackson worked this land produced a small log house, some cleared fields, and enough crops to feed his family. But the labor exacted in this enterprise broke the unfortunate man; after only two years in the country, he died suddenly in March 1767,[9] his wife pregnant with his third child. A rude farm wagon bore the body to the Waxhaw churchyard, where it was buried in the presence of relatives and neighbors, among them his sons, Hugh, now four, and Robert, aged two. After the funeral, Elizabeth went to the home of her sister, Jane Crawford; there, a few days later, on March 15, 1767, she gave birth to a third son, whom she named Andrew in memory of her late husband.

Something of a controversy exists about the birthplace of President Jackson—specifically, whether he was born in North or South Carolina. (There are also claims that he was born on the high seas and in Ireland, but there is no reliable evidence to support these contentions.) The problem of the birthplace turns on Elizabeth's actions following the death of her husband. If she went to the Crawfords and had her child in their house, then Jackson was born in South Carolina. However, there is a tradition in the Leslie branch of the family, accepted by some biographers,[10] that Elizabeth went to the home of George McCamie and there gave birth to Andrew, in which case Jackson's birthplace was North Carolina. According to the Leslie tradition, Elizabeth was on her way to the Crawfords when she stopped for a visit with the McCamies, and while there she went into labor. Not until after the child was born and she was able to travel—approximately three weeks later—did she continue her journey to the Crawfords. Since the Crawford house was located in South Carolina and the McCamie home in North Carolina, the two states have never given up trying to certify Elizabeth's physical location at the time of her son's birth.

The evidence advanced for both claims is inconclusive, but the better case is offered by South Carolina if for no other reason than that Jackson himself believed it was his birthplace. Presumably each person at some early period of his life asks and learns where his life began, and Jackson repeated many times that he was born in South Carolina. In response to an inquiry by James H. Witherspoon of South Carolina in 1824, Jackson wrote: "As to the question asked, I with pleasure answer, I was born in So Carolina, as I have been told at the plantation whereon James Crawford lived about one mile from the Carolina road and of the Waxhaw Creek, left that State in 1784, was born on the 15 of march in the year 1767."[11] Furthermore, Jackson constantly referred to South Carolina as his "native State" during the nullification crisis in 1832, and this, in the absence of concrete evidence, must be the decisive factor in awarding the state that Jackson threatened to drench in fraternal blood the honor of claiming him as its own.[12]

In any event, Elizabeth abandoned the farm her husband had worked himself to death to till and took up permanent residence with the Crawfords. As Jane Crawford seems to have been a semi-invalid, Elizabeth became housekeeper and poor relation. She had eight Crawford children to look after along with her own three. Later she was remembered as always knitting or spinning, always busy, always working—as she had been trained from early childhood. She was a stout woman and exceedingly pious, in many respects very much like President Jackson's wife, Rachel. She was a woman of extraordinary interior strength whose life was nearly as heroic as that of her famous son.

She had one pious little hope: that her youngest boy, Andrew, would become a Presbyterian minister. To fulfil that hope she would see to it that he got the liberal education he needed for the ministry. Then, with God's grace, he would go forth and help men to save their souls!

CHAPTER 2

Revolutionary Soldier Boy

FOR THE FIRST TEN OR TWELVE YEARS of his life Andrew Jackson lived at the Crawfords' and enjoyed the comfort and support as well as the turmoil and confusion of a large family. Since his mother ran the household, it is unlikely he felt like an outsider. Indeed Andrew was accorded many advantages. When he grew to age, he attended an academy conducted by Dr. William Humphries, which indicates that there was some financial support for his education. Later he went to a school run by James White Stephenson, a Presbyterian minister. His two older brothers did not share his advantage. They went to a "common country school."[1] Because Elizabeth Jackson was intent on rearing Andrew for the ministry, he had the benefit of a more expensive education.

At Humphries's academy Andrew learned to read, write, and "cast accounts." He later told a biographer that he also studied the "dead languages," by which he presumably meant Latin and Greek.[2] Exposure to the classical languages had no particularly profound effect on him. On occasion he could spout Latin phrases with the best of them—*delenda est Carthago, e pluribus unum,* and *sine qua non* were said to erupt from him at appropriate moments—but nothing much beyond these tired clichés. That he was exposed to the "dead languages" indicates that he attended better than ordinary academies, schools run by clergymen in which languages were emphasized and students were prepared for college and the clergy.[3]

If Elizabeth Jackson hoped the education she struggled to give Andrew would steer him into the ministry, she was mistaken. She soon

6

spotted signs that his interests and instincts were far removed from matters ecclesiastical. To begin with, even at a tender age, he swore a blue streak—fine, lovely, bloodcurdling oaths that could frighten people half to death—hardly the language of a budding clergyman. Indeed he used this art very effectively throughout his life to scare his victims into doing what he wanted. Which is to say that there was something of the bully in Andrew Jackson, both as man and boy. Sometimes he feigned anger as an excuse to release a flood of expletives, thereby terrorizing those around him. He had a mean, vicious temper that frequently exploded into ugly language and acts, although it now seems clear that his temper was more often than not under complete control and was displayed only for effect. As he matured he grew less insanely excitable, probably with his wife's help and encouragement.

Poor Elizabeth. Andrew never developed into the boy she wished him to be. After a while she probably knew he would never become a Presbyterian minister. Although her ministerial intention for him failed to quicken, there was yet a strong, distinctive religious streak in Andrew Jackson, no doubt rooted by his mother and later nurtured by his wife. It is too often assumed that the grown Jackson was a street brawler, duelist, gambler, and all-around ruffian. Any notion of him as being religious is dismissed as absurd—except as he might cynically use it for political purposes. But to deny his genuine religious faith is a mistake. True, he attended church services on an irregular basis, but he believed in organized religion and regarded himself as a practicing Christian. Late in life he formally joined a Presbyterian church.[4]

Despite his better-than-average education, better at least than that of his brothers, Andrew did not acquire a secure academic background. His education simply did not take, and he himself later recognized his deficiencies. Of history, political science, grammar, literature, mathematics, and science he knew little. Not that this bothered him particularly since he was absolutely confident of his instincts and talents. His consummate ego dispelled any anxiety he might have felt about his limitations. James Parton, an early and critical biographer, said his "ignorance of . . . everything which he who governs a country ought to know, was extreme. . . . His ignorance was as a wall round about him—high, impenetrable. He was imprisoned in his ignorance, and sometimes raged round his little, dim enclosure like a tiger in his den."[5] Parton got carried away; this is a gross distortion.

It was also said—again unfairly—that the only "secular" book Jackson ever read from cover to cover was *The Vicar of Wakefield*. True, he prized the *Vicar* above all other books after the Bible, but the extent of the library he left upon his death raises doubts about his reading limitations. He rarely talked about books in his correspondence, though on one occasion he counseled his nephew about "having a good library."[6] And he himself was a voracious reader of newspapers, like all good politicians, and subscribed to a wide range of journals from all parts of the country, particularly after he emerged as a national figure. His poor spelling and fractured syntax are glaring when compared to the writings of the early Presidents, like Jefferson, Madison, and the Adamses, but when compared to most contemporaries they are better than average.

Jackson wrote with a vigorous scrawl that reflected the strength of his character. Admittedly, his sentences collide with each other, running on line after line in a wild "Ciceronian" style; ideas crowd against each other in a rapid, free flow of thought; commas, dashes, or pauses replace periods; and all manner of grammatical mayhem savage the English language. Nonetheless, despite these lapses, he commanded a powerful style of writing. His prose sometimes vibrated with all the energy and aggressiveness of his forceful and explosive personality. He wrote as he talked: strong, assertive, self-confident. His imagery, especially when he got himself worked up, conveyed enough raw power to jolt readers even a hundred and fifty years after it was written. When he communicated with Spanish governors or Indian chieftains, for example, he frequently summoned an eloquence of unparalleled thrust and drive.

Jackson understood the value of academic subjects in later years. History especially. He once told one of his wards to amuse himself occasionally with history, "amongst which if to be had, I would recommend to you the history of the Scottish chiefs." Considering his background, this recommendation was hardly unexpected. He always regarded Sir William Wallace as "the best model for a young man. . . . we find in him the truly undaunted courage, always ready to brave any dangers, for the relief of his country or his friend."[7] Actually, Jackson could have been talking about himself.

In specifying the limits of his formal education—and they are not to be denied—there is danger of implying more than the actual truth, of suggesting (as did James Parton) that Jackson was a total ignoramus or something approaching it. And that would be absolutely false. Despite his limitations, Jackson was neither ignorant nor illiterate. He was in fact a man of genuine intellectual power, formidable in speech and writing, and, later in life, an excellent conversationalist.

Jackson's actions, more often than not, were inspired by instinct and intuition rather than knowledge or information. Supremely confident of himself, he was not afraid to rush forward and translate his impulses into action, declaring (as though the words provided justification) that he was taking full responsibility for whatever he did. Sometimes his impulses got him into trouble, but on the whole he had particularly keen instincts as a politician, and he developed along the way a strong sense of the popular will. Highly educated men, with few exceptions, tend to be notoriously feeble politicians; Andrew Jackson's limited education never proved a political liability.

As a youth, Andrew was a "wild, frolicsome, willful, mischievous, daring, reckless boy." He was especially fond of foot races or jumping matches. He also liked to wrestle, but since he was quite slender he was more active than strong and as a consequence was usually thrown. "I could throw him three times out of four," said one classmate, "but he would never *stay throwed.* He was dead game, even then, and never would give up."[8]

To those who competed with him and were his equals or superiors, Andrew was a difficult boy to get along with. He was easily offended, irascible, self-willed, and somewhat overbearing. From an early age he showed unmistakable signs of being a bully, although an unusual sort of bully in that he could be a generous protector of younger boys provided they never questioned his ability or challenged his leadership.[9] As one early writer put it, Andrew Jackson was a fighting cock all his life who was very kind to the hens who clucked about him, giving them many a nice kernel of corn. But he flared up in a rage and savaged with beak and spur any other cock who dared to challenge his domain.[10] As a mature man he brooked no opposition to his will. Disagreements or differences of opinion he tolerated only if they posed no threat to his authority or reputation. It is possible that these early, unpleasant traits—traits that were modified but not appreciably altered during his later years—were the result in large measure of his living with the Crawfords as a poor relation and lacking the guidance of a strong father who could ween him from his bullying inclination. His insecurity forged a terrible need to assert himself against those of demonstrated superior ability.

Because Andrew was so competitive and overbearing, some boys gave him a gun one day, loaded to the muzzle, and dared him to fire it. They wanted the delicious pleasure of watching him get kicked to the ground by the discharge. Never one to refuse a challenge, Andrew grabbed the gun and fired it. The recoil sent him sprawling. Infuriated by the joke, he jumped to his feet and in a near frenzy screamed, "By G-d, if one of you laughs, I'll kill him!"[11] There was silence. No one uttered a sound. No one dared.

With all his youthful petulance, Andrew liked to have fun, play games, indulge in outrageous practical jokes. "Frolic . . . not fight, was the ruling interest of Jackson's childhood." He had a bit of gibberish to accompany his frolicking, the meaning of which suggests a great deal about his character and personality. The gibberish was remembered by a second cousin who heard it from his father. It went like this: "Set the case: you are Shauney Kerr's mare, and me Billy Buck; and I should mount you, and you should kick, fall, fling and break your neck; should I be to blame for that?"[12] So, as he playfully knocked someone over or tripped him or wrestled him to the ground, Andrew would singsong his little piece about being the buck and mounting his opponent and asking whether it was his fault if calamity befell his opponent for resisting his advances.

The need to dominate. The need to have his will accepted without question. The warning that resistance could bring disaster. And whose fault was that? Certainly not Andrew Jackson's. Better to accept the yoke than chance a frightful consequence. If there be sexual meaning or connotation in the gibberish, it is for those with professional knowledge and skill at such analysis to suggest the possibilities.[13]

During the early years there were several indications that Andrew experienced emotional problems of one kind or another. An early writer mentions one without elaborating upon it or identifying the source of his information. He writes: "But the boy [Andrew], it appears, had a special cause of irritation in a disagreeable disease, name unknown, which induces a habit of—not to put too fine a point on it—'slobbering.' Woe to any boy who presumed to jest at this misfortune! Andy was upon him incontinently, and there was either a fight or a drubbing."[14] What this slobbering signified is difficult to fathom. A modern historian suggests it was precipitated by Andrew's relationship with his mother and occurred when he was excited and could not express himself coherently.[15] Like Billy Budd, who stuttered, Andrew could not defend himself verbally and therefore flew into a wild rage when tormented.[16] Living on the frontier, where passions were easily inflamed and invariably led to violence, Andrew experienced emotional outbursts of such intensity that he literally choked with rage. He slobbered. And a fight or a drubbing ensued.

To what extent Andrew's relationship with his mother was the cause of this "disagreeable disease" is a matter of conjecture. A measure of parental responsibility is invariably present in the emotional traumas children suffer. Was the slobbering an expression of rage against the mother for reasons that may be totally unknown? Elizabeth Jackson later abandoned her son in a patriotic cause. Did this separation signify rejection? Is this, then, a contributory factor of the slobbering and the devouring violence?

Elizabeth Jackson was said to have dominated her son. An early historian—one Augustus Buell, whose veracity is highly questionable[17]—tells the story that "Aunt Betty Jackson" found the five-year-old Andrew crying one day. "Stop that Andrew," she commanded. "Don't let me see you cry again! Girls were made to cry, not boys!" The young Andrew replied, "Well, then, mother, what are boys made for?" "To fight!" she snapped.[18] Elizabeth is also supposed to have advised her son against lying, stealing, or suing for slander or assault—an account which a true man would settle on the field of honor. According to one John Trotwood Moore, who cited no source for his story, Andrew Jackson on his birthday in 1815, immediately following his military victory over the British at New Orleans, said to several friends gathered around him, "Gentlemen, I wish she could have lived to see this day. There never was a woman like her. She was gentle as a dove and as brave as a lioness. Her last words have been the law of my life." Those supposed last words were these:

> Andrew, if I should not see you again, I wish you to remember and treasure up some things I have already said to you: in this world you will have to make your own way. To do that you must have friends. You can make friends by being honest, and you can keep them by being steadfast. You must keep in mind that friends worth having will in the long run expect as much from you as they give to you. To forget an obligation or be ungrateful for a kindness is a base crime—not merely a fault or a sin, but an actual crime. Men guilty of it sooner or later must suffer the penalty. In personal conduct be always polite but never obsequious. None will respect you more than you respect yourself. Avoid quarrels as long as you can without yielding to imposition. But sustain your manhood always. Never bring a suit in law for assault and battery or for defamation. The law affords no remedy for such outrages that can satisfy the feelings of a true man. Never wound the feelings of others. Never brook wanton outrage upon your own feelings. If you ever have to vindicate your feelings or defend your honor, do it calmly. If angry at first, wait till your wrath cools before you proceed.[19]

The final sentences of this passage, concerning what the law can and cannot remedy, have been repeated in other versions in other places.[20] They seem to support Augustus Buell's story of Aunt Betty's reminding her son that boys were made to fight. More reliable sources find Elizabeth Jackson considerably less combative, although the admonition against instituting suit for assault remained. John H. Eaton, a longtime associate of Andrew Jackson, wrote a campaign biography of his friend and recounted an incident in which Jackson spoke of his mother and her famous last words. "One of the last injunctions given me by her," said Jackson, "was never to institute a suit for assault and battery, or for defamation; never to wound the feelings of others, nor suffer my own to be outraged; these were her words of admonition to me; I remember them well, and have never failed to respect them; my settled course throughout life has been, to bear them in mind and never to insult or wantonly to assail the feelings of any one; and yet many conceive me to be a most ferocious animal, insensitive to moral duty, and regardless of the laws both of God and man."[21]

Perhaps the injunction to fight when assaulted is implied, but it is not specifically stated in this passage spoken by Andrew. And the tone of the whole is not one of violence but—quite the contrary—of respecting the rights and sensibilities of others. The record, therefore, does not demonstrate a relationship between mother and son in which the mother conditioned the son to fight or prodded him to violence. That distorts the relationship.

Elizabeth Jackson was a strong-minded woman who had a powerful influence on her son. In speaking of her in later life—on the few occasions he did so—Andrew seems to have remembered her with affection. He reflected most on her courage and the strength she displayed in losing her husband and having to face the rigors of harsh frontier life with three sons to raise, the youngest of whom never knew his father. It has been reported that Andrew sometimes clinched a remark or an argument by saying, *"That* I learned from my good old mother."[22] All the earliest accounts of his life insist that Andrew "deeply loved his mother, and held her memory sacred to the end of his life."[23] Time no doubt erased the most painful memories and left only those remembrances Jackson could accept of the one person who most influenced his early life.

The danger of reading great psychological meaning into Andrew's early behavior should be obvious: little hard evidence exists to support such speculation. The "slobbering" is a case in point. The mid-nineteenth century writer who used the term did not explain what he meant by it, nor could he imagine what dire traits of character would be found in that single word by later interpreters. Is it not possible that the slobbering was a simple and not unusual childhood dysfunction that accompanied momentary emotional outbursts and that Jackson easily outgrew in the course of time?

The same writer who mentioned the slobbering also insisted that "frolic . . . not fight" best described Andrew's ruling interest as a child. "No boy ever lived who liked fun better than he, and his fun . . . was of an innocent and rustic character, such as . . . gives a cheery tone to the feelings ever after." Surely "slobbering" is incompatible with a fun-loving boy when the word is made to freight deep psychological problems raging within the young man.

There was indeed one raging passion deep inside the fun-loving Andrew: horses. He loved everything and anything about them—riding them, racing them, tending to their needs. There was probably nothing unusual about this interest; most frontier boys came to know and appreciate the value of these animals almost as soon as they could walk and talk.

Nor was his delight in cockfighting any more unusual. Living on the frontier, he had an early initiation to this grisly sport. Like dueling, cockfighting was a fact of life in the south and west in the late eighteenth and nineteenth centuries, and Andrew absorbed the one as readily as the other. Interestingly, the earliest dated document in the collection of papers preserved by Jackson (it is not written in his hand) is titled, "A Memorandum How to Feed a Cock Before You Him Fight." It gives this advice:

> Take and give him some Pickle Beaf Cut fine 3 times a Day and give him sweet Milk Instead of water to Drink give him Dry Indien Corn that hase been Dryn Up in smoke give him lighte wheat Bread Soken in sweet Milk feed him as Much as he can Eat for Eaight Days Orrange Town in Orange County
> March the 22d 79
> Mr. Mabee Merchant[24]

It is fair to say that things athletic, rather than matters academic, interested Andrew most during his early school years. An older classmate remembered him as being "remarkably athletic" but also recollected that Andrew was impulsive, "ambitious, courageous and persevering in his undertakings."[25] At the time he attended school Andrew was a tall, extremely slender boy, whose most distinguishing features were his bright, intensely blue eyes—how they blazed when passion seized him!—and a shock of long, bushy, sandy-colored hair. If he got little out of school he nonetheless developed talents for absorbing what he needed and wanted. Over these early years he became uncommonly self-reliant. He had to. It was necessary for survival, particularly after the death of his mother. Moreover he frequently refused help or assistance from those who offered it. The strong urge to do things himself, to rely on his own resources, was a constant in his life, and he seemed to think all men should be guided by this principle. He was never afraid of responsibility. Indeed he hotly pursued it as though to satisfy some powerful inner need. No matter the circumstances, no matter the crisis, Andrew Jackson always prefaced his actions with "I take the responsibility"—as though that somehow put everything to rights.[26] Political opponents grew weary of his incessant "I take the responsibility." His defensiveness, they insisted, sought only to obscure the degree of his culpability.

Along with his self-reliance, Andrew developed an enormous sense of self-esteem, a protective coating that got thicker as he grew older and provided the daring and willingness to take risks that helped bring him many of his political and military successes. It was one of his greatest strengths. More important, it clothed him with an ambiance of authority that served him well—even when he was dead wrong—and encouraged men to follow him and to submit to his will.

Andrew's education, such as it was, may have failed to equip him with the knowledge and tools he would need as a well-informed public official, but it was better than most and it may have been sufficient to prod him toward a professional career in law. Certainly it did not hamper his swift and spectacular rise to fame and power. What invites conjecture are the accomplishments and heights he might have reached had his full intellectual strengths been cultivated.

Andrew's education took a different and very radical turn with the outbreak of war between the American colonies and the British Crown. Andrew was nine years of age when delegates to the Second Continental Congress, meeting in Philadelphia, signed a Declaration of Independence from Great Britain and in support of that Declaration mutually pledged their lives, fortunes, and sacred honor. There is a story that when the great document was received in the Waxhaw district, Andrew was called upon to read the Declaration aloud to the community. It is a charming story and deserves to be true—it would make a fitting complement to the story of Andrew's mutilation by a British officer after he was captured—but unfortunately the story is a fiction by a twentieth-century writer who made it up, probably to add color and excitement (as well as material) to his account of Jackson's early life.[27]

The revolutionary war did not touch the Waxhaw settlement until several years after the adoption of the Declaration. Then, suddenly, the British burst into South Carolina. Savannah fell, and Charleston appeared to be the next target. American troops hurried to Charleston to strengthen the defenses, but they were no match for the trained professionals opposing them, and the city capitulated on May 12, 1780. South Carolina was now helpless.

Following the capture of Charleston, bands of Tories and redcoats ravaged the Carolina countryside. In the spring of 1780 a force of 300 British horsemen, commanded by Lieutenant Colonel Banastre Tarleton, surprised a detachment of patriot soldiers in the Waxhaw vicinity, killing 113 and wounding 150. Because many bodies were mangled in the fighting, with a dozen or more wounds inflicted upon each one, and because the butchery and the pillaging of homes were so extensive, the engagement was rightly called a massacre. The wounded were left to the Waxhaw townspeople to attend, and the old log meeting house was converted into a hospital where Elizabeth Jackson, assisted by her sons

Robert and Andrew, treated the most desperate cases.

Then tragedy again touched the Jackson family. Hugh, at sixteen the eldest son, joined the regiment of William Richardson Davie when hostilities reached South Carolina, and he fought at the Battle of Stono Ferry. Immediately after the battle Hugh Jackson died, not from wounds but from the "excessive heat of the weather, and the fatigues of the day."[28]

After the grisly massacre of the Waxhaw inhabitants, Colonel Tarleton passed through the settlement and headed toward the Catawba Nation, where he hoped to enlist the Indian tribe in his war against the Carolina settlers. As Andrew Jackson later remembered it, Tarleton himself passed within a hundred yards of where Andrew and his cousin Crawford were hidden. "I could have shot him," Jackson recalled.[29]

Immediately after the Tarleton massacre came the grim report that an even larger corps of royal troops under Lord Rawdon was headed for the Waxhaw with the intent of devastating the region unless every inhabitant formally promised not to take part in the war thereafter. Elizabeth Jackson, her sons, the Crawfords, and most of their neighbors fled their homes rather than submit to this oath of allegiance. They retired to the north and waited until the enemy retreated. Soon it became a seesaw operation: the Waxhaw people moved back and forth from a northern sanctuary each time the British lunged at them. During the summer of 1780 there were so many alarms of troop movements by "murderous tories" that the people of the Waxhaw lived in a state of perpetual fright, ready to flee the area in an instant to escape the certain fury.

By this time both Andrew and Robert were fairly well acquainted with "the manual exercise, and had some idea of the different evolutions of the field."[30] Their mother had encouraged them to attend the drills and general musters of the local militia. No doubt her encouragement stemmed from a practical necessity and perhaps pride, but more particularly it arose from her violent hatred of the British, a hatred that stretched back many years. During winter evenings she frequently gathered her sons around her and chilled them with stories of the sufferings of their grandfather during the siege of Carrickfergus and the oppression imposed by the Irish nobility on the laboring poor, impressing upon her children, as their first duty, the necessity of "defending and supporting the rights of man."[31] The young and impressionable boys trembled at the horror of her tales, a horror that was never forgotten. Andrew absorbed a near-permanent hatred for the British not only because of his mother's instruction but as a result of his own revolutionary war experiences as well.

Thus at a relatively early age Andrew Jackson became familiar with the militia. He learned its drills and exercises and, far more important, he discovered its social and political assets. The militia did more than simply maintain the peace. It was an instrument for social advance within a community. It provided something one could join to find fraternal companionship and a sense of belonging. If a man belonged to any organization in his town (other than the church), that organization was the militia. There were no others. And participation in the protection of the community brought recognition of one's presence as well as the gratitude of those being protected. The militia provided men with a legitimate opportunity to get together on a regular basis, to talk, to exchange information, to dress up, carry a gun, and perhaps wear a sword, to parade, and to exude pride and presence and strength. To give it added attraction, the militia was run on somewhat democratic lines. Officers were elected by the rank and file, and this engendered competition, a drive for self-improvement to win recognition, and the acquisition of political skills to influence the way men voted. Andrew was exposed to this at the age of ten or twelve, and the exposure continued over a long period of his life. The association taught him much about politics—the art of dealing with individuals and groups—and it awarded him the social standing that a person of his origins desperately wanted. Further, his membership in the militia ultimately brought him a kinship with an enormous number of male Americans in every part of the country. He and they could identify with one another. It was the one advantage Andrew Jackson had as a national leader several decades later that none of his rivals could match—membership in a nationwide organization committed to the protection and safety of the United States.

With the Tories rampaging throughout the region, murdering, burning, and pillaging, a constant call for help sounded from the Waxhaw settlement. Finally, down from the north came Colonel William Richardson Davie and Colonel Thomas Sumter, two of the ablest light-horse leaders of the patriot cause during the entire war, seeking revenge for the Tarleton massacre. And they almost won it, too. At the Battle of Hanging Rock, on August 1, 1780, the American soldiers half gained the day—but finally lost it by beginning too soon to celebrate their victory by drinking the rum they had captured from the enemy. Colonel Sumter's plan called for his troops to rush in on horseback near the enemy line, then dismount and complete the attack on foot. But because of the rum the plan went awry. The Americans were slightly inebriated as the action commenced. Then, as they started to dismount, the enemy fired and so startled the tipsy patriots that they panicked and rode off in wild confusion. It was a pathetic (if slightly hilarious) operation.

Davie's cavalry suffered heavy losses in the engagement. Lieutenant James Crawford was among the badly wounded. Thought to be near death, he was placed on a river bank with his coat folded under his head for a pillow. Friends found him there the next day, still alive, but robbed of his coat by "Tory relatives." He was taken home, where he recovered.[32]

The Battle of Hanging Rock was Andrew Jackson's "first field."[33] He rode with Colonel Davie during the action. He was thirteen at the time, and while it is unlikely he did more than attend the troops or perhaps carry messages, he had the opportunity to observe Davie as he conducted the campaign. Like the future General Jackson, Davie was bold in planning his moves but extremely cautious in executing them. He was swift but wary, sleeplessly vigilant but untiringly active. Too much can be made of what a thirteen-year-old saw and remembered, but early writers and biographers all insisted that insofar as General Jackson had any model for soldiering, that model was Colonel William Richardson Davie.[34]

Following the Battle of Hanging Rock, Andrew and Robert rejoined their mother at the Waxhaw settlement, and there they learned of the devastating defeat on August 16 of General Horatio Gates at Camden, South Carolina. The victor, Lord Cornwallis, now steered his army toward the Waxhaw, and once again the settlers fled to the north for safety.

At a place about five miles below Charlotte, North Carolina, a fourteen-year-old named Susan Smart stood at the window of her home as duty prescribed and watched for travelers coming from the south. If she spotted any, she was supposed to run out and meet them and to inquire for news of the army, particularly of the corps in which her father and brother served. Late in the afternoon of a hot, dusty September day in 1780, she suddenly spied a tall, slender, gangling fellow riding a pony, his legs almost long enough to meet under the pony's belly. A worn yellow wide-brimmed hat flapped over his face. The lad was exhausted and covered with dust, "the forlornest apparition" Susan had ever seen. She ran out to greet the distressed youth and to ask if he knew anything of her father's regiment.

"Where are you from?" she asked in great anxiety.

"From below," came the answer.

"Where are you going?" she continued.

"Above."

"Who are you for?" asked the wary Susan.

"The Congress."

"What are you doing below?"

"Oh, we are popping them still," replied the boy.

Susan thought it must be mighty poor popping if such a skinny lad as this was involved.

"What's your name?" she finally asked.

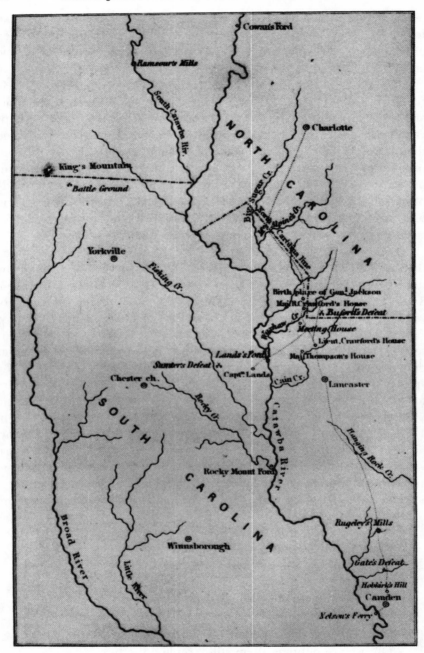

WAXHAW DISTRICT

(This map was prepared from two maps sent to Jackson for his correction and approval by Amos Kendall. It was subsequently published in Kendall's *Life of Andrew Jackson* in 1843. *Courtesy of the Tennessee State Library and Archives.*)

"Andrew Jackson," came the quick reply.[35]

Susan asked about the army and her father's regiment, and Andrew told what he knew, most of which was bad. Gates's army was gone, he said, the settlers in flight. Lord Rawdon had moved to the Waxhaw and taken over the home of Major Robert Crawford, the brother of James Crawford. Robert Crawford owned a substantial amount of land at the crossing of Waxhaw Creek, and now his home served as headquarters for the British commander-in-chief.

His woeful tale completed, Andrew galloped away toward Charlotte while Susan returned to her house to repeat what she had just heard from the scrawny-looking boy. Andrew headed for the Wilson home near Charlotte to stay with the family until it was safe to return to the Waxhaw. (Mrs. Wilson was a distant relative of Elizabeth Jackson.) Andrew boarded with the Wilsons for several weeks, earning his room and food by doing small chores around the house and farm. He brought in wood, "pulled fodder," picked vegetables, milked the cows, went to mill, and took farm tools to be sharpened or mended. One of the Wilson boys later remembered that Andrew never went to the shops without returning with some new weapon with which to kill the enemy. Sometimes it was a club or tomahawk, sometimes a spear forged while waiting for the blacksmith to complete his job. Once he fastened a scythe to a pole and cut the weeds that grew around the house, slashing them with fury and snarling, "Oh, if I were a man, how I would sweep down the British with my grass blade!" Mrs. Wilson's chief recollection of her young guest was his willingness to go with her into the garden and pick beans for dinner. She supposed he did it because of his obliging disposition, but she added, "Andy did like corn and beans, though."[36]

Whether Elizabeth Jackson and Robert also lived with the Wilsons during this autumn and winter is uncertain. Probably they did, although the Wilsons later could not remember. In any event, by February 1781 all three Jacksons were back at the Waxhaw, the British having departed and the countryside calmed.[37]

It did not last. Within a month intense fighting broke out again and developed into a vicious civil war that pitted Whig against Tory, neighbor against neighbor, and even father against son. "Men hunted each other like beasts of prey, and the savages were outdone in cruelties to the living and indignities to the dead."[38] As long as he lived Andrew Jackson remembered the horror of those days, and particularly the case of one man who laid about him like a madman, butchering twenty neighbors before the madness left him and he realized the enormity of his actions. Jackson also remembered a woman who assisted in the burning of her own home—one of the finest in the district—rather than allow it to become a command post for the British army.

Andrew and Robert were now engaged, more or less regularly, in the fighting operations in the Waxhaw area. One evening they were assigned to the house of Captain Land (or Lands) as guards, along with several others. Land was a "staunch whig," and so a group of a hundred or more Tories decided to kill or capture him.

The guards were stretched out on the floor, sound asleep—except one, a British deserter, who was restless and only slept fitfully. There was a noise. The deserter went outside to investigate and spotted Tories stealthily approaching the house. He ran back inside and grabbed Andrew by the hair.

"The Tories are upon us!" he screamed.

Andrew dashed outside, placed his musket in the low fork of an apple tree near the front door, cocked the gun, and yelled his challenge.

No reply.

A second challenge and still no reply. Andrew then fired his musket into the darkness and was answered by a volley that killed the deserter. Andrew retreated into the house where he and his comrades took up stations at the windows and set up a constant round of fire. One guard, James Crawford, took a hit and died by Andrew's side. Another received a wound, though less severe. Just as the situation became desperate a bugle was heard sounding the cavalry charge. The Tories dashed for their horses and fled the scene. But no cavalry appeared. Instead, out of the shadows emerged a neighbor, Major Isbell, bugle in hand, who had heard the firing and thought that just such an old trick might work again and frighten off the attackers.[39]

Shortly thereafter, Lord Rawdon, the British commander-in-chief, dispatched a small body of dragoons under Major Coffin to the Waxhaw to aid the Tories. The patriots learned of the approach and gathered at the meeting house, about forty in all, armed and mounted. With them were Andrew and his brother Robert. The British attacked in a swift action, captured eleven men, and scattered the others. Andrew rode off at the side of his cousin, Lieutenant Thomas Crawford, with a dragoon in close pursuit and several others coming rapidly on. They headed for a swamp. Andrew splashed across, but Crawford's horse sank in a mire. Before Andrew could turn to assist his cousin, Crawford received a severe head wound that forced him to surrender. Later in the day Andrew found his brother, who had escaped unhurt, and the two boys took refuge in a thicket where they passed a hungry and anxious night.

In the morning they looked for food. The nearest house belonged to Lieutenant Crawford. Leaving their muskets and horses in the thicket, the boys crept toward the house and reached it without being observed.

Meanwhile a Tory neighbor discovered the muskets and horses and notified the dragoons. A search immediately began. Soon the Crawford house was investigated. Before the family knew what was happening the place was surrounded, the doors secured, and the boys taken prisoner.

Then mayhem broke out. The soldiers started wrecking the house—breaking glasses, smashing furniture, and tearing clothes to shreds. While this destruction was in progress, the officer in command of the dragoons ordered Andrew to clean his boots—a rather curious command in view of what was happening. Curious or not, that was what the officer wanted, and he wanted it done immediately. It was like so many earlier experiences in which another boy, a superior, would give Andrew an order just to see how far he could push him.

Andrew struggled to control himself. In a calm voice he replied, "Sir, I am a prisoner of war, and claim to be treated as such."[40] Incensed by this retort, the officer lifted his sword and aimed it straight at Andrew's head. Instinctively the boy ducked, throwing up his left hand in time to break the full force of the blow. He received a deep gash on his head and fingers, the marks of which he took through life as a constant reminder of British affection.[41]

The officer then turned to Robert and ordered him to clean his boots. Again a refusal. The officer raised his sword a second time and struck Robert a blow on the head that one early historian claims "afterwards occasioned his death."[42] As further humiliation, Andrew was ordered to guide the soldiers to the house of a prominent patriot, one Thompson, and threatened with instant death if he misled them. Andrew submitted because he knew that Thompson would be on his guard so that if he led the British through a field, rather than by the usual road, they could be seen half a mile away. Thompson did in fact see them as they approached. Leaping on his horse, he escaped by fording a swollen creek.

Andrew and Robert, with Thomas Crawford and twenty other prisoners, were then taken on horseback to Camden, a distance of forty miles. It was a long and painful journey for the wounded boys and their cousin. Neither food nor water was permitted them, and when they tried to scoop up a little water from the streams they crossed to quench their thirst, they were ordered to stop.[43] Almost fifty years later Andrew Jackson could remember most vividly how "Harshly & inhumanly" he and the other prisoners were treated.[44]

At Camden they were thrown into a jail along with 250 other prisoners. Confined on the second floor, they had no beds, no medicine, no dressings for their wounds. The only food available was a small supply of bad bread. The two boys and their cousin were separated as soon as their relationship was discovered. They were robbed of some of their clothing, Andrew losing his jacket and shoes. They sickened and turned gaunt and yellow. Soon smallpox broke out among the prisoners, killing about a tenth of them and disfiguring most of the others. "I frequently heard them groaning in the agonies of death," Andrew later recalled, "and no regard was paid to them."[45]

For a time Andrew escaped the pox, but he shared the misery.[46] Then one day he was sitting in the sun near the entrance of the prison, trying to warm himself, when an officer of the guard engaged him in conversation. Andrew complained about the food, describing the condition of the prisoners with such animation and excitement that the officer promised an investigation—which subsequently proved that the contractors were robbing the prisoners of their rations. Lord Rawdon was informed, and he ordered that the full rations "be regularly Issued . . . as humanity [required]."[47] From the day of Andrew's appeal to the British officer, the condition of the prisoners improved, if only a little. They received meat and better bread and were otherwise treated more decently.

Hope of deliverance suddenly rose among the prisoners when General Nathaniel Greene and a brave little American army of 1200 men encamped a short distance from the jail, on Hobkirk's Hill, where they were clearly visible to the men confined to the second floor of the prison. A few days after witnessing Greene's approach, as Andrew later remembered, "an american soldier in the evening was seen coming in from the american lines, to the redoubt, where we were confined, supposed to be a deserter." The activity that ensued led the prisoners to think that the British were getting ready to retreat. But about sunset "a carpenter with some soldiers came into our room with plank, and nailed up the windows looking toward Genl Greens encampment; some tories who were in company, abused us very much, told us Green was on their lines without artillery, and they intended to make a second Gates of him, and hang us all."[48]

Anxious to witness the impending battle and having only a razor blade by which the prisoners divided their rations, Andrew "fell to work to cut out a pine knot, out of the plank nailed over the windows . . . and with the aid of a fellow prisoner, compleated my object before day, making an aperture about an inch and a half in diameter which gave a full view of Genl Greens situation." Through the knothole the "British army was seen drawn up in a column, under cover of the stockade." A little after sunrise it moved out, circling toward the woods to surprise the Americans and, on reaching the woods, wheeling to the left and drawing up at the foot of Hobkirk's Hill.

Andrew watched intently as the British began their advance. Greene, stationed on the heights, waited patiently for them to come within firing range. "The British supposing Green had no artillery, the officers in front lead on their men encourageing them, when Greens battery opened upon them with great effect, many horses coming in, with out riders, and many with the wounded upon them and the noncombatants running, helter, skelter, for safety . . . never were hearts elated more than ours, as the glitter of the americans swords, wielded by the american arm so success-fully which promised immediate release to us."[49]

But their joy ended abruptly. Greene was unable to maintain himself in this position. Soon the hilltop cannons ceased their roar, "our small arms appeared retiring, and the cavalry appeared to be attacked in front vigorously." The British swept over the hill and vanished from Andrew's sight. The Americans retreated.

Despair gripped the prisoners, Andrew in particular. He slumped to the floor, a desolate, weary, and heartsick boy. Over the next few days, as his spirits sank and his other general miseries pressed in on him, he began to show the first symptoms of the smallpox.[50] He sweated and shivered and burned with fever. But his brother was worse off. Not only was Robert down with smallpox but he suffered a "severe bowel com-plaint."[51] Further, his head wound had never been treated and an infec-tion had set in. Another week in prison and the two boys would probably have expired.

Fortunately their mother arrived just as an exchange of prisoners was being arranged between Lord Rawdon and Captain Walker of the Ameri-can militia. She had learned of her sons' plight and their location and had ridden from the Waxhaw to Camden, where with the help of Captain Walker and an eloquence born of desperation she persuaded the British to include Robert and Andrew in the exchange. The two boys, along with five Waxhaw neighbors, were freed in return for thirteen British soldiers surrendered by the American captain.

Elizabeth blanched when she saw her sons, so wasted were they by disease and malnutrition. Robert, in serious condition, could neither stand nor sit on horseback without support. Elizabeth procured two horses, placed the dying Robert on one and rode the other herself, keeping careful check on Robert to prevent him from collapsing to the ground. Poor Andrew had to walk the forty-five miles home barefoot and without a jacket, his body throbbing with pain. On the last leg of the journey a driving rain drenched the trio. And that was the final blow. The smallpox that had been raging within Andrew burst out in the loathsome sores so typical of the disease. Somehow Elizabeth got her two sons home and put them to bed. Two days later Robert Jackson was dead and his brother delirious and in mortal danger.

His mother's nursing and medical skills, the attention of a Dr. Tongue, and Andrew's essentially strong constitution eventually brought the young man around, although it was a slow recovery.[52] In fact Andrew was a feeble, desperately ill invalid for several months. Then, when her son was finally out of danger, Elizabeth Jackson decided to travel to Charleston, a distance of 160 miles, along with two other ladies from the Waxhaw, to nurse prisoners of war held in prison ships, among whom were her nephews, William and James Crawford. Although Lord Cornwallis had moved out of South Carolina and was now in Virginia fortifying Yorktown, the British still occupied Charleston, where prison conditions were so ghastly that word of them spread clear up to the Waxhaw. Knowing first hand what the sufferings of prisoners were, moved to compassion for the nephews she had helped raise, and believing she could ameliorate the living conditions of the prisoners if not assist in their deliverance, Elizabeth determined to leave her home and her sole surviving son and do what she could for her countrymen and her nephews. She was an extraordinary woman, a woman of courage, high purpose, and incredible interior strength. Tradition has it that she and the two ladies who accompanied her traveled to Charleston on foot, but more probably they rode on horseback, carrying with them the medicines, clothing, and other essentials available to them.

The ladies arrived at Charleston without incident and gained admission to the prison ships, where they tried to comfort the inmates of those floating horrors of disease and death. A short time later, while visiting William Barton, a relative who lived two and a half miles from Charleston, Elizabeth Jackson was taken ill with the cholera (or ship fever, as it was sometimes called) and died after a brief illness. It was then the fall of 1781, shortly after the surrender of Cornwallis at Yorktown.

Elizabeth was buried in an unmarked grave in the suburbs of Charleston, about one mile from Governor's Gate.[53] A small bundle of her possessions was sent to Andrew at Waxhaw as a kind of notice of her death.

On the few occasions that the mature Andrew Jackson talked about his mother he made no comment about her decision to leave him and go to Charleston to nurse the sick on the prison ship. He simply stated the fact as though it were perfectly natural and to be expected.[54] Probably he later interpreted her action as one of patriotism, heroism, and devotion to duty. But, as recent writers have insisted, it must have had a traumatic effect upon him, whether he realized it or not. He was fifteen at the time of his mother's death and still recovering from a serious illness. Did he resent his mother's departure? Did he regard it as abandonment? as rejection? as punishment? Did he think she cared more about her nephews than her own son to leave him when he still needed her? One writer contends that it produced in him a buried rage against his mother for having abandoned him and removed her protection, that Andrew consequently developed "an assertive self, mistrustful of dependence and suspicious of the world."[55]

One thing is certain: he suffered a staggering blow, one he probably never understood, one he could never mention or discuss. If he did feel rage against Elizabeth, he disguised it or rechanneled it. Nothing in his writings suggests resentment against her. Nowhere does he blame her for deserting him. Early biographers claim that he "deeply loved" his mother, which may or may not be true. But they noticed something else which was definitely true: he "imbibed a reverence for the character of woman."[56] He respected women and treated them courteously—far beyond what was expected of him as a proper gentleman. If he hated his mother, would he so revere "the character of woman"? Would he treat them with such marked respect and kindness?

The entire revolutionary war was one long agony for Andrew Jackson. Maybe there were moments when he felt like a patriot and hero, but most of the time Andrew experienced hardship, pain, disease, and finally the extinction of his immediate family. He emerged from the Revolution burdened with sorrow, a sorrow inflicted by "British tyranny." And because he subsequently saw himself as a participant "in the struggle for our liberties," he also emerged marked with deep patriotic and nationalistic convictions.[57]

At the age of fifteen Andrew was a veteran of war and a veteran of intense personal suffering. The scars remained with him through life.

CHAPTER 3

The Law Student

A SEVERE DEPRESSION, relieved at times by a scalding anger, settled over young Andrew. His face, creased by pain and the recent bout with small-pox, registered the profound suffering he felt during the weeks and months following the death of his mother. Almost immediately it was agreed that he would continue to live at the home of Major Thomas Crawford.[1] Unfortunately, this seemingly appropriate arrangement did not work out to anyone's satisfaction. Andrew was very difficult to handle. Resentment and anger of the most extreme kind flashed into the open at the slightest provocation. Something of his mood can be gauged by an incident that occurred after he took up residence in Crawford's house. Another soldier, one Captain Galbraith, who had charge of commissary stores and ammunition for the American army, was also living at the home of Thomas Crawford. Andrew later remembered that Galbraith had a "very proud and haughty disposition." For some unknown reason the captain took offense at something Andrew said or did and threatened to chastise the young man. As Galbraith raised his hand to strike, Andrew went wild. He showered the captain with obscenities and swore that if the hand struck him, Galbraith was a dead man. Reconstructing the scene for a biographer many years later, Jackson remembered his oath very clearly: "I had arrived at an age to know my rights, and although weak and feeble from disease, I had courage to defend them, and if he attempted anything of that kind I would most assuredly Send him to the other world."[2]

However Andrew phrased his promise of homicide, Galbraith under-stood his intent. The hand drooped. But such bad feeling continued between the two that Andrew soon went to live at the house of Joseph White, an uncle of Mrs. Crawford, whose son had recently established himself in the saddler's business.

Andrew's illness continued long after his mother's death. He suffered recurrent fever on account of the smallpox, on top of which he came down with ague. Physically and mentally Andrew was a rather sick young man for many months.[3] What may have saved him was his effort to assist in the saddler's shop. Since he loved horses and everything about them, Andrew was naturally drawn to the trade. For the next six months he helped out "as much as the fever and ague . . . would allow me," he later remembered, and learned a great deal about the saddler's craft.[4] More important, his work in the shop rescued him from his profound depression. It got him through one of the most difficult periods of his life.

Another release came in the presence of a number of socially prominent young men from Charleston whose families had fled to the Waxhaw settlement while awaiting the British evacuation of the city. They were a wild bunch, up to all sorts of devilment, and Andrew fell in with them almost at once. His energies found release in a series of escapades that won approval from his new friends and dismay from his relatives. Drinking, cockfighting, gambling, mischiefmaking, he seemed determined to go as far as possible in leading an "abandoned" life. He was almost manic. His relations took a decidedly dim view of his activities and probably thought him a ne'er-do-well headed for an early and unfortunate end. He was never particularly close to his surviving relatives, and his irresponsible behavior only alienated them further. A complete and permanent rupture eventually resulted. Once Andrew left the Waxhaw he never returned. Nor did he have much communication with his many cousins living in the Carolinas. For the remainder of his life he seems to have disassociated himself with his blood relations. After he gained national fame he would occasionally hear from one of these cousins who seemed anxious to renew ties of kinship. Jackson answered their inquiries in a tone that discouraged further correspondence.

When the British finally evacuated Charleston in December 1782 and all his sporting friends returned home, Andrew followed. Life in the Waxhaw would be mighty dull without them, he figured. So he mounted a "fine mare"—which he had probably earned by his work in the saddler's shop—and rode off to Charleston. In one last, glorious spree he "burned up the town"—or at least as much of Charleston as a fifteen-year-old could manage to ignite. It was a life of almost complete abandonment. He dissipated a small inheritance from his grandfather and piled up a debt to his landlord. He was headed for real financial trouble when he noticed some of his "acquaintances" at the tavern amusing themselves in a crap game called rattle and snap. One of the players offered to stake $200 against Andrew's horse—all on the throw of the dice. Andrew thought a minute, sensed the thrill of the risk, and accepted the challenge. He picked up the dice, warmed them with his will and his need to win, and then let them fly. And he won. That simple, final display of bravado seemed to jolt him out of his present mood and state of mind. Andrew decided to end his wasteful life in Charleston. With the money he won in the wager he paid his debts and headed home. "My calculation," he reportedly said, "was that, if a loser in the game, I would give the landlord my saddle and bridle, as far as they would go toward the payment of his bill, ask a credit for the balance, and walk away from the city; but being successful, I had new spirits infused into me, left the table, and from that moment to the present time I have never thrown dice for a wager."[5] Perhaps he never gambled with dice again, but he certainly gambled in other ways.

Andrew's departure from the city, infused with new spirit, marked a turning point in his life. The desolation of his personal losses and the kind of life it had generated now ended. He had spent the better part of 1782 in wild, carefree, dissolute behavior, trying to appease the demons within him. Those demons remained—probably to the end of his life— but now he no longer needed to allow them constant reign, and he began to think about what he wanted to do with his life. In quiet moments he probably swore he would make good as a kind of revenge for his unlucky past. As his dissoluteness diminished, it was replaced by a driving need to succeed. Andrew Jackson became fiercely ambitious—ambitious for place, for recognition, for attention. The tragedies of his early life did not break him, however low they brought him. Instead they toughened him and then spun him forward into the scramble for position and distinction.

When he returned to the Waxhaw after his sojourn in Charleston, Andrew resumed his studies under Robert McCulloch in a school then known as the New Acquisition, near Hill's iron works. He divided his time between languages and a "desultory course of studies."[6] When he completed this training he taught school himself. For a year, possibly two, he conducted classes near the Waxhaw Methodist Episcopal Church in South Carolina. Preparing lessons, keeping ahead of his students, learning in order to teach, he undoubtedly improved his own skills. But he soon realized the limitations of his profession for an ambitious man, and he left it.

With the Revolution ended, the peace treaty signed with Great Britain, and a new nation launched, it was the legal profession before all others that would shape the future course of the country. Many of the old Tory lawyers were gone, leaving to Whig lawyers a lucrative business. For an ambitious young man the legal profession held real promise. Since Andrew was both young and ambitious it hardly took him much time or thought to decide to become a lawyer.

In December 1784, when he was a ripe seventeen, Andrew gathered his money and belongings and rode north to Salisbury, the seat of Rowan County in North Carolina, seventy-five miles from the Waxhaw. He never returned to the place of his birth. In leaving it he had a sense of beginning a better life of hope and promise. It was a farewell to the past.

Andrew no sooner arrived in Salisbury when for some reason not quite clear—perhaps he met no encouragement—he turned west and rode sixty miles to Morgantown, North Carolina, to the home of a very distinguished lawyer, Colonel Waightstill Avery, who had one of the best law libraries in that part of the country. Andrew asked Avery for instruction in the law and for board in his home. But there was no room in the house, and Andrew, much against his will, had to return to Salisbury. There he was accepted as a student by Spruce McCay, an eminent lawyer and later a judge of some distinction. Andrew found quarters in the town's modest tavern, the Rowan House, where he joined a couple of other students studying with McCay, one of them a bright, engaging fellow named John McNairy.

So began Andrew Jackson's training in the law. The tall, gangling seventeen-year-old labored to comprehend the mysteries of the profession. For two years Andrew diligently copied papers, ran errands, cleaned the office, read law books, and did whatever McCay required of him so that one day he might win admission to the bar. How much law he really learned is questionable. Andrew Jackson was never a student of the law —or of any other academic subject for that matter—but he applied himself.[7] That was his nature. And in that sense he was a successful student and got what he needed from his studies.

For a young man of Andrew's fun-loving spirit the chores of tending a law office and reading briefs could never exhaust the tremendous energies pulsating within him. With the other students in Rowan House he began a rollicking life, full of fun and high spirits, and repeated many of those antics that had upset his relatives in Waxhaw when he took up with the Charleston swells. But this time it was different. It was not dissolution or the acting out of some inner rage. He was simply letting off steam after long and probably monotonous days. It was adolescent exuberance, if an exuberance that sometimes got out of hand. Almost every night, when the business at McCay's ended, Andrew and his friends dashed off to entertain themselves in the most unbridled manner they could devise. Andrew soon gained a reputation as the leader of this hooligan gang, and one resident of the town later remembered that "Andrew Jackson was the most roaring, rollicking, game-cocking, horse-racing, card-playing, mischievous fellow that ever lived in Salisbury." He did not trouble with the law books overly much, it was reported, and he "was more in the stable than in the office."[8] Between horses and girls, Andrew enjoyed a merry life. He was often away on "parties of pleasure" and was known as "quite a beau in the town," a lively fellow, fun-loving, a sport with young ladies but ever careful not to provoke a scandal that might bring social disgrace.[9] He was given to cardplaying, drunken sprees, and practical jokes. One of his favorite tricks was moving outhouses to remote places. Others included stealing gates and signposts.

There was a dancing school in Salisbury, and naturally Andrew attended it regularly. He was so constant in his attendance and so interested in the school that he was asked to manage the Christmas ball. As a practical joke—a cruel and vicious one—he sent invitations to Molly Wood and her daughter, Rachel, the town's fanciest prostitutes. The women, not realizing it was a joke and that they would be unwanted among respectable folk, showed up at the ball dressed in their fineries. Respectable young ladies, seeing the two doxies, stopped in their tracks, mouths agape, and withdrew to the side of the room, giggling and pretending outrage. Older women were appalled that Andrew had dared bring his *"mistress"* to the ball.[10] The two unwanted women were escorted from the room posthaste, and Jackson was tongue-lashed for his impertinence and rudeness. Jackson apologized, insisting it was all a joke and that he never for a moment thought the sporting ladies would take the invitations seriously and come to the ball.

On another occasion Andrew and his roommates were celebrating in the tavern, the hilarity becoming wilder and noisier as the evening progressed. About midnight it was agreed that the glasses and decanters that had witnessed and contributed to the joy of the evening should never be profaned by future use. They were smashed, carefully and solemnly. And if the glasses, which made such a beautiful mess, why not the table? Away went the table, shattered beyond repair. Then the chairs were attacked, and the bed. Finally, clothes and curtains were torn and piled into a heap. To conclude the ceremonies the entire debris was set afire. Oh, it was a tumultuous night, one that was remembered in the town for decades. Indeed, years later, when it was reported that Andrew Jackson was running for the presidency of the United States, some people in Salisbury could scarcely believe it. "What!" exclaimed one. "Jackson up for President? *Jackson? Andrew* Jackson? The Jackson that used to live in Salisbury? Why, when he was here, he was such a rake that my husband would not bring him into the house! It is true, he *might* have taken him out to the stable to weigh horses for a race, and might drink a glass of whiskey with him *there.* Well, if Andrew Jackson can be President, anybody can!"[11]

With all the drinking Andrew did—and there are accounts that he bought liquor by the pint, quart, and gallon[12]—he would surely have gone bankrupt had he not regularly engaged his landlord in bets that kept him solvent.[12] Sometimes it was horseraces, sometimes cards; but Jackson won enough to stay one step ahead of financial trouble.

Besides horseracing, Andrew enjoyed footraces, which were popular at the time and much in vogue. Andrew was extremely agile and very fast, and he made quite a reputation for himself in Salisbury. In one contest he was matched against Hugh Montgomery, a fellow law student noted for his size and strength, who proposed to run a quarter of a mile with a man on his back, Andrew to give him a start of half the distance. The challenge accepted, the race was run with half the town in attendance. And what a sight! Here was this huge hulk of a man sweating and grunting as he pounded down the track with a dead weight on his back, and here was the lanky Jackson coming full speed to overtake him and go on to win by two or three yards. The townspeople roared with laughter and burst into applause as Montgomery crossed the line. But the poor fellow on Montgomery's back was so shaken, clutched, and knocked about that he collapsed to the ground when Montgomery released him.

For all his wildness it would appear that Andrew was a popular figure in Salisbury. His exuberance was appealing. And perhaps his partygoing taught him some of the social graces that so characterized his later years. As a grown man he had the style and dignity of a born gentleman; his bearing and conduct on state occasions gratified the most fastidious. Those who expected to meet a coarse, untutored backwoodsman were quite surprised to find him an elegant and commanding presence. If his active social life in Salisbury did not provide the polish that later dazzled observers, it certainly contributed invaluable experience.

Moreover, Andrew Jackson had to struggle most of his early life. Consequently he was fiercely ambitious and therefore highly motivated. As a southerner he understood the importance of manners, grace, and bearing. No doubt he was always conscious of the need to be regarded a gentleman.

During the Salisbury years Andrew also began to show distinct signs of a charismatic presence. There was a quality about him that commanded attention, respect, awe, and occasionally fear. Whenever something happened, he was invariably a prime mover. His leadership of the law students on their nightly prowls and highjinks was only one example. It was said at the time that if Andrew Jackson joined a party of travelers and the party were attacked by Indians, he would instinctively take command, and the company would just as instinctively look to him for leadership.

Part of Andrew's charisma was his appearance. Erect in posture and slight of build—indeed cadaverously thin—he exuded rawboned toughness and strength. A ramrod, he stood six feet one inch in height and had a long, thin face accentuated by a strong shaft of jaw. His nose was slender and flared a little at the tip. But there was considerable dramatic play about the eyes, those remarkable, deep blue eyes that could shower sparks when excited by passion. Anyone could tell his mood by watching his eyes; and when they started to blaze it was a signal to get out of the way *quickly.* But they could also register tenderness and sympathy, especially around children, when they generated a warmth and kindness that was most appealing.

Jackson at twenty was a fair, clear-complexioned young man despite the attack of smallpox.[13] His high, rather narrow and sloping forehead was topped by a shock of long, sandy, almost reddish colored hair. As he grew older his hair became very dry and bristling, standing nearly as straight as he did and adding to his height and appearance of strength. At short range he projected strong features set on a long, narrow, sinewy shaft topped off by a touch of red. It was a powerful appearance.

Andrew Jackson was not handsome. But because his presence signaled authority, his glance coming quick and direct, he attracted attention. His height forced him to look down at most people, his eyes gripping their object. People were very flattered by the way he talked with them, clutched as they were by the intensity of his gaze. He always seemed absorbed in what they were saying to him. He was one of those men, wrote an early biographer, "who convey to strangers the impression that they are 'somebody.' "[14]

Tension and tremendous energy also seemed tightly wound within that spindly frame. He was an uneasy coil that might suddenly release an explosion of anger or outrageous behavior. Yet the anger that lurked just below the surface, constantly at the ready, was not an unbridled force. Indeed it was observed many times that Jackson more often than not feigned anger for the paralyzing effect he knew it had. Rarely was his temper out of control; rarely did he release all the stops on his emotions. There was indeed a fierce, explosive side to Jackson's personality, but it was usually under considerable control, more so than most people believed or suspected. *"No man,"* said a close associate, *"knew better than Andrew Jackson when to get into a passion and when not."*[15] On those occasions that he chose to summon a passion the performance could be devastating in its impact, cowing everyone within the sound of his voice. It was a skill that proved extremely useful to him in the military and political wars ahead.

Jackson was a cautious and prudent man. "If there ever lived a *prudent* man," said an early writer, "Andrew Jackson was that individual."[16] He dared a great deal during his lifetime but never what his nimble brain warned him was beyond his grasp. He did not court danger as something delicious in itself. He did not take risks if it meant losing control. Fundamentally he was a conservative, cautious man whose ambition and determination to succeed conditioned everything he did or said.

Jackson learned enough law at McCay's to suit his needs. The study did not have a profound effect on his mind, but it did provide a profession, the right to practice law, and the opportunity to hold legal office from time to time. It has been said that from schools Jackson derived little, from law books less than that, and from fortune nothing. He was the absolute personification of the self-made man: no father, no family to speak of, no education worth a lick, and certainly no money. In fact lack of money probably forced him out of Salisbury when he completed his training. Late in 1786 Andrew packed his belongings and bade McCay and Salisbury a quick but not indifferent farewell.

Jackson spent the next six months in the office of Colonel John Stokes, a brave revolutionary soldier, who was considered one of the best lawyers practicing before the North Carolina bar. Stokes had lost a hand at Buford's Defeat and may even have been nursed in the old Waxhaw meetinghouse by Elizabeth Jackson and her sons. In place of the hand he wore a silver knob, and in court he would bang the knob on a table to emphasize each point of his argument. Under the mentorship of this learned but eccentric man, Andrew completed his legal training. Little is known of this period of his life except that on September 26, 1787, he appeared for examination before Samuel Ashe and John F. Williams, two judges of the Superior Court of Law and Equity of North Carolina. Since the judges found him a man of "unblemished moral character" and competent in the knowledge of the law, they authorized Jackson to practice as an attorney in the several courts of pleas and quarter sessions within the state.

For a year after his admission to the bar Jackson seems to have drifted around North Carolina, doing little that was remembered or recorded. Except to get arrested. The circumstances are not clear, but Jackson, Hugh Montgomery, the beefy footracer, William Cupples, Daniel Clary and Henry Giles—all of them young attorneys from Salisbury— were charged with trespassing. Lord only knows what they did in their escapade, but the damages came to five hundred pounds. All five men were "held and firmly bound unto Lewis Beard Sherriff of Rowan /County/" and put up a recognizance bond of one thousand pounds by which they guaranteed to appear at the county courthouse on the first Monday of November, 1787 "and thare to Answer Unto John Ludlo &

Andrew Baird on a plea of Trespass on the Case &c." And to think only a month before Jackson had been found a man of "unblemished moral character."[17]

The record does not reveal what happened in court but presumably the case was settled to everyone's satisfaction. And maybe Jackson learned something about the price of his foolish highjinks. In any event he moved on to Martinsville, Guilford County, North Carolina, and stayed with two friends, Henderson and Searcy, who ran a store. To fill his time Jackson assisted his friends in operating the establishment and in the process learned still another trade, one he later turned to account in Tennessee. There is a tradition that he accepted a constable's commission while at Martinsville, but his activities and the extent of his duties remain unknown.

Jackson began practicing law during this period of drift and uncertainty. He obtained a license to practice in Surry and Randolph counties. While visiting the Surry Court he is said to have stopped at a tavern operated by Jesse Lister and run up a small bill. Lister claimed that Jackson failed to pay the bill but that he rather magnanimously canceled the debt twenty-eight years later. "Paid at the battle of New Orleans," he wrote against the account in 1815.[18] Jackson also visited Anson County, probably on legal business, which would indicate that he was practicing law in a circuit more than a hundred miles long.[19] As he traveled about the state he did a little gambling, a little horseracing, and a little socializing.[20] But his practice did not take hold, and he seemed bored and uncertain of his future.

Then Jackson heard that his old gaming companion and fellow student at McCay's, John McNairy, had just been elected by the legislature to be Superior Court judge for the Western District of North Carolina—a district that stretched clear to the Mississippi River. McNairy had the authority to appoint the public prosecutor for the district, and he offered the post to Jackson. It was a thankless position, certainly an unpopular one as it was practiced in the wilderness. But Jackson was getting nowhere in eastern North Carolina, and he saw, or thought he saw, a future in the West. So he accepted the job. Life in the wilderness might be exciting and rewarding. His law practice—which he would continue while serving as public prosecutor—was certain to become more lucrative now that a great many people were heading over the mountains. They would need law and government and assistance in conducting their business affairs. There would be few lawyers in the wilderness and perhaps Jackson could make a contribution. The risk seemed inviting. He sensed that his opportunity had arrived.

Attracted by the west, Jackson also felt a need to escape the east. He had no desire to return home now that his immediate family were all dead.[21] And the drifting around the state for the past year had convinced him he would not find a new home or develop a lucrative practice where he was. Better to start all over again. Better to take the prosecutor's job and see what he could make of it in the wilderness beyond the mountains.

In the spring of 1788 he made his move. Jackson, John McNairy, Bennett Searcy[22] (an old friend and fellow student at McCay's who had received the appointment of clerk of the court), and three or four other acquaintances agreed to rendezvous at Morgantown and then move as a band across the mountains into what is now eastern Tennessee.

The region they planned to enter lay west of the Allegheny Mountains. During the previous ten years or so, it had been undergoing settlement in two general areas: the eastern section, around the Wataugh, Holston, Nolichucky, and French Broad rivers, extending as far west as the community of Knoxville; and the western section, located in the rich Cumberland River valley, whose center was Nashville. The region between these two settlements was a wilderness infested by hostile Indians that divided the western country of North Carolina into two parts, each suspicious and watchful of the other.[23]

The Cumberland colony was settled in 1779 by a group of explorers commanded by Captain James Robertson. Colonel John Donelson had followed and guided the families of the explorers to the Cumberland settlement. For many years it was touch and go. The Indians were the most immediate and persistent problem; they were incited to attack the settlers first by the British during the American Revolution and later by the Spanish, who sprawled to the south and west across the Florida and Louisiana territories. It is important to remember that from the beginning of Tennessee history there were three continuous, stubborn, and savage enemies with which the settlers had to contend: England, Spain, and the Indian nations. The existence of these terrors shaped the thoughts and actions of all westerners. They also influenced Andrew Jackson once he arrived on the frontier, and through him altered significantly the course of American history.

At times the Indian menace grew so great that the Cumberland settlers were forced to flee many miles to safety, sometimes as far north as Kentucky. Eventually forces from the eastern and western settlements delivered devastating blows to the Indian tribes that temporarily quieted them and forced their withdrawal from the white communities.[24]

In the eastern settlement of Tennessee a movement toward independence from North Carolina developed shortly after the Revolution. A new state was ripped out of the old and named Franklin. The great hero of the Battle of King's Mountain during the Revolution, John Sevier (or

Nolichucky Jack, as he was popularly known), won election as governor of the new state. North Carolina took violent exception to this presumptuous act and labeled it treason. After lengthy quarreling and bickering the settlers were finally persuaded to return to their former allegiance. Although Sevier had been discredited, his many friends rallied to his support and elected him to the upper house of the North Carolina legislature, where he was permitted to take his seat. In the same year, 1789, he was chosen to sit in the convention that ratified the Constitution of the United States and made North Carolina a state within the new Union.[25]

In August 1788 the North Carolina legislature consolidated the settlements around the Cumberland to form the district of Mero (an incorrect spelling of Miró, the name of the Spanish governor of New Orleans). The name was conferred at the insistence of James Robertson in the hope that it would flatter the governor into granting commercial advantages to the Cumberland settlers and prod him as well into a more humane Indian policy.[26] The Spanish always posed a serious threat to these settlers—the "hated Dons" Jackson invariably called them—and much of the activity of the Cumberland centered around thwarting that threat.

With the difficulties between North Carolina and her western countries presumably settled, Mero was now sent a contingent of law-enforcement officers in the persons of McNairy, Jackson, Searcy, and the others. The team started west early in 1788, following the Wilderness Trace across the mountains, each man equipped with a horse, a few personal belongings, a gun, and a wallet containing letters from distinguished citizens of the old community to the settlers of the new. They headed first for Jonesborough, the principal town of east Tennessee. Then they would push on to the Cumberland.

The cavalcade journeyed in double column through an area fairly clear of hostile Indians, once the domain of Nolichucky Jack. By the time they reached Jonesborough it was obvious to them that they could not get to Nashville at the time appointed for the session of the court, so they decided to remain in Jonesborough until fall.[27]

As it turned out, the stay almost cost Jackson his life.

CHAPTER 4

Frontier Gentleman and Lawyer

WHEN THE McNAIRY-JACKSON LAW-ENFORCEMENT TEAM reached Jones-borough they found a settlement of approximately sixty log cabins. The community was ten years old and boasted a new courthouse. Nashville was almost 200 miles to the west; the area between the two towns was so infested with hostile Indians that even if Jackson and the others had wanted to push on to their destination they would have needed the escort of a larger party. So now it was settled. They would remain temporarily in Jonesborough. Perhaps they could drum up a little legal business.[1]

There is a tradition that when Jackson came riding into town he trailed behind him a second horse and a pack of hound dogs.[2] It was almost a grand entrance, as if his new life must begin with style, a style the people of the west would appreciate and respect. Indeed he meant to begin his new career with as many of the outward marks of a gentleman as he could muster. On the frontier, as has been shown by an eminent Tennessee historian, a gentleman was one who played the part, not necessarily one who could claim it by virtue of family or education.[3] And not only could Andrew Jackson play the part—or kill himself trying—but he looked it as well despite his youth.

A gentleman needs a servant. So shortly after Jackson arrived in Jonesborough he bought a female slave, Nancy, aged eighteen or twenty.[4] It is not clear whether the choice of a young woman was deliberate or dictated by the circumstance of availability.

A gentleman also frequents the racetrack, and Jackson not only at-

37

tended several horseraces in Jonesborough but apparently participated in them as well.[5]

A gentleman must stand ready to defend his honor—to the death if need be. Jackson fought his first known duel in Jonesborough against Waightstill Avery, the man he had sought as his law instructor when he first left the Waxhaw in search of a legal career.

Avery, like McCay, made frequent court visits to Jonesborough. As early as 1782, with the establishment of the first court in town, Avery served as attorney for the state. Jonesborough was located within Washington County, and when Jackson arrived, despite his intention to move on to Nashville, he obtained a license to practice in Washington County. That gave him something to do in Jonesborough until he departed for Nashville and a chance to earn a little money. While trying a case of no particular importance Jackson came up against Avery as a legal opponent. It is not entirely clear what happened to trigger the duel, but at one point Avery resorted to sarcasm to rebut Jackson's argument. (It must have galled the older man to be challenged by a student he had rejected and with arguments he regarded as trivial and flimsy.) The sarcasm coming from a superior who had once turned him away sparked an angry outburst from Jackson. In a rage he tore a leaf from a law book, scribbled a few lines on it, and hurled it at Avery. It is not known what he wrote, something provocative no doubt, but it was certainly not a formal challenge; Jackson needed time to consider whether he wanted to risk his life over this insult.

He spent the night in contemplation and by morning had definitely decided to demand satisfaction. Perhaps he thought the odds were in his favor; perhaps he reckoned the circumstances required him, as a gentleman, to issue a formal challenge; probably what really made up his mind was the knowledge that the insult had been public—in the presence of the court—and he had no choice but to deliver a public rebuke.

The next day Avery received this letter:

Agust 12th 1788

Sir: When a man's feelings and charector are injured he ought to seek a speedy redress; you recd. a few lines from me yesterday and undoubtedly you understand me. My charector you have injured; and further you have Insulted me in the presence of a court and larg audianc. I therefore call upon you as a gentleman to give me satisfaction for the Same; and I further call upon you to give Me an answer immediately without Equivocation and I hope you can do without dinner untill the business done; for it is consistent with the charector of a gentleman when he Injures a man to make a spedy reparation; therefore I hope you will not fail in meeting me this day. from yr obt st

Andw. Jackson

Collo. Avery
P.S. This Evening after court adjourned[6]

Avery was no duelist and he was not about to get himself killed by a young upstart acting out some "crazy" notion about his honor. Yet, on the frontier, he could not lightly dismiss a formal challenge. Reluctantly he agreed to meet Jackson in a hollow north of the town just a little after sundown. The distance was measured, the duelists took their positions, the signal was given, and the two men fired simultaneously—both into the air! Neither had any intention of getting hurt. A solution satisfactory to both sides had been worked out. (Perhaps they agreed to the suggestion of their seconds that the shots be thrown away.) Anyway, now that Jackson's honor had been technically restored by this convenient arrangement, he strode up to his adversary, announced he had nothing further to settle, shook hands, and walked away.

Such was Jackson's first known duel. It was hardly typical of his reputation as later described by friends and enemies, journalists and historians. But it was typical of the man, and it says much about his character. Jackson was sensitive about his honor and his reputation. As a gentleman and a youth of twenty-one, ambitious for recognition and acceptance, he understood his duty. At the same time he was certainly not a trigger-happy hothead oblivious to the possibility that he might get himself killed or wounded. When a tidy and sensible charade was proposed by which his honor could be satisfied and a possible danger avoided, Jackson readily accepted. He was a cautious man responsive to workable compromise when it suited his interest. Not that he was incapable of a genuine duel with intent to kill, but the circumstances—and his self-interest—would have to be of greater consequence than this fandango with Avery. When all was said and done, Jackson assured himself that his actions had been totally appropriate and proper and that he proved himself a man of honor and character.

Within a relatively short time Jackson had made something of a name for himself in Jonesborough. He had tangled with a man of legal eminence and held his own—western style. Actually it was a trifle, hardly worthy of notice. But he was only twenty-one and just beginning his career.

A few months later Jackson and his party, with a sizable escort and a number of settlers, left Jonesborough and headed for Nashville.

They traveled through dangerous frontier country.

It was night and the company asleep, except for the sentinels—and Andrew Jackson. He sat on the ground, his back against a tree, smoking a corncob pipe. At about ten o'clock he began to doze off, barely conscious of the hooting of owls in the forest around him. Strange to hear owls in this country, he thought. Just as he started to drop off, he heard another hoot, only louder—and there was something strange about its sound. In an instant he understood. He grabbed his rifle, bolted to his feet, and crept swiftly but cautiously to where his friends were sleeping.

"Searcy," hissed Jackson, "raise your head and make no noise."

His friend stirred to consciousness.

"What's the matter?" asked Searcy.

"The owls—listen—there—there again. Isn't that a little *too* natural?"

"Do you think so?" said Searcy.

"I know it," came the quick reply. "There are Indians all around us. I have heard them in every direction. They mean to attack before daybreak."

The other members of the company were quickly awakened. Jackson urged that they break camp immediately. No one questioned his advice; everyone responded speedily to his direction. The party fled the camp and plunged deeper into the forest, neither hearing nor seeing a sign of Indians for the remainder of the night. Unfortunately, a few hours later, a party of hunters stumbled upon the abandoned camp and decided it was a good place to spend the night. Before the day dawned the Indians attacked and killed all but one of their number.[7]

This story is appropriate to the Jackson legend, however exaggerated some of its details. It is one of the earliest in a long series of incidents recounted to demonstrate Jackson's emergence as a leader under frontier conditions. Despite the presence in the company of experienced and older guides who continued directing the movements of the party after their brush with disaster, it was Jackson who was credited with recognizing the danger and having the presence of mind to take charge and speed the group to safety.

The remainder of the journey to Nashville was uneventful, and the company arrived at their destination on October 26, 1788. As they neared the frontier town they could see a gently undulating, fertile country watered by the great Cumberland River. So rich in hardwood and livestock was this valley that tribes of Indians had fought over it for decades, fought until they exhausted themselves. Then white men appeared to settle the dispute by snatching the land for themselves.

The original settlers numbered 120 men, women, and children, among them John Donelson and his wife and eleven children—the youngest girl, Rachel, only thirteen years of age. Against constant harassment and attack by the Indians they planted their colony and sustained it. Still the Indians would not yield, and for many years the settlers were forced to live in fortified "stations" scattered along the Cumberland River.[8]

In 1785, after a particularly long winter in which an unexpectedly large number of new settlers arrived, placing a heavy strain on the community supply of corn, John Donelson moved his family to Kentucky and remained there until the corn reserves had been replenished. During the sojourn in Kentucky his daughter Rachel married Lewis Robards, and when Donelson returned to the Cumberland he left Rachel behind. Not long afterward he was murdered while surveying in the woods. Two men who were with him found his body near a creek, but it was never officially determined whether the murderers were white or red men. His daugher Rachel always believed that white men committed the crime because she knew her father was too crafty in the ways of Indians to be ambushed by them.

When Jackson, Judge McNairy, and the others arrived at the cedar bluff overlooking Nashville in 1788 the town contained a few hundred persons and boasted a courthouse, two stores, two taverns, a distillery, and a number of houses, cabins, tents, and other nondescript shelters. The Indian menace was still real and several more years would pass before the people of Nashville could spread freely over the countryside and build separate cabins for themselves.

In seeking a place to live, Jackson chose the best he could find. The widow Donelson was living in a blockhouse that was somewhat more spacious than any other dwelling in the neighborhood. She was obviously a woman of property as well as a notable housekeeper and so, almost immediately, Jackson decided to move in with the Donelson family as a boarder. The widow was happy to have him because it meant another man in the house for additional protection against the Indians. Several other friends joined the Donelson menage, occupying one cabin while the family resided in the blockhouse just a few steps away. One of the boarders Jackson met at this time was John Overton, another lawyer. They soon became fast friends.[9]

The widow's daughter, Rachel, had also come back to live with the family. Her stay in Kentucky had been an agony, her marriage shattered in a storm of violent quarrels. Although of good family and undoubtedly much in love with his wife, Robards was neurotically suspicious of her coquettish ways and began to believe all sorts of improprieties about her. The marriage was a mistake from the very beginning, for Rachel was a lively, vivacious girl, just the sort to drive her husband to madness simply by being herself. She was described as the "best story-teller, the best dancer, the sprightliest companion, the most dashing horsewoman in the western country."[10] She was a "rattle," a high-spirited, insouciant, frivolous charmer. The break in the marriage came when Robards caught Rachel talking with a Mr. Short in a manner that he felt exceeded ordinary politeness. The violence that ensued—it is possible Rachel was mistreated—ended with Robards writing his mother-in-law and demanding that she take her daughter back because he could no longer live with her. Shortly thereafter Rachel's brother Samuel fetched her home to Nashville.

But Robards soon relented. He found he could no more live without his wife than he could live with her. He pleaded with Rachel to take him back. He promised to mend his ways. Friends and family also intervened to effect a reconciliation.[11] Eventually Rachel agreed to give Robards a second chance and consented to resume their marriage. She suppressed her doubts in the knowledge that she had little choice given the social mores of the 1780s. They were reunited and bought property only five miles away. However, they continued to live with Rachel's mother until such time as the Indians had been sufficiently subdued to permit them to move into their own home.

It was at this juncture that the fun-loving, frolicking, rollicking, girl-chasing Jackson came on the scene. He had just the temperament and gaiety to insinuate himself into Rachel's affections. Undoubtedly he did everything possible to amuse and delight both mother and daughter. Naturally chivalrous and something of a gallant in the approved western fashion that was the mark of a gentleman, he quickly ingratiated himself with the Donelson household.[12] So here was Rachel, a lively, delightful, fun-loving young woman, who liked to dance and ride horses and tell amusing stories to an appreciative audience married to an agitated, suspicious, antisocial husband, and here was Jackson of commanding presence, who could match Rachel's gaiety and bounce and then spice it with a little wildness of his own—certainly all the ingredients for an explosive domestic quarrel.

It was not long in coming. Time and time again Robards "caught" Andrew and Rachel talking with one another, and this inevitably led to shouting and bickering between husband and wife. Sometimes the widow Donelson became involved as she sought in vain to mediate the quarrels. "Amidst tears of herself and her mother," Rachel pleaded her innocence. Robards refused to believe her.[13]

The many stories of the final breakup of the Robards marriage sometimes portray Jackson in a favorable light, as an honorable man caught in a difficult situation, desperately attempting to prove his innocence and to spare everyone further pain. Other accounts see him as a deliberate troublemaker, goading and taunting Robards with threats and in general acting so provocatively as to arouse the husband's worst suspicions. Both interpretations of his behavior need to be considered for a perspective both of the man and of what happened in the Donelson household.

On one occasion, during an afternoon stroll beyond the stockade, Robards remarked to one of the guards escorting the ladies to a blackberry patch that he believed Jackson was "too intimate with his wife."[14] The guard liked Jackson and at the first opportunity told him what Robards had said. The newcomer confronted Robards and warned him that if he ever again connected his name "in that way" with Rachel, "he would cut his ears out of his head, and that he was tempted to do it any how."[15] Frightened by the threat, Robards went directly to the nearest magistrate and swore out a peace warrant.

Jackson was promptly arrested. Guards were summoned from the blockhouse to escort him to the magistrate, Robards trailing behind. As they went, Jackson asked one of the guards for his butcher knife. Jackson was refused at first, but after pledging his honor to do no harm he was given the knife. Clearly he wanted it to bully and intimidate poor Robards. With his finger he examined the point and edge of the weapon, periodically glancing at Robards to see if he understood his meaning. Suddenly the frightened husband dashed for the canebrake, Jackson at his heels. In a moment or two the prisoner reappeared alone and proceeded to the magistrate. Since the complainant had disappeared, the warrant was dismissed.[16]

Another story shows Jackson under better circumstances. When the situation at the Donelson blockhouse became intolerable, John Overton suggested to Jackson that they find other quarters. Jackson agreed but questioned where they might go. He decided to speak to Robards first; he said he was totally innocent of the husband's worst suspicions and wanted to tell him so to his face.

The confrontation occurred near the orchard fence. It began agreeably enough. Quietly but firmly, Jackson argued that Robards was unjust toward Rachel. As the conversation continued Robards became visibly agitated, then angry, and finally abusive. He threatened to whip Jackson and even made a show of doing it right there. Jackson replied that he did not have the "bodily strength" to fight Robards, nor would he want to if he could because he was innocent of the charges.[17] However, if Robards insisted on fighting him, he would "give him gentlemanly satisfaction."[18] That remark convulsed the outraged husband. Cursing Jackson and Rachel for making him so miserable, he swore he would never live with Rachel again.

It is probable that Jackson's love for Rachel began as sympathy for
the cruelties and unjust suspicions she suffered and then intensified as he
became aware of the extent of Robards's misbehavior. The husband
regularly "cheated" on his wife; the incidents were so flagrant that most
boarders at the Donelson home knew of them. Everyone pitied poor
Rachel. "I resided in the family," one boarder recalled many years later,
and Robards's conduct toward Rachel "was cruel, unmanly & unkind in
the extreme." Specifically, "Lewis Robards was in the habit within my
knowledge of leaving his wife's bed, & spending the night with the negro
women." Robards's sister-in-law "fully corroborates all I have said. She
states . . . that the breach arose from Robards own cruel & improper
conduct."[19] Guilty himself of adultery, Robards suspected his wife of his
own misdeeds.

Not much later Jackson moved out of the Donelson home and found
new quarters at Kasper Mansker's station. Robards remained a short time
with his wife, then he too packed up and returned to Kentucky, leaving
the field wide open to the smitten Jackson. In no time the young lawyer
was deeply, perhaps passionately, in love with Rachel Donelson Robards.

Such was Jackson's introduction to Nashville life and the Donelson
family. He made quite a splash. But if his personal affairs began badly his
professional life, by comparison, was a total success. Almost immediately
he acquired a license to practice law in Nashville, arranged through his
good friend Judge John McNairy of the superior court. McNairy found
him of "unblemished Moral character, and from a previous examination
before me had likewise appears to possess a competent degree of law
Knowledge."[20] McNairy also appointed Jackson an attorney for the entire
Mero District, which included the counties of Davidson (Nashville was the
county seat), Sumner, and Tennessee. Since the law made no provision
for filling the post of district attorney, Jackson served without pay. Frequently the legislature retroactively reimbursed the attorney for his services. The North Carolina legislature was notified of the problem in 1789
and Jackson was eventually granted a regular appointment—sans salary.[21]

Thus Jackson functioned as both public prosecutor and licensed
lawyer in western Tennessee.[22] In the opinion of the propertied class of
the district, his arrival in Nashville occurred at a most opportune moment. Debtors had refused to pay legitimate obligations and had banded
together to defy the law. They had bribed the only licensed attorney in
western Tennessee, and, to make matters worse, the sheriff was incompetent. Merchants and other creditors deluged Jackson with requests to
help them collect their bills. He enthusiastically obliged. An engine of
inexhaustible energy, he issued seventy writs to delinquent debtors

within a single month, much to the delight of the creditors. Demand for his services soared, and within sixty days his practice before the bar of Tennessee was off to a flying financial start. Indeed his career progressed so rapidly that Jackson decided to remain indefinitely in Nashville. At first it had not been his intention to settle permanently in the western wilderness but he was such an immediate success as a frontier lawyer that he changed his mind.

Some debtors had moved to Sumner County and forgotten what they owed. Jackson pursued them. His persistence so infuriated these debtors that one of them walked up to him one day and to show his anger deliberately stepped on Jackson's foot. Without batting an eye, Jackson turned, picked up a piece of wood, and calmly knocked the man out cold.[23]

Early court records of Davidson County show that Jackson handled between one-fourth and one-half of all cases on the docket during the first few years of his arrival—an extraordinary record.[24] During a single session in April 1789 a total of thirteen suits were argued, principally for debt, and Andrew Jackson was counsel in every one of them. Most of his business involved land titles, debts, sales, and assault, and in trying these cases he traveled regularly, principally between Nashville and Jonesborough. In the first seven years of his residence in Tennessee, Jackson shuttled the 200 miles between the two towns a total of twenty-two times —and this when the Indian menace still discouraged such journeys.[25]

Like all frontiersmen, Jackson helped maintain the community posture of strength against the hostile Indian. Within six months of his arrival he was conscripted into an expedition to punish the "savages" following their bold attack on Robertson's station. A twenty-man team pursued the Indians to their camp on the south side of Duck River. Through most of the night the white men, hidden by the thick cane that grew in the region, watched their quarry. In the morning they attacked and drove the Indians across the river. Although most of the "savages" escaped, the team captured sixteen guns, nineteen shot pouches, and all the Indian baggage—moccasins, leggins, blankets, and skins.[26] This was Jackson's first formal expedition against the tribes of Tennessee and he held the low rank of private. Nevertheless, he was cited by his comrades as "bold, dashing, fearless, and *mad upon his enemies.*"[27] He literally vibrated with a "great ambition for encounters with the savages," and for the next several years he indulged this passion to his "hearts' content."[28]

On another occasion a group of Tennesseans accidentally stumbled upon the recently abandoned campsite of a particularly large party of hostiles. Retreat was obligatory, and Jackson immediately assumed leadership. Reaching a swollen stream and finding a place to ford it, they bound logs and bushes together with hickory withes to form a raft, and Jackson and a companion started across the stream with all the guns and equipment. They no sooner shoved off than a strong undercurrent seized the raft and drove it downstream toward a cataract. Jackson struggled to aim the raft toward the bank. He wrenched one of the oars from its fastenings, braced himself at the stern of the raft, and held the oar out to his friends on shore who grabbed it and pulled the raft to safety. It was a close call and his companions chided him for the risk he had taken. Jackson laughed. "A miss is as good as a mile," he said; "you see how near I can graze danger. Come on, and I will save you yet." The party resumed the march, found a suitable ford, and crossed to safety some forty miles to the rear of the Indians.[29]

At another time Jackson was tracking through the woods to reach a party of friends who were crossing the wilderness. Arriving late at the rendezvous, he found the party had left. He also discovered Indian tracks, a great many of them. It was obviously a war party intent on slaughtering Jackson's unsuspecting friends. There was only one thing to do: race ahead and warn his friends of their danger.

There was still time. The Indians had left the road and taken to the woods in order to circle ahead and set an ambush. Jackson plunged forward, propelled by a throat-clutching fear for the safety of his friends. He reached them by dark, just after they had crossed a deep, nearly frozen river. They were drying their clothes. Jackson burst into the camp shouting his warning, and the march was instantly resumed. All that night and most of the next day they hurried forward, not daring to stop or rest, until they finally reached the cabins of a party of hunters. They begged for shelter but were summarily refused for fear that they would steal the provisions. Incredibly, they were forced back into the night, lashed by a driving storm of wind and snow. Finally they were obliged to stop and rest, utterly exhausted and unable to move another step. Jackson, who had not slept for sixty hours, wrapped himself in his blanket and fell to the ground. The next morning he awoke to find himself covered with six inches of snow.

The relentless Indians pursued. Their blood was up and they were intent on a killing. Discovering the cabins of the hunters, the Indians butchered every last man of them. Then, satiated by their savagery, they turned back. Jackson and his friends proceeded unmolested.[30]

The Indian menace made the early Tennessee settlers a daring and reckless lot.[31] According to early chroniclers, they placed little value on life—their own or that of the Indians. They prized horses and rifles above all other property. Yet, in the midst of their trials and sufferings, they enjoyed themselves. They played cards, ran footraces, pitched quoits, and wasted hours in "idle chat." They could amuse themselves with the violin and the dance even though the Indian war whoop could be heard distinctly above the sprightly music.[32]

The presence of the Indians and the danger they constituted shaped much of the early political policy of Tennessee.[33] The Cumberland settlers even stooped to intrigue in order to protect themselves from Indian assault. They courted the Spanish ranged along their southern border, intimating secession from the United States as an inducement to the Spanish governor in New Orleans to discourage Indian attacks.[34]

They courted the Spanish for economic reasons as well. The situation was this: Spain received the Louisiana Territory from France at the close of the French and Indian War; at the conclusion of the American Revolution the British restored Florida to her. Thus, in 1790, Spain controlled a vast empire that stretched from Florida to Louisiana and Texas, up the west bank of the Mississippi to some indefinite point close to Canada, and westward to the Pacific Ocean north of California—an empire that reached from ocean to ocean across a continent.

The peace treaty ending the American Revolution fixed the southern boundary of the United States at the thirty-first parallel from the Atlantic to the Mississippi River. But Spain did not recognize this boundary. Spanish troops and Spanish officials continued to administer a wide area north of Baton Rouge that included Natchez on the east bank of the Mississippi. The expansion of the United States to the west and south was therefore stalled by the Spanish. Expansion to the north was blocked by the English in Canada.

For Tennesseans the worst aspect of this situation was the presence of the Spanish at the mouth of the Mississippi. The frontiersmen had the right of passage down the Mississippi until they collided with the Spanish somewhere north of the thirty-first parallel. If they wanted to continue south to sell their produce at Natchez or New Orleans, or to ship it east via the Gulf of Mexico, they had to have Spanish approval. Thus Spain was a collar around western economic and territorial expansion. At any moment the Spanish could squeeze the very life out of them.

Dr. James White, a congressman from North Carolina and a land speculator in Tennessee, approached the Spanish minister to the United States, Diego de Gardoqui, and poured into his ear the intrigue common among the Cumberland settlers. He assured the minister that the western country would surely secede from the United States and unite with Spain or England in order to obtain access to the entire length of the Mississippi River. He slyly added that if Spain would open the river to westerners, the crown would win western allegiance forever. James Robertson confirmed this judgment. "In all probability," he wrote, "we cannot long remain in our present state, and if the British or any commercial nation who may be in possession of the mouth of the Mississippi would furnish us with trade, and receive our produce there cannot be a doubt that the people on the west side of the Apalachian mountains will open their eyes to their real interest."[35]

Between the economic obstacle presented by the Spanish presence in the Mississippi valley and the constant complaints of westerners like James Robertson, John Sevier, and Anthony Bledsoe that Indian attacks on American settlements were instigated by Spanish officials in Florida and Louisiana, a situation developed that invited conspiracy, intrigue, and even treason. Some westerners—Sevier, for example—were so frustrated and so certain that the Spanish could never be expelled from the south that they indicated a willingness to place themselves under the protection of the King of Spain.[36]

As a gesture of good will and a means of inducing secession, the Spanish encouraged western settlers to migrate to Louisiana. Immigrants were assured favorable grants of land and a measure of religious freedom provided they took an oath of allegiance to Spain.[37] There was another reason for this liberal policy: Spain had no success in stimulating the settlement of the southern borderlands by her own nationals, and she was obliged to look north for settlers. That was her undoing.

As an additional inducement to immigration to Louisiana, it was decreed that Americans could ply the full length of the Mississippi River subject to a 15 percent duty—unless they migrated to Louisiana, in which case the duty was rescinded.

But what of the Indians, especially the Creeks and Chickamaugas? The "savages" continued their determination to drive the Americans from their ancestral lands, and this resolve did not require Spanish encouragement or instigation. A war directed by the Creek chieftain, Alexander McGillivray, flamed across the southern and western frontier beginning in 1786. After two years of intense and savage conflict, Robertson (who had lost a son in the war) appealed to McGillivray, and through him to the Spaniards, to end the fighting. There was such heartbreak and misery from the raids that the Tennesseans were prepared to accept any condition to obtain peace—even Spanish citizenship.[38] So disillusioned were they with the American government and its failure to protect them or to safeguard their trade and property that they were determined "to free themselves from a dependence on Congress."[39]

Robertson and Brigadier General Daniel Smith, one of the earliest settlers in the Cumberland and a man of considerable social and political prominence, wrote directly to Miró in New Orleans to appeal for his assistance in terminating the Indian raids and to urge again the establishment of more favorable commercial relations between the Americans and the Spanish. At approximately the same time a young French captain, André Fagot, arrived in Nashville, ostensibly to engage in trade but actually to serve as courier between the Cumberland settlers and Miró. Jackson met Fagot, was favorably impressed, and offered to arrange an interview between Fagot and General Smith. He wrote to Smith:

> Sir:—I had the pleasure of seeing Captain Fargo [sic] yesterday, who put me under obligations of seeing you this day, but as the weather seems dull and heavy, it prevents my coming up: but I commit to you in this small piece of paper the business he wants with you: he expresses a great friendship for the welfare and harmony of this country: he wishes to become a citizen and trade to this country by which means, and through you I think we can have a lasting peace with the Indians: he wishes you to write to the Governor informing him the desire of a commercial treaty with that country. He will then importune the Governor for a privilege or permit to trade to this country, which he is sure to obtain, as he is related to his Excellency. Then he will show the propriety of having a peace with the Indians for the purpose of the benefit of the trade of this country: and also show the Governor the respect this country honors him with by giving it his name: he bears the commission of Captain under the King of Spain, which is an honorable title in that country, and can, in my opinion, do a great deal for this; and hopes you will do him the honor as to see him upon this occasion before he sets out for the Orleans, and I think it the only immediate way to obtain a peace with the Savage. I hope you will consider it well, and give me a few lines upon the occasion by Colonel Donelson, who hands you this, as I have the good of this country at heart, and I hope also if you will do Mr. Fargo the honor as to go and see him upon the occasion, as you go down you will give me a call, as I think I could give you some satisfaction on this subject. This, sir, from your very Humble Servant,

> Andrew Jackson[40]

It is a remarkable letter. Aside from its grammatical problems—a constant in Jackson's early correspondence—it shows an extremely energetic and aggressive young man, only four months on the frontier, presuming to insinuate himself into the controlling political circle of the western country. No sooner had he arrived in Nashville than he was courting the power brokers in the community and plunging deep into the Spanish intrigue. In fact he became one of the "chief agents in the intrigue."[41] He probably knew Smith at the time he wrote this letter and was now attempting to improve the relationship. He was a shrewd observer of the frontier situation, a man on the make who calculated his actions with concern for future advantage.

"I have the good of this country at heart," he wrote, which may have caused Smith to smile at the pretentiousness of one so young and so new in the country. Still, Jackson did care about the country, and he was actively involved in its troubles with the Indians and the Spanish. From the time he arrived in Tennessee Jackson absorbed powerful sentiments against all barriers to westward expansion and economic prosperity—be they Indian, Spanish, British, or whatever. Eventually he annihilated those barriers. More than any other man, Jackson was responsible for the removal of the Indians to the remote reaches west of the Mississippi River.[42] More than any other man, he kept the British from returning to the Gulf Coast. More than any other man, he expelled the Spanish from their southern stronghold and made possible the transformation of the United States into a continental power.

Writing to General Smith, Jackson not only got the Frenchman's name wrong but somehow mistakenly thought Miró and Fagot were related. As Smith already knew Fagot, Jackson's blunders must have amused him.[43] In any event Fagot subsequently became Smith's agent, was sent to Miró as a representative, and told the Spanish governor that the Cumberland people planned to ask permission from the North Carolina legislature to separate from the state.[44] Whatever happened the settlers seemed determined to detach themselves from their present allegiance.

But westerners had no real desire to become citizens of Spain except as a last resort. In spite of Spain's liberal land policies that encouraged migration, Americans played a dishonest game with the Spaniards, intimating much but delivering little. Their intrigue was a means of using Spain to force immediate objectives. For some the objective was a change in Indian policy or the opening of the Mississippi River; for others it was a scheme to frighten North Carolina into first ratifying the federal Constitution and then ceding the western territory to the United States.[45] And to a large extent the intrigue eventually worked. Miró succeeded in getting the Indians to lessen the intensity of their attacks, the Mississippi was partially opened, and North Carolina both ratified the Constitution and ceded her western lands to the new Union.

Within six months the Congress of the United States organized the North Carolina cession into the Southwest Territory. On May 26, 1790, the country between Kentucky and the present states of Alabama and Mississippi was officially designated the Territory of the United States South of the River Ohio. Since the Northwest Ordinance provided that prior to statehood a territory be governed by appointed officials—a governor, a secretary, and three judges—President George Washington named William Blount of North Carolina as governor, Daniel Smith of the Mero District as secretary, and John McNairy, David Campbell, and Joseph Anderson as the judges.

Blount was an original. An early version of the wheeling and dealing, land speculating, sharp-nosed manipulator, politician, and financier, he knew how to get what he wanted—and usually by the shortest route. He campaigned for the appointment of territorial governor because, he baldly admitted to his brother, it was of "great Importance to our Western Speculations."[46] In another letter he elaborated: "The appointment is truly important to me more so in my opinion than any other in the Gift of the President could have been, the Salary is handsome, and my Western Lands had become so great an object to me that I should go to the Western Country to secure them and perhaps my presence might have enhanced their value. I am sure my present appointment will."[47]

Blount snagged the appointment because he inveigled a number of influential friends, including Hugh Williamson, Timothy Bloodworth, John B. Ashe, Benjamin Hawkins, and Daniel Smith, to petition the President on his behalf. He brought enough pressure by the right people to force the appointment; it was an old and highly effective political technique, one that Jackson quickly learned after he met Blount. The only potential difficulty with the appointment was the fact that the position of territorial governor also included the post of superintendent of Indian Affairs, and that meant supervision of the four Southern tribes: the Cherokees, Creeks, Choctaws, and Chickasaws. This duty, he admitted frankly, would be "laborious and disagreeable."[48] Still there were his land speculations to think about and they more than made up for the trouble of attending to "savages."

To establish the territorial government, Blount received extensive appointive powers that helped him initiate personal rule in the territory. These appointments included justices, sheriffs, constables, clerks, registrars, and militia officers of every rank below general. He boasted, with obvious delight, that no lawyer could plead in the Southwest Territory without a license from him.[49] "The Writing the Commissions for every officer of the Government both Civil and Military," he said, "I find a great Task and that I have to do for every officer even to a Constable receives his Appointment from me."[50] His two private secretaries assisted him in establishing control: Willie Blount (his half brother) and Hugh Lawson White were both young, energetic, loyal, dependable men. Archibald Roane and David Allison, friends of Jackson who may have traveled with him to Tennessee, helped to reinforce the administration's position. Roane became attorney general of the Washington District and Allison served the governor in a semiofficial and semiprivate capacity as his business manager.[51] In addition to his post as secretary, Daniel Smith received appointment as surveyor of the territory. Finally, Blount recommended James Robertson and John Sevier as brigadier generals, and their commissions were duly approved by the federal government in 1791.

The appointments guaranteed Blount absolute control of the Southwest Territory. He was a shrewd politician who knew all the clever little devices for retaining the loyalty and support of his appointees; and he knew particularly how to play upon the vanities of his superiors in the federal government. He called his capital Knoxville after Henry Knox, the secretary of war and his immediate superior in Indian Affairs. Two new counties were named Jefferson, after Thomas Jefferson, secretary of state, and Hamilton, after Alexander Hamilton, secretary of the treasury. There was already a Washington County; presumably the President needed no additional flattery. Blount had the kind of political style that could keep him in office (and in the good graces of important men) for quite some time.

Together with his brothers, Governor Blount had acquired more than a million acres of western land, and much of his policy as chief executive of the Southwest Territory revolved around protecting and advancing his landed investments. This meant getting rid of the Indians —or at least pacifying them. With the help of federal troops, Blount had hoped to inaugurate a policy of suppression, particularly against the four great Southern tribes. But he failed to get the necessary cooperation from the federal government. The Washington administration had its hands full with the Northwest Indians, who inflicted a crushing defeat on General St. Clair in November 1791. Blount was told by Knox to bide his time and pursue a defensive policy against the Southern tribes. The local militia was to be used only to ward off attacks.

The defensive policy Blount was forced to adopt after he assumed his duties as governor, along with the great victory of the Northern tribes over federal troops, encouraged the Southern Indians to renew their raids on American settlements in Tennessee. And the Spanish reversed their policy. Under a new governor at New Orleans, the Baron de Carondelet, who reckoned Miró's efforts at conciliation self-defeating, the Spanish adopted an aggressive Indian policy and prodded the Southern tribes into active warfare with the frontier settlers.[52]

For his part Blount hounded the federal government for greater aid in responding to the renewal of Indian-Spanish warfare. In terms of his own investments, the destruction of the Indian menace was an absolute necessity. In a letter to the secretary of war he declared that "the Creeks, if not the Cherokees must be chastised by the hand of the Government before they will desist from killing and robbing the Frontier Inhabitants of the United States."[53] The government's responsibility was clear, he said. To procrastinate only invited further killing and robbing. In an apparent effort to placate Blount (at least to the extent of lessening his constant nagging) Knox authorized David Allison, "the storekeeper and paymaster," to purchase goods in the amount of $5,784.70 to combat the Indians.[54] This limited aid could not end the war, but it did sting the Indians with a series of raids that achieved a temporary truce.

Blount's absolute control of his administration attracted to his cause all ambitious men within the territory, including Jackson. Without Blount's aid, career advancement in Tennessee was virtually impossible. Jackson had several entrees to the governor, including McNairy, Smith, and Allison, any one of whom may have provided the introduction. No doubt all these men in time affirmed the young lawyer's loyalty and dependability. And Jackson had an excellent record as a successful and hard-driving prosecutor; it behooved the governor to enlist the support of such an obviously talented and rising young lawyer. The two men were introduced in due course, Jackson's measure taken, and on February 15, 1791, the position of attorney general of the Mero District was offered to him and accepted.[55] The duties of this office were not unlike those he had discharged as prosecuting attorney, but Blount had additional responsibilities in mind for Jackson in terms of resolving the Indian problem. He informed General Robertson that he wanted a recent treaty with the Cherokees "preserved inviolate and if this can not be done I beg you to make examples of the first violators of it. It will be the Duty of the Attorney of the District Mr. Jackson to prosecute on Information in all such cases and I have no doubt but that he will readily do it."[56] When Blount heard that a number of white settlers had violated the treaty, he demonstrated what he meant, at the same time indicating further confidence in his newest appointee. "Let the District Attorney Mr. Jackson, be informed," he said; "he will be certain to do his duty, and the offenders will be prosecuted."[57]

As a matter of fact Jackson's reputation as a dependable hardworking, and loyal official was frequently observed and reported.[58] Consequently he received additional appointments over the next few years, all intended to advance his career and reputation. On September 10, 1792, Blount named him judge advocate for the Davidson County cavalry regiment commanded by Lieutenant Colonel Robert Hays. This was Jackson's first military appointment; although it was conferred solely because of his legal talent, it was the beginning of a long association with the Tennessee militia, one that proved highly significant in the success of his later political career.

Blount's pleasure with Jackson's handling of the office of attorney general, especially the energy and zeal with which he performed his tasks, prompted him in October 1792 to suggest a promotion within the military—perhaps the best way of rewarding an aspiring talent on the frontier. "Can't you contrive for Hay to resign," he wrote Robertson, "and I will promote Donelson and appoint Jackson second Major."[59] Implementing the suggestion at the expense of Robert Hays was both unwise and impractical; Blount was advised that the necessary resignation could not be arranged.

But first and foremost Blount was the complete political animal. Jackson's legal ability alone would not move him to acts of recognition and reward. Somewhere along the line he came to regard Jackson as one of his strongest supporters in the Cumberland, someone he could trust and rely on. Sometime around the middle of 1792 his confidence was completely won. And it was mutual, as those things usually are. Said Jackson: "Any Transaction of . . . Governor Blount with Respect to My Business will be perfectly pleasing to me as I know from experience that My Interest will be attended to."[60]

Robertson was another loyal Blount partisan and the major political force in the Cumberland region. He too appreciated Jackson's obvious energy and determination to get ahead, and he unstintingly encouraged the young man. This double-barreled support further advanced Jackson's career. The promotions when they came (regularly, almost every few years) not only documented the confidence of Tennessee's political leaders and his own fierce ambition for recognition but they surely indicated Jackson's success as an able and industrious frontier lawyer.

He was also making money—slowly at first, then more quickly as his reputation spread. Like all westerners he acquired land as rapidly and as avidly as possible. Land was the principal attraction for western settlement and its acquisition the quickest route to financial success and social advance. Land speculation dominated the thoughts of every man who journeyed west seeking a better life. It enriched the shrewd and skillful; it bankrupted many more, sending them to debtor's prison to rot away their lives in disgrace. It was a contagion, the intensity of which lured successive generations across a continent to establish what Thomas Jefferson hoped would be "an empire for liberty." Land fever determined negative American attitudes toward Indians, Spanish, English, and anyone else who hindered the steady availability of this seemingly limitless source of wealth. Though it poisoned and corrupted, it also fashioned a nation of republican institutions and democratic attitudes.

Jackson contracted the fever like everyone else. Alert to any scheme that would augment his income, and aided by association with an ever-increasing number of western power brokers, he engaged in a series of speculative (and mostly successful) land ventures over the next dozen years. In addition, his expanding legal activities frequently brought fees in the form of land; also he was asked to arrange transactions of land for which he received land as a commission.[61]

But land speculation and his law practice were not Jackson's only business interests. Earlier, when the Spanish moderated their Indian policy and liberalized their land policy in order to "draw off the settlers" and "make them desirous of a Spanish alliance," Jackson was one of the first of the Cumberland settlers to be attracted.[62] As early as 1789 he was regularly visiting Spanish-held Natchez, the leading city on the Mississippi after New Orleans and the mecca for American emigration to the Spanish domain. Whether Jackson ever obtained land in this area is difficult to determine, but he did get to know a great many Natchez businessmen and through them began an extensive trading operation.[63] Most of these men were transplanted Americans, successful entrepreneurs among whom were Abner Green and his brother Thomas Marston Green, Stephen Minor, Melling Wooley, George Cochran, Joseph Ballinger, Ralph Humphreys, and John Potter. Between court terms in Tennessee, Jackson frequently dropped down to Natchez where he brought these men such items as cotton, furs, swan skins and feathers for bedding, lime, pork, beef, boats, and slaves.[64] It was later reported that Jackson also engaged in horse trading, horseracing, and breeding in the Natchez area and at one point attempted to establish a tobacco business.[65] Surviving accounts show considerable evidence that enough liquor was transported into the district to enliven significantly the horseracing and betting among these Americans. On occasion the wild scenes of Salisbury may have been reenacted with a vengeance. George Cochran, a former Tennessean and Jackson's agent in the Natchez district, recollected "many agreeable hours" spent with Jackson at "Your friendly retreat at Bayou Pierre" near the Mississippi. And, quite possibly, Cochran was a suitor for Rachel's hand until he lost her to the "more fortunate scenery of the Cumberland," as he gracefully put it.[66]

There is also evidence to suggest that Jackson engaged periodically in slave trading during his early years in Tennessee. The business was extremely lucrative and impossible to avoid in the course of regular trade between two distant points such as Nashville and Natchez. His friends frequently asked him to transport slaves as a courtesy, and Jackson was never one to deny his friends. On one occasion he returned a runaway slave to the Spanish governor of Natchez, Manuel Gayoso de Lemos, for James Robertson.

In terms of slaves, Jackson's own steadily improving financial worth as of 1790 can be estimated by a document in the Jackson papers that lists his human "property." The list, signed and approved by David Allison, involved a division of slaves and indicated those allotted to Jackson.

One Negroe fellow Daniel about 28 years old sawyer		£250.
One Wench Kate	32	150.
One Boy Joe	11	150.
One Boy Bob	9	100.
One Boy Pompey between one and two years		60.[67]

These were not Jackson's only slaves. His surviving records and papers show constant purchases, at least sixteen slaves bought between the years 1790 and 1794.[68] They measured his steady progress toward economic security. For, within two years of his arrival in Nashville, Jackson's legal and business careers were firmly established. He seemed well on his way toward ultimate financial success.

But as his professional status soared, bringing recognition and social distinction within the community, Jackson's personal life became more entangled. Then, in one of the boldest, shrewdest, most passionate moves of his life, he decided to marry Mrs. Rachel Donelson Robards.

CHAPTER 5

Marriage

WHEN, IN RAGE, LEWIS ROBARDS abandoned his wife and stormed back to Kentucky it was "really his determination . . . never to return or live with his wife again, but to desert her forever"—at least that was the official version of Robards's intentions given by the Nashville Central Committee when Jackson ran for the presidency in 1828.[1] Following this desertion Rachel lived with her mother and periodically stayed with her elder sister, Jane, who was married to Robert Hays, the commander of the Davidson County regiment and one of the more substantial citizens of the community by virtue of the large land grant he had received for his services in the revolutionary war.

Thomas Crutcher, who accompanied Robards back to Kentucky, claimed there was a "tender and affectionate" farewell between husband and wife, but that during the homeward journey Robards's mood turned ugly. He became upset over the loss of a riding horse, and when Crutcher suggested that the horse would be found and returned to him "as he moved down," Robards responded in an angry outburst. "He made a very harsh reply," Crutcher reported, "he said he would be damned if ever he would be seen in Cumberland again, with many other quite angry and ilnatured remarks. I observed to him that the friends of Mrs. Roberts [sic] would not like, and perhaps would not consent for her to go back to Kentucky to live; he said he did not care what they liked, or disliked, he should do as he thought proper."[2]

One Jackson biographer is inclined to believe that Robards and Rachel reconciled a second time and that she returned to Kentucky with her husband despite her fear of the consequence. This biographer argues that the quarreling resumed immediately and Rachel was forced to flee her husband again, this time accompanied by Andrew Jackson.[3] If the story is true, it provides damaging evidence that Robards's jealousies were not unfounded and that Rachel and Jackson acted improperly; but it cannot be substantiated. On the contrary, the earliest accounts all agree that once Robards quit Tennessee, the marriage terminated.[4] Rachel never returned to her husband.

The subsequent events were apparently set in motion by Robards himself. In the fall of 1790 a rumor of unknown origin began to spread that Robards intended to return to Nashville and take his wife back to Kentucky—by force if necessary. Rachel, on hearing the rumor, became extremely agitated and since she was convinced "after two fair trials . . . that it would be impossible to live" with her husband, she decided to flee Nashville. "In order to keep out of the way of Captain Robards, as she said he had threatened to *haunt* her," Rachel made plans to escape to Spanish-occupied Natchez on the Mississippi River, where she may have owned property, and where she could find devoted friends and relatives and protection from her husband.[5]

This new development made Jackson very uneasy, according to the account later written by his friend, John Overton. "And this will not appear strange to one as well acquainted with his character as I was," Overton said. "Continually together during our attendance on wilderness courts, whilst other young men were indulging in familiarities with females of relaxed morals, no suspicion of this kind of the worlds censure, ever fell to Jackson's share. In this—in his singularly delicate sense of honor, and in what I thought, his chivalrous conceptions of the female sex, it occurred to me, that he was distinguishable from every other person with whom I was acquainted."[6]

When Jackson learned of Rachel's decision to flee to Natchez he expressed his tremendous sorrow to Overton, claiming he was "the most unhappy of men, in having innocently and unintentionally been the cause of the loss of peace and happiness of Mrs. Robards, whom he believed to be a fine woman."[7] Soon thereafter Jackson announced his decision to accompany Rachel to Natchez! Colonel Robert Stark,[8] "a venerable and highly esteemed old man and friend of Mrs. Robards," had already agreed to escort Rachel to Natchez.[9] But because the route was perilous and liable to Indian attack, Stark prevailed upon Jackson to accompany them and serve as escort. It seems strange that he would invite Jackson, the third party of this marital triangle, when members of the Donelson clan could have obliged. There were certainly brothers and brothers-in-law enough to see to her protection. There were Alexander, the eldest;

Captain John Caffery, married to her eldest sister, Mary; Colonel Thomas Hutchings, married to sister Catherine; Stockley; Colonel Robert Hays, married to sister Jane; John; William; Samuel; Severn; and Leven—almost a platoon. Jackson, by now a suitor, may have explained his intention to marry Rachel once she obtained her freedom—and thereby won their consent. It is hardly likely they would agree to anything that might further humiliate Rachel and embarrass the family; any scheme directed by Jackson that did not include marriage would surely have been vetoed by the brothers.

Jackson's decision to accompany the Stark party to Natchez was absolute folly or absolute calculation. His actions confirmed Robards's worst suspicions and involved him in a sequence of events that could be used as evidence of moral delinquency. Why did he do it? Why risk his own and Rachel's reputation further? It was probably a deliberate and calculated move to give Robards the evidence he needed to commence divorce proceedings—and thereby free Rachel so she could marry Jackson. It was intended to provoke a divorce.

Jackson's critics later pilloried him for falling in love with a married woman and, by his act of rescue, forcing the dissolution of the Robards marriage. The criticism is well taken. But Rachel was a woman in acute distress, and her dreadful situation tugged at his sympathy and gallantry. Most of his life Jackson acted the role of rescuer; in this instance he was especially challenged to do something positive to assist this stricken woman.

If Jackson bears a degree of responsibility for the breakup of a bad marriage, so too does Rachel. She did not fall in love with Jackson *after* her marriage to Robards broke up. Her illicit love affair preceded that collapse. Like Jackson, and despite the provocations of her husband's infidelities with slave women and his insane jealousy, she allowed herself to become emotionally entangled while legally joined to someone else. The difficulties of extricating herself from a marriage in the 1790s were enormous. She knew that. And the impact on her reputation of a divorce in which adultery would be the principal charge was certainly clear to her. But, obviously, she could not help herself. She had been cruelly mistreated. Desperately unhappy, she reached out for comfort and aid from a gallant and chivalrous young man. And he responded. Although her personal conduct was probably "irreproachable"[10]—testimony on that score seems irrefutable—she indulged herself to the point that she compromised her position. She generated enough scandal to provide wicked tongues with a lifetime of vicious talk.

As she grew older, Rachel became extremely pious. It was not the ordinary kind of piety that may result with advancing age, but a rousing, evangelical, near-fanatical piety that permeated her entire life. It is possible that Rachel later suffered great torment and remorse over her youthful and illicit love for Andrew Jackson. It is possible her later life constituted one long act of expiation.

According to the official version of what happened, written by John Overton in 1827 and issued by the Nashville Central Committee, Rachel's decision to flee to Natchez came in January 1791. The dates are important because Overton later offered them as proof that Jackson and Rachel were innocent of the charges of adultery and bigamy brought by Lewis Robards. And Overton's account of the events leading to the marriage of Rachel and Jackson, which follows, remained unchallenged for more than a hundred and fifty years.

According to Overton, it was "in the winter or spring of 1791," almost six months after Rachel heard the rumor of Robards's intentions, that Rachel, Jackson, and Stark and his family floated downriver from Nashville to Natchez.[11] After delivering his charge, Jackson returned to Nashville in time to attend superior court in May 1791.[12] Meanwhile Rachel resided with the families of Colonel Thomas Green and Colonel Bruin in Natchez.

Hardly had Jackson returned to Tennessee than word reached Nashville that Robards had obtained a divorce in Virginia (he was living in a district of Kentucky which was then a part of Virginia) through the good offices of his brother-in-law, Major John Jouett, a member of the Virginia legislature. Another member of that legislature later remembered that a request for divorce was almost unheard of at that time. It was only the second instance of such a request coming to that body.

Actually Robards had no divorce, something Jackson did not comprehend at the time. All Robards had was an enabling act, dated December 20, 1790, permitting him to bring suit against his wife in Supreme Court of the District of Kentucky. The act, introduced by Burwell Ronald on behalf of a nine-man committee (of which Robards's brother-in-law, John Jouett, was a member) and passed by the Virginia General Assembly, specifically declared: "A jury shall be summoned who shall be sworn well and truly to enquire into the allegations contained in the declaration, or to try the issue joined, as the case may be, and shall find a verdict according to the usual mode; and if the jury in the case of issue joined, shall find for the plaintiff, or in case of enquiry into the truth of the allegations contained in the declaration shall find in substance, that the defendant hath deserted the plaintiff, and that she hath lived in adultery with another man since such desertion, the said verdict shall be recorded, and thereupon the marriage between the said *Lewis Roberts* [*sic*] and *Rachel* shall be totally dissolved."[13]

When word of the so-called divorce reached Nashville, according to Overton, Jackson, a lawyer, made no attempt to determine its truth. Instead he hastened back to Natchez as soon as his business permitted —probably in the summer of 1791—and married the woman he had "innocently & unintentionally" caused much "loss of peace & happiness."[14]

Who performed the marriage is uncertain. Overton does not say. And no record of the marriage survives.[15] Overton merely says, "In the Summer of 1791, Genl. Jackson returned to Natchez, & *as I understand,* married Mrs. Robards."[16] Natchez was under Spanish rule in 1791, which meant that all legal marriages had to be performed by the Catholic Church under the supervision of a duly ordained Catholic priest. During the spring and summer of 1791 the spiritual needs of the people in the Natchez area were ministered to by Father Guillermo Savage, an Irish priest who took up his duties in May 1791. It is unlikely that he performed the marriage; he would have recorded it if he had, and no such record exists. Furthermore, Rachel was a married woman (albeit thought to be divorced), and no Catholic priest would solemnize a marital union while the husband of one of the partners still lived.

Both Rachel and Andrew were Protestant. Even so, the Spanish would not have permitted a contractual obligation to take place within their jurisdiction without their knowledge and approval. And such approval, if given, would have been recorded. Thus this "marriage"—if one took place—was doubly illegal; not only was Rachel still married to Robards but the civil authority in Natchez did not give its permission for a marriage service to take place. Jackson's failure to obtain legal sanction from a civil authority was on a par with his failure to investigate the report of Robards's divorce.

Although Natchez was officially Catholic and only Catholic marriages were permitted, Protestant ministers did live in the district and they did on occasion perform marriage ceremonies, for which they frequently got into trouble. But on the whole the Spanish pursued a liberal policy toward non-Catholics as part of their effort to attract Americans to the district. Protestants were neither persecuted nor required to convert to Catholicism; they were not disturbed in the practice of their religion unless they attempted to preach in public. But a marriage performed by a Protestant minister would, in the eyes of the Spanish, be illegal. The situation was regularized in 1792, when a royal decree required that Catholic priests officiate at all baptisms and marriages, including those of Protestants. A Protestant couple, to be legally married in Natchez in the 1790s without the benefit of a Catholic priest, would have had to leave the district and have their marriage solemnized in the United States.[17]

It is possible that a Protestant minister in Natchez did in fact marry Rachel and Andrew. Such a marriage would have been considered perfectly legal in frontier communities where jurisdictions were sometimes so confused that no one could tell where legal authority resided. A theory has been advanced that Rachel and Andrew were married by Colonel Thomas Green, acting as a magistrate of Georgia, at the home of his son, Thomas Marston Green.[18] If such a ceremony was performed, it too was illegal.

The circumstances were these: Georgia claimed the Natchez area in the mid-1780s as within her legal boundaries and attempted to exercise sovereignty over the district by forming it into the county of "Bourbon" and assigning justices of the peace to administer it. Several members of the Green family received appointments in this county, much to the distress of the Spanish. At one point Thomas Green landed in a Spanish jail, was forced to transfer his property to his sons, and was sent into exile. In 1788 Georgia renounced the Bourbon County scheme, thereby terminating the authority of all its appointees. Thomas Green was permitted by the Spanish to return to Natchez in December 1789, provided he renounce all connection with the earlier Georgia scheme and take an oath of loyalty to the Spanish government, following which he was allowed to live with his sons. Thus it is unlikely that Green performed a wedding service. If he did—an action that would put him in great jeopardy in light of his oath and the abandonment of the Bourbon County scheme by Georgia—his action was totally illegal.

To continue Overton's story: The "married" couple probably lived for a short time at Bayou Pierre—possibly on property owned by Rachel[19] —and then returned to Nashville in the fall of 1791 where together they took up a respectable life that won the admiration of their neighbors.

It was not until *two* years after the Natchez "marriage" that they learned the awful truth. There was no divorce, at least not in 1791. It was on September 27, 1793, that Robards finally received a decree of divorce from the Court of Quarter Session of Mercer County at the courthouse of Harrodsburgh. Since Rachel and Andrew had been living together for more than two years, there was no problem in convincing a jury that "Rachel Robards, hath deserted the plaintiff, Lewis Robards, and hath, and doth, Still live in adultery with another man." Accordingly, "it is therefore considered by the Court that the Marriage between the Plaintiff and the Defendant be disolved."[20]

It is difficult to explain why Robards waited so long to exact his revenge. He certainly did not need two years of evidence to prove desertion and adultery. As early as January 9, 1791, just twenty-one days after receiving permission from the Virginia Assembly to institute divorce proceedings in court, Robards wrote in a friendly manner to Rachel's brother-in-law, Robert Hays, indicating that the divorce was under way and that he expected an equitable partition of his property holdings. "I shall depend on you and Mr. Overton," he wrote, "That theire is no advantage taken of me in My Absence at Cumberland you will plase to Right by the first Opportunity if the Estate is devided as I may no how to proseed to get my [due?] if theire is any Opportunity Offers of selling my land you will please to let me no my price is 260 will give long credit For one half I will take Negroes if theay are Young and likely."[21] It would appear that Robards was winding down his Nashville operations in prospect of an imminent divorce. Still he did nothing. He simply waited. Perhaps he hoped for a reconciliation, as unlikely as that was; perhaps he sought to share the estate of Rachel's late father; perhaps it was his way of getting even, of punishing Jackson and Rachel for offending his honor and pride. It is also possible that the wretched man was becoming irrational. A letter written by him a few years later strongly suggests that he was mentally unbalanced.[22]

The shocking news of the delayed divorce reached Jackson in December 1793, while he and Overton were on their way to Jonesborough on law business. Overton was astounded—or so he said. He had been in Kentucky during the summer of 1791 and even stayed at old Mrs. Robards's home, and never once was anything said to indicate that the action of the Virginia legislature was not final. "I need not express to you my surprise," Overton wrote when he learned the truth.[23] Immediately he suggested to Jackson the propriety of obtaining a marriage certificate and going through another wedding ceremony.

Jackson too was "surprised," according to Overton. He could hardly believe his friend. He *was* married. Everyone in the territory knew that; everyone knew that he and Rachel had lived as man and wife for two years. To go through the marriage ceremony again would be tantamount to admitting the charge of adultery. What Jackson did not seem to understand was that the question of adultery had already been determined by a court of law. Even if he and Rachel were morally innocent, they were technically guilty and had been so declared in court.

It took Overton a long time to convince Jackson.[24] Finally, on January 17, 1794, on his return home from Jonesborough, Jackson obtained a license. The following day Rachel and Andrew were married by the justice of the peace of Davidson County, Robert Hays, Rachel's brother-in-law.[25]

Those were the "facts" presented to the American people in 1827 when Jackson ran for the presidency. They constitute a plausible account —if one wants to believe in Jackson's innocence and is prepared to overlook the circumstances that Jackson, a lawyer, did not bother to obtain legal proof of divorce before "marrying" his beloved, that no record of the 1791 "marriage" or who performed it exists, and that it took two years for the couple to learn that no divorce had been granted. While these difficulties place an enormous strain on the credibility of the story, they are not insurmountable, particularly for those predisposed to believe this account.

Far more damaging is the fact that Overton's narration cannot be reconciled with several pieces of evidence that contradict his story in significant ways. The first of these concerns the time of arrival of the Stark party in Natchez. The Spanish kept precise records. Upon entry to Natchez all foreign subjects (and that included Americans) were required to take an oath of loyalty to the Spanish Crown if they wished to remain. According to Spanish records, Stark arrived in Natchez on January 12, 1790—not 1791.[26]

The second piece of evidence is a letter written by George Cochran in Natchez to Jackson, dated November 3, 1790, which he concludes, "My best respects Wait of Mrs. Jackson."[27] Could Jackson have been "married" in the fall of 1790 as this letter suggests? But Robards did not obtain legislative approval to begin divorce proceedings until December 20, 1790. Did Jackson "marry" even before the Virginia legislature acted? If so, it was bigamy on Rachel's part.

A second letter from Cochran to Jackson, dated October 21, 1791, states that Jackson's letter of the previous April 14 was the only communication Cochran had received from him since his "departure from this country." If the marriage occurred in Natchez in the summer of 1791, as Overton contended, Cochran would hardly have made this statement.[28]

Another piece of evidence indicating that Andrew and Rachel "married" a full year earlier than was later claimed, "married" even before Robards received legislative approval to initiate divorce proceedings, is an inventory of the estate of John Donelson, Rachel's father. The July and October 1790 terms of the Davidson County court list Rachel as "Rachel Donelson," but the January 1791 term lists her as "Rachel Jackson."[29] (There is no mistaking the date; it is given twice: January 28, 1791.) Thus, at the approximate time Overton said she fled to Natchez, she was already officially referred to as "Rachel Jackson."

It would appear that Overton's dates are off by one year. Instead of marrying *after* Robards received legislative approval for the divorce proceedings, as alleged in 1827, Andrew and Rachel were "married" months before, earlier than November 3, 1790, when Cochran referred to Rachel as "Mrs. Jackson," and probably sometime in late October 1790. If this is true, they "married" when Rachel was still legally bound to another man—unless, of course, they did not marry at all (which would explain the absence of documentation) and simply lived together as common-law husband and wife. This would not have been unusual on the frontier. Indeed cohabitation often preceded formal marriage in the west because a minister or a justice of the peace was not always available when needed.

Such behavior seems untypical of Jackson, considering his ambition and his desire for the status of gentleman. But it is possible that he was forced to participate in this charade because he loved Rachel and wished to protect her reputation and because it was required of him as a gentleman and a man of honor.

There are several possible explanations of what happened. None of them can be proved absolutely, and all require a stretch of the imagination.

One involves legal guilt on the part of the couple: Jackson fell in love with Rachel—deeply, passionately. He wished to marry her and tried to force Robards to initiate divorce proceedings. This was the reason for the trip to Natchez in the winter of 1789–90. When that tactic failed, Rachel and Andrew took the extreme action of running off and "marrying" (or perhaps living together as common-law husband and wife), believing such action would surely produce the desired effect—which it did. If they "married" sometime around October 1790, as assumed, Robards started legal action almost immediately and had his legislative approval within two months. And, it should be remembered, that Robards, in his complaint, accused his wife of desertion "and that she hath lived in adultery with another man since desertion."[30] Of course, once the couple had begun to live together they were forced to pretend marriage to preserve their respectability in the community no matter what Robards did. When the divorce was finally granted in a court of law on September 27, 1793, Andrew and Rachel married immediately thereafter.

It is also possible that the original "marriage" occurred in July 1790 despite the fact that Rachel was still referred to as "Rachel Donelson" in the October term of the Davidson County court. According to hostile newspapers during the presidential election of 1828, the jury found for Robards in the divorce action on evidence of desertion and adultery committed in July 1790. This date as a possible time of the "marriage" is substantiated somewhat by Jackson's recorded whereabouts throughout the year. He was present in various courts in Tennessee during the January, April, May, October, and November terms in 1790 (and throughout 1791), but he was noticeably—and, for him, most unusually—absent from court during the summer of 1790. Ten cases came to trial in the July 1790 term in connection with which Jackson had earlier pleaded on behalf of the defendants. In the trials of these defendants

Jackson did not appear. For him to fail to follow a client's case through to final disposition was most uncharacteristic. Particularly striking was the large number of such cases at this single term. It would take something extremely important to account for his absence.[31]

"In the summer of 1790," the Cincinnati *Gazette* reported on April 24, 1827, "Gen Jackson prevailed upon the wife of Lewis Roberts of Mercer county, Kentucky, to desert her husband, and live with himself in the character of a wife." Assuming for the moment that this accusation was correct Jackson's action of "marrying" Rachel was bound to provoke scandal—something he dreaded with a passion. But—the argument can be made—he really had no choice. It would have been worse, less honorable, had he done otherwise. His relationship with Mrs. Robards had exceeded the bounds of strict propriety; as a man of honor, he had to protect the woman he loved. As he said many times, he deeply regretted the "loss of peace & happiness" he had "innocently & unintentionally" caused Mrs. Robards. Characteristically, then, Jackson acknowledged the responsibility and made Rachel his wife.

There is yet another possible account of what happened: Jackson escorted the Stark party to Natchez in the winter of 1789–90, deposited Rachel, and returned to Nashville. Perhaps a year later, when the notice of the December 20, 1790, action by the Virginia legislature reached Tennessee, Jackson immediately dashed down to Natchez and married Rachel in time for the January term of the Davidson County court to list Rachel as Mrs. Jackson on January 28, 1791. The problem with this theory —apart from the Cochran letter of November 3, 1790—is that a great deal of ground must be traversed in a comparatively short period of time. Between December 20, 1790, and January 28, 1791, word of the action by the Virginia legislature must travel from Richmond to Nashville, Jackson must get to Natchez and marry Rachel and yet appear at least twelve times in the January sessions of various county courts in Tennessee. That would be quite an accomplishment. Besides, it requires belief that word of Virginia's legislative action could whip across the country in a matter of weeks but that an explanation of its true meaning took two years.

One thing is certain. Whatever Rachel and Andrew did, and whenever they did it, their actions did not outrage the community. This in itself is an important consideration in determining what happened. Community acceptance of their behavior is proven in the fact that within the next few years the people of the state conferred a number of honors on Jackson that they would never have given had they believed him guilty of acting improperly. As William B. Lewis, Jackson's neighbor, later wrote, "I would ask how it is possible that any man could have been held in such high estimation by a whole community if he had acted as has been alledged? Could any man, so destitute of moral virtue, and even setting at defiance the common dreams of life, no matter what his talents, and acquirements might be, maintain so high a standing? The thing is impossible and the mere supposition of its possibility is a vile slander upon the whole population of this State." In another letter Lewis wrote, "The Genl and Mrs. Jackson both perhaps acted imprudently but no one believed they acted criminally—the whole course of their lives contradicts such an idea."[32]

Because they were in love and trapped in an impossible situation, Andrew and Rachel handled the problem as best they could. And they handled it badly from start to finish—even Lewis admitted that. For the very reason that they were not criminals they were required to cover up the questionable start of their marriage in order to live a respectable life together. When Jackson ran for the presidency it was imperative that they move the date of the first "marriage" forward a year (although it is entirely possible that after thirty-seven years—from 1790 to 1827—they honestly confused the dates).

Whatever the circumstances of this marriage, the union of these two remarkable people sobered their lives. The wildness in each dissipated. Jackson's ferocious temper was considerably subdued; he became more tender and considerate of Rachel over the years, perhaps in part because of the realization that he had been the cause of her anguish and humiliation. If possible he became more chivalric. She in turn became extremely pious; religion came to be a near obsession with her. But the bitterness and the quarrels that had disfigured her marriage to Robards were absent from her marriage to Jackson. The love Rachel and Andrew bore each other matured over the years, tested by his long absences and strengthened no doubt by the villainy of those who pricked them with vicious taunts about the origins of their marriage. Throughout their life together no one ever heard them address each other in a disrespectful, irritated, or angry fashion.

They were formal with each other, as was the custom in those days. He called her "Mrs. Jackson" or "wife," never Rachel. His letters to her (the few that survive[33]) frequently began *"My Love."* Her letters to him sometimes began *"My Dearest Life."* He remained "Mr. Jackson" to her always, not "General" much less "Andrew." And nobody called him "Andy." That affectionate nickname came after he was dead.

When Andrew and Rachel returned to Tennessee after their "marriage" in Natchez, they established their home on a small plantation called Poplar Grove, located on a hairpin turn of the Cumberland River, with the house nestled at the center of the turn. As Jackson's law practice increased, payment coming frequently in the form of land, he gradually laid the foundations of a large estate. He acquired a lovely plantation, Hunter's Hill, about thirteen miles from Nashville and near the home of his brother-in-law, John Donelson.[34] The extent of Jackson's landholdings increased dramatically during the next ten years, although much of it involved speculation in which he hoped to realize a sizable profit.

The marriage automatically promoted Jackson's social standing despite the divorce and the charge of adultery. He was now linked to the Donelsons, and perhaps, after the Robertsons, no family held higher distinction in western Tennessee. Shortly after his announced marriage to Rachel, Jackson was elected a trustee of the Davidson Academy. Trustees were selected to represent the "first" men and clergymen of Nashville, and Jackson took the appointment seriously, playing a leading part in the affairs of the institution and serving until 1805. The Academy later became Nashville University.

Little evidence survives of Jackson's experiences with the Academy except for the usual stories that are more concerned with his reputation for violence and ignorance. For example, at one meeting of the board of trustees, General Daniel Smith commented on the fact that the ferry across the Cumberland River had been leased for the sum of $100 per annum. "Why, this is enough to pay the ferriage of all the trustees over the river Styx," Smith said with a chuckle.

"Sticks?" Jackson cried. "I want but *one* stick to make *my* way."[35]

The anecdote is probably apocryphal; it is repeated here only as an example of the surviving fictions that render Jackson a stereotyped, carboard figure and, as a consequence, mask the complexities and contradictions fused within his character. To depict him simply as all sound and fury, willful and ignorant, smashing his way to victory in the cause of country and female virtue is a distortion of the character of a complex man who deserves better.

His marriage not only added to his social stature—something Jackson surely understood and anticipated—but provided a partner who proved indispensable in the management of his growing estate. Jackson was away on business much of the time, even before the start of his military and political careers, so Rachel was obliged to run the plantation —which, incidentally, Jackson always called his "farm." He later acknowledged that without her their estate would have gone to ruin. Some historians are of the opinion that the ultimate success of the Jackson plantation was in large measure due to Rachel's extraordinary administrative talents.[36]

Jackson's philosophy of marriage was revealed partially in a letter he wrote to his ward, Andrew J. Hutchins, many years later. He said that a man must have more than romance on his mind when he seeks a wife.

"One word to you as to matrimoney," he wrote, "—seek a wife, one who will aid you in your exertions in making a competency and will take care of it when made, for you will find it easier to spend two thousand dollars than to make five hundred. Look at the economy of the mother and if you find it in her you will find it in the daughter. recollect the industry of your dear aunt [Rachel], and with what economy she watched over what I made, and how we waded thro the vast expence of the mass of company we had. nothing but her care and industry, with good economy could have saved me from ruin. if she had been extravagant the property would have vanished and poverty and want would have been our doom. Think of this before you attempt to select a wife."[37] Apparently Andrew Jackson had thought about it many times during his life. He owed a great deal to Rachel—more than he could ever possibly acknowledge.

CHAPTER 6

Creating a New State

THE INDIAN PROBLEM PERSISTED. Despite treaties, despite punitive actions taken by settlers, despite savage barbarities inflicted on both white and red men, the killing and raiding and terrorizing continued. And the federal government did nothing—or next to nothing. American lives were constantly being sacrificed, argued the settlers, to a policy of indifference. Governor Blount was told most emphatically that Tennesseans were furious with this policy and wanted something done about it.[1]

The Cumberland sites were especially hard hit. The Chickamauga Indians, a branch of the Cherokees living in the five lower towns near Chattanooga, joined the Creeks in orchestrated raids up and down the Cumberland River, burning and pillaging in a desperate, futile effort to drive the intruders from their land. But the settlers dug in their heels and snarled their defiance at the outraged "savages," all the while promising terrible retribution if they were not permitted unlimited access to the vast wilderness.

The anger and resentment, the threats and solemn oaths of revenge, the craving desire for Indian removal, and the bitterness toward a disinterested federal government all infected Andrew Jackson, as they probably did most young men who had come to the frontier in search of a better life. Some of his earliest letters seethe with a passion to punish the Indians. The red men murder; they deceive and cheat; they dishonor their pledges.

70

The Late Express that proclaimed peace to our Western Country; attended with the late Depredations and Murders Committed by the Indians on our frontier has occasioned a Great Clamour amonghst the people of this District and it is Two Much to be dreaded that they Indians has Made use of this Finesse to Lull the people to sleep that they might save their Towns and open a more East Road to Commit Murder with impunity; this is proved by their late conduct, for since that Express, not Less than Twelve Men have been killed and wounded in this District: one Question I would beg leave to ask why do we now attempt to hold a Treaty with them; they have attended to the Last Treaty; I answer in the Negative then why do we attempt to Treat with Savage Tribe that will neither adhere to Treaties, nor the law of Nations.[2]

Indians cannot be reasoned with, argued Jackson. They must be told. They cannot discipline their behavior in accordance with their solemn oaths. Their promises are deceptions to trick the unwary settler into relaxing his guard—and facilitating his execution. Indians are children—cruel and vicious children—who need the stern punishment of a wrathful parent to force their compliance with civilized conduct. Treaties with them are useless; all they understand is the harsh command of the gun and the stick.

Over the next few years Jackson emerged as a fire-breathing frontiersman obsessed with the Indian presence and the need to obliterate it and contemptuous of Congress for failing to help. Jackson railed against the Indians and against Congress. Because of them, innocent settlers were murdered, treaties violated, the frontier splashed with blood. "I fear that their Peace Talks are only Delusions," he wrote in 1794, "and in order to put us off our Guard; why Treat with them does not Experience teach us that Treaties answer No other Purpose than opening an Easy door for the Indians to pass through to Butcher our Citizens." And Congress was no better. "What Motives Congress are governed by with Respect to their pacific Disposition towards Indians I know not; some say humanity dictates it; but Certainly she ought to Extend an Equal share of humanity to her own Citizens; in doing this Congress would act Justly and Punish the Barbarians for Murdering her innocent Citizens." The entire Indian nation "ought to be Scurged for the infringement of the Treaty," Jackson snorted, especially for failing to surrender the murderers of American settlers. "I dread the Consequence of the Ensuing Summer. the Indians appear Verry Troublesome the frontier Discouraged and breaking and numbers leaving the Territory and moving to Kentucky, this Country is Declining fast, and unless Congress lends us a more ample protection this Country will have at length to break or seek a protection from some other Source than the present."[3]

Did he mean the Spanish? Whatever he meant, he talked like many other Tennesseans who were not above conspiracy or threats to get what they wanted. Their justification was their concern that "this Country will have at length to break."[4]

Finally, in 1794, a secret arrangement was worked out. In direct defiance of federal orders (the government had forbidden all but defensive operations) a detachment of troops under General Robertson attacked the Chickamauga towns. Known as the Nickajack Expedition, the raid was highly successful. Many Indian villages were burned to the ground, and the Cumberland settlers gained a period of relief. But Governor Blount had given Robertson explicit orders—in seeming compliance with federal directives—to employ troops for defensive tactics only. Undoubtedly Blount knew the real plan and probably authorized it. His orders were conveyed with a wink of the eye.

Robertson was ultimately forced to resign his military commission on account of the raid, so flagrant was its violation of the government directive. "If I have erred I shall ever regret it," Robertson told Blount; "to be a good citizen, obedient to the Law is my greatest pride, and to execute the duties of the Commission with which the President has been pleased to honor me, in such manner as to meet his approbation & that of my Superiors in rank has ever been my most fervent wish."[5] This frontier highhandedness, combined with sentiments of citizenship and obedience to the law, typified western behavior with regard to the Indians and the Spanish. It was something Andrew Jackson absorbed almost upon arrival in Nashville.

In any event, the federal government seemed disinclined to discipline its insubordinate generals in the performance of their duties; when no successor was named to replace him, Robertson simply continued to perform his military duties as though nothing had happened. As a result the central government inadvertently encouraged frontiersmen to scorn federal orders whenever they felt so inclined.

Blount now found himself in a dilemma: On the one hand he faced continued restrictions by the federal government in dealing with the Indians and on the other the mounting demands from the settlers to take vigorous action.[6] Continuation of this situation could only weaken his position—either with the government, or the people, and most probably both. Then, in a flash of inspiration he discovered a route of escape that was bound to strengthen his own position in Tennessee. In a bold and electrifying action he proposed the admission of the territory as a new state of the Union. Once a full-fledged state, Tennessee could manage the Indian problem any way it saw fit.

For Blount this was a turnabout; his entire career in Tennessee had been dedicated to blocking representative government within the territory. From the moment he became governor he had kept administrative control tightly within his grasp. Even when the earliest census showed that the territory was filling up with settlers and that some form of representative government short of statehood could be inaugurated, Blount dragged his feet. Representative government would almost surely undermine his control. But his footdragging stirred public resentment; the people wanted representation, and Blount was forced to give way. Reluctantly, in December 1793, he ordered the election of thirteen men to constitute a House of Representatives. This body met at Knoxville and nominated ten men from whom President Washington chose five to serve as the upper house of the legislature. The five were Stockley Donelson (Jackson's brother-in-law), John Sevier, James Winchester, Griffith Rutherford, and Parmenas Taylor, most of whom were Blount's associates in land speculation.[7] Rutherford was chosen presiding officer and Dr. James White was dispatched to Congress as territorial delegate.

But territorial status was a far cry from statehood and all that it implied. When Blount finally determined that admission into the Union would not only solve the Indian problem and release him from his dilemma but also advance his own land speculation (never far from his mind), he joined the clamor for statehood. Moreover, he knew that the popular patriot John Sevier was ambitious for higher office and could cause trouble if he were not advanced. Statehood would solve this problem and permit a satisfactory arrangement: Blount could go to the United States Senate (a strong position from which to maneuver his financial empire) and Sevier could take the governorship.[8]

In a series of carefully thought out moves Blount demonstrated his skill as a political operator. He laid the groundwork by informing his henchmen throughout the territory of his intent. This was done via the Knoxville *Gazette,* which served as his personal organ, on August 25, 1794. "Would it not be wise in the approaching General Assembly," the newspaper asked, "to take measures that this territory may, as speedily as possible, become a member state of the federal union?" The signal escaped no one. Next, Blount contacted his many lieutenants, informing them of his intentions and telling each what they most wanted to hear. Blount wrote to Robertson: "The Cherokees I believe sincerely wish peace but the Creeks must be humbled before you can enjoy peace and I fear that wished for period will never arrive until this Territory becomes a State and is represented in Congress for this and other Reasons I am clearly determined that it is the true interest of this territory to become a state as early as possible and I hope that will be the opinion of the majority of the people."[9] There was no better way of securing the support of the Cumberland settlers for statehood than promising a final solution to the Indian problem. Then, in a final act, Blount nudged the General Assembly into passing a joint resolution requesting him to order a census to determine popular sentiment for applying for admission to the Union.

Having arranged to be prompted to action by the legislature, Blount speedily complied. Besides, he believed he was the only person who could initiate the process of transformation; certainly the United States Congress could not be relied upon. "I am disgusted of the rascally Neglect of Congress," he said.[10]

Straight off, Blount contacted James White, the territorial delegate to Congress, to inquire as to the fastest way of arranging Tennessee's acceptance as a state. There were few precedents to follow; no territory had yet become a state. But the Northwest Ordinance (adopted under the Articles of Confederation in 1787) described a procedure, and White relayed this to Blount. The first step was the application for statehood on the part of the territory plus the submission of a written constitution prepared by a convention elected for that purpose. Blount reckoned in addition that a glowing report of the territory's financial health, prepared by a committee of the legislature, would favorably influence popular opinion on the question of statehood. (When this report was published —showing the treasury in such good condition that a tax reduction could be recommended at the following session—it convinced the public to favor the change of government from territory to state.[11])

Moving with impressive speed—the territorial legislature only met for thirteen days—Blount guided the General Assembly into planning a census, calling for a plebiscite on the question of statehood, arranging a constitutional convention, and preparing a financial report to the people that would prove fiscal solvency. It was a stupendous performance. For Blount was acting pretty much without guidelines, having only what the Northwest Ordinance decreed and what friends in Congress advised.

The Ordinance stated one qualification precisely: There had to be 60,000 people in the territory before it could apply for admission to the Union. So the census was conducted with extreme care, and Blount officially reported the results in November 1795. The territory had an aggregate population of 77,263, of which 65,776 were free white males and females, 10,613 were slaves, and 973 were free Negroes. The eight eastern counties of the territory had a population of 65,338; the three western counties totaled 11,924. Davidson County tallied 728 free white males over sixteen years of age, 695 free white males under sixteen, 1,192 free white females, 6 free Negroes, and 992 slaves—for a total of 3,613 persons.[12]

In the plebiscite for statehood, 6,504 voted for statehood and 2,562 against, a ratio of 13 to 5 in favor.[13] Davidson County voted overwhelmingly against statehood, 96 to 517. The domination of the eastern counties probably explains the lopsided vote. Delay in the statehood process could conceivably mean the eventual admission of the western counties as still another state of the Union.[14]

It can be presumed that Andrew Jackson was one of the 96 who favored statehood, responding to the advice and recommendation of his mentor, William Blount. His social, professional, and political situation singled him out as one of the western country's most promising young men among those who favored statehood. Some evidence of this can be seen in a letter Jackson received from Joseph Anderson. "By the enumeration it appears," Anderson wrote, "that there is in the Territory, 77,508 Souls, by which it [would be] entitled, to two Representatives in Congress. My Choice (as well as a number of others) [for one of these posts] is yourself."[15]

Blount immediately called for the election of delegates to the constitutional convention, to meet in Knoxville on January 11, 1796. Each county would elect five delegates. He also pulled political strings again to insure a pro-statehood delegation to the convention. A flurry of letters to his friends across the territory announced his intent. In one letter he urged James Robertson to stand for election. "You *must be* a member of the convention," he pleaded. "Take care of your popularity as will be necessary to punish your & my Enemies upon the change of Things."[16] He then asked Robertson to use his influence to help General Daniel Smith win election in Sumner County. It is possible he also requested that Jackson be named a delegate, but whether he did or not and whether he aided Jackson's candidacy in any way cannot be demonstrated by direct evidence.[17]

The election was held on December 18 and 19, 1795, and Blount's stringpulling paid off. A totally pro-statehood assemblage of delegates won popular support, and enough of Blount's close friends were included to steamroller him by a unanimous vote into the chair of the convention when it convened. Blount seemed utterly invincible.

The five members of the convention designated by Davidson County were John McNairy, James Robertson, Thomas Hardeman, Joel Lewis, and Andrew Jackson. Other distinguished delegates included Jackson's friends, Joseph Anderson and Archibald Roane from Jefferson County; Dr. James White, the territorial delegate to Congress; John Adair, George Rutledge, John Tipton, and General Daniel Smith from Sumner County; and the future governors and congressmen W. C. C. Claiborne, Joseph McMinn, and John Rhea. Rhea, who was later to play a small but significant role in Jackson's life, was named doorkeeper of the convention.

The delegates met in a small building in Knoxville that afterward served as a schoolhouse. James White coordinated the local arrangements and was later reimbursed $10.00 for seats, $2.62 for an oilcloth to cover the president's table, and $22.50 for candles, firewood, and stands. The legislature had allowed each member $2.50 per diem expenses, which the delegates voted to reduce to $1.50. The difference, they agreed, should be given to the secretary, the printer, and the reading and engrossing clerk, who had not been provided for by the tightfisted legislature.

As soon as the convention was organized, the delegates voted to appoint two members from each county to draft a preliminary constitution, each county naming its own members. Most of the delegations chose their brightest, ablest, most "learned" colleagues. Davidson County members chose Judge McNairy and Andrew Jackson. The drafting committee was also asked to prepare a bill of rights.

Unfortunately, none of the convention debates were recorded, not even in the official *Journal* of the proceedings.[18] It is therefore impossible to follow the constitution-making process in the way that one can with the federal Constitution through the notes kept by James Madison and others. The entire session of the convention lasted twenty-seven days. The deliberations were "said to have been marked by great moderation and unusual harmony . . . with singular courtesy, good feeling and liberality."[19] The speeches were probably few and brief, as one might expect in a frontier community.

Although the Blount forces controlled the proceedings to a large extent, an opposition of sorts developed within the convention that advocated the creation of a unicameral or single-house legislature. The arguments that were advanced remain unknown; however, a motion to establish a House of Representatives and a Senate eventually passed. This motion was seconded by Andrew Jackson, obviously a staunch supporter of the Blount faction.

Jackson appears to have taken an active though not an important part in the convention proceedings. He was vocal enough to be noticed favorably by the friends of Blount. There was a later tradition—totally wrong in fact—to the effect that Jackson suggested the name of the state, Tennessee, which was derived from Tinnase or Tenase, the name of a Cherokee chief. But the name was already in general use at the time of the convention as a result of General Daniel Smith's *Short Description of Tennessee Government,* published in 1793 and reissued two years later. The delegates liked the name because it had a smoothness and an attractiveness that captured the beauty and strength of their land. And it sounded

American!—not at all like Carolina, Virginia, and Georgia, all of which were English in origin and sounded like it.

When the original version of the constitution was submitted to the other delegates by the drafting committee it was proposed from the floor that a "profession of faith" be required of all officeholders—an affirmation that they believe in God, a future life, and the divine authority of the scriptures. This was a typically Presbyterian profession of faith that Jackson might be expected to support; in fact, he opposed it, played a prominent role in fighting it, and succeeded in winning the deletion of its final section.

The original draft also excluded clergymen from civil or military office or position of trust within the state. Jackson disapproved such a far-reaching act of proscription and seconded a motion to limit the ban to the legislature, and this carried. Jackson also supported a property qualification of 200 acres and a three-year state residency requirement to hold a seat in the General Assembly and a one-year county residency to represent a county. In addition, he won the right of judges of inferior courts to issue writs of certiorari to bring evidence into their own court.

Like many western frontiersmen, Jackson had ideas about government that varied according to the issue. He would be very conservative with respect to property rights and slavery and he would resent (if not resist) any interference by government in these matters. On the question of Indians, however, he would take the opposite view, demanding full government participation (if not leadership) in eliminating the Indian presence.

In the matter of suffrage, Jackson was consistently democratic all his life—as were many westerners. He advocated simple residency for all freemen as the sole condition for the franchise. If men were to be bound by laws and subject to punishment under them, he later said, then they "ought to be entitled to a voice in making them." For officeholders, however, he supported a property qualification.[20]

The final document approved by the convention was a workable, democratic instrument. The preamble stated a desire to become a free and independent state and hinted that if Congress refused admission, Tennessee would attempt to exist as an independent commonwealth. As for suffrage, any white man could vote after six months' residence in the state, while a freeholder could vote as soon as he entered a county. In effect the delegates adopted universal manhood suffrage that included free Negroes. Those who owned 200 acres of land could be elected to the legislature but only those who possessed 500 acres could serve as governor.[21]

Legislative power was vested in a General Assembly consisting of a

House and a Senate; this power was extensive and unhampered by gubernatorial veto. The legislature had the right of appointment for all offices except those otherwise designated by the state constitution. Since Blount was headed for the United States Senate—or thought so—and was turning over the office of governor to John Sevier, these provisions did not particularly disturb him; in fact he may have devised them. The provisions represented the general attitude among Americans at the end of the eighteenth century, not just the people of Tennessee, though it was particularly strong among those living on the frontier. Americans feared despotism, especially within the executive branch, and wished to see most power lodged with the legislature. Representative government meant legislative government; executive government meant monarchical government. The United States Constitution, as originally framed, reflected this commitment to legislative government. Ironically, it was President Andrew Jackson, the man from the frontier, who transformed the federal system and began the process of creating a strong executive government.

In Tennessee the original state constitution lodged executive power in the governor, who was elected by the people for a two-year term but could not serve more than three consecutive terms. He was designated commander-in-chief of the militia but could appoint only the adjutant general (though he was allowed to fill vacancies). As no provision was made for a lieutenant governor, the successor to the governorship was the speaker of the Senate.

The judiciary was also appointed by the legislature and served during good behavior. Justices of the peace were in charge of the county governments and constituted the county courts. These justices in turn appointed sheriffs and other county officers.

A Bill of Rights proclaimed that "all power" resided in the people, reaffirming the basic philosophy of the American Revolution. Religious freedom, trial by jury, and freedom of speech, press, and assembly were guaranteed. As part of the Bill of Rights, Blount cleverly had inserted a statement that an equal participation of the free navigation of the Mississippi is "one of the inherent rights of the citizens of this State; it cannot, therefore, be conceded to any prince, potentate, power, person or persons whatever."[22] Let Spain beware!

The Bill of Rights also stated that the people who had pioneered this country and had spread themselves like a barrier between the "savage hostiles" and the older settlements—to be precise, those residing south of the French Broad and Holston rivers and between the Tennessee and Big Pigeon rivers—were entitled to the right of preemption and occupancy. Because these settlers had lived in the region without benefit of land and exposed to pillage, starvation, and massacre, it was felt that preemption was richly deserved.

Their work done—work that would last until 1834 without significant amendment—the convention adjourned on February 6, 1796. Jackson received $53.16 in salary and expenses for his efforts. His modest but respectable role in the convention unquestionably helped his reputation and advanced his image as a leading figure of the western community. He certainly improved his standing within the Blount clique; they knew he could be relied upon as a valued lieutenant on the Cumberland. Several times during the convention proceedings Jackson led or participated in a fight for something Blount and his friends advocated. All of which indicated that he was developing steadily as a credible politician and one of the more important men in western Tennessee.

Many years later Jackson's political skills caught the attention of shrewd observers who asked where he had learned them. Although no satisfactory answer could be given at the time, his education in the art of politics may have begun as he watched and studied the activities of that remarkable Tennessean, William Blount. Some of Blount's actions were highhanded, and devious. But all in all he was an effective operator—not a bad example for someone who wanted to learn the political trade.

One reason Blount appreciated Jackson was that the young man had strong western views, just the sort of views that the Cumberland settlers liked to hear. On the questions of the Indians, the Spanish, and the English, for example, Jackson regularly thundered imprecations for their assorted criminalities. He had a reputation as a forceful, vigorous spokesman. "You have loud speach," one man told him bluntly.[23] They especially liked it when he lambasted Congress. Thus, when Jackson heard of the treaty signed by John Jay with Great Britain opening West Indian ports to American shipping (provided certain severe restrictions were enforced), he erupted in a torrent of passionate, almost incomprehensible language to Nathaniel Macon, the able conservative congressman from North Carolina.

> What an alarming Situation; has the late Negciation of Mr. Jay with Lord Greenvill, and that Negociation (for a Treaty of Commerce it cannot be properly Called, as it wants reciprocity) being ratified by the Two third of the senate & president has plunged our Country in; will it End in a Civil warr; or will our Country be relieved from its present ignominy by they firmness of our representatives in Congress (by impeachments for the Daring infringements of our Constitutional rights) have the insulting Cringing and ignominious Child of aristocratic Secracy removed Erased and obliterated from the archives of the Grand republick of the united States.

Here is the wild, threatening, supernationalist Jackson slamming around the frontier in hot temper, glibly invoking the menace of civil war, shouting impeachment, posturing defiantly. Sensitive to the point of violence when it came to what he interpreted as the rights and dignity of the "Grand republick," Jackson fearlessly (and sometimes recklessly) demanded appropriate action, however extreme, to assert national pride. As a vocal and active force on the frontier, poised close to the "hated Spanish Dons" and their allies the "savage hostiles," he could become an exceedingly dangerous man.

The Jay treaty was unconstitutional, he protested. Unconstitutional because the President must have the advice and consent of the Senate, which he did not get "previous to the Formation of the Treaty." It was also "inconsistent with the Law of Nations," he argued in his best legal manner. "Vatel B2, P. 242 S325 says that the rights of Nation are benefits, of which the sovereign is only the administrator, and he ought to Dispose of them no further than he has reason to presume that the Nation itself would dispose of them therefore the president (from the remonstrance from all parts of the Union) had reason to presume that the Nation of america would not have ratified the Treaty, notwithstand[ing] the 20 aristocratic neebobs of the Senate had Consented to it."[24]

Jackson's constitutional argument was as shaky as his knowledge of the law of nations. But there was much in this long, angry, inchoate, confused, wrongheaded letter that bespoke the essential character and ideology of Andrew Jackson. This outburst of a western lawyer and politician, contemptuous of the Congress for failing to protect the dignity and honor of the country, sneering at the aristocratic "neebobs" of the Senate, who were, of course, the real culprits, basically argued a narrow interpretation of the federal Constitution. Frontiersmen of the southwest naturally tended toward a strong states' rights philosophy as a result of their being left to their own devices when it came to safeguarding their economic and political interests. Although it may seem trivial it is significant that Jackson always wrote "states" with a capital S but invariably wrote "united" (referring to the United States) with a lowercase u. He also tended to write the word "union" with a small u. Too much can be made of this, of course, in view of his haphazard spelling and punctuation. Still it does provide a small clue to his thinking. For, Jackson, as for many others on the frontier, the state was the important and immediate thing. The federal government in Philadelphia was a remote, impersonal operation that not only failed to assist the beleaguered westerners in coping with the Indian problem but frequently disgraced itself abroad by consenting to treaties that negated American commercial rights or land claims, thereby humiliating a proud and free people.

Thus, Jackson understood the necessity of statehood for Tennessee in terms of community self-interest. Perhaps a separate state encompassing the three western counties would be preferable in providing adequately for frontier needs. But that was impractical; it meant delay for a period of years until the present population of 12,000 could be swelled to the necessary 60,000. The best recourse for the western counties, as Jackson probably recognized, was to hold with the eastern counties and win immediate admission into the Union. To what extent Jackson actively participated in generating support for the new constitution and in providing for its implementation after he returned home from the convention in Knoxville is not clear.[25] What is known is the haste with which the constitution was put into operation. Without approval from Congress— or from anyone else—Tennessee immediately commenced to function as a state. March 28, 1796, was fixed as the day for the territorial government to go out of business. John Sevier, the popular Indian fighter and revolutionary war hero, was elected governor. The General Assembly was elected and the members began their first session toward the end of March. As one of its first acts, the legislature provided for the election of two members to represent the state in the federal House of Representatives and then proceeded to name William Blount of Knox County and William Cocke of Hawkins County to the United States Senate. It was all arbitrary (and illegal) yet it said something about western temper and style. Much of early United States history starting with the Revolution lacked legal authority; besides, the admission of a new state fashioned from the national domain was still a novelty. Who understood how such things worked? Who could provide counsel? Tennessee marched forward, oblivious of all but the need for immediate recognition as a full-fledged state.

Then came the jolt. Congress was not about to rubberstamp the acts of a group of hasty westerners. To allow people living in a territory to simply set aside the government established over them by Congress and proceed to initiate state machinery without a by-your-leave was totally unacceptable. So when Blount and Cocke arrived in Philadelphia prepared to take up their duties in the Senate, they were unceremoniously denied their seats. While the matter remained under debate, they were told to cool their heels somewhere else.[26]

The problem was complicated further by the fact that 1796 was a presidential election year. George Washington had had enough after eight years in office; the verbal abuse he had suffered over the Jay treaty was more than he chose to endure. The Federalist party put forward John Adams for the presidency and the Republican party nominated Thomas Jefferson. Since the Republicans were popular along the frontier because of their strong states' rights position and their commitment to the needs of the farmer, the Federalists recognized that Tennessee's admission to the Union would automatically increase Jefferson's electoral count. There was also sectional rivalry in the presidential contest. Adams came from New England, Jefferson from the South, and Tennessee, a southern as well as western state, would upset the balance.

Within Congress there were further objections to Tennessee's statehood. It was argued that the initiative in creating a new state must come from Congress, that the census decreed by the territorial legislature was both improper and inaccurate, and that the constitution was poorly drawn and in several particulars conflicted with the United States Constitution.[27]

In rebuttal, the friends of Tennessee in Congress insisted that the territorial government, as the creature of the national government, had indeed the authority to conduct the census and to call for a convention; that the people wanted statehood and were entitled to have their wishes regularized as a matter of right; and that Congress must be liberal in its policy toward statehood by encouraging new admissions, not thwarting them.

On April 12, 1796, a select committee of the House of Representatives reported a bill favorable to admission. Full-scale debate commenced May 5. Nathaniel Macon and Thomas Blount of North Carolina, along with Albert Gallatin of Pennsylvania (one of Jefferson's strongest and most valued supporters in the House), argued long and hard in favor of the bill. Because Republicans held a majority in the House the friends of Tennessee squeezed through a victory by a vote of 43 to 30. All but three Federalists opposed the bill, and only one representative living south of the Potomac said no to admission.[28]

In the Senate the bill received rougher treatment. There a committee chaired by Rufus King of New York reported unfavorably on the bill although it conceded that the territory might be admitted at some future time provided a more satisfactory census was taken under congressional authority.

The ploy was obvious. Delay would postpone admission until after the presidential election and Jefferson would be denied additional electoral votes. The House refused to accept the Senate proposal and offered as a compromise the immediate admission of Tennessee with representation in the House reduced to one (instead of two) until the federal census (required every ten years under the Constitution) was completed in 1800. This compromise was meant to appease the critics of the census just completed in Tennessee; moreover, the reduction in representation reduced Tennessee's presidential electoral votes from four to three because the number of electoral votes is determined by the number of a state's senators and representatives. After some haggling the compromise was accepted by both houses of Congress. On June 1, 1796, President Washington signed the measure making Tennessee the sixteenth state to be admitted to the Union.

The Tennessee legislature promptly reelected Blount and Cocke to the Senate, annulled the election of its four electors and replaced them with three (who of course voted for Thomas Jefferson and Aaron Burr), and arranged for the popular election of a single member of the House of Representatives. In an angry letter to the legislature Senator Cocke expressed the "deepest concern to see our dearest rights invaded by the supreme legislature of the nation. We are by them made subject to the payment of taxes, while we have been unjustly deprived of representation."[29] According to many Tennesseans, it was the same old story: western rights disdained by a feckless Congress. The politically adroit Senator Blount offered a shrewder appraisal. In a letter which both he and Cocke signed and sent to Sevier he wrote: "It is generally believed that the State of Tennessee would have experienced no difficulty . . . if it had not been understood . . . that the State would throw its weight into the Southern Scale against Mr. Adams whom it seems the northern people mean to run at the approaching Election."[30] Adams was elected President by a majority of three votes. Jefferson, who had the next highest number of votes, became Vice President.

The opposition of the Federalist party in Congress to statehood finished off whatever trace of that party still lingered in the state of Tennessee. Blount himself had begun as a Federalist in order to maintain friendly relations with the Washington administration and keep his job as territorial governor, but he led the movement for statehood in part to escape his dependence on the federal government. Once Tennessee was safely tucked inside the Union as a state, Blount quickly and wisely shifted to the Republican party under the leadership of Thomas Jefferson.

As territorial governor, Blount had run an efficient operation with strong lines of support to all parts of the territory. He also kept tabs on several of the younger men who were obviously rising fast, and Jackson was one of these. By the time Tennessee was admitted to the Union Jackson had achieved a degree of distinction; he had proven his ability as attorney general, and Blount repeatedly mentioned a desire to do more for him. In 1796 Blount decided the time had come to advance Jackson's career in a significant way; he determined to run Jackson for Tennessee's single seat in the United States House of Representatives.[31]

There were compelling reasons for this decision. Of all the men in the western country, Jackson was obviously a comer, well connected, loyal, and dependable—and he was popular at home.[32] Since Blount and Cocke were both from the eastern part of the state, it made a great deal of political sense to select the third federal legislator from the west. And if from the west, then someone from an area that had opposed statehood —yet someone who had himself favored it. Such balancing and compromising was typical of Blount and it all added up to Andrew Jackson. The more Blount thought about it the more he was certain of his choice. Davidson County opposed statehood, but Jackson had not. Jackson had impeccable connections among the Cumberland settlers as well as strong ties to the Blount operation. Blount wanted a westerner who would speak up in Congress for the rights of the frontiersmen, especially in their continuing war with the Indians—and Blount was pretty sure that Jackson would be loud enough to be heard in the furthest parts of Tennessee. The Indian question constantly produced political thunderclaps to which a westerner—particularly a passionate, fiery-spoken westerner—could best respond. And it would be good for the westerners, who had opposed statehood, to know there was someone in Congress who would battle for their interests. Finally, Blount wanted someone his faction could depend on, someone who understood the value of party loyalty and cooperation.[33] And Jackson had written, "Any Transaction of . . . Governor Blount with Respect to My Business will be perfectly pleasing to me as I know from experience that My Interest will be attended to."

There might be one hitch, however. Joseph Anderson, one of Jackson's political friends, explained. "I shall make a point of informing my fellow Citizens generally and Specially," he wrote Jackson, "of your intention of holding a pole as a representative to Congress. If Blount and Cocke Shou'd be again elected Senators—you will be most certainly elected. if only one of them, and the other Senator Shou'd be Doctr. White—I cannot answer so certainly—but in either event—you may count upon my interest, and that of all my friends."[34] Anderson's hesitation reflected Blount's need to do something for Cocke in order to maintain a political balance within the state. If Cocke failed to win election to the Senate, he might demand the House slot. As it turned out, both Blount and Cocke were reelected and Jackson was given the nod of approval. In the fall of 1796, with little serious opposition, Jackson at the age of twenty-nine was elected to Congress as Tennessee's sole representative in the lower house.[35] John Overton had written him, "I must beg leave to congratulate you on your interest and popularity in this country. Your election is certain and I believe that there is scarcely a man in this part of the Territory that could be elected before you."[36]

Although Jackson was elected without incident, there were signs of an emerging opposition to the Blount operation and its tightfisted control of the state. Sevier, the new governor, was annoyed that a man of his distinction and popularity should be overshadowed by a political land jobber. And he was restless; a scuffle with Blount might have a salutary effect on the state by forcing the people to choose between a revolutionary war hero and a political operator. Something of this incipient opposition appeared when Jackson presented the Tennessee legislature with a "remonstrance" stating that money he had received as attorney general of the district had been expended for other purposes—perfectly legitimate, let it be said—and therefore he wished the legislature to "appropriate other publick monies within the District of Mero, to the payment of the Debt" which was due him.[37]

A committee on claims looked into the request and decided to insert it into a general compensation bill that was then brought before the assembly. Before anyone knew what was happening a motion had been introduced and carried to strike out Jackson's claim. One of Blount's henchman had been pricked to see how loud a cry he would make and how many would respond to it. A few days later the committee on claims attested to the reasonableness of the request and in the name of justice recommended that it be paid. A lengthy debate ensued; when the vote was finally taken the claim squeaked through by the narrowest of margins —the vote of the speaker.

However small, the incident was a sign that political conditions in Tennessee were about to change. And the changes would please neither William Blount nor Andrew Jackson.

CHAPTER 7

Land Speculator and Congressman

WHEN JACKSON ARRIVED IN PHILADELPHIA, the nation's capital, in the fall of 1796 to participate in the deliberations of the Fourth Congress, second session, it was not his first trip to the great city. In March 1795 he had come to Philadelphia to sell a large tract of land in Tennessee—and here begins the strangest, most convoluted, most potentially dangerous sequence of events in Jackson's long, complicated, sometimes hidden personal history. This is the story of Jackson as land speculator. And it nearly landed him in prison.

The story begins with the surrender of western land by individual states to the national government at the time of the adoption of the Articles of Confederation. North Carolina had to be prodded to cooperate—but not before she passed a Bonus Act that set aside a military reservation in Tennessee from which veterans of the revolutionary war could be paid in land for their service. The land grants rose on a graduated scale from 640 acres (one section) for a private soldier to 12,000 acres for a brigadier general. Between 1784 and 1799, some 5,312 military warrants were issued for eligible veterans, although fewer than one-fourth of this number were redeemed by the veterans themselves.[1] North Carolina also passed in 1783 the infamous land grab act, largely at the behest of William Blount and his brother John Gray Blount, which opened all of the Tennessee land for purchase even though Indian claims had not yet been extinguished. The Blount family became the largest beneficiary of this act, gaining possession of millions of acres of land stretching from South Carolina to Arkansas, though most of it lay within Tennessee.[2]

The Blount allies also benefited. One of them, John Rice, obtained a choice grant in the western district of Tennessee that included the fourth Chickasaw Bluff, the site of present-day Memphis. In 1792 Rice was killed, and in the settlement of his estate John Overton emerged with a considerable amount of the Rice grant, including the fourth Chickasaw Bluff. At approximately the same time, on May 12, 1794, Overton and Andrew Jackson signed an agreement to establish a partnership for the purchase and sale of land "within and without" the military reservation.[3] Whether Jackson bought into Overton's holdings of the Rice grant or was Overton's partner at the time the grant was acquired is not clear. By 1795 Jackson and Overton shared 50,000 acres of land, part of which was the Rice grant.

Other allies shared in the land grab. David Allison, a Blount appointee and business manager for the family, was one of them. In the latter capacity he took up residence in Philadelphia where he became a partner in the firm of John B. Evans and Co., a mercantile establishment that conducted a substantial amount of business with the settlers of the Cumberland. So good were Allison's business connections in Philadelphia that Tennessee acquaintances had little difficulty establishing credit with mercantile firms in the capital. But it was land speculation rather than mercantile goods that engaged Allison's real interest. Together with William Blount he bought and sold hundreds of thousands of acres.[4]

And there was Andrew Jackson. He probably immersed himself in land speculation almost on his arrival in Tennessee, for land was the surest and quickest way to riches in the west. Also, he may have been a partner with Thomas Green in the Natchez District to acquire land in the Bourbon County conspiracy.[5] Unquestionably Jackson was a willing participant in any land scheme that seemed promising; however, it is difficult to follow his business transactions in this regard because the documentation is incomplete. But it is no exaggeration to suppose that at the age of thirty he was speculating in tens (maybe hundreds) of thousands of acres of land.[6]

When Jackson traveled to Philadelphia in 1795 it was with the purpose of selling 50,000 acres held jointly with his partner, Overton, and another 18,750 acres he had been commissioned to sell by a member of the Rice family. Shortly after arriving in Philadelphia Jackson received a memorandum from Overton with explicit instructions. "Be candid and unreserved with the purchasers," Overton wrote. "If you sell Lands and get money that you can spare, it will be best that you purchase, somewhere in the lower part of the eastern States such Negroes we may want for Rice, and also a likely Negroe Boy which I want for a Servant. . . . If you purchase Negroes in any of the northern States, be careful in so doing not to subject yourself to the penal Laws of the State." Good advice of which the cautious Overton felt obliged to remind his sometimes reckless friend. He also warned Jackson against taking goods in payment for their land.[7]

When Jackson arrived in Philadelphia he encountered unexpected problems. No one was interested in his property. He presumed he could easily dispose of his land in Philadelphia and yet one day followed another without his finding a buyer. For twenty-two days he fretted and fumed. He went "through difficulties such I never experienced before," he told Overton.[8] Then, at that moment, that singularly unfortunate moment, he met up with his old friend, David Allison.

Allison was prepared to buy the property and offered a fifth of a dollar (twenty cents) per acre. Under the circumstances, Jackson jumped at the offer. His directive from Rice with respect to the 18,750 acres was that he must not sell the land for less than twelve and one-half cents per acre for which he would receive a 10 percent commission. He was well over that mark. So Jackson agreed to sell both the 50,000 acres and the Rice property, and in exchange he accepted three promissory notes from Allison.[9]

Jackson had been running a trading operation from Tennessee north to Kentucky and south to Natchez, Mississippi, and he planned to open a regular store on the Cumberland River to consolidate these activities and place them on a more businesslike footing. In preparation for this he took his brother-in-law, Samuel Donelson, as a partner.[10] His experience as a storekeeper in North Carolina encouraged him in this venture almost as much as his need to consolidate his business operations. Thus Jackson now functioned as lawyer, land speculator, government official, and storekeeper.

To stock his store Jackson made purchases from Meeker, Cochran and Co., a Philadelphia firm, and presented Allison's notes, which he endorsed, in payment. Allison also took Jackson to John B. Evans and Co., where Allison was a partner, to purchase additional supplies. With Allison's avouchment Jackson was allowed to "have goods to any amount I thought proper to take out."[11] When the invoice was presented, Jackson again offered Allison's notes, which Evans accepted after they had been properly endorsed. Later Jackson admitted he did not realize at the time that in signing the notes he "stood security for the payment" of the notes "or that Mr. E. expected me to do so, or then contemplated such a thing."[12]

This is a remarkable admission. What businessman or lawyer enters financial transactions involving thousands of dollars without knowing his responsibilities and the degree of his involvement? Sometimes Jackson behaved quite stupidly. He lamely excused himself to Overton by declaring that he "was placed in the Dam'st situation ever man was placed in."[13] Nevertheless, Evans warned him as a matter of course that the notes must be redeemed or he would bring suit. When Jackson returned to Tennessee he felt really depressed by the experience. He said he was "fatigued even almost unto death."[14]

But the real blow came two months later. Jackson had no sooner set up his trading post on the Cumberland than he received a short business letter from Meeker, Cochran and Co.

> We are sorry so soon after your departure, to follow you the advice, that any notes or acceptances of David Allisons now falling due are not generally or regularly paid, and that there is little reason to expect he will be more punctual hereafter, as his reasons is no doubt must suffer; in his want, of punctuallity. We take this early opportunity to make known to you that *we* have little or no expectations of getting paid from him, and that we shall have to get our money from you, which we shall expect at maturity, as the orriginal cr. was longer, than we usual gave, assuring you of our perfect regard we remain Dear sir you very ob servants[15]

Allison bankrupt! That really shocked Jackson. And the shock was repeated a few months later when he received a letter from John B. Evans and Co. stating that Allison's notes, endorsed by Jackson, were due on February 13 and, since Allison could not meet them, Jackson was responsible.[16] Jackson immediately sold his store to Colonel Elijah Robertson for 33,000 acres of land, realizing a slight profit.[17] Then he dashed over to Knoxville and sold the land to James Stuart for twenty-five cents per acre, of which $2,800 was to be paid within sixty days to Jackson's Philadelphia creditors and the remainder within two years.[18] This happened at the time Jackson was attending the Tennessee constitutional convention and he probably offered the land to Stuart through William Blount, who served as Stuart's agent.

In February 1796 Jackson and Overton revalidated their partnership and took protective action against their liability by agreeing to bear an equal share in any loss incurred in the Allison transaction "under penalty of $100,000 each."[19] The following month Jackson began picking up large parcels of land all over Tennessee, from Powell's Valley in the eastern district to the Obion River in the western district. Much of this land was probably intended for sale in Philadelphia.[20] At this time he also purchased the Hunter's Hill plot, 640 acres on the south side of the Cumberland River, formerly owned by Lewis Robards.[21] (This was the property Robards had purchased to begin his married life with Rachel but which he was unable to occupy because of the Indian menace.) Over a period of two months in the spring of 1796, Jackson obtained 29,228 acres of land for sale in Philadelphia, of which 11,760 acres was purchased from Stockley Donelson and 5,000 at a sheriff's sale.[22]

When Jackson arrived in Philadelphia in June 1796 he met William Blount, his political mentor and James Stuart's agent. According to the terms of the land sale to Stuart, the first payment was due in Philadelphia within sixty days. But the cash could not be scraped together. Instead Blount agreed to assure the amount Jackson owed his creditors, and Jackson in turn deducted this amount from the price of the land sale.[23] Twenty-four years later Jackson ruefully noted that the land he sold Stuart was then worth $200,000.[24]

Jackson had nearly 30,000 additional acres for sale when he reached Philadelphia in June 1796. Again he had trouble finding a buyer. And again—incredibly—he turned to Allison and Blount. He sold 28,810 acres to the two, taking two notes from Allison for $5,000 and $676.73 and one note from Blount for $4,539.94.[25] Blount promised this money plus interest within two years.[26]

With the Blount security Jackson was out of immediate danger, but the problem remained of what to do about Allison, who owed him the price of the original land sale—which, with interest, Jackson later estimated came to $20,000. Moreover, on May 13, 1795, Allison gave Jackson an additional note for $1,101.[27] Allison was deeply in debt to the young congressman—and going deeper each year because of the interest. But there was nothing Jackson could do to get his money. Just wait and hope that Allison would soon set his financial house in order.

It was a pious hope. The Allison affair dragged on for several more years and almost ended with Jackson sitting in debtor's prison.

Having accepted notes from Blount and Allison, Jackson purchased $4,800 worth of merchandise in Philadelphia (probably for resale in Tennessee) and returned home.[28] A few months later he obtained another 1,000 acres in Sumner County from Elisha Rice. So the process of buying and selling land went on year after year. Even as Jackson headed for Philadelphia to begin his career as a member of Congress, his brother-in-law, Stockley Donelson, signaled him about further land sales. "I should have written to you before this but heard you were Elected a Member of Congress and was on your way there," Donelson wrote. "I want to purchase yours and Brother Samls. right of Land on duck river that you purchased of William Purnell. . . . I want you to make enquiry and get all the Millitary Land Survey that you possible can. . . . I will make it worth your trouble."[29] Whatever Jackson was doing, wherever he was going, land speculation was never far from his mind.

Heading for Philadelphia in 1796, Jackson was beginning a period of long absences from home. These absences would be very difficult for him—and more so for Rachel. Frequently he wrote her long, fond letters that show a side of the man infrequently seen. One of the earliest letters that survives, written in 1796, conveys a tenderness quite remarkable for Jackson.

My Dearest Heart

It is with the greatest pleasure I sit down to write you. Tho I am absent My heart rests with you. With what pleasing hopes I view the future period when I shall be restored to your arms there to spend My days in Domestic Sweetness with you the Dear Companion of my life, never to be separated from you again during this Transitory and fluctuating life.

I mean to retire from the Buss of publick life, and Spend My Time with you alone in Sweet Retirement, which is My only ambition and ultimate wish.

I have this moment finished My business here which I have got in good Train and hope to wind it up this Touer, and will leave this tomorrow Morning for Jonesborough where I hope to finish it, and tho it is now half after ten o'clock, could not think of going to bed without writing you. May it give you pleasure to Receive it. May it add to your Contentment until I return. May you be blessed with health. May the Goddess of Slumber every evening light on your eyebrows and gently lull you to sleep, and conduct you through the night with pleasing thoughts and pleasant dreams. Could I only know you were contented and enjoyed Peace of Mind, what satisfaction it would afford me whilst travelling the loanly and tiresome road. It would relieve My anxious breast and shorten the way—May the great "I am" bless and protect you until that happy and wished for moment arrives when I am restored to your sweet embrace which is the Nightly prayer of your affectionate husband,

Andrew Jackson

P.S. My compliments to my good old Mother Mrs. Donelson, that best of friends. Tell her with what pain I reflect upon leaving home without shaking her by the hand and asking her blessings.

A.J.[30]

Though painful—increasingly so over the years—the separations necessitated by "publick life" could not be avoided, and late in 1796 Jackson began his new career as a member of Congress in Philadelphia. Albert Gallatin, Swiss born and French accented, remembered seeing Jackson on his arrival and later described him as "a tall, lank, uncouth-looking personage, with long locks of hair hanging over his face, and a queue down his back tied in an eel skin; his dress singular, his manners and deportment those of a rough backwoodsman."[31] Gallatin never could abide this western upstart, and his description is a distortion. To depict Jackson as uncouth, ill-mannered, and dressed in a bizarre costume is more fancy than reality. In fact Jackson had a Philadelphia tailor, Charles C. Watson, who provided him before the start of the congressional session with a black cloth coat with velvet collar, a pair of florentine breeches, and sundry other items of apparel.[32] There may have been rough spots in Jackson in 1796, but he had been to a big eastern city before and he knew how gentlemen dressed. As one of the first men of Tennessee and the state's single representative, he would no more walk into Congress outlandishly rigged than he would deliberately outrage Cumberland society. As an early biographer noted, Gallatin's baleful description was unrecognizable to Jackson's friends.[33]

Philadelphia! The nation's capital, a city of 65,000 people, and the center of all that was elegant and civilized and agreeable in American society. It was a rare opportunity for a young westerner as intelligent, ambitious, and socially mobile as Andrew Jackson. In Philadelphia the young congressman lived with a man by the name of Hardy. Since he was on very close personal terms with Blount, who had extensive connections in the city, Jackson probably enjoyed a rich social life in the capital—or as much of one as he cared to sample.

Unlike many congressmen, Jackson was present on the opening day of Congress and found himself in the company of such distinguished American statesmen as James Madison of Virginia, Albert Gallatin and Frederick Muhlenberg of Pennsylvania, Nathaniel Macon of North Carolina, Edward Livingston of New York, Fisher Ames of Massachusetts, Roger Griswold of Connecticut, Abraham Baldwin of Georgia, and Robert Goodloe Harper of South Carolina, many of them Founding Fathers. Not until the third day of the session, when the Senate finally had a quorum, were both houses of Congress ready to begin business.

Just a few months earlier, in his Farewell Address, President Washington had called for the gradual creation of a navy to protect American commerce in the Mediterranean, suggested government aid to manufactures in order to free the country from foreign dependence in time of war, recommended a national university and military academy, denounced the spoliations of American ships by French cruisers, and ended with a wish that the government they had instituted for the protection of American liberties would be perpetual.[34]

A committee of the House of Representatives was appointed to write a formal reply to the President's address. This reply, full of extravagant praise, was intended as an appropriate farewell to the Father of His Country. On December 11 the reply was formally reported out of committee and debated for two days. It soon became apparent that not every representative approved the encomiums heaped by the committee on the Great Man. Thomas Blount of North Carolina, the brother of William, asked for a vote with the yeas and nays recorded so that posterity might know that not everyone in Congress approved so extravagant a tribute.

Posterity has kindly forgotten Thomas Blount—but not all of the representatives who voted nay. Among those who rejected the salute to Washington were Edward Livingston, Nathaniel Macon, and Andrew Jackson.[35] Years later, when Jackson himself ran for the presidency, this vote was remembered and used against him; it caused Jackson great embarrassment since it was felt that anyone showing the slightest disrespect to the great Washington during his lifetime was practically a traitor and certainly one who did not deserve to follow Washington into the White House.

Jackson's vote took courage and independence, even if it showed a lack of courtesy and judgment. Jackson believed that the Jay treaty with Great Britain, concluded by the Washington administration and submitted to the "aristocratic" Senate, was a stain on the honor of the Republic. For that alone Washington deserved no thanks. Then, too, the present administration had been impossibly tolerant of Indian massacres in Tennessee. To repeated pleas for help the administration had responded with a thundering silence. And Jackson did not especially care for the administration's sympathy with England against France. A hint of this slipped out in a letter to his brother-in-law, Robert Hays. The President's supporters, Jackson wrote, "wish to Cultivate a close friendship with Britain at the expense of a war with the French Republick. . . . The British are daily Capturing our vessels [and] impressing our seamen . . . but from the presidents speech it would seem that . . . all the Depredations on our commerce was done by the French."[36] Jackson's anglophobia had less to do with the position of Thomas Jefferson and his Republican friends (whose ideology and sentiment favored France) than it did with his revolutionary experiences and his western antagonism toward and suspicion of the British and Spanish. England and Spain surrounded the United States north, south, and west, thwarting further American expansion and confining the nation to the status of a hemmed-in island. Moreover, they constantly fomented Indian attacks along the frontier.

Jackson's disapproval of President Washington went beyond the administration's handling of foreign affairs. Several of his letters during the session registered his complaints. He claimed that those who professed "republican principles" were being removed from office "if they do not think exactly with the Executive." If a man cannot be led to believe, he said, "as the President believes in politics (and God forbid a majority should) he is not to fill an office in the United States. This, sir, I view as more dangerous than the establishment of religion."[37] (This is a remarkable statement in view of Jackson's own behavior as President.) In another letter to John Overton the young congressman said, "the Executive of the Union has Ever Since the Commencement of the present Government, been Grasping after power, and in many instances, Exercised powers, that he was not Constitutionally invested with."[38] (Still another criticism later leveled at President Jackson.)

In voting against the reply to Washington, Jackson teamed with several other congressmen committed to a conservative philosophy of government. They interpreted the Constitution narrowly; they were concerned for the privileges of the states; and they opposed all but the most necessary appropriations by the central government. In identifying himself with these men—men like Nathaniel Macon of North Carolina and Henry Tazewell of Virginia—Jackson reinforced his own native conservatism, one that reflected western concern for the rights and sovereignty of the states. The conservatives in Congress welcomed him into their ranks, and several of them corresponded with him regularly on very familiar terms.[39]

"The Legislature of the Union progress slowly in business," Jackson wrote a month after the session had begun. "The greater part of the time as yet have been taken up in committee prepareing business for the house. It is much Talked of to increase the salaries of the officers of Government and to lay a direct Tax, neither of which I hope will take effect. It is strongly urged the necessity of a direct tax, it appears necessary by the Secretarys Report to raise for the next year a further sum than is annually raised of 1,200000 Dollars to meet the exigencies of Government. this is urged in favour."[40]

As he had promised, Jackson voted against the direct tax when it came up for final legislative action. He also opposed an appropriation to aid the sufferers of a disastrous fire that had nearly destroyed Savannah. These votes confirmed his conservative, states' rights commitment, though he took no part in the discussions of the issues. Indeed he was for the most part a quiet freshman congressman, content to hold his tongue and take his lead from his more distinguished conservative colleagues in the House.

Then, when a petition was received from Hugh Lawson White asking compensation for his services in an offensive attack against the Indians led by General Sevier in 1793, Jackson sprang to life. President Washington had steadfastly refused to honor the petition, claiming he needed special authorization from Congress to do so. On December 29, 1796, the Committee of Claims came to the full House with the petition. The committee reported that the Indians had "greatly perplexed and harassed" the settlers of Tennessee by "thefts and murders" but asked the House itself to judge how far these "agressions . . . constitute a case of imminent danger, or the expedition a just and necessary measure."[41] The attack was offensive, undertaken without presidential approval, and in defiance of general orders from the War Department not to wage war against the Indians unless attacked.

The report infuriated Jackson.[42] It clearly implied that the Tennesseans had acted improperly. Worse, it seemed to sympathize with the Indians! Gaining the floor, Jackson spoke concisely and immediately to the point raised by the committee: whether the expedition was a just and necessary measure. Indeed it was just, said Jackson, and necessary. "When it was seen that war was waged upon the State," he said in a loud voice, "that the knife and the tomahawk were held over the heads of women and children, that peaceable citizens were murdered, it was time to make resistance."[43] He disputed a report of the secretary of war, mentioned in the statement of the Committee of Claims, because some of its particulars were not based on fact, he said, such as the remark that the Sevier expedition was undertaken "for the avowed purpose of carrying the war into the Cherokee country."[44] As an "inhabitant of the country," Jackson claimed full knowledge of the business. From June to October, he asserted, the militia acted entirely on the defensive. Then, despite their peacekeeping efforts, some 1,200 Indians suddenly assaulted them, drove them from their position, and "threatened to carry the Seat of Government." In such a dangerous situation, Jackson asked, "would the Secretary (upon whom the Executive power rested, in the absence of the Governor) have been justified, had he not adopted the measures he did of pursuing the enemy?" Certainly not, he said. Thus the expedition was necessary and the claim of Hugh Lawson White legitimate.[45]

But Jackson did not stop there. He moved that since the expedition was just and necessary all expenses for everyone involved—not just White's—should be paid by the government. Jackson may have been unsympathetic and niggardly with the victims of the Savannah fire, but with the Tennessee expeditionary heroes he was generous to a fault. And his motion, an expression of Jackson's heartfelt sentiments, was one that was certain to spark gratitude and appreciation in Tennessee.

There was considerable debate over the original committee report, and several representatives argued that the entire matter should go back to the committee for further consideration. Sending it back to committee would temporarily dispose of it, perhaps get rid of it permanently. Jackson jumped to his feet again, protesting that he did not know the rules of the House very well, "but from the best idea he could form, it was a very circuitous way of doing business."[46] Why refer the matter back to committee, he asked, when all the facts were known and there was nothing further the committee could learn? The House adjourned for the day without taking action on the report.

When the session reconvened the following afternoon Jackson asked for recognition. As the first order of business he presented the petition of George Colbert, one of the chiefs of the Chickasaw Nation, complaining of the government's failure to provide full compensation for supplies furnished by the tribe to a detachment of Tennessee volunteers commanded by Colonel Mansker.[47] The Chief demanded congressional relief.[48] As Jackson said in a subsequent letter, "I named to you the steps I had taken to Bring into view the subject of Col Manskers and men who marched to the Chickasaw nation in my last, by preferring a petition in the name of G. Colbert, to obtain pay for the provissions and relieve [Captain David] Smith, but I think the Claim will be negatived."[49] The House referred the petition to the Committee of Claims and then returned to the petition of Hugh Lawson White. Jackson's resolution of the previous day was read again and then Jackson asked to address the full House.

The rations provided the troops on the expedition, Jackson began, had already been paid for by the secretary of war, and he (Jackson) could see no reasonable objection to the payment of the entire expense of the expedition. Did not the payment of part imply obligation for the whole? Moreover, Jackson continued, the troops were called out by a superior officer and had no right to doubt his authority. "Were a contrary doctrine admitted," he declared, "it would strike at the very root of subordination."[50] It would be tantamount to saying to soldiers, "Before you obey the command of your superior officer, you have a right to inquire into the legality of the service upon which you are about to be employed, and, until you are satisfied, you may refuse to take the field."[51]

This is madness, Jackson said. No one can act on such a principle. General Sevier was bound to obey the orders he received to undertake the expedition; so too were the officers under him. They participated in this perilous campaign with "full confidence that the United States would pay them, believing that they had appointed such officers as would not call them into the field without proper authority." Even if the expedition was "unconstitutional"—which he did not believe for a moment—"it ought not to affect the soldier, since he had no choice in the business being obliged to obey his superior." Indeed, he concluded, since the provisions had already been paid for by the government, and the rations and payrolls were always considered a check upon each other, he hoped his resolution would be approved by the House.

For a freshman congressman it was a strong speech, nearly outstanding, and it earned him the respect of his colleagues at the very outset of his brief career in Congress. He had done nobly by the heroes of Tennessee, and the speech was bound to generate considerable enthusiasm at home—provided he could get his resolution approved. Embedded in the speech were a number of basic principles that were constants in Jackson's life, principles that were later reasserted rather forcefully during his military career. They had to do with authority and responsibility, subordination and obedience, discipline and loyalty. Jackson's ideas were strict and allowed no room for compromise: Soldiers obeyed orders properly authorized and governments supported and defended their soldiers regardless of the expense or the risk of embarrassment.

In the deliberation that followed Jackson's speech it was pointed out that the petition actually before the House came from a single individual, whereas Jackson had moved a resolution to pay the *entire* expeditionary force. Surely there was a discrepancy; was the House expected to act on the petition before it or to disregard it and respond to the resolution introduced by the representative from Tennessee?

Jackson regained the floor. If the members would refer to the committee report, he said, it will be noticed that the secretary of war admitted that in allowing White's petition the House would establish a principle that would apply also to the entire militia engaged in the campaign. If White's petition was just, so too was that of every man in the expedition, and it would not be necessary for the militiamen to apply personally to the House for compensation.[52]

A long debate followed. Representative Robert Rutherford of Virginia observed that Jackson had set the matter in "so fair a light" that it was really not necessary to say anything further.[53] Nevertheless, James Madison of Virginia felt compelled to add his voice of support to Jackson's position, agreeing that the government had made a commitment that extended to every man who served in the campaign. Finally the matter was turned over to a select committee, chaired by Jackson and including Jeremiah Smith of New Hampshire, Thomas Blount of North Carolina, George Dent of Maryland, and Robert Goodloe Harper of South Carolina. A month later the committee issued a long, clear, and dispassionate report, the language of which was clearly not Jackson's. After describing the events that occurred during the expedition the report stated that there were two questions before the committee: Was the expedition essential for the defense of the frontier? and was the authority of the governor of the territory (or the secretary in his absence) such as to oblige the militia to obey his orders? The committee replied affirmatively to both questions and therefore recommended full compensation to the entire militia. Without a word of debate the recommendation was approved by the House and sent to the Committee of Ways and Means to be introduced into the federal appropriations for expenditure in 1797. The amount granted was $22,816.[54]

Hardly a month in Congress and Jackson, against some odds, had realized a very respectable achievement. He had not simply won compensation for a detachment of Tennesseans; in a sense he had won a victory over the national government. He had struck a blow for westerners in their continuing struggle to survive on the frontier. And he had produced a cash settlement, the best possible expression of his achievement.

This early success virtually assured Jackson's reelection to Congress should he decide to stand for a second term.[55] It was buttressed by Jackson's attentiveness to his constituents in Tennessee, for at the very outset of his congressional career he understood the ingredients of political longevity.[56] Some of this was expressed in a letter he wrote at the time of his initial victory in the House.

> I am the only representative from the State. Consequently all the business of the State in the house of representatives devolve on me, on all Committees, before whom business is brought that is of a general Nature I am appointed and have to serve, and also upon Many select ones, wherein the Interest of the Individuals of My state are Concerned. the Committs meet general at 6 oclock in the Evening and sit to 9, and then on Saturdays. This they are Compelled to do from the shortness of the Session, having to attend to the Committees and the business of the house I have not Much time to wa[s]te and I am well Convinced that My Constituents would rather have Justice done, and their demands paid then receive letters from me and as I am Compelled to Neglect one or the other My duty dictates to Me to attend closely to the interest of My Country.[57]

Attending to the "demands" of his constituents, Jackson did not forget his family or the friends of the Blounts. He told his brother-in-law, Robert Hays, that Hays would win appointment as marshal but he was not certain who would be chosen district court judge of Tennessee—although he thought John Rhea might get it, "the senate being in his Interest."[58] President Washington subsequently named Hays as marshal but appointed John McNairy as judge. Both nominations received quick confirmation.

With understandable pride, Jackson wrote to Governor Sevier and informed him that he and his army would be recompensed for their services against the Indians in 1793. He also commented on the direct tax proposal and conjectured that "it will be verry unpalatable to the Tennesseans in their present Situation, therefore will be opposed to it."[59]

He said the situation of American commerce was given as the reason for the tax. He railed against the administration because of its favorable policy toward Britain, which necessarily hurt the French. "I am sorry to see our Country by the Conduct of our Government," he wrote, "involved in such a situation with the republick of France, who are now struggling to obtain for themselves the same B[l]essings (liberty) that we fought and bled for, we ought to wish them success if we could not aid them. How the present difference with France May terminate is for wiser politicians than Me to Determine."[60]

In the same letter Jackson articulated his strong commitment to states' rights, a position, he said, "I long Entertained" and which was "founded on mature deliberation. . . . My oppinion is so firmly invested in the sovereignety of the State, both by Constitutional principles and by the law of nations added to that the Sovereignety, reserved by the state, in forming the federal Constitution, that nothing but the act of the strong hand of power itself, can divest us that right."[61] A clear, straightforward statement—one that characterized Jackson's "philosophy of government" throughout his early political life. Indeed a powerful states' rights strain can be observed in his thinking and writing throughout his entire career, even when as President many of his actions buttressed and strengthened the central government.

Although the responsibilities of representing Tennessee in Congress took much more time than he had anticipated, Jackson faithfully performed his duties. At all but two roll call votes he was present (one mark of a responsible congressman). He voted in favor of completing three frigates for the navy, and he opposed the continuance of bribes to the pirates of Algiers to keep them from attacking American ships in the Mediterranean; both votes were predictable given Jackson's supercharged patriotism and his sense of the nation's dignity and honor. He also voted against an appropriation for the purchase of furniture for the presidential mansion then being constructed in the District of Columbia, the new national capital to which the government would repair in 1800. And Jackson opposed the removal of the restriction which confined public expenditures to specific objects for which each sum was appropriated.[62] Like his basic political creed, Jackson's fiscal philosophy was fundamentally conservative; yet, like all good politicians, he could on occasion compromise his principles. Although he opposed excessive expenditures of federal money and voted against a raise in salary for the secretary of war (which may have been pique at the secretary's reaction to the Sevier expedition), he had no hesitation about reversing himself when the question of increasing the salary of the district judge in Tennessee came up. A long debate developed over reducing the salary from

$1,000 to $800. Jackson argued for the higher figure, claiming it was necessary to induce men of ability to serve. Moreover, Tennessee was an expensive place to live; every article must be imported at considerable expense, he said, because of the state's distance from the major centers of commerce. Furthermore, the judge must travel through the wilderness four times a year at great personal risk given the constant threat of Indian attack.[63] But Jackson's efforts were unavailing. The other congressmen turned him a deaf ear and reduced the salary.[64]

At the conclusion of his first session in Congress, Jackson's performance could be summed up as modestly successful—nothing extraordinary, nothing outstanding, but solid nonetheless. He served on five committees, chaired one, presented two petitions, introduced one resolution, made five speeches, and voted twenty-four times with the majority out of a total of thirty-nine votes. He proved himself a diligent, hardworking representative, devoted to the interests of his state and his constituents. And although he was committed to the rights of the states in principle, his voting pattern demonstrated a pragmatic concern for the needs of Tennesseans. As a politician, Jackson developed fast.

Congress adjourned on March 3, 1797, and Jackson was glad to quit the hectic capital and return home. Not that politics ceased to engage his attention; now that the Sevier crowd was active as a faction separate from the Blount clique, he was sucked inevitably into the political conflicts developing within the state.[65] Jackson had to be careful of Sevier because of the older man's popularity with the people—especially those of east Tennessee. And it was only by a hair that an open and serious quarrel between the two was avoided in 1797. It all began with Jackson's decision to seek election as major general of the militia in 1796, an office that could advance his name, reputation, and political ambitions throughout the state, for there was no surer way of gaining popularity with Tennesseans than military success—particularly against the Indians.

Under the territorial government Sevier held the office of major general; now that Tennessee was a state, Sevier as governor was commander-in-chief of the armed forces—and Jackson thought he should relinquish the militia post. Sevier was ready to do it, but he was disturbed about Jackson succeeding him, probably because of Jackson's youth and inexperience. After all, commanding troops to combat the Indians required more than legal training and political ambition. And Sevier may have been jealous of Jackson's new popularity in the state and fearful of what he might accomplish as general.

Holding high rank in the militia provided powerful leverage for political advancement within the state. In the late eighteenth and early nineteenth centuries, most men belonged to the militia if they belonged to any organization at all; to stand at the top of this organization would certainly accelerate Jackson's career with dazzling speed. Thus Jackson's decision to seek the post of major general—the highest military rank in the state—when he was not yet thirty years of age indicates the gargantuan size of his ambition.

But John Sevier stood in his way. The governor preferred George Conway.

The operation of the militia and the selection of the commanding officers were essentially democratic processes. There were three militia districts within Tennessee (one of them was Mero). Each district had a brigade and each county a regiment; one cavalry regiment was attached to each brigade. Regimental and company officers were elected by members of the militia regardless of rank, brigadier generals were elected by the field officers of each district, and the field officers of all three districts plus the brigadier generals elected a major general who commanded the militia of the entire state. In the event of a tie vote in the selection of the major general, the governor cast the deciding vote.

The election was held in November 1796. According to law, the brigadier generals and the field officers were to meet in their respective districts and cast their ballots. Just prior to the election Sevier sent some blank commissions to Brigadier General Robertson with instructions to use them to appoint cavalry officers. But his real intention was obvious. At the same time Sevier wrote Joel Lewis of Mero to recommend Conway as major general. When the Mero officers gathered to vote there was a general discussion of some of the candidates, and Jackson was present as a "private citizen."[66] At one point Lewis spoke against Jackson's candidacy and in favor of Conway's, reading from the governor's letter for support.

The hot-tempered Jackson bolted to his feet. The governor had no business sending blank commissions to Robertson, he said; that clearly exceeded his constitutional power. Worse, Sevier was attempting to control an election that ought to remain free from executive interference. Jackson also said a few other intemperate things, the tenor of which was quickly communicated to Sevier. The governor took exception to what he called Jackson's "scurelous" remarks and the implication of wrongdoing. But what did he, a man of achievement and distinction, care about the language of a *"poor pitifull petty fogging Lawyer"*?[67] The danger of an open split between the two men was now very real, and such a rupture would surely damage Jackson's reputation throughout the state.

Conway edged out Jackson in the election, and the defeat taught Jackson an important lesson: He must prepare his way, he must build his personal strength within the militia before announcing another candidacy.[68] Thereafter Jackson took keen interest and active participation in the militia elections, and slowly over the years he built his political strength within the organization.

Meanwhile his relations with Sevier worsened. After Jackson's return from Philadelphia in the spring of 1797 an angry exchange of letters passed between the two men. But six months had passed since the election and while they were still jabbing at one another with the business end of their quills, they had calmed down considerably. Besides, mutual friends, among them General Robertson, intervened with soothing words. Both were reminded that a public quarrel was self-defeating. Soon Sevier was saying that "I never was nor am I yet, either your private or political enemy"[69] and Jackson, matching these words, said that it was "with pleasure sir that I now remark to you that I think you had no *malicious* design to injure my reputation."[70]

It was a narrow squeak; still a tension remained. For, despite his disavowal, Jackson continued to harbor the suspicion that Sevier was bent on injuring his reputation, and nothing infuriated him more than that. Later the tension would mount to an uncontrollable level and burst into open conflict.

The quarrel also soured Jackson's relationship with Judge McNairy, who he felt was a little too pro-Sevier to suit his sense of loyalty.[71] Jackson believed that friendships should be absolute—no in-between, no playing both sides.

The Blount people were extremly pleased with Jackson and the way things had developed over the past year, not simply because he had dared to take on the popular Sevier by running for major general but because his fine performance in Congress justified their faith in him and signaled the beginning of an important new political career within their clique. Even Senator Cocke went out of his way to comment favorably on Jackson's record in the House. In a letter to the Knoxville *Gazette* he said to the people of Tennessee: "Your representative, Mr. Jackson, has distinguished himself by the spirited manner in which he opposed the report [of the secretary of war concerning the petition of Hugh Lawson White]. Notwithstanding the misrepresentation of the Secretary, I hope the claim will be allowed; if it is, a principle will be established for the payment of all services done by the militia of the Territory."[72] Blount himself, who had been constantly promoting Jackson's interests for the past five years,[73] broadly hinted that he would support the young man for the United States Senate in the next election.[74]

The opportunity came soon enough. It developed because of a conspiracy which resulted in Blount's expulsion from the Senate. The intrigue began with rumors that the Spanish, after agreeing to the Pinckney treaty of 1795 (which opened the entire Mississippi River to American trade and allowed Americans a right of deposit for storing goods at New Orleans), were about to return part of Louisiana to France as the price of a new treaty of friendship and that France would not be bound by the Pinckney treaty and would close the river. Worse, it was feared in the American capital that Napoleon, the master of France, would seize the opportunity to foment revolution in the West. Even Jackson got wind of the cession. "I believe it to be a fact," he wrote, "that France has acquired by Barter From the Spaniards the East and west floridas and part of Louisiana in exchange for part of St. Domingo, therefore the[y] will be masters of the mouth of the Mississippi, but I hope they will be good neighbors."[75]

If true, the presence of the French in the lower Mississippi valley would create an extremely dangerous situation. (The hated Dons had again acted to kindle western fears and apprehensions!) With Napoleon forcing his way into their lives on behalf of his own imperialistic designs, Tennesseans and other westerners were no longer dealing with a second-rate antagonist (Spain) but with a powerful and clever statesman who would not hesitate to cripple them if it suited his purposes. Since Napoleon was locked in war with England the possibility of his meddling in western affairs for military advantage was frighteningly real. Under the circumstances there was one obvious course of action: turn to Britain; turn to the only real military power in the world who could block Napoleon. And justification quickly followed. Had not England agreed to concessions in the west? Had she not guaranteed the free navigation of the Mississippi in the treaty of 1783 that ended the Revolution? This reversal of attitude toward Britain on the part of some westerners was predicated totally on who controlled access to the Mississippi. Economic self-interest determined friend and foe.

The threat of active French intervention in the old southwest was clearly inimical to the land-speculation interests of the Blounts. Senator Blount and his brother were overextended when land values began to fall on account of the rumors—thereby further depressing their financial situation. To Senator Blount's way of thinking it made sense to invite the British to active participation in American affairs in the southwest: Since England was at war with both Spain and France, she should finance American and Indian filibusters against Florida and Louisiana (the United States would not do it) and then take possession of them.[76] As compensation England would make generous land grants to the American "conspirators," guarantee free navigation of the Mississippi, and make New Orleans a free port. All of this was certain to raise Blount and his friends to high popular standing throughout the western country, for it would mean the expulsion of the Spanish and the advancement of American economic interests in the southwest. It would also mean immediate improvement for the Blount financial empire because the success of this plan would increase land values. So many of their land deals were on the shady side that the Blounts reckoned that *any* alteration of the political scene meant money in their pockets.

The operations of the Blounts were not much different from the efforts and aspirations of a great many other westerners; they were merely on a larger, more lavish, more ambitious scale. If necessary, they would signal nations to war or reverse political alliances. They dreamed in terms of empire, and they found many westerners who understood their dreams and would join their conspiracy to make them come true.

But the conspiracy came a cropper, collapsing before it had barely gotten under way. A letter—a foolish, blunt, candid letter—written by Blount on April 21, 1797, to one James Carey knocked the conspiracy in the head. The letter came into the possession of the Adams administration and was turned over to the United States Senate on July 3 for appropriate action. In the letter Blount admitted his part in the conspiracy and warned Carey about letting word of it leak out, particularly to Benjamin Hawkins, agent to the Creek Indians and acting superintendent of Indian Affairs. "I have advised you, in whatever you do," Blount wrote, "to take care of yourself; I have now to tell you to take care of me too, for a discovery of the plan would prevent the success, and much injure all parties concerned." If the Indians, who were part of the plan to instigate hostilities in the southwest, gave Carey any trouble over the treaty that Blount had negotiated earlier but whose boundary line had just been surveyed, the letter instructed Carey to throw the blame "upon the late President, and, as he is now out of office, it will be of no consequence how much the Indians blame him."[77]

The extraordinary lengths to which the conspirators were willing to go to initiate their scheme of conquest and to cover up the evidence of their manipulations indicates the pervasive, almost relentless expansionist fervor of frontiersmen to control the southwest. Their economic needs and ambitions powered an incredible drive. River rights to the Mississippi and access to the port of New Orleans were so essential that they were even prepared to conspire against the United States if necessary.[78] This fact of life remained a constant for a generation or more. It formed the background to the Blount conspiracy, to the Burr Conspiracy and, still later, to Jackson's activities in Florida and Louisiana—which, in a sense, constituted a "conspiracy" against both the English and the Spanish.

Thus, early on, a tradition of conspiracy developed in the southwest. But the Blount and Burr conspiracies failed in large part because they were motivated by personal ambitions; Jackson's "conspiracy" succeeded because it took into account the necessary and important presence of the United States. To be sure, Jackson's "conspiracy" served the economic ambitions of western Americans; but it also served the expansionist and imperial ambitions of the entire people of the United States.[79] And that essential ingredient separated success from failure and hero from traitor.

In 1797 the Blount conspiracy unraveled with all deliberate speed once the incriminating letter to Carey had been disclosed. A select committee of the House of Representatives initiated an inquiry and reported that Blount "did conspire, and contrive to create, promote, and set on foot within the jurisdiction of the United States—a military hostile expedition against the territories and dominions—the Floridas and Louisiana, or a part thereof—for the purpose of conquering the same for the King of Great Britain."[80]

Upon receiving the report of the select committee, the House adopted impeachment charges against Blount and asked that his seat be "sequestered." But the Senate did not bring him to trial; instead the members expelled him from the Senate, an action which made a successful impeachment trial virtually impossible, for he could not be tried and removed when he no longer held a seat in the Senate.[81]

The conspiracy was badly handled in Congress. But then the government had had no experience in dealing with impeachable offenses against the United States. Still the possibility of a Senate trial on the conspiracy charges passed by the House remained alive even though its practicality (and legality) worried some lawyers in Congress. Meanwhile, Blount wasted no time in taking advantage of the congressional action against him. He admitted his letter was unfortunate. "It makes a damnable fuss here," he wrote from Philadelphia. "I hope, however, the people upon the Western Waters will see nothing but good in it, for so I intended it —especially for Tennessee."[82] Blount knew there was sympathy and understanding in the west for his conspiratorial actions; he also knew there was resentment against "eastern" hostility to western economic and political aspirations as expressed in the impeachment charges.

Awaiting possible trial in the Senate, Blount posted bond and returned to Tennessee. Some of his friends at home were cautious about expressing their loyalty to him. Not Jackson.[83] Committed mind and will to the entire conspiratorial design against the Spanish in Florida and Louisiana, and fiercely loyal to his friends as a matter of principle, he stoutly defended his political mentor at every opportunity and sought to explain and justify the conspiracy in terms of its advantages to westerners. It was not difficult. The west needed the Mississippi, it needed New Orleans, it needed the removal of any presence in the southwest that might halt or slow the physical and economic progress of Americans along the frontier. That included both foreigners and Indians.

Jackson was particularly eloquent in conjuring for western minds what might have been accomplished for them had the conspiracy succeeded. Blount, their paladin, was simply a victim of party prejudice engineered by the Adams administration. Tennesseans could believe this charge against a President who continued to apply Washington's Indian policy and to forcibly remove white settlers living on Indian lands. They believed the President hated the west.

Blount could have run for reelection to the United States Senate to show easterners that they were not going to push westerners around and get away with it. And no doubt he would have been reelected.[84] Instead, with impeachment charges still hanging over him, he decided upon a plan (he was an inveterate intriguer) whereby he would succeed Sevier as governor of Tennessee. The plan was simplified by Sevier's desire to resign his office once he had been appointed brigadier general of a provisional army that was being recruited in anticipation of war with France. Given Napoleon's depredations of American commerce and shipping and the shooting war on the high seas between the two nations during the late 1790s, a formal declaration of hostilities by the United States against France seemed imminent.[85] Such a war meant further military glory for Sevier and he was quite prepared to exchange the robes of executive leadership for the uniform of military leadership. For Blount it was a matter of getting himself elected to the state senate and then getting himself chosen speaker—for as speaker he would automatically succeed as governor when Sevier resigned.

But war with France never came and Sevier continued as governor. Blount was elected to the Tennessee senate, where he remained despite the decision of the United States Senate to bring him to trial late in 1798. His defense, conducted by counsel without benefit of Blount's presence, was based principally on the technical question of whether senators were included within the meaning of the impeachment clause of the Constitution. In any event, said his lawyer, Blount was no longer a senator and therefore could not be tried, much less removed. The more serious charges drawn up by the House of Representatives—that he conspired to violate American neutrality, to seduce an official from the performance of his duty, and to undermine Indian relations with the United States— were largely ignored. The Senate acquiesced to this charade and on January 11, 1799, it decided it had no jurisdiction in the case and dismissed the impeachment.

With Blount out of the United States Senate and unwilling to stand for reelection it was necessary to select someone to replace him. The

Blount clique also decided to terminate William Cocke's tenure in the Senate (he had been elected to a two-year term) as punishment for Cocke's vote to expel Blount from the Senate. Cocke no longer belonged to the Blount faction, having sensed that his career would make better progress in another direction. His act of "treachery" in the Senate completed his divorce from his former friends.

Joseph Anderson stood for Blount's seat in the Senate and was elected without opposition.[86] Since Cocke had every intention of running for reelection, the Blount forces had to find someone who could muster strong support against him. They nominated Jackson on the basis of his excellent record in the House of Representatives, his successful defense of Tennessee interests, and the consequent approval he won among the voters. "He was a valuable and highly respected member of Congress," Blount declared.[87] And loyal, too. His defense of Blount when the conspiracy unraveled was heroic. As a final "blessing," Blount publicly added his own endorsement and then let it be known in the Knoxville *Gazette* that "it was as certain as the Decrees of Heaven that Cocke would not be elected a Senator."[88]

The election by the Tennessee legislature involved a six-year term. Cocke received 13 votes (one cast by his son and another by "one who would have voted against him if necessary to insure Jackson's Election"[89]) and Jackson received 20. Blount was delighted. "Jackson Ele[ction] had my most hearty Concurrence," he wrote. He was also pleased to learn that Cocke "has written to all his Senatorial Friends that I prevented" his election. "That was doing as I could have wished him to have done."[90] William C. C. Claiborne received the nod as Jackson's replacement in the House of Representatives. Blount exulted over all three results. "Congress will find in the two Senators & the Representative of Tennessee Three warm Republicans."[91]

Then, about to leave for Philadelphia to commence his new duties, Jackson got into a vicious row with Cocke—and he was quite ready to shed blood to settle his grievance. The immediate cause of the quarrel was what Jackson regarded as Cocke's "baseness" in betraying a confidence by revealing the contents of a private letter Jackson had written him, a letter that, in print, did not exactly flatter Jackson's political image. In fact the real cause of their bitterness was the recent election. Both took the election very seriously, and Cocke was particularly aggrieved by its outcome.

Jackson vented his rancor over the incident in a letter to Cocke dated November 9, 1797.

Your sacrificing all private confidence by making publick my private letter merits & receives my utmost indignation, Sir the baseness of your heart in violating a confidenc reposed in you in an hour of intimate friendship, should as I conceive it was between you and me, by the most solemn obligation will bring down the indignation of the thinking part of mankind upon you & the thunderbolt you were preparing for me will burst upon your own head, it will occasion that part of mankind, that heretofore view'd you worthy of publick confidence to pause a moment & reflect how far a man is worthy of publick confidence who has violated all kind of *private* at the Shrine of malice occasioned by goaded disappointment, the Western world will think for themselves like freemen as they are & view the man who has made such sacrifice as you have done, capable of betraying all publick confidence to private interest.[92]

Six months later Jackson was still braying at Cocke. "My feelings & justice," he wrote, "demand that the opproprium that has been attached to my character upon false evidence must be publickly washed away by an open declaration that I did not merit the stigma, this is what justice demands, and which I will obtain at the risque of my blood. . . . my friend Mr Sweetman is authorized to name the time & place to meet me to give me that satisfaction that the wounded feelings of a Gentleman requires."[93] Fortunately a duel was avoided when both men agreed—since both claimed the other had received and credited "false information"— to have the dispute arbitrated by a panel of men they both respected.[94] Jackson was no fool. He was as quick as the next man to disengage from a potential duel, provided his honor and his reputation suffered no critical whispers. Apparently the findings of the panel satisfied Jackson— he was ready and anxious to be satisfied—and a bloody encounter was avoided.

The tone of Jackson's letters in this dispute and his seeming readiness to shoot a man over what can only be described as a shallow pretext give some indication of his general mood during the winter of 1797–98. When he departed Tennessee to begin his senatorial duties he left a wife distressed by his absence and resentful of his willingness to go. The "Situation in which I left her—*(Bathed in Tears),*" he wrote his brother-in-law, "fills me with woe. Indeed Sir, It has given me more pain than any Event in my life—but I trust She will not remain long in her dolefull mood,. but will again be Cheerful. Could I learn, that, that was the case I could be Satisfied."[95] Rachel always resented his departures and invariably created a hysterical scene when he left home.

In Philadelphia Jackson was one of the walking wounded. His generally angry, unhappy mood prevailed throughout his entire senatorial term, brief as it was. Vice President Thomas Jefferson, who had no great love for Jackson once he got to know him, later recalled the young senator's arriving to take his seat. He remembered the anger. "His passions are terrible," Jefferson said. "When I was President of the Senate, he was Senator, and he could never speak on account of the rashness of his feelings. I have seen him attempt it repeatedly, and as often choke with rage. His passions are, no doubt, cooler now; he has been much tried since I knew him, but he is a dangerous man."[96]

There was something terribly wrong with Jackson that winter, and it showed. One of his agonies was certainly financial. Every few years his involvement with David Allison came back to plague him. Jackson complained and threatened, but it did him little good. Finally Allison was thrown into debtor's prison in Philadelphia (where he died a little over a year later, on September 30, 1798). Still Jackson fumed, despite the poor man's incarceration. "On the Subject of Mr. Allison," he wrote John Overton, "I can assure you there are no hopes of Payment, I believe he is in funds. If he was only Possessed of honesty, but this is wanting. I happened to be Security for his appearance, at Jonesborough in '88. Judmt. last court has passed against me as his Bail for upwards of Two Hundred Dollars, and D--n the Rascal, he will not Evan convay me land in the amount. This Shews the Principle of the man."[97] Jackson had expected William Blount, from whom he had accepted a draft, to make good the money, but he soon discovered that Blount was himself in tight financial straits, worsened by his many business connections with Allison and the recent collapse of his conspiracy.[98] "You will have heard probably," Blount wrote, "that I am much embarrassed by my security paper for David Allison which is unfortunately too true. I shall however pay every just debt first and such others of them as have appealed to the law by law shall be paid."[99]

Another sign of Jackson's distress at this time—if not a cause of it— was his inactivity in the Senate. His senatorial record is nearly blank. Although he responded to a number of roll calls, his participation in debate was nil. He chaired one committee, introduced one bill, and twice called for the yeas and nays. As something of a sign of his disaffection, he voted with the majority only 13 times out of a total of 34 votes. He opposed the nomination of General Arthur St. Clair as governor of the Northwest Territory and voted against the nomination of John Quincy Adams as commissioner to Sweden. On the question of the Blount impeachment he was strictly partisan. He voted to postpone consideration of the reports of the impeachment proceedings, voted against the reports themselves, and finally voted to deny payment for the expenses incurred by the house committee on impeachment.[100]

Clearly Jackson did not belong in the Senate, and he probably knew it. He was too young, too inexperienced. Sitting in that quiet chamber, hearing men of considerable experience and national distinction discuss momentous issues of war and peace, freedom and liberty, Jackson may have been intimidated. And if Jefferson was correct in his recollection that Jackson tried repeatedly to express himself on the floor and failed because of an emotional block, it is small wonder that his participation dwindled to nothing. It must have been very disheartening, very frustrating.

Still, Jackson had an enormous sense of duty so he regularly attended the Senate sessions and kept himself informed of national issues and conveyed his opinions about them to his friends and relatives in Tennessee. Especially grave were the negotiations in progress with France, as some Congressmen were determined on a war policy. But Jackson thought this belligerence was declining and that a treaty with France would eventually result. "France has finally concluded a treaty with the Emperor and the King of Sardinia," he told James Robertson, "and is now turning her force toward Great Britain. Bonaparte, with one hundred and fifty thousand troops (used to conquer), is ordered to the coast, and called the army of England. Do not then be surprised if my next letter should announce a revolution in England. Should Bonaparte make a landing on the English shore, tyranny will be humbled, a throne crushed, and a republic will spring from the wreck, and millions of distressed people restored to the rights of man by the conquering arm of Bonaparte."[101] Some of this rhetoric reflected Jackson's admiration of Napoleon; but much of it was wishful thinking stemming from his long hostility toward the British.

Jackson was also very conscious of President Adams's use of patronage—which, he said, was just like Washington's. He thought it an "execrable system." The "American mind" should be roused from its lethargy, he declared, over the determination of the President to force every man holding public office within the executive branch "to think as the Executive does" or lose his job.[102] (He was not so critical of the system when he himself became President thirty years later.)

Like President Washington, President Adams proved a great disappointment to Senator Jackson. On several occasions the entire Tennessee delegation in Congress felt compelled to complain directly to Adams about the administration's Indian policy. Repeated failures to conclude essential treaties with the Indians were driving settlers "to the Spanish Dominions."[103] Worse, the federal government was guilty of the grossest violation of personal liberty in carrying out its Indian policy. The action was so monstrous that Jackson and his colleagues Joseph Anderson and William C. C. Claiborne sent a blistering letter to the President.

By last post, we receiv'd letters from the Governor of the State of Tennessee, informing us, that Colonel [Thomas] Butler, the Commanding Officer of the Federal Troops, in that State, had caused the Honoble David Campbell (Who is one of the Judges of the State of Tennessee) to be taken from his bed, about ten O Clock at night by a Military force [on the charge of trespassing on Indian lands without a passport], and in that ignonimous manner, Conducted a prisoner to the Camp—where the Judge was detaind, until Some time the next day, before he was liberated. . . .

Representing as we do, the Sovereignty of the State of Tennessee, and Considering that Sovereignty as haveing been Outrag'd by the Conduct of Colonel Butler, on the person of one of the Supreme Judges of the State, as also the rights of Civil Liberty, most unwarrantably Violated. To you Sir, as the Guardian of the Constitution, and the Supporter of the Laws, we appeal for redress—and trust, that you will take Such measures, as will not only hereafter, protect the Citizens of our State, from Such wanton Violence; but will cause, the most ample attonement to be made; for the integrity offered to the State—Which we conceive, can only be done, by removing from his Command, the auther of Such Military Tyranny.

In a former letter, we intimated to you, that the Conduct of Some of the Military, was rather calculated to irritate than Conciliate, the minds of our Suffering fellow Citizens. Instances of an unwarrantable exercise of Military power, had at that time, been Communicated to us, but little did we then expect, that any of the Officers, wou'd have proceeded to the Commission of so dareing an Outrage against the Dignity of the State, and the rights of Civil liberty. We request that you will please to give us, an answer to this adress; in order that we may be enabled, to Communicate to our State and its Citizens, your determination upon this Subject.[104]

It was a grand letter. Jackson and his colleagues never spoke more splendidly. Although President Adams responded satisfactorily and a new and improved Indian treaty was soon concluded, Jackson was "disgusted with the administration of the government."[105] Bored, too, by the inactivity of Congress and wearied by letter writing, which he found "Irksome."[106] He did manage to rouse his interest in "compensations of Marshals and attornies" and similar financial legislation that might prove important to Tennesseans.[107] In one instance he functioned effectively for his constituents by assisting the government in drawing up a treaty with the Cherokees that gained additional land for white settlers.[108] Neither as settler nor as congressman did Jackson defend or protect Indian rights. But he would have been a most uncommon frontiersman had he behaved differently.

Everything considered, Jackson failed completely as senator although Tennesseans thought otherwise since they liked the way he attended to their interests. The office suited neither him nor his temperament. He was too young and inexperienced to serve satisfactorily—and too wise not to recognize it. He was moody and angry. He was plagued by debts. He was inarticulate in debate and stammered into frustration and silence. In February he fell on the ice and injured his left knee; this confined him for many days. He spent the "best hours of every day for seven successive months quiescent in a red morocco chair."[109] That was no life for Jackson, particularly when he could not function. And what with being bored and unhappy and concerned about Rachel and harassed by debts and disgusted with the government he was in no mood to act his senatorial role. Indeed, one session of the Senate was all he could stomach, and so in April 1798 he asked for and obtained a leave of absence for the remainder of the session. On his return to Nashville he resigned his seat without apology or explanation. It was a flat rejection of a job that he could not handle.[110]

CHAPTER 8

Mr. Justice Jackson

ONE REASON FOR JACKSON'S DECISION to resign from the Senate was the possibility of another office, one that would keep him close to his interests in Tennessee without requiring him to leave the state for months on end, one that would pay more than any other office in the state with the exception of the governorship, and one that would advance his political and military ambitions by taking him to all parts of Tennessee and bringing him into contact with the people and the leaders of the various sections of the state. He had his eye on election by the legislature to a seat on the bench of the state superior court, often called the supreme court because its judges sitting together comprised Tennessee's highest tribunal. The post carried an annual salary of $600, which was $150 less than the salary of the governor.

It is not clear whether Jackson initiated the move toward a judgeship or whether he was first approached by a friend or a member of the Blount faction. Whatever the circumstances, he was elected without opposition to the bench in 1798 at the age of 31, shortly after his return to Tennessee. With his distinguished reputation and standing in the state, his affiliation with the Blount organization, and his large circle of friends, many of whom were well connected, there was no difficulty in arranging his election by the legislature. Previously, Blount had spoken with Jackson and gained his acceptance of the post if the appointment should be tendered. Said Blount to Governor Sevier: "Your excellency will recollect that some days past I suggested to you that I had reason to believe Mr. Andrew Jackson would accept the office of Judge . . . A letter from him which I had received in answer to one I had written to him, in which I had informed him it was the wish of many people in this quarter of the State that he should do so if by you appointed had authorized me to make to you the suggestion above alluded to towit: that he would accept if appointed."[1] In a subsequent letter to the governor, Blount said it was the definite wish of the people from the western country "that Andrew Jackson should be appointed."[2] Sevier wrote to Jackson on August 29, 1798, saying "that your Acceptance of the office, I have reasons to believe will give general Satisfaction." If you are willing to serve, Sevier continued, "you will please Consider yourself as Already appointed."[3] Formal election by the Tennessee legislature followed a few months later.[4]

Jackson served on the bench for six years, holding his court in the principal communities of Tennessee such as Knoxville, Jonesborough, and Nashville. From all indications he was a good judge, one who believed in a strong judiciary. Just a few years earlier he had told William Blount, "I am of opinion that a good Judiciary lends much to the dignity of a state and the happiness of the people. When on the Contrary a bad Judiciary involved in party business is the greatest Curse that can befall a Country."[5] Considering how little law Jackson actually knew to qualify as a jurist, he earned a respectable reputation and record.

There were several reasons for Jackson's subsequent success. He was a man of the highest integrity; his decisions were swift and devoid of prejudice or discrimination; he was courageous and he spoke without fear or hesitation. Moreover, he had a fierce sense of justice, however wrongheaded it might be at times. It was this sense that sustained his impartiality under most circumstances. "Tradition reports," an early biographer said, "that he maintained the dignity and authority of the bench, while he was *on* the bench; and that his decisions were short, untechnical, unlearned, sometimes ungrammatical, and generally right."[6] If his decisions were indeed generally right, then surely justice and the people of Tennessee were well served—with or without the supporting niceties of legal scholarship.

Recorded decisions did not become general practice in Tennessee until after Jackson left the bench in 1804. Consequently, only five of his written decisions survive, each signed by Jackson and the other members of superior court.[7] Judicial proceedings in Tennessee at this period were neither primitive nor makeshift. Early judges were careful to establish proper courtroom practice and decorum, and they insisted on strict compliance with accepted procedures. Disrespect for the law, rowdy behavior, and legal highjinks brought severe penalties. Jackson knew what was proper and what was expected of him. He wore a judicial gown in court —perhaps a reflection of his enormous sense of dignity and self-importance, perhaps an indication that he felt the office dictated the wearing of a gown—and for the most part he performed with distinction.

It was widely said that no backlog ever clogged the Jackson court. Cases were dispatched with a swiftness that would stagger more learned jurists. In fifteen days Jackson went through fifty cases.

On one occasion Jackson was holding court in a little village, "dispensing justice in large and small doses," when a great, hulking fellow named Russell Bean, who had been indicted for cutting off the ears of his infant child in a "drunken frolic," paraded before the court, cursing judge, jury, and all assembled, and then marched out the door. "Sheriff," Judge Jackson intoned in his most solemn voice, "arrest that man for contempt of court and confine him." The sheriff went to collar the offender—and soon returned emptyhanded with the excuse that it was impossible to apprehend the culprit.

"Summon a posse, then," the judge commanded, "and bring him before me."

Off the sheriff went again, and again he returned without a prisoner. No one dared lay a hand on the armed man; Bean threatened to shoot the "first skunk that came within ten feet of him."

At this Jackson "waxed wroth." "Mr. Sheriff," he stormed, "since you can not obey my orders, summon me; yes, sir, summon me."

"Well, judge, if you say so, though I don't like to do it; but if you will try, why I suppose I must summon you."

"Very well," Jackson said, rising and walking toward the door, "I adjourn this court ten minutes."

Bean was standing a short distance from the court, in the center of a crowd, cursing and flourishing his weapons and vowing death and damnation to all who might attempt to molest him.

Mr. Justice Jackson walked straight toward the man, a pistol in each hand. "Now," he roared, staring into the eyes of the ruffian, "surrender, you infernal villain, this very instant, or I'll blow you through."

Bean stood perfectly still, watching Jackson's blazing eyes. Then, as though reading something terrible in those eyes, he quietly surrendered his weapons. "There, judge," he said, "it's no use, I give in." He was completely cowed and surrendered meekly.

A few days later Bean was asked why he gave up to Jackson after having defied an entire posse. "Why," he said, "when he came up, I looked him in the eye, and I saw shoot, and there wasn't shoot in nary other eye in the crowd; and so I says to myself, says I, hoss, it's about time to sing small, and so I did."[8]

Thus Jackson made a very effective backwoods judge. There was no fooling with him. There was "shoot" in his eyes, and sane men did not argue with that.

Jackson was careful about the dignity of his court and jealous of his reputation as an honest judge. When one man reportedly impugned his honesty, Jackson called him to account. The man denied the charge, but the judge was not satisfied until an affadavit had been duly sworn and attested to.

June 15, 1800

State of Tennessee, Davidson County.

Whereas a report has been in circulation that I Michael Glieves of the county and state aforesaid should have on the sixth day of June in the year of our Lord Eighteen hundred and at the House of John Bosley utter and speak the following words of his honour Judge Jackson (to wit) As honest a man as Andrew Jackson was called he had stolen his Bull and he could prove it. I do therefore certify that if I did speak the above named words they were groundless and unfounded and further I do certify that I never did suspect Andrew Jackson of a dishonest act in my life. Given under my hand this fifteenth Day of June 1800.

Michel Gleave

Test
Saml Johnson[9]

Ordinarily Jackson would have demanded "satisfaction." Now that he was a judge such a demand might appear unseemly. He must be satisfied with an affadavit that was legally recorded and could be displayed publicly if necessary.

As good as Jackson was on the bench, many friends kept after him to run for Congress and to engage in a more active political life. "I have been importuned," he wrote Robert Hays, "nay I may Say pressed by Some to let my name run [for Congress]. On the other hand I am pressed by the Barr to remain upon the Bench. One event has taken place, that I believe will determin me to remain where I am—and you may believe me when I Say it is motives of Publick good."[10] Hugh Lawson White, a very able lawyer who was soon to be elected to the bench, gave as condition for his own election that Jackson not leave the judiciary. The election of White, said Jackson, "is and ought to be the wish of every Citizen— and nothing can be of greater importance to the State. To have this done is my greatest wish—and If my remaining on my present Seat will be conducive to the object it is a duty I owe my country to do."[11]

White's testimonial was repeated by others.[12] Jackson must remain on the bench. He was an asset to the judicial process and his resignation would be a distinct loss to the people of Tennessee. Pleased and convinced, he bowed to their will.

As Jackson moved about Tennessee dispensing justice, he observed the many transformations that had occurred in the state since his arrival in 1788, some dozen years earlier. New towns dotted the landscape almost to the Mississippi River; frame houses replaced rude log cabins; dancing masters, dressmakers, and other artisans were setting up shop in the leading settlements; stores carried silks and brocades as well as homespun and buckskin. Civilized society had arrived, and the frontier was moving on—although vestiges of it would linger for many years.

During his tenure as a superior court judge, Jackson helped organize a lodge of the Order of Freemasons in Tennessee. The grand lodge of North Carolina on September 5, 1801, provided the necessary dispensation to "open the Lodge in due form on the first Degree of Masonry." Jackson, the "Right Worshipful George W. Campbell Master Jenkin Whiteside Senior Warden John Rhea Junior Warden," and others met at the home of Daniel Harrison, where the lodge was opened. Jackson was named senior warden pro tem, and on his motion a committee was formed to prepare the bylaws for the governance of the lodge.[13]

It also developed during Jackson's judicial career that his longsmoldering feud with Governor John Sevier broke out into violent conflict. And it could only happen in the west that the governor of the state and a justice of the supreme court would end up shooting at one another. This new train of events began in 1797 when Jackson journeyed to Philadelphia for the congressional session. Along the way he met John Love, who told Jackson of a remarkable land fraud in which a company of speculators in Tennessee were forging North Carolina land warrants and selling Tennessee lands to which they held no right. Much of the fraud operated through the office of James Glasgow, secretary of state for North Carolina. At first Jackson did not know the extent of the conspiracy or the names of the principal agents. He knew only that the agents in Nashville were William Terrell Lewis and William Tyrell.[14]

Because he was an upright and honorable citizen who knew "the duty I owed to my country," Jackson informed the governor of North Carolina of the conspiracy so "that the fraudulent plans of those two Villians might be arested, regardless of who might be implicated with them." Then he learned the names of some of the others involved in the fraud. To his shock and dismay he discovered his wife's brother, Stockley Donelson, implicated. Nevertheless Jackson felt compelled to expose the plot.[15]

He turned his information over to the governor of North Carolina along with a written statement about the origin of his discovery, and these were relayed to the state assembly. On March 24, 1798, after an extended investigation by a legislative committee, a report was issued that detailed an enormous conspiracy involving more than four million acres of land —about one-sixth of the state of Tennessee.[16] Shades of William Blount! But the plot went deeper. It included forgeries of papers which entitled revolutionary war soldiers to lands in the west and "under cover" of which the state had been cheated of vast tracts of land.[17]

The governor of North Carolina asked Governor Sevier for the extradition of some of the accused. Sevier refused. Then a letter was found in Glasgow's office that seemed to implicate Sevier himself in the fraud. Under the Confiscation Act of 1779, which permitted patriots of the Revolution to purchase Tory property, Sevier had obtained a number of land warrants in an area east of the mountains which he wanted shifted to the Cumberland region because the land was more attractive to settlers and he could make a greater profit. Sevier also wanted the price on the face of the warrants increased from fifty shillings per hundred acres to ten pounds. This would give him the benefit of an act passed in 1783 that fixed the ten-pound figure for lands that lay beyond the mountains. To help him arrange the substitution Sevier found a willing accomplice in James Glasgow who was empowered to issue grants to rightful claimants. For this favor Sevier gave Glasgow three of his warrants (for 640 acres each), stating in a letter that he hoped the warrants were sufficient to pay the fees to which Glasgow was entitled. Glasgow made it appear as though the land had been taken under the 1783 law rather than under the 1779 law.[18]

Beginning with what John Love had told him in 1797, Jackson slowly pieced together the facts of the conspiracy. Most of the information he subsequently gathered was pried from a county land agent by threatening to expose the agent's father, who was also involved in the fraud.[19] After he had reconstructed the main outline of the fraud Jackson did something extraordinary when he submitted his evidence to the governor of North Carolina. He failed to name Sevier.

There were good reasons for his silence, all of them political. Sevier and Jackson had just eased past one potential difficulty when Sevier raised no objection to Jackson's election to the Senate. The governor repeated this courtesy when Jackson stood for election to the bench. Sevier was an important power in Tennessee, especially in the eastern section of the state, and Jackson dared not challenge that power—yet. For the moment it made a great deal of sense to cooperate with that power as much as possible. More important, Jackson still hungered for the rank of major general in the militia—indeed it became a passion—and the one man who could successfully block him, as proved in the last election, was John

Sevier. Perhaps the next time, if Sevier did not interfere, Jackson could win that election. Finally, by keeping the information quiet, he retained a secret weapon that he might use against the governor at any time. He had, in effect, the makings of political blackmail. So Jackson bided his time and maintained friendly relations with Sevier. He even expressed a willingness to perform any service in the Mero District that the governor might wish. "I thank you sir," Sevier wrote him, "for your Very polite offer, to be the bearer of Any commands that I might have to Mero."[20]

Only the election of the major general could shatter this friendly truce—and eventually it did. Sevier had run out his constitutional limit of three successive terms as governor of the state and could run again only after the interval of another term. He had been succeeded by Archibald Roane, a member of the Blount faction and Jackson's friend.[21] Sevier, out of a job, decided to take over the militia again. But Jackson wanted the post, and for years he had been working diligently to arrange his election. So successful was he in these efforts that the officers of the militia not only put him forward but made it appear that his election was "unsolicited."[22]

Sevier was shocked to learn he had been challenged for the post by a lawyer with no known military experience. His shock turned to outrage when the results of the election, held on February 5, 1802, were announced. Both he and Jackson received seventeen votes while Brigadier General James Winchester got three. That Jackson could achieve such a feat against an immensely popular war hero demonstrates how far his political skills had advanced and how well he had used them. Over the previous few years he had assiduously cultivated the friendship of many of the officers of the militia. He became particularly popular with the young officers. They liked his style and they imitated it. Whatever Jackson did or said or wore quickly became fashionable among them. Jackson would have triumphed overwhelmingly in the election had he not been running against someone as popular and powerful as John Sevier.

A tie existed, and the final selection lay with the new governor. Governor Roane broke the tie in favor of his old friend, Andrew Jackson. Thus, at the age of thirty-five, Mr. Justice Jackson became Major General Andrew Jackson of the Tennessee militia. It was one of the most important and decisive events in his life.

According to some Tennessee historians, Jackson presented his evidence of land fraud against Sevier to Roane "on the day when the Governor cast the deciding vote."[23] He presented an affidavit by John Carter, entry taker for Washington County, and documents that supported the charges of fraud. Since Roane intended to seek reelection as governor the following year, and since Sevier would undoubtedly challenge him, this evidence, when published, could damage if not destroy Sevier's reputation. In turning it over to Roane, Jackson practically guaranteed the governor's reelection. Supposedly, in appreciation, Roane then broke the tie in Jackson's favor.

Whatever the exact day of transfer, Jackson did in fact give his evidence to Roane. In challenging the great revolutionary war hero and providing the issue to wreck Sevier's career, Jackson in effect claimed political preeminence in West Tennessee.[24] Since William Blount had died suddenly on March 21, 1800, his leadership in the west was now assumed by Andrew Jackson.

In the following year, 1803, Sevier announced his candidacy for governor. Roane thereupon released his information, and the political explosion followed. Naturally Jackson had to substantiate the charges, and on July 27, 1803, he authored a communication published in the Knoxville *Gazette* charging Sevier with fraud. The three warrants given to Glasgow, he said, constituted a bribe to commit a crime. Jackson claimed the warrants were worth $960 and were given for a service that, had it been legal, would have cost no more than one dollar.[25]

Sevier was livid. That a pettifogging lawyer (as he called Jackson) would dare to compete for military office with a revolutionary war hero was bad enough; that he would accuse him of fraud was monstrous. Furious at the outcome of the militia election and seething with indignation over the fraud charges, Sevier's friends in the legislature rushed through a bill on November 5, 1803, dividing the military command and creating two militia districts, one in the east and one in the west, and allowing Jackson to retain command over the western district.

Sevier responded to Jackson's newspaper attack on August 8, 1803, insisting in the *Gazette* that he had committed no crime in "consolidating" his landholdings or in paying Glasgow a reasonable free for a legitimate service. Obviously, he said, the charges were politically motivated in an attempt to discredit him with the people.

As the controversy intensified the danger of violence also increased. Not much later, Jackson was informed of a "combination" to mob him on his arrival at Jonesborough. He had been quite ill for several days, and when he arrived at Jonesborough he took to his bed with a high fever. A friend came to his room with a warning that a regiment of men commanded by Colonel Harrison had assembled in front of the house to "tar and feather" him. The friend begged him to lock his door. Instead, Jackson rose from his bed, threw open the door, and said to his friend, "Give my compliments to Colonel Harrison, and tell him my door is open to receive him and his regiment whenever they choose to wait upon me; and that I hope the colonel's chivalry will induce him to lead his men, and not follow them." The message was delivered. As soon as they heard the slightly menacing words the mob quietly dispersed.[26]

But a showdown could not be avoided indefinitely. On the first day of October 1803, Mr. Justice Jackson arrived in Knoxville to hold court and ran into Sevier in the public square.[27] It was a dramatic moment. Seeing the cause of his present embarrassment, Sevier slashed at him with stinging words about daring to challenge and humiliate a great man. Who did Jackson, a pitiful nothing of a lawyer, think he was? Sevier sneered at him and his "pretensions." Caught off guard, and confused by the torrent of abuse, the judge stammered a defense by citing his considerable services to the state.

"Services?" Sevier laughed, his voice soaring with sarcasm. "I know of no great service you have rendered the country, except taking a trip to Natchez with another man's wife."

Jackson blanched. He was transfixed, then went wild. "Great God!" he screamed, "do you mention *her* sacred name?"

Pistols were drawn. The crowd scattered. Shots rang out and one bystander was grazed by a bullet. Fortunately the antagonists were separated before a general melee could begin; but thereafter the expression "Great God" became a favorite saying with the young men of Knoxville.[28]

As soon as he could lay hands on pen and paper Jackson scratched out a challenge.

> Knoxville, October 2, 1803
>
> *Sir,* The ungentlemanly expressions, and gasgonading conduct of yours, relative to me on yesterday was in true character of yourself, and unmask you to the world, and plainly shews that they were the ebulitions of a base mind goaded with stuborn proof of fraud, and flowing from a source devoid of every refined sentiment, or delicate sensation. But Sir the voice of the people has made you a Governor, this alone makes you worthy of my notice, or the notice of any Gentleman. For the Office I have respect, and as such I only deign to notice you, and call upon you for that satisfaction and explanation that your ungentlemanly conduct and expressions require, for this purpose I request an interview, and my friend who will hand you this will point out the time and place, when and where I shall expect to see you with your friend and no other person. my friend [Captain Andrew White] and myself will be armed with pistols—you cannot mistake me or my meaning.
>
> I am etc. etc.
>
> Andrew Jackson[29]

Sevier accepted the challenge to meet at any time and place, provided it was not on the sacred soil of Tennessee.[30] To Jackson that was "a mere subterfuge. Your attack was in the Town of Knoxville," he wrote Sevier. "Did you take the name of a lady into your poluted lips in the Town of Knoxville? Did you challeng me to draw, when you were armed with a cutlass and I with a cane, and now sir in the neighborhood of Knoxville you shall atone for it or I will publish you as a coward and a poltroon. . . . I shall expect an answer in the space of one hour."[31]

Sevier did not respond.

Jackson wrote again, and now he was willing (since Sevier was so squeamish) to preserve Tennessee soil from desecration and to fight in Georgia, Virginia, North Carolina, or the "Indian boundary line." To prod Sevier to a response, Jackson added, "I have spoke for a place in the paper [*Gazette*] for the following advertisement, and I have named publickly that you are the greatest coward I ever had an[y]thing to do with. the advertisement as follows, To all who shall see these presents Greeting. Know ye that I Andrew Jackson, do pronounce, publish, and declare to the world, that his excellency John Sevier, Captain General and commander in chief of the land and naval forces of the state of Tennessee, is a base coward and poltroon. He will basely insult, but has not courage to repair the wound. *Andrew Jackson.*"[32]

Sevier shot right back:

> Sir
> I am again perplexed with your scurilous and paltroon language. You now pretend you want an interview in this neighborhood; this evening, or tomorrow Morning!! And all this great readiness After you have been so repeatedly informed that I would not attempt A thing of the kind within the State of Tennessee. I have constantly informed you I would cheerfully wait on you in any other Quarter and that you had nothing to do but Name the place and you should be Accommodated. I am Now constrained to tell you, that your conduct, during the whole of your pretended bravery, Shews you to be a pitiful paltroon And Coward, for your propositions are such as you and every other person of common Understanding do well know is out of my power to Accede to,—especially you a *Judge!!*
> Therefore the whole tenor of your pretended readiness is intended for nothing more than a cowardly evasion.
> Now Sir, if you wish the interview accept the proposal I have made you, and let us prepare for the Campaign.
> I have a friend to attend me. I shall not receive another letter from you, as I deem you a Coward.
>
> *John Sevier*[33]

When Jackson's "advertisement" appeared in the *Gazette* on Monday, October 10, 1803, the sound and fury the two men had poured upon paper was finally translated into action; they agreed to meet on Wednesday in the Indian territory in the neighborhood of South West Point. Without a moment's delay Jackson rode straight to the rendezvous, impatient to be in position and ready when his antagonist arrived.

He waited for days. No Sevier. Not a sign.

Furious, Jackson started back to Knoxville determined to force the coward to a showdown. He had not gone a mile when he spotted his man riding toward him in the company of mounted men. Jackson drew a pistol, dismounted, and drew a second pistol. Seeing the armed judge before him, Sevier leaped from his horse, a pistol in each hand.

The two men glared, then began to curse and abuse each other as though it was essential to experience the delight of tongue-lashing before shooting one another. The verbal assault was so therapeutic that for the moment they put away their pistols.

Then Jackson lunged at Sevier, threatening to cane him. Sevier drew his sword, which "frightened his horse and he ran away with the Governor's Pistols." Not to lose an opportunity, Jackson drew a pistol, whereupon Sevier ducked behind a tree to get out of the line of fire. At that point Sevier's son drew on Jackson and Jackson's second drew on the son.

It was quite ridiculous. Jackson's second was aiming at Sevier's son, who was aiming at Jackson, who was aiming at Sevier, who was hidden behind a tree. Even the antagonists must have recognized the absurdity of it all. Finally members of Sevier's party rushed forward making friendly signs, and soon the two men, still cursing each other, put away their guns and—after some persuasion—agreed to end their murderous feud. The entire party rode together peaceably to Knoxville. Although Jackson and Sevier did not reconcile, their disagreement never flared again into open combat.[34]

Sevier won election to the governorship despite the accusations of wrongdoing. The people of Tennessee simply could not believe the charges leveled against their hero. To them, Sevier was synonymous with Tennessee, and they could no more vote against Sevier than vote against their own state. In all likelihood the scandal did more to harm Jackson's reputation than that of anyone else—which may in large part explain his furious verbal assaults on Sevier. Indeed the challenge to a duel may have been an *unconscious* attempt at political assassination. Jackson's party had failed in the election and would later fail in impeachment charges against Sevier; moreover, Jackson knew that as governor Sevier had it in his power to deprive him of any opportunity to distinguish himself as a general and Indian fighter. Why not, then, kill him?

Most historians generally agree that the quarrel between Jackson and Sevier marked the beginning of political sectionalism between East and West Tennessee. After William Blount's death in 1800, Jackson assumed political leadership of the Cumberland region and Sevier that of the eastern counties of the state.[35] Now the governor's election victory, the failure to prove the charges of land fraud, and Sevier's public insult to Jackson—and the fact that he got away with it—all combined to wreck what there was of the judge's political organization. It would take Jackson years to recapture the esteem he had once enjoyed among the people of Tennessee. The irony here is that if Sevier had been elected major general of the militia in 1802, he would probably never have become a candidate for governor and Roane would have won reelection without opposition.[36] But furious over his defeat by Jackson, Sevier announced his candidacy, the rivalry flared into the open and the state split in two.

Sevier's final judgment was that Andrew Jackson was "one of the most abandoned rascals in principle my eyes ever beheld."[37]

Jackson had also become estranged from his old friend and colleague, Judge John McNairy. A coolness had grown up between them since the year of the constitutional convention, when McNairy listened to stories of troublemakers who claimed that Jackson opposed his election as a delegate.[38] The two men became increasingly touchy with one another as McNairy drew closer to Sevier. The breach nearly became permanent when McNairy caused the removal of General Robertson from the Chickasaw Indian agency—which in turn produced the removal of their old friend Bennett Searcy as clerk of the agency. Indignant over these removals, Jackson expressed his anger to McNairy in language that almost severed their relationship permanently.

Although Jackson was generally recognized as the leading man in West Tennessee and had strengthened his position by allying himself with John Tipton, one of Sevier's earliest rivals,[39] Willie Blount, William's half brother, assumed nominal leadership of the Blount faction around the state. Although a man of some talent, Willie did not have his brother's political skills. Sevier had no trouble winning a second series of three terms as governor, from 1803 to 1809, after which Willie Blount replaced him. By 1809 Blount had constructed a respectable organization that helped him defeat William Cocke, Jackson's onetime rival for election to the United States Senate. The organization also provided two additional gubernatorial victories for Blount in 1811 and 1813.

The two events most critical to Jackson's military career—his election as major general of the militia and the outbreak of the War of 1812 —came at times when Sevier was out of office and the administration of the state was in the hands of Jackson's political friends. And while there is no question that Jackson was a man of considerable ability, ambition, and connections, yet there is much to be said in explaining his subsequent fame as a soldier and politician to just plain luck.

CHAPTER 9

The Duel

DURING THE PERIOD OF JACKSON'S early military career he received few calls for action from the federal government. The earliest alert came in 1803, immediately following the purchase of Louisiana.

The pressure to secure New Orleans and drive the foreigner from that strategic location built to an intolerable level once Napoleon forced the Spanish to return Louisiana to France. The southwest seethed with conspiracy.[1] Treason against the United States became an open invitation.

President Jefferson understood the danger. "There is on the globe one single spot," he wrote to Robert R. Livingston, American envoy to France, "the possessor of which is our natural and habitual enemy. It is New Orleans, through which the produce of three-eighths of our territory must pass to market. . . . The day that France takes possession of New Orleans . . . from that moment, we must marry ourselves to the British fleet and nation."[2] But instead of marrying the British nation, Jefferson secured the purchase of Louisiana from Napoleon, who needed the money and whose position in America and the Caribbean had weakened to the point where ridding himself of the territory became a practical necessity. In selling Louisiana to the United States, however, Napoleon violated an earlier treaty obligation never to alienate the territory except to return it to Spain.

Although Jefferson had grave doubts about the constitutionality of the purchase, he knew the alternative should any foreign power control New Orleans; it included the possibility of rebellion or treason by citizens of the southwest. "To lose our country by scrupulous adherence to written law," he reasoned, "would be to lose the law itself, with life, liberty, property and all those who are enjoying them with us; thus absurdly sacrificing the end to the means."[3] Burdened with fears that he was reducing the Constitution to a scrap of paper, he went ahead with the purchase anyway. But he had no choice. The safety of the Union dictated it.

Jefferson got more than he bargained for, much more than the crescent city and the mouth of the Mississippi River. The enormous stretch of land to the northwest that was part of the purchase flung the United States across the Mississippi River and propelled the nation further westward.

But the Spanish remained. Though forced out of Louisiana by Napoleon's treachery, they still occupied East and West Florida, Texas, Mexico, and the adjacent lands reaching as far west as California. And, like the Indians, the Spanish continued to be a threat and a menace to all Americans along the southern frontier. Indians and Spaniards both continued to inspire conspiracies.

The French, who had never actually occupied the territory but permitted the Spanish to administer it on their behalf, were now gone, but the question remained whether Spain would respect the purchase or declare it a violation of her treaty rights and refuse to surrender the territory. This troubled President Jefferson, and he sent an alert to the command in western Tennessee to stand ready to march in case it became necessary to expel the Spanish from Louisiana. Jackson responded promptly with a general order to the militia. It had the ring of authority and command.

The late conduct of the Spanish Government, added to the Hostile appearance and menacing attitude of their Armed forces already incamped within the limits of our government, make it necessary that the militia under my Command, should be in complete order and at a moments warning ready to march.

This armed force under the sanction of their government, have imprisoned and transported five of the good citizens of the U. states to the dominion of Spain. They have cut down and carried off the flag of the U. states, which was erected in the Cado nation of indians and within the limits of the U. States. They have compelled by force men in the employ of Government when exploring the red river to desist and come home and they have taken a unjustifiable and insulting position on the East side of the river sabine and within the Territory of New Orleans!!! Acts thus daring as well as degrading to our national Character and constituted rights demand prompt satisfaction and cannot fail to excite that resentment so becoming and so natural on the occassion.

Demanding "prompt satisfaction," Jackson sounded as though he would like nothing better than to summon the Spanish to the field of honor. Their presence was "degrading to our national Character." Jackson chose provocative words that would appeal to the sentiments of western Americans.

He told his soldiers to be ready to move if the opportunity presented itself. "Our good *materials, our best of men,* must be properly deciplined . . . to meet the wishes of the Genl. and the exegencies of our Country. Inspired with the laudable ambition of avenging our countries wrongs and impelled by the most cogant necessity of defending our national dignity and liberties, it is calculated that but one voice will be heard among us and that, that will be for *preperation and decipline.*" Accordingly, "You are . . . ordered, without delay, to place yr. brigade on the most respectable footing and be in readyness to furnish the quota required of you at the shortest notice."[4]

For a man of little military and command experience, Jackson suffered no sense of inadequacy about leading troops into combat. He had absolute confidence in himself. And he later transmitted that confidence to his men.

The treaty of cession between Napoleon and the American government was respected by the Spanish, and it was unnecessary to prod them out of Louisiana with a show of military force. Jackson clearly regretted missing a chance of humiliating the "hated Dons." The expulsion of foreign control from the Mississippi was a mighty deed in the minds of westerners, one that further endeared them to their new President. General Jackson told President Jefferson, "all the Western Hemisphere rejoices at the Joyfull news of the cession of Louisiana, an event which places the peace happiness and liberty of our country on a lasting basis, an event which generations yet unborn on each revolving year, will hail the day, and with it the causes that give it birth."[5] Later in the year General James Wilkinson and a detachment of regular army troops floated down the Mississippi and hoisted the American flag over the city of New Orleans.

The danger past, General Jackson returned to his judicial duties and his several business interests. But thoughts of Louisiana remained; it would need a government and a firm hand to guide it deftly into the American system—and surely no hand could be firmer than his own. Jackson soon saw himself governor of the territory and began to prepare an application for the appointment. Remembering William Blount's way of doing things, Jackson proceeded on the assumption that winning the appointment lay in the supportive efforts of others. He began by gathering the entire Tennessee delegation in Congress and getting them to sponsor his cause. That was an absolute prerequisite. And despite some hostile feelings (on account of the Sevier business) Jackson won the consent of the members for several reasons: because they knew he would do everything possible to assist Tennesseans' business interests in the region; they knew he would exercise firm control over the Indians; and they knew he could deal with the Spanish abrasively, if necessary, and that was an important consideration. They reckoned that Jackson was precisely what Louisiana needed, so the delegation enthusiastically signed a petition on his behalf to President Jefferson, requesting that he be appointed governor. It was a respectable beginning.

Jackson then turned to loyal and important Republicans, men whom Jefferson could not afford to ignore. During his years in Congress Jackson had met a number of distinguished men from whom he could request letters of recommendation. To give his petition a special touch he arranged a personal appeal from Matthew Lyon, one of the so-called martyrs of the Republican party who had been sent to prison for violating the Sedition Law during the Adams administration. Finally, to complete his application, Jackson journeyed to Washington, D.C., the nation's new capital, in the event Jefferson wanted to learn more of him in person. But Jackson could not bring himself to confront Jefferson face to face. He could not humiliate himself by asking the President for the appointment. He told John Coffee, his friend and business partner, "Under present circumstances my feelin could not consent to pay my respect to him [Jefferson] least it might be construed into the conduct of a courteor, and my vissit might have created such sensations in his mind. I therefore passed on without calling. of all ideas to me it is the most humiliating to be thought to cringe to power to obtain a favour or an appointment, feeling calculated to bend to those things, are badly calculated for a representative Government, where merrit alone ought to be road to preferment."[6]

Jefferson passed over Jackson's application. He probably gave it little consideration, knowing what he did of the Tennessean and his performance in the Senate. Jefferson appointed W. C. C. Claiborne, who had accompanied General Wilkinson to New Orleans to receive the transfer and serve as provisional governor of Louisiana. It was a natural, perhaps an obvious decision, but it staggered Jackson. In that single act relations between Jefferson and Jackson collapsed. It galled Jackson to be refused. It humiliated him to be passed over. In the following years Jackson became increasingly anti-Jefferson. He veered closer to the more extreme states' rights wing of the Republican party, taking his political direction from such doctrinaire Republicans as John Randolph of Roanoke and Nathaniel Macon of North Carolina.

Jackson's campaign for appointment demonstrated continued development of his political skills. What he had learned from the Blounts and the techniques he had applied to win command of the militia had been employed with deftness and decorum. In no way did his failure reflect discredit on him or on the manner of his campaign. Despite his setback, he had become a fairly skillful politician.

All his life Jackson liked to imagine that he had not pursued office, that office had pursued him in recognition of his manifold services to the people and the Republic. To some extent this was true; it was also true —and far more important—that like all successful politicians he was first and foremost a man in imperious pursuit of his star, a man whose ambition and political dexterity powered his ascent to fame.

On July 24, 1804, shortly after losing the Louisiana post, Jackson resigned his judicial office because of bad health—or so he said.[7] There may have been other reasons, however. It is possible that he reached this decision because a number of cases growing out of his disclosures of land fraud were likely to come before his court within the coming year. Resignation was preferable to further embarrassment in the matter.[8] And he could no longer afford the luxury of judicial life with its limited salary and its enormous demands on his time. His financial situation had deteriorated appreciably in the last few years; if he was to escape the possibility of bankruptcy, he must devote more time and energy to his personal affairs.

One major problem was the wretched Allison business, which had left Jackson in a very precarious position. It soon worsened. In 1794 John Gray Blount and his brother Thomas Blount sold 85,000 acres of land on the three forks of the Duck River to David Allison. On January 1, 1795, Allison mortgaged this property to Norton Pryor, a Philadelphia merchant, for $21,800.[9] After Allison's death, Pryor engaged Jackson to bring suit to foreclose the mortgage and gain clear title to the property. However, Jackson had just been elected judge of the superior court; he felt constrained not to involve himself in the proceeding and asked John Overton to prosecute the foreclosure case for him, offering to split the fee. Overton agreed.

On October 27, 1801, suit was brought in United States District Court to foreclose the mortgage on 85,000 acres of land to satisfy Allison's indebtedness of $21,800 to Pryor. The land was ordered sold and sixty days' notice was given in the Tennessee *Gazette*. On April 14, 1802, the sale took place. Jackson, acting for Pryor, purchased the land in three parcels: 40,000 acres for $730.50, another 35,000 acres for $638.50, and the final 10,000 acres (Jackson's fee for the transaction) for about $160.[10] Half of the 10,000-acre tract he purchased in his own name, the other half he transferred to Overton in accordance with their agreement. In disposing of this land just a few years later Jackson sold one tract for $1,666.66 —a profit of 2,000 percent![11]

On July 13, 1802, Jackson's brother-in-law, Robert Hays, the marshal of West Tennessee, issued deeds to the property. After splitting with Overton, Jackson proceeded to sell his share in small sections, "believing it to be a good tittle. . . . I never once thought of a defect in the decree, or the want of Jurisdiction in the court."[12] So certain was he of the deed that Jackson offered warranted titles to those who bought the land from him, thereby binding himself to buy back the land if the title proved defective—and to buy it back not at the original price but at the current value of the land when any defect in the title should be discovered. "I never once thought on the subject," Jackson moaned at a later date.[13]

Years passed and the land quadrupled in value with houses, barns, and cotton gins being added to the property. Within ten years the land was selling for $3 to $14 per acre, depending on improvements. In another ten years the minimum price was $5 an acre.[14]

In 1808 Andrew Erwin bought Pryor's land and went to Tennessee to sell it to individual purchasers. After receiving assurances from Jackson (who acted as legal agent for Pryor) that the title was good, Erwin took possession of the land, marked its boundaries, and initiated suit against squatters.

Then, in 1810 or 1811—Jackson could not remember the exact date —George W. Campbell told Jackson he had been examining the proceedings in the original suit in 1801 and had found that the decision was invalid because it had been handed down by a federal court that did not have jurisdiction. If Campbell was correct, Jackson faced ruin. The 85,000 acres were now worth hundreds of thousands of dollars. "I became alarmed," said Jackson—the more so when he learned "that the heirs of David Allison had it in their power at any time to redeem."[15]

With a desperation born of panic, Jackson galloped through the Indian wilderness into Georgia in search of the Allison heirs.[16] He found them in Wilkes County and begged them to sign over to him "all their rights to any property within the state of Tennessee that they were invested with by descent as heirs of David Allison."[17] He said he was willing, in exchange, to give up their father's notes to him—he estimated that Allison owed him approximately $20,000, including interest—and to make a small cash settlement of $500.[18] The $500 proved powerfully persuasive; Jackson convinced them to go along with his scheme. Alexander Allison, John Allison, and William Allison (for himself and for Peggy deceased) executed a deed to Jackson, who gave them a release against Allison's debt.[19]

Now the situation was reversed. Jackson held the only legal deed (if Campbell was correct in his opinion) not only to the 5,000 acres he had sold but to the entire 85,000 acres originally mortgaged to Pryor. He returned to Tennessee, gave clear title to those who had purchased from him and to John Overton, and tried to negotiate with Andrew Erwin for the land Erwin had purchased from Pryor. Erwin absolutely refused to bargain. He would not give the General a dollar, not a penny.

Shrewdly, Jackson bided his time. Later, when he had won a great victory over the Indians and felt himself in a strong position, he filed suit against Erwin. He argued that Erwin had conspired against his assuming title to the property and asked the court to grant him the land by virtue of the Allison deed.[20] For refusing to bargain in the first place, Erwin would be stripped of the entire property.

The case dragged on for ten years, while Jackson became a national hero. Erwin wrung his hands in dismay. Over a hundred subpoenas were served on the persons who had purchased land from him, and he himself was reported by Jackson to the President of the United States as trafficking illegally in slaves. The case was finally settled in the January 1824 term of the court of equity. Erwin agreed to pay Jackson $10,000, and Jackson conveyed to Erwin a deed of release for all of Allison's lands.[21]

When it came time to pay Jackson the $10,000, Mrs. Erwin went to the General and begged him to forgive the debt. She said her husband faced ruin as a result of the judgments that had piled up against him over the last few years. And Jackson did so. Having won his case in court, he graciously and generously waived payment.[22] It was all a matter of principle. And it was typically Jackson, vindictive one minute and generous to a fault the next.

The thirty-year history of the Allison land deal scarred Jackson for life with fearful marks of fiscal conservatism. He hated debt; paper money represented dishonest money; banks that manipulated debts and loans were an abomination. Felix Robertson, son of General James Robertson, reported that Jackson said "he would pay what he owed; he would do what he said he would."[23]

To pay what he owed, Jackson returned full time to his business interests in 1804. He resigned the judgeship, sold his plantation at Hunter's Hill (where for a time he had operated a small store and from a narrow window sold goods to the Indians), disposed of an additional 25,000 acres he held in various parts of the state (he continued his land speculation despite the Allison disaster), and moved with his wife and slaves to a 420-acre place about ten miles from Nashville which he came to call the Hermitage.[24] He expected to retire here and live out the rest of his days with Rachel. Through consolidation and liquidation he managed to pay off all his debts. It meant starting all over again financially, and it meant living in a log cabin once again.

Rebuilding his fortune took time, effort, and considerable sacrifice. Fortunately, he had the help of Rachel and the Donelsons. Curiously, he did not resume his law practice. As far as can be determined, he ceased practicing law in 1796 when he went to Congress. The last case he argued in Davidson County was *James Bosley* v. *James White,* October 11, 1796, a case he won. One reason for his failure to return to the law may have been the number of cases, particularly those involving land purchases and sales, with which he was involved during his six years as a judge.

The first thing he did to get back on his financial feet was to expand his mercantile interests. On February 16, 1802, he had formed a partnership with Thomas Watson and John Hutchings. Hutchings was Rachel's nephew and the son of Catherine and Thomas Hutchings. Together the three men operated a cotton gin and distillery as well as stores in Gallatin, Lebanon, and Hunter's Hill. The gin was located on Watson's property, the distillery on Jackson's. A dispute between Jackson and Watson over the amount of cotton received and freighted for the years 1802 and 1803 brought a dissolution of the partnership on August 6, 1803.[25] Early in April 1804 Jackson and Hutchings formed a new partnership with John Coffee, who had been engaged in business in a neighboring town and who would soon marry Rachel's niece, Mary (Polly) Donelson.[26] The firm, called Jackson, Coffee & Hutchings, was established at Clover Bottom, the site of a racecourse, four miles from the Hermitage and seven miles from Nashville. The store was a blockhouse standing next to Stone's River. Coffee lived in the house and each morning Jackson rode over from his cabin at the Hermitage and worked all day in the store. In all, the establishment included the store, a boatyard, a tavern—a "house of entertainment," according to the documents—and a racetrack.[27]

The firm sold dry goods for the most part—blankets, calico, cowbells, grindstones—all of which were purchased in Philadelphia and sold for triple the price on the Cumberland. Jackson also sold coffee, rum, gunpowder, salt, and whatever else his neighbors wanted and he could obtain. In return he usually received not money but cotton (ginned and unginned), wheat, tobacco, corn, pork, skins, and furs. These items were floated down the Cumberland, Ohio, and Mississippi rivers to Natchez, where they were sold for the New Orleans market. In 1802 cotton sold for $28 per 100 lbs in New Orleans, flour was $9 per barrel, and bar iron went to the highest bidder, so great was the demand for it.[28] Their location on a branch of the Cumberland River allowed the firm to build riverboats for other traders, a business that was managed by Coffee; and because he had agents in Natchez and regularly sent down boatloads of produce, Jackson occasionally engaged in slave trading as a service for a friend or a client.

The company prospered. It prospered because Jackson was a reasonably shrewd businessman, one who was honest, who knew the value of an article, and who made up his mind quickly and set the price. There was no bargaining with him. "I will give or take so much," he would say, according to Felix Robertson. "If you will trade, say so, and have done with it; if not, let it alone."[29] Soon the company expanded. A branch was opened at Gallatin, the capital of Sumner County, twenty-six miles from Nashville. It was followed by stores in Lebanon and at the Cantonment on the Tennessee River (a military establishment about 300 miles north of Mobile and close to Muscle Shoals).[30]

While Jackson tended store his farm was cultivated by slaves superintended by Rachel. Over a period of years Jackson had accumulated many slaves. In 1794, according to a list of his taxable property, he owned 10 slaves.[31] The Davidson County tax books show that the number rose to 15 in 1798. The 1820 census reported that he held 44 slaves, of whom 27 were male and 17 female. By the time Jackson became President of the United States there were 95 slaves at the Hermitage.[32] A few years later that number totaled 150.[33]

Jackson treated his slaves decently and tried to make certain his workers were not abused. "My negroes shall be treated humanely," he wrote later. "When I employed Mr Steel [his overseer], I charged him upon this subject, and had expressed in our agreement that he was to treat them with great humanity, feed and cloath them well, and work them in moderation. if he has deviated from this rule, he must be discharged."[34] In another letter, to Andrew J. Hutchings, Jackson repeated his concern. "I thank you for the information you have given me of my family and concerns. It has dispelled many anxious thoughts. I could not bear the idea of inhumanity to my poor negroes. yours has dispelled my anxiety on this score."[35]

Yet he could be very severe with his slaves. If he felt punishment were merited, he had them whipped and on occasion chained. When his wife informed him that her maid, Betty, had been "putting on some airs, and been guilty of a great deal of impudence," Jackson directed that the woman be publicly whipped. He may have ordered fifty lashes—which would be extreme cruelty—but the number is not clear. Certainly he threatened fifty lashes if her disobedience or impudence continued or if she washed clothes "for any other person but the family without the express permission of her Mistress." Jackson admitted it was "humiliating" for him to have to resort to such punishment.[36]

With runaway slaves Jackson had little mercy. They were chained and later gotten rid of. While Jackson was on a business trip to Alabama in 1822, four of his slaves ran away. All four were recovered, and "although I hate chains," he was "compelled to place two of them in irons, for safekeeping untill an opportunity offers to sell or exchange them."[37]

Under the watchful eye of Rachel the Hermitage workforce produced a variety of crops, the most profitable of which were cotton, corn, and wheat. Jackson was one of twenty-four men in the county who boasted a cotton gin, on which there was a special tax of $20 per annum. The gin de-seeded Jackson's crop and serviced that of his neighbors as well—for which he usually took a fee in goods. He had had a distillery, but it had burned down in 1801 together with the copperware, stills, caps, worms, and the rest of the equipment. Worse, 300 gallons of whiskey were destroyed.[38]

Jackson bred horses, cows, and mules. He raced horses, and he bet on them, too. One of his great passions was the breeding and training of horses, horses that sometimes won him thousands of dollars. Shortly after he resigned from the bench, Jackson took a long tour of Virginia in an effort to find an improved breed. He returned from that journey with Truxton, a stallion 15 hands 3 inches high, which he bought for $1500, one of the greatest racehorses Jackson ever owned and one of which he was justly proud.[39]

Jackson also loved cockfighting and frequently took his birds to the cockpit in the public square near the old Nashville Inn. He would cheer on his favorite birds with wild cries and demands for bets.

"Hurrah! my Dominica! Ten dollars on my Dominica!" or "Hurrah! my Bernadotte! Twenty dollars on my Bernadotte! Who'll take me up? Well done, my Bernadotte! My Bernadotte for ever!"[40]

Although Jackson, Coffee & Hutchings prospered at first, the firm eventually failed. There were several reasons for the failure, among them an economic depression, bad debts and a breakdown in communications between Nashville and the lower country which made it impossible to figure prices and transportation costs.[41] Sometimes the firm's boats would reach a glutted market and there were heavy losses. The high cost of transporting goods from Philadelphia absorbed large amounts of cash and narrowed the margin of profit. When the store started to fail Jackson decided to get out. He sold his share to Coffee, taking notes payable at long intervals. Coffee continued to operate as long as he could; eventually he too gave up and resumed his old profession of surveyor. There is a tradition that when Coffee married Rachel's niece Polly, Jackson, on the wedding day, took Coffee's notes from his strongbox, tore them in two, and with a gracious bow handed the fragments to Polly. If the story is not true, it ought to be, for Jackson was extraordinarily generous to his wife's relatives, and Coffee, he later claimed, was his best friend.[42]

Although Jackson was badly shaken by the Allison misadventure and came to loathe debts and notes in the form of paper money, he nonetheless continued to speculate in land as a means of rebuilding his fortune. Through speculation he helped to found several towns, the most important of which was Memphis. Among his and Overton's properties was the fourth Chickasaw Bluff overlooking the Mississippi, where eventually the city of Memphis was founded. Jackson later disposed of part of his interest to General James Winchester and John C. McLemore, retaining only a one-eighth interest.[43] As soon as the Indians were forced to surrender their claim to the tract, the town was laid out, lots were sold, and Overton, the most active promoter of the combine, sought to have Memphis designated the county seat. Thanks to Overton's efforts, Memphis, after a slow start, developed into an important river town. Jackson sold his remaining interest in 1823 when he became a presidential candidate, believing that speculative interests did not enhance his stature as a statesman.

Jackson joined a group of investors in founding Florence, Alabama, at the foot of Muscle Shoals. This was the Cypress Land Company, which had been formed by a group of Tennessee land speculators under the direction of John Coffee, the principal surveyor, and James Jackson, a rich Nashville merchant and General Jackson's agent and partner in a number of business deals.[44] Although Jackson was neither an active member of the company nor an important stockholder, he did own shares and land in the enterprise and kept in close contact with its promoters.[45] When Florence was first laid out and the auction of land announced, Jackson put in a bid for one town lot. By this time he was a famous man and a national hero. Out of respect, no one bid against him. Out of embarrassment, the General placed no other bid.[46]

It is impossible to judge with any accuracy the overall success of Jackson's land speculations; it is even less possible to trace all his activities as a speculator.[47] With the help and advice of a number of businessmen, most notably Overton, Coffee, and James Jackson, the General probably realized a respectable profit on his land dealings, possibly as much as $100,000 in all. By 1823 he had reduced his operations considerably on account of his presidential aspirations, but by that time he was a fairly rich man. Even so, he remained interested and involved in land speculation almost to the moment of his death.

One thing needs to be emphasized concerning the land speculations: Jackson's scrupulous honesty. Though many Tennesseans were charged with fraud over the years, no suspicion was ever voiced against him. Stockley Donelson, William Tyrell, William T. Lewis, Joshua Hadley, and John Sevier were all accused of improper activities. Jackson and Overton never were. Jackson swore he would clear title to the land he sold under the Allison title even if it ruined him financially. Indeed the Erwin suit cost him $2,000 in court costs for which he got nothing but Mrs. Erwin's tearful gratitude when he forgave her husband the $10,000 debt. In financial transactions Andrew Jackson was an unusually honest man throughout his life.

Several years after paying off his debts and selling his farm at Hunter's Hill, Jackson returned to financial prosperity. Rachel and her family assisted, and there were steady profits from the sale of his cotton, fees for the use of his gin, and frequently large sums won by his great racehorse, Truxton.

Horseracing! Jackson's great passion. And because of a horserace he became embroiled in the most lamentable sequence of events in his life. The racecourse was located at Clover Bottom, near Jackson's store, and here the General trained and raced his horses. In the autumn of 1805 a spectacular race was arranged between Jackson's five-year-old Truxton and Captain Joseph Ervin's mighty stallion, Plowboy. The stakes were $2,000, payable on the day of the race, and an $800 forfeit payable in a list of specified notes should the race be canceled by one side or the other. Six persons were closely interested in the race: on Truxton's side, Jackson; Major John Verell, from whom the General had purchased the horse; Major William P. Anderson; and Captain Samuel Pryor, Truxton's trainer; on Plowboy's side, Ervin and his son-in-law, Charles Dickinson.

Just before the day of the race Plowboy went lame, the race was canceled, and Ervin paid the forfeit. Ervin at first offered a variety of notes (the list of specified notes previously agreed to was in Dickinson's possession) and Jackson refused to accept them, claiming the right to select from the notes described in the 'list. The list was finally produced, the selection made, and the affair presumably settled.

At about this time, Jackson experienced some difficulty with Dickinson, who was a lawyer and a speculator in produce, horses, and (it was rumored) slaves.[48] It was reported to Jackson that Dickinson, when drinking, had taken the "sacred name" of Rachel into his "polluted mouth" and pronounced it in a most lascivious way. There was a wild side to Dickinson—like Jackson in his youth—that occasionally burst into reckless boasts and drunken orgies. But Dickinson was well connected, charming, affluent, something of a dandy, and known to be one of the best shots—if not *the* best shot—in Tennessee.

Jackson confronted the twenty-seven-year-old dandy. Eyes aflame, voice rasping, he demanded an explanation and an apology. The response came quickly. If true, said Dickinson, he was drunk at the time; under no circumstance was his intent malicious. He apologized. Jackson wanted no truck with him and nodded acceptance of the explanation.

Some time later Captain Patten Anderson, a friend of Jackson, entertained a gathering of acquaintances at George and Robert Bell's store in Nashville with local gossip. He declared that the notes offered by Ervin to pay the forfeit on the Truxton-Plowboy horse race were different from those Jackson had agreed to accept. Naturally this was repeated, and when Dickinson heard it he asked Thomas Swann, who was present at Anderson's storytelling session, to confirm it. A few days later Swann met Jackson at the General's store and queried him about Anderson's story. Jackson replied that the notes of forfeit were supposed to be due on demand but that Ervin had offered notes which were not due and therefore not according to the list agreed upon.

It is incredible that this slight misunderstanding over the "merest word-play"[49] should lead to tragedy. But the triviality of cause leading to murderous quarrels on the frontier was more often the rule than not. Anyway, Swann took it upon himself to act as go-between, carrying statements back and forth between Jackson and Ervin and Dickinson, perhaps misunderstanding or misrepresenting what was told him as he went his meddling way from the one to the other. At one point he got caught in the cross fire. Dickinson told him that Jackson implied that Swann was a "damned lyar" for misinterpreting what was said to him.[50]

Swann did not have the sense to duck for cover. Instead he grew indignant and fired off a letter to Jackson expressing his outrage. "The harshness of this expression has deeply wounded my feelings," he wrote; "it is language to which I am a stranger . . . I shall expect an answer."[51]

Jackson tried to be gentle with the youthful Swann. "Let me, sir, observe one thing, that I never wantonly sport with the feelings of innocence; nor am I ever awed into measures. If incautiously I inflict a wound, I always hasten to remove it; if offence is taken when none is offered or intended, it gives me no pain." As for Dickinson's interpretation of what Jackson had said, the General used sharper language. A gentleman and a man of truth, he wrote, when he hears "harsh expressions applied to a friend . . . will immediately communicate it"; but *"the base poltroon and cowardly tale-bearer, will always act in the* background. you can apply the latter to mr. Dickinson, and see which best fits him. I write it for his eye."[52]

Swann rejected this response. Spoiling for a fight, he said he would demand the satisfaction that a gentleman was entitled to receive. Jackson answered that he would cane Swann first and then give him satisfaction.[53]

A short time later, in Nashville, Jackson and Coffee stopped at Winn's Tavern to have a few drinks. Swann walked in. When Jackson spotted him he got up from his chair, walked over to Swann, said he was glad to see him, and then struck him "a very severe blow" with his cane. About to strike again, he got his foot tangled in the legs of a chair and fell backward, almost into the fireplace.

Swann's hand shot into his coat as though he were reaching for a pistol. In a flash Jackson whipped out his own gun, while the crowd in the tavern raced to get out of the line of fire. When Swann withdrew his hand to show it was empty, Jackson doused him with a stream of abuse for being a stupid meddler, "that such was the treatment he deserved, and such he would always give young men, conducting themselves as he had done." At that Swann fled the tavern.[54]

The incident was immediately relayed to Dickinson, who posted a letter to Jackson calling him a coward and an equivocator. "And do you pretend to call a man a tale-bearer for telling that which is truth and can be proved?" he asked. "I shall be very glad when an opportunity serves to know in what manner you give your anodines [something Jackson had promised in an earlier letter], and hope you will take in payment one of my most moderate cathartics."[55] Dickinson had a delightful sense of humor. It was part of his charm.

When Dickinson wrote this letter he was preparing for a trip to New Orleans, and he was well on his way downriver when the General received it. Friends of Jackson later swore that Dickinson target-practiced all the way down the river and back, certain the General would call him out on his return.[56]

The controversy worsened, at least for Jackson, when Swann charged into the columns of Nashville's only newspaper, the *Impartial Review and Cumberland Repository,* on March 1, 1806, and labeled the General a boastful, falsifying coward. Now it had become a public scandal, one the General could not easily escape without irreparably damaging his reputation.

Ever a fierce guardian of his name, Jackson never permitted a public rebuke to escape unchallenged or unpunished. A week later he responded in the columns of the same newspaper. Swann, he said, was no gentleman; rather "he has acted the puppet and lying valet for a worthless, drunken, blackguard scoundrel."[57]

That did it. That single sentence had enough shot in it to produce an instant gunfight. But there was more. Jackson taunted friends of Swann and Dickinson with sneering asides. Nathaniel A. McNairy, the younger brother of Judge McNairy, had supported some of Swann's contentions, and Jackson rapped him for it. McNairy responded in the following week's *Review.* "General! Come out. You can make boys fight at six feet distance; risk yourself for once on equal terms, at least at ten yards. The risk is not great when you consider that your opponent will be under the impression that he has come in contact with the *brave, magnanimous, invincible and honorable Major General Andrew Jackson,* of Tennessee, *but not commander of the navies.* Let this suffice as a relish for the *gentleman General* until I shall have time to answer the charges exhibited by the *braggadocio General;* especially as it regards his honorable certifier, Mr. Coffee."[58]

Now Coffee was involved, and he promptly challenged McNairy to a duel. The two men consented to meet in Kentucky rather than pollute Tennessee. They met, assumed the appropriate positions, and agreed to wait for the count of three and the word "fire" before blasting each other.

The seconds took their positions.

"One," came the call.

"Two."

McNairy fired, hitting Coffee in the leg. Coffee then fired, but his shot went wild. The seconds raced over to McNairy and screamed that he deserved to be shot on the spot for firing ahead of time. McNairy insisted it was an accident.

Accidents are inadmissible in a duel, Coffee's second scolded. McNairy's second intervened, pointing out that Coffee also fired before the proper signal. False, Coffee shouted. His pistol went off when he was struck by McNairy's bullet.

At that point Coffee hobbled over to McNairy. "G-d d--n you," he cried, "this is the second time you have been guilty of the same *crime.*"

Shocked, one of the seconds reprimanded Coffee for his coarse language. After all they were gentlemen, and gentlemen should speak courteously to one another, especially on the dueling grounds. Finally the two men were prevailed upon to admit that each had been accorded satisfaction. That done, they retired from the field of honor.[59]

Dickinson returned from New Orleans in May 1806, and straightaway he prepared a written attack on Jackson and submitted it to the *Review.* Choice phrases from the piece were repeated to General Thomas Overton (brother of John Overton), who immediately rode out to the store at Clover Bottom and relayed them to Jackson. Jackson asked Overton to bring him more details about the contents of the article.

"It's a piece that can't be passed over," Overton insisted. "General Jackson, you must challenge him."

"General," replied Jackson, "this is an affair of life and death. I'll take the responsibility *myself.* I'll *see* the piece and form my own judgment of it."[60]

Jackson rode to the office of the *Review* and asked to see the article. He was handed a statement that was published on May 24, 1806.

Nashville, May 21, 1806

Mr Eastin, In looking over the tenth number of your Impartial Review, I discover that *a certain Andrew Jackson* has endeavored to induce the public to believe, that some inconsistency has been attempted by me, relative to his dispute with Mr Thomas Swann. My letter to *Andrew Jackson,* published by Mr John Erwin, is (I consider) a sufficient answer, with any impartial person.

I should never have condescended to have taken any notice of Andrew Jackson, or his scurrilous publication, had it not been promised by Mr John Erwin, when he published my letter at length, which Mr Jackson, for some cause, unknown but to *himself,* had not the generosity to have published but in part.

I shall take notice, but of those parts of his publication which are intended for myself. . . . [One] part of his publication . . . is as follows. "He (alluding to Mr Swann) has acted the puppet and lying valit, for a worthless, drunken, blackguard, scoundrel", etc etc. Should Andrew Jackson have intended these epithets for me, I declare him (notwithstanding he is a major general of the militia of Mero District) to be a worthless scoundrel "a poltroon and a coward", A man who, by frivolous and evasive pretexts, avoided giving the satisfaction, which was due to a gentleman whom he had injured. . . .

Yours etc

Charles Dickinson[61]

A glance at the article convinced Jackson that he must challenge Dickinson. He could have fought Swann or McNairy, both of whom had sullied his character and reputation in the public press. But Swann was a nobody and McNairy a puppy. Clearly Dickinson was the man to challenge. He had position and prominence in the community, and he must give satisfaction.

Within an hour General Thomas Overton placed a letter from Jackson in Dickinson's hands. It read in part, "Your conduct and expressions, relative to me of late have been of such a nature and so insulting, that it requires and shall have my notice. Insults may be given by men, and of such a kind that they must be noticed and treated with the respect due a gentleman, altho (as in the present instance) you do not merit it. . . . I hope, sir, your courage will be ample security to me that I will obtain speedily that satisfaction due me for the insults offered, and in the way my friend who hands you this will point out. he waits upon you for that purpose, and with your friend will enter into immediate arrangements for this purpose."[62]

After months of hedging and stalling and verbalizing they were finally going to get on with it. The challenge came clear, formal, and direct. Dickinson accepted promptly, and it was agreed (after some haggling, since Jackson was anxious to fight as soon as possible) that they would meet on Friday, May 30, at Harrison's Mills on the Red River in Logan County, Kentucky, which was just beyond the state border north of Nashville. It was further agreed that the distance separating the two men would be set at 24 feet, the parties facing each other, their pistols down at their sides. When ready, the word "fire" would be given, at which time they were free to fire when they pleased. Should either fire before the signal, as McNairy had done, the seconds pledged to shoot down the offender immediately. Choice of position and the person to give the signal to fire were to be chosen by lot.

Within a day all Nashville knew of the approaching duel. Since it was something of a sporting event, bets were freely made, most of which went against Jackson because Dickinson was clearly the better shot.

Thursday morning, before dawn, Dickinson left for Kentucky, a long day's ride from Nashville. He kissed his young wife farewell. "Good bye, darling; I shall be *sure* to be at home tomorrow night." Off he went with his second and half a dozen "gay blades of Nashville," all in high spirits and delighted to be spectators of the match. It was like a pleasure party, with Dickinson amusing the company by displaying his shooting skill each time they stopped to rest or eat. Several times he cut a string with his bullet at a distance of 24 feet, and at one tavern he left a severed string with the innkeeper and said, "If General Jackson comes along this road, show him *that!*"[63]

Jackson's trip north was very different. No merrymaking, no showing off. He and Overton discussed strategy almost every mile of the way, considering how to act and how to proceed once the signal to fire had been given. They finally determined that it would be best to let Dickinson fire first since he was an expert shot and a quick one and would probably fire first anyway. Jackson, they figured, was sure to be hit; if he fired quickly himself his aim would be ruined by the impact and shock of Dickinson's bullet as it struck. Once he took the shot—presuming he was still alive—he could take careful aim before firing. And Jackson, having heard most of his opponent's boastful wagers, was determined to "hit" Dickinson.[64]

Thursday night Jackson stayed at a tavern kept by David Miller. After a hearty dinner he smoked his usual evening pipe and talked freely with his companions. The next morning he and his party, which included a surgeon, rode to the designated spot in a poplar forest that had been partially cleared and cultivated. They waited quietly for the Dickinson party.

"How do you feel about it now, General?" one man asked after a long silence.

"Oh, all right," Jackson replied. "I shall wing him, never fear."[65]

Dickinson arrived, and lots were drawn. Dickinson's second, Dr. Hanson Catlett, won the choice of position and Overton the count. The distance of eight paces was measured. The men took their positions.

"Are you ready?" asked Overton.

"I am ready," said Dickinson.

"I am ready," replied Jackson.

"Fere!" cried Overton in his old-country accent.

Dickinson quickly raised his pistol and fired. The ball struck Jackson in the chest. As it hit a puff of dust rose from the breast of his coat and Jackson slowly raised his left arm and placed it tightly against his throbbing chest. He stood very still, "his teeth clenched."

Dickinson, horrified to see Jackson still standing, drew back a step. "Great God!" he cried, "have I missed him?"

"Back to the MARK, sir," shouted Overton as he aimed his pistol at the dumbstruck man.[66]

Dickinson regained his composure, stepped back to the mark, and waited for Jackson's return. He was at the General's mercy. Jackson could have been magnanimous and refused the shot or fired into the air, but he had promised to hit Dickinson and nothing could dissuade him. "I should have hit him," he said, "if he had shot me through the brain."[67]

Slowly and deliberately Jackson raised his pistol and took aim. He squeezed the trigger. There was no explosion, only a click as the hammer stopped at half cock. The pause was an eternity. Dickinson waited. Jackson drew back the hammer, aimed again, and fired.

The bullet struck Dickinson just below the ribs. He reeled. His friends rushed forward and caught him as he fell. They stripped off his clothes to try to stop the flow of blood. But there was nothing they could do. The bullet had passed clean through his body, leaving a gaping hole. Charles Dickinson bled to death.

Overton looked quickly at the prostrate Dickinson and then walked over to Jackson. "He won't want anything more of you, General," Overton said, and with that he led Jackson away. About a hundred yards on, the surgeon saw that one of Jackson's shoes was full of blood.

"My God! General Jackson, are you hit?" he asked.

"Oh! I believe that he has pinked me a little," Jackson replied. "Let's look at it."[68]

He opened his coat. The bullet had shattered two ribs and buried itself in his chest. It could not be removed because it was lodged close to Jackson's heart, so it remained right where it was. More than a month passed before the General could move around without difficulty. The wound did not heal properly, and his discomfort was considerable. For many years Jackson suffered intense physical pain on account of his gunfight with Charles Dickinson.

Townspeople in Nashville were aghast at what had happened, particularly when they learned how poor Dickinson was made to stand defenseless while a wrathful man took his time to slaughter him. His funeral was attended by many people and was followed by a mass meeting that drew up a memorial to the *Review* requesting that the editor dress the paper in mourning at its next issue "as a tribute of respect for the memory, and regret for the untimely death of Mr. Charles Dickinson."[69] Seventy-three signatures appeared on the petition.

From his bed Jackson demanded the publication of these names. "The thing is so novel," he wrote the editor, "that names ought to appear that the public might judge whether the true motives of the signers were 'a tribute of respect for the deceased,' or something else that at first sight does not appear."[70] When the editor agreed to honor Jackson's request, twenty-six names were quickly withdrawn.

Many men said the duel was a scandal, a brutal, cold-blooded killing. Not murder, although some of Dickinson's friends argued that the shooting of a defenseless man was practically the same as murder. There was no need for Jackson to claim a life, they said. He had several options. Killing should not have been one of them.

Jackson's friends attributed his lack of magnanimity to his fear that his own wound might be fatal, that he might die without exacting revenge from his enemy. After all, a gentleman had to have satisfaction. Everyone knew that. Jackson himself put it differently. Dickinson meant to kill him; he "marked the genl on a tree and boosted how often he had hit him. and when Setting out to meet the genl left 300$ with Mr. Wagaman to bet he would kill the genl."[71] Dickinson wanted a killing, and that is precisely what he got.

Coming on the heels of his quarrel with Sevier, the duel did Jackson great harm and saddled him with a reputation as a fearful, violent, vengeful man. For the next few months Andrew Jackson was virtually a social outcast in western Tennessee.

CHAPTER 10

The Burr Conspiracy

For several years Jackson was at pains to recoup his political and financial losses. Most of his attention was given to developing his plantation (he called it his "farm" despite its size and workforce) and increasing his landholdings. He and Rachel lived in a square two-story blockhouse of three rooms, one room on the ground floor and two upstairs. Later he built a second house, smaller than the first and standing approximately twenty feet from it, and connected the two with a covered passageway. This was their home until he built the stately Hermitage mansion in 1819.

Despite limitations of space the Jacksons entertained widely and generously. They were known as a very social family—this helped somewhat to rehabilitate him after the Dickinson affair—who brought to their home a great number of people, from the rich and affluent to the poor and itinerant. When he entertained Jackson was unreserved in conversation, speaking quickly and with great animation but always with dignity and self-possession. He consciously tried to impress visitors by demonstrating an interest in a variety of subjects and by exuding an air of superiority. He regarded himself as a leader of Nashville society and acted accordingly.

Jackson enjoyed the company and conversation of women and preferred to sit between two ladies at the dinner table rather than at its head. He was easy and graceful in conversation, turning from one guest to another but always keeping an ear cocked to the conversation at the other end of the table in case he need comment or give an opinion. He spoke freely, often playfully, never without dignity, never forgetting his station in society and as major general of the militia. Sometimes he misused or mispronounced words—and gave the impression that it was deliberate, to emphasize a point or produce an effect. He could be very definite in what he was saying, coming down hard on a word or phrase to buttress an argument, but he did it politely, never rudely, always in the southern, aristocratic tradition of gentlemanly behavior. Andrew Jackson in 1805 had come a long way from the Waxhaw settlement.

Into his fashionable if unostentatious frontier home in May 1805 came a very distinguished visitor who stayed for several days. None other than Aaron Burr, former Vice President of the United States and slayer of Alexander Hamilton. Burr had tried to slip past Thomas Jefferson to snatch the presidency in the election of 1801 but he failed in his outrageous scheme and was then read out of the Republican party.[1] Westerners forgave him his highjinks because he had generally favored their interests and had been particularly powerful in advocating the admission of Tennessee to the Union. His killing of Alexander Hamilton in a duel at Weehawken, New Jersey, in 1804 restored Burr's standing in the Republican party as far as westerners were concerned because Hamilton had long been identified with the Federalist party and eastern interests.

Out of office and out of favor, Burr sought new opportunities for his clever and ingenious mind beyond the Appalachian Mountains. In 1805 he began to sport himself among westerners, enjoying their hospitality and affection and dropping hints that some delectable tragedy might soon engulf the hated Spanish to the southwest. On his arrival in Nashville, people from many miles came into town to see him; flags appeared, cannons fired a salute, and dinners were tendered in his honor. Aaron Burr was a great man to the frontiersmen, and they treated him accordingly. The fact that he stayed with the Jacksons during his five-day visit to Nashville increased community respect for the social standing of the Jackson family.[2]

Aaron Burr had long been considering ideas for an adventure in the west whereby he might restore his depressed fortunes. Precisely what he planned to do remained unclear; he told different stories to different men, depending on his evaluation of their character and personality. He may have been unsure himself and planned to play it by ear, simply taking advantage of whatever developed once he had set his "coup" in motion. Perhaps this was his one fatal mistake, that his plans only served his own personal interest. Had he been able to formulate his goals in accordance with the ambitions of westerners and their perceived destiny of their section, like Jackson after him, he might have succeeded—and in the process achieved the status of hero. Instead he pursued a private need.[3]

Like any number of men in the early days of the Republic, Burr was capable of treason against the United States if that was the price of success. Not that he broadcast it. He simply insinuated all sorts of things, one more appealing than the next. Among westerners he could expect an attentive and appreciative audience for his plans and intimations—treason or no—since for decades they had engaged in plots and conspiracies against the Spanish, against the English, against the French, even against their own government. Any scheme was a good one—indeed a patriotic one—if it advanced western land and trading interests. Any scheme was a good one if it expelled the Indians and Spanish.

Burr's versatility and flexibility (to say nothing of his audacity) expressed themselves in his efforts to wheedle both the English and the Spanish into financing his plans. They were led to believe that his scheme would check American expansion further west. But neither the English nor the Spanish responded to his alluring propositions with the financial support he required, and his Spanish dalliance was a mistake that showed how little he understood the mood and temper of settlers along the frontier. The very fact that he had approached the Spanish, whatever the likelihood of engaging their support, foredoomed his project. No matter. He would find others and tailor his proposals to their interests.

Burr's trip to the west was intended to scout general conditions, consult friends, meet possible allies, and try out some of his schemes on the local settlers. Whether he was plotting the establishment of a personal empire at the expense of Spanish and American territory, as later reported, can probably never be determined with certainty. (Given his opportunism, he would not have opposed it.) He did espouse the possibility of settling a colony on the Red River and using it as a staging area against Mexico in the event of war between the United States and Spain. When he learned of western hunger for Mobile he blithely included the seizure of Florida in his schemes. At the same time, he was assuring the Spanish minister in Washington of his regard for the integrity of the Spanish empire.[4]

In casting his net as widely as possible, Burr was bound to come up with a shark. General James Wilkinson, the commanding general of the United States army in the lower Mississippi valley, surfaced almost immediately. He and Burr had known one another during the Revolution, and a reunion was eventually arranged on Burr's initiative. Wilkinson was a double agent. He spied for the Spanish, accepting their gold while commanding American forces in the southwest.[5] Money commanded his allegiance and to obtain it he stooped to anything, including conspiracy and treason.[6] In the winter of 1804–05, following their reunion, Burr and Wilkinson spent much of their time in Washington copying maps of Florida, Louisiana, and adjacent Spanish territories, including Mexico.[7] They kept their options opened wide.

Burr's western trip in 1805 was a huge personal success. He said and did all the things that were guaranteed to captivate westerners. Leaving Nashville in an open boat provided by Jackson, he sailed down to Natchez, where he talked with the governor of the Mississippi Territory, and on to New Orleans, where he was cordially received by the governor of the Louisiana Territory, W. C. C. Claiborne. By August he was back in Nashville, again residing with the Jacksons (as he had promised) and acknowledging in his diary that he found his host "a man of intelligence, and one of those prompt, frank, ardent souls whom I love to meet."[8] In their private conversations the two men discussed at length the presence of Spain on the continent. Both agreed to the need for her expulsion. During one of their talks Burr assured Jackson that the secretary of war, Henry Dearborn, was secretly in league with him.[9]

Jackson was utterly charmed by the suave and cultivated Burr. He went out of his way to present his guest to Nashville society and to make it appear that he and Burr were linked in affection and friendship. These visits occurred shortly after the duel with Dickinson and Jackson found they helped enormously in restoring his social standing in western Tennessee. He knew how to use them to advantage. "Col. Burr is with me," he wrote to one man. "I would be happy if you would call and see the Colonel before your return. Say to Gen. O[verton], that I shall expect to see him here tomorrow with you. Would it not be well for us to do something as a mark of attention to the Colonel—he has always [been], and still is, a true and trusty friend of Tennessee."[10]

At Jackson's call the leading men of the district rode out to the Hermitage to pay their respects to Burr and to invite him to their homes. They thanked Jackson profusely for giving them the opportunity of meeting the distinguished visitor and hearing him expound on ways of walloping the Spanish. The General also arranged a splendid ball in Burr's honor, and for years afterward many in Nashville remembered "the hush and thrill attending the entrance of Colonel Burr, accompanied by General Jackson in the uniform of a Major General."[11] The invited company lined the sides of the room and looked on intently "while the two courtliest men in the world" circuited the room. Jackson introduced his guest "with singular grace and emphasis. It was a question with the ladies which of the two was the finer gentleman."[12]

Drawing his new ally ever deeper into his plot, Burr asked Jackson to provide him with a list of officers for one or two regiments, from colonel to ensign, who were fit for the business of war and with whom the General could trust "your life and your honor."[13] Supposedly the names would be transmitted to the War Department and held in reserve in case of an emergency. Burr also asked him to build five large boats on Stone's River at Clover Bottom, to be used for descending the river, and to purchase a large quantity of provisions to be transported in these boats. The orders were accompanied by $3,500 in Kentucky banknotes. Jackson accepted the money and notified his partner, John Coffee, to contract for the building of the boats and to arrange for the purchase of the provisions.

Jackson was now an accomplice. He knew the purpose of the orders —or thought he did. Jackson never revealed precisely what Burr said to him (other than to insist it in no way involved treason), but he clearly believed the orders for the boats and provisons were intended for an assault on the Spanish in Florida and beyond the Louisiana Territory. For Jackson, as for many Americans in the southwest, an undeclared war against the Spanish posed no problem; they were totally committed in their minds to further expansion southward and westward. For some, including Andrew Jackson, even Mexico was an object of this ambition.[14]

On October 4, 1806, as the conspiracy took shape and gained wider acceptance, Jackson issued a proclamation (which appeared in the *Impartial Review*) to the generals of the second division of the Tennessee militia. "The late conduct of the Spanish government," the proclamation began, "added to the hostile appearance and menacing attitude of their armed forces already encamped within the limits of our government, make it necessary that the militia under my command, should be in complete order and at a moment's warning ready to march."[15] Then, word for word, Jackson reiterated his orders to the militia of three years before—about how the Spanish had imprisoned and transported five American citizens into "the dominion of Spain," "cut down and carried off the flag of the United States," and expelled a government party exploring the Red River east of the Sabine River and clearly within the Louisiana Territory. Again he cited these acts as "degrading to our national character" and demanding "prompt satisfaction." He wanted his officers to be prepared to fill their quotas at the "shortest notice" and "when the government and constituted authorities of our country require it, they must be in readiness to march."[16]

For Jackson the present Spanish danger was similar to that at the time of the Louisiana Purchase, when President Jefferson had alerted the western militia. Without changing a word, Jackson lifted entire paragraphs from the proclamation of 1803 and reissued them in 1806.

Where his public pronouncement bristled with threats, his private remarks went further and revealed the full dimension of Jackson's intended aggression against Spain. He sent a copy of his proclamation to James Winchester, attaching to it a letter that cited the "Hostile and menacing attitude of Spain" as the reason for his decision to issue the proclamation. "You no doubt have seen from the late papers," he continued, "that the negociation for the purchase of the Floridas has failed." This means war, he said. Our moment of opportunity. With "less than two million [dollars we] can conquer not only the Floridas, but all Spanish North America."

All Spanish North America! Here, then, was Jackson's dream of American empire, explicitly stated, a dream he never significantly altered. "I have a hope," he revealed, that with two thousand volunteers commanded "by firm officers and men of enterprise [we] . . . will look into Santa Fe and Mexico, give freedom and commerce to those provinces and establish peace, and a permanent barrier against the inroads and attacks of foreign powers on our interior, which will be the case so long as Spain holds that large country on our borders."

That large country on our borders must be surrendered to us, he said. And it will be—from the Floridas to Mexico!

War could bring other delights. "Should there be a war," Jackson enthused, "it will be a handsome theatre for our enterprising young men, and a source of acquiring fame."[17]

The immediate cause of Jackson's issuing the new alert was the reappearance of Aaron Burr in Nashville the week before. Again a sumptuous banquet was given him at Talbot's Hotel, where "many of the most respectable citizens of Nashville and its vicinity" came to honor him. At the banquet "there appeared an union of sentiment. . . . Many appropriate toasts were drank, and a few of the most suitable songs given, when the company retired quite gratified."[18] The local newspaper reminded its readers that Colonel Burr is "the steady and firm friend, of the state of Tennessee."[19]

The opportunity Burr offered Jackson for military action and its attendant glory was extremely enticing to someone as eager and anxious as the General, and Jackson had been waiting for the opportunity for years. Only one thing could give him pause, the thing that separated him from Burr, Wilkinson, and other conspirators. He was not capable of treason against the United States, even to get a shot at the Spanish. As he told Governor Claiborne in New Orleans, "I love my Country and government. I hate the Dons. I would delight to see Mexico reduced, but I will die in the last Ditch before I would yield a foot to the Dons or see the Union disunited."[20]

Jackson had no reason to suspect a plot against the United States. All he knew was that he might soon have the opportunity to drive the Spanish from the southwest, to avenge "our national character" and maybe reduce Mexico. And he was ready. If it ever crossed his mind that a conspiracy against the United States might be in train, he blanked it out.

Not until November 10, 1806, was he forced to consider the unthinkable. A week or so after Jackson accepted Burr's money and agreed to provide boats and provisions for the enterprise, a young man, Captain Fort, called at the Hermitage with an introductory letter. After a stay of a night and part of a day he casually mentioned Burr's plans, one of which was to take New Orleans.

New Orleans! Fort had spoken incautiously and realized it immediately. When Jackson questioned him, Fort "attempted to take [me in]," Jackson wrote, "to explain etc., etc., but from circumstances I was in Possession of, it flashed upon my mind that plans had been named of settling new countries, of Punishing the Dons, and adding Mexico to the united states etc., etc., [that] were only mere coverings to the real designs."[21] Now it dawned on him that perhaps the "real design" was the dismemberment of the Union.

How was it to be done? Jackson asked Fort. The young man stammered a reply that staggered the general. In addition to the seizure of New Orleans, the bank would be captured, the port closed, Mexico conquered, and the western part of the United States joined to the conquered territory to form a great southwestern empire.

And how would all this conquering come about? Jackson asked. Federal troops, Fort responded, led by General Wilkinson.[22]

Jackson loathed Wilkinson. Three years earlier his good friend, Colonel Thomas Butler, then serving in New Orleans under Wilkinson, was dismissed from the army on charges of disobedience and neglect of duty for refusing to have his queue of long hair cut. Jackson protested to Prsident Jefferson and later presented a petition on Butler's behalf signed by Nashville citizens.[23] Nevertheless Jefferson refused to intervene.[24]

Jackson readily believed the charge that Wilkinson was engaged in a conspiracy to commit treason. The man was an obvious scoundrel. And to think that President Jefferson had refused the pleas of honest citizens. It was another example of his incompetence.

Jackson renewed his questioning. Had Fort gotten his information directly from Wilkinson?

No.

Burr?

Fort said he hardly knew Burr and that he had received his information from Colonel Samuel Swartwout of New York, one of Burr's lieutenants.

Now it "rushed into my mind like lightning," Jackson later reported, "that Burr was at the head [of a conspiracy], and from the coulourings he had held out to me Genl Robertson and Overton, and the hospitality I had shown him, I viewed it as base conduct to us all and hightened the baseness of his intended crimes if he really was about to become a traitor."[25]

Dismissing Fort, Jackson rushed off a flurry of letters, one of them to Daniel Smith, his successor in the U.S. Senate, outlining the details of the plot as he understood it, but mentioning no names.[26] Another letter went to Governor Claiborne, warning him to "keep a watchful eye on our Genl. [Wilkinson], and beware of an attack as well from your own Country as from Spain. I fear there is something rotten in the State of Denmark. You have enemies within your own City that may try to subvert your Government and try to seperate it from the Union." It was not a direct accusation—just a warning. "This I write for your own eye and for your own safety—profit by it—and the Ides of March remember."[27] (The tone and mood of conspiracy definitely colored his language.)

Although Jackson was alarmed at the possibility of a conspiracy to divide the Union, he was cautious enough to refrain from accusing anyone directly or mentioning the name of the chief conspirator or the source of his information. He dared not risk embarrassment by making unsubstantiated accusations—at least until he had more evidence than Captain Fort had given him. To protect himself, Jackson wrote a carefully worded letter to President Jefferson in which he professed his loyalty. Without specifically mentioning a conspiracy, he offered the services of the citizens of Tennessee—provided, of course, they were mustered under his command. "In the event of insult or aggression made on our government and country FROM ANY QUARTER," he wrote Jefferson, "I am well convinced that the public sentiment . . . within the State . . . are of such a nature . . . that I take the liberty of tendering their services, that is under my command."[28]

What a strange letter, Jefferson thought when he received it. What a strange proposal. Was Jackson suggesting war against Spain? In reply, he told the general he was a friend of peace and therefore unwilling to see it disturbed as long as the rights of the nation were preserved. "But whenever hostile aggressions on these [rights] require a resort to war," he said, "we must meet our duty, and convince the world that we are just friends and brave enemies."[29]

While Jackson furiously signaled an alarm in several quarters, thereby covering himself with a paper shield, Burr was arraigned before a grand jury in Frankfort, Kentucky, on charges of raising troops for illegal purposes. His activities in the west had finally stirred official attention. Jackson heard he had been arrested for a plot to invade Mexico.[30] A young lawyer named Henry Clay—who also served as legal representative in Kentucky for Jackson's trading firm—defended Burr.[31] At length the grand jury dismissed the charges, declaring that "no violent disturbance of the Public Tranquility or breach of the laws" had come to their knowledge.[32] President Jefferson, who had hoped Burr had at last taken a fatal tumble, was so annoyed by the dismissal of the charges that he had the federal district attorney who prosecuted the case removed from office.[33] He was out for blood, and the disappointment further excited his blood lust.

Jackson, who held $3,500 of conspiracy money, wrote to Burr about his suspicions and declared that until they were erased "no further intimacy was to exist between us."[34] According to Jackson, Burr responded immediately "with the most sacred pledges, that he had not nor never had any views inimical or hostile to the united States, and whenever he was charged with the intention of seperating the union, the idea of insanity must be ascribed to him."[35]

Burr followed his letter with a quick trip to Nashville to check on the boats and provisions. He called at the Hermitage, but Jackson was away. Rachel received him coolly and did not invite him to stay. Burr found lodging at the Clover Bottom tavern, where Jackson and General Overton visited him several days later. The three men talked at great length, Jackson repeating what he had heard and what he suspected. Burr swore that his suspicions were unfounded. He said he had no goals that were not sanctioned by legal authority, that he would produce orders from the secretary of war, and "that he wanted but young men of *habits* to go with him. with such he wanted to make his settlement and it would have the tendency to draw to it wealth and charector."[36]

Ultimately Jackson accepted Burr's oath of allegiance. He wanted to believe him. He wanted the Spanish expelled from the continent and Mexico reduced, and he was keenly aware of Tennessee's enthusiasm for a filibuster in the southwest and what it would mean to the careers of those who commanded it. Furthermore, his own name and reputation had been closely linked with Burr's from the latter's first appearance in Nashville. Jackson could ill afford Burr's disgrace, particularly in the aftermath of the Sevier and Dickinson fiascoes. Most important, Jackson habitually judged other men's loyalty according to their personal commitment to him. Since Burr had always been deferential, had treated him with marked respect, Jackson summarily cleared him of suspicion.

The General delivered the boats and provisions that Burr had ordered. Since the order had been reduced to two boats by the former Vice President, a balance of $1,725.62 was returned in the same banknotes the partners had received. Jackson permitted the seventeen-year-old Stockley D. Hays, one of Rachel's many nephews, to accompany Burr to New Orleans in the belief that the association and the experience would aid the young man's education. But the ever-cautious Jackson gave his nephew letters to Governor Claiborne and warned the young man that, should he discover Burr's actions to be treasonable, he must abandon him immediately and place himself under Claiborne's protection.

On December 22, 1806, Burr left Clover Bottom with the two boats and a few followers, expecting to rendezvous at the mouth of the Cumberland River with a flotilla of boats and men coming from an island in the Ohio River owned by Harman Blennerhassett, one of his chief lieutenants. The entire expedition, when it finally assembled, numbered approximately 60 men. Not long after Burr's departure from Clover Bottom, word reached Nashville that President Jefferson had just issued a proclamation declaring a military conspiracy in progress in the west and calling for the apprehension of those involved.

Conspiracy against the United States! And the proclamation was official. The President himself declared it in progress. Jefferson had been alerted by General James Wilkinson who began having doubts about the ultimate success of the conspiracy and what might happen to him as a consequence. In a panic of fear and uncertainty, Wilkinson betrayed the plot to the President. He informed Jefferson that a conspiracy existed to seize New Orleans, revolutionize the Louisiana Territory, and invade Mexico. With this evidence before him, and predisposed to believe it, Jefferson called for the arrest of the conspirators.[37]

Nashville panicked. Rumors about the intent of the conspiracy and the persons involved circulated everywhere. Men swore their innocence and their loyalty to the Union. Frightened at the possibility of implication in the plot, "distinguished" citizens who had once jostled one another to be seen in Burr's presence now rushed to disassociate themselves from him. They hardly recollected meeting him.

Jackson had no need to worry. After all he had warned both the President and Governor Claiborne, and he had kept copies of his letters. On January 1, 1807, he received orders from Jefferson and Secretary of War Henry Dearborn to hold his command in readiness and be prepared to march to frustrate the conspiracy.

The long-anticipated moment had arrived. The opportunity to lead a great expedition down the river to save his country from treason and disunion now seemed at hand. Jackson summoned the militia to duty and notified Dearborn that twelve companies would be mustered and ready to move within a few days. "Nothing on my part," he assured Dearborn, "shall be wanted to promote the interest of the government, and quell the conspiracy."[38] Having helped to launch Burr's expedition, Jackson was now arranging to scuttle it.

One thing troubled Jackson: the necessity of dealing with Henry Dearborn. He did not trust the secretary and rather suspected him of implication in Burr's schemes. Even Dearborn's order to him was a fright.

"It is the merest old-woman letter . . . you ever saw. . . . The Secretary of War is not fit for a granny." What "we ought to have," he said, is "a little of the emperor's [Napoleon] energy."[39]

A little Napoleonic energy was already in evidence: Jackson had committed himself to raising twelve companies in four days and another thirty in twenty days.[40] The first troops mustered were the Nashville companies. Jackson reviewed them in town, amid the enthusiasm and vocal approval of a large body of citizens. The *Review* of January 17 expressed its "satisfaction at the promptness with which this rendezvous was attended, and the patriotism displayed by the major general. . . . The unity of sentiment which pervaded every breast on this occasion, and the general flame of indignation which burst forth on all sides at the recollection of the traitorous conduct of the individuals whose expedition gave rise to the orders that called them together, is a pleasing momento of our fellow-citizens generally, that neither the intrigue of restless ambition, nor the efforts of disorganizing demagogues, can withdraw our affections from that Union on which our prosperity and happiness depend."

Jackson's vigor in mustering and displaying a show of military force in support of the Union calmed the people of Nashville, ended the panic, and restored a sense of peace and order. Jackson had a flair for playing the part of the great commander even without a jot of military experience.

The terror that had gripped Nashvillians now seems odd in view of their past involvement with conspiracies. But this conspiracy was different. This one brought a proclamation from the President of the United States shouting treason, and the wild rumors that this shout released predicted a wide range of possible disasters, all of them involving military subjugation. Rumor insisted that a large force of armed men was preparing to attack the western settlements and pluck them out of the Union— action that guaranteed bloody civil war on the frontier.

No large military assembly existed. Dispatches Jackson sent to locate Burr's expedition returned with assurances that the force was small. Burr had been seen floating down the Mississippi with ten boats, each with six men, and they had "nothing on board that would even suffer a conjecture more than a man bound to a market; he has descended the river towards Orleans."[41] There was no cause for alarm. The conspiracy, like Burr, had simply floated away.

General Wilkinson, meanwhile, lay about like a demon, jailing dupes and issuing orders for the movement of troops, as though he were smashing a great plot to dismember the United States. He generated noise and clatter enough to distract attention from his own involvement in the conspiracy. The sounds carried straight to Burr and frightened him into deserting his boats and men and fleeing into the Mississippi wilderness.

With the steady flow of information coming to him, Jackson soon realized that his chance for military glory had vanished down the river. The conspiracy, such as it was, had evaporated. It was now senseless to pretend otherwise. With a nice regard for the feelings of his men Jackson sent them back to their homes. But he did it with a flourish. He assembled the troops and delivered an address so patriotic, so lavish in its praise of his officers and men, that the troops "with one voice demanded its publication."[42] A superb politician, Jackson utilized his skills to win approval of his generalship, even without the true test upon the battlefield. That would come later. For the moment he knew how to employ language to establish his fame. His patriotic, supernationalistic rhetoric included repeated and exorbitant praise of his troops. "Return, fellow-soldiers," he concluded in his address, "to the bosom of your families, with the best wishes of your General, until your country calls, and then it is expected you will march at a moment's warning."[43]

Great generals are necessarily great politicians—and can be as dangerous. At this point in his military career Jackson was a superb politician. Astride a horse and decked out in a handsome uniform, he delighted his troops by his manner and colorful speech. He exuded the presence of command. He was dashing within bounds, for he handled himself with great dignity. He won immediate approval of his men because he looked and acted like a great commander. But he soon demonstrated he possessed other qualities of leadership. He was decisive, energetic and forceful. He exercised absolute and total command over his troops, yet he did it with obvious concern for their interests, and he did it as a natural expression of his authority by virtue of his office and position. He surrounded himself with officers whose loyalty and commitment to his leadership were unquestioned, and he reciprocated by giving them his utmost confidence and support. There was mutual respect and regard. Jackson spoke and acted as though the patriotism and fighting potential of his troops were a foregone conclusion.

Despite Jackson's efforts to protect his neighbors and calm their fears, many people had doubts about his loyalty and were uncertain about his part in the conspiracy. Who had been more visible as companion and friend of Aaron Burr? Who more zealous in advocating western and southern expansion? Rumors connecting Jackson (and his militia) with Burr reached Washington. The Richmond *Enquirer* of December 30, 1806, hinted at it. "We are happy to hear," it said, "that General Wilkinson had been tampered with *unsuccessfully;* we must acknowledge that we have entertained involuntary suspicions of him as well as of a military general in Tennessee, who some time past issued a thundering proclamation, rousing the resentment of the people against the Spaniards."

Secretary Dearborn conveyed these suspicions to Jackson in language so baldly offensive and accusatory that the General had no choice but to reply in white heat. "The Tenor of your letter," he said, "is such and the insinuations so grating—The ideas and tenor so unmilitary, stories alluded to, the intimations, of a conduct, to stoop, from the charector of a general to a smiling *assasin.* "[44] Jackson fumed as he struggled to fix the words to paper. Remembering his efforts to warn the administration and to expose Wilkinson only to learn that this traitor had the confidence of the President, and now finding himself under suspicion, Jackson boiled with rage. The more he thought, the more he was convinced that Wilkinson was the true scoundrel, not Burr. Poor old Burr was devoted to western interests and wanted only the expulsion of the Spanish from the southwest. But Wilkinson was a traitor conspiring to revolutionize the Louisiana Territory and dismember the Union. And if Jefferson and Dearborn defended him, surely that meant they had collusive knowledge of the conspiracy.[45]

Two months later Jackson was still seething, and he let Dearborn have the full blast of his fury.

> I will, in the first instance, take the liberty Sir of asking you, whether you did or did not, from this *Story in circulation,* believe me conserned, with any citizens of the U. States, in a *criminal attempt contrary to law, to carry on, a military expedition against the Government of Spain?* And if you did, was it your belief at the time you honored me with your address of the 19th Dmr., that you could, by inviting me to the commission of a treacherous act utter such views and effect the purposes intended?
>
> You say Sir that it is industirously reported amongst the adventurers that they are to be joined at the mouth of cumberland by two regiments under the command of Gnl. Jackson. . . . If Sir *stories* are to be attended to, recd. and acknowledged as evidence of a mans' innocence or guilt, you stand, convicted at the bar of justice, of the most notorious and criminal acts, of dishonor, dishonesty, want of candour and justice.

These were hardly the respectful words an officer addresses to his superior. But more followed. Jackson referred to the persecution his friend Colonel Butler had suffered under Wilkinson and Dearborn. "The later Colo Thos Butler . . . under the combined influence and villanous treatment of yr. self and yr. much loved Genl. Wilkinson, died the death of persicution. . . . and in consequence of the part which I took in favor of the Colo. your spleen your hatred of me became settled and fixed. . . . The first opportunity of gratifying yourself, was afforded and under the garb of official security and importance, you have sought yr. revenge."[46]

It takes a base mind, Jackson rasped, to listen to such base accusations, much less transmit them. As for his connection with Burr, the General proudly admitted it. He came to my house from time to time, Jackson said, and never uttered one solitary treasonable syllable. "He was an old acquaintance and a gentleman that I highly respected and was by me treated as such." Jackson admitted he sold Burr two boats and added that Burr "could have had ten more" if he had asked for them.[47]

Dearborn did not dignify this insubordinate outburst with a reply. But Jackson never forgot, and his need for revenge nearly consumed him. For years he worked to prove Wilkinson's guilt, no doubt with the hope of implicating Jefferson and Dearborn. As in his earlier persecution of Sevier in the land fraud, the General diligently and laboriously gathered documentary evidence wherever he could find it and passed it along to influential friends. Some of the evidence was forwarded to members of Congress with the demand that it be shown to the President.[48] Jackson could hate with a passion, and his hate could be relentless and vindictive.

Burr, meanwhile, suffered the fury of Jefferson's persistent malice. Shortly after stumbling into the Mississippi wilderness he was captured in disguise a few miles from the frontier of Spanish Florida. Charged with treason, he was taken to Richmond, Virginia, for trial in United States Circuit Court, presided over by Chief Justice John Marshall. John Randolph, a bitter enemy of Jefferson and another of Jackson's mentors of sorts, served as foreman of the jury. Unfortunately, the trial degenerated into a political duel between Marshall and Jefferson.

During the entire conspiracy and the subsequent trial Jefferson acted badly. His spite and his desire for revenge—not fear for the safety of the Union—drove him to persecute Burr. He overreacted to the conspiracy; he claimed more in the way of potential danger than actually existed. From start to finish his was a disgraceful performance.[49]

Jackson, loyal and reckless, journeyed to Richmond to testify on Burr's behalf. He was examined by a grand jury along with approximately fifty other witnesses.[50] But his appearance in court did not have the impact of the verbal bombshells he detonated on the steps of the capitol building before an appreciative crowd. His remarks were so provocative and his rage so uncontrolled that defense counsel decided against placing him on the witness stand in the trial that was scheduled to begin several months later. It was feared his violent outbursts would offend the jury and injure Burr's case. "I am more convinced than ever that treason never was intended by Burr," Jackson said; "but if ever it was you know my wishes that he may be hung."[51]

The decision to dispense with his presence before the jury infuriated

Jackson, who had hoped to use the witness box as a platform from which to accuse Wilkinson of conspiracy and treason. The country should know the character of the man guarding the border, he fumed. Yet each time the whisper of suspicion was heard, Jefferson defended Wilkinson and refused to order an investigation into his conduct. "I have no doubt," Jackson wrote to his friend, Senator Daniel Smith, "nor have I had of the guilt of Wilkingson; from the proofs I see exhibitted against him at Richmond," which included evidence that he was "a pensioner of Spain." Jackson wrote to Smith because the senator was a "real friend of Mr Jefferson and the republican cause." The President should "shake off this viper," he said, for the honor of the nation. "I have loved Mr Jefferson as a man, and adored him as a president," he protested, but if the President continues to "support such a base man with his present knowledge of his corruption and infamy, I would withdraw that confidence I once reposed in him and regret that I had been deceived in his virtue."[52]

Jackson's public pillorying of the administration offended not only Jefferson but his secretary of state, James Madison. They tagged him a willing tool of a cabal in Congress—which included John Randolph of Roanoke—who assailed Wilkinson in order to embarrass the administration and force the country into war with Spain. Madison had not forgotten this rudeness when several years later, as President, he sought generals to fight the war against Great Britain.

Disgusted, Jackson returned home, still maligning Jefferson, still branding Wilkinson a traitor, still demanding the administration cease its defense of "this viper," this "Spanish hireling." Later it was generally understood that Jackson represented the anti-Jefferson, anti-Madison faction in Tennessee and that he would not support Madison's candidacy for the presidency in 1808. Instead he backed James Monroe, who was favored by Randolph and other leading advocates in Congress of states' rights. Jackson admired Monroe because he had vigorously protested England's Orders-in-Council when he was minister to the Court of St. James's. More important, the General disliked the clique running the Republican party that had dictated Madison's nomination. Jackson probably realized he was wasting his time supporting Monroe. He put little effort behind his campaign in Tennessee and he certainly did nothing to risk his political influence in a cause that was hopeless from the start.

Burr was eventually acquitted of treason, thanks to the assistance of the presiding judge and his ruling on what constituted treasonable acts. Jackson never totally escaped the suspicion that he had helped Burr in his scheme to divide the Union, and that suspicion hounded him for years. In providing boats and provisions, Jackson clearly had participated in the conspiracy. He justified it as a legitimate enterprise to expel the

Spanish from the continent and reduce Mexico. He simply acted out his western prejudice and commitment. But the charge that he intended to divide the Union or injure his country is patently ridiculous. What Jackson failed to realize was that error of judgment can sometimes produce the same effect, intended or not.

The failure of the conspiracy and the humiliation of Burr in no way lessened Jackson's faith in the ultimate expulsion of the Spanish or his need to persist in efforts to bring it about. What he learned from the Burr Conspiracy—and he demonstrated that he had indeed learned from it— was that western expansion could not be undertaken for personal and private needs. To be successful, it must be done in the name and authority of the United States. It needed regular armed forces under proper direction, not a haphazard collection of dreamers dependent upon the sympathy and support of western expansionists. It would take determination and military prowess—some of the things that lay buried deep within Major General Andrew Jackson.

There was another lesson. The recent conspiracies against the Spanish going back through Burr to Blount enjoyed the approval of most westerners. But the settlers could not be counted on. Let someone cry havoc and they scurried for cover. Therefore a successful conspiracy must not be dependent on frontier approval and contributions. All the more reason for military action, directed by a bold commander, under the aegis of the United States government.

His hope for military glory extinguished for the moment, Jackson retired to his farm for the next several years and tended his crops, bought and sold land and slaves, and improved his racing stable. Truxton won over $20,000 in prize money over the next several years and his stud fee of $30 in ginned cotton brought additional revenue. With careful and attentive management of the farm, enterprising land speculations that netted handsome returns, and a series of excellent cotton crops, Jackson completely recovered from the Allison debacle and began living the life of a well-to-do southern planter. He entertained often and became known as the most public private man in the state. "His house was the seat of hospitality," wrote Thomas Hart Benton, a young officer in his militia, "the resort of friends and acquaintances, and of all strangers visiting the State."[53]

The visits and the entertainments kept him in constant touch with important politicians in Tennessee and elsewhere, for no person of consequence came to Nashville without enjoying the hospitality of Rachel and Andrew Jackson. To some extent he strengthened his political standing in western Tennessee through these social activities; and it was during this period that he formed a strong alliance with John Tipton, an original settler in Tennessee and one of John Sevier's earliest rivals. Before long Jackson had an extraordinary following of devoted and loyal friends and allies. He was especially adept at attracting the admiration of young men, always encouraging them, asking about their background, offering help. When Thomas Hart Benton proposed keeping a journal devoted to the operation of the army he wrote Jackson, "You Sir, who feel a generous wish to see young men come forward by their own intrinsic strength, will not smile at this presumption."[54]

The General also maintained close rapport with his militia, which he boasted came out in full quota whenever he called. "My pride," he said, "is that my soldiers has confidence in me, and on the event of a war I will lead them on, to victory and conquest. Should we be blest with peace, I will resign, my military office, and spend my days, in the sweet calm of rural retirement."[55]

By 1810, despite a brief depression occasioned by "many unpleasant occurrences" such as his recent financial difficulties, the Dickinson and Burr episodes, and a momentary impulse to move to Mississippi, Jackson was living in handsome style, replete with "delightful farm," slaves, a position of prominence in the community and state in which he was "highly esteem'd" by the "respectable and well informed part of the Country," and, most important, family.[56] Jackson exalted family. Like many other Americans in the early nineteenth century, he believed that family constituted the bulwark of society, the moral force that perpetuated the noble principles upon which the nation was built.

Jackson's family consisted of Rachel and the Donelson kin. He and Rachel had no children of their own, however much they desired them. But there were children at the Hermitage constantly, young nieces and nephews visiting for long or short periods and adding warmth and gayety to the Jackson home. Several times the General served as guardian for children whose fathers had died. First there were four children of Edward Butler: Caroline, Eliza, Edward, and Anthony. Shortly thereafter Butler's brother, Colonel Thomas Butler (the man arrested by Wilkinson), asked Jackson to look after his children. Thomas Jr. was twenty years old and a lawyer in Louisiana at the time of his father's death in 1805. The second son, Robert, became Jackson's adjutant during the War of 1812 and married Rachel Hays; Lydia, the daughter, married Stockley Donelson Hays; and William Edward Butler became a medical doctor and married Martha Hays.

After the Butlers came John Samuel and Andrew Jackson and Daniel Smith Donelson, the sons of Samuel Donelson, whom the General raised and schooled following the death of their father. And, at approximately the same time, there was William Smith, a neighbor's unwanted burden.

Some years later Andrew Jackson Hutchings, the son of Jackson's business partner, became Jackson's ward at the age of six. And Mary Lewis, daughter of William B. Lewis, and Mary Eastin, the granddaughter of Rachel's brother John, were Jackson's wards. The two Marys had White House weddings: Mary Lewis married Joseph Pageot, secretary of the French legation, in a Catholic ceremony, and Mary Eastin married Lucius Polk in a Protestant ceremony.[57]

Jackson frequently meddled in the romantic affairs of his friends; on a few occasions he encouraged elopements against stiff parental opposition. He assisted the elopement of Mary Smith (the daughter of Daniel Smith) and Samuel Donelson. Mary climbed down a tree from her second-story window to reach her beloved—and her father was so angry with all concerned (including Jackson who tossed up the grapevine ladder used to swing her to the tree) that he chopped down the tree and boarded up the window.[58] On another occasion Richard Keith Call and Mary Kirkman were married at the Hermitage over her mother's violent opposition. The mother was the sister of James Jackson, the General's business associate; as a result of the marriage James Jackson broke with Andrew and Mrs. Kirkman disowned her daughter. Later, when the General tried to intervene on the daughter's behalf, the mother ordered him out of her house. An intense romantic, if not a meddling busybody, Jackson found no contradiction to his strong opinions about family in his assisting these couples in their escape to wedded bliss.

In 1809, through legal adoption, Rachel and Andrew finally obtained a child of their own. They were permitted to have one of the twin boys born December 22, 1809, to Severn Donelson and his wife, Elizabeth. The natural mother was in poor health and could not nurse two children, so she willingly allowed Rachel to take one of them three days after his birth.[59] The child was legally adopted and christened Andrew Jackson, Jr. He brought joy to the family, particularly to Rachel, who resented the prolonged separations from her husband and now found a measure of comfort and happiness in caring for her own son.

Jackson himself mellowed somewhat on becoming a parent. Although he could still produce fits of uncontrolled rage, he now displayed great tenderness and meekness bordering on shyness in the presence of his wards and his son. The contrast was sharp. Observers often commented that there were two Jacksons, one fierce and militant, the other compassionate and generous. And the speed with which he could flash from one to the other was stupefying. The story was frequently told of his riding with his wife one day when some careless wagoners drove their cart accidentally against his carriage, giving Rachel a violent lurch. Jackson splattered them with curses and blood-chilling oaths. The wagoners, pretty rough customers themselves, shrank involuntarily under the wagon as if to ward off the terrible blows of his language. They rode off without a word, outmatched and "outdone in their own speciality."[60]

Yet this bravura performance was mere playacting. Jackson was not one whit as angry as he pretended. When he pulled the string of his temper and released a flood of sound, he usually did it deliberately, whether or not it represented his true feelings. And he could extinguish the tantrum in an instant. His temper, so furious and startlingly sudden, intimidated his victims by its abruptness and its noisiness. Unfortunately, Jackson could not resist playing the bully when it suited his purpose. And like all bullies he intruded in the affairs of others on the slightest pretext.

A very close friend of his, one Patten Anderson, was shot to death by David Magness in a feud over a land title, and Jackson vowed that Magness must hang. (Magness had shot Anderson when he saw Anderson attack his father.) The trial lasted two weeks and involved some of the best lawyers in the state: Felix Grundy for the defense and Thomas Hart Benton for the prosecution. Jackson roared into town and drunkenly delivered a wild harangue in the public square about how Magness was a coward and had assassinated Anderson. In utter amazement, someone in the crowd said "Pshaw!"—which Jackson heard.

"Who *dares* to say *pshaw* at me?" he bellowed. "By ————! I'll knock any man's head off who says pshaw at me!"

The offender slipped away.

After that Jackson strode into the courtroom to give testimony and to tell the jury its duty. His manner and tone—the sheer arrogance of the man!—produced an effect opposite to the one intended. The clever prosecutor followed up his advantage by seeking to force Jackson into testifying that Anderson was a troublemaker. Had not Anderson frequently been in "difficulties"? Grundy pointedly asked.

Jackson could not deny it, but he also saw the lawyer's game.

"Sir," the General said, his most Jacksonian look fixed upon the lawyer, "my friend, Patten Anderson, was the NATURAL ENEMY OF SCOUNDRELS!"

The jury did not appreciate that snappy reply and found the prisoner guilty of manslaughter—a milder verdict than had been expected—and sentenced Magness to be branded on the hand.[61] The infuriated Jackson responded to this "miscarriage of justice" by shaking his fist under the nose of one of the jurors.[62]

On another occasion the General heard about a United States agent to the Choctaw Indians, one Silas Dinsmore, whose agency house in the Mississippi Territory was used to detain every slave traveling with a white man. Jackson decided to interfere and teach Dinsmore his duty. The

agent's house was located on the great road between Nashville and Natchez and was meant to serve as a station to prevent runaway slaves from
taking refuge with the Indians. Dinsmore was very tolerant toward runa-
ways. Worse, he required each master to show documentary proof of
ownership before he would let him pass with his slaves. If proof were
lacking, he took the slaves into custody. Obviously there were many
complaints to the secretary of war about the highhandedness of this
official.

At the time Jackson was an inactive partner of a business firm that
traded in slaves to the lower country. To instruct Dinsmore on the proper
execution of his duties, the General rode down to Natchez and picked up
several slaves to march back to Nashville. He expected to encounter
Dinsmore and deliberately failed to carry the necessary documents to
prove ownership. Instead he armed two of the more trusted blacks and
purchased a rifle for himself.

An incident was averted because Dinsmore was absent when Jackson
got to the agency. After leaving provocatively worded messages for the
agent, stating what he had done and what the agent could expect in the
future if he persisted in his behavior, the General proceeded home. In
Nashville again, he won applause by swearing he would burn both agent
and agency if any more slaves were detained. Meanwhile he roused his
friends in Congress to press for Dinsmore's removal.[63]

But the agent was not to be intimidated. A short time later he not
only detained ten slaves owned by a lady who was passing through the
Choctaw country but he published in the Nashville newspaper, on September 11, 1812, a card announcing his action and his intention of stopping anyone in the future who did not obey the rules of his office.

Jackson exploded. *"My God!"* he wrote George W. Campbell. "Is it
come to this? Are we *freemen, or are we slaves? Is this real, or is it a dream?*
. . . Can the Secretary of War, for one moment, retain the idea that we
will permit this petty tyrant to sport with our rights . . . and sport with
our feelings by publishing his *lawless tyranny exercised over a helpless and
unprotected female?* If he does, he thinks too meanly of our patriotism and
gallantry."[64]

Jackson's position was a popular one, as well he knew. The Dinsmore
affair "irritated the public mind," he wrote, "and are now ready to burst
forth in vengeance."[65]

Ultimately Dinsmore was removed. He happened to be away from his
post during the war with Great Britain, when a crisis arose. Another agent
was needed, and the Tennessee authorities appointed a replacement who
performed his duties to their satisfaction. After the war they wanted to
keep him and prevent Dinsmore's reappointment. Jackson, now the great

hero of the war and a considerable influence in the War Department, shielded the new agent. Poor Dinsmore was reduced to wandering in poverty among the Indians he had once protected. Several years later Dinsmore tried to effect a reconciliation with the General, but the stern, unbending Jackson simply glared his contempt and turned away.

Jackson did not always refuse reconciliation. When it suited his purposes—particularly his political purposes—he could be coaxed into letting bygones be bygones. Of course the niceties of southern manners in arranging such things had to be observed, but he liked to be known as a man of unflinching loyalty toward his friends and implacable hatred toward his foes.

Once, at a great outdoor banquet, Jackson was engaged in conversation at one end of the table when it sounded as though a close friend was under attack at the far end of the table. Rather than try to force his way through the crowds on either side of him, Jackson jumped on top of the table and strode toward his friend, wading through dishes and knocking food aside.

"I'm coming," he shouted, "I'm coming," and his hand reached inside his coat.

When the crowd saw the motion of his hand they began screaming. "Don't fire," they begged. "Don't fire."

When he realized that his friend was safe, Jackson halted in his tracks. And there he stood, like some "mad Colossus," atop the table, amid the wreckage of dishes, the spectators drawn back in terror and expecting him to start firing at any moment.[66]

He drew his hand from his pocket. It held a tobacco box. With a loud click he shut the lid and returned to his place.

CHAPTER 11

"Who Are We?"

ANDREW JACKSON WAS FORTY-FIVE YEARS OF AGE when Congress formally declared war against Great Britain in 1812. He had been living fairly quietly with his family at the Hermitage, where he now owned 640 acres of land.[1] His only excitement away from the plantation—not including public brawls—occurred at the racetrack. He had desperately wanted fame as a military chieftain, but here it was ten years after his election as major general of the militia and still no sign of war. Despite the efforts of some, both in and out of Congress, hostilities with Spain never materialized and a genocidal war against Indians remained undeclared. In those ten years there had been few calls by the government for his services, although he offered them speedily every time he thought he heard the beat of a war drum.

Then came war with Great Britain. The causes were many, but the most important one was psychological. Although Britain, over a period of many years, had seized American ships, impressed American sailors, tampered with American trade, and encouraged Indian raids along the northern frontier, perhaps the most compelling reason driving the United States to war was the urgent need to prove its inalienable right to liberty and independence. Since winning its freedom from England the country had been subjected to a series of humiliations by the major powers of Europe. France and England, locked in struggle in the Napoleonic wars, disregarded American rights and sovereignty as though they did not exist. To many in America there was a frightful, overpowering urge to prove once again that the independence they had gained in the

Revolution was no mistake. Predictions that the States would eventually return to British rule had to be refuted by yet another demonstration of America's determination to be free. It was as though the nation could not find collective peace of mind until it established again the legitimacy of its freedom. There were many reasons for an American war against Napoleonic France in view of the Berlin and Milan decrees and the subsequent seizure of American ships. But such a war could not provide the country with surcease from its fierce, almost pathological craving to show Great Britain—and the world—that its liberty had been truly and fairly earned. In a real sense the War of 1812 was part of a search for national identity.[2]

There was another reason, almost as important and far more pragmatic. American expansion! For years Americans dreamed of taking Canada from England. They tried to do it during the Revolution and failed. The seizure of Canada would add the great St. Lawrence River valley to the nation, and the combination of that seaway with the Great Lakes promised a future of unparalleled economic possibilities for all Americans. The capture of Canada would not only swell the size and prosperity of the nation it would rid the continent of a dangerous foe who might swoop down from the north at any moment to extinguish American freedom. Furthermore, it would end the British provocation of Indian raids on the frontier. "I should not wish to extend the boundary of the United States by war," Representative Richard M. Johnson of Kentucky said, "if Great Britain would leave us the quiet enjoyment of independence; but considering her deadly and implacable enmity, and her continued hostilities, I shall never die contented until I see her expulsion from North America, and her territories incorporated with the United States."[3] Only war with England could realize this ever-beckoning dream of conquest.

There was more. War with Britain meant probable hostilities with her ally, Spain—southerners and westerners realized that—and war with Spain could provide the Floridas. In foreign hands the Floridas posed a constant threat to the peace and safety of the Republic. People living along the southwestern frontier used to say that whoever owned the Floridas held a pistol at the heart of the United States.[4] The expulsion of the Spanish, therefore, was an absolute necessity dictated by self-preservation. And a war of conquest might bring, in addition to the Floridas, Mexico and the creation of a tremendous American empire stretching from ocean to ocean.[5] In terms of geographic expansion, war in 1812 made a great deal of sense to many Americans.

Within Congress there was a contingent of young militants who actively urged a declaration of war against Great Britain. The War Hawks, as they were called, included some of the best young talent in the country, north and south, men like Johnson, Henry Clay of Kentucky, John C. Calhoun of South Carolina, Peter B. Porter of New York, and Felix Grundy of Tennessee. This second generation of Americans since the founding of the Republic were anxious to prove their worth as successors to the illustrious patriots who were their forebears. They demanded the restoration of American honor through the chastisement of war. They plotted to force President Madison to ask Congress for a declaration. Their demand was constant, their tone strident. Congressmen G. M. Troup and William H. Crawford of Georgia joined the cry for the Floridas while Porter and John A. Harper of New Hampshire added their voices to the call for Canada.⁶ John Randolph of Roanoke, one of Jackson's conservative friends in Congress, described the passion for expansion. "Ever since the report of the Committee on Foreign Relations came into the House," he said, "we have heard but one word—like the whippoorwill, but one eternal monotonous tone—Canada! Canada! Canada!"⁷

It might be "Canada! Canada! Canada!" to the north, but to the south it was "Florida! Florida! Florida!" Both territories could be bagged in a war that succeeded in expelling the nation's two foreign enemies. Thomas Jefferson, hearing of a British attack on an American ship, said, "If the English do not give us the satisfaction we demand, we will take Canada, which wants to enter the Union; and when, together with Canada, we shall have the Floridas, we shall no longer have any difficulties with our neighbors."⁸ The conceit of Americans in believing that Canada "wants to enter the Union" encouraged northern expansionists to demand a declaration of war. The moment seemed propitious. The conquest of Canada and Florida—at last—seemed at hand.

Henry Clay was chosen Speaker of the House of Representatives, and he used his position to fill important committees with men who were as militant as he. Grundy, on the foreign relations committee, wrote Jackson in the fall of 1811 that if the opinion of that committee prevailed, the "Ruebicon" was already crossed. "I firmly believe," he said a few days later, "that G Britain must recede or this Congress will declare war. If the latter takes place the Canadas & Floridas will be the Theatres of our offensive operations."⁹ To prepare for the emergency, Grundy's committee recommended the addition of 10,000 regular soldiers to the present military establishment, the call of 50,000 volunteers, and the arming of the merchant fleet.

As the fervor of war mounted within the country, Jackson burned with a need to call his troops and lead them into battle. He was ready for any foe—British, Spanish, Indian. When William Henry Harrison, commanding the Indiana and Kentucky militia, attacked a confederation of

Indians led by the Shawnee chief, Tecumseh, and his brother, the Prophet, Jackson wrote pleadingly to Harrison to volunteer his services.[10] But victory over the Indians at Tippecanoe dashed his hopes. Next Jackson wrote to the new governor of Tennessee, Willie Blount, who had succeeded Sevier after Sevier completed his second string of three terms, offering to have 4,000 men ready within ten days to march against Quebec. Congressmen were "talking a great deal about *taking Canada*"—even the newspapers commented on it[11]—and Jackson wanted a share of the action. Blount passed his offer on to the secretary of war, but nothing came of it.[12]

In February 1812, just a few months before the actual declaration of hostilites, Congress authorized the enlistment of 50,000 volunteers. The announcement was greeted with wild enthusiasm all along the frontier, and the ecstatic Jackson immediately responded with a ringing call for enlistments.

Hermitage, March 7, 1812

VOLUNTEERS TO ARMS!

Citizens! Your government has at last yielded to the impulse of the nation. Your impatience is no longer restrained. The hour of national vengeance is now at hand. The eternal enemies of american prosperity are again to be taught to respect your rights, after having been compelled to feel, once more, the power of your arms. War is on the point of breaking out between the united States and the King of great Britain! and the martial hosts of america are summoned to the Tented Fields! . . .

A simple invitation is given to the young men of the country to arm for their own and their countries rights. On this invitation 50,000 volunteers, full of martial ardor, indignant at their countries wrongs and burning with impatience to illustrate their names by some signal exploit, are expected to repair to the national standard.

Could it be otherwise? Could the general government deem it necessary to force *us* to take the field? We, who for so many years have demanded a war with such clamourous importunity—who, in so many resolutions of town meetings and legislative assemblies, have offered our lives and fortunes for the defence of our country—who, so often and so publickly, have charged this verry government with a pusillanimous deference to foreign nations, because she had resolved to exhaust the arts of negociation before she made her last appeal to the power of arms. No under such circumstances it was impossible for the government to conceive that compulsion would be wanting to bring us into the field. . . .

But another and nobler feeling should impell us to action. *Who are we? and for what are we going to fight?* are we the titled Slaves of George the third? the military conscripts of Napolon the great? or the frozen peasants of the Russian Czar? No—we are the free born sons of america; the citizens of the only republick now existing in the world; and the only people on earth who possess rights, liberties, and property which they dare call their own.

For a badly educated man this was an impressive statement. Having asked *Who are we?* and answered it, Jackson turned to the question, *For what are we going to fight?*

We are going to fight for the reestablishment of our national charector, misunderstood and vilified at home and abroad; for the protection of our maritime citizens, impressed on board British ships of war and compelled to fight the battles of our enemies against ourselves; to vindicate our right to a free trade, and open a market for the productions of our soil, now perishing on our hands because the *mistress of the ocean* has forbid us to carry them to any foreign nation; in fine, to seek some indemnity for past injuries, some security against future aggressions, by the conquest of all the British dominions upon the continent of north america.

That meant Canada. "Should the occupation of the canadas be resolved upon by the general government," Jackson continued, "how pleasing the prospect that would open to the young volunteer, while performing a military *promenade* into a distant country. . . . To view the stupendous works of nature, exemplified in the falls of Niagara . . . to tread the consecrated spot on which Wolf and Montgomery fell, would of themselves repay the young soldier for a march across the continent."[13]

A march across the continent! It was a dazzling offer, and the response Jackson received from his "young men" delighted him.

Finally President Madison capitulated to the inevitable and asked for a declaration of war against Great Britain. Congress obliged on June 18, 1812.

Jackson was overjoyed. At last the nation's honor had been restored. Immediately he offered the President 2,500 volunteers, a small army ready to fight and die for their major general and the United States of America. He expected a prompt reply, praising him for his patriotism and calling him and his troops into battle. Instead he received a polite if perfunctory acceptance of his offer but no call to duty. It was a shock. Months passed, and still no call. At first he could scarcely believe or understand it. Then the truth dawned on him: The administration remembered his involvement with Burr and his support of James

Monroe, and therefore had no wish to favor him with an active command. Henry Dearborn was sent against Quebec and Brigadier General James Winchester, along with two of Jackson's regiments, was ordered to assist General Harrison in the north. Nothing for Jackson. Nothing for the old friend of Aaron Burr.

Meanwhile General William Hull surrendered Detroit to a combined force of British soldiers and Indians. The invasion of Canada to advance American territorial expansion northward was a disaster. Along the northern frontier one defeat followed another. No general of any ability emerged. No general of any ability was summoned. The only good general sat idle in Tennessee, and no one but Andrew Jackson knew it.

He raged at home against the "old grannies" in Washington who risked the safety of the nation by failing to recognize him. He talked publicly of conquering Florida and of raining death and destruction upon the Creek Nation.[14] He proposed slicing through Alabama to the Gulf of Mexico and capturing the Spanish-held port of Mobile, an act all Tennesseans cheered. "Turn your eyes to the south," he exhorted his volunteers. "Behold in the province of West Florida, a territory whose rivers and harbors are indispensable to the prosperity of the western. . . . It is here that an employment adopted to your situation awaits your courage and your zeal; and while extending in the quarter the boundaries of the Republic to the Gulf of Mexico."[15] But Jackson was no fool; the Burr conspiracy had taught him the importance of the approval of responsible authority. There was nothing to do but wait and carry on his silly little war with Silas Dinsmore. Not until October 1812 was Governor Blount asked to provide 1,500 volunteers to support General Wilkinson in the defense of New Orleans. Although the administration wished to protect the country against the possibility of a southern invasion, the President also hoped to build a strike force that would seize eastern Florida and keep it after the war as reparation.

In requesting volunteers for the New Orleans expedition, the administration indicated to Blount that it could do without Andrew Jackson, but it did not impose this sentiment as an obligation. Blount, who was politically allied to Jackson and had received his principal support in West Tennessee from the Jackson forces, hesitated only briefly before deciding to disregard the administration's hint. He felt authorized to appoint whoever he believed best qualified to command the expedition, and after obtaining legal support for his interpretation he filled in Jackson's name on one of the seventy blank commissions that Washington had forwarded. Henceforth Andrew Jackson was a major general of *United States* volunteers. Blount forwarded the commission to Jackson along with the general order directing the volunteers to New Orleans.[16]

Now, at last, Jackson had an active command. Now, at last, he might begin his search for military glory.

But a problem existed. The troops were called to support General Wilkinson! Blount appreciated Jackson's feelings about serving under Wilkinson after all that had happened, but he urged him to accept the command nonetheless. "At a period like the present," Jackson replied, ". . . it is the duty of every citizen to do something for his country." Still, there was "a sting to my feelings," he said. He had read the orders of the secretary of war and it seemed clear to him that the intention of the administration "was either to exclude me from the command, or if I did command by an apparent willingness and condesension on my part to place me under the command of Genl Wilkinson."[17] Much more likely was the administration's unwillingness to bring together two men who so thoroughly detested each other. That would explain the administration's hint to Blount. Whatever the administration's motivation, Jackson concluded, "viewing the situation of our beloved country at present, should your Excellency believe that my personal service can promote its interests in the least degree, I will sacrifice my own feelings, and lead my brave volunteers to any point your excellency may please to order."[18] It was bitter medicine to serve under that "publick villain" General James Wilkinson, but it was that or nothing. Jackson had no choice.

Blount instructed him to call out two divisions and have them ready in Nashville on December 10, 1812. Since the troops were to proceed to the lower country, Jackson was told to procure the necessary boats for transportation and to requisition the supplies and "Camp equipage" he needed. The troops were expected to bring their own arms, including rifles, although the government would supply those who had none.[19] Jackson issued an address to his soldiers that was full of patriotic pride and the strong "feelings of a soldier."[20] He advised his troops that the expedition would last a good five or six months and that they should have clothing for winter and spring "in quantity and quality of both seasons."[21]

The winter of 1812–13 was particularly brutal, and the day set for the rendezvous saw snow a foot deep on the ground. The quartermaster, William B. Lewis, had obtained a large quantity of wood, but every stick of it was burned on the first night to keep the men from freezing. Jackson and Lewis roamed among the troops from dusk to morning that first night, checking on the condition of the men and hauling those unconscious from liquor within the reach of the fire. At about six o'clock in the morning Jackson entered the local tavern to rest. As he walked in he overheard a civilian (who had passed the night comfortably in bed) complain about the stupidity of the authorities for having massed troops without providing adequate shelter. It was monstrous, he said, that the men should be outside in the cold while the officers had the best accommodations in town. The civilian had barely gotten the words out of his mouth when Jackson cut him down with a verbal assault.

"You d---d infernal scoundrel," he cried, "sowing disaffection among the troops. Why, the quartermaster and I have been up all night, making the men comfortable. Let me hear no more such talk, or I'm d---d if I don't ram that red hot handiron down your throat."[22]

It was a mark of Jackson's leadership that he personally supervised the care of his men and concerned himself with their well-being. He had great pride in them, as he had in himself, and was extremely solicitous of their welfare. The men knew this, and they reciprocated with respect and devotion. They realized he could be tough and unyielding, arbitrary and rigid; they knew his anger could be a terrible burden to them; but they also knew he cared about their comfort more than his own and would tend to their needs as his first priority.

A few days later the cold spell broke and the troops were organized into an army and readied to march. For the general staff, Lewis, the General's friend and neighbor, was named assistant deputy quartermaster; William Carroll, a bright young man from Pennsylvania, was appointed brigade inspector; Thomas Hart Benton, the clever young lawyer whom Jackson had met on the circuit and recognized as a man of talent and industry, was chosen first aide-de-camp; and John Reid, who came from Virginia and was probably recommended to Jackson by Benton, was named second aide and secretary to the General. Reid showed unusual intellectual ability and became an immediate favorite. (He later wrote an early narrative of Jackson's military career that was completed after Reid's death and converted into a campaign biography by John H. Eaton.) John Coffee, a simple, brave and modest man, who was Jackson's former business partner and absolutely devoted to him, received command of the cavalry. A giant, Coffee stood well over six feet and weighed 216 pounds.[23] His round face framed in a helmet of black hair, his prominent nose, and his firm jaw projected a physical presence of enormous strength and stamina. He proved a superb field commander and Jackson's ablest associate.

Colonel William Hall and Benton received command of two regiments of infantry comprising 1,400 men. The troops came from every station and from every corner of the state. They were businessmen, planters, and yeomen, most of them descendants of revolutionary war veterans. Finally, on January 7, 1813, the army was ready to move in defense of the lower country. On orders from Governor Blount the infantry and riflemen were to be transported by boat (via Natchez) to New Orleans and the cavalry and mounted infantry were to proceed by land. On his arrival in New Orleans, Jackson was instructed to await the orders of President Madison.

In sending him off, Blount congratulated Jackson on his skill and energy in raising and organizing the volunteers. The General demurred. It was my duty, he said. I was "brought up under the tyrany of Britain," and although very young at the time I "embarked in the struggle for our liberties, in which I lost every thing that was dear to me, *my brothers and my fortune.*" But "I have been amply repaid by living under the mild administration of a republican government." To maintain that government and the independent rights of the nation "is a duty I have ever owed to my Country to myself & to posterity, and when I do all I can . . . I have only done my duty."

Duty to his country and its republican government—that, more than anything else, bespeaks the quintessential Jackson at the outset of his military career. Duty to protect a free society. Duty to preserve its "independent rights." He concluded his letter by "praying that the God of Battles may be with us, and that high Heaven may bestow its Choice Benedictions on all engaged in this Expedition."[24]

With a few taps of a drum, the firing of a cannon, and a burst of huzzas from a crowd standing on the wharf, the fleet moved away from its mooring and headed down the Cumberland toward the Ohio and Mississippi rivers. His army finally in motion, Jackson notified the secretary of war that he was under way at the head of 2,071 volunteers and if the government so ordered they would rejoice at the opportunity of placing the American eagle over Mobile, Pensacola, and St. Augustine.[25]

At last Jackson had reached the moment he had anticipated for more than a decade. Opportunity lay before him, and he eagerly reached for it. "Do not, my beloved husband," wrote Rachel, as he set off on his expedition, "let the love of country, fame and honor, make you forget you have [a wife]."[26] He did not forget. On the trip down the river he paused to write her.

> *My Love:* I have . . . your miniature. I shall wear it near my bosom; but this was useless for without your minature my recollection never fails me of your likeness.
>
> The sensibility of our beloved son has charmed me. I have no doubt from the sweetness of his disposition, from his good sense as evidenced from his age, he will take care of us both in our declining years. From our fondness toward him, his return of affection to us, I have every hope, if he should be spared to manhood, that he will, with a careful education, realize all our wishes. Kiss him for his papa

and give him the nuts and ginger cake sent him by Dinwiddie.

I thank you for your prayers. I thank you for your determined resolution to bear our separation with fortitude. We part but for a few days—for a few fleeting weeks when the protecting hand of Providence, if it is His will, will restore us to each others arms.[27]

Ice clogged the Ohio River. A series of earthquakes along the Mississippi changed the course of the river. Three men and a boat were lost during the long voyage, but thirty-nine days later and one thousand miles down the river from Nashville the expedition arrived in Natchez, where Coffee and the cavalry awaited them.

There was also a letter from Rachel.

My thoughts are forever on thee. Where'er I go, where'er I turn, my thoughts, my fears, my doubts distress me. Then a little hope revives again and that keeps me alive. Were it not for that, I must sink; I should die in my present situation. But my blessed Redeemer is making intercession with the Father for us to meet again, to restore you to my bosom, where every vein, every pulse beats high for your health, your safety, and all your wishes crowned. . . .

Our little Andrew is well; the most affectionate little darling on earth. Often does he ask me in bed not to cry, papa will come again and I feel my cheeks to know if I am shedding tears. On Thursday last, he said, "Mama, let's go to Nashville and see if he's there." I told him where you had gone. He said, "Don't cry, sweet mama." You can't think how that supported me in my trials. . . .

May the Almighty God of heaven shower down his blessings. His mercy on you, assist you in the ways of life, in the ways of righteousness, be your shield in time of danger, support you in the paths of wisdom—the ways thereof in peace afar. Think of me your dearest friend on earth.[28]

In addition to Rachel's gentle letter there were several communications from General Wilkinson. Each one reiterated a single theme: stay away! Jackson and his volunteers were to remain in Natchez.

Several reasons for this abrupt command were given: that Wilkinson had received no instructions from Washington; that he had no provisions in New Orleans to share with Jackson's troops; that if the expedition was intended against Florida it would be best if the army were stationed at some point on the river above New Orleans. There was also the matter that Jackson had "not done me the honor to communicate with me" about "your command." In any event Wilkinson wanted one thing clear: "I . . . must repeat my desire, that you should halt in the vicinity of Natchez."[29]

So Jackson halted. He moved his army four miles from Natchez and took a position where there was enough wood and water and which would allow him to move quickly once he received his orders. Weeks passed without further instructions, just strained but polite exchanges between himself and Wilkinson concerning his status and authority. Jackson worried about the effect that inactivity would have upon his troops. "Indolence creates disquiet," he wrote.[30]

On top of everything else Jackson was distressed by the news of General Winchester's disastrous defeat at the battle of Frenchtown in Canada. Those were Tennessee troops, his troops, and their humiliation evoked his deepest sympathy. "My heart bleds for the disaster that has lately befel Genl Winchester in the North West," he wrote to Rachel. "If true; what an ocean of blood, from the chocest viens of the Western sons has been spilt. It appears that fate has destined our best heroes to perish in those deserts, or can these misfortunes arise, from want of Judgt. incaution, or is it from a fixed destiny of heaven."[31]

The "fixed destiny of heaven" had also prepared a blow for Jackson. On March 15 he received an order from the new secretary of war, John Armstrong, that convulsed the General and left him shaking with rage.

War Department, February 5, 1813

> *Sir,* The causes embodying and marching to New Orleans the Corps under your command having ceased to exist, you will on receit of this letter, consider it as dismissed from public service and take measures to have delivered over to Major General Wilkinson all articles of public property which may have been put into it's possession. You will accept for yourself and the Corps the thanks of the President of the United States.
> I have the honor to be Sir, With great respect,
> Your Most Obedient Servant[32]

Dismissed! Jackson could scarcely believe his eyes. Here he was with over two thousand men, five hundred miles from home, cast loose in the wilderness without pay, without transport, without medicine, and told to return home with a simple thank-you for your patriotism and loyalty. Dissolving an army in Indian country! The order was insane. Surely Armstrong did not know where the troops were. Surely he believed them to be waiting in Nashville.

Small wonder the war was going so badly, thought Jackson, when idiots in Washington had the authority to issue such orders. Or was this repayment for his friendship with Burr and his support of Monroe? Neither, Jackson concluded. It must be that "traitor" Wilkinson. He had already received a number of letters from the "publick villain" telling him that he would "render a most acceptable service to our Government by encouraging" his troops to enlist in the regular army. Since his troops were without food and far from home, they would probably join Wilkinson once they were dismissed. Thus Wilkinson and the imbeciles in Washington would get rid of him, take his army, and humiliate him by forcing him to return alone to Nashville.[33] What a disaster! What a tragic end to the glorious expedition he had earlier promised his troops.

Jackson invariably interpreted his difficulties on a purely personal basis. There was always an enemy lurking somewhere, trying to do him in. Actually the administration had found Congress ill-disposed toward an invasion of East Florida—which would constitute an act of war against Spain. Spain was allied to Russia, and the Czar was now attempting to act as mediator between the United States and Great Britain. To avoid further international complications the administration decided to abandon the project against East Florida, and consequently Armstrong dismissed the intended strike force. (But Congress did authorize the seizure of what was left of West Florida, and in the spring of 1813 American forces easily captured Mobile and forced the Spanish garrison to withdraw to Pensacola.)

None of which Jackson knew. All he had was an order that said he was finished. Go home. Snorting his fury, Jackson called in Benton and told him he would not obey Armstrong's order.[34] He would not dismiss his volunteers; instead he would lead them back to Tennessee himself, at his own expense if necessary. He sketched a "very severe" reply to the secretary that his aides—who were as adamant as he about keeping the army together and marching it back to Nashville—convinced him to revise.[35] He toned down his anger on paper, but he still let Armstrong know that "these brave men . . . deserve a better fate and return from their government." At the call of their country they "voluntarily rallied round its insulted standard. They followed me to the field; I shall carefully march them back to their homes."[36]

Jackson also wrote a restrained letter to Madison, expressing the pain it gave him to record the events of the last month "when the misfortunes of our Country and the loss of our military reputation, requires every nerve to support the contest in which we are engaged" and hoping that funds would be available at Nashville to pay for the discharge of his troops when they arrived.[37] To others he expressed his true feelings. "Is this the reward of a virtuous administration, to its patriotic sons, or is it done by a wicked *monster*, to satiate the vengeance, of a combination of hypocritical Political Villains, who would sacrifice the best blood of our Country, to satiate the spleen of a villian who their connection with in acts of wickedness they are afraid to offend."[38]

Then he wrote his wife to tell her what had happened. He ended the letter with a sigh. "Kiss my little andrew for me tell him his papa is coming home."[39]

CHAPTER 12

Old Hickory

IRONICALLY, THE DISASTROUS JOURNEY TO NATCHEZ and back proved a personal triumph for Jackson. All the things the volunteers admired about their General were amplified before their eyes: the determination, the fortitude, the personal courage, the strength of leadership, the personal identity with their small successes and many hardships, the consideration, patience and understanding. What it all added up to was the fact that they admired him and trusted him, and so if he said they would walk from Natchez to Nashville, then they would do it.

But something else emerged on that painful road back home. It was a quality in Jackson's character that is essential to an understanding of his subsequent military successes. The quality had probably always been there but now it suddenly billowed out into full view. That quality was will power. Not the ordinary kind. Nothing normal or even natural. This was superhuman. This was virtually demonic. This was sheer, total, concentrated determination to achieve his ends. So if he determined to march his men back to Nashville he would get them there even if it meant carrying every last one of them on his back.

Andrew Jackson was not a great general. He was better than most of the commanders available in 1812, but that hardly does him credit. What distinguished him and basically made the difference between victory and defeat on the battlefield was his absolute determination to win—at whatever cost. As a consequence he was capable of extraordinary feats of courage and daring and perseverance in the face of incredible odds. Nothing less than victory was acceptable. Defeat was unthinkable.

This fierce exercise of will, supported by supreme self-confidence and genuine military talent, although unexceptional, shaped repeated triumphs over the Indians, the British and the Spanish. He swept them out of the south and west. Had his talent been employed along the northern frontier he would have spearheaded an invasion of Canada that might ultimately have succeeded in aiming American expansion in a more northerly direction. Granted conquering Canada was quite different and infinitely more difficult than removing the Indian-Spanish-British power in the southwest. But if any man could have pulled it off during the War of 1812 that man was Andrew Jackson—or so he always believed.

Starting with the overland journey from Natchez to Nashville a Jackson emerged whose whole existence and purpose in life was to achieve military victory. His men recognized it and were awed by it. On occasion they rebelled when his demands upon them transcended human capability. But most times they realized that such a commander wins battles and carries his men to victory and undying fame and so they obeyed him and fought hard for him.

At his command the Tennessee volunteers marched back to Nashville. And it was an agony. In organizing the march Jackson had to accommodate 150 men on the sicklist, of whom 56 could not sit upright or raise their heads from their pillows. And there were only eleven wagons to convey the sick back home. For many, therefore, it was a long, difficult, painful journey that they would never forget. Jackson ordered his officers to turn their horses over to the sick, and he surrendered his own three horses for this duty. Trudging alongside his men day after day, never showing weariness or fatigue, he cheered the men with a word, a gesture, a sign of his pride in them. His concern for their safety and comfort was instinctive; it was rooted in his sense of leadership. "It is . . . my duty," he told his wife, "to act as a father to the sick and to the well and stay with them untill I march them into Nashville."[1]

Once it began, the march moved quite rapidly, averaging eighteen miles a day. Jackson prodded the men along in the gentlest possible way. When a delirious invalid lifted himself in a wagon and asked where he was, Jackson responded, "On your way *home!*" whereupon all the soldiers cheered.[2] As the army lurched forward, Jackson was everywhere, moving up and down the column, watching for any incident that needed his attention, overseeing the distribution of rations, encouraging his men to keep going. When a recruiting officer from Wilkinson was found hanging around the camp, Jackson favored him with one of his celebrated glares and warned him that if he attempted any word or action to seduce the volunteers, he would be drummed out of the camp in the presence of the entire corps.

Jackson's sternness at one moment contrasted sharply with his gentleness at the next. As General there was only one word to describe him: indomitable. His men said he was "tough," tougher than most anything they knew. Tough as hickory, someone ventured, which was about as hard as anyone could suggest. Soon his men started calling him Hickory. And because they deeply admired him as a commander they added the prefix "old," thereby giving him his everlasting nickname: Old Hickory.

Within a month the army had pulled itself back to Tennessee. And when the troops arrived in Nashville, word was soon broadcast of Jackson's heroic conduct and how the men had knighted him. Some of the stories were exaggerations, but all repeated the strength and quality of his character and leadership: his toughness and perseverance, his towering presence at all times, his regard for the comfort and safety of his men, his pride in their accomplishment, his total command of the entire operation. "Long will their General live in the memory of his volunteers of West Tennessee," the Nashville *Whig* pronounced, "for his benevolence, humane, and fatherly treatment to his soldiers; if gratitude and love can reward him, General Jackson has them. It affords us pleasure to say, that we believe there is not a man belonging to the detachment but what loves him." [3] The soldiers loved him, the newspapers said, and they were not ashamed to admit it.

Almost overnight Jackson's character defects vanished from the minds of frontier Americans. No longer was he the murderous slayer of Dickinson or the quarrelsome hothead who dared besmirch the reputation of the heroic Sevier. Now he was "the most beloved and esteemed of private citizens in western Tennessee."[4] It was a miraculous conversion. At the age of forty-six Jackson had become a father figure, protector of his men as well as guardian of the people of the frontier.[5] Henceforth Jackson nurtured that image, speaking and acting in accordance with its recognized and required characteristics.

But periodically he battered that image, always straining the limits of popular affection and loyalty toward him. The frightful delinquencies of character—the savage hatreds, the readiness to violence—he never completely dissolved or totally banished. Even now, with his newly acquired reputation, he allowed himself to be drawn into an unseemly affair of honor that had people shaking their heads in wonder over the fearful, conflicting qualities fused within his singular personality.

The origins of the affair are cloudy, but they apparently developed during the homeward march of the volunteers from Natchez. Jackson was rather fond of his brigade inspector, William Carroll, whom he thought an exceptionally capable young man and destined to carve for himself an important military and political career. As he usually did when he reached such conclusions, Jackson showed Carroll every favor and interest—thereby exciting the jealousies of other junior officers. Carroll had only recently arrived in Tennessee from Pennsylvania, and some men thought he displayed a decidedly superior air. In addition to being personally unpopular, Carroll had a difficult job to do as inspector, and no doubt his efficiency only worsened his already poor relations with his fellow officers.

At some point Carroll and Littleton Johnston quarreled. The matter was serious enough for Johnston to challenge Billy Carroll to a duel. Haughtily, Billy refused to fight on the ground that Johnston was no gentleman. Johnston tried again, this time asking Jesse Benton, the brother of Thomas Hart Benton, to carry the challenge. Billy still refused. He only fought gentlemen. Thereupon Jesse offered himself as Johnston's surrogate, and his social standing was such that Billy could not again refuse without being labeled a coward.[6]

By this time the army had arrived in Nashville. The duel was set and drew keen interest among the junior officers. Billy needed a second and soon discovered that no one would oblige him. So he rode out to the Hermitage and asked Jackson, who had shown him so many favors on their recent expedition, to act as his "friend."

"Why, Captain Carroll," said Old Hickory. "I am not the man for such an affair. I am too old. The time has been when I should have gone out with pleasure; but, at my time of life, it would be extremely injudicious. You must get a man nearer your own age."[7]

Good advice, and a pity that Jackson did not resolutely heed his own words. But Billy persisted and argued that a conspiracy existed to run him out of the country. There were people, he said, who envied him his commission and resented his good relations with Jackson. That struck a responsive chord. Jackson understood conspiracies. He believed in the conspiracy theory to explain human behavior and events. How else, for example, could he account for the administration's actions toward him?

"Well, Carroll," he finally said, "you may make your mind easy on *one* point: they sha'n't run you out of the country as long as Andrew Jackson lives in it. I'll ride with you to Nashville, and inquire into this business myself."[8]

Initially Jackson hoped to talk the two men out of their quarrel. And at first he succeeded. Jesse was a hothead, like his more talented brother, and prone to get himself into awkward situations that he later regretted. Thus a few soothing words from Jackson were enough to bring Jesse around and get him to forget the whole affair.

But the junior officers were itching to see Carroll called to account, and they prevailed on Jesse to renew the quarrel. Disgusted, Jackson agreed to act as Billy's second and in fact carried the note that provoked the formal challenge.

Because Billy had "never shot much" and Jesse was a "first rate marksman," Billy insisted that the firing distance between them be reduced to ten feet (rather than thirty) to eliminate Jesse's advantage and "equalize" their situations. Jesse objected, but since Billy had been challenged he had the right to determine the distance. It was further agreed that they would take a back-to-back position—which meant they had to wheel around and face each other in order to fire. Jackson explained to Jesse the three wheeling modes permitted: "that he might place his left heel in the hollow of his right foot—that he might stand with his feet close together or that he might stand with them apart and wheel in either of those positions." Jackson then demonstrated "with his body perfectly erect."[9]

The duel took place on Monday, June 14, 1813, at six o'clock in the morning. The participants assumed their proper positions, Billy and Jesse standing back to back.

"Prepare!" called John W. Armstrong, the other second.

"Fire!"

Jesse wheeled "with great quickness" but "came round to a very low squatting position with his body considerably prostrated." He fired and hit Carroll in the thumb.

Billy also fired. And the bullet caught Jesse in the act of squatting. It inflicted a long, raking wound across both cheeks of his buttocks.

Surprised at Jesse's unfortunate "maneuver," Billy asked Jackson if it was "correct or honorable."

"No, sir," replied the outraged Jackson. "Mr. B. did not wheel erectly." But he thought Jesse "mortally wounded" and therefore advised Billy to say nothing about it. If he died, "the disgrace of his conduct" ought to die with him, said the General.[10]

Thomas Hart Benton was in Washington when this foolishness transpired. He was trying to square away Jackson's military accounts and to induce the War Department to pay the expenses involved in the expedition to Natchez. He also carried letters of recommendation from Jackson to the secretary of war that were intended to win him (Benton) a colonel's commission in a new regiment of regular troops to be raised in Tennessee. Benton had no real prospect of immediate active service; at best he hoped to recruit a new regiment with John Williams of Knoxville as colonel and himself as lieutenant colonel. As for the claims, Benton handled them efficiently. Eventually an agent was appointed to audit and approve the accounts in Tennessee, which was exactly what Jackson wanted.[11]

Returning from Washington full of the good news he bore Old Hickory, Benton learned of the humiliation of his brother. The stories, exaggerated by troublemakers, clearly staggered him. Here he had been working hard in the General's interests only to have it repaid with this crushing disgrace to a member of his family. Of course troublemakers worsened the account of the duel and the suffering and plight of poor Jesse. Beside himself, Thomas threatened vengeance. Hotheaded like his brother, he swore things he would soon regret.

The words and threats carried to Jackson. As usual he immediately wrote to Benton and asked if they were true. He had extended friendship, he said, but "rumors and information has reached me of some conduct, expressions and threats of yours as they relate to me of the basest kind." Did Benton speak disrespectfully? Had he "threatened to make a Publication against me . . . and lastly have you or have you not threatened to challenge me."[12]

Benton was a straightforward, honest man. No coward, he. His complaint, he replied, could be reduced to four specifics.

> 1. That it was very poor buisness in a man of your age and standing to be conducting a duel about nothing between young men who had no harm against each, and that you would have done yourself more honor by advising them to reserve their courage for the public enemy.
> 2. That it was mean in you to draw a challenge from my brother by carrying him a bullying note from Mr. C. dictated by your self, and which left him no alternative but a duel or disgrace.
> 3. That if you could not have prevented a duel you ought at least to have conducted it in the usual mode, and on terms equal to both parties.
> 4. That on the contrary you conducted it in a savage, unequal, unfair, and base manner.[13]

Some of Benton's points were well taken. Jackson had no business mixing in this fight, even if he thought Jesse wrong in going back on his word. His position and age dictated the role of peacemaker.

But that was no longer the issue. Jackson only cared to know if Thomas Benton had threatened to challenge him. Nothing else.

Thomas denied it. "I have not threatened to challenge you," he wrote. "On the contrary I have said that I would not do so; and I say so still. At the same time the terror of your pistols is not to seal my lips. What I believe to be true, I shall speak; and if for this I am called to account, it must even be so."[14]

Although Benton's answer was satisfactory with respect to the challenge, Jackson did not like the stories that continued to circulate about

Benton's pronouncements in public places. Benton supposedly repeated his claims that the duel was savage and unfair, that his brother did not understand the back-to-back business or wheeling and that this "French" way of dueling had been deliberately imposed to confuse him. He said many other things, all duly reported to Jackson.

Benton's accusations were serious enough, but what really infuriated Old Hickory was the fact that they were repeated in public places, over and over, in every major town in Tennessee. Jackson had just recaptured popular favor and he was not about to see his reputation endangered by Benton's reckless charges. Now a fierce guardian of his fame and image, Jackson had become extremely sensitive to public criticism. The trouble with Benton, Jackson said, was his inability to keep his mouth shut, and Jackson promised to horsewhip Thomas the first time he saw him.

Immediately the word went out to all Nashville: General Andrew Jackson would thrash Thomas Hart Benton on sight. It was only a matter of time. Not if, but when. For his part, Benton was not looking for trouble and probably regretted his initial rashness. But he was no coward; he would not run away. So when he arrived in Nashville, full of outward wrath and defiance, he took only a single precaution. There were two taverns in Nashville: the Old Nashville Inn, which Jackson and his friends used, and the City Hotel. To avoid trouble, Jesse (now recovered) and Thomas registered at the City Hotel.

Early in September, Jackson, John Coffee, and Jackson's nephew, Stockley Hays, rode into town and put up at the Old Nashville Inn. The next morning Jackson and Coffee walked to the post office to pick up their mail, both of them armed and Jackson carrying a riding whip. The route they chose led them past the City Hotel—a fair indication that they were hoping for a confrontation, the news of the Bentons' arrival having been previously circulated. As they crossed the square, Coffee saw Thomas Benton standing in the doorway of the hotel, "looking daggers" at them.

"Do you see that fellow?" Coffee asked Jackson in tones barely above a whisper.

"Oh yes," replied Jackson, "I have my eye on him."

For some reason Jackson did not attack Benton immediately but continued walking toward the post office to get his mail. It may be that he wanted more time to plan his move; or he may have wished to catch Benton off guard. In any event Jackson and Coffee collected their mail and started back, walking along the sidewalk that would bring them to the door of the City Hotel.

Both Bentons were waiting, their pistols loaded with two shots each. As Jackson came abreast of Thomas he suddenly turned toward him, brandished his whip, and cried, "Now, you d———d rascal, I am going to punish you. Defend yourself."[15]

Benton reached into his pocket as if fumbling for a gun. Instantly the General drew his own gun and backed Thomas into the hotel. Jesse, meanwhile, ducked through the barroom to a door that opened into a hallway that led to the rear porch overlooking the river. From that position he raised his pistol and fired at Jackson, hitting him in the arm and shoulder with a slug and a ball. Old Hickory pitched forward, firing at Thomas as he fell. The shot missed. Thomas then fired twice at the prostrate figure, and Jesse faced forward to shoot again but was interrupted by a bystander, James Sitler.[16]

Now Coffee came dashing in from the street. Seeing Jackson lying in the doorway, his left arm and shoulder gushing blood, Coffee lunged at Thomas and fired but missed. He then tried to club Benton with his pistol, but Thomas retreated quickly and in his haste fell backward down a flight of stairs at the rear of the hotel.

Stockley Hays, hearing the shooting, raced into the hotel. Like Coffee, he was gigantic in stature. When he saw Jesse he tried to run him through with a sword cane, but the point of the weapon struck a button and broke. Hays then wrestled Jesse to the ground and repeatedly stabbed him in both arms with a dirk. Desperately Jesse struggled to avoid the dagger thrusts; finally he got his hand on his second pistol and shoved its muzzle into Hays's body "to blow him through," but the charge failed to go off.[17] Bystanders rushed forward, pulled the men apart, and brought the gunfight to an end.

Half unconscious from loss of blood, Jackson was lifted and carried to the Nashville Inn, his shoulder shattered by the slug and his arm pierced by a ball which lay embedded against the upper bone of his left arm. He soaked through two mattresses before the doctors could stanch the flow of blood. Every physician in Nashville worked over the wounded General, and all but one recommended the amputation of the shattered arm.

"I'll keep my arm," ordered the General. With that, Jackson slipped into unconsciousness. The doctors did not dare to contradict him and they made no effort to remove the metal; it remained in his arm for nearly twenty years. Both wounds were dressed with poultices of elm and other wood cuttings, as prescribed by the Indians. Jackson was utterly prostrate from the great loss of blood; it was three weeks before he could leave his bed.

Down in the street the Bentons remained for an hour or more, recounting to the crowd what happened and denouncing Jackson as an assassin—a defeated assassin at that. Thomas Benton recovered a small sword that Jackson had dropped in the hotel and after brandishing it in the public square broke it in two, shouting defiance in his booming voice as he paraded back and forth across the plaza.

Jackson's many partisans appreciated neither the defeat of the General nor the accompanying theatrics. It soon became obvious that Nashville was not a safe place for the Bentons. "I am literally in hell here," wrote Thomas; "the meanest wretches under heaven to contend with—liars, affidavit-makers, and shameless cowards. All the puppies of Jackson are at work on me. . . . I am in the middle of hell, and see no alternative but to kill or be killed; for I will not crouch to Jackson; and the fact that I and my brother defeated him and his tribe, and broke his small sword in the public square, will for ever rankle in his bosom and make him thirst for vengeance. My life is in danger . . . for it is a settled plan to turn out puppy after puppy to bully me, and when I have got into a scrape, to have me killed somehow in the scuffle."[18] To escape the vengeance of Jackson's "puppies," Thomas returned to his home in Franklin and, after the war, resigned his commission in the army and headed west to Missouri.[19]

Thomas Benton and Jackson never saw one another again until 1823, when both men became United States senators and both realized it was to their mutual political benefit to forget their ancient feud. A handshake dissolved the ten-year hatred and signaled the beginning of an eventful political alliance.

Jesse Benton, unlike his brother, never forgave General Jackson. Nor could he forgive Thomas for his later desertion to the enemy. He went to his grave cursing Andrew Jackson.

This was the last of Jackson's great gunfights. Like the others, there was something petty about it. None of Jackson's quarrels did him credit; all diminished him.

CHAPTER 13

The Creek War: Disaster

WHILE JACKSON WAS RECOVERING from his gunfight, tended by the faithful Rachel, news reached Tennessee that the Creek Indians had massacred white settlers at Fort Mims in Alabama, then a part of the Mississippi Territory. William Weatherford, known as Chief Red Eagle, led the attack —and with it commenced the Creek War that finally placed Jackson on the road to national fame.

They called themselvs the Muskogee Nation, but white men dubbed them Creeks because they roamed among so many streams and tiny rivers. They ranged from the Atlantic to the Tombigbee River, living in parts of Florida, Georgia, Alabama, and Mississippi. When Colonel Benjamin Hawkins was appointed agent for the Southern tribes he attempted to coax the Creeks into assimilation with whites by teaching them the arts and skills of modern farming and industry. Some Creeks responded enthusiastically—mostly those in the lower Creek region (east Alabama and west Georgia around the Chattahoochee River), who understood the advantages of cooperating and living harmoniously with white men. Other, younger Creeks rejected contact with white society and the consequent abandonment of their Indian culture. These were the Indians living in the upper Creek region (central and southern Alabama on the Coosa and Tallapoosa rivers). In the ensuing war some Creeks remained neutral and others fought alongside whites as allies.

But all Creeks, upper and lower, had many grievances against Americans, principally the relentless encroachment on their land. The Spanish in Florida encouraged Creek resistance and promised arms and supplies if the Indians would declare war. Then when the United States government built roads from Georgia to the Alabama settlements, sending more whites streaming into Creek country, the collision of the two cultures made conflict inevitable.[1]

Red Eagle, leader of the militant Red Sticks (so called because they painted their war clubs a bright red color), planned to commence the war against the Americans with one mighty and bloody stroke. He was a remarkable chief. The son of a Scot trader, he preferred his mother's people, she being the half sister of the great Creek chieftain, Alexander McGillivray, himself a mixed blood.[2] Red Eagle fell under the sway of another extraordinary Indian chieftain, Tecumseh, a Shawnee who conceived a plan to organize the Northern and Southern tribes from the Great Lakes to the Gulf of Mexico into a great confederation and with it hurl the white man back into the sea from whence he had come.[3]

Like the Spanish in the south, the British in Canada aided and organized Indian resistance to Americans along the northern frontier.[4] Tecumseh's scheme, therefore, seemed to promise enormous material support from the two foreign powers in their efforts to stifle further American expansion. Indeed the Shawnee leader later promised his southern allies that weapons would be made available at St. Marks, Pensacola, and other Spanish ports.[5]

In October 1811 Tecumseh visited the Creeks and with his matchless eloquence stirred the old fears and hatred of the whites. "Let the white race perish!" he cried. "They seize your land; they corrupt your women; they trample on the bones of your dead! Back whence they came, upon a trail of blood, they must be driven! Back—aye, back to the great water whose accursed waves brought them to our shores! Burn their dwellings —destroy their stock—slay their wives and children, that the very breed may perish. War now! War always! War on the living! War on the dead!"[6]

Tecumseh was particularly anxious to convert to his cause Big Warrior, a powerful Creek chief. Big Warrior resisted. Enraged, Tecumseh thrust a finger into the chief's face and uttered a fearful vow: "Your blood is white. . . . You do not believe the Great Spirit sent me. You shall believe it. I will leave directly and go straight to Detroit. When I get there I will stamp my foot upon the ground and shake down every house in Tookabatcha."

And it happened just as Tecumseh promised. A mighty rumble of the earth occurred soon after and every house in Tookabatcha tottered and fell. The people ran about in a state of shock and fear. "Tecumseh has got to Detroit," they cried. "We feel the shake of his foot!"[7]

The earthquake, at that propitious moment, seemed to signal divine approval for Tecumseh's call to war; so, too, the formal declaration of hostilities between England and the United States that came the following spring. Benjamin Hawkins pleaded against war but the braves would not listen to him. Only the older, more "enlightened" chiefs knew that he spoke for their own good.[8]

Late in 1812 a party of Creeks journeyed to Canada and participated in a massacre. On their way home, near the mouth of the Ohio River, they killed some white men. The Chickasaws, fearing they would be held responsible for the murders, demanded that the Creeks themselves punish the murderers. It was done. But the executions split the Creek Nation, and bloody civil war broke out between the upper and lower tribes.

Thus, it needs to be remembered that from start to finish the Creek War was essentially an Indian civil war. And, most important of all, that it was General Andrew Jackson who took supreme advantage of this internal strife. He not only strengthened the military posture of the United States and enlarged its territory but he also virtually annihilated the Creek Nation.

Desultory raids along the American border by the upper tribes widened the split within the Creek Nation during the following months. The raids ignited the southern frontier and hurried settlers from exposed areas into blockhouses and stockades. Then, at Burnt Corn, less than a hundred miles due north of Pensacola, white settlers attacked a party of Red Sticks led by Chief Peter McQueen, a mixed blood. The Indians escaped, claiming victory despite the loss of most of their ammunition. The settlers, having bumbled their mission, took refuge in the fortified residence of Samuel Mims.[9]

Mims, a well-to-do merchant and part Creek, lived as a white man. He had built his stronghold (located about forty miles north of Mobile) by enclosing an acre of land with upright logs pierced by two heavy gates and 500 portholes three and a half feet from the ground. The stockade was protected by 120 militiamen commanded by Major Daniel Beasley, a lawyer from the Mississippi Territory with little military experience. Besides the militia there were nearly 300 whites, mixed bloods, and friendly Indians within the fort and probably an equal number of black slaves.[10]

August 30, 1813, was hot and muggy. Children played within the stockade and soldiers sauntered about. Both gates were open. At noon a drum in the fort beat a summons to dinner and soldiers laid aside their guns to respond to the call. But the beat had another signal. With the first tap of the drum, a thousand Creeks screaming their fury rushed from the forest, across the open fields surrounding the fort, and toward the yawning gates. Major Beasley raced desperately to shut the gates but the Creeks battered their way inside, clubbed Beasley to death, and systematically slaughtered the settlers despite a brave defense. A few whites escaped; the rest, almost 250 persons, "were butchered in the quickest manner, and blood and brains bespattered the whole earth. The children were seized by the legs, and killed by batting their heads against the stockading. The women were scalped, and those who were pregnant were opened, while they were alive, and the embryo infants let out of the womb."[11] Red Eagle, who led the attack, tried to stop this savagery, but many clubs were raised over his head and he was forced to withdraw to save his own life. Most of the blacks were spared to serve as slaves.

This senseless massacre brought the United States into the Creek civil war. And the horror of it rolled over the western states like a shock wave. Anger and fear and a need for revenge gripped the settlers of West Tennessee, who hourly expected an attack by the upper Creeks. Instinctively they turned to Jackson. Without considering the need for government authority they appealed to him to rescue them from their danger. He must hurry to Alabama and destroy the Creeks before they swarmed into Tennessee and repeated the Fort Mims massacre.

Even before Fort Mims, Jackson had warned of the need to respond to the frontier raids by attacking the Creeks before they could "be supported by their allies the British and Spaniards."[12] His appeal to Governor Blount to authorize this expedition went unheeded; now they must all suffer the consequence.[13]

When the report of the Fort Mims massacre reached Nashville, Jackson was still recovering from his wounds and was too weak and unsteady to commence a campaign. But he had no choice; he recognized that his long-awaited opportunity for military glory had at last arrived. If he failed to assume leadership now he might not get another chance; he must begin a campaign at once even if he had to drag himself from bed and tie himself to his horse. Even without proper authorization he must respond—though he knew Governor Blount would back him, so he was not terribly concerned on that score. And he reckoned that by the time it took to gather and move an army he would be swamped with directives ordering him to pursue and crush the hostile Indians.

Loudly trumpeting his call that it might reassure Tennesseans, Jackson gave general orders to his militia to rendezvous at Fayetteville for immediate duty against the Creeks. "The late attack of the Creek Indians . . . call a loud for retaliatory vengeance. Those distressed citizens of that frontier . . . implored the brave Tennesseans for aid. They must not ask in vain. . . . They are our brethren in distress and we must not await the slow and tardy orders of the General Government. Every noble feeling heart beats sympathy for their sufferings and danger, and every high minded generous soldier will fly to their protection."[14] Since everyone knew he had been gunned down in Nashville by the Bentons, he felt obliged to mention his physical condition. "The health of your general is restored," he said, "he will command in person."[15]

As anticipated, Governor Blount responded immediately to the crisis. Empowered by the legislature to raise 5,000 men (including 1,500 regulars enrolled in the service of the United States) for a three-month tour of duty, he ordered Jackson to "call out organize rendezvous and march without delay" 2,500 volunteers and militia "to repel an approaching invasion . . . and to afford aid and relief to the suffering citizens of the Mississippi Territory."[16] A similar force of 2,500 men from eastern Tennessee, commanded by Major General John Cocke, was also ordered against the Creeks. Fortunately, John Sevier was safely entombed in Congress or there might have been a popular cry to give him supreme command of the operation.

Jackson planned to slice through the Creek Nation, hewing a road through the wilderness as he marched, until he reached Mobile on the coast. Such a march would provide a magnificent highway across the southwestern heartland for future American settlers, at the same time shredding Creek power in the area. After that he would "strike at the root of the disseas": he would invade Spanish Florida and capture Pensacola, thereby exterminating the Creek potential to make war.[17] In one great operation he would destroy the Creeks, open an important road and permanent line of communication to the coast for western settlers, and expel the Spanish from the American continent. There was no question in Jackson's mind that the removal of Spanish and British influence in the area (and British influence was known to exist in the south) was essential to the final solution of the Indian problem.[18]

Certainly by 1813, if not earlier, Jackson's course of action was fixed. He intended to eliminate all foreigners along the southern frontier as a necessary prelude to the systematic destruction of the Indian menace and the territorial expansion of the American nation. To this task he brought a fierce determination that never wavered or faltered and—something that no one imagined since it had not yet been tested—a military and command competence by which he would implement his imperial design. As no one of like determination and military skill had command on the northern frontier, the course of American expansion for the immediate future was directed southward.

For the civilian authorities, however, the present danger was the Creek Nation. To defeat the Indians a basic strategy was devised in which four armies would enter the Nation and merge where the Tallapoosa and Coosa rivers joined to form the Alabama River. Two armies, one from East Tennessee under General John Cocke and one from West Tennessee under Jackson, would merge in northern Alabama and, commanded by Jackson, advance to the juncture of the Coosa and Tallapoosa rivers. These forces would be met by two other armies, one from Georgia under General John Floyd, the other consisting of the Third Regiment of U.S. Army regulars and the forces of the Mississippi Territory led by Brigadier General Ferdinand L. Claiborne.

In the usual muddled tradition of the Madison administration, a problem of command arose because the Creek Nation straddled the Sixth and Seventh Military Districts, with the Sixth headed by Major General Thomas Pinckney with headquarters at Charleston, South Carolina, and the Seventh by Brigadier General Thomas Flournoy with headquarters at New Orleans. The secretary of war tried to resolve the problem by placing the entire Creek War under General Pinckney while reserving Flournoy's authority within his own district except in matters dealing with the Creeks. The secretary's decision only increased the friction between the two generals, and eventually Flournoy resigned.

Although details of this strategy were modified slightly in the course of the war, the overall plan never changed. All four armies were expected to kill the Red Sticks, burn their villages, and destroy their crops; they were instructed to build forts about one day's march apart in order to divide the Creeks from north to south and east to west with lines of blockhouses that would permanently dismember the Creek Nation. The entire operation was expected to take no longer than two or three months.[19]

On October 7, 1813, still pale and weak, with his arm in a sling, Jackson took command of his West Tennessee army at Fayetteville. Three days later he broke camp and headed south to link up with Coffee's cavalry, which he had sent ahead to Huntsville to prepare a camp for the main army.[20] Clipping along at the astounding speed of 36 miles a day, the army joined Coffee's cavalry, moved into Creek country, and arrived at the southernmost tip of the Tennessee River, where Jackson built Fort Deposit as a depot for supplies at the mouth of Thompson's Creek. After waiting several days for supplies and reinforcements from Tennessee that never came, the impatient Jackson decided to move ahead. "I am determined to push forward," he told his friend and quartermaster, William B. Lewis, "if I have to live upon acorns."[21] He sent Lewis back to Nashville to see about the supplies and ordered Coffee to forage among friendly Indian villages.

A less ambitious and more cautious commander might have paused before leading a winter campaign across the Lookout Mountains in Alabama, particularly when he had neither sufficient supplies nor an organized commissary to obtain them. Not Jackson. He could not wait. "With his soldiers [your commander] will face the danger of the enemy," he told his troops; "and with them he will participate the glory of a conquest." Jackson pushed south to the Coosa River, cutting a road over the mountains as he went, and established a base at Fort Strother (not far from Ten Islands) that became his advance supply depot. He had barely a week's rations, but he expected to be joined momentarily by General Cocke from East Tennessee.

Meanwhile Jackson encouraged friendly Creek tribes to "hold out obstinately" if attacked by Red Sticks and "I will come to your relief." He supported this promise with strong guarantees. "If one hair of your head is hurt," he told Chief Chennabee, "or of your family or of any who are friendly to the whites, I will sacrafice a hundred lives to pay for it. Be of good heart, & tell your men they have nothing to fear." He repeated this admonition to Chief Pathkiller of the Cherokees after learning of Red Eagle's threat to punish all Indians who failed to aid the Red Stick cause. When he got through with the hostile Creeks, Jackson told Pathkiller, they will have no thought of molesting anyone else ever again.[22]

At Fort Strother, Jackson came within striking distance of the Red Sticks. Thirteen miles to the east lay the hostile village of Tallushatchee with its nearly two hundred warriors. Jackson ordered General Coffee and his cavalry and mounted riflemen to destroy it, and Coffee "executed this order in elegant stile." On the morning of November 3, 1813, a thousand men encircled Tallushatchee and systematically slaughtered most of the warriors. It was a massacre. "We shot them like dogs," attested Davy Crocket.[23]

So horrible was the killing that Lieutenant Richard Keith Call became almost physically ill. "We found as many as eight or ten dead bodies in a single cabin," he wrote. "Some of the cabins had taken fire, and half consumed human bodies were seen amidst the smoking ruins. In other instances dogs had torn and feasted on the mangled bodies of their masters. Heart sick I turned from the revolting scene."[24] Coffee lost five men killed and forty-one wounded in the attack; he slew 186 braves (every man in the village) and brought back to Jackson's camp 84 women and children as captives.[25] "We have retaliated for the destruction of Fort Mims," Jackson wrote triumphantly to Governor Blount. He expected to follow this victory with an even greater slaughter of Creeks further south, but much depended on the speedy arrival of food. "If we had a sufficient supply of provisions, we should in a very short time, accomplish the object of the expedition."[26]

On the bloody battlefield a dead Indian mother was found still clutching her living ten month old infant. The child was brought to Jackson's camp along with the other captives, and the General asked some of the Indian women to care for the child and give him nourishment. They refused. "No," they said, "all his relations are dead, kill him too."[27] As they spoke the words, "all his relations are dead," something responded inside Jackson. He was reminded of himself little more than thirty years before, his family wiped out by war, he an orphan. Brusquely he dismissed the women and had the child taken to his tent where he dissolved a little brown sugar with water and coaxed the boy to drink. Afterward the General sent him to Huntsville to be nursed, clothed, and housed at his expense until the end of the campaign, when he was sent to the Hermitage.

The child was named Lyncoya and given almost every advantage a planter's son enjoyed, including an education. When the child arrived at the Hermitage, Jackson was anxious to know how his own son responded to the addition to the family. "Please write me how my little Andrew . . . [has] taken to him . . . & what he thinks of him." Jackson gave explicit orders how Lyncoya should be treated. He wanted the boy kept in the house and not treated like a servant—or an orphan. "I therefore want him well taken care of," he told Rachel, "he may have been given to me for some valuable purpose—in fact when I reflect that he as to his relations is so much like myself I feel an unusual sympathy for him."[28]

Despite his immersion in white society from an early age, Lyncoya remained true to his race and heritage. "His tastes were always Indian," an early Jackson biographer wrote. "He delighted in rambling over the fields and through the woods, sticking into his hair and clothes every gay feather he could find. He was always anxious to return to the Creek nation with the chiefs who, for many years after the war, continued to visit the Hermitage." So anxious was Lyncoya to return to the Creek Nation that he ran away from home several times. "My Dear Father," Andrew Jr. complained several years later, "no one will fetch my Lyncoia I have a thought of going my self for him . . . my Mother thinks highly of his understanding she treats him as well as any person on Earth could."[29] As Lyncoya grew up, he wanted to be a saddler—the one occupation Jackson himself had favored as a youth. Unfortunately, he contracted tuberculosis and, though nursed "with a father's and mother's tenderness," he died on July 1, 1828, a few months before his seventeenth birthday. "By the general and Mrs. Jackson he was mourned as a favorite son, and they always spoke of him with paternal affection."[30]

After the Tallushatchee victory, many Indian villages wisely switched their allegiance to Jackson. One of these was Talladega, a small Indian community of 154 people which lay thirty miles south of Fort Strother across the Coosa River. Red Eagle surrounded the town with a thousand braves and planned to destroy it for its treachery. So tight was the siege

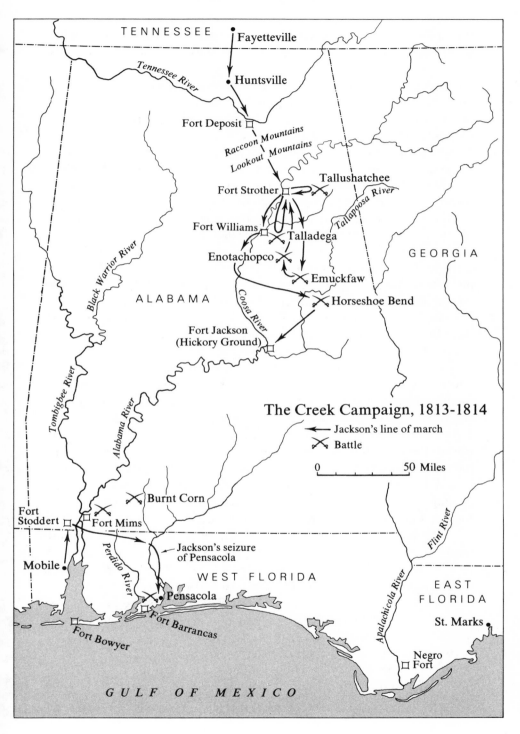

The Creek Campaign, 1813-1814

→ Jackson's line of march

✗ Battle

0 ————————— 50 Miles

that it was almost impossible to get a messenger to Jackson to inform him that the village was in danger of capture. Finally a chieftain wearing the skin of a hog crept through the lines of the besiegers and reached Jackson's camp.

The General now had his chance to destroy a large hostile force, but he faced a dilemma. General James White, who commanded the advance of General Cocke's East Tennessee army, had just been ordered to rejoin Cocke. Cocke was not anxious to see his troops fall under Jackson's command; moreover, he too was low on provisions and a juncture of the two armies would not help the situation. Jackson had counted on White to protect Fort Strother, where there were two hundred sick, all his baggage, and the remaining provisions. To march ahead before White arrived meant abandoning the sick to the mercy of roving Indian raiders; to stay put meant the destruction of Talladega and a blow to American prestige among friendly Indians. Jackson chose to move. At twelve o'-clock midnight the General set his men in motion. Invariably he moved his army in three columns. He had 1,200 infantry and 800 cavalry, just double the number of Weatherford's warriors besieging Talladega. He left only a token force at Fort Strother because he did not want to risk defeat by weakening his main attacking force. As a commander, Jackson believed in outnumbering the enemy.

It was dawn on November 9, 1813, when the army deployed for battle within a half mile of the Red Sticks surrounding Talladega. The infantry advanced in two lines, militia on the left and volunteers on the right. The cavalry formed two extreme wings on the flanks and were ordered to advance in a crescent-shaped "curve," the points thrown toward the town and the rear connected to the advance lines of infantry. A mounted reserve was placed behind the main line. Jackson's plan directed that an advance guard move ahead to initiate an engagement; after making contact, it was to fall back and join the main force, drawing the Indians into the curved arms of Jackson's army.[31]

The maneuver began beautifully. The vanguard moved out. Suddenly the Red Sticks came "screaming and yelling" from cover and took four or five rounds of shot.[32] The guard fell back. The Indians, nearly a thousand of them, swarmed into the trap and the two curving arms of troops snapped shut around them. The Tennesseans fired at the Red Sticks at point-blank range. The destruction would have been complete had not a portion of the infantry on the right, for some unaccountable reason—perhaps a confusion of orders—suddenly retreated instead of advancing. The line broke, a hole widened, and soon the Indians found it and poured through the gap by the hundreds to escape the withering fire. The reserves were quickly dismounted and thrown into the gap, once again closing the ring. The Indians trapped within the circle were shot to death in a steady rain of fire. Later, Coffee's cavalry pursued the fleeing Red Sticks for three or four miles, killing and wounding them as they ran. Unfortunately for Jackson, some 700 Indians escaped to renew the war at a later time. This "faux pas of the militia," he reported, which forced him to dismount the reserves, prevented total destruction of the Red Sticks.[33] Nevertheless, 300 Indians lay dead on the battleground. Jackson's losses amounted to 15 dead and 85 wounded.[34]

After burying his dead, providing litters for the wounded, and gathering what food was available, Jackson swung his army back to Fort Strother, hoping to find there the long-awaited supplies from Nashville on his return. Nothing. Not only had the provisions failed to come but the sick had eaten what little remained of Jackson's private stores brought at his own expense. (They had permission to take these stores; before leaving for Talladega Jackson had ordered the surgeons to distribute his provisions should it become necessary.) Now, returned to the fort, the army had only a few dozen biscuits and a small supply of meat. So the remaining cattle were slaughtered and distributed among the troops. Jackson and his staff made do with the offal.[35] One story, often repeated and later published in the newspapers, told how a soldier who was nearly starving approached Jackson and asked for something to eat. "I will most cheerfully divide with you what I have," said Old Hickory. With that, he put his hand in his pocket and drew out a few acorns. "This is the best and only fare I have."[36]

Days passed. Still no supplies. The troops grew angry and mutinous. Jackson, himself starving and ill with dysentery, railed at the contractors who could not get him his provisions. Also he quarreled with General Cocke, whom he accused of sabotaging the campaign. Field officers held a meeting and presented Jackson with a petition requesting that the army be permitted to return home. They were starving and were forced to subsist on inadequate rations—less than two meals for the past five days. Furthermore, they argued, the frontier was now safe and they needed to return home for winter clothing.[37] From first to last the petition was rational and respectful; clearly the army was in a frightful state and the General was simply being asked to return to Tennessee before conditions became worse. Perhaps a commander less rigid than Jackson would have been more sympathetic; perhaps one less anxious for military glory would have heeded the plea. Not Jackson. He rejected the petition with haughty disdain, reminding his men what was expected of them as soldiers and frontiersmen.

The situation collapsed when the militia broke camp and started home anyway. They did not get far. Jackson drew up the volunteers in front of them and forced them back to the camp. The next day the roles were reversed; the volunteers attempted to march off and were halted by the militia.[38] It was one of the lunacies of war.

In the face of the dissolution of his command, Jackson exhorted his field and platoon officers to remain loyal. He extolled their patriotism, deplored the conditions of the camp, and promised imminent relief. He reminded them of their recent victories and the dreadful consequences should they now retreat. "I have no wish to starve you—none to deceive you," he said. Then he made a promise, having heard that supplies had already reached Fort Deposit. "Stay contentedly," he pleaded; "and if supplies do not arrive in two days, we will all march back together, and throw the blame of our failure where it should properly lie."[39] It was a stirring appeal, and it produced the desired effect: The officers and men agreed to wait a few more days.

Two days passed and still no relief. Now the troops insisted Jackson keep his word and allow them to return home. Overwhelmed by the thought of leading a retreat, Jackson threw up his hands and cried out in desperation, "If only two men will remain with me, I will never abandon this post."[40] A Captain Gordon stepped forward. "You have one, general, let us look if we can't find another."[41] One hundred nine men volunteered to remain at Fort Strother. His hopes renewed, Jackson brightened. He reformulated his plans in accordance with his promise. The volunteers would guard Strother while he and the remainder of the army set off for Fort Deposit. Jackson's understanding was that on meeting the supply train the troops would return to Fort Strother and renew the campaign.[42]

On November 17 the order to march was given. The haggard, weary, hungry men eagerly broke camp, desperately praying that they might never meet the supply train and thus march all the way home. To their dismay and Jackson's great joy, they met 150 "beeves" of cattle and nine wagons of flour not twelve miles from camp. The men gorged themselves. Then, their hunger appeased, they were ordered to head back to camp.

Audible grumbles greeted the command. One company formed and moved off—in the direction of Tennessee. As they did so Jackson mounted his horse and detoured ahead of them. At a point one half mile in advance of the mutinous troops Jackson met Coffee, who had halted with a few of his cavalry. Forming these soldiers across the road, Old Hickory ordered them to shoot any deserter who refused to turn back. Then he took his position in front of them.

As the mutineers approached Jackson presented quite an awesome sight. A shaft of implacable determination stretched high on the saddle of his horse, eyes flashing, grizzled hair bristling on his forehead, Jackson roared a threat to kill any man who defied him. To brave this fury was madness. After a moment the company slowly, grudgingly turned around.

But the rebellion was worse than Jackson realized. When he returned to the main body of the army he found an entire brigade in the act of deserting. This was no small gesture of rebellion. This was mass desertion. This was the supreme challenge to his leadership.

Snatching a musket and resting it on the neck of his horse (his left arm was still useless), Old Hickory positioned himself in front of the brigade. Slowly, deliberately, he aimed his gun directly at the mutineers. There was "shoot" in his eyes, just as there had been when, as a judge, he had arrested Russell Bean.

General Coffee and Major Reid galloped forward and placed themselves beside Jackson. The troops, sullen and silent, stared at the trio. His voice hoarse from his earlier screaming at the company of deserters, Old Hickory croaked out an oath. The first man who advanced toward Tennessee would get a bullet through the brain.

Minutes passed. The tableau did not change. No one moved. No man had the courage to tempt the "shoot" in Jackson's eyes. Then a few loyal companies formed behind Jackson to block the road. And that did it. Several mutineers peeled off and returned to their posts. More followed. Then others. Finally the remainder of the brigade saw the hopelessness of their situation and backed away. The rebellion ended. And it ended with Jackson in even greater command of his troops. For days and months afterward the soldiers recounted what had happened and tried to understand how Jackson, almost singlehandedly, had overcome the rebellion of a full brigade. Later it turned out that the musket he had used so effectively was too ancient a weapon to be fired.[43] Had they risked his challenge they might have walked away scot-free.

Jackson thought the worst was over. His army marched back to Fort Strother without further incident. Supplies continued to arrive, thanks to Major Lewis, and Jackson expected General Cocke to join him momentarily. Together they would move swiftly against Weatherford and the Red Sticks, annihilate them, and return home to the applause of the state and the nation. "Nothing can be more gratifying to a true patriot," he wrote Governor Blount, "than the unanimous approbation of his country."[44]

But the army had other ideas. The volunteers made no secret of their intention to break camp on December 10, 1813, when their one-year enlistment expired. They counted as part of that year the time they had spent at home, where they were at the call of the government, ready to respond when summoned. Jackson, on the other hand, held the view that a year's enlistment meant 365 days of actual service. The men reminded him that after the Natchez expedition he had discharged them on their promise to return to active duty when he called. Jackson denied it; or, rather, he quibbled. He had not discharged them—only the President could do that—he had dismissed them, so the time away from service did not count. But Jackson was on shaky legal ground, trying to repudiate what he had obviously done, and finally he offered to refer the dispute to Governor Blount and the secretary of war, promising to abide by their decision. This ploy would give him a few months of service, Jackson thought, since the government could be expected to delay a decision. Meanwhile he sent Colonel Carroll and Major Searcy to Tennessee to raise more troops. Hopefully they could round up additional reserves by the time the government decided.

Jackson kept insisting to his men that with their support he could end the war in a few weeks. But the troops were obviously weary of the promises he never kept, weary of their hunger, and weary of fighting Indians. They had a legal right to go home when their enlistments expired and they intended to exercise it. "You can have no idea of the clamours of the men," one officer wrote; "all disorder here and daily desertions etc etc."[45]

As the day of reckoning approached, Jackson grew more determined to hold his troops, even if it meant shooting them one by one. "The disquietude of the volunteers has grew to a hight," he wrote General Coffee, "that it is impossible to tell in what it may end. I have been on yesterday threatened with disagreable events on the 10th. unless they are discharged. . . . What may be attempted tomorrow I cannot tell, but should they attempt to march off in mass, I shall do my duty, should the mutineers be too strong, and you should meet any officers or men, returning without my written authority, you will arrest and bring them back in strings, and if they attempt to disobey your order you will immediately fire on them and continue the fire until they are subdued, you are to compel them to return."[46]

On the evening of December 9 General Hall went to Jackson's tent to report that his entire brigade planned to slip away during the night. Instantly Jackson wrote out an order commanding the first brigade to parade on the west side of the fort. At the same time he posted the artillery company fore-and-aft of the rebellious troops, their two small fieldpieces trained on the mutineers. The loyal militia were strung along an adjacent "eminence" commanding the road to Tennessee and ordered to prevent by any means necessary the departure of the brigade.[47] Then Jackson mounted his horse and rode along the line of the mutinous volunteers. He spoke to them, quietly at first, almost pleadingly. He

This, one of the better likenesses of Jackson, was painted by Samuel L. Waldo within a few years of the Battle of New Orleans. *Courtesy of the Addison Gallery, Phillips Academy*

A miniature watercolor on ivory by Anna Claypoole Peale in something of the French or Napoleonic tradition. *Courtesy of the Yale University Art Gallery, the Mabel Brady Garvan Collection*

A romantic portrait of Jackson in uniform painted shortly after his invasion of Florida in 1818 by John Wesley Jarvis. *Courtesy of the Metropolitan Museum of Art, Harris Brisbane Dick Fund, 1964*

This miniature of Rachel Jackson painted on ivory by Anna Claypoole Peale in 1819 was reputedly worn by Jackson over his heart after her death in 1828. *Courtesy of the Ladies Hermitage Association*

General John Coffee, Jackson's friend, business partner and military associate in the Creek War and at the Battle of New Orleans. This portrait hangs in the Hermitage. *Courtesy of the Ladies Hermitage Association*

John Overton boarded with Jackson at the Donelson home, became Jackson's partner in land speculation and served as a judge of the Superior Court of Tennessee following Jackson's resignation from the bench. *Courtesy of the Travellers' Rest Historic Site*

John Sevier, revolutionary war hero, Governor of Tennessee and Jackson's rival for the post of Major General of the Tennessee militia. Their quarrel ended in a street brawl and politically split the state east and west. *Courtesy of the Library of Congress*

General Jackson quells a mutiny during the Creek War by threatening to shoot the first man who heads home. An engraving in Amos Kendall's biography of Jackson. *Courtesy of the Library of Congress*

William Blount, land speculator and territorial governor, exercised an enormous influence on Jackson's early career. *Courtesy of the New York Public Library*

General Jackson at the Hickory Ground just prior to the negotiations with the Creek Indians which resulted in the Treaty of Fort Jackson. *Courtesy of the Library of Congress*

The interview, as imagined by an artist, between General Jackson and William Weatherford (Chief Red Eagle) at the conclusion of the Creek War. *Courtesy of the Library of Congress*

This poor likeness of a Napoleonic Jackson by Jean François Vallee was nonetheless presented to Edward Livingston by the General. The inscription, in Jackson's handwriting, reads: "Mr. E. Livingston is requested to accept this picture as a mark of the sense I entertain of his public services, and a token of my private friendship and Esteem. Headquarters N. orleans, May 1st, 1815. *Andrew Jackson*" *Courtesy of the Library of Congress*

This excellent visual representation of the Battle of New Orleans by Hyacinthe Laclotte, one of Jackson's engineers, depicts Rennie's troops attacking along the river road while Keane's men cross the field in front of the rampart to support Gibbs's troops. The large house behind the Rodriguez Canal is Jackson's headquarters. *Courtesy of the Library of Congress*

A dramatic representation of the confrontation in court between General Jackson and Judge Dominick Hall. From a painting by C. Schusselle. *Courtesy of the Library of Congress*

Shelocta, the Creek chief, who at the Hickory Ground movingly but vainly appealed to Jackson to reduce his demands for Creek lands in Alabama and Georgia. *Courtesy of the Newberry Library*

Billy Bowlegs, the Seminole chief, whose town of over 600 houses on the Suwannee River in Florida Jackson burned during the First Seminole War. *Courtesy of the Newberry Library*

Pushmataha, the Choctaw chief and general, who fought with Jackson at New Orleans and later participated in the treaty negotiations between the Choctaw Nation and the United States at Doak's Stand. *Courtesy of the Newberry Library*

praised their former good conduct and the esteem it had won them; he reminded them of the disgrace that would befall them and their families if they were branded mutineers and deserters. But they would never leave, he said in a matter-of-fact tone of voice, except over his dead body. Reinforcements were expected at any moment. They must not leave— nay, could not leave—until replacements arrived. Then and only then would he let them go. He gave them his word. "I have done with in- treaty," he said, his voice rising in a studied display of anger; "it has been used long enough. I will attempt it no more."[48]

No one stirred. "It was a scene," Jackson later told his wife, "that created feelings better to be Judged of than expressed . . . a whole Brigade whose patriotism was once the boast of their Genl and their country . . . turning their backs on an enemy fifty miles in advance."[49]

Jackson demanded an answer from them. Still no response. Old Hickory then ordered the artillery gunners to light their matches, he himself remaining motionless before the brigade, within the line of fire. The men had seen enough of Andrew Jackson to know that he would give the order to fire without a pause for second thoughts. Whispers ran along the lines of the volunteers: Better to return to duty than have an artillery piece explode in your face. Abruptly the officers stepped forward and pledged themselves and their men to remain at the fort until the arrival of reinforcements or the answers to the General's inquiries about their term of service. The men nodded their consent and were dismissed to their quarters.

My volunteers, Jackson sadly informed his wife, had sunk from the "highest elevation of patriots—to mere, wining, complaining, Sedioners and mutineers—to keep whom from open acts of mutiny I have been compelled to point my cannon against, with a lighted match to destroy them. This was a grating moment of my life. I felt the pangs of an effectionate parent, compelled from duty to chastise his child—to prevent him from destruction & disgrace and it being his duty he Shrunk not from it—even when he knew death might ensue."[50]

Later that evening Lieutenant Richard Keith Call went to Jackson's tent and found the General lost in brooding thought. The young man roused his superior by offering to resign his lieutenant's commission and serve as Jackson's bodyguard with the rank of private. It was just what the General needed. He gratefully rejected the offer but said that "if I had 500 such men I would put an end to the mutiny before the sun sets." Many young officers felt as Call did. They idolized their General. "Never did a man labour more incessantly in the cause of his country & of those who have abandoned him," wrote one of them, "than he has done. Day & night his whole soul has been devoted to the honor & the welfare of both. And yet this man has been traduced by those who have abandoned the campaign. He is represented as a tyrant & a despot. Never was there a milder man, when mildness could possibly succeed—never a more energetic one, when energy was necessary; but at all times never did a general love his army so much or labour so much to promote their interest."[51]

On December 12 General Cocke and 1,500 men arrived at Fort Strother. Jackson had no choice but to keep his pledge and allow the First Brigade to return home. In winning release as a group they could refute any criticism of their patriotism or loyalty; nevertheless, once they reached Tennessee, the officers published an elaborate and cogent defense of their conduct and that of their men.[52]

The brigade had barely left the fort when it was discovered that the term of service for a majority of Cocke's men would also expire within a few days—and for the remainder a few weeks after that. Nor did the men have suitable clothing for a winter campaign. Disgusted, Jackson ordered Cocke to march his troops back home and discharge them. Before they left, however, Old Hickory begged the volunteers to reenlist when they got home and return to him at once.

Then disaster struck again. No sooner were Cocke's men out of the camp than Jackson received a letter from General Coffee informing him that the cavalry had deserted. Previously, Jackson had sent the cavalry to Madison County, Tennessee, to recruit horses and procure clothing; they were due back on December 8.[53] But at Huntsville they met the First Brigade on its way home and, learning what had happened at the fort, the cavalry turned around, recrossed the Tennessee River, and galloped away. Poor Coffee was recovering from a severe illness when he learned of the desertion. Chagrined and humiliated, he mounted his horse and rode after his men in the hope of persuading them to return. In vain. They listened to his speech and then rode on. "I am really ashamed to say any thing about the men of my Brigade," Coffee wrote Jackson. "They are now lying encamped with that holy body of Infantry that deserted you and their country in the hour and moment of danger. . . . In such company I have no hopes of ever reclaiming them."[54]

Jackson was now left with the Second Brigade, which consisted of militiamen enlisted for three months under a resolution of the Tennessee legislature. But when they entered the service of the state they were also received into the U.S. Army—which prescribed a six-month tour of duty. Jackson carefully informed his men of the distinction and their obligation to remain with him, but all they knew was that their three-month enlistment ended on January 4, 1814, and that they would then be free to go home. Thus, in a matter of a few weeks, Jackson's army would virtually evaporate. When the men pressed him for a discharge, Jackson refused, though he did agree to submit the matter to Governor Blount for an opinion.

Then came a series of hammer blows that almost finished Jackson's military career. Blount sided with the militia in their interpretation of their term of service; the secretary of war also agreed with the volunteers and ordered their honorable discharge.[55] On top of that Blount advised Jackson on December 22 to abandon Fort Strother and retreat to the Tennessee frontier. There Jackson could do one of two things: await the order of the national government or stand by until such time as Blount felt authorized to call together a new force. Retreat seemed the wisest course of action, he told the General, in view of what had happened to Jackson's army. Blount had called up all the troops permitted by Congress and the Tennessee legislature. For the present there was nothing more he could do.[56]

Jackson sagged. His one great ally had deserted him. During all his disputes with the administration over his attempts to sustain an army and protect the frontier, Jackson had had the support of Governor Blount. Now that too seemed gone. Yet with everything falling apart, his army disintegrating, Blount advising retreat, Jackson seemed to gain interior strength by his many misfortunes. He was one of those extraordinary men who flourish with adversity. The more he was opposed, the more determined he became. A strong, obstinate streak surged within him whenever his situation seemed hopeless. His emotional and physical resources were supplied from reserves of confined desperation.

In the middle of the night of December 29 he sat down and wrote a long letter to Blount in a desperate attempt to renew the governor's spirit and courage. The words were sharp, the tone bitter; still he was sure Blount would understand his feeling of "personal regard and public good."

"Is the campaign ended?" he asked. "Is protection afforded to the frontiers of the Territory as contemplated by the act of assembly? Is the creek nation exterminated or conqueored? . . . The answer is plain, is it not? . . . And are you my Dear friend sitting with yr. arms folded under the present situation of the campaign recommending me to retrograde to please the whims of the populace and waiting for further orders from the Secy war. Let me tell you it imperiously lies upon both you and me to do our duty regardless of consequences or the opinions of these fireside patriots, those fawning sycophants or cowardly poltroons who after all their boasted ardor, would rush home or remain at those fireside and let thousands fall victims to my retrograde."

Jackson spoke candidly. He told Blount flat out that it was his obligation as governor to maintain 3,500 men in the field until the Creeks were either "exterminated or conqueored." "It is yr duty," and whenever the number falls below that level the militia of the state should be called out. President Madison believes, and has a right to believe, said Jackson, that 5,000 men serving for six months are protecting the frontiers of Tennessee and the Mississippi Territory, and unless this is done the Cherokees, Choctaws, and the friendly Creeks will join the cause of Red Eagle and his Red Sticks. "The Chocktaws are wavering and in these circumstances I am advised to retrograde. . . ."

> For what purpose? To please the people of the present moment which in a short time bring down upon our heads the imprecations of those very vile reptiles in the Community who are seeking for popularity and self agrandizement, and now wishing to wear the name of patriots, and what is still worse the just indignation of our government and thousands yet unborn.
>
> Arouse from yr. lethargy—despise the fawning smiles or the snarling frowns of such miscreants—with energy exercise yr. functions—the campaign must rapidly progress, or you are forever damned, and yr country ruined. Call out the full quota authorised— execute the orders of the Secy war, and arrest the officer who omits his duty—or a draft for the deficiency occasioned by the desertion of the volunteers, and let popularity perish for the present—let the miscreant who never thinks of his country or its dangers . . . feel the weight of the orders of the Government. Save Mobile—save the Territory—save yr frontier from becoming drenched in blood—and yourself from being damned for it by these monsters these sychophantic complainers. What retrograde under these circumstances. I will perish first. . .'. I have long since determined when I die I will leave my reputation untarnished. You have only to act with a little energy for which you will be applauded by your Government. Give me a force for 6 months in whose term of service there is no doubt . . . and all may be safe. Withhold it, and all is lost and the reputation of the state and yrs. with it.[57]

It was a powerful letter, one very typical of Jackson. It throbbed with determination and resolution to save the frontier and the nation. It contained many Jacksonian sentiments: the relentless patriotism; the energy to face down adversity; the will to prevail. The language hit hard—and tellingly. With all his faults—and they were legion—he was a tenacious, courageous, formidable man.

While his letter was on its way to Blount, Jackson informed his troops of the governor's recommendation and gave them the choice of staying with him and completing the campaign or returning home. To his dismay, they chose to return. As they streamed away, Old Hickory wished them each "a smoke tail in their teeth, with a Peticoat as a coat of mail to hand down to there offspring."[58] It was his way of branding them all cowards.

The fort was now practically deserted. Only one regiment separated Jackson from the ferocious Red Sticks a few miles away. On January 14, 1814, the term of service for this regiment would expire. Then he would be alone.[59]

CHAPTER 14

The Creek War: Victory

THE WAR WENT JUST AS BADLY for Americans in other parts of the Creek country. In November 1813 the Georgia militia under General John Floyd attacked and destroyed the Creek village of Auttose on the left bank of the Tallapoosa River. In reprisal the Red Sticks struck Floyd's camp and killed or wounded nearly 200 soldiers before they were driven off. Discouraged, Floyd abandoned further offensive action, his command was discharged, and Georgia virtually withdrew from the war.

At the same time an expedition into southern Alabama of volunteers from the Mississippi Territory led by General Ferdinand L. Claiborne also proved a failure. Despite a victory at Enotachopco there were mass desertions when enlistments terminated. Claiborne was forced to withdraw, leaving the Creek War in the hands of General Jackson and his single regiment at Fort Strother.[1]

But the war at the end of 1813 was not a total disaster. Nearly a thousand Creek warriors had been killed in the various engagements, and a large part of the hostiles' food supply was destroyed. Unfortunately, the Americans failed to follow through with a knockout blow. They withdrew. They virtually abandoned the war.

Except Jackson. As he sat in his fort waiting for reinforcements, he was practically alone. If his report on the size of his force to General Thomas Pinckney, commander of the regular army for the department of the south, is accurate, it would appear that at one period he had no more than 130 men under his command at Fort Strother.[2]

Then, suddenly, Governor Blount acted. Stung by Jackson's strong language, he ordered a new levy of 2,500 troops—and was surprised and delighted to find not only popular support for his call but approval by the War Department.[3] He gambled on popular resentment against the Indians and won, just as Jackson had predicted. Some of the officers of the disbanded companies who had served under Old Hickory now began to raise new companies, and General Pinckney offered the use of the Thirty-ninth Regiment. By the middle of March 1814 several thousand men were available to General Jackson.

But that was March. In January 1814 all Fort Strother could muster against the Indians was a handful of men and the indomitable will of their commander. Then, on January 14, 800 raw recruits marched into the fort. Their unannounced arrival startled Jackson. He could scarcely believe his eyes. But he accepted his blessing joyfully and immediately spun into action. Before any of them could discover the hazards of life in the wilderness with Old Hickory or the ordeal of fighting "savage" Indians under his command, the recruits were marched into Creek country. The action verged on rashness, and Jackson nearly paid a terrible price for it.

Jackson headed directly for the important and heavily fortified encampment of Tohopeka, or the Horseshoe Bend, a 100-acre peninsula formed by the looping action of the Tallapoosa River. On January 21 he camped at Emuckfaw Creek, three miles from the fortification, and dispatched his spies. About midnight they returned with a report that the Indians were encamped some three miles distant; their whooping and dancing indicated that they probably knew of Jackson's presence and were planning an attack.

At dawn the Red Sticks struck. Jackson was ready. The action raged for an hour with the heaviest fighting on the left wing. After the Creeks had been repulsed Jackson sent Coffee, who had rejoined him, together with 400 men and some friendly Creeks, to destroy the Red Stick encampment. But Coffee found it too strongly fortified to risk an assault and returned to Jackson's camp. On his return the Red Sticks struck again, this time on the right wing. With great difficulty the Indians were repulsed. During the action Coffee was wounded and Jackson's brother-in-law and aide, Major Alexander Donelson, was killed. Then came the main attack, again on the left side, where Jackson expected it. The Creeks peppered the army with "quick irregular firing, from behind logs, trees, shrubbery, and whatever could afford concealment."[4] Lying prone behind logs the Indians loaded their guns, rose, fired, and then ducked down again to reload. To dislodge them Jackson ordered a charge led by Billy Carroll which "broke in on them, threw them into confusion," and eventually drove them off.[5] The Creeks had devised an excellent plan of attack—to hit three different points of the American line at once—but the execution went awry. One of the tribes designated to strike Jackson's front line decided instead to retire to their village.[6] Had they cooperated in the general assault, Jackson's army might have been cut to pieces.

It was a close call, and Jackson decided against taking further chances with his raw troops and wisely ordered a return to Fort Strother. Red Eagle was stronger than he imagined; 900 troops were not enough to proceed to Horseshoe Bend.[7] Retreat was the only sensible course, and the General did not hesitate to order it.

As Jackson pulled back the Creeks followed stealthfully. When he reached Enotachopco Creek and started across, the hostiles attacked just as the artillery was entering the water behind the front guard and the flank column. Jackson immediately ordered the rear guard to engage the Indians; at the same time he called for the left and right columns to wheel around, recross the creek above and below the Red Sticks, and surround them—in imitation of the Talladega strategy. "But to my astonishment and mortification," Jackson later reported to General Pinckney, "when the word had been given to Colo. Carroll to halt and form . . . I beheld . . . the rear guard precipitately give way. This shameful retreat was disastrous in the extreme."[8] The raw troops plunged back into the creek in their effort to escape the Indians. Only Carroll and about twenty-five men held their ground while Constant Perkins and Cravan Jackson fired the six-pounder, using a musket butt as a rammer and the musket ramrod as a picker. "The brave Lieutenant Armstrong just after the first fire of the cannon . . . fell . . . exclaiming as he lay, my brave fellows some of you must fall but you must save the cannon."[9]

Jackson, screaming orders in his high-pitched voice, managed to reform his columns and throw them hard against the Indians. He landed a solid blow. Detachments were hurried across the creek in strength, and after several minutes of intense fighting they drove off the Indians. In the action the Tennesseans proved themselves men of courage and fortitude despite their inexperience, and they earned their commander's highest praise.

Jackson during the engagement was described by a friendly observer as a "rallying point" even for the brave. "Firm and energetic, and at the same time perfectly self-possessed, his example and his authority alike contributed to arrest the flying, and give confidence to those who maintained their ground. . . . In the midst of a shower of balls, of which he seemed unmindful, he was seen . . . rallying the alarmed, halting them in their flight, forming his columns, and inspiriting them by his example."[10] In the engagement 20 Americans were killed and 75 wounded, some of whom died afterward; approximately 200 dead Indians were counted on the ground and in the creek. Jackson's gallantry and skill succeeded in extricating the army from the depths of Creek country and the danger of annihilation had they remained.

Although the Emuckfaw and Enotachopco skirmishes in no way constituted victories, or demonstrations of superior tactical ability on the part of Jackson (they might easily have ended disastrously), they were important. For one thing, the Red Sticks had suffered a severe mauling, so severe in fact that they abandoned their aggressive policy and withdrew into their strongholds—particularly the seemingly impregnable fortress at Horseshoe Bend.[11] For another, a good route into the heart of Creek country had been explored by Jackson's army and in that sense the raid was a reconnaissance in force and valuable for future campaigns. For a third, enlistments in Tennessee surged because reports of the skirmishes sounded like genuine victories and, as a result, more Tennesseans wanted to share the final honor and glory of destroying the Indian menace. Lastly, Emuckfaw and Enotachopco were important for Jackson personally. They proved he could lead an army and preserve it in the face of devastating defeat. He had earned the right to command. In searching for generals who could win battles, the administration no longer dared to disregard him. General Pinckney, his superior, carefully drew the attention of the secretary of war to Jackson's exploits. "Without the personal firmness, popularity and exertions of that officer," Pinckney wrote, "the Indian war, on the part of Tennessee, would have been abandoned at least for a time. . . . If government think it advisable to elevate to the rank of general other persons than those now in the army, I have heard of none whose military operations so well entitle him to that distinction."[12] Compared to the other military news Washington had received in recent months, Emuckfaw and Enotachopco sounded like stupendous victories. They brightened Jackson's name in the capital and dispelled the curse of the Burr episode.

Jackson, too, was pleased with the outcome of the raid, and he was almost ecstatic at the large number of recruits who joined his army following his return to Fort Strother. He wrote to Rachel, detailing everything that had happened in the recent campaign and expressing his hope that the war would soon be over. In reply he received a nearly hysterical letter by an obviously tormented woman.

Hermitage, February 10, 1814

My Dearest Life. I received your Letter by Express. Never Shall I forget it. I have not Slept one night Since. What a dreadfull scene it was—how did I feel. I never Can disscribe it. I Cryed aloud and praised my god For your safety. how thankfull I was—Oh my unfortunate Nephew [Alexander Donelson] he is gon how I Deplore his

Loss his untimely End. My Dear pray Let me Conjur you by every Tie of Love of friend ship to Let me see you before you go againe. I have borne it untill now it has thrown me into feavours. I am very unwell —my thoughts Is never Divirted from that dreadfull scene oh how dreadfull to me—the mercy and goodness of Heaven to me you are Spard perils and Dangers so maney troubles—my prayers is unceasing how Long o Lord will I remain so unhappy. no rest no Ease I cannot sleepe. all can come home but you. I never wanted to see you so mutch in my life . . . I must see you pray My Darling never make me so unhappy for aney Country. . . . You have served your Country Long Enough you have gained maney Larells you have Ernd them . . . you have been gon a Long time six monthes in all that time what has been your trails daingers and Diffyculties hardeships oh Lorde of heaven how Can I beare it. Colo Hayes waites once more I Commend you to god his providential Eye is on you his parental tender Care is garding you. . . . our Dear Little Son is well he sayes maney things to sweet papa which I have not time to mention. . . . health and happy Dayes untill we meete. Let it not be Long from your Dearest friend and faithfull wife untill Death.

Rachel Jackson[13]

Jackson had absolutely no thought of returning home. He had a war to conclude.

Early in February the General received word that 2,000 east Tennesseans would soon join him, and on February 6 the Thirty-ninth Regiment of U.S. Infantry, commanded by Colonel John Williams, marched into Fort Strother. Soon after a part of Coffee's old cavalry brigade and a troop of dragoons appeared. By March Old Hickory had nearly 5,000 men under his command, a force large enough to "exterminate or conquor" the Creeks.

Discipline was essential. Enotachopco proved that. Jackson could not march his men into Creek country as he had in January and expect to overwhelm the hostiles by a mere show of force. Now that he had regular troops to serve as a nucleus of authority, he could train an effective fighting unit. And there could be no exception to the strictest discipline. Mutiny would be dealt with severely. Not like the last time, arguing and cajoling the men, pleading with them to be good soldiers and to remain at their posts. Now, by God, they would obey orders and act as military personnel should or they would suffer the supreme penalty. Thus, slowly and deliberately, Jackson set about training his men and completing the formation of a professional army.[14] Such a force powered by his iron will would be unbeatable. First the Indians would be smashed, then the Spanish.

"There never was so thorough going a man, nor one who so well knew how to inspire his men with ardor & enthusiasm as our general," wrote one young officer. "Had he been appointed to the command of the armies in the North I am well assured the war had long ago been at an end. He will not be delayed or trifled with by the contractors. He *makes* them do their duty. . . . Indeed every officer & every soldier—every man . . . connected with the army, is here, compelled to the strictest observance of whatever appertains to his duty." In the field the army was required to rise at 3:30 A.M., the staff at 3:00 A.M. This precaution Jackson insisted upon in order to prevent a surprise attack since the Indians frequently struck early in the morning.[15]

Jackson put his troops to work improving the road between Fort Deposit and Fort Strother and banned the transportation of whiskey and every other dispensable item. When he heard that Generals Cocke and Isaac Roberts were unsympathetic to his brand of discipline and were attempting to sabotage it, Jackson sent them home under arrest. With General Roberts he was particularly angry. Roberts tried to force him to agree that Roberts's men would not serve more than three months. When he refused and the men assembled to begin their march home, Old Hickory arrested Roberts and declared the unit deserters. Later he relented and promised pardons if the men returned to duty. Eventually most of them did.

During the period of Jackson's determination to instill absolute discipline in his troops there occurred an incident that would haunt Jackson throughout his military and political life, an incident that convinced people, and indeed engraved it forever in their minds, that Andrew Jackson could be a ruthless, pitiless killer. John Woods was hardly eighteen years of age when he enlisted in the militia. He belonged to a company that had caused considerable disciplinary problems, although apparently Woods himself took no part in the trouble. In any event, the young man was standing guard one cold, rainy February morning. After obtaining permission from an officer to leave his post, he went to his tent for a blanket. There he found that his comrades had left him his breakfast, and he calmly sat down to eat it. A few minutes later an officer entered the tent and, using abusive language, ordered him to return to his post. Woods, who had received his permission to leave his post from a different officer, refused to obey the order. An argument ensued and the officer ordered Woods's arrest. Then the young man went berserk. He grabbed his gun and swore he would shoot the first man to lay a hand on him. As the quarreling intensified, someone informed Jackson that a "mutiny" was in progress. The cry "mutiny" was electrifying. Jackson bolted from his tent. "Which is the ----- rascal?" he shouted. "Shoot him! Shoot him! Blow ten balls through the ---- villain's body!"[16] In the meantime Woods had been persuaded to give up his gun and submit to arrest.

Most soldiers thought nothing much would come of the incident. Such things had happened before and the offender was usually dismissed without pay or drummed from the camp. Then, too, militiamen were special; they had rights no others enjoyed—such as freedom from capital punishment for mutinous actions. But Jackson was determined to make an example of Woods. He had Woods courtmartialed on a charge of mutiny. The young man pleaded not guilty, but the court found unanimously against him and ordered his execution.[17] Several efforts were made to win clemency for Woods, but the stern commander turned a deaf ear. On March 14, two days after the trial, John Woods was shot to death by a firing squad in the presence of the entire army.

Jackson's aide, John Reid, believed the execution had a "most salutary effect" on the other men. "That mutinous spirit," he wrote, "which had so frequently broken into the camp, and for a while suspended all active operations" had to be crushed once and for all and "subordination observed." "Painful" as the execution was to Jackson, "he viewed it as . . . essential to the preservation of good order." It produced "the happiest effects," Reid reported. "That opinion, so long indulged, that a militia-man was for no offence to suffer death, was, from that moment, abandoned, and a strict obedience afterwards characterized the army."[18]

Many years later, when Jackson sought the presidency of the United States, the circumstances of Woods's death were recounted in newspapers around the country in attempts to prove that Old Hickory was a butcher who could have imposed a milder sentence for Woods's momentary rebelliousness but chose instead to snuff out his life. The punishment was indeed harsh. Under different circumstances Jackson might have been more lenient—although he was most unpredictable—but his experiences of the previous December and January left his mood and temper strict and unyielding in matters of discipline. Which was understandable. He had kept a force in the field despite massive desertions and the worst possible hardships. That experience toughened him. As far as he was concerned, the troops must be made to understand their duty whatever the circumstances—even if it meant the sacrifice of a young man's life.

An Iron General had been fashioned by painful experience. If possible Jackson's already cold will and steely determination intensified. He became a relentless, driving, indefatigable machine devoted to one solitary purpose—the destruction of his country's enemies.

Out of the pain, including the Woods incident, Jackson forged an army. Now he could get on with the war.

The same day Woods was executed Jackson commenced the campaign that he passionately believed would annihilate the Red Sticks and end the Creek War. His plan, now that his army numbered several thousand men who behaved like disciplined soldiers, called for him to move southward along the banks of the Coosa River, then eastward toward Emuckfaw in the vicinity of Horseshoe Bend, where he knew many tribes of the Creeks were gathering for self-protection. After destroying this "confederacy" he would march to the Hickory or Holy Ground, which was approximately in the geographic center of the Creek Nation (at the junction of the Coosa and Tallapoosa rivers). This was the sacred meetingplace of the Indians; they believed that it was protected by the deities and that no white man could violate it and live.[19] General Andrew Jackson saw himself as the appropriate white man to disprove that Indian superstition.

On March 14, 1814, Jackson moved. He left 450 men behind to guard Fort Strother and sent Colonel John Williams and his Thirty-ninth Regiment downriver in flatboats to establish an advance post that would provide lines of communication and protect provisions. The post, built on the Coosa approximately 30 miles to the south, was named (by the topographical engineer) Fort Williams for the commander of the Thirty-ninth Regiment.

At first Jackson moved cautiously, but once he received assurances from General Pinckney that men and supplies would be sent from Mobile to meet him at the Hickory Ground, he felt confident enough to strike straight out from Fort Williams, heading almost due east toward the strong encampment of Indians some sixty miles away at Horseshoe Bend. He now commanded a force of nearly 4,000 men, including many Creek allies. His intelligence forces (an asset he used with extraordinary skill throughout the war) informed him that tribes from the Oakfusky, Newyorka, Hillabees, Fish ponds, and Eufaula towns had gathered their strength in anticipation of Jackson's attack at the Bend. A thousand Indian braves and nearly 300 women and children were already locked within the fortress.

The stronghold at Horseshoe Bend was actually a 100-acre wooded peninsula almost completely surrounded by water and with a stout breastwork running across its 350-yard neck. The breastwork was made of "large timbers and trunks of trees" laid "horizontally on each other, leaving but a single place of entrance."[20] It ran five to eight feet high and had a double row of portholes "artfully arranged" to give the defenders "complete direction of their fire." Because of the curvature of the breastwork no army could advance upon it without being exposed to deadly crossfire. It was an engineering feat that surprised some white men who did not believe "savage" Indians capable of such skill. It was "a place well formed by Nature for defence & rendered more secure by Art," said Jackson.[21]

Stationing a strong force at Fort Williams to protect his rear, Jackson marched eastward on March 24 with an army numbering between 2,000 and 3,000 men, headed for the Tallapoosa by way of Emuckfaw.[22] The numerical odds were completely in his favor (by more than two to one) —something the General always tried to secure. Furthermore, he took every precaution to protect his army as he pulled it forward to meet the enemy. Everything was done with care and precision. There was nothing rash or impulsive about any of his actions. He had too much to lose.

At ten o'clock on the morning of March 27 Jackson arrived at the Bend. He was flabbergasted by what he saw. "It is impossible to conceive a situation more eligible for defence than the one they had chosen," he reported to General Pinckney; "and the skill which they manifested in their breast work, was really astonishing."[23] Several hours earlier Jackson had detailed Coffee and his cavalry, along with the companies of spies and the entire force of friendly Cherokees, to occupy the side of the river opposite the Bend in order to prevent the Red Sticks from escaping. In addition, Coffee was told to make some feint or maneuver to divert the enemy from the principal point of attack. The plan was to contain the Creeks inside their fortress, where Jackson would smash through the breastwork to overpower and destroy them.

Jackson planted his artillery, one six-pounder and one three-pounder, on a small eminence about 80 yards from the closest and 250 yards from the furthest points of the breastwork. At 10:30 A.M. he opened fire. The balls thudded harmlessly into the thick logs or whistled through "the works without shaking the wall." Whenever the Indians peeked over the breastwork to pepper the gun crews, Jackson raked them with musket and rifle fire. For two hours the firing continued, the artillery pounding the defenses without inflicting appreciable damage and the sharpshooters futilely searching the wall for targets. As they watched the frustrated whites attempting to rupture the line of defense, the Indians whooped their derision. Several medicine men, their heads and shoulders decorated with the plumage of many birds, danced and howled their incantations to the sun to bring death and damnation to the invaders.

Meanwhile Coffee sent a group of swimmers across the river to cut loose the Creek canoes and bring them back to be used to ferry soldiers in an assault on the rear position of the encampment. Then a party of soldiers under Captain Morgan crossed the river to set fire to the huts clustered at the turn of the Bend and to attack the Indians within the compound. Morgan's force was too small to inflict serious damage, but it provided the diversion Jackson wanted; when the General saw the smoke from the burning huts and realized what was happening he ordered his troops to storm the breastwork.

The order brought a shout from Jackson's men. The Thirty-ninth Regiment, led by Colonel Williams, charged forward under a withering fire of Indian bullets and arrows. The soldiers reached the rampart and thrust their rifles through the portholes. For a time it was point-blank shooting, muzzle to muzzle, "in which many of the enemy's balls were welded to the bayonets of our musquets."[24] Major Lemuel P. Montgomery of the Thirty-ninth was the first to reach the breastwork. Leaping on the wall, he called to his men to follow—but no sooner had he spoken than a bullet struck him in the head, and he fell lifeless to the ground.[25] Ensign Sam Houston mounted the wall and renewed Montgomery's cry. An arrow pierced his thigh but Houston jumped into the compound followed by a large contingent of regulars who poured over the wall. The breastwork was breached; the troops scaled the rampart in force.

The Indians, stunned and frightened, backed away to conceal themselves in the thick brush that covered the ground. But the troops were after them and had the advantage of pursuit. The killing became savage, but the Indians asked no quarter and continued to fight even though they were hopelessly outnumbered. As the Red Sticks retreated they took a devastating round of fire. "The *carnage* was *dreadful,*" Jackson reported.[26] Some headed for their canoes to escape, splashing across the river when they found them gone, only to run headlong into Coffee's troops. Others leaped down the river bluff and concealed themselves among the cliffs that were covered with brush and fallen trees. Hour after hour throughout the afternoon the fighting continued, the troops flushing the Indians from their hiding places and shooting them when they frantically sought new cover. Now the Red Sticks were in total disarray, scampering wildly from place to place. The whites systematically slaughtered them.

Still the Creeks would not surrender. When Jackson sent a flag and an interpreter to their last stronghold on the bluffs to ask them to throw down their weapons, the Indians responded with a blast of gunfire that killed one member of the party. At that Jackson leveled his artillery at them, pounding the cliffs with cannonballs. To no effect. The Indians would not surrender. Jackson then ordered lighted torches thrown down the cliffs. The brush and fallen trees quickly caught fire; the area became an inferno. As the Indians dashed from their hiding places, the soldiers picked them off one by one. The killing continued through the late afternoon and into the evening; it stopped only when the light disappeared and the soldiers could no longer see their targets. A few Indians, under cover of darkness, managed to cross the river and escape.

The next day Jackson ordered a count of the dead. Some 557 Indians were found on the ground; Coffee estimated as many as 300 Creeks dead in the river; and a few dozen bodies were later discovered in the woods —a total of approximately 900 Indians killed. Few warriors escaped the carnage; Jackson figured that no more than fifteen or twenty braves got away, but the number may have been higher. As they counted the slain hostiles, the soldiers cut off the tip of each dead Indian's nose in order to keep the count accurate. Many also cut long strips of skin from the bodies of the dead Indians to make bridle reins.[27] As the counting progressed, an eighteen-year-old Indian was brought before Jackson. He had been severely wounded in the leg, and a surgeon was summoned to dress the wound. While the operation progressed, the proud Indian looked at the General and asked, *"Cure 'im, kill 'im again?"* Jackson assured him he would not be killed. He was so struck by the youth's "manly behavior" that he sent him to the Hermitage and after the war bound him out to a trade in Nashville, where he married a "colored woman" and established himself in business.[28]

In picking over the dead, the soldiers discovered three prophets, one of whom was the famous Monahoee, "shot in the mouth by a grape shot," reported Jackson, "as if Heaven designed to chastise his impostures by an appropriate punishment."[29] Three hundred captives were taken, all but four of them women and children. Jackson said he regretted to learn that two or three women and children were accidentally killed.[30] He never made "war on females"; only the base and cowardly do that, he said. His own casualties amounted to 47 dead and 159 wounded, along with an additional 23 friendly Creeks and Cherokees killed and 47 wounded.[31]

Jackson was not satisfied with his incomparable victory. He grieved at the loss of Major Montgomery, and he regretted something else: William Weatherford, Chief Red Eagle, had escaped him. The Indian chief was away from Horseshoe Bend on the day of battle—and Jackson desperately wanted his head as tribute for the massacre at Fort Mims. Nevertheless the power of the Red Sticks was irreparably broken. Jackson expected them to sue for peace immediately. "Should they not," he told his wife, " . . . I will give them, with the permission of heaven the final stroke at the hickory ground."[32]

The Battle of Horseshoe Bend was one of the major engagements of the War of 1812. Apart from the incredible number of men killed, it crushed the Indian will and capacity to levy war just when the British were about to land troops in the south and provide the hostiles with an enormous supply of arms and ammunition. Had the Creeks not been defeated so decisively they would have become a force of incalculable danger to the entire southern half of the United States.

Jackson sank his dead in the river to prevent their being scalped by the "savages." Then he collected his wounded and returned to Fort Williams, burning and destroying Indian villages as he went. At "my approach," he informed Rachel, "the Indians fled in all directions. . . . I have burnt the Verse Town, this day that has been the hot bed of the war, and has regained all the Scalps, taken from Fort Mims."[33] The destruction of the Creek food supply had been so systematic over the last year that the Indians, both friend and foe, now verged on starvation. With famine a real prospect, many Red Sticks laid down their weapons or fled to Florida.

On his return to the fort, Jackson gathered his army on parade and published a short address which praised their valor and the extent of their victory. They had redeemed the character of the state, he said, and were entitled to the gratitude of their country. They had destroyed the Creek confederacy, and consequently the "fiends of the Tallapoosa" would never again disturb the quiet of the frontier or "murder our women and children." Never! "By their yells, they had hoped to frighten us, and with their wooden fortifications to oppose us. Stupid mortals! their yells but designated their situation the more certainly; whilst their walls became a snare for their own destruction. So will it ever be, when presumption and ignorance contend against bravery and prudence."[34]

After resting his army for a few days, Jackson set out on April 5 for the Hickory Ground at the juncture of the Coosa and Tallapoosa rivers, intending to pulverize whatever remained of Creek resistance. He was also anxious to link up with the Georgia and North Carolina militia, which General Pinckney was sending him to strengthen his forces. But the Creek War was really over. As Jackson advanced southward, the principal chiefs of the hostile tribes came to his camp with a flag of truce, making professions of friendship and stating their desire to end the war and live in peace. The Iron General rudely informed them that the only way they could have peace was to retire to the rear of the army and settle them-selves north of Fort Williams, where they would be cut off from Florida (and British and Spanish assistance) and where they might more easily become wards of the federal government. When they had relocated they would learn his final terms for ending the war and establishing peace. Nothing else was acceptable as proof of their good intentions. Lacking any choice, the Indians stoically consented.

Preceded by detachments sent to scour the country and flush out hostile Creeks, Jackson continued his march toward the Hickory Ground. On April 18 he raised the American flag over the old Toulouse French Fort, which was rebuilt and renamed Fort Jackson after the Commanding General. Here many more Creek chiefs surrendered to Old Hickory, agreeing like the others to removal. But where were the remaining chiefs?

Jackson asked. Where was William Weatherford? He was told that many of the Creeks had fled to Pensacola to seek the protection of the Spanish. Weatherford, too? They could not say. To test their good will, Jackson directed the chiefs to bring Weatherford to his camp, tied as a prisoner, so that he could be dealt with as he deserved.[35]

Weatherford spared the chiefs the further humiliation of turning him in. A few days later he walked into Jackson's camp and calmly claimed the protection that had been extended to the other chiefs, at the same time expressing his desire for peace for himself and his people. Jackson was astonished at Weatherford's daring and his presumption of asking protection after what he had done at Fort Mims. "I had directed that you should be brought to me confined," growled Jackson; "had you appeared in this way, I should have known how to have treated you."

"I am in your power," replied Red Eagle. "Do with me as you please. I am a soldier. I have done the white people all the harm I could; I have fought them, and fought them bravely: if I had an army, I would yet fight, and contend to the last: but I have none; my people are all gone. I can now do no more than weep over the misfortunes of my nation."[36]

The speech deeply impressed Jackson. He tried to look grave and solemn, but he could not hide the admiration he felt for this courageous leader who walked bravely into a camp swarming with white men whose one desire was to torture and kill him. Still, Jackson had a role to play as commander and conqueror; no amount of admiration could change that.

"The terms on which your nation can be saved," Jackson said, "and peace restored, has already been disclosed: in this way, and none other, can you obtain safety." If Red Eagle wanted a continuation of war, Jackson was prepared to fight on.[37]

The Indian replied quietly, but his voice was strong and his pride clearly apparent. He said he desired peace so that his nation might be relieved of their sufferings and the women and children saved from destitution and death. "There was a time," he continued, "when I had a choice, and could have answered you: I have none now—even hope has ended. Once I could animate my warriors to battle; but I cannot animate the dead. My warriors can no longer hear my voice: their bones are at Talladega, Tallushatchee, Emuckfaw and Tohopeka. I have not surrendered myself thoughtlessly. Whilst there were chances of success, I never left my post, nor supplicated peace. But my people are gone, and I now ask it for my nation, and for myself. On the miseries and misfortunes brought upon my country, I look back with deepest sorrow, and wish to avert still greater calamities. If I had been left to contend with the Georgia army, I would have raised my corn on one bank of the river, and fought them on the other; but your people have destroyed my nation. You are a brave man: I rely upon your generosity. You will exact no terms of a conquered people, but such as they should accede to: whatever they may be, it would now be madness and folly to oppose. If they are opposed, you will find me amongst the sternest enforcers of obedience. Those who would still hold out, can be influenced only by a mean spirit of revenge; and to this they must not, and shall not sacrifice the last remnant of their country. You have told us where we might go, and be safe. This is a good talk, and my nation ought to listen to it. They shall listen to it."[38]

So ended the interview. Weatherford pronounced and accepted his defeat. Jackson, though awed by Red Eagle's courage and his stature as a leader of his people, made it clear that the Creeks could find safety only in submitting unconditionally to his authority. Weatherford agreed to do what he could to convince any holdouts that they should surrender. A few days later he left the camp with several followers to fulfill his pledge. But his career as a Creek leader was over; when the War of 1812 ended he retired to a large farm in Monroe County, Alabama, and became a respected planter. Occasionally he visited Old Hickory at the Hermitage.[39]

Apart from Jackson's admiration of Red Eagle, which was genuine, the General determined he had more need of the Indian alive than dead or locked in a stockade. Whatever the chief could do to immobilize hostiles would be advantageous to him, for greater enemies still needed to be reckoned with: the British and the Spanish.

Of course Jackson did not rely on Weatherford to end the Creek War; the mopping-up operations were the duty of his army. Dispatching detachments on a regular basis, he scoured the Coosa and Tallapoosa river basins and the intervening country "to scatter and destroy any who might be found concerting offensive operations."[40] He commissioned spies and emissaries to pass the word that all Indians who failed to retire to the north of Fort Williams—and thereby cut themselves off from communication with Florida—would be treated as enemies and punished accordingly. "Every hour brings in more" Creeks, said Jackson, "all thankful to be received upon unconditional submission."[41] So thorough was this operation that Jackson reported to Governor Blount on April 18 that the Creek War was virtually ended.[42]

Not quite. A number of hostile Creeks still preferred to fight; with the help of the British they regrouped themselves in Florida and merged their forces into the larger conflict between the United States and Great Britain.[43]

Still in April 1814 the Indian problem in the southwest appeared settled, thanks to Jackson and his army, and so the secretary of war appointed General Pinckney and Benjamin Hawkins as commissioners to arrange a peace treaty with the Creek Nation.[44] The principal condition:

indemnity for the cost of the war. Otherwise Pinckney was given wide discretion in deciding the terms of settlement. The appointment of these two men, particularly Hawkins who had a reputation for liking and protecting Indians, infuriated many westerners who believed these commissioners would not punish the Indians severely enough. Protests fluttered into Washington. Unless a huge cession of land was demanded from the Creeks as indemnity, they said, the government could expect further trouble from the west.

Jackson totally agreed with this sentiment. Indeed he was its principal spokesman. He favored stripping the Creeks, both friend and foe, of all their land west of the Coosa and north of the Alabama rivers in order to insure complete separation of the Creeks from the Spanish in Florida.[45]

For the moment, however, he continued his military assignment of subduing hostiles. With the rebuilding of Fort Jackson a string of posts stretched down the center of Alabama, straight through the heart of Creek country, forming a line of protection from Tennessee and Georgia to Alabama and Mississippi. On April 20 General Pinckney arrived at Fort Jackson to assume command of the area and commence negotiations with the Creeks. He was unstinting in his praise of the Tennessee troops and their brave commander. Indeed he delighted in Jackson's triumph as though it were his own. Banquets were given to celebrate the stupendous victory. When it was no longer possible to propose yet another toast to the bravery and skill of the Tennesseans, Pinckney directed Jackson to march his troops back home and discharge them.[46]

Although the War of 1812 still raged and the presence in the south of the British and the Spanish needed attention, there was something to be said for Jackson's marching his victorious army back to Nashville. There were the glory and the honor to be savored. More important, his attitude toward the volunteers' terms of service had always been questionable; his willingness to release them now, after their colossal victory at Horseshoe Bend, would prove his good intentions and erase his previous reputation for obstinate disregard of the rights of ordinary soldiers.

Within two hours of receiving Pinckney's order Jackson assembled his troops, and three days later they were back at Fort Williams, a distance of sixty miles. There he issued a parting address to his soldiers.

Jackson never missed an opportunity to speak directly to his men. Skillfully written, these addresses helped strengthen his hold on the army. They invariably expressed his pride in their gallantry, skill, loyalty, and stamina. And that was the keynote now: his enormous pride in them. For the troops believed, via these addresses, that Jackson not only appreciated their trials and suffering but would proclaim to the world the price of the victory they had purchased in terms of blood and hardship. The addresses were always fatherly, almost patronizing. "Your general is pleased with you," and "he salutes you" and "he compliments you"— these were favorite expressions. Jackson's salutes had a way of getting back home, especially after a victory, and they often carried an emotional impact that vastly enhanced his reputation.

In the parting address to his soldiers at Fort Williams, Jackson told them that they deserved the undying gratitude of their country. "Within a few days," he said, "you have annihilated the power of a nation, that, for twenty years, has been the disturber of your peace. Your vengeance has been glutted. Wherever these infuriated allies of our arch enemy assembled for battle, you pursued and dispersed them. The rapidity of your movements, and the brilliancy of your achievements, have corresponded with the valour by which you have been animated. The bravery you have displayed in the field of battle, and the uniform good conduct you have manifested in your encampment, and on your line of march, will long be cherished in the memory of your general, and will not be forgotten by the country you have so materially benefited."[47]

The army turned north. When it reached the vicinity of Fayetteville it was discharged from further service. At this parting Jackson again addressed the troops and again praised their bravery and devotion. He would never forget them.

Old Hickory proceeded to Nashville, where an excited and near-frenzied mob waited to greet him. Hundreds of people lined the streets to get a glimpse of the hero and to shout their appreciation for his noble victory over the "savages." An arrangements committee escorted him to the courthouse, where Felix Grundy spoke for the entire community in expressing joy at having found a commander who could so thoroughly and devastatingly purge the frontier of the Indian menace. A state banquet followed at the Bell Tavern where Old Hickory was presented with a ceremonial sword. Responding to the presentation, he spoke plainly and forthrightly, without vanity or mock modesty. It was a magnificent speech, one that underscored his superb gifts as a politician. He praised his officers and men; he reminded his listeners how intense their sufferings, how enormous their accomplishment. "The success which attended our exertions," he said, "has indeed been very great. We have laid the foundation of a lasting peace to those frontiers which had been so long and so often infested by the savages. We have conquered. We have added a country to ours, which, by connecting the settlements of Georgia with those of the Mississippi Territory, and both of them with our own, will become a secure barrier against foreign invasion, or the operation of foreign influence over our red neighbors in the South and we have furnished the means not only of defraying the expenses of the war against the Creeks, but of that which is carrying on against their ally Great Britain." He ended by invoking the memory of those Tennesseans who had died in the war. They were worthy of being called Americans, he said. They were true "descendants of their sires of the Revolution."[48]

Throughout Tennessee the name of Andrew Jackson now brought unstinted praise. All the old enmities and quarrels faded. Those who still harbored grudges kept them to themselves, and those who had reservations about Jackson's character and personality glossed over his faults to praise his staggering contribution to the state and the nation. Even Sevier's friends spoke of him "with affection" and went so far as to mention him as the next governor. The state was prepared to give him whatever he required, so universal was the approbation.

He had come a long way. Barely eight months before he had struggled out of a sick bed after a disgraceful gunfight and by sheer determination forged an army and kept it in the field. He had enemies on all sides who did not miss an opportunity to injure his reputation. Now they were silent or, like everyone else, had joined in the chorus of praise.[49]

Even the administration in Washington had to take note of Jackson's formidable presence. In view of the many defeats suffered by other American generals—especially those favored by the administration—it was gratifying to have one general who knew how to fight and win battles. Thus, when General Wade Hampton resigned after failing in Canada, the administration offered Jackson a brigadier generalship in the U.S. Army with the brevet of major general and command of the Seventh Military District, which included Louisiana, Tennessee, the Mississippi Territory, and the Creek Nation.

The offer galled Jackson, who anticipated a higher rank. He expected to be a major general—the rank he held in the militia. Secretary of War John Armstrong said it was the best they could do.[50] Another affront! Still, it was a generalship in the U.S. Army and that unquestionably had value, so on June 8 Jackson accepted it. Meanwhile, General William Henry Harrison, after a long dispute with the administration, resigned his commission in disgust. Armstrong was so angry with Harrison that out of pique he offered the vacant major generalship to Jackson. The offer went out on May 28; Jackson accepted it on June 18.[51]

Now Jackson had what he wanted: a first-class rank in the U.S. Army —and, as it turned out, a valuable command, though the administration did not think so when they offered it to him. In addition, there was a not inconsiderable salary. Jackson's base pay was $2,500 a year; with allowances for servants, rations, transportation, and miscellaneous expenses the total salary came to $6,500, a rather handsome amount. The war brought Jackson many benefits, not the least of which was financial.

As gratifying as these honors may have been, they were in a sense undeserved. Or, rather, they had not yet been earned. After all, Jackson had not demonstrated extraordinary military skill, nor had his soldiers; all they had proved was that they could overwhelm Indians who could not match them in numbers or in firepower. True, they broke the Red Sticks' will to pursue the war, but the Red Sticks were only one part of the Creek confederation—the less civilized part at that—and did not represent the true strength and might of the Creek Nation. In effect, the Tennesseans had only demonstrated that superior numbers and firepower could subdue an undersized "savage" force fighting mostly without muskets.

Jackson's distinction at this stage—a significant distinction—was his proven ability to command an army, maintain it in the field, and deploy it effectively to pacify the frontier. He was not a great tactician, nor were his battles brilliantly executed; but he commanded the confidence of his officers and the obedience of his men, even under terrible adversity. When necessary he moved his army rapidly, and he understood and could evaluate the importance of intelligence reports. And welding all of this together was his titanic determination, his stupendous will to overcome the enemy and achieve total victory.

There are two reasons for the extravagant praise heaped on Jackson and his men in the spring of 1814. First, there had been so few victories and so many disasters in the War of 1812 that anything remotely approaching success on the battlefield was wildly applauded across the country. Second (a fact more appreciated in the west), the smashing blow inflicted on the Indians showed what could be done with the "savages" whenever the white man so determined and whenever they had someone like Andrew Jackson to lead them.

For Jackson personally there was something more. He mirrored in splendid excess the westerner's yearning for heroics, drama, storm. After 1814 he was altogether unique and special to frontiersmen—their "beau ideal"—and that feeling never changed appreciably for the rest of Jackson's life.

His reputation as general, as westerner, as frontiersman, as symbol, was made by the Creek War. But the war did something more to him. It permanently shattered his health. In the relatively short space of eight months his constitution was devastated by chronic diarrhea and dysentery brought on by wilderness conditions, lack of adequate food and medicine, and his own indifference to his physical suffering. When he began the campaign he was still recovering from the gunfight with the Bentons. For months he could barely move his arm because of the shattered bone. Then pieces of the bone "came out of my arm" (and he sent them to

Rachel as a souvenir). Once they were gone the arm seemed to get better and to strengthen so he could get it into his sleeve unassisted. "I hope all the loose pieces of bone is out," he wrote, "and I will not be longer pained with it."[52] Then, once he contracted dysentery he could not shake it off, and his body took a fearful beating. When the attacks were particularly severe in the field he doubled over the branch of a tree; in camp he pressed his chest against the back of a chair. Somehow this physical labor gave him a measure of relief—or at least helped him through the worst of the spasms. For nourishment, when eating was unthinkable, he swallowed weak gin and water. Throughout the war he suffered many days of pure agony when he thought he would collapse because of the pain. Yet he forced himself to keep going. He would not indulge his body. It, too, must respond to the demands of his sovereign will. By the end of the war his constitution was half wrecked but his will power had grown to monumental proportions.

When Secretary Armstrong notified Jackson of his appointment in the regular army, he informed him that it was the President's wish that he proceed without delay to Fort Jackson and arrange the peace treaty with the Creek Nation.[53] Jackson was to be guided by the instructions previously given General Pinckney: that an indemnity in land equivalent to the government's expenses, a guaranteed right to open roads through the Creek country, the termination of intercourse with any Spanish post, garrison, or town, and the surrender of the Creek prophets who had fomented the war should be part of the treaty. Armstrong also suggested that the treaty might take a military form in the nature of a "capitulation."[54]

As everyone suspected Pinckney and Hawkins offered the Indians the easiest terms imaginable, all in accordance with their instructions from Washington. Land-hungry westerners were appalled by the terms and demanded better representation.[55] Once Jackson replaced Pinckney and Hawkins in response to the outcry and assumed the responsibility of concluding the peace agreement, no one doubted the outcome. For himself, Jackson was delighted with the assignment. He feared the long-range effects of leniency toward the Creeks. And with the presence of the Spanish in Florida and the recent arrival of the British along the coast to initiate attacks against the United States, the Indians would never submit to American domination. Already a large number of Red Sticks chiefs had taken refuge in Florida, where they felt the Americans would not pursue them. Jackson wrote to Armstrong that according to his information some 300 British had landed at the mouth of the Apalachicola River and were arming and inciting the Indians to acts of hostility against the United States. "Query—*If the Hostile creeks have taken refuge in East Florida,*" he wrote, *"fed and armed there by the Spaniards and British . . .* Will the government say to me . . . proceed to ----------* and reduce it. If so I promise the war in the south has a speedy termination and British influence forever cut off from the Indians in that quarter."[56]

Jackson had always been committed to the destruction of Spanish power in Florida. And now he argued that the solution of the Indian problem was contingent on the expulsion of all foreign influence from the area. He would gladly plunge across the Florida border and send the Dons swimming to Cuba, but he wanted official authorization. (The memory of Aaron Burr was still quite vivid.) It need not actually be spelled out in detail. Any pretext would suffice to set in motion the further territorial expansion of the American nation.

No reply from Washington. Not for months. Not until January 17, 1815—nearly ten days after the Battle of New Orleans—did Jackson receive a response to his "query." Yet the response was dated July 18, 1814, and no reason was given for the mailing delay.[57] As to Jackson's request, the letter hedged. "The case you put is a very strong one," it said, but "there is a disposition on the part of the Spanish government, not to break with the United States." If that is true, the administration must be extremely careful in deciding a course of action. However, if the Spanish "feed, arm and co-operate with the British and hostile Indians, we must strike on the broad principle of self-preservation:—under other and different circumstances, we must forbear."[58] Had Jackson received this letter in July instead of the following January he would have taken immediate action. His army would have slammed into Florida without another moment's delay.[59]

Jackson arrived at Fort Jackson on July 10, 1814, and promptly notified the Indian agent, Benjamin Hawkins, that he was calling a general meeting of the Creek chiefs—friendly and hostile—to meet with him at the fort on August 1. He wanted Hawkins to attend and to use his influence with the Indians that they might accept the invitation. And he made his mood perfectly clear. "Destruction will attend a failure to comply with those orders," Jackson told Hawkins.[60] He repeated this warning to General Coffee. "If they do not come in and submit, against the day appointed which is the first of next month, a sudden and well directed stroke may be made, that will at once reduce them to unconditional submission."[61]

His tone frightened. His intent seemed clear: the destruction of the Creek Nation. Sensitive to the land greed of westerners, and conditioned

*Jackson obviously meant Pensacola. See Reid and Eaton, *Jackson,* p. 196.

by environment and heritage to disregard Indian rights, Jackson prepared to strip the Creeks of their property. His logic was simple: Indians were savage and warlike because they possessed too much land to roam in and therefore pursued "wandering habits of life." If the range of their activities were sharply restricted, their errant habits would gradually subside "until at last, necessity would prompt them to industry and agriculture, as the only certain and lasting means of support."[62] And by being industrious like white men, Indians would eventually share the blessings of civilized life. Thus, for the Indians' own safety and welfare, it was necessary to seize their property and restrict their movement.[63]

It can easily be argued that this logic is a fraud, a ready justification for theft—and that is true. But it is also true that Jackson and westerners like him believed the argument. Later, in precisely the same way, they would justify the removal of the Indian beyond the Mississippi River. The argument was never simply invented to serve as a coverup. It was always there, a part of their creed, a doctrine of incontestable truth.

Commanded to appear before the imperious presence of their conqueror, the chiefs of the Red Sticks assembled at the fort on the appointed day. A larger number of friendly chiefs also appeared as instructed, although it was not yet clear to them why their presence was demanded—unless they were to be rewarded for their aid and loyalty. The Red Sticks would surely be punished for their treachery, but they— the friends of the Americans—expected gifts and praise. Yet when they arrived at the fort they saw the first indication that they would be treated no differently than the Red Sticks: All the chiefs, friendly and hostile, were ranged together at one side of a spacious canopy that had been erected for the occasion. On the other side stood Jackson, his aides, officers, and secretary, and the venerable Hawkins. And standing around watching the proceedings was a large concourse of Indians, both Creek and Cherokee, and a number of regimental troops.

Jackson opened this first peace session by faintly acknowledging the help of the friendly Creeks. That done, he turned to the Red Sticks and admonished them for listening to evil counsel. For their crime, he said, the entire Creek Nation must pay. He demanded the equivalent of all expenses incurred by the United States in prosecuting the war, which by his calculation came to 23 million acres of land. He wanted more than half the old Creek domain—roughly three-fifths of the present state of Alabama and one-fifth of Georgia![64] Jackson required all the territory lying south and west of a line to be drawn from the point where the Coosa River crossed the Cherokee boundary line, down the Coosa to the Big Falls (approximately seven miles north of Fort Jackson), and east to the Georgia boundary. He permitted the Creeks to keep their lands north and east of this line, an area of 150,000 square miles.[65] Thus the entire Creek Nation, even the Indians who had fought on Jackson's side, must pay this enormous indemnity.

The Indians were shaken by his words, but their faces betrayed no sign of outrage. The demand was clearly excessive, although Jackson maintained that he merely executed the government's instructions as he understood them. Actually he was less the government's agent than the agent of westerners, all of whom wished the treaty to both punish the Indian and reward the white man.

After allowing a moment or two to pass so that his words registered, Jackson proceeded to enumerate the other demands: the Creeks must cease all communication with the British and Spanish; they must acknowledge the right of the United States to open roads through Creek country and to establish military and trading posts wherever necessary; and they must surrender the instigators of the war.[66]

Despite the explanation given the Indians, the punishment of the Creeks was clearly Jackson's own idea, one he believed compatible with western (and particularly Tennessean) interests. All his later life the General was extremely sensitive about this punitive treaty. To his mind the Creeks had been conquered at considerable expense and loss of American lives; what other nation, he asked, would have treated the vanquished "savages" with such justice and leniency? Moreover, the treaty removed the threat of attack from the borders of Tennessee and Georgia and confined the Creeks to a manageable area where they could be watched and guarded and where they were separated geographically from the evil influence of the Indians and Spanish in Florida. For the protection of the citizens of the United States he had no choice. Finally, by the extent of the land cession, he had obtained a valuable highway from western Tennessee to the Gulf of Mexico. The natural and rightful expansion of the United States required the additional access to the sea.[67]

But Jackson wanted more than territory. He was out to destroy the Creek Nation once and for all. Consequently the entire Nation had to pay the indemnity, even those Creeks who had fought with him as allies. What he proposed by this masterful, yet cruel, political stroke was the virtual annihilation of a once powerful Indian tribe.

When the interpreters finished translating Jackson's words, the chiefs retired to a private council to discuss the monstrous terms imposed on them by the man they now called Sharp Knife or Pointed Arrow.[68] The following day they tried to convince Sharp Knife that his terms were harsh and unjust. Big Warrior, a friendly chief and the most eloquent, was the first to speak. He narrated the causes of the war, admitted that the American army had saved them from destruction, and agreed that an indemnity was just. But he also argued that Jackson's demands were premature because many members of the war party had fled to Florida and might return to continue the struggle. Moreover the indemnity was excessive and would reduce the entire Nation, not simply the Red Sticks, to penury. "The president, our father," the chief concluded, "advises us to honesty and fairness, and promises that justice shall be done: I hope and trust it will be! I made this war, which has proved so fatal to my country, that the treaty entered into, a long time ago, with father Washington, might not be broken. To his friendly arm I hold fast. I will never break that chain of friendship we made together, and which bound us to stand to the United States." Then he pointed at the Indian agent, Benjamin Hawkins. "There sits the agent he sent among us. Never has he broken the treaty. He has lived with us a long time. . . . By his direction, cloth was wove, and clothes were made, and spread through our country; but the red sticks came, and destroyed all—we have none now. Hard is our situation, and you ought to consider it."[69]

Next, Shelocta, another friendly chief, addressed Sharp Knife. Having fought alongside the Americans and won Jackson's confidence, he spoke freely and sincerely of his deep feeling for his white brothers and with what zeal he had tried to keep their friendship and maintain peaceful relations with them. He allowed that the lands lying to the south along the Alabama should be yielded as indemnity because that would sever communications with the Spanish in Florida, who were a potential threat to peace. But to demand the country west of the Coosa was something else. That was not punishment, that was annihilation. The lands were needed if the friendly Creeks were to survive. In a moving conclusion the chief appealed to Jackson's feelings, reminding him of the dangers they had shared and of his loyalty and support. With dignity, yet with genuine emotion, he pleaded with Jackson not to strip the Creeks of their homeland.[70]

He spoke to a stone wall. Loyalty was something Jackson profoundly admired, and without question Shelocta, Big Warrior, and most of the other chiefs assembled around him had been faithful not only to him but to their earlier pledges to keep the peace. But how could he destroy the Indian menace on the southern frontier, how could he strengthen the military might of the United States, unless the entire Nation paid the indemnity? Later, in an official biography, a ready excuse was manufactured to explain Jackson's repudiation of the friendly chiefs. The General, it was claimed, despised them for having entered "the ranks of an invading army" and by their efforts assisted in the destruction of their own people. In his eyes they were "as traitors to their country, and justly deserving the severest punishment."[71]

When Shelocta had concluded his talk, Jackson returned to the speaker's stand. He reminded the friendly chiefs that they had not always acted properly. Had they not allowed Tecumseh to visit their villages and raise the war cry? Had they not allowed him to incite young braves to raise the tomahawk against peaceful settlers?

But what could they do? they asked. What recourse did they have?

They should have seized him instantly, stormed Sharp Knife, and sent him bound as a prisoner to their father, the President. "Or," he cried, his voice rising to a crescendo, they should have "cut his throat."[72]

The words paralyzed the chiefs. They just stood there, awestruck.

Jackson continued. Since they did neither, they must bear the punishment. As for Shelocta's plea for the land west of the Coosa, that must be denied—for everyone's sake, Indian as well as white man. "You know," said Sharp Knife, "that the part you desire to retain is that through which the intruders and mischief-makers from the lakes reached you, and urged your nation to . . . acts of violence. . . . That path must be stopped. Until this is done, your nation cannot expect happiness, nor mine security. . . . This evening must determine whether or not you are disposed to become friendly. Your rejecting the treaty will show you to be the enemies of the United States—enemies even to yourself."[73]

It was a crushing response. But the Indians had one last card to play. Appealing to Jackson's sentiment and gratitude would obviously get them nowhere. They tried another tack. A letter written by General Pinckney to Hawkins several months earlier, and known to the chiefs, contained promises of indemnity to the friendly Indians for the losses they sustained in fighting the Red Sticks. Pinckney, a kindly old gentleman from Charleston, had been disposed to recognize the contribution of the friendly Creeks. "You may likewise inform them," he wrote Hawkins, "that the United States will not forget their fidelity, but, in the arrangements which may be made of the lands to be retained as indemnity, their claims will be respected; and such of their chiefs as have distinguished themselves, by their exertion and valor in the common cause, will also receive a remuneration in the ceded lands, and in such manner as the Government may direct."[74] In view of Pinckney's commitment, surely this indemnity should be taken into consideration in drawing up the terms of the treaty. What say Sharp Knife?

Jackson glowered. These promises, he retorted, were unauthorized; they were not contained in the letters sent to Pinckney by the American government and therefore could not be included in the treaty. This was true. He had been directed by Armstrong to follow the directions contained in the letter previously sent to Pinckney, and nothing in that letter said anything about indemnity for friendly Creeks.

The chiefs persisted. A commitment had been made by the commanding general, a commitment he expressly told Hawkins to pass on to the friendly Creeks. Would Sharp Knife repudiate that commitment? It was a powerful argument forcefully presented, and Jackson admitted he had "considerable deficulty in making the arrangement with them in consequence of [the] letter written by General Pinckney."[75]

At length Jackson agreed to send Pinckney's letter and Hawkins's reply to President Madison for his consideration—a decision that inevitably meant delay and protracted dispute.[76] Meanwhile he insisted that the Indians sign the treaty as he proposed it. "Here is the paper," he said; "take it, and show the president who are his friends. Consult, and this evening let me know who will sign it, and who will not. I do not wish, nor will I attempt, to force any of you;—act as you think proper."[77]

The chiefs withdrew to council. Unjust and harsh as Jackson's treaty was in crushing the power of the Creek Nation and divesting them of their lands, the alternative to submission was to renew the war. Sharp Knife's overwhelming military strength and their own weakness necessarily dictated their decision. As Jackson told the secretary of war, "The whole creek nation is in a most wretched State, and I must repeat, that they *must* be *fed* and *clothed* or necessity will compel them to embrace the proffered friendship of the British."[78]

On August 9, 1814, the Creek chiefs surrendered themselves to Jackson's vengeance.* But they were still cunning enough to attempt two ploys to lessen the sting of their humiliation. One was a claim that some of the land Jackson demanded really belonged to the Cherokees who had established a number of settlements along the Tennessee River. But Sharp Knife had no difficulty disposing of that fraud. The other was more subtle. In an attempt to save face by making it appear that they had not been coerced into accepting the treaty—and perhaps to embarrass Jackson by their generosity—they offered the General and Benjamin Hawkins a gift of three square miles each, and the interpreters, George Mayfield and Alexander Cornells, a gift of one square mile each. Hawkins, who advised the chiefs to accept the terms even though he himself disapproved of them, graciously accepted the land saying "I esteem it the more highly by the manner of bestowing it, as it resulted from the impulse of your own minds, and not from any intimation from the General or me."[79] The Iron General responded stiffly that he would accept the gift if the President approved but that he would sell it and use the proceeds for the benefit of needy Creek women and children.

The chiefs shook their heads. That was unacceptable. "They did not give to General Jackson the land to-day," they said, "to give it back to

*See map, page 396.

them in clothing and other things; they wanted him to live on it, and when he is gone his family may have it; and it may always be known what the nation gave it to him for."[80]

With these words the chiefs concluded their remarks. The treaty was placed before them and thirty-five chiefs, under protest, signed it. Only *one* of those who signed was a Red Stick. They then withdrew from the fort to carry the word of their disgrace and ruin to the other members of the tribe.

"I have just finished the business with the creeks," Jackson informed his wife the following day; "the convention was signed yesterday at 2 oclock P.M. and tomorrow at 12 I embark for Mobile. . . . Could you only see the misery and wretchedness of those creatures perishing from want of food and picking up the grains of corn scattered from the mouths of the horses and troden in the earth—I know your humanity would feel for them, notwithstanding all the causes you have to feel hatred and revenge against."[81]

But Jackson was talking about his friends. These were not hostiles. These were law-abiding Indians. What Jackson had done had the touch of genius. He had ended the war by signing a peace treaty with his allies! Most of the Red Stick chiefs by this time had fled to Florida and planned to continue their warfare. Thus Jackson converted the Creek civil war into an enormous land grab that insured the ultimate destruction of the entire Creek Nation.

Justification for the peculiar circumstances of the treaty presented no problem. Since the Creeks constituted a Nation—or so they claimed—the hostiles alone could not sign a separate peace. The entire Nation must capitulate.

Jackson never received the gift of land. President Madison turned the matter over to Congress in 1816, but the Senate failed to act and it was forgotten save for a slight derogatory notice of it when Jackson ran for the presidency in 1828. Hawkins accepted his land but never lived on it.

The Creek War and the resulting Treaty of Fort Jackson were the beginning of the end not only for the Creek Nation but for all Indians throughout the south and southwest. What Blount, Burr, and hundreds of others had failed to do, Andrew Jackson accomplished. Millions of acres of choice land had been ripped out of the Indian domain and placed under the auction hammer of the land speculator. And the Indians must remove to get out of harm's way—for their own good. So the pattern of land seizure and removal was established. Within twenty-five years the entire family of red men, Creeks, Cherokees, Chickasaws, Choctaws, and Seminoles, were swept from the south and either buried under the ground or banished to the remote western country beyond the Missis-sippi River. And from start to finish the man most responsible for this expansion of the American empire was Andrew Jackson.

In the long history of Indians in North America the Creek War was the turning point in their ultimate destruction. The certain, the inevitable, the irreversible turn toward obliterating tribes as sovereign entities within the United States now commenced. The Creek Nation was irreparably shattered. All other tribes would soon experience the same melancholy fate.

Exultant, Jackson hurried his treaty to Washington and sent copies as well to friends and officials in Tennessee. "I finished the convention with the Creeks," he told John Overton, his partner in land speculation, " . . . and [it] cedes to US 20 million acres of the cream of the Creek Country, opening a communication from Georgia to Mobile."[82] The General was enormously proud of his accomplishment. He had savaged the Indians to a degree that would enrapture westerners. The treaty, he believed, had been fashioned with justice and understanding for the needs of white men and red men alike. As it turned out, Jackson was right about one thing at least. The Indians learned only through punishment. The harsher the treatment, the less likely they were to cause trouble. Fear of swift and terrible retaliation insured Indian neutrality in the continuing war with Great Britain, for Jackson's treatment of the Creeks served as an example of what would happen to red men who sided with the British. As a consequence most of the Southern tribes, out of fear, kept to the American side for the remainder of the war.

Still, there was a danger which Jackson recognized. The Creeks were in desperate need and might be pushed beyond endurance. The best strategy in removing them as a danger was to make them wards of the federal government. "To clothe the whole number [of approximately 8200 Creeks] will cost a considerable sum," he told the administration, "but this sum would be very inferior to the Value of the territory ceded to the United States: in addition to which I may observe, that the cession . . . will in future effectively prevent their becoming our enemies." He added another word of advice: The boundary line must be run immediately and the land sold to settlers as quickly as possible. This, too, guaranteed Indian submission. Jackson proposed that Congress pass the necessary legislation to provide "to each able bodied man who will settle upon this land a section at two dollars per acre, payable in two years with interest—this measure would insure the security of this frontier, and make citizens of the soldiers who effected its conquest."[83]

So much for the Indian menace. But that of the British and Spanish remained. "Retaliation and vengeance" had characterized his treatment of the Creeks. The Europeans deserved no less. "I owe to Britain a debt of retaliatory vengeance," he told Rachel, perhaps thinking of his own experience during the American Revolution; "should our forces meet I trust I shall pay the debt—she is in conjunction with Spain arming the hostile Indians to butcher our women & children."[84] Jackson had no doubt of his ability to administer a severe military chastisement to both England and Spain. But a technicality existed. Although an armed attack against the British was quite in order in view of Congress's declaration of hostilities against that nation, the United States was not at war with Spain. Indeed the Madison administration had indicated, and would continue to indicate, a willingness to respond favorably to Spain's desire to maintain peaceful relations between the two countries.[85] Even so, Jackson felt no compunction about attacking the Spanish, operating on the broad principle later approved by the administration that if Spain cooperated with the British and the Indians, then the United States must take appropriate countermeasures.[86] So General Jackson took it upon himself to write to the Spanish governor of Pensacola, Don Matteo González Manrique, and instruct him in the terror he could expect if Jackson's complaints were not immediately and satisfactorily resolved.

It was a provocative and insulting letter. There were "refugee banditti from the creek nation" crowding into Florida, Jackson informed Manrique, and "drawing rations from your government and under the drill of a British officer." They should be arrested, confined, and tried for their crimes. "Such should be your Excellencys conduct toward Francis, McQueen Peter and others forming that matricidical band for whom your christian bowels seem to sympathise and bleed so freely." The United States had retaliated and would do so again if further provoked. Be warned, said General Jackson, of my creed: "An Eye for an Eye, Toothe for Toothe and Scalp for Scalp."[87]

Thus spake Sharp Knife to the Spanish governor of Florida.

CHAPTER 15

"I Act Without the Orders of the Government"

A REMARKABLE STRING OF GOOD FORTUNE trailed Jackson throughout the War of 1812, some of it earned, most of it entirely accidental. More often than not it was simply a matter of his being in the right place at the right time. His new command, which eventually led to a confrontation with the British at New Orleans, was a case in point. A number of generals had to be gotten rid of before Jackson could take over. First there was the notorious General Wilkinson, the darling of the administration. Since he was expected to perform nobly in battle he was sent north to win victories in Canada—and of course he failed spectacularly, as did all his successors. In his place to command the Seventh Military District went General Thomas Flournoy, and although General Pinckney was directed to command the Creek War, Flournoy's authority in the area had not been superseded. In fact Flournoy ordered the expedition of the Mississippi volunteers against the Creeks in southern Alabama. But the War Department's inept handling of the two commands offended Flournoy, and he finally resigned in the spring of 1814 and left New Orleans early in July. General Hampton might have replaced him, but he too resigned following an abortive effort to capture Montreal. Then Harrison resigned. Finally General Benjamin Howard of Kentucky was directed to succeed Flournoy, but he died before reaching his post. Now, with virtually no one left to compete with him, the assignment went to Jackson. Not that the administration wanted to block any longer his road to higher command. By the close of the Creek War President Madison recognized that he had a superior general in the south and planned to take every advantage of

234

his talent. Indeed the command of the Seventh District was a testament to Madison's newfound confidence.

Poor Madison needed a victory after so many defeats, if only to support his unshakable belief in the justice of his country's cause. His secretary of state, James Monroe, shared his creed—and its corollary, that justice always prevails. He was positive that the final terms of the peace treaty would be dictated by the United States; accordingly, he instructed the American ministers in Europe assigned to writing the treaty to demand from Great Britain all of Canada![1] Unfortunately, the northern frontier lacked an Andrew Jackson. And although the United States desperately hungered for Canada, the repeated invasion failures in the last two years turned that fierce desire into national shame.

Unbelievably, the shame worsened late in 1814. As Jackson headed south from Fort Jackson to smite the Spanish in Florida, the British prepared to launch a mighty assault in the Gulf to drive the Americans out of West Florida and Louisiana. The war in Europe was over, Napoleon had been captured, and the British were now free to concentrate their forces in America and deliver the final blow that would bring the United States to heel.

Already the offensive had begun. British troops under the command of Sir George Cockburn invaded the Chesapeake, marched on Washington, burned the President's mansion and the Capitol, and then shelled Baltimore. Another army plunged into New York from Quebec but failed to secure Lake Champlain and dared not advance until its rear could be protected. Meanwhile Vice Admiral Sir Alexander Cochrane, commander of the North American station, recommended to his government an expedition to invade the United States from the Gulf. Only a few thousand troops were necessary, he contended, for they would be joined by Indians and Spanish in routing the Americans and driving them back from the coast and up the Mississippi valley.[2] Control of the valley would produce a linkup with Canada that at the very least would reduce the United States to an island surrounded and contained by Great Britain in the north, west, and south.

In documenting his cause, Cochrane forwarded to the Admiralty a report he had received from Captain Hugh Pigot, who on May 10, 1814, anchored his ship *Orpheus* at the mouth of the Apalachicola River. Pigot had consulted with numerous Indian chiefs and reported that 2,800 Creek warriors were prepared to assist a British invasion of the Gulf. Impressed with Pigot's report, Cochrane dispatched Major Edward Nicholls of the Royal Marines to lead a party of more than 100 marines to Pensacola (thereby violating Spanish neutrality) to arm the Indians, to enlist Negroes who could be persuaded to flee their captivity, and then to recapture Mobile. Once Mobile was taken it would be relatively easy for a few thousand invading troops to cut across to the Mississippi River at some point north of Natchez, thereby isolating New Orleans and rendering its capture a simple landing operation.[3] Subsequently they could proceed straight north to Canada.

Cochrane's excellent plan persuaded the Admiralty.[4] In addition to Pigot's report he submitted a letter signed by several Creek chiefs confirming their readiness to assist a general invasion. The Admiralty formally approved Cochrane's plan and authorized the use of the troops from the Chesapeake area which would be supplemented by more than 2,000 additional men to be sent from Europe. These troops could be expected in Jamaica by mid-November 1814.[5]

While the British developed their plans for a massive invasion of the United States from the Gulf of Mexico, General Jackson hurriedly moved his army from Fort Jackson down the Coosa and Alabama rivers to Mobile, where he arrived on August 22. This splendid strategic move thwarted British intentions and forced an important alteration in their invasion plans. Cochrane originally intended to use the Mobile route to reach the Mississippi valley—clearly the most feasible plan for invasion because it involved linking up with the Indians and Spanish in the area before pushing on to the Mississippi. But when he learned that Jackson had occupied Mobile with a large army and that New Orleans was entirely unprotected—as indeed it was at the time he received his information—Cochrane decided to strike instead at New Orleans. That was his first big mistake.

Jackson traveled 400 miles through the wilderness in eleven days to reach Mobile. There his first action—an obvious and astute strategic move—was to send Major William Lawrence and 160 men to repair Fort Bowyer, which stood on a long sandspit commanding the entrance to Mobile Bay, approximately thirty miles from town. Working around the clock, Lawrence had the fort in an acceptable state of defense within two weeks. Equipped with 20 guns mostly of the nine- and twelve-pounder class plus two heavier guns, the fort occupied a strong position for guarding the town.

While these hurried preparations continued, Jackson dispatched scouts and spies to discover the place and nature of British landings on the coast. (His intelligence operation was quite advanced and extremely valuable.) Since Spain was supposedly neutral and its ports open to trade, Jackson sent Captain John Jones to Pensacola to study its defenses. Jones's notes later became one of Jackson's secret weapons.

The more Old Hickory learned of the activities of the British in Pensacola and their preparations for launching an invasion, the more he seethed at the failure of the administration to permit the invasion of Florida. "I can but regret," he told Secretary Armstrong, "that permission had not been given by the government to have seized on Pensacola, had this been done the american Eagle would now have soared above the fangs of the British Lyon."[6]

Instead of worrying about the right to invade Florida, Jackson should have been worrying about New Orleans. For the city was totally unprotected, its militia disaffected and reluctant to take the field. Jackson knew this; Governor Claiborne had described conditions in the city and warned him that New Orleans could be the principal point of a British attack.[7] The highest officer in charge of the city's military forces was a lieutenant colonel. All Jackson did was to order him by letter to put the city's fortifications in the best possible state of defense. In reply he was told that Forts St. Charles and St. John were badly in need of repair and that Fort St. Philip, which was 60 miles below the city, had 28 guns in good condition but that the barracks were old and decayed and could be set afire easily by enemy shells.[8]

It was, of course, essential to hold Mobile; it would provide the best route for a general invasion from the Gulf. But it was also essential to do something about New Orleans. Instead Jackson delayed at Mobile, appealing to various governors for militia, warning of an imminent invasion, and suggesting that 25,000 of Wellington's troops would be involved. Within a month the British and Spanish expect to take Mobile and the surrounding country, he said. "There will be bloody noses before this happens."[9]

Because of Jackson's threats, the Spanish governor, González Manrique, invited the British to land at Pensacola—a clear and palpable violation of Spanish neutrality.[10] He acted on his own, feeling compelled to respond to what he believed was the immediate danger of an American invasion.[11] However, when Major Nicholls arrived at Pensacola on August 14, he assumed complete control of the town and otherwise acted so highhandedly that some of the inhabitants actively engaged in spying for Jackson.[12] They detested the British.

Slowly, then, the pieces of the great invasion began coming together in accordance with the original plan: first the arrival at Pensacola; then the capture of Mobile; finally the attack by the major invasion force. But by the time Nicholls and his men finally sailed from Pensacola to invade Mobile, to begin the second phase of the operation, Old Hickory was prepared for battle and had infused his troops with a sense of dedication and a determination to repel the invaders.

On September 12 Admiral Sir William Percy reached Mobile Bay commanding four ships—the *Hermes*, *Carron*, *Sophie*, and *Childers*—with a total of 78 guns. This constituted more than triple the firepower of Fort Bowyer. The ships also carried Nicholls's marines and 130 Indians, all of whom were put ashore six miles east of the fort. But the American long guns kept Nicholls's force at a distance during the principal naval attack, which began on September 15. Thus the joint land and sea operation by the British—a fundamentally sound idea—got nowhere.

At four in the afternoon on September 15 the *Hermes* and *Sophie* sailed within range of the fort's guns, but because of the shallowness of the channel and a dying wind the other ships were unable to get into position. Then the firing began with a thundering cannonade. Broadside after broadside poured out of the ships, the fort returning the fire in quick bursts that improved in aim as the battle progressed. For an hour the battle continued with the fort and the ships enveloped in huge clouds of smoke. Then a lucky shot from the fort severed the *Hermes's* anchor cable, and the current pulled her toward shore and placed her under the American guns. The fort tattooed the ship with shot and shell. Although Percy managed to swing the ship around, he could not haul her from the range of the fort because her sails were shredded and her rigging shot away. She grounded. Quickly, Percy transferred his men to the other ships and at seven o'clock set the crippled ship ablaze. For hours the *Hermes* burned. Then at eleven o'clock she blew up with a deafening roar that was heard by Jackson thirty miles away in Mobile.[13] It signaled the end of the engagement. No further effort was made to capture the fort; the squadron sailed away and Nicholls and his men also returned to Pensacola. The *Hermes* lost 22 killed and 20 wounded, the *Sophie* 9 killed and 13 wounded, and the *Carron* 1 killed and 4 wounded. Major Lawrence lost only 4 killed and 5 wounded.[14]

During the engagement Jackson attempted to send reinforcements, but they could not get through. It was several days at least before he knew that his men had won a victory. And an important victory it was, too. For it nullified all Nicholls's plans for an expedition into the interior to win Indian allies to bolster the principal invasion. As a consequence Cochrane's plans had to be completely revised to eliminate any idea of capturing Mobile and the surrounding country. Had the British committed adequate forces to this battle, Fort Bowyer most likely would have fallen and with it Mobile. At least the defeat taught them some respect for American firepower.

The battle brought one clear advantage to the British: it immobilized Jackson. Now more than ever he was convinced that Mobile would be the principal point of attack. So he waited. Weeks went by. Nothing. He sent proclamations to the citizens and free Negroes of Louisiana asking them to resist the British, and he called for troops and heavier guns to defend

New Orleans.[15] Otherwise he sat and frittered away time when he should have been attending to the defense of the crescent city. Even if the main attack came at Mobile, he needed to do more to protect New Orleans and the lower Mississippi valley.[16]

On October 10 the new secretary of war, James Monroe (who also continued as secretary of state), informed Jackson that he had received intelligence from the American ministers in Ghent (who were working on a treaty to end the war) that a British expedition to take New Orleans had sailed from Ireland in September. The invasion must be repelled, said Monroe, and therefore he had ordered the governors of Tennessee, Georgia, and Kentucky to make 12,500 troops immediately available to him.[17]

Still Jackson sat. He had his eye fixed on the British in Florida, where he believed (correctly) their intelligence operation was centered. Florida! —that was where he wanted to go. Not only could he carry the offensive to the British and dismantle their spy system but he could also punish the Spanish for violating their neutrality. With any luck he might sweep all of them into the sea.

To his wife, Jackson breathed patriotic fire. He hoped she was reconciled to "our separation, the situation of our country require it for who could brook a British tyranny, who would not prefer dying free, strugling for our liberty and religion, than live a British slave."[18]

While Jackson was convincing himself that he must invade Florida, the administration in Washington, long aware of his intentions, decided to warn him off. On October 21 Monroe wrote Jackson that the President had directed that for the present he must take no measure which would involve the United States in a contest with Spain.[19] Having recently appointed a minister plenipotentiary to Spain, it would be indelicate for the administration to authorize an invasion of Florida; thus the instructions were written to provide a cover. However, Madison and Monroe probably hoped the instructions would fail to reach Jackson in time.

Simultaneously with the writing of these instructions, General Jackson finally made up his mind to invade Florida without waiting for specific authorization from Washington. He later had the "broad principle of self-preservation" as an excuse.[20] At the moment he believed he had private assurances that Madison would approve the Pensacola expedition.[21] Thus the long history of intrigue and conspiracy that colored American-Spanish relations in the southwest would now be climaxed by this Jacksonian stroke of conquest.

It is extraordinary how little it took for Jackson to convince himself and others that the invasion was proper and necessary. But he needed more troops if he were to risk such an attack. Happily, the always dependable General Coffee came to his aid by bringing more than 2,000 cavalry southward from West Tennessee, picking up several hundred more troops along the way. Learning of Coffee's approach and the size of his force, Jackson quit Mobile on October 25. When he rendezvoused with Coffee, his army swelled to over 4,000 men (including 1,000 regulars) plus some Indian allies.

Jackson had not yet received Monroe's instructions. Now that the decision to invade Florida was settled, he decided to inform the new secretary of war of the reasons for his action. Writing from Pierce's Stockade (or Mills) on the Alabama River, where he had joined Coffee, Jackson explained to Monroe that he could safeguard the Gulf region only by driving the British and their Indian allies out of Pensacola and then capturing Fort Carlos de Barrancas, which was situated below Pensacola on the west side of the bay. "This will put an end to the Indian war in the south," he said, "as it will cut off all foreign influence." Jackson frankly admitted he had no specific official authorization for his contemplated action, but he repeated again and again the reasons for his decision, as though mere repetition might somehow legitimize his action and provide the authorization he needed.

> As I act without the orders of the government, I deem it important to state to you my reasons for the measure I am about to adopt. First I conceive the safety of this section of the union depends upon it, The Hostility of the Governor of Pensacola in permitting the place to assume the character of a British Territory by resigning the command of the Fortresses to them, Permitting them to fit out an expedition against the U.S. and after its failure to return to the Town refit, and make arrangements for a second expedition. At the same time making to me a declaration that he (the Governor) had armed the Indians and sent them into our Territory. Knowing at the same time that these very Indians had under the command of a British officer captured our citizens and destroyed their property within our own Territory. I feel a confidence that I shall stand Justified to my government for having undertaken the expedition. Should I not I shall have the consolation of having done the only thing in my own opinion which would give security to the country by putting down a savage war, And what to me will be an ample reward for the loss of my commission.[22]

Jackson clearly understood what the penalty might be should he proceed. Yet he had not the slightest hesitation of going ahead. He knew his invasion plan was strategically sound; he knew southerners and westerners supported all military actions against the hated Dons; and he knew he had reliable information from Washington that he could expect administration support for any offensive he initiated against the Spanish.[23]

Of course Jackson did not acknowledge that the Pensacola situation was one he himself had generated, that his threats had caused González Manrique to invite British protection.[24] Now Jackson was using what he had himself provoked as an excuse to launch an invasion. Burr would have been proud.

Monroe never responded to the letter. What could he say? The administration was forced to play along and see what would happen. Florida, like Canada, had long been an object of American expansion. Madison had been after it since the beginning of the war, had authorized the seizure of West Florida (claiming it as part of the Louisiana Purchase) and had been stopped from going ahead with East Florida by the reluctance of Congress. Now he had a general willing and anxious to implement his own and the nation's ambition. But between Jackson's first request for approval of his invasion, for which he eventually received a hedging reply, and his second request, the administration had been forced to back away from overt aggression in view of the recent appointment of a new minister to Spain. But that hardly changed the desire or need for Florida—not by Madison, Monroe or Americans along the southern frontier.

Madison and Monroe always knew the kind of general they were dealing with when it came to the Spanish presence in Florida. Jackson was their best hope that the conspiracy so long in being would finally culminate in the acquisition of all Spanish territory east of the Mississippi River. They probably counted on it.

On the afternoon of November 6, 1814, Jackson reached the defenses of Pensacola. Pensacola was hardly more than a village dominated by two small forts, St. Rose and St. Michael; its real strength lay in Fort Barrancas, which guarded the entrance to the bay. Under a flag of truce the General sent his demands to Governor González Manrique. "I have come not as the enemy of Spain," declared Jackson, "but I come with a force sufficient to prevent the repetition of those acts so injurious to the U.S. and so inconsistent with the neutral character of Spain." Then he cracked out his demand: possession of Barrancas along with its fortifications and munitions "until Spain can preserve unimpaired her neutral character." He ended his letter with a threat. If my demands are rejected, he said, "I will not hold myself responsible for the conduct of my enraged soldiers and the Indian warriors."[25]

The governor never received the letter. The flag of truce was fired on, probably by the British, as it neared the town. "Turn out the troops," was Jackson's sole comment when he heard what had happened.[26] And before daylight on November 7 his men were armed and in motion.[27] The assault force consisted of four columns, three of Americans and one of Choctaw Indians; it caught the Spanish completely by surprise.

Jackson sent one column of 500 mounted men to make a noisy attack on the west side of the town while he led the main force from the east side. After a sharp exchange of fire (two cannons made and manned by the British were used in the defense) the Americans poured into the town and through its streets, driving Spanish soldiers from houses and gardens. Jackson expected the British ships anchored in the harbor to open fire on him, "but they remained silent from a dread of our Artillery." In fact their guns were posted to repel an attack on the usual western approach to Pensacola and the battle proceeded too swiftly for the fleet to change its position.[28] Indeed the assault was so swift that resistance collapsed within minutes. "There never was more universal and deliberate bravery displayed, by any set of troops," Jackson said, "than by those I had the honor to command and stormed Penscola with on the 7th instant."[29]

Appalled at the speed with which Pensacola was occupied, Governor González Manrique tottered forward with a white flag and surrendered the town and its fortifications. A delay in the actual surrender of Forts St. Rose and St. Michael had Jackson fuming again over "Spanish treachery" —particularly after he realized he must take Fort Barrancas by storm because it was held by the British.[30] The following morning, just as he was preparing the assault, "a tremendous explosion" rocked the earth and a column of smoke rose over Barrancas. Colonel Nicholls, the British garrision, and hundreds of Indian allies retreated to their ships and sailed off leaving Jackson with the wreckage of the fort. At least, Jackson said, "I had the Satisfaction to see the whole British force leave the port and their friends at our Mercy."[31]

American casualties in the engagement were 7 dead and 11 wounded. The Spanish suffered 14 killed and 6 wounded. No document records British and Indian losses, but it can be presumed that they too were light.[32]

Although the destruction of Fort Barrancas disappointed Jackson, who relished the idea of taking British prisoners, it was probably another lucky break for him. There was no temptation to hold the fort or to remain in Pensacola. In fact he dismissed thoughts of garrisoning the town since it was defenseless against future British attack. Thus, for strategic reasons, Jackson decided to give the whole thing back to González Manrique and return to the United States. His mission was a total success. He told James Monroe that he believed he had "broken up the hot bed of the Indian war" and convinced the Spaniards that the United States would no longer tolerate violations of their neutrality that jeopardized American safety.[33] He also felt he had seriously disrupted the British plan of operations against the southern section of the nation.[34]

The invasion of Florida and the capture of Pensacola was a stategically sound move. His action sealed off potential avenues of invasion, avenues that made more military sense than a frontal assault up the Mississippi River to New Orleans. A dash from Mobile or somewhere in East Florida, across Louisiana to a point above the crescent city, was so obvious a move that even Jackson with his limited knowledge of warfare could apprehend it. Such a dash, if successful, would cut off New Orleans from supplies—particularly with a British fleet patrolling the Gulf; the city would be defenseless and easily captured. Then it was a simple matter to drive north to Canada.

Thus, by securing his eastern position, Jackson added immeasurably to the security of the country. True, he was forcing an invasion of the country through New Orleans, but that was the worst possible site for a military action of this kind with its bayous, streams, creeks, and soggy ground—all treacherous to the movement of heavy invasion equipment and large armies. The pieces of his grand strategy fitted together right from the beginning—and maybe in some extraordinary way only Jackson understood it. Had he not conquered the Creeks, Mobile could not have been held; and if Pensacola had not been taken, the British would have used it as an invasion route into the United States and then across to the Mississippi. The invasion would have been infinitely simplified.

There were other advantages. The British, dismayed by the ineptitude and indecision of the Spanish in defending Pensacola, no longer planned their strategy with Spanish cooperation in mind. The Spanish, horrified by the behavior of the British who kidnapped almost all the slaves in Pensacola and "liberated" other property, wanted nothing more to do with the British. And Jackson's invasion terminated once and for all any desire by the Indians to aid the British. Henceforth the British would have to rely solely on themselves for the conquest of the United States. No Spanish. No Indians.

The glorious penetration of Spanish territory enraptured the west. Its profound impact on the Indians was applauded, and Jackson's status as hero escalated. The invasion of Florida also vastly improved his own talents in handling the army. The speed with which he could now maneuver his men was truly extraordinary. The victories necessarily improved morale among the troops, strengthening their confidence in themselves and their commander.[35] They also stiffened resistance in New Orleans, where the governor had previously reported a deep lassitude on the part of the inhabitants with respect to defending their city.[36]

With a small flourish—he could never resist a dramatic display—

Jackson returned his conquest to González Manrique. The "enemy having disappeared and the hostile creeks fled to the Forest, I retire from your Town, and leave you again at liberty to occupy your Fort."[37] The governor, who had witnessed the abysmal performance of his British allies, replied to Jackson in extremely friendly terms, asking "God to preserve your life many years."[38] With that Old Hickory headed back to Mobile.

On his return Jackson learned that Colonel Nicholls had established a fort on the Apalachicola River which separated East from West Florida. The fort was intended as a staging area for raids on the frontier settlements of Georgia as well as a point of attack on Fort Jackson to cut off American supplies from the Alabama area. Jackson sent Major Uriah Blue of the Thirty-ninth Regiment and approximately 1,000 men to harass the Indians in the area, destroy their crops, and insure their loyalty. This was one of his many spoiling operations intended to obstruct British activity. Meanwhile he strengthened Fort Bowyer, increased the troop allotment in Mobile, and turned the whole over to Brigadier General James Winchester before setting out at long last for New Orleans.

In mid-November 1814, while in Pensacola, Jackson received definite information from his intelligence (which had picked up a leak in Jamaica) that the British were about to launch a full-scale assault on New Orleans. Still worried that Mobile was the real invasion site, he heavily defended the town—probably employing many more troops than necessary—before turning toward New Orleans. He cautioned Winchester to keep Mobile secure, repeating his belief that the original British plan called for an invasion in that area followed by the ascent of the Mobile and Alabama rivers. The British, he said, would rouse the Indians, slice across the Mississippi Territory, produce insurrection among the slaves, cut off supplies from the upper country, and consequently compel the lower country and New Orleans to surrender. Should the British attempt a landing at Pensacola, he continued, Winchester must make every effort to cut their lines of supply and communication before they penetrated very far into the country. Jackson gave his subordinate wide discretion in posting troops "in the best positions to give security to the country committed to your care."[39]

At the same time that he strengthened his eastern flank, Jackson sent General Coffee with 2,000 men of his brigade to cover New Orleans by riding to Baton Rouge and there meeting the newly mustered militia said to be on their way from Tennessee and Kentucky. From this point Coffee could be easily summoned either to New Orleans or to Mobile, depending on the focus of the British invasion. In fact it is surprising that Jackson himself did not take up this position, given his conviction that the invasion would come through Mobile.

While Coffee rode to Baton Rouge, Jackson's inspector general, Colonel Arthur P. Hayne, was sent to the mouth of the Mississippi to discover sites on which batteries might be erected that would command the river and prevent the British from crossing the bar. After completing these arrangements, Jackson with 2,000 troops finally set out for New Orleans himself on November 22, 1814, allowing himself twelve days to reach his destination in order to view at first hand all those places at which the British might attempt a landing.[40]

He also summoned Rachel to New Orleans. He told her to bring beds, bedsteads, tables, carriage, servants, Andrew Jr., and a nurse—not Lyncoya, however. He needed her desperately; he was close to total physical collapse. Before leaving Pensacola "I was taken verry ill," he said, "the Doctor gave me a dose of Jallap & calemel, which salavated me, and there was Eight days on the march that I never broke bread. My health is restored but I am still verry weak."[41]

Debilitated, but nonetheless determined to throw back the invasion, Jackson struggled to his horse and headed west to New Orleans.

CHAPTER 16

"We May...Have a Fandango"

NEW ORLEANS IS A DREAMY, SLEEPY CITY that comes awake periodically with great bursts of raucous noise and joyful shouts. It lies slightly more than one hundred miles from the mouth of the winding Mississippi and curves along the eastern bank of the river in an area of swamps and bayous and great trees festooned with Spanish moss. Because the river is broad and almost unfordable the city is virtually invulnerable to attack from the west. Consequently invasion must come from the south or the east. An attack up the long river was difficult but possible, although the route was protected by Fort St. Philip, a military post sixty-five miles downstream that was garrisoned by regular troops manning twenty-eight 24-pounders. Further up the river, approximately twenty-five miles below New Orleans, Fort St. Leon was situated at a sharp looping bend in the river, known as the English Turn. Sailing vessels were obliged to stop here to wait for a change in wind direction in order to navigate the bend. Invading ships that stopped at the bend were sitting ducks; the guns of the fort could easily pick them off.

Clearly invasion from the south would be extremely difficult. That left two eastern approaches: the land route through Mobile (which Jackson always feared because it made more sense than any other) and the water route from the Gulf into Lake Borgne and Lake Pontchartrain. The lakes were connected by a narrow, shallow strait called the Rigolets, situated only a few miles to the north and east of New Orleans. Bayou St. John flows out of Pontchartrain and comes within two miles of the city limits, but Fort St. John—a small brick fort in a rather bad state of repair

246

—guarded the entrance to the bayou. The land between the lakes and the city was generally swampy, flat, dotted with bayous, and virtually road-less. Sweeping northeastward from the city, however, was a narrow ridge of dry land called the Plains of Gentilly; a road, Chef Menteur, followed this ground and connected the Rigolets with the city. Most citizens of New Orleans believed the invasion would come along this route, but they also believed it could be defended easily because of the extensive swamps on either side of the plains. If an invading force decided against the Chef Menteur, it could attempt to follow any one of seemingly hundreds of bayous that fingered their way between the east bank of the Mississippi and Lake Borgne.[1]

At about the time Jackson began to give serious thought to the problems involved in defending New Orleans he received a frantic letter from Secretary Monroe. The administration had received intelligence from Cuba that a large invasion force under Admiral Cochrane had departed for New Orleans. Monroe hoped Jackson had already taken up a suitable position of defense. New Orleans was where he must be. "Mobile is comparatively a trifling object with the British government," he continued. "Your presence at such a point, on the river, with the main body of your troops will be of vital importance." Then, in a quieter tone, Monroe sought to rouse his commander to great feats of arms. "All the boasted preparation, which the British government has been making thro' the year, with veteran troops from France and Spain, after having been gloriously foiled, in attacks on other parts of our Union, is about to terminate in a final blow against New Orleans. It will, I hope, close there its inglorious career, in such a repulse as will reflect new honor on the American arms."[2]

Monroe was indeed correct. On November 27–28 an armada of sixty British ships—frigates, sloops, gunboats, and various other transports—carrying 14,000 troops put out to sea commanded by Admiral Cochrane aboard his flagship *Tonnant,* with Major General John Keane in tempo-rary command of the troops. It was a grand display of military and naval might. Indeed it was practically a colonizing expedition, so fully equipped was the fleet. The ships abounded with lighthearted merriment, music, dancing, and dramatic entertainment, thanks to the efforts of the officers' wives who accompanied the expedition. They even carried printing presses for a newspaper. Cochrane still had the choice of landing at Mobile or striking directly for New Orleans. He chose New Orleans not only because of its apparent weakness but the money to be found in the city.[3]

When Jackson rode into New Orleans early in the morning of December 1, he was beginning to show the effects of many long months of

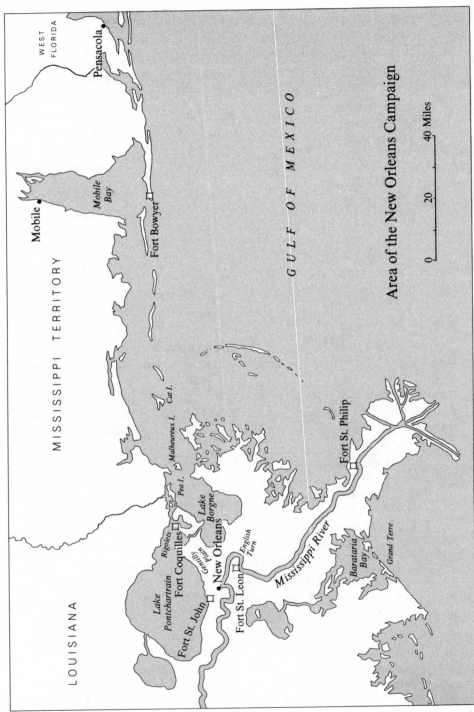

Area of the New Orleans Campaign

campaigning and his most recent illness.[4] His frame was long and gaunt, indeed emaciated like someone who had been suffering a protracted and painful sickness. His complexion was sallow and unhealthy but his carriage was very erect and the strength—if not the fierceness—of his countenance bespoke a spirit that willed mastery over his damaged body. Steely determination lay coiled within that emaciated shell. He was forty-seven years of age, his hair iron grey; in his manner he radiated confidence, stern decision, and enormous energy. One observer described him at the time as "erect, composed, perfectly self possessed, with martial bearing. . . . One whom nature had stamped a gentleman."[5]

With Jackson rode Robert Butler, his adjutant general; John Reid, his aide; and Major Howell Tatum, his chief topographical engineer. The party was greeted by the governor of Louisiana, W. C. C. Claiborne, who after ten years still had not mastered the language of the Creoles. His tenure was also troubled by a running quarrel with the legislature, fears of a slave revolt, and the charged emotions of the city generated by the imminent invasion. With Claiborne was Commodore Daniel T. Patterson, the commandant of the naval district, a stout, compact man who showed the signs of gracious living in New Orleans. Also present was the mayor, Nicholas Girod, a pleasant old French gentleman, and Edward Livingston, formerly of New York City, who served with Jackson in the Congress back in 1796 and was now the sharpest legal talent in New Orleans. Tall, ungainly, and rather homely, Livingston quickly renewed his friendship with Jackson and won the General's admiration for his intelligence and good judgment and soon became Jackson's secretary, translator, and confidential adviser. He also found himself forced into the role of mediator between the haughty commander and the equally haughty citizens of New Orleans.[6]

After a short welcoming address by the governor before a large crowd, Jackson responded in typical fashion. He had come to save the city and its inhabitants, he said, and he would drive the enemy into the sea or die in the attempt. He called on the people to unite with him in the effort, to put aside their feuding and bring honor rather than disgrace to their city.

As Livingston translated Old Hickory's remarks into French the people began to stir with excitement. They caught the fervor of his words and responded enthusiastically; they were impressed by the heroic stance of his commanding presence; they felt new confidence that this man would indeed save the city despite the internal turmoil and external danger. A sigh of gratification seemed to pour out of the crowd and wrap Jackson in a brief embrace.[7]

The ceremony finished, a cavalcade formed; Old Hickory entered a carriage and rode to 106 Royal Street, where in one of the few brick buildings in the city he established his headquarters.[8]

Livingston, who as chairman of the committee of public safety had been in correspondence with the General for several months, was named aide-de-camp, and when the reception ended he invited Jackson to his home for dinner. Livingston's wife, a beautiful Creole lady and something of a leader of New Orleans society, was a trifle distressed when she learned of the imminent arrival of her husband's guest. At the time she was giving a dinner party for a small group of young ladies. "What shall we do with this wild General from Tennessee?" they whispered among themselves. Then, as they fluttered with apprehension, he entered the room. Dressed in a uniform of coarse blue cloth and yellow buckskin, his high dragoon boots badly in need of polishing, he nonetheless appeared "the very picture of a war-worn noble warrior and commander."

Jackson bowed to the ladies seated around the room. It was done gracefully despite the awkward need to acknowledge those sitting in distant corners and in widely separated groups. He turned to Mrs. Livingston, escorted her back to her sofa, and sat conversing with her for several minutes. The ladies were astonished at his poise and gratified by his grand manner. At dinner the General continued his conversation in a free and relaxed style, discussing the invasion, assuring the ladies he would save the city, and urging them not to trouble their pretty heads about the matter. In the presence of lovely ladies, Jackson the Fierce suddenly became Jackson the Gallant. When the General finally rose from the table and left the house with Mr. Livingston, the ladies descended on their hostess. "Is *this* your back woods-man? Why, madam, he is a prince."[9]

Once back at headquarters, the General began preparations for the defense of the city.[10] Although New Orleans was eminently defensible because of its location amid swamps, bayous, and a wide, twisting river, it was correspondingly difficult to plan a defense ahead of time because of the many possible invasion routes into the city. Like most citizens of the city, Jackson mistakenly came to believe that the Chef Menteur road was the likeliest possibility. But he wanted to keep his troops mobile until he knew the exact location of the invasion; if anything typified Jackson's generalship, it was his ability to maintain a high degree of mobility of his army, and in this situation he knew he must move his troops quickly, within a limited time, in order to concentrate his forces at the precise point of the British invasion.

Another task requiring immediate attention was the blocking of the many bayous that served as highways to the outskirts of the city. He also appreciated the need to strengthen the forts along the river, although a quick inspection of the lower Mississippi convinced him that the British would not attempt to ascend the river and run the forts.

Jackson carefully studied the maps provided him by Major A. Lacarrière Latour, the chief engineer for the New Orleans district. Seeing the many bayous and coulées, or creeks, that connected Lakes Borgne and Pontchartrain with the Mississippi, the General directed Governor Claiborne to close all water routes leading into the city, a task Claiborne assigned to the chief of his militia, General Jacques Villeré.[11] In addition Jackson ordered a guard posted at the mouth of every bayou to give warning if the enemy approached. Unfortunately, Jackson's excellent scheme for blocking these passages was negated by his failure to inspect the completed task or to delegate a responsible official to do so. Next, Jackson ordered additional batteries erected at Fort St. Philip. After inspecting the site firsthand and examining diagrams provided by Major Latour, he suggested specific alterations in the fort to improve its capability to defend the river. Earlier, at Patterson's direction, a fleet of five gunboats consisting of twenty-three guns and 182 men under the command of Lieutenant Thomas Ap Catesby Jones was stationed on Lake Borgne. Lieutenant Jones was ordered to retire if attacked and to try to lead the British ships into the Rigolets in front of Fort Petites Coquilles.

The defensive force within New Orleans numbered—on paper— only 700 men, many of whom were absent from duty. To complicate matters there were justified fears of the loyalty of the French and Spanish inhabitants. Worse, the troublesome legislature seemed more intent on creating internal dissension in order to embarrass the governor than on aiding the city.

Another problem was the pirates who operated out of Barataria Bay, a large body of water some seventy miles southwest of New Orleans that provided a series of water routes to the great river at a point opposite the city. The chief of the pirates was Jean Lafitte, who with his brothers Pierre and Dominique and a corps of freebooters lived on the island of Grand Terre in Barataria Bay, where they had built houses, erected rude fortifications with heavy guns, and engaged in the lucrative if unlawful practice of privateering and smuggling, much of it at the expense of the Spanish in Mexico and Florida. With the help of the merchants and prominent citizens of New Orleans, who traded in the stolen merchandise, the pirates flourished and grew rich. Even the renowned Livingston served as legal adviser to the Lafittes. In fact the Lafitte brothers were frequently seen parading "arm in arm with Livingston's brother-in-law, Davezac" along the streets of New Orleans, bold as you please.[12]

The situation was so scandalous that the governor of Florida, in his many exchanges with Jackson, reproached him and the United States for allowing the piracy to continue.[13] The unlawful activities unquestionably violated the neutrality obligations of the United States; thus, when Jackson tried to lecture the Spanish on their responsibilities with respect to the Indians and the British, they promptly responded by pointing to the pirates. The charge of hypocrisy nettled Jackson because it was true. And he sounded off to Governor Claiborne. "Permit me to express my extreme regret and astonishment," he wrote the previous September, "that those wretches, the refugees from Barataria and its dependencies, should find an asylum in your city; that they should even be permitted to remain in it, without being strictly scrutinized under your existing vagrant laws."[14] More often than not Jackson called the pirates "hellish banditti."[15]

For his part, Lafitte was a shrewd operator. Fluent in English, French, Spanish, and Italian and an energetic and efficient businessman, he calculated his advantages before committing himself or undertaking a financial venture. Formerly a New Orleans blacksmith with a forge at the corner of Bourbon and St. Philip streets, Haitian born, a man of great courage, adventurous, totally unnautical but highly successful as a practicing pirate, he demonstrated the cunning qualities of a born robber baron.[16]

Early in September the sloop *Sophie,* commanded by Captain Nicholas Lockyer, appeared at Barataria with letters from Colonel Nicholls that invited the pirates to support the British. In return for their ships and supplies, along with a promise not to prey on Spanish or British shipping, the pirates were offered land according to rank and a guarantee that their property and persons would be protected.[17] The cagey Lafitte asked for two weeks' time to think it over, realizing that the offer and the letters could be turned to advantage with the Americans. Aware that his brand of racketeering had a limited future and determined to make the best deal possible, Lafitte sent Lockyer's letters to Governor Claiborne with a note offering his services in the defense of Louisiana in return for a general amnesty for himself and his followers.[18]

Claiborne received the extraordinary propostion while planning an invasion of Barataria. He already had Pierre, one of Lafitte's brothers, in jail, and he hoped to imprison the rest of the pirate crew. Thus Claiborne's military advisers saw the proposition as a plot by Lafitte to spring Pierre from prison and abort the contemplated attack on his stronghold. They believed Lafitte had learned of the governor's plans through his many friends in New Orleans. Since this conceit sounded typical of Lafitte, the governor hastened the expedition against the pirates. As a precaution he also sent copies of the letters to Jackson.

On September 13 the American expedition under Patterson sailed for Barataria. It reached Grand Terre three days later. Lafitte and most of his men managed to slip away aboard his best ships, but Patterson captured nine vessels, about 80 pirates, and a hoard of valuable merchandise valued at half a million dollars. Then he destroyed the pirates' lair. Despite this ungracious act Lafitte still preferred the Americans over the British because of his many friends in Louisiana and because so many of his followers were born in the United States. In the long run he figured he had more to gain by fighting alongside the Americans.[19]

When Jackson reached New Orleans in December he found strong sentiment in favor of accepting assistance from the pirates, many of whom were now operating out of Cat Island near the mouth of Bayou La Fourche. Livingston was a powerful advocate; a legislative committee headed by Bernard Marigny urged acceptance;[20] and in December the Louisiana legislature passed a series of resolutions asking Jackson to use his good offices to procure amnesty for the pirates if they agreed to lend their aid in fighting the British.[21] A group of distinguished citizens added their petition to the others and reminded Jackson of the talents of the cutthroats as gunners and marksmen. As a final strategic move, the citizens consulted Judge Dominick A. Hall of the United States District Court —since the offenses of the pirates violated federal law more than anything else. The judge agreed to release those pirates from jail who promised to enlist in the defense of the city, and he granted a safe conduct to Lafitte so he could come to New Orleans and plead his case with General Jackson.

There is no account of the subsequent interview, only the brief statement of Major Latour that Lafitte simply asked the honor "of proving that if they had infringed the revenue laws, yet none were more ready than they to defend the country and combat its enemies."[22] Undoubtedly Lafitte's aggressiveness, his enthusiasm for fighting, and his bravery—so reminiscent of William Weatherford—impressed Jackson. The General appreciated the help the pirates could provide in the defense of the city: powder, shot, flints, a thousand men, and incomparable marksmanship. The offer was irresistible. Jackson accepted it and ordered Lafitte to assist in the defenses between Barataria and the city.[23] The pirates later proved very useful in manning two batteries below New Orleans during the British invasion and in serving with one of the companies of marines. The charges against them were later dropped in recognition of their contribution and their loyalty.[24]

Jackson also accepted the aid of free blacks in the city. The suggestion was initially forwarded to him by Governor Claiborne, who received in reply an enthusiastic response. "Our country," Jackson wrote, "has been invaded and threatened with destruction. She wants Soldiers to fight her battles. The free men of colour in your city are inured to the

Southern climate and would make excellent Soldiers. They will not remain quiet spectators of the interesting contest. They must be for, or against us—distrust them, and you make them your enemies, place confidence in them, and you engage them by every dear and honorable tie to the interest of the country who extends to them equal rights and priviledges with white men."[25] Jackson directed that they be officered by white men (noncommissioned officers might be blacks) and treated identically with other volunteers. He placed Pierre Lacoste in command of the black battalion. Later, when a second battalion of refugee Santo Domingo blacks was formed, he assigned Major Jean Daquin to command it. The General also published a proclamation to the freemen that promised them the regular bounty (160 acres of land and $124) if they served, along with the regular pay, rations, and clothing furnished to every American soldier.[26]

Many Louisianians were not happy with Jackson's decision, fearing a bloody revolt if guns were placed in the hands of "men of colour." When the assistant district paymaster questioned the General's authority to enlist blacks into the service, Old Hickory blasted him. "Be pleased to keep to yourself your opinions upon the policy of making payments of the troops with the necessary muster rolls without inquiring whether the troops are white, black or tea."[27]

One of the first things Jackson did in New Orleans was to review the two black battalions, demonstrating to the citizens his regard for the units. He also reviewed the city militia, which was composed of the young men from the best New Orleans families and commanded by Major Jean Plauché, just to show how democratic he was. But he really wanted his Tennesseans. They were his favorites. At the moment these troops waited in Baton Rouge while General Billy Carroll slowly descended the Mississippi with an additional 2,000 men from West Tennessee. Jackson hoped they would all be reunited in the near future; he told Coffee to hold his brigade "in compleat readiness to march at a moments warning. We may, or may not have a fandango with Lord Hill* in the christmas holidays. If so you and your Brave followers must participate, in the frolic. I hope the west Tennessee militia and the Kentuckians will reach here in due time to participate."[28]

---

*Lieutenant General Lord Rowland Hill, Wellington's second in command, was originally expected to lead the British invasion of Louisiana.

CHAPTER 17

The Invasion Begins

NEARLY TWO WEEKS AFTER JACKSON arrived in New Orleans—on December 13, 1814, to be exact—the British armada was sighted off Cat Island at the entrance to Lake Borgne. As the British advanced westward into the lake, soundings warned against further penetration by the deep-draft vessels. But before landing troops it was imperative to clear the lake of the small force of American gunboats commanded by Lieutenant Jones that hovered ahead of them, trying to coax them toward the Rigolets.

Admiral Cochrane ordered an expedition of barges commanded by Captain Lockyer to pursue the American vessels. There were 45 boats in this expedition; they carried 42 cannons and were manned by 1,000 sailors and marines picked from the crews of the other ships. With the barges aimed toward him, Jones and his gunboats tried to retreat to the straits as Patterson had ordered, but during the night the gunboats were becalmed and the strong current at the western end of the lake drew them toward Malheureux Island (a prophetic name), where several of them got stuck in the mud.[1]

On the morning of December 14, after resting from their severe rowing and after breakfasting, the British bore down on Jones's squadron, forming a line abreast extending nearly from the mainland to Malheureux Island. It was quite a sight: An unbroken front of barges, six oars on each side dipping into the water with metronomic regularity, the red shirts of the sailors, the shining muskets of the marines, and the stubby noses of the short-range cannons protruding over the bows—a picture of supreme naval power about to blow five American gunboats right out of the water. Cornered and unable to maneuver, the Americans put up a barrage of gunfire but were clearly outnumbered and outgunned. The enemy soon clambered up the sides of the flagship, captured her, and turned her guns on the other ships. Shortly after noon all the American gunboats had been captured. Both Jones and Lockyer were badly wounded; on the American side 6 were killed, 35 wounded, and 86 captured; on the British, 19 were killed and 75 wounded.[2] The lake was now free of any American force.

The British victory was an American disaster. It extinguished Jackson's watch on the lakes and prepared the way for the invasion of the mainland.[3] Yet it did have one salutary aspect. The American sailors taken prisoner all swore that Jackson's army in New Orleans numbered four times its actual size.[4] That gave the British pause. Consequently Cochrane decided, as a preliminary and precautionary action, to move all troops to Pea Island, just to the east of the Rigolets, at the mouth of the Pearl River as it flows into Lake Borgne. Once the soldiers were safely transferred to the island they could be moved to the mainland. So, because of the shallow water, a gigantic ferrying operation began. Day after day the barges rowed back and forth, from the anchorage at the western end of the lake to the island.[5] It was a tedious, difficult, and time-consuming operation, the sailors pulling against wind and tide to carry thousands of soldiers to the island. To make matters worse the weather grew cold and unpleasant; sudden rains lashed the invaders and stiff winds hampered their progress. The British found Pea Island an insect- and reptile-ridden sandspit, as inhospitable a stretch of bleakness as anyone might imagine. It rained practically every afternoon, and at night the frost was so severe that the wet clothing of the soldiers froze to their bodies.

This painful operation lasted nearly a week, took the troops no further than a sandspit, and necessitated still another move to the delta proper. But it gave Jackson the time he needed to hurry his troops into the city once he learned of the landing. And, indeed, he heard of it soon enough. Witnesses of the battle between the gunboats and the barges raced to the city with the news. Jackson had just returned to New Orleans from Chef Menteur, where he had been inspecting the site and trying to calculate the best strategy of defense. Topography indicated it was the likely invasion route—provided the British could navigate the shallow waters from Lake Borgne and the Rigolets into Lake Pontchartrain in their oceangoing ships. The lack of light-draft vessels, more than any other reason, explains Cochrane's ultimate decision against penetration into Lake Pontchartrain and in favor of an immediate landing at the most favorable site and a swift march to New Orleans via the quickest route.

Once Jackson learned of the sighting and had positive evidence that

New Orleans and not Mobile was the immediate target of the invasion, he summoned all available troops to the city. An order went forward to Coffee: "You must not sleep until you arrive within striking distance," he commanded. Furthermore, Coffee must send an express to Carroll, inform him of the invasion, and order his presence in New Orleans by the fastest route possible. The ever-reliable Coffee responded that although some of his regiments were dispersed in a foraging operation he would round them up immediately and swing down to the city to "reach you in four days."[6] Actually Coffee arrived in New Orleans early in the morning of December 20, a day earlier than he anticipated, and was joined the following day by Carroll and almost 3,000 Tennessee recruits, along with Colonel Hinds and a regiment of Mississippi dragoons. The streets of New Orleans teemed with armed men, giving the impression that a stupendous army now guarded the city.

When the news of the sighting of the British first reached New Orleans the inhabitants panicked. Although by this time they had acquired enormous confidence in Jackson, the alarm produced a shock wave that left confusion and terror in its wake. Old Hickory instinctively considered proclaiming martial law—a move heartily endorsed by the governor, who feared the legislature and knew the city swarmed with spies. When Patterson had suggested the suspension of habeas corpus in order to round up enough sailors in the city to man his two armed vessels, the *Carolina* and the *Louisiana,* the legislature turned him down and instead offered a bounty to those who would serve. Annoyed, Claiborne recommended that the legislature prorogue itself for a couple of weeks. Again the legislature refused.

In these circumstances Jackson felt he must *take* control of New Orleans. If he was to defend the city, halt the invasion and drive the British back into the sea, he had no alternative. The decision came quickly. On December 16 he proclaimed martial law throughout New Orleans, turning it into an armed camp and making all its citizens potential soldiers. The proclamation directed that every citizen entering the city must report to the adjutant general's office and that no person might leave without permission in writing signed by the General or one of his staff. Ships must have passports to clear the port, and a curfew was ordered for nine o'clock. Any unauthorized person found in the streets after that hour would be arrested as a spy.[7]

To reassure the populace that they were in safe hands and to inspirit them with self-confidence, Jackson ordered a review of the city militia for Sunday, December 18. The city, as he knew it would, turned out *en masse* for the colorful ceremony. The square before the cathedral was jammed with people dressed in their Sunday best, as though the event were a kind of mardi gras prior to the imminent lent of invasion and battle. And, because Jackson had learned in his youth about the orations addressed to Greek soldiers on the eve of battle and how essential they were to victory in rousing the fighting spirit, he prepared an address to the armed forces that rang with Jacksonian fervor, encouragement, and enthusiasm. Although specifically directed at the troops, the language was deliberately chosen to stir the polyglot people of New Orleans. It was all part of Jackson's ceremonial ablution prior to battle.

Thus, when the impressive review ended, Edward Livingston stepped forward to read, in his deep, sonorous voice, Jackson's call to heroism, sacrifice, and ultimate victory.

> *Fellow-Citizens and Soldiers:* The general, commanding in chief, would not do justice to the noble ardour that has animated you in the hour of danger . . . if he suffered the example you have shewn to pass without publick notice. . . .
>
> Natives of the United States! they [the British] are the oppressors of your infant political existence, with whom you are to contend —they are the men your fathers conquered whom you are to oppose. Descendants of Frenchmen! natives of France! they are the English, the hereditary, the eternal enemies of your ancient country—the invaders of that you have adopted, who are your foes. Spaniards— remember the conduct of your allies at St Sebastiens, and recently at Pensacola, and rejoice that you have an opportunity of avenging the brutal injuries inflicted by men who dishonor the human race.
>
> Fellow citizens of every description! remember for what and against whom you contend. For all that can render life desirable— for a country blessed with every gift of nature—for property, for life —for those dearer than either, your wives and children—and for liberty, dearer than all, without which country, life, property, are no longer worth possessing: as even the embraces of wives and children become a reproach to the wretched who could deprive them by his cowardice of those invaluable blessings. You are to contend for all this against any enemy whose continued effort is to deprive you of the last of those blessings—who avows a war of vengeance and desolation, proclaimed and marked by cruelty, lust, and horrours unknown to civilized nations.
>
> Citizens of Louisiana! the general, commanding in chief, rejoices to see the spirit that animates you, not only for your honor but for your safety. . . . He salutes you, brave Louisianians, as brethren in arms. . . . Continue with the energy you have began, and he promises you not only safety, but victory over the insolent enemy who insulted you by an affected doubt of your attachment to the constitution of your country.

Livingston paused. He wanted the words to penetrate the consciousness of everyone within the range of his voice. Then he turned to the
Batallion of Uniform Companies and began again to read Jackson's
words.

> When I first looked at you on the day of my arrival I was satisfied
> with your appearance, and every day's inspection since has
> confirmed the opinion I then formed. Your numbers have increased
> with the increase of danger, and your ardour has augmented since
> it was known that your post would be one of peril and of honour.
> This is the true military spirit! this is the true love of country! you
> have added to it an exact discipline, and a skill in evolutions rarely
> attained by veterans; the state of your corps does equal honour to
> the skill of the officers and the attention of the men.

It was a typical Jacksonian exhortation, full of extravagant praise and
high promise for the future.

Now it was the turn of the "men of colour." Livingston's voice rang
out.

> *Soldiers!* From the shores of the Mobile I called you to arms—
> I invited you to share in the perils and to divide the glory of your
> white countrymen. I expected much from you, for I was not unin-
> formed of those qualities that must render you so formidable to an
> invading foe—I knew that you could endure hunger and thirst, and
> all the hardships of war—I knew that you loved the land of your
> nativity and that, like ourselves you had to defend all that is most
> dear to man—but you surpassed my hopes; I have found in you,
> united to those qualities, that noble enthusiasm which impels to
> great deeds.

And finally to the entire assemblage of soldiers as well as the listening crowd, Jackson concluded:

> Soldiers—the President of the United States shall be informed
> of your conduct on this occasion, and the voice of the representatives
> of the American nation shall applaud your valour, as your general
> now praises your ardour. The enemy is near; his "sails cover the
> lakes"; but the brave are united; and if he finds us contending among
> ourselves, it will be for the prize of valour and the rewards of fame.[8]

The people applauded their approval. The soldiers stood rigid with
pride. Then Old Hickory spoke briefly, dismissing the troops and granting them the rest of the day to visit with their families and instructing
them as to their stations upon their return.[9]

Two days after this pageant the British completed their landing on

Pea Island. By this time, too, Admiral Cochrane had learned from a number of fishermen and Spaniards who were former residents of New Orleans that approximately thirty miles due west of Pea Island a bayou, Bayou Bienvenu, stretched from Lake Borgne to within a dozen miles of New Orleans and was navigable for large barges. Cochrane sent Captain Robert Spencer and Lieutenant John Peddie to explore the bayou. With the help of Spaniards and Portuguese who lived in Fisherman's Village a quarter of a mile from the entrance of the stream, they soon discovered that the route was indeed practical and clear and virtually unattended. They reported this to Cochrane.

Just why this bayou remained unobstructed—in violation of Jackson's precise orders—has never been explained and probably never will be. Whether it was negligence, oversight, or treachery, the effect nearly delivered New Orleans into British hands.[10]

At nine o'clock on the morning of December 22 an advance army of 1,800 men under Colonel William Thornton, who had led the successful assault on Bladensburg in the Chesapeake area, entered the boats and headed for Bayou Bienvenu. General Keane, who would make all of the wrong decisions for the expedition, accompanied the advance, and the flotilla moved with perfect order into the wide, flat expanse of swamp covered with reeds. By dawn the next morning they reached the mouth of the bayou, their movement accomplished in complete secrecy. The pickets stationed at Fisherman's Village to sound an alarm should anything suspicious occur were easily captured, although one American managed to break away and escape into the swamp, where he wandered for three days before he reached the American camp.[11] For the remainder of the day the British moved up the bayou—which was 100 to 150 yards wide and 6 to 9 feet deep, depending on the tide—until they discovered a narrow strip of solid land along the bank. The troops debarked in single file. As they moved inland the ground became firmer, the path more distinct. Gradually the swamp gave way to stunted cypress trees, then canebrakes, and finally the open, cultivated fields that formed the plantation of General Jacques Villeré of the Louisiana militia.

Forming his front into companies, Thornton moved quickly toward the plantation houses, which were not more than a thousand yards from the Mississippi. Major Gabriel Villeré, son of the general, had been charged with guarding the Bienvenu approach and was sitting on the porch of the main house smoking a cigar and talking with his brother Celestin when he suddenly saw redcoats flashing through the orange grove, heading toward the river. He jumped from his chair and ran into the house to escape by a rear door—and encountered several armed men, one of whom was Colonel Thornton. Forced to surrender, he was taken

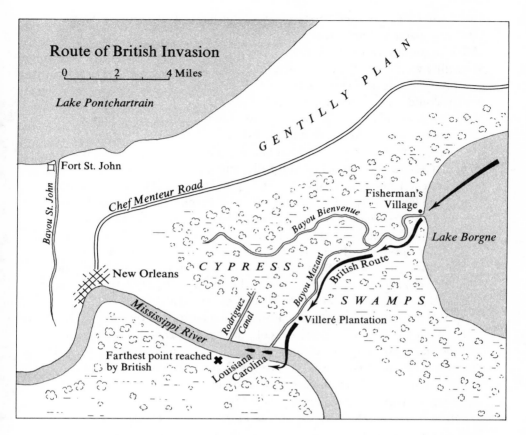

Route of British Invasion

0   2   4 Miles

Lake Pontchartrain

Fort St. John

Bayou St. John

Chef Menteur Road

GENTILLY PLAIN

Fisherman's Village

Bayou Bienvenue

Lake Borgne

New Orleans

CYPRESS

British Route

Bayou Mazant

SWAMPS

Mississippi River

Rodriguez Canal

Villeré Plantation

Farthest point reached by British

Louisiana

Carolina

under guard to another room to await the arrival of General Keane. Villeré realized he must escape and sound the alarm. With a daring born of fear and desperation he suddenly sprang from his captors and leaped through a window.[12] Dashing across the yard, he hurdled a picket fence and plunged into the cypress forest that fringed the swamp before the British could take after him.

"Catch or kill him," Thornton shouted to his men as they fanned out in pursuit of the fleeing Creole.[13] Crashing through the cypress forest with a speed that quickly separated him from his attackers, Villeré finally located a neighbor, Colonel de la Ronde, and together they rushed to the river, boarded a boat, and rowed to the opposite bank. There they found Dussau de la Croix, a member of the New Orleans Committee of Public Safety. The three men saddled horses and hastened toward the city.

It is possible that young Villeré was the person responsible for failing to obstruct the bayou. Perhaps he wished to avoid the cost and damage to his father's property. By relying on the pickets to warn him of the enemy's approach in time to summon the militia, he may have felt the intent of Jackson's instructions had been carried out.

In any event the British were now formed alongside the Mississippi. When General Keane joined the column he ordered the troops into battalion formation, wheeled right along the levee road which paralleled the river, and marched by Villeré's house to the upper line of the planta- tion, where he halted in a position between the river and a cypress swamp, throwing a strong advance toward New Orleans. Thornton urged Keane to continue the march and seize the obviously defenseless city. Since they had moved without opposition, without even the knowledge of the Americans, it seemed a safe bet that New Orleans could be taken with the troops at hand.

He was undoubtedly right. Jackson had no notion of the British location, nor did he have adequate defenses to stop a surprise attack. He would have been reduced to street fighting, guerrilla fashion, which would have had devastating effects on the city and its people.

But Keane was a cautious man. The pickets he had captured at Fisherman's Village told him the city was crawling with soldiers, maybe as many as 20,000 of them. This preposterous figure was substantiated by prisoners Keane had questioned earlier, notably the sailors from the American gunboats and some of Lafitte's men. Moreover, Keane feared his lines of supply and communication with the fleet were too tenuous; he believed he should wait until the main body of his command caught up with the advance column. His timid decision undoubtedly saved the city from capture.[14]

While the British busily established their position on the bank of the

Mississippi roughly ten miles south of New Orleans, Jackson was in the parlor of his headquarters on Royal Street reading reports and dispatching orders, trying desperately to determine where the invaders might strike and how best to respond. According to one early historian of the approaching battle, it was half past one o'clock in the afternoon of December 23 when the sentry notified the General that there were three gentlemen to see him who had important information. De la Croix, Villeré, and de la Ronde were ushered into the room, all nearly breathless from the pace of their ride.

"What news do you bring, gentlemen?" Jackson asked.

"Important! Highly important!" de la Croix gasped. "The British have arrived at Villeré's plantation nine miles below the city and are there encamped. Here is Major Villeré, who was captured by them, has escaped, and will now relate his story."[15]

Villeré babbled his account in French, de la Croix translating as he spoke. When he finished the General rose, his eyes smoking with anger at the treason that had allowed the British to slip from the lake to the river undetected. "With an emphatic blow upon the table with his clenched fist," Jackson cried: "By the Eternal, they shall not sleep on our soil!" His fury spent in that brief outburst, the General courteously invited his guests to join him in a glass of wine, at the same time summoning his secretary and aides. "Gentlemen," he said as the officers entered the room, "the British are below; we must fight them to-night."[16]

No Keane, he. Jackson was spoiling to fight. "I will smash them," he allegedly said, "so help me God!"[17] Jackson understood the urgency of making immediate contact with the enemy and keeping them from moving directly into the city. There was nothing precipitous or rash in his decision to fight that night; it was a rational, sober judgment, dictated by the fast rush of events.[18]

Hurriedly orders were dispatched to assemble the regulars, the battalions of city guards, the Mississippi dragoons, the free black battalions, and Coffee's cavalry and to move them quickly down the river. Carroll's Tennesseans and the Louisiana militia under Governor Claiborne were left behind to guard the Chef Menteur in case Jackson's original hunch was correct and the British were only feinting as they moved up the Mississippi.

As usual, Jackson planned a pincer tactic. He directed Coffee to move along the cypress swamp on the left and hit the British on the flank while the main force would strike along the river. Jackson also ordered Patterson to have the *Carolina* drop down the river to a point opposite the British camp and open fire at half past seven o'clock. That would be the signal for the start of a general attack. Meanwhile, General David Morgan, commanding the Louisiana militia at the English Turn, was ordered to create a diversion from the rear. In conducting this hastily assembled operation, Jackson had a little better than 2,000 troops to throw against the invaders, slightly more than Keane's force by a few hundred men.

As these preparations took shape, news of the enemy's arrival whipped through the city like a fearful pestilence. Soon Jackson heard a crowd of women weeping openly in the streets, for there was much talk about British desire for "Booty and Beauty" or "Loot and Lust" when they entered New Orleans. Jackson turned to Livingston and told him to speak to the women and tell them that "he was there, and that the British should never get into the city, so long as he held the command."[19] That had been his constant refrain since arriving in New Orleans: Fear not. I am here. I will rescue the city.

At seven o'clock it was dark and the *Carolina* stood in position some three hundred yards from Keane's position. The enemy campfires, blazing brightly on account of the cold, beautifully silhouetted the British and made them splendid targets for the American gunners. At half past seven the *Carolina* opened fire with a broadside that roared over the delta and took the British completely by surprise. For ten minutes or so Keane's men stumbled about in total confusion, grabbing for guns, extinguishing fires, running for the protection of the levee. Then, as the *Carolina* slackened her fire and the enemy began to breathe a little easier, Jackson ordered a frontal assault. For several hours the fighting was a confused tangle of men frequently fighting hand to hand. The American line weaved back and forth as the British regulars struck at them again and again. According to Jackson the invaders were also aided by a thick fog that suddenly came up from the river and "occassioned some confusion among the different [American] Corps."[20] It was now nine thirty, the fog heavy and the moonlight gone. "Fearing the consequences, under this circumstance, of the further prosecution of a night attack with troops then acting together for the first time," Jackson later reported, he disengaged, pulled back his men several hundred yards away from the enemy, straddled the road leading to the city, and waited for daylight.[21]

It was a wise decision. Shortly after eight o'clock Keane began receiving reinforcements from Bayou Bienvenu. Fresh, disciplined troops would have given Jackson's unseasoned men a bad time of it; they would have been outnumbered in short order. Clearly Jackson needed to back away.

The Americans, by their own count, suffered 24 killed, 115 wounded, and 74 missing or captured. The British admitted to 46 killed, 167 wounded, and 64 missing.[22] Both sides lost over 10 percent of their men, a very high casualty count. At best Jackson got away with a draw, although in a real sense the British could—and did—claim victory, for the Americans failed to destroy their advance guard. Still, Jackson had taken the offensive, returned a surprise invasion with a surprise counterattack and frightened the British into staying where they were. Always aggressive, Jackson brought the invasion to an abrupt halt. Indeed his action saved New Orleans; for had he not attacked so quickly and with such "impetuosity," the British would have immediately marched against the city after the arrival of reinforcements and undoubtedly taken it.[23]

The following morning, December 24, 1814, the very day American and British ministers in Ghent signed a treaty of peace ending the war, Jackson decided to move his army back another mile and set up his defense behind an old millrace called Rodriguez Canal, a ditch four feet deep and ten feet wide that ran from the eastern bank of the Mississippi to a cypress swamp about three quarters of a mile inland. The trench afforded the best natural protection in the area for making a stand. Rather than risk another engagement, as he was inclined to do, Jackson saw the wisdom of crouching behind a strong defensive line. Shovels were brought from the city and the work begun of digging, widening, and strengthening the position. Earthen ramparts were thrown up at the northern rim of the canal (that closest to the city) and artillery pieces were installed at regular intervals. Jackson also ordered his engineer, Latour, to cut the levee and flood the ground immediately in front of the line. This was done, but it proved ineffective because the temporary swell of the river subsided.[24] The fickle Mississippi refused to take sides in this contest of strength and will.

When Jackson retreated to the canal he left a small company behind to watch the enemy and report their movements. At the same time he ordered the *Carolina,* now joined by the *Louisiana,* to lob cannonballs at the enemy at regular intervals to keep them from initiating an attack. Night and day the two vessels pitched fire and lead into the enemy camp. While they caused little physical damage, they had a devastating effect on the morale of the invading troops.

For their part the British strengthened their position by hurrying reinforcements from the fleet—John Reid estimated they now had 7,000 troops "against our 3,000"—until by the end of the day all the troops at the anchorage had been drawn into position. The camp was formed between two parallel levees to provide protection against the cannonading of the *Carolina* and *Louisiana* and the possibility of a land attack.[25]

On Christmas day there was a stir in the British encampment. A salvo of artillery summoned the attention of Jackson two miles away. It was not the start of an attack but a salute to the new British general who had arrived to assume command of the invasion. Not the Duke of Wellington (as the Americans feared at first) but his wife's brother, Lieutenant General Sir Edward Michael Pakenham, who had at last caught up with his new command. (General Robert Ross was the original choice for this expedition, but his death during the Chesapeake action necessitated a new appointment.) Pakenham was a skilled officer who had risen rapidly through the ranks. A bad wound suffered at St. Lucia had given him a pronounced cock of the head, but he sustained another wound at Martinique that conveniently corrected the defect. During the Peninsula War against Napoleon he achieved military distinction when he broke open the French line in a daring but costly attack. Now thirty-seven years of age, he was considered by some to be one of the very best officers in the British army.

Pakenham surveyed the position of his troops along the Mississippi, his initial annoyance turning to cold fury as he realized he was cramped into a narrow defile between a swamp and a river. Before him was an enemy entrenched in a fortified position with armed river vessels guarding the flank and catching his left column in a crossfire whenever it attempted to move forward.[26] Before doing another thing, Pakenham decided he must silence the *Carolina* and *Louisiana* or drive them away. At his command, nine fieldpieces were dragged to the river bank—two 9-pounders firing hot shot, four 6-pounders firing shrapnel, two 5.5-inch howitzers, and a 5.5-inch mortar—along with furnaces for heating shot.[27] Once in place the battery opened up on the *Carolina* in a devastatingly accurate display of firepower. On the second round of hot shot the ship caught fire; because the shot lodged in her main hold under her cables and could not be removed, the fire soon raged out of control.

The crew tumbled over the sides. And none too soon. The *Carolina* suddenly blew up with a tremendous roar, shaking the ground for miles and raining burning fragments in every direction. Jackson, from his command post at the Macarté house two hundred yards behind the mud rampart, ordered the *Louisiana* out of range—not that Patterson needed the advice. To move the *Louisiana*, sailors were piled into boats to assist the operation. While hot shot fell hissing into the water around them, the sailors, with much exertion, succeeded in towing the ship out of the range of Pakenham's guns.[28]

The escape of the *Louisiana* could have been avoided. Had Pakenham directed his fire first upon the *Louisiana*, which was further away, he probably could have destroyed both ships. To get out of range the *Louisiana* only had to move half a mile, while the *Carolina* had at least two miles to sail to enter a safety zone. Once the heavier and better armed vessel, the *Louisiana*, was fired, Pakenham would have had plenty of time to play with the smaller ship. The *Louisiana* now took station across the river, in position to rake lengthwise any column of troops that advanced on Jackson's barricade. Except for 1 killed and 6 wounded, the *Carolina* crew were saved to join the American line, where they helped man the artillery.

On December 28 Pakenham ordered a general advance. Formed into two columns, the British moved swiftly, driving Jackson's advance observation corps before them. From the window of his headquarters Jackson watched the brilliant array of soldiers marching smartly toward his mud ditch, one column close to the river and the other near the cypress swamp. The "red coats," as Jackson liked to call them, were about to show the "dirty shirts," as the British called their American foes, what real soldiering was all about.[29] To the "dirty shirts," who had never seen professionals in action, "it was certainly a formidable display of military power and discipline."[30]

Under a shower of Congreve rockets (a new and frightening pyrotechnic) and continual fire from their artillery, the British column crossed the open plain in front of Jackson's rampart. When the soldiers got within 600 yards of the ditch, the American batteries opened up in a stupendous roar of cannonading, supported by deadly fire from the *Louisiana*. The American crossfire between ship and artillery was so devastating as it raked the advancing redcoats that the invaders dove into ditches for protection. Those closest to the river had to wait until nightfall before they could withdraw; those further away retreated as best they could. Near the swamp, out of the range of the *Louisiana* and the American artillery, the British column might have chewed up Coffee's troops and reached Jackson's line at its weakest point had not Pakenham ordered a general retreat. The British commander mistakenly assumed that since the column along the river was doing badly, the column near the cypress swamp must be in equal danger. Slapped back by the sharp American firepower, Pakenham moved his troops two miles from the rampart and threw up two advance redoubts, known as the artillery and forward redoubts. Now perhaps he understood the error of letting the *Louisiana* get away. Having failed to advance, the British lost the opportunity to break through Jackson's line and march on New Orleans.[31]

During the assault Jackson was informed that members of the Louisiana legislature were so fearful of the city's capture and destruction that they were ready to offer terms of capitulation to the enemy and surrender. Immediately the General alerted Claiborne to the report. He instructed him to watch the legislators and at the first sign of treating with the enemy to arrest the members and hold them subject to his further orders.[32] Claiborne went one step further: He closed the legislature and put a guard at the doors of the capitol.[33] Then a committee of the legislature confronted Jackson and demanded to know what he would do in the event of a general retreat.

Old Hickory blistered them. He knew they were more concerned about the safety of New Orleans than the destruction of the invading army. They cared only for their city, not the nation. "If I thought the hair of my head could divine what I should do," he told the committee, "forthwith I would cut it off; go back with this answer: say to your honorable body, that if disaster does overtake me, and the fate of war drives me from my line to the city, they may expect to have a very warm session."[34] His intent did not escape them.

He was more precise when asked the same question by Major John H. Eaton at a later time. "I should have retreated to the city, fired it, and fought the enemy amidst the surrounding flames. There were with me men of wealth, owners of considerable property, who, in such an event, would have been among the foremost to have applied the torch to their own buildings, and what they had left undone I should have completed. Nothing for the comfortable maintenance of the enemy would have been left in the rear. I would have destroyed New Orleans, occupied a position above on the river, cut off all supplies, and in this way compelled them to depart from the country."[35] Without batting an eye, Andrew Jackson would raze an entire city to achieve his purpose.

The obvious intent and bluster of his remarks to the committee outraged the Louisiana legislature. Bernard Marigny went to the General and complained that he and his fellow legislators had been misunderstood, maligned, and abused, that they had no intention of betraying their country or surrendering to the enemy. It was just another attempt on the part of Claiborne and his friends to discredit them. Marigny's defense was so spirited and so obviously sincere that Jackson accepted his word and ordered a halt to further interference in the functioning of the legislature. It was a necessary truce to quiet the disorder in the city's internal operation.[36]

After Pakenham failed to tear through Jackson's line on December 26 and had withdrawn two miles to build his redoubts, the British commander decided to treat the American position as a fortification and erect breaching batteries to knock out their guns. For the next three days he had heavy naval cannons dragged to his position rather than wait for the siege train of field artillery that was still somewhere at sea. It was a horrendous task and involved moving four 24-pound carronades and ten 18-pounders through the swamp. Admiral Cochrane cheerfully cooperated. The guns and their ammunition were ferried from the ships, floated up a canal, and then transferred to carts and dragged nearly a half mile to their emplacements.

While this staggering operation proceeded with the help of many boatloads of sailors, Jackson worked to reinforce the rampart. He dug the ditch deeper and mounded the mud bank higher. At the suggestion of Jean Lafitte, whom Jackson now rather admired, the line was extended on the left from the cypress woods into the swamp, thereby strengthening the entire line tremendously. By this time Jackson knew that he faced the invasion itself, not a mere ruse to distract him from Chef Menteur. Accordingly, Carroll and his Tennessee division had been recalled to the city, and some of these troops were assigned to the reinforcement operation. The number of gun emplacements along the ditch was increased from five to twelve. Cotton bales were sunk into the ground and wooden platforms built over them to hold the thirty-twos and twenty-fours and to keep them from miring in the mud. Across the river, on the west bank of the Mississippi, Patterson placed a 24-pounder and two 12-pounders behind the levee just opposite the British batteries, at a distance of three quarters of a mile. Latour constructed a defensive line at this point, and General Morgan and the Louisiana militia were assigned to defend the line and protect Patterson's guns. Meanwhile New Orleans was scoured for every pistol, musket, sword, flint, ramrod, and any other weapon that could be found.[37]

Pakenham's three-day interruption of the invasion gave Jackson just enough time to reinforce completely his position on both sides of the river. It was another blunder of delay that Jackson turned to good effect.

By the evening of December 31 the British commander had completed his preparations for bombarding and assaulting the American position. His string of five batteries ran from the levee to the swamp and was protected by barrels of sugar found on a plantation. The barrels substituted for sandbags, which were impossible to obtain because of the swampy conditions of the area. The batteries were capable of throwing over 300 pounds of lead per salvo. (The American artillery could heave 224 pounds per salvo.) That evening, after the preparations had been completed, the British army moved forward and took cover about 500 yards from Jackson's rampart, waiting for their artillery to breach the American line the following morning. But what the British did not know in planning their attack for the next day was Jackson's decision to conduct a grand review of the entire army on the open ground between the front line and his headquarters at the Macarté house.[38] Jackson was again using the strategy of military review to bolster the morale of his troops—and that of visiting dignitaries, magistrates, and ladies from the city. An important factor in the final outcome of the invasion was the steady rise of American morale, fostered by Jackson, and the equally steady decline of British morale, left unattended by General Pakenham.

On New Year's morning 1815, a thick fog rose from the river and shrouded the open plain, cutting visibility to a few yards. The British waited, hoping the sun would burn the fog away. The Americans turned out at an early hour in clean clothes, with flashing swords and polished arms and regimental and company standards unfurled, to parade their pride and might. Toward ten o'clock the fog slowly lifted; the British, to their amazement, saw a brilliant scene: colors floating in the air, bands playing, mounted officers riding through the ranks of the regiments formed on parade. Then, suddenly, the main British battery smashed into the colorful tableau. Congreve rockets screamed their alarm as the Americans fled in every direction. Ranks came apart; lines of smartly dressed troops dissolved; precision and order degenerated into confused crowds. Had the British charged at that moment, or had antipersonnel ammunition rather than demolition ammunition been used, the invaders might have breached the American line and carried through to New Orleans.[39]

The first fire was aimed directly at the Macarté house, which the British knew was Jackson's headquarters.[40] The General and his staff were finishing breakfast when the house was shaken by the crash of rockets; balls and shells shattered masonry, splintered furniture, and tore the plaster from the walls.[41] Miraculously, no one was hurt, "though for ten minutes after the batteries opened, not less than a hundred balls, rockets and shells struck the house."[42] Jackson scurried to the rampart where the troops, following their initial confusion, were assembling to return the artillery fire. He inspected each battery, hurrying to the left and waving his hat to the men as they cheered him.

"Don't mind these rockets," he cried, "they are mere toys to amuse children." Later the British acknowledged, reported John Reid, "that ours is the first . . . army that was not thrown into confusion by their rockets."[43]

Within minutes the American line thundered its response to the attack. For an hour and a half the cannonading was constant, the entire delta shaking from the impact of the explosions. Dominque You, brother of Jean Lafitte, stood on the end of the embankment shouting to his men to fire more rapidly and to cram their pieces to the mouth with chain shot, ship cannister, and any other destructive missile they could find. As the firing continued the Americans improved their accuracy by watching where their shots fell and adjusting the range to come right down on target. Captain Humphrey, commanding number one battery, patiently straddled his targets to find the exact range and direction. Patterson's naval batteries located the British artillery mounted on the levee and knocked it out. "Too much praise," Jackson later informed Monroe, "cannot be bestowed on those who managed my artillery."[44]

On the left, Coffee and his cavalry dismounted and anchored their position knee-deep in mud. Jackson had given special attention to this segment because of the experience of December 28. Coffee ordered his men to drive the British into the swamp and then drown them. They performed most satisfactorily.

But the Americans took a pounding too, although at first the British seemed indifferent about range and threw much of their fire beyond Jackson's line.[45] Still, the carriage of Dominque's 24-pounder was broken, the 32- and 12-pounders were put out of commission, and two caissons, one of which contained a hundred pounds of powder, blew up. When the ammunition exploded the British infantry let out a cheer in the hope that the American line had been breached; but they soon learned otherwise when more intense fire from the rampart rained down on them.

Within two hours it was clear the British had failed in their objective. Indeed, the bombardment was a poor demonstration of professional standards. Many of the sugar casks stacked around the gun emplacements for protection burst and disabled the guns. Some batteries had inadequate flooring and after a few salvos drove themselves into the mud and out of operation. Several fieldpieces were damaged by the Americans, and casualties among British gunners were particularly heavy.[46]

By noon the invaders slackened their fire. An hour later the guns on the left and center ceased firing, and by three o'clock the levee guns also fell silent. British casualties included 44 killed and 55 wounded; Americans suffered 11 dead and 23 wounded.[47] Toward evening it began to rain, and the British were forced to drag their guns back to camp through mud. Unfortunately, Jackson made no attempt to capture these guns or drive the British away from them—something he might have accomplished without exposing his force to the numerically superior British army.

Back at headquarters after his abysmal failure to penetrate the American line, Pakenham cursed the imbecility that had confined him to this narrow plain. One thing now struck him as crystal clear: since he could not maneuver he must punch his way straight ahead through Jackson's fortification if he was ever to reach New Orleans. And that required additional troops. That also necessitated massive power hurled directly forward, committing thousands of men to a frontal assault in such depth that the Americans would be overwhelmed by sheer numbers. Considering the low morale among some of the British troops, particularly those unprepared and ill-equipped for the Louisiana weather, the plan had built-in disadvantages. In any event, Pakenham decided to wait for the reinforcements under Major General John Lambert that were expected daily. These troops included the crack Seventh Fusiliers and the Forty-third Regiment. In fact they had already arrived at the fleet anchorage and were on their way across the lake to join the main force. They reached Pakenham's position on January 6.

To lessen the burden of the frontal assault and to support his attacking soldiers, Pakenham planned to catch Jackson in a crossfire. He proposed to ferry 1,500 troops (under the brilliant Colonel William Thornton) to the west bank of the Mississippi, capture Patterson's guns, and turn them on Jackson. This enfilade, timed to coincide with the assault by the main force on the east bank, would rake Jackson's position and—hopefully—wipe him out. Only one problem existed: boats. Boats to ferry Thornton's men across the river. Barges were available, but they lay moored in Bayou Bienvenu. Admiral Cochrane suggested widening and deepening Villeré's canal to provide a navigable route from Bayou Bienvenu to the Mississippi. Once the canal had been improved and the levee breached, barges could move freely from their base to the river and then across the Mississippi.

In many respects Pakenham's basic strategy had great merit. The American defense on the west bank was perilously weak and could easily be captured, provided it was hit quickly and in strength. With Patterson's heavy guns trained on the American line, a murderous crossfire could be established and hole after hole drilled into Jackson's position.

Unfortunately, the difficult work of extending, widening, and deepening the canal took many days, delaying the invasion and giving Jackson additional time to reinforce his position. Not until January 7 was the canal ready for use. While inspecting it, Pakenham noticed that only one dam had been constructed to hold the force of the river, and he questioned his engineers about the advisability of a second dam as a precaution against the collapse of the first. The engineers dismissed his fears—and, sure enough, the dam collapsed, delaying the operation sufficiently to defeat Pakenham's crossfire scheme.

Jackson was not idle during the time the British so generously provided. Again the ditch was deepened, the mud rampart heightened. Rodriguez Canal was lengthened and a high parapet constructed along the northern edge and revetted with fence nails to keep it from sliding into the canal. The American line ran for more than half a mile from the river to the swamp, extending into the swamp for a short distance, then turning in a right angle toward the city. The rampart averaged five feet in height; it was twenty feet thick in some places but was so thin in others that cannonballs could easily puncture it. On the left side, for example, the breastwork was only thick enough to withstand musketfire. Reluctantly Jackson agreed to construct an advance redoubt near the river, but it was still incomplete when the major assault began on January 8. He also had commenced the construction of two additional lines of defense behind the canal, one closer to the city by two miles and the third closer still by a mile and a quarter. To assist in the difficult and time-consuming construction, Jackson had the help of a task force of slaves—something the British desperately needed.[48]

Time also swelled Jackson's army. On January 4 more than 2,000 Kentucky militiamen arrived in the city to bolster Old Hickory's defense. Unfortunately, many of them were without guns. A lack of weapons and ammunition had been plaguing Jackson for months; rifles requisitioned in August arrived in mid-January after the major battle had been fought. Covering himself, the General warned Washington that it was courting a disaster for which it would be solely responsible. "Depend upon it," he wrote Monroe, "this supineness, this negligence, this *criminality,* let me call it, of which we witness so many instances in the agents of Government, must finally lead, if it be not corrected, to the defeat of our armies, and to the disgrace of those who superintend them." The Kentucky troops had just arrived, he added, but "not more than one third of them are armed, and those very indifferently. I have none to put in their hands."[49] He assigned half of the new troops to Brigadier General John Adair (acting in place of General John Thomas, who had become ill) to support Carroll's Tennesseans in the center; the rest were held in reserve or sent to the west bank to reinforce Patterson's position.

.Jackson was slow to see the danger to his right flank across the river, despite the preparations of the British in digging their canal and breaching the levee. He blithely assumed that transit across the river in force would require many boats and that their assemblage would be observed in plenty of time to take appropriate action. Over the past week he had already ordered Brigadier General David Morgan to abandon his post at English Turn and assume a position on the west bank of the river. He had also directed Latour to help build a defensible line and an advance position. These commands were obeyed with dispatch. But the location of Patterson's gun emplacements and furnaces made it necessary to move Morgan's advance further south, and that required the deployment of many more troops than Jackson felt he could afford. The best Old Hickory could do was to send Morgan 500 Kentuckians, only 250 of whom were armed.[50] The rest of Morgan's troops included 500 Louisiana militiamen and a few hundred from the First, Second, and Sixth Regiments. The force was totally inadequate to its task; it was undermanned and underarmed. Its exposed position was approved by the commander, who refused to reinforce it adequately. Thus the disaster that occurred on the west bank was largely the responsibility of General Andrew Jackson.[51]

On January 7 Patterson walked along the western side of the river to a point directly opposite the British position and for several hours watched the enemy's movements. What he saw left him in a cold sweat. Villeré's canal had been stretched to the river, breaching the levee. Barges loaded with cannons were already floating in the Mississippi and preparing to ferry a large contingent of soldiers to the west bank. Then, when Patterson inspected Morgan's sorry position and saw the number of men assigned to defend it, his heart sank.[52] Straight off he sent Richard S. Shepherd to the General to beg him to reinforce Morgan's desperate situation.

Shepherd arrived at Jackson's headquarters at one o'clock on the morning of January 8 and found the General lying on a sofa trying to catch a few hours' sleep. Shepherd repeated Patterson's instructions, ending with Morgan's information that the main attack would be made on the west bank and his request for troops as quickly as possible.

"Hurry back and tell General Morgan that he is mistaken," replied Jackson. "The main attack will be on this side, and I have no men to spare. He must maintain his position at all hazards."

Then, seeing that it was one o'clock, the General aroused his sleeping aides, Reid, Butler, Livingston, and Davezac, and said, "Gentlemen, we have slept enough. Arise. The enemy will be upon us in a few minutes; I must go and see Coffee."[53]

Jackson was right about the main attack coming on his side of the river. Too many preparations bustled in front of him. And he was ready: He had 4,000 men on the front line and another 1,000 men in reserve.[54] Besides the artillery—set up in three groups, river, center, and swamp—the line consisted of the Seventh Regiment, commanded by Colonel George Ross, alongside the Mississippi; Plauché's battalion; Lacoste's and Daquin's battalions of black soldiers; the Forty-fourth Regiment; the Tennesseans under Carroll, supported by Adair's Kentuckians; and General Coffee's cavalry on the left, with Choctaws scouting in the swamp.

Against this impregnable line Pakenham planned to send a column of 2,200 men (the Fourth, Twenty-first, and Forty-fourth Regiments and three companies of the Ninety-fifth) under Major General Sir Samuel Gibbs to hit the America position slightly left of center, accompanied by a second column of 1,200 men (the Ninety-third, two companies of the Ninety-fifth, and two companies of the Forty-third) under Major General Keane to strike Jackson's right along the river. Simultaneously, a West Indian regiment of 520 men would skirmish in the swamp to distract Coffee and slice through his line if possible, while Thornton, having crossed the river, would capture Morgan's batteries as Gibbs and Keane moved up and then turn the batteries against Jackson. A third column of 1,500 men (the Seventh Fusiliers and the remainder of the Forty-third) under Major General Lambert was held in reserve near the center of the field.[55]

It was three o'clock in the morning when, after many delays because of cave-ins along the banks of the canal, Thornton and a third of his force started across the Mississippi. Then the river's current seized the flotilla and swept it a mile and a half further downstream. According to Pakenham's plan, Thornton and his men were expected to land three miles below the American line, move rapidly along the bank, and seize Morgan's and Patterson's position. But they landed further south than anticipated, which put them many hours behind schedule. It was nearly daylight when they finally got ashore on the west bank. Poor Thornton knew he had no chance of capturing the American batteries before the general attack began. In anger and sorrow he stared across the river and saw the flashes of gunfire that told him the attack had already begun.

CHAPTER 18

The Savior of His Country

FROM START TO FINISH THE ATTACK was a shambles. At 4:00 A.M. a column of redcoats stole to within half a mile of the mud rampart. This was the Forty-fourth Regiment, led by a particularly incompetent officer, Lieutenant Colonel, The Honorable Thomas Mullens, third son of Lord Ventry.[1] The Forty-fourth were ordered out in advance of Gibbs's column and instructed to carry fascines and ladders with them. The fascines were bundles of sugar cane to be thrown into the ditch in front of Jackson's line to fill it up. The sixteen ladders assigned for the operation were needed to scale the rampart. The fascines and ladders had to be in place in order for the advance to move forward smoothly once the attack began.

The Forty-fourth Regiment moved rapidly but quietly. They were almost in position when they realized their blunder.

They had forgotten the fascines and ladders!

Quicktime to the rear to pick up the bloody things. Then a race to get back into position before the signal to attack.

Too late. The battle had commenced.[2]

Sunday, January 8, 1815, dawned with a thick mist covering the ground separating the two armies. But, slowly, as the light of the new day spread across the plain, the mist thinned and rolled away, revealing the British army stretched across two-thirds of the field. Then a Congreve rocket rose with a screech on the left, near the swamp, and another ascended from the right, next to the river. "They announced to each other, that all was prepared and ready, to proceed and carry by storm" the entire American line.[3]

Immediately, Gibbs's column charged forward, directed at Jackson's left in order to have the cover of the woods. Drums beat a steady rhythm to accompany the advancing column.

Jackson surveyed his line with rapid glances to the left and right. He ordered all troops resting in the rear to move quickly to the rampart. Gun crews at the batteries tensed for action. The climactic moment of Britain's determination to seize and occupy the American southwest had arrived.

The army of redcoats, displaying dazzling military discipline, came within range of the defenders. The Americans cheered. They had been waiting for hours for this moment. Guns trained on their brightly colored targets. Suddenly the entire line illuminated with a devastating blaze of fire. The band of the Orleans Battalion struck up *Yankee Doodle* as artillery, rifles, and small arms emptied into the faces of the onrushing British. The initial roar of defiance no sooner echoed away than another thundering rebuke smashed into the scarlet ranks. The American ranks rotated, line after line: The first line delivered its destruction and stepped back to reload; the second line jumped forward, aimed, fired, and retreated as the third line appeared. There was not a moment's intermission in the musketfire.[4]

"Stand to your guns," cried Jackson, as he surveyed the line, "don't waste your amunition—see that every shot tells."[5]

The initial confusion of the British offensive, occasioned by the failure of the Forty-fourth Regiment to have the ladders and fascines ready, spread among Gibbs's men as they neared to within a hundred yards of the American line. Instead of rushing the rampart, as planned, they paused instinctively at the first blast of shot and returned the fire. That action proved fatal. In imitation the Forty-fourth also halted, threw down their ladders and fascines and started shooting too. And this hesitation of both the column and the Forty-fourth made them sitting ducks as volley after volley thundered from the rampart into their ranks. And with each volley, dozens of redcoats crumbled to the ground. Within moments the entire advance deteriorated into a reeling, confused army, verging on total disarray.

"Give it to them, my boys," called Jackson as he walked along the left of his line, cheering his men with words of encouragement. "Let us finish the business to-day."

"Fire! fire!" ordered General Carroll to the Tennessee and Kentucky sharpshooters in response to Jackson's command.[6] And the order was executed, not hurriedly or excitedly but calmly and deliberately. Hardly a shot was wasted by the skilled marksmen as row after row of riflemen shattered the British column. Major Harry Smith, an aide to Pakenham, said he never saw a more destructive fire poured upon a single line of men.[7] Every shot seemed to find its mark; scores of soldiers pitched to the ground, many of them falling on top of one another.

Seeing the British on the ground, Captain Patterson of Kentucky jumped on top of the breastwork and called to his men in his North of Ireland brogue, "Shoot low, boys! shoot low! rake them—rake them! They're coming on their all fours."[8]

Soon the British officers barked out commands to advance, and the disciplined column began to move again. Some of the men scrambled into the ditch, but they had no means of scaling the rampart. There was no sign of the ladders and fascines. They panicked. The men cried out their dismay.

"Where are the Forty-fourth? If we get to the ditch we have no means of scaling the lines!"

General Gibbs saw the disaster. He did what he could.

"Here come the Forty-fourth!" he shouted, swearing under his breath at the same time that if he lived he would see Mullens hanged from the highest tree in the cypress swamp. "Here come the Forty-fourth!"[9]

Reassured, the column pressed on. But the Forty-fourth did not come—at least not in strength—and there were not enough fascines and ladders. Again the column halted.

Then it happened: the psychological disintegration of the attack. The troops lost their nerve. "The horror before them was too great to be withstood."[10] They could no longer face the "flashing and roaring hell" in front of them.[11] They recoiled. And in that moment the battle was lost.

General Gibbs screamed at the men to reform and advance, but his commands went unheeded. The troops began a general retreat.

Pakenham rode forward from his position in the rear. "For shame," he cried, "recollect that you are British soldiers. *This* is the road you ought to take"—as he pointed to the fiery furnaces before them.[12]

Gibbs dashed up to him, his voice choked with emotion. "The troops will not obey me," he half sobbed. "They will not follow me."[13]

Removing his hat, Pakenham spurred his horse to the head of the wavering column, shouting reassurances to the men and pleading with them to follow him. A shower of balls from the rampart greeted his appearance. One shattered his right arm, another killed his horse. Mounting his aide's black Creole pony, Pakenham pursued the retreating column with cries to halt and reform.

They heard him. Once out of range of the fierce Tennessee and Kentucky rifles the column halted and turned, their spirits restored as they caught sight of the superb Highlanders commanded by General

Keane marching rapidly toward them to strengthen their column. The Highlanders, 900 strong, had made a successful feint on the right side of Jackson's line and were then ordered to cross the field and help their comrades on the left. As the tartan-trousered Highlanders obliqued to the right, exposing a flank to the enemy, the bagpipers began playing *Monymusk,* the regimental charge. The soldiers broke into a run when they heard the call. But the rampart also heard and responded. Round, grape, musketry, rifle, and buckshot raked the entire length of the Highlanders' line, the front as well as the left flank. The carnage was frightful.

Seeing the charge, the men under Gibbs's command dropped their knapsacks, reformed, and started back toward the rampart. When they again came within rifle range the mud ditch barked its command to halt. Round after round smashed into the British ranks. One 32-pounder, loaded to the muzzle with musketballs, crashed into the head of the column at point-blank range and leveled it to the ground, some 200 men killed or wounded in this single salvo.

"Order up the reserve," called Pakenham to his aide. And seeing the Highlanders still advancing toward the ditch despite the murderous fire, he saluted them with a wave of his hat and a cry, "Hurra! brave Highlanders."[14] In that instant the big guns of the Americans returned his salute with a terrible blast of grapeshot that struck down everyone standing near the commanding general. One of the shots ripped open Pakenham's thigh, killed his horse, and tumbled both to the ground. As his aides started to lift him, a second shot struck him in the groin and Pakenham instantly lost consciousness. He was carried to the rear out of gun range and propped up under an oak tree in the center of the field. Within minutes Lieutenant General Sir Edward Michael Pakenham died.[15]

Gibbs too was struck down in the devastating fire. He was carried from the field, writhing in agony. He lingered for another day before death released him from his torment. General Keane was also painfully wounded in the groin and was borne to the rear. Now not a single senior officer remained in the forward position to assume command and rally the dispirited troops.

The destruction of the high command in one blow "caused a wavering in the column which in such a situation became irreparable," General Lambert later reported.[16] The brave Highlanders halted in their tracks not one hundred yards from the rampart, taking round after round from the Americans until more than 500 of them lay on the ground. At last they too turned and fled in horror and dismay.[17] "Before they reached our small arms, our grape and canister mowed down whole columns," said General Coffee, "but that was nothing to the carnage of our Rifles and muskets."[18]

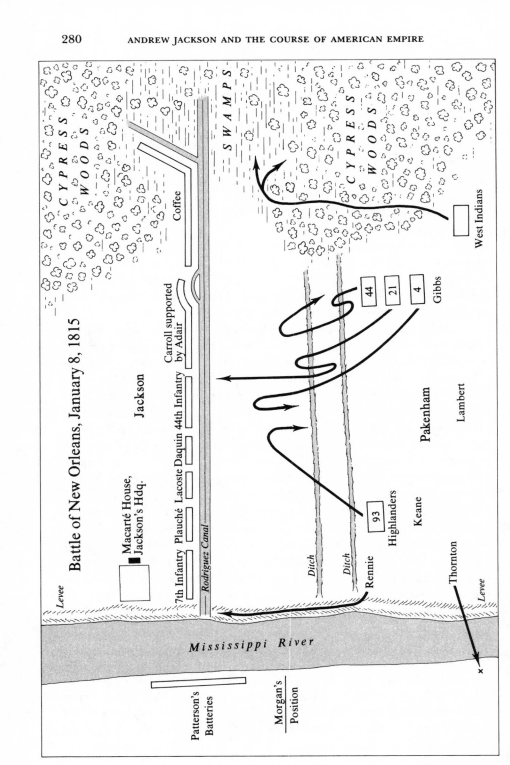

Battle of New Orleans, January 8, 1815

When the attack began General Jackson hurried back and forth behind his line, particularly on the left side, to assure himself that all necessary precautions had been taken. He called words of encouragement to his men. Those not occupied with loading or firing cheered him as he went by. Once the battle became a general engagement, Jackson took a position on slightly elevated ground near the center of the line in order to have a good sweep of the line and a general view of the entire scene. He looked absolutely calm and composed as he watched, as though he had no doubt about the ultimate outcome of the battle. Few spoke to him, unwilling to disturb his concentration or flow of thought.

When the British columns broke, Thomas Hinds, whose Mississippi dragoons were positioned slightly to the rear, dashed up to Jackson and requested permission to pursue the fleeing soldiers. It was a terrible temptation, one Jackson ached to indulge. But it had hazard written all over it. Reluctantly he shook his head. Permission not granted.

Far to the rear of the British attacking force, General Lambert waited with his reserves. When he learned of the death of Pakenham and the wounding of Gibbs and Keane he assumed command.[19] He ordered the reserve troops forward. But he moved slowly and cautiously, expecting the Americans to counterattack. Pakenham had ordered up the reserves earlier, but the bugler in the act of sounding the advance was struck in the arm and dropped his bugle. The charge never sounded. Now the reserves could do no more than cover the retreat of the fleeing column.[20] Fortunately Jackson decided against pursuit. His men would have run headlong into a powerful British reserve unit.

Successful as the Americans were on the left side of their line, the situation on the right (the side nearest the river) was completely different. Keane's brigade, commanded by Colonel Robert Rennie, crept up on the Americans so suddenly after the signal rocket exploded that the sentries at the American outposts had to scramble for their lives. Rennie's men pursued them and soon the troops of both sides were so intermingled that the American commander, Captain Humphrey, had to withhold his fire for fear of hitting his own men. At last the Americans managed to escape by racing over a plank stretched across the ditch to the rampart. Then Humphrey's batteries opened up. Rennie and two of his men reached the top of the rampart but were immediately cut down by the New Orleans sharpshooters, Rennie catching a ball in "one of his eyes."[21] Had the entire British column followed quickly behind Rennie's successful advance, Keane might have breached Jackson's line. But Pakenham ordered him to support Gibbs instead of Rennie.[22] It was a costly mistake. Keane led his men across the field to their subsequent destruction.

At the extreme left of Jackson's line, where Coffee and his men guarded the cypress swamps, a detachment of British West Indian troops skirmished in the woods. Some succeeded in getting quite close to Coffee's position but then became mired and were drowned or captured. These troops were astonished at the squirrel-like agility of the Tennesseans in jumping from log to log and their alligator-like facility for navigating the water, mud, and bushes.[23] Once again Coffee and his men demonstrated their courage and skill.

As the British beat a retreat and Jackson's officers surrounded and congratulated him on their astounding victory, Old Hickory seemed a trifle apprehensive. He cast an anxious glance across the river. Why no movement? Why such silence? The quiet distressed him.

Then, suddenly, General Morgan's guns spoke. Jackson sighed with relief. He mounted the breastwork and turned to his men. "Take off your hats and give them three cheers!" he commanded. The army obeyed as it tried to discern what was happening nearly a mile and a half away.

What was happening was disaster. Disaster for the Americans. The defeat on the west side of the Mississippi was as total as the victory on the east side. Jackson appeared oblivious to the needs and danger of his position across the river. He did not adequately reinforce it with troops when he could have spared at least one of his regular regiments. Nor does it appear that he even visited the location during the sixteen-day period in which the British were moving toward the city. Worse, he did not provide any boats for crossing the three-quarter-mile-wide river should reinforcements be necessary. The west bank defense—if it can be called that—was easily swept aside by the British once their offensive got under way.[24]

To prevent a landing on the west bank, 120 Louisiana militiamen, commanded by Major Jean Arnaud, were sent forward three miles below Morgan's main position. They bivouacked along the river road and went to sleep leaving a single sentry on guard. Thornton with 600 men and three gun-barges manned by 100 sailors landed at daylight on the west bank at a point about one mile downstream from Arnaud's men. A larger invading force had been intended but only a third of the boats needed for transport had been hauled into position on the night of January 7th, and Pakenham permitted Thornton to proceed with a reduced contingent. Upon reaching the opposite side, Thornton formed his men into columns, used the gun-barges to cover his flank, and rushed forward.

He just missed capturing the sleeping Louisianians, who awoke at the sentinel's alarm and quickly retreated.[25] About a mile from Morgan's line they met a detachment of Kentuckians under Colonel John Davis, sent to assist them. They joined forces and tried to check Thornton's advance. But the British officer easily turned their right, sending the Louisianians fleeing into the swamp, and then routed the main body of Kentuckians, who rushed back toward Morgan's line in great confusion. Thornton halted his advance within seven hundred yards of the Americans, reconnoitered, and completed preparations for a general assault.[26]

Morgan's line, unlike Jackson's, was badly positioned due to the need of protecting Patterson's batteries—batteries whose location was determined by the American and British positions on the opposite bank.[27] Morgan was crouched behind a sawmill race but the race was too long for the number of men available to defend it. And many of the men were badly armed, or not armed at all. The right side of Morgan's line was particularly weak, so the Kentuckians were assigned to it. But even with the Kentuckians, a section of the line running to the swamp was unprotected except for a picket guard of eighteen men. Thornton quickly determined the weakness of the American position and the ease with which the right could be turned.[28]

A bugler sounded the charge. Amid a shower of rockets British sailors and soldiers in two columns, against the center and extreme right of the line, charged on either side of the Kentuckians. Finding themselves hemmed in between two divisions, the Kentuckians fired one volley and then abandoned their position. Morgan rode to the right and called to Colonel Davis to halt his men. Davis said it was impossible.

"Sir," replied Morgan, "I have not seen you try."

And then, turning to the fleeing Kentuckians, Morgan shouted, "Halt, halt! men, and resume your position."

At the same time an adjutant ran after them. "Shame, shame! Boys," he cried. "Stand by your general."[29]

They did not listen. They ran in confusion and panic. Morgan followed them on horseback and succeeded in bringing a few back, but another shower of rockets renewed their fears and sent them scurrying in every direction. The British, meanwhile, rushed over the millrace, scaled the parapet, attacked the left side of the line, and forced it to retreat.[30]

Patterson, with his battery on the levee some 300 yards to Morgan's rear, witnessed the retreat. In a moment of rage he turned to a midshipman standing near a twelve-pounder trained on the road. "Fire your piece into the d----d cowards!"[31] But sanity quickly returned and he countermanded the order. Instead he directed the guns to be spiked and the ammunition thrown into the river. Unfortunately his orders were not properly carried out, for the British were able to restore half his guns to action. The American naval gunners boarded the *Louisiana* and escaped into the river. Patterson retired to the rear with an aide, alternately cursing the Kentuckians and the British.

Thornton and his men had just repaired many of Patterson's guns and were about to enfilade Jackson's line when news of the disaster on the east bank arrived from General Lambert, along with orders for Thornton and his men to retire, recross the river, and join the main body.[32] It was then ten o'clock in the morning.

Two hours earlier the battle in front of the Rodriguez Canal had ended. First the muskets stopped firing with the redcoats retreating out of range, then word was passed down the line to cease fire. The men rested on their arms. The entire assault had taken hardly more than two hours, the principal attack lasting only thirty minutes. Some of the Americans again pleaded to counterattack, but Jackson aware of the risk, would not permit it.

After accepting a round of congratulations from his officers and calling for his men to shout their encouragement to the troops on the west bank of the river, Jackson walked slowly down the line with his staff, stopping at the center of each command to congratulate the men on their bravery and skill. As he passed, the band played *Hail Columbia*. In fact the band had played throughout the entire action. It enlivened the proceedings! Now, with the last strains of *Hail Columbia* sounding in everyone's ears, the entire line for the first time burst forth with loud and prolonged cheers for their General. Jackson nodded and gestured his appreciation. The cheering continued for some time.

But the cheers soon died when the army scaled the parapet and wandered around the battlefield. The men were stunned by what they saw. The ground, one observer reported, was "covered with dead and wounded laying in heaps, the field was completely red."[33] The ground immediately in front of the rampart was so strewn with the dead, the dying, the horribly wounded that "you could have walked a quarter of a mile to the front on the bodies of the killed and disabled."[34] In the ditch itself there were forty dead and over one hundred wounded. In other places bodies were piled on top of other bodies, some wounded, some dead. Many of the mortally wounded pitched and tumbled about in the agonies of death. "Some had their heads shot off, some their legs, some their arms. Some were laughing, some crying, some groaning, and some screaming."[35] Many had ducked for protection behind the piles of dead. They now began to move and stir and rise up. "I never had so grand and awful an idea of the resurrection as on that day," Jackson later wrote. "After the smoke of the battle had cleared off somewhat, I saw in the distance more than five hundred Britons emerging from the heaps of their dead comrades, all over the plain, rising up, and still more distinctly visible as the field became clearer, coming forward and surrendering as prisoners of war to our soldiers. They had fallen at our first fire upon them, without having received so much as a scratch, and lay prostrate, as if dead, until the close of the action."[36]

From all parts of the field came "terrible cries for help and water." and the American soldiers assisted the wounded into the lines, where they could receive medical attention. Some of the soldiers lying in the ditch did not understand "the language of the free men of color" who went to their aid, and thinking they were about to be robbed or murdered fired at the blacks and killed or wounded a number of them.[37] Indeed one writer believed that more American casualties occurred after the battle than during it.[38]

Later Jackson reported to Monroe that his losses amounted to seven killed and six wounded, but these were battle losses that did not include the later casualties among the "men of color" or those injured during the minor skirmishing that continued for the next few days.[39] On January 14 Jackson directed a full report on casualties. It produced a total of 13 killed, 39 wounded, and 19 missing in the action on January 8.[40]

For their part the British admitted to casualties totaling 2,037. For the entire disastrous expedition the total was slightly in excess of 2,400 men.[41] Of the 2,037, 291 were killed, 1,262 wounded, and 484 captured or missing. Most of the casualties were wounded or missing; nevertheless the figures were staggering when compared to American losses. Even Jackson had trouble accepting them at first and realized there would be many in the country who would have difficulty believing the figures and might dismiss them as absurd. The British loss, he reported to Monroe, "was immense. I had at first computed it at 1500; but it is since ascertained to have been much greater. . . . My loss was inconsiderable. . . . Such a disproportion in loss, when we consider the number and the kind of troops engaged must, I know, excite astonishment, and may not, every where, be fully credited; yet I am perfectly satisfied that the amount is not exagerated on the one part, nor underated on the other."[42]

Later a Frenchman tried to account for the staggering British losses. "Ah!" he exclaimed after some moments of reflection, "I see how it all happened. When these Americans go into battle, they forget that they are not hunting deer or shooting turkeys and try never to throw away a shot."[43] Indeed it was massive firepower—a "most destructive fire, of ball, Grape and musquetry"—heavily concentrated at the precise point of the main enemy attack that accounted for the heavy toll among the British.[44]

As the British army coiled back on itself, the eager and aggressive Jackson was tempted to counterattack and destroy what remained of the enemy. But a counterattack meant abandoning the safety of the rampart; it meant engaging highly professional soldiers on an open field with his motley army of militiamen and regulars, pirates and "men of color." Lambert had over 6,000 soldiers to meet a counterattack, and easily outnumbered Old Hickory's ragtail army. And Jackson had a sense of the size of his opponent from the reports he received from British deserters —reports that generally agreed on the approximate number of yet uncommitted troops.[45] Wisely, then, Jackson and his counselors decided to sit behind their ditch and wait for the enemy's next move.[46]

Lambert's first communication to Jackson asked for a truce in order to bury the dead and attend the wounded.[47] Jackson had no objection to this, but his major concern in any truce arrangement was the need to reinforce his position on the west bank while keeping Lambert from doing the same. When he first learned of the disaster across the river he sent a detachment of 400 troops under General Jean Humbert to retake the lost position. Believing them safely across the Mississippi at the time Lambert asked for a truce, Jackson conditioned his acceptance of Lambert's request on a mutual agreement not to reinforce their armies on the west bank beyond the existing numbers. Jackson also questioned whether protocol allowed his corresponding with Lambert instead of the commander in chief. "As you have not in our Correspondence Designated yourself as Such," he wrote, "Allow me Sir to ask whether I have now the honor of Addressing the Commander in Chief." Lambert hesitated to report Pakenham's death, but he had little choice. He admitted the fact. He also asked for a little time to consider Jackson's stricture about the west bank since he had approved a request from Colonel Alexander Dickson for permission to countermand the order for the withdrawal of Thornton's troops until he could learn firsthand whether they might exploit their success there. When Dickson reported that a force of several thousand was necessary to capitalize on the position, Lambert repeated his order for withdrawal and then accepted all of Jackson's requirements for a truce. Once the British withdrew from the west bank the Americans promptly reoccupied the position, and within a few days Patterson unspiked his guns and retrained them on the enemy across the river.[48] In the days following the truce Lambert buried his dead in mass graves and began careful preparations for the difficult task of withdrawing through the swamp to the ships of the fleet.

Like so many of his preceding victories, Jackson's incredible triumph over the British at New Orleans was again compounded of extraordinary luck. He himself acknowledged it although he did not call it luck but providence. "It appears," he wrote Colonel Robert Hays, "that the unerring hand of providence shielded my men from the shower of Balls, bombs and Rocketts, when every Ball and Bomb from our guns carried with them the mission of death."[49] A letter to James Monroe indicated the same understanding of his good fortune. "Heaven, to be sure, has interposed most wonderfully in our behalf, and I am filled with gratitude when I look back to what we have escaped."[50]

What he escaped, if nothing else, was the consequence of his own folly in mishandling the defenses of the west bank—a blunder that could have cost him the battle. Perhaps because of his towering ego and pride, he could not accept the blame for his own mistakes. From the moment he received word of the disaster on the opposite side he screamed imprecations across the water for this affront to his victory and reputation. In his "Address to His Troops on the Right Bank" of January 8, 1815, he stooped to an invidious and wholly unjustifiable comparison of his own and Morgan's commands.

> While by the blessing of heaven directing the valour of the troops under my Command, one of the most briliant Victories in the annals of the War was obtained, by my immediate command; no words can express the mortification I felt at witnessing the scene Exhibited on the oposite bank. I will spare your feelings and my own by entering into no detail on the Subject. To all who reflect it must be a source of eternal regret, that a few moments exertion of that courage you certainly possess was alone wanting to have rendered your success more compleat; than that of your fellow citizens in this Camp: by the defeat of the detachment which was rash enough to cross the river to attack you.
>
> To what cause was the abandonment of your lines owing? To fear? No! You are the Countrymen, the friends, the brothers of those who have secured to themselves by this courage the gratitude of their Country who have been prodigal of their blood in its defence, and who are strangers to any other fear than that of disgrace. To disaffection to our glorious Cause? No my Countrymen your General does justice to the pure sentiments by which you are inspired.
>
> How then Could brave men abandon the post committed to their care. The want of Dicipline, the want of Order, a total disregard to Obedience, and a Spirit of insubordination, not less distructive than Cowardise itself, this appears to be the cause which led to the disaster. And the Cause must be eradicated or I must cease to command, and I desire to be distinctly understood, that every breach of Orders, all want of discipline, every disattention of duty will be seriously and promptly punished.[51]

And on and on he went, blaming the troops for actions that stemmed in large measure from his own failures. He did not have the magnanimity to accept even a small portion of the blame he deserved. His later condemnation of Colonel Davis's Kentucky troops was similarly unjust; likewise his stout defense of Morgan and Patterson, whose personal bravery during the engagement deeply impressed him. As far as he was concerned, they did not share the disgrace of the west bank defeat. Later a court of inquiry, presided over by General Carroll, exonerated the Kentuckians from any conduct deserving censure but condemned the flight of Arnaud's men and criticized Morgan's choice of a defensive line.[52] Court findings or no, Jackson stuck to his own evaluation of guilt, and his disparagement of the Kentuckians not only produced a newspaper attack later on but it blemished his relationship with General John Adair, who commanded the Kentuckians at the Rodriguez Canal.[53]

While an uneasy truce operated on the plain below New Orleans, Admiral Cochrane, rather belatedly, attempted to run his fleet past Fort St. Philip on the lower Mississippi. It was a foolish and pathetic gesture; if the operation made any sense at all, it needed to be executed in conjunction with the general attack on the Rodriguez Canal. Instead the bombardment by Cochrane's ships began on January 9, continued to January 12, and succeeded only in killing one American and wounding three others. Finally the fort's commander, Major William Overton, ordered heavy mortar sent to him from the New Orleans Navy Yard. It was capable of long-range firepower. One salvo and the invading ships withdrew.[54]

There was no longer any question now that Lambert, would retire with his army. Instead of renewing the attack, he would withdraw, then revert to the original invasion plan and strike at Mobile. But the retreat was extremely difficult, complicated by the swamp and the lack of boats sufficient to embark more than half the army in one operation—thereby exposing the other half to attack. For nine days the British prepared a road to Fisherman's Village so that the entire army might retire as one unit. It was arduous work, and they never succeeded in constructing more than a rough trail covered with reeds and brush. At midnight on January 18, with fires still ablaze to fool the watchful Americans, Lambert's army silently decamped, leaving behind 80 seriously wounded men under medical attendance, two officers, fourteen pieces of heavy artillery, and a considerable quantity of shot. They destroyed most of their powder before they departed. As part of their baggage, the British carried the body of General Pakenham encased in a hogshead of rum to be shipped to the Caribbean for reshipment to London.

The following day, January 19, Jackson and his staff inspected the abandoned camp. Again the dark thought of pursuit teased the General's mind. Had he known of Agincourt and Crécy, Jackson would have understood that a large British army with its mind on retreat is not something to sting to battle. Fortunately, his advisers dampened his romantic enthusiasm. As Edward Livingston had said to him earlier, "What do you want more? Your object is gained. The city is saved. The British have retired. For the pleasure of a blow or two, will you risk against those fearless troops your handful of men, composed of the best and worthiest citizen, and rob so many families of their heads."[55] To his superior, Secretary Monroe, the General explained why he had not attacked the retreating enemy. "Such was the situation of the ground which he [the enemy] abandoned, and of that through which he retired, protected by canals, redoubts, entrenchments and swamps on his Right the river on his Left, that I could not, without encountering a risque which my true policy did not seem to require or authorize, annoy him much on his retreat."[56]

With all his faults as a commander, Jackson always had a sense of his true purpose and duty. And his duty was the salvation of the city and the repulse of the invading British army. Much as he may have desired further fame and glory, he was not seduced from his basic responsibility.

As Livingston said, Jackson had his victory: the city saved, the enemy gone. And it was his victory, one he earned and richly deserved. He was a brave, determined, untutored but innately skillful commander. He had inspired his men and officers to formidable acts of courage, and exceptional valor. No great strategist or tactician, he did not always recognize and understand quickly how a military situation was developing, as witness his slowness in concentrating his forces below New Orleans after the British landed and his ineptness in defending the western bank. Still he had true instincts of command; he radiated confidence and implacable resolution; he unerringly made all the right decisions in meeting the British on the east bank and fighting them as he did; he built an impenetrable wall and topped it with sheets of smoke and flame. And he did not jeopardize his colossal victory with an impetuous counterattack.

On January 25 the British fleet, with its cargo of defeated, wounded, and dead men, sailed out of Lake Borgne. A number of slaves in the immediate area gathered at Lambert's headquarters in hopes of escaping their servitude but were turned back. Cochrane launched an attack against Fort Bowyer and invested it on February 11. Major Lawrence surrendered his 400 men, an action which Jackson condemned as cowardice.[57] But the fort held out long enough to slow the preparations for the capture of Mobile; by the time the British were ready to invade the mainland again, the official news arrived announcing the end of the war. Early in March the ill-fated expedition sailed back to England. An American court of inquiry convened shortly thereafter, and Lawrence was absolved of all charges of misconduct in the surrender of Fort Bowyer.

Not until January 21 did Jackson find it prudent to remove the major portion of his army from behind the Rodriguez Canal. Two days earlier he had indicated to the Abbé Guillaume Dubourg, apostolic administrator of the diocese of Louisiana and the Floridas, that the return of the army to the city should occasion a public act of thanksgiving. "The signal interposition of heaven," he wrote, "in giving success to our arms against the Enemy . . . while it must excite in every bosome attatched to the happy Government under which we live, emotions of the liveliest gratitude, requires at the same time some manifestation of those feelings. Permit me therefore to entreat that you will cause the service of public thanksgiving to be performed in the Cathedral in token at once of the great assistance we have recd. from the *ruler of all Events* and of our humble sense of it."⁵⁸ The abbé heartily approved the idea and said he would begin immediately to "make the dispositions for the ceremony, the brightest ornament of which, will certainly be *yourself,* General, surrounded by your brave army."⁵⁹

On the morning of January 21 Jackson ordered the army drawn up behind the rampart for the last time. An address was read to the troops that described in glowing words the exciting events of the campaign and praised the men without stint for their bravery and skill. It was a typical Jackson production, an exultant shout of praise and gratitude. When the address ended the troops wheeled into marching order and headed back to New Orleans, the General with them. It was the first time he visited the city since the campaign began.

The old and the infirm, women and children, all turned out to hail the noble rescuers of their city. "Every countenance was expressive of gratitude—joy sparkled in every feature on beholding fathers, brothers, husbands, sons, who had so recently saved the lives, fortunes and honor of their families, by repelling any enemy come to conquer and subjugate the country. Nor were the sensations of the brave soldiers less lively on seeing themselves about to be compensated for all their sufferings by the enjoyment of domestic felicity. . . . How light, how trifling, how inconsiderable did their past toils and dangers appear to them at this glorious moment! All was forgotten, all painful recollections gave way to the most exquisite sensations of inexpressible joy."⁶⁰

The abbé, with Jackson's approval, postponed the religious service until Tuesday, January 23, in order to have time to make the necessary preparations. It had to be a stupendous jubilation.

On the day of the ceremony the streets were jammed. Balconies and rooftops came alive with spectators. People gathered everywhere: in the great square opposite the cathedral that fronted the river, in the streets leading to the square, along the levee. The uniformed companies of Plauché's battalion formed two lines from the entrance of the square (by the river) to the church. A temporary arch was erected in the middle of the square, opposite the main entrance of the cathedral. The arch was supported by six Corinthian columns, and on each side of it stood a young lady—one represented Justice, the other Liberty. Under the arch, standing on a pedestal, were two children holding a laurel crown. Between the arch and the cathedral "the most beautiful girls" took positions at regular intervals, each representing a different state or territory of the Union, all dressed in white with transparent blue veils and a silver star on their foreheads. Each held in her right hand a flag inscribed with the name of the state she represented and in her left hand a basket of flowers. A lance embedded in the ground behind each young lady carried a shield with the name of a state or territory. The shields, linked together with garlands of evergreens and flowers, filled the distance from the arch to the cathedral.[61]

Then, through the gate of the plaza, strode the Hero of the Battle of New Orleans, accompanied by his staff. An enormous cheer burst from the crowd. People waved to him and called him by name. Repeated salvos of artillery announced his presence and saluted his magnificent accomplishment. Entering the square, Jackson was requested to proceed to the cathedral by the walk prepared for him. As he passed under the arch the two children lowered the laurel crown to his head.[62] The eight-year-old daughter of Dr. David Kerr stepped forward and congratulated the Hero on his victory in the name of the people of Louisiana. A ballad written by Mrs. Ellery of New Orleans was sung to the tune of *Yankee Doodle*. The General was so touched by the words and actions of the children that he stopped and spoke to the young ladies and asked for a copy of the ballad (which he sent home to his nieces).[63] As he continued toward the church the young ladies strewed flowers in front of him and recited an ode.

> Hail to the chief! who hied at war's alarms,
> To save our threaten'd land from hostile arms;
> Preserv'd, protected by his gallant care,
> By his the grateful tribute of each fair:
> With joyful triumph swell the choral lay—
> Strew, strew with flow'rs the hero's welcome way.
> Jackson, all hail! our country's pride and boast,
> Whose mind's a council, and whose arm's an host;
> Who, firm and valiant, 'midst the storm of war,
> Boasts unstain'd praise—laurels without a tear:
> Welcome, blest chief! accept our grateful lays,
> Unbidden homage, and spontaneous praise;
> Remembrance, long, shall keep alive thy fame,
> And future infants learn to lisp thy name.[64]

At the porch of the cathedral the Abbé Dubourg, resplendent in his ecclesiastical robes, welcomed Jackson with a speech glowing with praise to the Almighty for having sent the country such a sublime savior. "In approving yourself the worthy instrument of Heaven's merciful designs," said the abbé, "the first impulse of your religious heart was to acknowledge the *signal interposition of providence*—your first step, a solemn display of *your humble sense of his favours*. . . . Immortal thanks be to his Supreme Majesty for sending us such an instrument of his bountiful designs." Then he handed the General a bough of consecrated laurel.[65]

Jackson, who was now something of a master at addressing assembled masses of people, responded to the abbé's glowing salute in carefully chosen words that sounded at once republican and imperial, stressing the heroism of his men without diminishing his own exalted accomplishment. "General Jackson knew well how to do a 'pretty thing,' " said one observer.[66]

The crowd hushed to hear him. "Reverend Sir," began Jackson with a courtly bow, "I receive with gratitude and pleasure the symbolical crown which piety has prepared; I receive it in the name of the brave men who have so effectually seconded my exertions for the preservation of their country—they well deserve the laurels which their country will bestow. For myself, to have been instrumental in the deliverance of such a country is the greatest blessing that heaven could confer. That it has been effected with so little loss—that so few tears should cloud the smiles of our triumph, and not a cypress leaf be interwoven in the wreath which you present, is a source of the most exquisite enjoyment."[67]

After a few more sentences in which he thanked the abbé for the prayers offered for his happiness, Jackson concluded by wishing the city wealth and happiness commensurate with its courage. Then he was escorted into the cathedral to a conspicuous seat near the altar. The cathedral was ablaze with light from "a thousand tapers." The *Te Deum* boomed forth with impressive solemnity, after which a guard of honor attended the General to his quarters. In the evening, the curfew suspended, the town and its suburbs were brilliantly illuminated; all New Orleans—in its own inimitable way—gave itself over to pleasure and feasting.[68]

In Washington, gloom and despair locked the nation's capital in hushed resentment and apprehension. Since the new year opened the inhabitants were unhappily conscious of the nation's shame and disgrace. From the very start the war had gone badly; now the capital was in ruins, burnt by the enemy, and the government humiliated by its flight from the British invaders. Congress indulged itself with ill-tempered accusations of blame for the war's misfortunes. Worse, rumors abounded that representatives from the Hartford Convention in Connecticut, which adjourned on January 5, 1815, were headed for Washington bearing constitutional revisions as the price of their continued acceptance of the Union. And what could James Madison, the poor appleseed johnny, do but bow to their demands?

There was yet another rumor and, if possible, a greater fear. It was generally known that an invasion force of monumental size had formed in the West Indies to strike a blow somewhere along the underbelly of the American Gulf Coast. Once New Orleans was picked off and the west lost, nothing could stop the British from returning to the Chesapeake with Wellington's veterans, capturing Baltimore and Washington, and marching on to Philadelphia and New York. A war that had begun with fantasies of conquest now appeared likely to conclude with defeat and subjugation.

Toward the middle of January the capital learned of the invasion before New Orleans and the night battle of December 23. Then followed ten days of silence.[69] To add to the gloom a severe snowstorm lashed Washington on January 23 and continued for three days, blocking roads in every direction until the last day of the month, when one mail delivery struggled through the snowdrifts. The mail was a disappointment. It brought only details of the gunboat battle on Lake Borgne.

Several more days passed. Still no word. Then, on February 4, came the report of the victory—and Washington went "wild with delight." The city erupted from its gloom and fear and general malaise. People thronged the President's mansion. They invaded the homes of the cabinet officers and the leading advocates of the war, saluting all with shouts of congratulation. The mayor issued a proclamation for the illumination of the city. Newspapers broke out their largest type to announce: ALMOST INCREDIBLE VICTORY!!! "Enemy . . . beaten and repulsed by Jackson and his brave associates with great slaughter. The Glorious News . . . has spread around a general joy, commensurate with the brilliance of this event, and the magnitude of our Victory."[70]

"Glory be to God that the barbarians have been defeated," shouted the *Niles Weekly Register.* "Glory to Jackson . . . Glory to the militia. . . . Sons of freedom . . . benefactors of your country . . . all hail!"[71]

The news shot further north as fast as it could be carried, "kindling everywhere the maddest enthusiasm." Cities turned night into day with spectacular illuminations to celebrate the unbelievable news of the nation's triumph. In Philadelphia parades were organized and transparencies constructed to depict the New Orleans battle as best they could conceive it. One man devised a transparency showing Jackson on horseback at the head of his staff, in pursuit of the enemy, with the motto, "This day shall ne'er go by, from this day to the ending of the world, but He, in it, shall be remembered."[72]

Then, nine days later, and certainly before Americans could catch their breath over this ecstatic event, came the announcement that the commissioners in Ghent had signed a treaty of peace with their British counterparts that ended the War of 1812. Never did such happy news have such an immediate and electrifying impact on the entire nation. Men raced through the streets crying, "Peace! Peace!" At night the same deep, throbbing anthem could be heard from town to town. No one wanted to be home alone, so with little preparation or organization men and women lighted torches and lamps and marched through the streets weeping with pride and happiness that this ugly war had at last been concluded.

Jackson's role in bringing honor and glory to the nation made him a popular hero for the remainder of his life. The country had entered the war with a desperate need to prove its right to independence, but the last two years seemed to prove the reverse, that the United States was only a temporary experiment in freedom, that its independence was undeserved.

Until New Orleans. New Orleans demonstrated that the nation had the heart and the will and the strength to roundly defeat its enemies and defend its freedom. "The last six months is the proudest period in the history of the republic," asserted one newspaper. "We . . . *demonstrated* to mankind a capacity to acquire a skill in arms to conquer 'the conquerors of the conquerors of all' as Wellington's *invincibles* were *modestly* stiled. . . . *Who would not be an American? Long Live the republic! . . . Last asylum of oppressed humanity! Peace is signed In the Arms of Victory!*"[73]

The nation's faith and confidence in itself had been restored by General Andrew Jackson. He alone was responsible for giving the country back its self-respect. He had "slaughtered" a magnificent British army— over 2,000 victims, a figure that seemed incredible at that time—and repelled the greatest armada in history.

The American people, their self-confidence restored, abandoned the need to prove their right to independence. Secure in the knowledge that their freedom had been permanently won, they turned to the important tasks of building a nation. Indeed "from that time on the Union had less of the character of a temporary experiment," something that might disappear in a stroke. "The country had also won respect abroad, and was recognized in the family of nations as it had not been before."[74]

In the public mind, all of this was associated with Andrew Jackson —not simply because of the magnitude of his victory over the British (although that was certainly important) but because the announcement of his colossal feat immediately preceded the announcement of the conclusion of the war. The tremendous boost to everyone's morale that his accomplishment on the battlefield provided was followed a few days later by the news of the peace treaty—and people tended to fuse the two events together. The result was the feeling that Andrew Jackson had come like some special messenger of the Almighty to rescue His people and preserve their freedom. Small wonder that Jackson's place in the pride and affection of the American people lasted until his death—and beyond. Small wonder that his popularity exceeded that of Washington, Jefferson, or Franklin.

Congress, upon hearing the details of the victory, unanimously adopted a set of resolutions bestowing special commendations on Jackson and the principal actors in the New Orleans drama.

> *Resolved,* By the Senate and House of Representatives of the United States of America in Congress assembled, That the thanks of Congress be, and they are hereby, given to Major General Jackson, and through him, to the officers and soldiers of the regular army, of the volunteers, and of the militia under his command . . . for their uniform gallantry and good conduct conspicuously displayed against the enemy, from the time of his landing before New Orleans until his final expulsion therefrom, and particularly for their valor, skill and good conduct on the 8th of January last, in repulsing, with great slaughter, a numerous British army of chosen veteran troops . . . and thereby obtaining a most signal victory over the enemy with a disparity of loss, on his part, unexampled in military annals.
>
> *Resolved,* That the President of the United States be requested to cause to be struck a gold medal, with devices emblematical of this splendid achievement, and presented to Major General Jackson as a testimony of the high sense entertained by Congress of his judicious and distinguished conduct on that memorable occasion.[75]

George M. Troup of Georgia introduced the resolutions from the Committee on Military Affairs and in his accompanying remarks congratulated the House "on the glorious termination of the most glorious war ever waged by any people. To the glory of it, General Jackson and his gallant army have contributed not a little. I cannot, sir, perhaps language cannot, do justice to the merits of General Jackson . . . ; it is a fit subject for the genius of Homer."[76]

Charles J. Ingersoll of Pennsylvania echoed these sentiments and repeated a question frequently posed in the newspapers. "Who is not proud to feel himself an American—our wrongs revenged—our rights recognized!" he asked. "For I repeat that no matter what the terms of the treaty may be [the terms of the Treaty of Ghent had not yet reached Washington], the effects of this war must be permanently prosperous and honorable. The catastrophe at Orleans has fixed an impress, has sealed, has consecrated the compact beyond the powers of parchment and diplomacy. . . . Let us then pass, let us vote by acclamation, the thanks of Congress to General Jackson and his companions in victory."[77]

Nearly every state in the Union passed similar resolutions. "We consider your defence of . . . New Orleans," read one, "as the most illustrious among illustrious deeds."[78] The President dispatched his congratulations via James Monroe. "I am instructed by the President to convey to you in strong terms," wrote the secretary, "his approbation of your conduct, and of that of the troops acting under you who have rendered such important services to their country. Your arrangements for the defence of the City, in selecting and fortifying the proper points at which to oppose the enemy, and in the disposition of your force in action; afford proofs of a talent for command which do you honor. By the example of your personal energy and distinguished gallantry, in the field, the more necessary and commendable with your troops, it is believed that the happiest effect was produced. By these important services you have merited in an eminent degree the approbation of the Government and the gratitude of your fellow citizens."[79]

By mid-February a number of songs had been composed to commemorate the great event. One of the most popular was *Jackson Is the Boy.*

> Come all ye sons of freedom
> Come all ye brave who lead 'em
> Come all who say God speed 'em
>   And sing a song of joy!
> To Jackson ever brave,
> Who nobly did behave—
> Unto Immortal Jackson,
> The British turn'd their backs on,
> He's ready still for action,
>   O Jackson is the boy. . . .
>
> Our Country is our mother,
> Then let each son and brother,
> Stand firm by one another,
>   And sing a song of joy!
> Let party spirit cease,
> Here's "Victory and Peace."
> And here's "Immortal Jackson,"
> The British turn'd their backs on,
> He's ready still for action,
>   O Jackson is the boy.[80]

Even Jackson now knew he had ascended to the ranks of the Immortals. He calculated correctly the impact of his victory on the country at large. And he had ego enough to see his triumph in fairly exalted terms. The "morning of the 8th of January," he wrote, ". . . will be ever recollected by the British nation, and always hailed by every true american."[81]

Thereafter Americans sang with one voice, "O Jackson is the boy."

CHAPTER 19

The Course of American Empire

JACKSON'S ROLE IN THE WAR OF 1812 was absolutely crucial to the future course of American expansion. Not only did he spare the nation an almost certain amputation of territory in the southwest but he prepared the way for the immediate future growth of the American nation.[1]

Under no circumstances did Great Britain recognize any American claim to territory along the Gulf Coast. In fact Britain disputed—correctly—the legality of the Louisiana Purchase. France had no right to sell it to the United States since the Treaty of San Ildefonso of 1800, by which Napoleon had forced Spain to surrender Louisiana to him, specifically stated that France would not sell or otherwise alienate the territory without first offering to return it to Spain. When Napoleon blithely ignored his own previous agreement with the Spanish government and sold Louisiana to the United States, many other nations regarded the action as illegal.

As far as England was concerned, none of the lower Mississippi, or New Orleans, or any of the Gulf Coast belonged to the United States. In invading Louisiana and seizing New Orleans, Britain probably intended ultimately to restore the area to its rightful owner, Spain. And in signing the Peace Treaty of Ghent, which ended the War of 1812, there was nothing that could be remotely construed as British acquiescence in the terms of the Purchase.[2] Louisiana, therefore, was not included in the Treaty of Ghent in any shape or form.

Nor Mobile. The United States had claimed West Florida as part of the Louisiana Purchase but did not dare seize it until hostilities commenced.[3] Thus Mobile, too, was not covered by the Treaty of Ghent as far as the British were concerned and most probably would have been restored to Spain if the invasion had established a solid base on the Gulf Coast.[4] In fact Spanish representatives claimed to have been assured that all of Louisiana and West Florida would be restored to Spain at the end of the war.[5] As late as April 1815 Spain, assuming Pakenham had defeated Jackson at New Orleans, asked Britain to retain what had been occupied —despite the Treaty of Ghent—and return it to her.[6]

Secretary Monroe stated the situation concisely to Madison:[7] Had Jackson lost the Battle of New Orleans, Britain would have insisted that the entire Gulf Coast belonged to Spain, arguing that the Treaty of Ghent did not apply and that American claims to this area were specious because Mobile had been illegally seized and Louisiana illegally purchased.[8] Thus Jackson's victory did more than simply demonstrate the excellence of American arms on the battlefield. It prevented the almost certain detachment of the entire Gulf Coast area (and maybe all of Louisiana as well) which would have been a major catastrophe for the United States had it happened. In a sense, then, Jackson's victory legitimized or legalized— if conquest ever legalizes—the Louisiana Purchase, which France had no business selling in the first place.

Fortunately for the United States the British did not capture Fort Bowyer until after the war had been concluded. For its seizure made certain the capture of Mobile, which could never have withstood a siege, much less a direct attack by a large invading force. General Winchester, who had been left in command of the Mobile forces and who had already surrendered one army to the British in Canada, resigned when he learned of the capture of Fort Bowyer rather than face the certain prospect of another humiliating surrender.[9] The fall of Mobile would have introduced a large British army to the American continent (Lambert had over 6,000 professional soldiers) that could then launch further assaults into the interior and perhaps even attempt another attack on New Orleans by an overland route. Since Britain did not consider Mobile to be covered by the Treaty of Ghent, she could have refused to surrender it. Conceivably she might have retained Mobile for herself as a kind of Gibraltar in the western hemisphere.

All of which is conjecture and of little historical significance since it did not happen—except that it helps to emphasize the fact that Britain did not regard Florida or Louisiana as areas covered under the terms of the treaty that ended the War of 1812. Jackson's victory, therefore, was not a futile exercise. Nor did it lack significance in terms of American territorial expansion.

It is generally agreed that the War of 1812 ended with no side having lost or gained—that the peace treaty established a *status quo ante bellum*. Actually a *status quo* was not established. In the eyes of the British a true *status quo* would have restored New Orleans and Mobile to Spain. Since Britain did not conquer these areas and the United States continued to hold them they were, in a manner of speaking, acquired as a result of the War of 1812.

Especially Mobile. Mobile was seized after hostilities commenced— a good year after. A real *status quo* would have required the restoration of this territory to Spain.[10] By keeping it, the United States expanded the nation's boundaries. The acquisition also whetted still further the country's appetite for the rest of Florida and facilitated the eventual annexation of the entire Gulf Coast.

Because a *status quo* had not been established and because the western part of Florida had been seized and retained by the United States, the Spanish again divided what remained into two sections, East and West, with the Suwannee River the dividing line between them. The Perdido River became the western boundary of the Floridas (and is the present boundary of the state). Also there was little Spain could do to protect this borderland against further American aggression. Over the past few years, and continuing for several more years—roughly 1810 to 1825—the Spanish empire was shaken by a series of revolutions in Central and South America, and Spain no longer had the resources to exercise any real authority along the American frontier.

The War of 1812 also triggered the ruination of the American Indian and the spoliation of his property—a process already in motion and now accelerated far beyond the imagination of the most rapacious speculator —thanks to the efforts and intentions of General Andrew Jackson. The war considerably enlarged the amount of Indian land available to American citizens, and the pace of that acquisition continued after the close of hostilities.

Had the British established themselves on the Gulf Coast even temporarily, an Indian buffer state would have been created in the southwest to block American expansion and provide protection for the Spanish in Florida. Even without establishing a coastal stronghold, the British furnished extensive military aid to the Indians and sought to engage their active support in the war with the United States.

To understand what happened to hasten the destruction of the Indians, it is necessary to recall a series of events that began in the spring of 1814. Admiral Cochrane ordered Captain Hugh Pigot aboard the frigate *Orpheus* to proceed with the vessel *Shelburne* to the mouth of the Apalachicola River and to open communication with the Creeks in an effort to win Indian assistance for the coming invasion. Pigot was also instructed to supply the Creeks with arms and ammunition, and he carried with him 2,000 stands of arms and 300,000 ball cartridges.[11] The ships anchored on May 10, 1814, a landing party scouted the area, and within ten days nearly a dozen Indian chiefs agreed to confer with Pigot. Out of the talks came an agreement to station on shore George Woodbine, brevet captain of marines, a sergeant, and a corporal of marines to organize the Indians and distribute arms. In his report to Cochrane, Captain Pigot emphasized the strong anti-American feeling among the Indians and estimated there were 2,800 Creeks ready to assist a British invasion, along with an equal number of Choctaws and 1,000 other Indians in the swamps around Pensacola, as well as black slaves in Georgia. These Indians offered their support on condition that Britain assure them the necessary arms and supplies. With their help and a small force of regulars, Pigot believed Mobile could be captured without difficulty; after that it would be relatively simple to take Baton Rouge and then New Orleans. He enclosed with his report a letter from the Creek chiefs confirming their desire to support a British invasion and drive the Americans from the coastal area. This letter was written just two months after their disastrous defeat at Horseshoe Bend and two months before the signing of the Treaty of Fort Jackson.[12]

Cochrane, on receiving Pigot's report, sent Major Edward Nicholls with four officers, 108 marines, and arms and ammunition to the Apalachicola area to begin training the Indians. Nicholls's instructions also included enlisting as many slaves as could be induced to flee the United States, reconnoitering the country west of the Apalachicola, discovering the problems involved in capturing New Orleans, and aiding the process of enlisting Indian support for the invasion. Woodbine was placed under Nicholls's command.

With respect to the Indians, Nicholls achieved notable success in his mission and armed over 4,000 braves. Something like 3,000 muskets, 1,000 pistols, 1,000 carbines, 500 rifles, and more than a million rounds of ammunition were distributed to the Creeks and Seminoles.[13] And there they were, a very powerful force, waiting to link up with a British army and destroy their American foe.

After the failure of the New Orleans campaign, Admiral Cochrane revived his earlier scheme to strike through Mobile and unite with the Indian confederation he had created and had been supplying for the past six months. But when he learned that the peace treaty had been signed he terminated the invasion.

In addition to supplying Indians with guns and ammunition, Nicholls also promised them, in Cochrane's name, that the King of England would protect their interests after the war.[14] This guarantee was written into the

Treaty of Ghent. At the insistence of the British government, an article was inserted into the treaty safeguarding the rights of their Indian allies.[15] It was quite specific. Article IX provided that the United States agreed to end hostilities with the Indians "and forthwith to restore to such tribes . . . all possessions . . . which they have enjoyed or been entitled to in one thousand eight hundred and eleven previous to such hostilities." This article automatically nullified the Treaty of Fort Jackson.[16]

Furthermore, since many Creek chiefs had refused to sign the Treaty of Fort Jackson and had instead fled to Florida where they continued fighting, they were still technically at war with the United States. But now that the United States had agreed to end the war and now that Washington and London had both accepted the restoration of Indian rights and property as of 1811, Cochrane left Nicholls and a body of marines at Apalachicola to protect and assist his allies until the full guarantees of Article IX had been implemented.[17] Moreover, Cochrane assured the Creeks that the United States was obligated *by treaty* to restore all the lands forced from them by Jackson at the conclusion of the Creek War.[18] With that he sailed away.

The Iron General had no intention of allowing the nullification of the Treaty of Fort Jackson. That was *his* treaty. The government of the United States might yield to the Indians under pressure from the British, but not Old Hickory, not Sharp Knife. According to Jackson, the Creeks agreed to peace with the United States under the terms of *his* treaty and were therefore exempt from the Treaty of Ghent. Article IX did not apply to them. It did not include them. No matter what anybody said, that was the way he saw it and that—by God—was the way it was going to be.

But could he get away with such an interpretation? The administration understood its treaty obligations—and already the Creek chiefs were complaining. "I am also desired to say to you by the chiefs," wrote Nicholls to Benjamin Hawkins in May 1815, "that they do not find that your citizens are evacuating their lands according to the 9th article of the treaty of peace." Dutifully, if begrudgingly, the United States government finally acknowledged its obligation in June 1815, and Jackson was duly notified. "Inclosed you will receive copies of communications from the commissioners appointed to make overtures of peace to the hostile Indians," the secretary of war wrote Jackson, "in pursuance of the stipulations of the 9th article of the treaty of Ghent. . . . The President . . . is confident that you will cooperate with all means in your power to conciliate the Indians, upon the principles of our agreement with Great Britain."[19]

Conciliate the Indians? Return their property? Not Andrew Jackson. He contemptuously dismissed the instructions, presuming a better knowledge of the proper attitude the American government should assume with respect to the obligations of the Treaty of Ghent. He simply decided that whatever the secretary of war intended by his instructions they did not apply to his treaty. So he continued to execute the terms of the Treaty of Fort Jackson. Despite repeated protests by the Creek chiefs, he continued expelling the Indians from their land. And nobody stopped him. Nobody dared, not even the administration. Apart from everything else, the administration feared western reaction to such a move; it feared attempting to bring a national hero to heel to please the Indians and Great Britain. So it did nothing. Rather it allowed Jackson to pursue uninterrupted his policy of removal.

But if for the sake of argument Jackson was right and the Creeks who signed the Treaty of Fort Jackson in 1814 were excluded from the terms of the Treaty of Ghent, what of the Creeks who rejected Jackson's treaty and continued their war against the United States? Sharp Knife had a ready answer. These Indians were not Creeks living within the jurisdiction of the United States, he claimed. Rather they were Creeks residing in Florida and consequently had lost no property under the terms of the Fort Jackson treaty.

A perfect answer, and completely self-serving. It totally harmonized with western views and expectations, and the government knew it. There was nothing for Washington to do, therefore, but grant official approval. So, in violation of its treaty obligations and in violation of the law, the United States government accepted Jackson's interpretation and his actions.

The violation of the Treaty of Ghent was not simply the product of the administration's recognition of western desire for the spoliation of Indian property and the danger of antagonizing a popular hero. The administration itself approved expansion. It wanted the Indian removed. The growth of the nation dictated the support of western claims; national policy precluded the protection of Indian property and rights.

Still, a problem existed. The government had given its word to Great Britain to guarantee Indian rights and restore all possessions taken after 1811. Surely the British would insist on this guarantee. Surely they would demand the enforcement of Article IX.

But they did not. England sold out. England betrayed both the Spanish and the Indians. England abandoned the south in order to protect her possessions in the north. Given American expansionist desires, north and south, it was better to allow the United States a free hand to expand at the expense of the Spanish and Indians in the south if, in return, the Americans would abandon their interest and desire for Canada.[20] If the United States would agree to respect the northern border, Britain could afford to look the other way when the Spanish and Indians were dispossessed in the south.

And the United States did agree. Within two years, Charles Bagot, His Britannic Majesty's Envoy Extraordinary, and Richard Rush, acting secretary of state, signed an agreement on April 28, 1817 neutralizing the Great Lakes and providing for an unfortified frontier between Canada and the United States. The two countries pledged disarmament on both land and sea. But they did more. For the British the agreement signaled abandonment of her resistance to American expansion along the Gulf Coast and in the Mississippi valley. For the Americans it signaled the end of northern expansion. Canada was forever relinquished.

Then, on October 20, 1818, the two nations took another step to lock each other in place. They signed the Anglo-American Convention of 1818. This Convention established a boundary line between the United States and Canada along the forty-ninth parallel from the Lake of the Woods to the Rocky Mountains. Beyond the western slope of the Rockies the territory was open to joint occupation. The line permanently froze a boundary between the two countries.[21] For the United States, the Rush-Bagot Agreement and the Convention of 1818 made a great deal of sense. They constituted pragmatic recognition that future seizure of Canada was impossible. After repeated and humiliating failures to annex the northern provinces, the United States abandoned its aggression. American expansion to the north came to an abrupt halt. It never again became a realistic possibility.

The British understood their betrayal. They knew the United States violated the Treaty of Ghent and they knew that they should protest. Lord Bathurst, the secretary for war and colonies, admitted as much.[22] He even tried to force his country to intervene on behalf of the Indians, but he was overruled.[23] The Indians were sacrificed to a greater need.

Edward Nicholls also tried to assist the Indians. After all it was he who provided all the guarantees and promised the Creeks that the King of England would protect their interests after the War. When he realized —after repeated arguments with Benjamin Hawkins—that the United States had no intention of honoring its word, he pleaded with his own government to protest this violation of the treaty. In desperation he attempted to effect formal British recognition of the tribe and establish a "regular Creek-British military alliance"[24] That would force his government to carry out its earlier promise to protect Indian interests. Again and again he pressed the authorities in London to guarantee Creek property as the Treaty of Ghent stipulated.[25] But his government ignored him. It would neither honor its obligations nor commit itself to an alliance with the Indians. In shame and disgust, Nicholls eventually abandoned his efforts and left Apalachicola for Bermuda.

The United States officially consented to the permanent loss of Canada. The Senate approved the Rush-Bagot agreement. And no one seriously protested this abandonment of American hope and expectation. No one objected.

In the south it was a different story. Andrew Jackson would not permit a similar sellout. He refused to allow the government to enforce Article IX of the Treaty of Ghent. The feeble effort of the administration to begin the process of restoring Indian possessions in accordance with the treaty was rudely turned aside. Thus, because England would not intervene and Jackson would not budge, the administration permitted the seizure of Indian property in deliberate violation of the treaty.

Nor would the Spanish get border guarantees similar to the Rush-Bagot agreement. For Jackson their expulsion from North America must proceed without delay. The safety and necessary growth of the United States, he believed, dictated the removal of Spain from Florida, Texas, and Mexico. American expansion might be closed to the north, but it would continue to the south and west—that is if Andrew Jackson had anything to say about it.

In forcing the federal government to adopt *his* policy toward the Indians and the Treaty of Ghent, Jackson accomplished two things: He initiated the first step in the removal of all Southern Indians from their lands and their ultimate transportation beyond the Mississippi River; and he destroyed a potential Indian buffer state that might have protected the Spanish in Florida. By eliminating that buffer an already weak Spanish presence in Florida was further weakened. Jackson had created a situation that assured the eventual acquisition of Florida.

The Indian buffer zone could have served the interests of the British and Spanish, thereby endangering the American frontier. Not all the Indians who sought British aid were Red Sticks; many had avoided the Creek War and waited patiently for their traditional ally, Great Britain, to arm and feed them. But Britain waited too long before intervening; meanwhile, Jackson destroyed the Red Sticks and sent starvation galloping among the Creek people, killing friend and foe alike. It has been suggested that if the Red Sticks had delayed their war and sought British assistance, as did the Creeks living near Apalachicola, the British could have captured the entire Gulf area, including New Orleans.[26] This is true. The Americans could never have coped with both a full-scale British invasion and a general Indian war. Such a disaster would have terminated American expansion to the south and west just as it was terminated to the north.

Thus the Creek War was an unmitigated disaster for both the British and the Spanish. It decimated the Indians, it created a large armed American force in the southwest, and it produced General Andrew Jackson. Unfortunately for the United States, no one of Jackson's caliber appeared on the northern frontier to serve his country and assist its expansion. Had Old Hickory and his Tennessee volunteers been sent to Canada, Jackson's aides later agreed, the physical shape of the United States at war's end would have been vastly different.[27]

Over the next several years General Jackson pursued his policy of Indian removal, arranging nearly half a dozen treaties that involved the acquisition of valuable land in virtually every southern state. One historian has already pointed out that Jackson's treaties acquired almost one-third of Tennessee, three-fourths of Florida and Alabama, one-fifth of Georgia and Mississippi, and perhaps one-tenth (or slightly less) of Kentucky and North Carolina.[28] He assembled a veritable kingdom. The Cotton Kingdom!

All told, Jackson's achievement in less than sixteen months was little short of miraculous. By his several victories he had blocked the return of Great Britain to the southwest, guaranteed continued American expansion in the area and destroyed Indian power. Considering what he had to start with and what was expected of him, the assignment was impossible. He had a small army and yet was given the entire Gulf Coast to defend against an enormous strike force that could land almost anywhere it chose. He understood the need to maintain a high degree of mobility in order to meet the invasion wherever it appeared. That he accomplished this feat and stationed himself in an impregnable position when the strike finally occurred, despite so many imponderables, speaks well of his leadership and generalship.

When the British retired from their fortified stronghold at Apalachicola, the Indians also evacuated the fort. But the Negroes remained —several hundred of them, with guns, cannons, and a large amount of ammunition. The Spanish were unhappy about the Negro fort, as it was called, because it invited American intervention to reduce it. But the Spanish were incapable of capturing it because it was strongly armed. So they did nothing. It just sat there, infuriating Americans. Settlers yammered at Jackson to do something. It was bad enough to have such a fort near the American frontier; worse that the fort was occupied by armed black men.

British abandonment of the Gulf Coast and their Indian allies following the war outraged the Spanish. Without engaging in any hostilities at all, Spain lost West Florida (including the important town of Mobile), witnessed the destruction of a protective Indian buffer state and the almost total erosion of her position along the Gulf Coast. Worse, the

Spanish fully recognized that an implacable enemy had emerged who was totally committed to their destruction.[29] General "Andres" Jackson, as they called him, made his intentions so obvious that they momentarily expected him to march into Florida and then turn west and take Texas and Mexico. Indeed Jackson was quite disposed to seize both Texas and Mexico—"all Spanish North America," as he once said. Much of it already belonged to the United States, he figured, as part of the Louisiana Purchase. For the rest it was a simple matter of commanding 2,000 volunteers and running off the hated Dons so that Americans could claim what was clearly intended for them.

But before Texas, Florida. That first.

CHAPTER 20

United States v. Major General Andrew Jackson

THE PEOPLE OF NEW ORLEANS had joyfully exploded after their long fearful watch. The nightmare was over. The restrictions and regulations and curfew and all the other limitations on their living habits would now be removed—or so they thought. But they thought wrong. They did not understand the character and will of Andrew Jackson.

The morning after the victory celebration when crowds had cheered and children had pressed a laurel wreath upon Jackson's brow, the city awoke to find martial law reimposed. The previous night had only been a moment of relaxation. Now the people learned they must return to a state of military preparedness. Jackson had his duty. He must safeguard New Orleans and with it the entire Mississippi valley. As far as he knew the war was still on, and the redcoats might return after a period of rest and reconnoitering to renew the fight. So in Jackson's mind a return to martial law was not a debatable matter. The militia must remain under arms; the people must submit to martial law.

What made the situation worse were the rumors that Jackson was prepared to destroy property indiscriminately, even to burn the city if necessary, to prevent it from falling into the hands of the enemy. The governor, the legislature, and other civil authorities feared the rumors and resented the prolongation of martial law. Within days their grumbling rose from whispers to shouts. Soon they were talking about the "rule of the tyrant"; soon Jackson had been verbally converted from hero to despot. The deterioration of relations was speeded by attempts on the part of both Jackson and the civil government to handle the problem of runaway slaves who had sought refuge with the retreating British army. Nearly 200 slaves were involved, necessitating a lengthy correspondence between Jackson and Lambert.[1] When the generals failed to resolve the difficulty, the governor and legislature thought they would intervene and try their hand.

Jackson flared. This amounted to unwarranted interference in a purely military matter. "I do hope that the Legislature nor yourself," he wrote Governor Claiborne, "will not attempt any thing like negotiating or having any communication with the Enemy, that is a subject on which you nor the Legislature as such has any power over. . . . Be assured if either the assembly or yourself attempt to interfere with subjects not belonging to you, it will be immediately arrested."[2]

To forestall the legislature from appointing a commission to treat with the British, Jackson hurried Edward Livingston, Manuel White, and R. D. Shepherd to Lambert to recover the slaves and arrange for an exchange of prisoners. Meanwhile, the legislature demonstrated its growing displeasure with Jackson by voting its thanks on February 2 to all the leading officers of the army during the Battle of New Orleans—except the Commander in Chief. To Adair, Carroll, Coffee, Hinds, and Thomas went the legislature's gratitude, conveyed through Governor Claiborne; to Jackson, nothing. Old Hickory took no notice of this crude insult, but no one missed its intent or its effect.

Jackson's troubles escalated during February and March. Early in February rumors reached the city that a peace treaty had been signed in Ghent that ended the war. Now, surely, martial law must end. But Jackson had received no official confirmation of the news and therefore sought to prevent newspapers from circulating the "inflammatory" report—an action that won him additional criticism for "muzzling" the press. By the end of the month the Louisiana militia verged on mutiny. Governor Claiborne appealed to the General to permit their discharge.[3] Jackson refused.

The Creoles hit upon another scheme. Registering themselves as French citizens with the French consul, Toussard, they demanded discharge from military service for reasons of their foreign nationality. Jackson reacted to this ploy in typically no-nonsense fashion. On February 28 he ordered all Frenchmen—and that included the consul—to leave New Orleans within three days and to keep to a distance of 120 miles from the city until news of the ratification of the peace treaty had been officially published.[4] The voter registration lists for the last election were used to determine who were American citizens and who were not. Those who had voted were compelled to serve in the militia; the others, claiming French citizenship, were ordered out of the city.[5] It was a sorry spectacle.

At this juncture an article appeared in the French language newspaper *La Courrière de la Louisiana* signed by "A Citizen of Louisiana of French Origin" which boldly and forcefully criticized Jackson's order of expulsion. "It is high time," the writer said, "the laws should resume their empire; that the citizens of this State should return to the full enjoyment of their rights; that, in acknowledging that we are indebted to General Jackson for the preservation of our city and the defeat of the British, we do not feel much inclined, through gratitude, to sacrifice any of our privileges, and, less than any other, that of expressing our opinion of the acts of his administration." Persons accused of crime should be brought before civil judges, the writer continued, not military or special tribunals. The moment for moderation has arrived. With the enemy gone, Jackson's acts of authority are "no longer compatible with our dignity and our oath of making the Constitution respected."[6]

Jackson ranted at the open defiance of his authority. The editor of the newspaper was hauled before him and made to reveal the name of the author of the article. He was Louis Louailler, a member of the legislature and a staunch supporter of the war. Two days later Jackson dispatched a file of soldiers to arrest Louailler for inciting mutiny and disaffection in the army. The writer was spotted walking along the levee opposite the Exchange Coffee House. The officer in charge of the detail tapped him on the shoulder, informed him he was under arrest, and advised him to go along peaceably.

Suddenly Louailler cried out in a loud voice to a group of bystanders that he was being taken against his will by armed men and that they were witnesses to this police-state tactic. A lawyer in the crowd, hearing him, offered his services and was retained. The lawyer sped to the residence of Federal District Judge Dominick Augustin Hall and requested a writ of habeas corpus for Louailler. Like everyone else in New Orleans, Hall felt that martial law must end, and he now found he had an excellent opportunity to reassert the prerogatives of the civil authority. He promptly granted the petition with an order that Louailler appear before the court at eleven o'clock the next day.

When the writ was handed to him, Jackson responded with an order of his own. "Having recd information that Domanic A Hall has been engaged in aiding abetting and exciting mutiny within my camp," he wrote Colonel Mathew Arbuckle, "You will forthwith order from your Regt a detachment to arrest and [confine] him, and make report of the same to head Quarters."[7] The statement was patently absurd. Nevertheless the order was immediately carried out, and by evening Hall was locked in the same barracks with Louailler.

All his life Jackson believed himself justified in imprisoning Judge

Hall. Later, in a biography written with his knowledge and active participation, the General defended his action through the words of his biographer. "He did it . . . to silence opposition, and satisfy the refractory and designing, that judicial interference should not mar the execution of his plans, or afford a screen, behind which treason might stalk unmolested. He did it, to make the example effectual, and to obtain, through fear, that security which could not be had through love of country."[8]

Through fear! On more than one occasion Jackson resorted to that tactic to achieve his purposes. And because of his demeanor, shrill voice and "hawk-like" eyes he was a master at terrorizing his victims.

There were several instances of his terror in New Orleans. Rumors of criticism brought a hundred soldiers with an order to arrest the offender for insubordination and mutiny. This occurred over and over. Jackson established a police state with no other authority but his own. He clearly overreached himself.

The city had become an armed camp even though everyone knew—still not officially—that the war was over. And the more the people cried out for a relaxation of the tyranny, the more Jackson turned the screw. Efforts were made to organize meetings to protest his violation of their constitutional rights, but because of his command of the military such meetings only invited further repression. There was talk of forming a secret military force to support the judicial authority, but this produced nothing but gossip for the coffeehouses and the destruction of a portrait of Jackson in a house of public entertainment.[9] The situation was so bad that when a courier from Washington brought "semi-official" word of the war's end—and even though Jackson himself was convinced a treaty had indeed been signed—Old Hickory would not yield.[10] He would not let go the reins of military power. There was nothing the people could do but continue to suffer the harshness of his implacable sense of duty.

The courtmartial of Louailler ended with his acquittal. Louailler contested the authority of a military court since he was not a member of the militia or the army, and the court allowed the plea. As for the charge of spying, the court thought it ridiculous that a spy would publish his views in a newspaper. But it was one thing for the court to dismiss the charges and quite another for General Andrew Jackson to do so. He most definitely disagreed with the court's judgment, and so he simply set it aside and retained Louailler in prison. Then, realizing the futility of trying to obtain a guilty verdict against Judge Hall, Jackson decided to hustle the jurist out of the city with orders that he not return until peace was officially announced or until the British had evacuated the southern coast. "I have thought proper to send you beyond the limits of my encampment," the General informed Hall, "to prevent you from a repetition of the improper conduct for which you have been Arrested and Confined."[11] On Sunday, March 12, a small detachment of troops marched Judge Hall four miles beyond New Orleans—the limits of Jackson's encampment—and set him free. The extent of Old Hickory's lunatic militarism had now reached comic proportions.

But it was not funny. Jackson behaved in a highhanded, bizarre and dangerous manner. Defending a city in the face of clear and imminent danger can justify a multitude of improprieties; Jackson's present disregard of civil and judicial authority—to say nothing of individual legal and constitutional rights—when he had all but absolute certification that the war was over cannot be justified by any stretch of the imagination. The only explanation for it involves his total sense of duty. Not until he was relieved of that duty by replacement or official notification of the war's termination was it possible for him to step aside and acknowledge an authority other than his own.

The following day, Monday, March 13, 1815, the long-awaited official information of the ratification of the peace treaty arrived from Washington, along with copies of the treaty and the ratification. Without an instant's hesitation Jackson laid down his dictatorial power. Military law was revoked, commerce released, military offenses pardoned, and all persons held in confinement for military crimes were discharged. It was one of the strange contradictions fused within Jackson's personality that he could ruthlessly seize and exercise absolute power and yet at the next moment lay it down and walk away from it without a hint of regret or a sense of loss.

Louailler was promptly released, and Hall and Toussard were returned to the city amid applause and acclamation. The next day the patient and long-suffering militia and volunteers of Tennessee, Louisiana, Kentucky, and Mississippi were dismissed with strong words of grateful praise from their commander.

"Go, then, my brave companions," said Old Hickory, ". . . full of honor, and crowned with laurels which will never fade. . . . Farewell, fellow soldiers. The expression of your General's thanks is feeble, but the gratitude of a country of freemen is yours—yours the applause of an admiring world."[12]

It had a nice turn, this farewell address. It was obviously sincerely felt. As far as his soldiers were concerned, Jackson was a hero, a great leader who won battles and who always shared the credit of those victories with them. Even the Louisianians admired him for that.

The officers of the city battalion extended Jackson a warm and glowing tribute, grateful that he had "allowed us the endearing title of your brothers in arms." They referred to the retention of martial law, although they deftly sidestepped the issue by leaving to others, they said, "the task of declaiming about *privileges* and constitutional rights; we are content with having fought in support of them."

Jackson, in reply, carefully selected each word.

> Whenever the invaluable rights which we enjoy under our happy constitution are threatened by invasion, privileges the most dear, and which, in ordinary times, ought to be regarded as the most sacred, may be required to be infringed for their security. At such a crisis, we have only to determine whether we will suspend, for a time, the exercise of the latter, that we may secure the permanent enjoyment of the former. Is it wise, in such a moment, to sacrifice the spirit of the laws to the letter, and by adhering too strictly to the letter, lose the *substance* forever, in order that we may, for an instant, preserve the *shadow?* . . . Private property is held sacred in all good governments, and particularly in our own, yet, shall the fear of invading it prevent a general from marching his army over a corn-field, or burning a house which protects the enemy? A thousand other instances might be cited to show that laws must sometimes be silent when necessity speaks.[13]

Jackson's coldly pragmatic defense of his actions articulated a soldier's contention that the good of his country transcended all other considerations. It is the sort of argument that can justify monstrous misdeeds as well as noble acts of patriotism. It was Jefferson's argument in overcoming his constitutional scruples about purchasing Louisiana, and now it was Jackson's argument in defense of his treatment of the inhabitants of Louisiana.

For the next few days the city of New Orleans joyfully celebrated its freedom. Freedom from General Andrew Jackson as well as the British. Now that the hardship was over and Old Hickory had voluntarily ended martial law, the people quickly forgave him his harshness and reminded themselves that after all he had saved the city and brought honor to them and to his country. Let the worse be forgotten.

Not Judge Hall. He did not forget. Waiting until most of the rejoicing had ended, he issued an order on March 21 to show cause why Andrew Jackson should not be held in contempt of court for refusing to obey the writ of habeas corpus issued in the case of Louis Louailler. Hall was clearly retaliating for his own arrest, imprisonment, and exile from the city. And here Jackson had a justifiable complaint. By "becoming the prosecutor and arbiter of his own grievances," Hall "placed himself in a situation, where reason could have but little agency, calculated to do injustice, and attach to his decision suspicion and censure."[14] Jackson believed a trial by jury the better instrument of justice, considering the judge's own involvement in the case. Nevertheless, on Friday, March 24, 1815, at 10:00 A.M., as directed, Andrew Jackson, dressed in civilian attire, appeared in court with his aide, Major Reid, and his legal counsel, Edward Livingston and Abner L. Duncan. A large crowd of people cheered Jackson's appearance and gave the judge cause for alarm. Dominique You sidled up to the Hero. *"Général,"* he whispered, "say the word and we pitch the judge and the bloody courthouse in the river." Jackson shook his head. Then he reassured the judge in a typical Jacksonian pronouncement. "There is no danger here," he intoned, ". . . the same arm that protected from outrage this city . . . will shield and protect this court, or perish in the effort."[15]

So began the celebrated trial, *United States* v. *Major General Andrew Jackson.* As soon as the court had come to order the defense raised objections to the propriety and legality of the proceedings, all of which Hall overruled. Nor would the judge permit the reading of a prepared statement explaining why Jackson could not validly be held in contempt. "The ears of the court were closed against everything, of argument or reason," complained Old Hickory.[16]

The case was put over until the following Friday, when Jackson again appeared before Judge Hall and was asked nineteen specific questions concerning his actions in handling the writ. The two strongminded, willful men glared at each other. Then, very deliberately, Jackson replied, speaking guardedly but firmly.

"I will not answer interrogatories," he said. "When called upon to show cause why an attachment for contempt of this court ought not to run against me, I offered to do so. . . . You would not hear my defense. . . . Under these circumstances I appear before your Honor to receive the sentence of the court, and with nothing further to add. Your Honor will not understand me as meaning any disrespect to the court by the remarks I make; but as no opportunity has been furnished me to explain the reasons and motives which influenced my conduct, so it is expected that censure will form no part of that punishment which your Honor may imagine it your duty to perform."[17]

It was a dignified and astute protest, one that the wise and urbane Hall appreciated. The judge responded in like manner, imposing a fine of $1,000—which he found an unpleasant duty in view of the General's services to the country.[18] In consideration of those services, he would not send Jackson to jail. Then he said something fundamental about the institutions of American government. "The only question," Hall said, "was whether the Law should bend to the General or the General to the Law."[19] But Jackson never claimed that the law should bend to his will. Under martial rule he was the law, and he believed himself justified in what he had done.

Jackson paid the fine, much as it may have distressed him to do so. He was not prepared to defy Hall; he was unwilling to blemish his victory with a quarrel he was certain to lose. This business had already run on too long, and the General was anxious to have done with it. In a final display of spirit, he refused to accept $1,000 raised by popular subscription and requested that the sum be distributed among the families of soldiers who died in defense of the city. Jackson had style. Always did have.

When the courtroom proceedings ended, friends of Jackson crowded around him and hurried him to his carriage. A knot of people formed, unhitched the horses, and dragged the carriage to the coffeehouse "amidst the huzzas" and approving shouts of a large gathering of people who trailed behind him.[20] His brief role as Tyrant had been forgotten; once again he was the Hero of New Orleans.

"Relieved by this display of the public regard and gratitude for his exertions in their defense," Jackson turned to the crowd and gestured for silence. "I have," he said, "during the invasion exerted every one of my faculties for the defense and preservation of the constitution and the laws. On this day I have been called on to submit to their operation under the circumstances which many persons might have thought sufficient to justify resistance. Considering obedience to the laws, even when we think them unjustly applied, as the first duty of the citizen, I did not hesitate to comply with the sentence you have heard, and I entreat you to remember the example I have given you of respectful submission to the administration of justice."[21] It was sound, fatherly advice, the words of a true civilian, which Jackson inherently was, but with none of the thunder the crowd expected.

When the administration in Washington learned of Jackson's brush with the civilian authority it mildly reproved him for it. "The President instructs me to take this opportunity," wrote the new acting secretary of war, Alexander J. Dallas, "of requesting that a conciliatory deportment be observed towards the State authorities and citizens of New Orleans."[22] Jackson took no notice of this rebuke, and the entire matter was soon forgotten. Thirty years later a grateful (and partisan) Congress remitted the fine and Jackson was pleased to accept both principal and interest.

The General's final days in New Orleans, prior to his return home, were spent quietly in the relaxed company of his family. A few days after the announcement of peace, Rachel and their adopted son, Andrew, finally arrived in New Orleans, much to the General's delight. Rachel was now an extremely stout, dark-complexioned, forty-seven-year-old woman, religious to the point of fanaticism yet warm and gently beguiling. During Jackson's long absence from the Hermitage she had been forced to manage the plantation, and her appearance now reflected the many hours she had spent outdoors under the Tennessee sun. Homely in dress and speech, every inch the farmer's wife, she hardly seemed the mate of so elegant and commanding a figure as Andrew Jackson. On occasion the General reminded her of her new status and its obligations. "You must recollect," he told her, "that you are now a Major Generals lady—in the service of the U.S. and as such you must appear, elegant and plain, not extravagant—but in such stile as strangers expect to see you." She felt uncomfortable and inhibited among the elegant Creole ladies of New Orleans; indeed she confessed to Mrs. Livingston that she was ignorant of fine clothes and fine company, for she had never before visited a city larger than Nashville. In time she came to regard New Orleans as a veritable "Babylon-on-the-Mississippi," given over totally to "disipation" and the delights of the flesh. "Oh, the wickedness, the idolatry of this place! unspeakable the riches and splendor." "So much amusement balls Concerts Plays theatres &c &c but we Dont attend the half of them" she told one of her relatives in Tennessee.[23]

Mrs. Livingston kindly took Rachel under her wing and arranged a selection of suitable dresses for the wife of the city's distinguished Hero. Shortly after Jackson lifted his censorship of the press, an editorial cartoon depicted a short and stout Rachel standing on a table while Mrs. Livingston tugged at the strings of her stays, trying to create a waist where a waist had once existed. The fashionable ladies of New Orleans were rather amused by Rachel's country ways and tastes, but they later warmed to her gentle disposition and kindliness. Their conversion from sly amusement to genuine affection was marked by their presentation to her of a set of topaz jewelry. To the General the ladies awarded a handsome and quite valuable diamond pin. Gallant to a fault, Jackson gushed his thanks. "The world heaps many honors on me," he said to them, "but none is greater than this."[24]

At one grand ball, complete with transparencies, flowers, colored lamps, a sumptuous dinner, and dancing, Rachel could scarcely believe such splendor possible this side of the heavenly throne. At supper she was placed opposite a transparency that read "Jackson and Victory: They are but one." When the meal ended, Jackson and his lady led the way to the ballroom and there treated the guests to "a most delicious *pas de deux,*" country style. "To see these two figures, the General, a long, haggard man, with limbs like a skeleton, and Madame la Generale, a short, fat dumpling, bobbing opposite each other like half-drunken Indians, to the wild melody of *'Possum up de Gum Tree,'* and endeavoring to make a spring into the air, was very remarkable, and far more edifying a spectacle than any European ballet could possibly have furnished."[25]

These final days in New Orleans were relatively happy ones for Jackson. He could relax and enjoy playing the role of Hero and Savior. The old animosities toward the Tyrant had dissipated with hardly a trace; only a few continued to harp on his former highhandedness in ruling the city. The presence of little Andrew also cheered him. Having been an absent father for so long, Jackson spent every leisure moment with him and of course denied him nothing. On one occasion a crowd of soldiers congregated outside his headquarters and shouted to him to come to the window and acknowledge their cheers. Just then little Andrew, who had been asleep in an adjoining room, heard the noise outside and started to cry. The General, on his way to the window to greet the soldiers, heard his son's cries and paused for a moment, unsure which summons to obey. Then he rushed to the child's bedside, caught him in his arms, quieted his fears, and carried him to the window where he bowed to his men, all the while distracting the child from his fright by laughing over the noisy actions of the soldiers below.[26]

Jackson undoubtedly felt guilty about his long absences from home and the limited time he could devote to the child when they were together. Already he had begun to spoil his son; in later years young Andrew had trouble developing into a mature, responsible adult. Jackson's own fatherless early life, the lack of sustained parental guidance, and the resulting aimlessness of his formative years encouraged him to dote on the child, to spoil him with extravagances. Moreover, he was an older man, just turned forty-eight, and his instincts about how to minister to the needs of a five-year-old had long since dulled. Then, too, Jackson was now a famous man, accustomed to command and deference and surrounded constantly by aides and hangers-on. To the child his presence was almost a happening, full of attention and scenes of agitation and activity, cheering crowds and saluting soldiers. Under these circumstances a normal father-son relationship would be difficult to achieve at best. The child was certainly awed by his father and was properly respectful and obedient. He found favor when "he behaved like a soldier," and he was always reminded to act like one.[27] But, as with many children of famous fathers, the son could not handle the notoriety and the obligations of distinction. He grew up irresponsible and ambitionless, a considerable disappointment to his father.

Before leaving New Orleans, Jackson presented his aide, Edward Livingston, with a miniature of himself and a letter of appreciation for his personal services and his invaluable assistance in the defense of the city. To Livingston's daughter, the General presented a brooch and a pretty note full of gallant remarks about how much she had brightened his stay in New Orleans. There were other gifts expressive of his gratitude as he prepared to depart the city. Arrangements were made to turn over the detail work of his command to Edmund P. Gaines, and on April 6, 1815, together with his family, Jackson boarded a ship and headed home.

It was difficult to leave New Orleans. The city was the scene of his greatest triumph, and the acknowledgments he had received for his stupendous feat amply gratified his need for recognition and applause. "We left Orleans on the 6th amid the lamentations & benedictions of Whites, Blacks and Half Breeds, of men, women & children," John Reid reported. "A hundred dinners" were tendered the General and his staff, "consisting of 40 dishes each, & many & many a bottle of wine."[28] But the victory was over. It was time to move on.

The first leg of the river journey took him to Natchez, where he was delayed for a time in settling a small dispute with Harman Blennerhasset, who sued Jackson for what he thought was the unreturned balance of the money given the firm of Jackson and Coffee by Aaron Burr for the building of several boats in 1806. The money had in fact been returned; both Jackson and Coffee testified to this in court, whereupon the case was dismissed.

Except for this slight unpleasantness, Jackson's homeward trip was one long, exhilarating ovation. One town after another vied to express its gratitude for the honor he had achieved for the nation. "He is everywhere hailed as the saviour of this Country," reported Reid. He has been "feasted, caressed & I may say idolized. They look upon him as a strange prodigy; & women, children, & old men line the road to look at him as they would at the Elephant. This is a sort of business in which he feels very awkwardly. . . . He pulls off his hat—bows graciously but as tho his spirit were humbled & abashed by the attention which is shown him."[29]

Everyone in Nashville turned out to welcome the Hero when he arrived on May 15. A procession escorted him into town in a wild, enthusiastic demonstration full of joyous shouts at having this magnificence home again. At the courthouse Felix Grundy, the great War Hawk, welcomed him in a long speech that recounted glowingly the highlights of Jackson's last campaigns. When Grundy concluded there was a pause as everyone looked to the General.

"I am at a loss to express my feelings," Jackson said simply. "The approbation of my fellow-citizens is to me the richest reward. Through you, sir," he said to Grundy, "I beg leave to assure them that I am *this day* amply compensated for every toil and labor."[30]

The students of Cumberland College then recited an appropriate ode, which was mercifully short. Jackson acknowledged their good words "with lively feelings of pride and joy."[31] With that the ceremonies ended.

Jackson continued to the Hermitage, where a large number of friends and neighbors gathered to pay him tribute. But the principal event of the homecoming was a grand banquet given in Nashville on May 22, attended by the most distinguished citizens of Tennessee and presided over by Governor Blount. During the feast an appropriately elegant and ornate sword voted by the Mississippi legislature the year before was presented to the General. Further speeches assured the Hero that he was the first man of the state of Tennessee and always would be.

Every vestige of former bitterness, hurt, anger, jealousy, resentment, or indignation generated by Jackson's past misdeeds wafted away on the breezy sentiments of love and gratitude that his fellow Tennesseans assured him were his forever. In every way the homecoming was the triumph Jackson wanted—and earned. He was properly humble before the adulation and hysterical praise. At times he almost sounded like a politician, but then the many months he spent at war, raising, training, and deploying an army, had taught him something about the diplomatic and political arts. In the ensuing months and years—again, like a politician—he nurtured his national reputation and kept himself in the public eye. The slightest criticism of his behavior at New Orleans, particularly from within the administration, and he sprinted to Washington to face down his critics. He also began touring the country to receive his due, accepting invitations from this town or that to attend a banquet or some other public activity commemorating the New Orleans victory. And always the militia turned out to salute him and parade in his honor. Militiamen acknowledged him as their chief and identified with him. If there was one organization that could be said to have formed the earliest base of his political strength throughout the country, it was the militia. Every state had one, and the members almost universally acknowledged him as their head.

Soon newspapers traced Jackson's movements around the country and detailed his activities, much to the delight of their readers. "Tho I have not had the honor of hearing from you since your Departure," wrote Edward Livingston to the General, ". . . yet your progress has been so distinctly traced by the expression of public gratitude that your friends have not lost sight of you for a moment."[32] And not just the major urban centers claimed him. "In every little town," John Reid reported, "the citizens seem exceedingly desirous to demonstrate their regard for the general."[33]

In the late fall of 1815 Jackson dutifully journeyed to Washington to receive official recognition of his tremendous accomplishment. It was a great state occasion. The President, the cabinet, sundry other officials, and their ladies formally acknowledged the nation's pride in him at a magnificent reception in the presidential mansion. The attention and flattery accorded Jackson signaled his arrival as the first man in America.[34]

Only one thing marred the triumph: Jackson's health collapsed and he nearly died. President Madison was so alarmed that he insisted on summoning the celebrated Dr. Physick from Philadelphia to attend the General. Jackson's arm caused him great discomfort during this crisis and it took several weeks before the pain subsided. Probably he suffered a general infection which accompanied the flareup of his old wound. In addition, he caught a particularly bad cold in the fall and could not shake it off. His incessant coughing wracked his emaciated body. Each cough brought up blood. Each spasm prostrated him. Not until spring did he fully recover.

It was during this trip to Washington, prior to his collapse, that Jackson had occasion to ride through Lynchburg, Virginia, and the entire town turned out *en masse* to greet him. The militia proudly lined up for his inspection and approval, and prominent citizens congregated to extend their welcome. In the afternoon a grand banquet attended by 300 people honored the conqueror, and among the distinguished guests was Thomas Jefferson, now seventy-two years of age, who lived a long day's ride from Lynchburg. Although Jackson harbored distinct reservations about the former President, he was profoundly impressed to learn that Jefferson had made the long and tiresome journey to participate in the tribute. It helped to wipe away all the asperities of the past. During the banquet, Jefferson was asked to give a toast and most willingly obliged. "Honor and gratitude," he said, "to those who have filled the measure of their country's honor." Jackson responded gracefully and pointedly. He toasted James Monroe, secretary of war at the time of the Battle of New Orleans, a Virginian, Jefferson's friend, and a recognized candidate in the forthcoming presidential election. Everyone at the banquet thought Jackson's toast most gracious and properly modest. They were not a little surprised that a man from the back country could be so urbane, so aristocratic in his bearing, so gallant in his speech.[35]

Before long Jackson became quite proficient at playing the role of modest hero. And he was sincerely modest—as long as no one *else* described his victory in modest terms. The few persistent murmurs about his activities in New Orleans following the battle, such as his being a tyrant, gently fluttered away in succeeding months.[36] All that remained was a fantastic image of an impossible hero to whom the American people were eternally indebted. There could be "little doubt," he was told, that "with the proper management of your friends that you might be elected to the highest Office in the American Government."[37]

CHAPTER 21

"Brothers Listen . . . I Am Your Friend and Brother"

IN THE MONTHS IMMEDIATELY FOLLOWING HIS RETURN to the Hermitage Jackson relaxed at home and tried to readjust to the relative calm of plantation life in a quiet southern community. The transition went well, largely because everyone went to great pains to accommodate him. In fact when the U.S. Army was reorganized in the spring of 1815 into the northern and southern divisions, with Jackson commanding the southern and Jacob Brown the northern, the government allowed the Hero to name the Hermitage his headquarters and this permitted him the luxury of attending to military business while managing his plantation and generally enjoying the life of a country gentleman. Moreover, a major general's pay of $2,400 a year, together with $1,652 in allowances, gave him a dependable income that substantially eased his life-style. He had achieved the good life in every possible way.

The General's staff lived with him, becoming practically part of his family. At various times the staff included Sam Houston, Richard Keith Call, Andrew Jackson Donelson, Robert Butler, James Gadsden, John and Samuel Overton, Dr. James C. Bronaugh (his personal physician), and John H. Eaton.[1] In addition he had his immediate family and a large number of close relatives clustered about him as the center of their lives and interests, a profitable plantation (thanks to Rachel), a splendid command that included all military forces south of the Ohio River, and a national reputation that immediately set off demonstrations wherever he appeared. There was hardly anything more he required.

While this conqueror capitalized on his triumphs and savored the

321

results of his victories, another conqueror, one with a better claim to the title, went down to crushing defeat. For the summer of 1815 was the summer of Waterloo and the end of Napoleon Bonaparte. Jackson's sympathies lay totally with the Emperor, perhaps because in some ways they were kindred spirits, perhaps because of Jackson's anglophobia or his admiration for Napoleon's military prowess. In any event Jackson watched the declining fortunes of the Emperor with regret. When the news arrived in 1814 that Marmont had surrendered Paris and Napoleon was forced into exile, he not only decried the betrayal but revealed the full dimension of his own capacity for annihilation to serve a military end. "It was not Marmont that betrayed the Emperor," he exclaimed; "it was Paris. He should have done with Paris what the Russians did with Moscow —burnt it, sir, burnt it to the ground, and thrown himself on the country for support. So *I* would have done, and my country would have sustained me in it."[2] As a military commander Jackson could be totally ruthless and yet absolutely certain of his country's approbation for whatever he did.

Jackson's major military concern after the withdrawal of British forces from American soil was the protection of the southern border, a task complicated by the continued hostility of the Creeks despite their crushing defeat and the annoying presence of the Spanish. As long as the Spanish remained in Florida, the Indians had an ally to encourage and subsidize their hostilities against the Americans. But in his mind Jackson had solved the problem long ago; the expulsion of the "foreign" elements was simply a matter of time. Another complication was the continued activities of Colonel Nicholls and Captain Woodbine, who encouraged the Creeks to believe that their lands would be restored in accordance with the Treaty of Ghent.[3] These annoyances and complications only stiffened Jackson's will—if it needed stiffening—to treat the Indians in a stern and arbitrary manner.

To the Creeks, any excuse to avoid running (marking) the boundary line established by the Treaty of Fort Jackson excited them. The northern and western limits of the cession were fuzzy—perhaps a deliberate move, according to one historian, to encourage white surveyors to defraud the Indians.[4] Congress provided for three commissioners to run the boundary, and Jackson insisted that his close friend General John Coffee be appointed one of them. Coffee, without waiting for the other commissioners to arrive and assist the operation, ran the boundary line on his own. Between the two Tennesseans and their commitment to the strict enforcement of the Treaty of Fort Jackson, they insured the destruction of Creek landholding in the southwest. The ultimate physical removal of the Indians would therefore create little difficulty.

One of the many arguments the Creeks advanced against the Treaty of Fort Jackson was the claim that some of the lands appropriated by the United States under the treaty actually belonged to the Cherokees and had been recognized in a treaty of 1806 between the federal government and the Cherokee tribe. This argument infuriated Jackson, possibly because it was true. In question was a fifty-mile-wide tract south of the Tennessee River in northern Alabama, stretching from the Coosa to what is now the Mississippi boundary. One of Coffee's outstanding accomplishments was the collection of affidavits from various Indians and whites certifying that the land had been loaned to the Cherokees by the Creeks.[5] The presumption of the Indians in daring to defy his will prompted Jackson to visit the various tribes (Creeks, Cherokees, Chickasaws, and Choctaws) in the area, hold ceremonial talks with them, and force their agreement to a land settlement once and for all. But to the Creeks he sent a stern warning. Actually it was a threat.

> *Friends and Brothers.* You know me to be your friend, you remember when your nation listened to the advice of bad men, and became crasy by the prophecies of your, wicked prophets raised by the machinations of Great Britain and spain. . . . You remember I destroyed your enemies, put those wicked prophets to death and to flight, and by the Capitulation and Treaty at Fort Jackson gave peace to your nation. . . .
>
> *Brothers* Listen, did I not send my men and warriors . . . and destroyed upwards of two hundred of the Hostile Indians and did the British dare to land any men to protect them. Listen, did not the British after exciting them to war, after promising them protection flee like cowards and leave the Indians to perish, and is there any of your nation after all this so crasy as to Listen to their wicked talks again.
>
> *Friends and Brothers* I hear with sorrow that some of your people has been listening to the wicked Talks of Colo Nicholls again, and that he has directed you to oppose the running of the line agreeable to the Treaty of Fort Jackson. . . .
>
> *Brothers* Listen did I ever tell you a lie. Listen I now tell you that line must and will be run, and the least opposition brings down instant destruction on the heads of the opposers. Brothers Listen, My men are ready to crush all the enemies of the U. States. . . . I am your friend and Brother.[6]

Jackson's trip south was burdened with the news of the sudden death on January 15, 1816, of his aide, John Reid.[7] The General felt very close to this gifted young man and had arranged for Reid to write his biography. Only four chapters had been completed when the author died of a fever in Virginia after an illness of only eighteen hours. John Henry

Eaton, a young lawyer with respectable writing skill, was chosen to re-place Reid. The biography, *The Life of Andrew Jackson*, based entirely on primary materials that included interviews with the General himself, was published in 1817. It described Jackson's life from birth through the Battle of New Orleans and is a valuable historical account; the chapters by Reid contain critical analyses of exceptional merit.[8] Later editions, in 1824 and 1828, diminished that merit by enlarging Jackson's already outsize characteristics of leadership for purposes of political gain.

On his southern tour Jackson swung through New Orleans, where he reviewed the city militia and made peace with Judge Hall. "It being the wish of some of my friends that I should meet Judge Hall in friendship," he later wrote, "their wishes I could not forgo. When he offered me his hand I received it and . . . my mind . . . tells me I have done right. I have in some measure added peace to his bosom, tranquility to my own, and restored him to the social circle of his former friends and acquaintances. On my part the hatchet is buried in oblivion."[9] This burying of the hatchet was not unique. Any number of times Jackson chose to forgive and forget, particularly when the advantages were compelling and the desire for reconciliation mutual. More than that, Jackson had no real fondness for everlasting enmities despite his volatile temperament. As he said sincerely on several occasions, "It is the first wish of my heart to be in friendship with all good men."[10]

Jackson's efforts to intimidate the Indians into yielding to his de-mands were somewhat hobbled by the decision of the new secretary of war, William H. Crawford, to accept the argument of the Cherokees and to return four million acres of land that the Treaty of Fort Jackson claimed for the United States. This action was concluded in a treaty signed on March 22, 1816. To add injury to insult the secretary agreed to compensate the Indians in the amount of $25,500 for war damages (destruction of crops and livestock) inflicted by the Tennessee militia-men.[11]

Jackson raged. And he was not timid about sounding off to the secretary of war—or the President of the United States. He practically threatened to disobey any order requiring him to restore land to the Indians, and he predicted that Tennessee would never stand by and watch the disputed territory handed over to "savages."[12] What a humilia-tion, he said, for him to be told he must return land already ceded under a legitimate treaty. How could the secretary agree to the surrender of these millions of acres? "On the principle of right and justice," Jackson lectured Crawford, "the surrender ought never to have been made." The Indians, "I mean the real Indians, the natives of the forest" had little quarrel with his treaty. Rather, the demand for restoration was a "strategem" by "designing half-breeds and renegade white men" for their own gain. (Jackson invariably faulted half-breeds and renegade white men whenever the Indians resisted his demands.) "Were I disposed to throw off the military garb and assume the character of a politician, I think it susceptible of argument if the President and Senate have not just as much right in hasty convention to cede away West Florida to Spain as to do what has been done." Again and again his anger stabbed the paper he scribbled over, blotting from his mind the fact that he was addressing his immediate superior. And it is interesting how readily and naturally he referred to the Spanish in Florida when arguing the need to dispossess the Indians.

Having signed a convention in direct conflict with the interests of the American people, Jackson asked, how did the government propose to acknowledge the rightful claims of its citizens living within the disputed territory? When and how will the Indian presence on the border—a presence constantly tempting the Spanish to foment trouble—be extinguished? A title is no sooner procured from one tribe, Jackson contended, than another claims it, and as soon as this second claim is resolved yet another tribe presents itself as legal owner. "An Indian . . . will claim everything and anything," he pontificated. Give them a single acre and they will demand the entire territory. It is high time that the government of the United States stop worrying about rapacious Indians and start earning the confidence of its own citizens.[13]

Crawford had badly miscalculated. His recognition of the justice of Cherokee demands infuriated westerners and provoked them to threats of political retaliation. In the face of recrimination he finally yielded. He agreed to the appointment of three commissioners to conclude treaties with the Cherokees, Choctaws, and Chickasaws. Under the circumstances he dared not exclude Jackson as one of the members. The other two appointees included General David Meriwether of Georgia and Jesse Franklin of North Carolina and they were instructed to arrange agreements with the Indians that would determine the limits and validity of tribal territorial claims.[14] For Crawford it was a neat political escape hatch; and once again the Indians were turned over to the tender mercies of General Andrew Jackson.

Naturally the Hero dominated the commission. In the negotiations that followed he had solid support from General Meriwether, whom he described as "a fine old fellow."[15] And Franklin, although delayed in attending the initial negotiations because of the illness of his son, also followed Jackson's lead once he joined the team. Soon Sharp Knife was "managing the whole business" and acting pretty much in the double capacity of commissioner for Tennessee and for the United States.[16] So the "talks" with the Indians went exactly as Old Hickory dictated—and he knew precisely how red men should be treated and what westerners expected of him. He once said that Congress had the right to "occupy and possess" any part of Indian territory "whenever the safety, interest or defence of the country" dictated.[17] It was one of the earliest arguments justifying sweeping governmental power under the umbrella of "national security." But Jackson had no need to rely on this principle of higher national priority; when it came to Indian lands the red men had virtually no rights, according to Jackson, except by sufferance of Congress to hunt and fish and otherwise sustain themselves. After all, they did not constitute a sovereign nation with the rights and privileges appropriate to a free country. They were dependent. They were subject. "If they are viewed as an independent nation, possessing the right of sovereignty and domain," Jackson told Monroe, "then negotiating with them and concluding treaties, would be right and proper. But this is not the fact, all Indians within the Territorial limits of the United States, are considered subject to its sovereignty, and have only a possessory right to the soil, for the purpose of hunting and not the right of domaine, hence I conclude that Congress has full power, by law, to regulate all the concerns of the Indians."[18]

Jackson also believed that the Indians occupied more land than they actually needed and that because they roamed within it at will they got into trouble. Their land mass should be reduced sharply, he said, to the precise amount required to feed, clothe, and house the tribe. Excessive landholding only foments wars with white men. "Their territorial boundary must be curtailed," he said.

Jackson had other guidelines for negotiating with Indians, which he gratuitously forwarded to John Coffee to assist him and his team of commissioners, who were meeting with the Choctaws to arrange a final land settlement with that tribe. First, said Jackson, it is essential to take a definite position at the beginning and stick to it. No hesitation. No indecisiveness. Let them know your position when the convention commences and stand firm thereafter. Next, remember the sort of person you are dealing with. "An Indian is fickle, and you will have to take the same firm stand and support it and you are sure of success."[19] Moreover, the "Treachery of the Indian character will never justify the reposing of confidence in their professions. Be always prepared for defence and ready to inflict exemplary punishment on the offenders when necessary."[20] Finally, "it may be necessary . . . to make the chiefs some presents" to ease the negotiations along.[21] But a word of caution: It is always wise to have authority for such bribes and to know precisely where the money is coming from.

Unfortunately bribery was an accepted instrument of negotiation with the Indians, and Jackson regularly practiced it. In January 1815 alone, some $60,000 in goods was sent to him to distribute among the tribes, and the government never did learn how he dispensed these "presents."[22] Fortunately, Jackson was a scrupulously honest man. On several occasions he indicated that the practice of bribery was most distasteful to him. He frequently informed his superiors that he was "compelled, not from choice, but from instructions" to bribe chiefs into surrendering their land.[23] "It is high time the Legislature should interpose its authority and enact Laws for the regulation and control of the Indian Tribes," he wrote. This, along with circumscribing Indian territory and providing the Indians with "instruments of agriculture . . . would be more humane and just, than by corrupting their Chiefs to acquire their Country, which is the only means by which it can be effected."[24]

Before meeting with the Cherokees and Chickasaws, Jackson took the precaution of advising Crawford that "presents" to the Indians might be required and asked what "source" they were to be drawn from.[25] He had had long experience with government financial inefficiency, and he wanted written authority before involving himself in the disbursement of funds or merchandise.

On September 6, 1816, the Cherokees began arriving at the Chickasaw Council House to meet with Jackson and Meriwether. Two days later the conference began. The Indians, great warriors and proven friends of the United States, stood proud and majestic before the two commissioners. But they had not anticipated Jackson's absolute determination to bend them to his will. Nor did they realize how gargantuan his demands would be. He came as a conqueror resolutely committed to their destruction as sovereign nations living within the confines of the several states. He had decided "that the people of the west will never suffer any Indian to inhabit this country again." They must vacate the territory.[26]

It would not be easy to drive the Indians from their ancestral home. It would take every ounce of Jackson's skill and determination to force the land cession he wanted. But his expansionist fervor and devotion to western interests made him a formidable adversary.

The Chickasaws also attended this initial convention, and they insisted that each individual had to be consulted before any settlement could be reached. It was an annoyance—but then Jackson suffered several annoyances during this convention, one of them occasioned by a letter Crawford had written to an Indian agent that provoked multiple interpretations among the Chickasaws of its precise meaning. Jackson did not hesitate to inform Crawford—whom he thoroughly detested by this time for his wrongheaded actions toward the Indians—that his letter "caused much embarrassment."[27]

The convention opened with an address by Jackson. Splendidly outfitted in his general's uniform, looking every inch the bold commander, he stepped forward, gestured a salute to the chiefs, and began to speak. The Indians listened quietly.

"Friends & Brethren," he began, "The President of the U States has instructed General Meriwether, the Hon. Jesse Franklin & myself to meet you here this day, shake you by the hand, brighten the chain of Friendship & greet you with the pleasing tidings that Peace & Friendship exists between the People of the U States & all their red Brethren." It was a cordial beginning, and the chiefs nodded their pleasure at hearing such expressions of friendship. Then, his introduction out of the way, Jackson's tone and words darkened. When the Creek Nation, he said, "listened to the tongues of lying Prophets," went crazy and raised the hatchet, and "stained it with the blood of our innocent women & children," your Father, the President, sent his warriors against them and the hostile Creeks were conquered and forced to yield their land to pay the expenses of the war. Now you claim part of that ceded land. "That a good understanding may continue to exist between the U. States & the Cherokees, Chickasaws & Choctaws," Jackson continued, "it is absolutely necessary that the right to this land should be fairly & friendly investigated & settled." To this end "Our Father the President of the U States has charged us to make some propositions to you . . . which he believes will be to your interest to accede." First, however, the Indians would be given the opportunity of presenting the grounds for their claims. After that they would hear the President's propositions. But Jackson warned the Indians against losing the friendship of their Father, the President, and assured them that their approval of the propositions would prevent that calamity. "Relinquish then your claim," he urged. "Receive the offering of your Beloved Father the President of the U States, Give him proof that you return his love & that you wish to join hearts and heads & live like our People, one Family in Peace & Friendship."[28]

With the conclusion of this address, or "talk," the convention adjourned until the next day. Besides, Jackson decided to treat the Indians separately. By dividing the tribes he believed he could weaken their resistance to his demands. He began with the Cherokees because he anticipated "much difficulty" with the Chickasaws on account of a guarantee or charter they had received from President Washington in 1794 that was later confirmed by treaty in 1801. An initial success with the Cherokees, therefore, would strengthen his negotiating stance with the Chickasaws.

When the convention reconvened the next day, Jackson invited the Cherokees to argue their right of possession. That done, he proposed that they yield their claims to the lands on the north and south sides of the Tennessee River. The Cherokees respectfully refused. They steadfastly insisted that they could not cede their land on the north side. "They would be too much confined," they said, "and if they would agree to such surrender they would be put to death by the nation." Clearly Jackson had gone too far. For the Cherokee representatives to agree to his demand would mean their execution at the hands of the rest of the tribe. So he took a map and drew a line from Camp Coffee on the south side of the Tennessee River, opposite Chickasaw Island, south to the ridge dividing the Tennessee and Tombigbee rivers and then east to the Coosa River and down the Coosa. The Cherokees must cede all their lands to the south and west of that line, he commanded. In return the United States would grant $6,000 annually for ten years and $5,000 to be paid sixty days after the treaty was ratified.[29]*

It was an enormous land grant, one that involved millions of acres even without a cession on the north side of the river. But, Jackson said, it was the price of peace and friendship with the United States. Still the Cherokees resisted. They begged him to reduce the size of the cession, to propose some other means of proving their friendship and desire for peace. To no avail. Finally Jackson resorted to bribery. And between these bribes—"a few presents to the chiefs and interpreters," Jackson called them—and Sharp Knife's absolute determination to sweep them from "this country," Cherokee resistance was overcome. The treaty was signed on September 14, 1816, and ratified by the entire Nation at Turkey Town. It promised peace and friendship between the United States and the Cherokee Nation forever.[30]

The seeming ease with which Jackson imposed his imperious will upon the Indians sent shock waves through the Council House. The treaty "alarmed and seemed to irritate the Chickasaws," said Jackson. "Confusion amongst them was visible." The sudden death of one of the principal chiefs of the tribe, the Factor, also appeared to distract them.[31] Nevertheless Jackson felt confident that he could compel their consent to his demands. "I have a sanguine hope," he told Rachel, "we will be fully successful with the chikesaws and once more regain by tribute what I fairly . . . purchased with the sword."[32]

The Chickasaws assembled before Sharp Knife to hear the pronouncement of their cession. It came like a thunderclap: They must cede all land on the north and south side of the Tennessee River and east of a line from Caney Creek to Gaines's Road, south to Cotton Gin Point on

*See map, page 396.

the Tombigbee River, and down the west bank of the Tombigbee to the Choctaw boundary. In effect this cession would connect the white settlements of Tennessee with those of the Gulf of Mexico, combining the military and economic needs of the "people of the west" with those of the entire nation.[33] As compensation, the United States would grant $12,000 per annum for ten successive years and $4,500 in sixty days for any improvements to the lands surrendered.[34] It was another incredible land grab, and the Indians howled their dismay. They invoked the name of President Washington and the guarantees which they said "bound the u states to prevent intrusions of every kind whatever." They also begged time to deliberate—anything to stall the engine of their ruin. Finally the commissioners were compelled, much as it distressed them, to "apply the sole remedy in our power. It was applied, and presents offered to the influential chiefs, amounting to $4,500 to be paid on the success of the negotiation." Jackson not only resorted to bribery, he did it surreptitiously. "Secrecy was enjoined as to the names," he wrote. "Secrecy is necessary, or the influence of the chiefs would be destroyed, which has been, and may be, useful on a future occasion."[35]

The presents worked. The treaty was signed on September 20, 1816.[36]* For a little less than $200,000 Andrew Jackson acquired for the United States a land mass nearly a quarter of the amount taken from the Creeks by the Treaty of Fort Jackson. It was a formidable purchase.

The necessity of bribing the chiefs to obtain their land disgusted Jackson. It was not his style. He much preferred having the United States step in and impose its authority over the tribes, simply telling them what they must do. If this could not be done, he said, then he wanted no part of such negotiations. They revolted him.

The Choctaws, like the Cherokees and Chickasaws, also capitulated when confronted by John Coffee, John Rhea, and John McKee, the commissioners sent to arrange the provisions of their land settlement. Through his influence with and instructions to John Coffee, Andrew Jackson dominated the proceedings. At the Choctaw Trading House on October 24, 1816, the Indians ceded land east of the Tombigbee River, in return for which the United States agreed to an annual payment of $16,000 for twenty years and $10,000 in merchandise on signing the treaty.[37]

The land obtained by these three treaties, plus the millions of acres taken from the Creeks in the Treaty of Fort Jackson, opened an enormous country, running hundreds of miles north and south, east and west, to white settlement. Jackson appreciated the size and value of his acquisition as well as its importance to the continued expansion and defense of the

*See map, page 396.

American nation. After all, he had been anticipating it for some time. "The whole southern country from Kentucky and Tennessee to Mobile," he boasted, "has been opened by the late treaties and . . . I know of no situation combining so many advantages . . . as the lower end of the Muscle shoals."[38] The latter was a particularly choice acquisition that provided, he said, unobstructed navigation to the Ohio River all year round. Its falls could be "adapted to any machinery"; it contained iron, saltpeter and flint; and it allowed excellent military access to the lower country, the better to attack the Spanish.[39]

Jackson recounted the benefits of his accomplishment to a number of senior officials in Washington. There was no need to bludgeon westerners with the obvious. They knew he had implemented effectively their wish that no Indian "inhabit this country again."

In arranging the land cessions, Jackson's mind dwelt constantly on the military question and its importance to American expansion. His present concern was the need to acquire from the Indians those lands that would make possible the running of a good military road from Tennessee to the Gulf of Mexico. Such a road would prepare the way for an assault on Spanish possessions in the area. Within a year Jackson had mapped plans with Coffee for such a road, and then he supervised its construction. Built between June 1817 and January 1819, it ran "483 miles from Nashville to Madisonville on Lake Ponchairtrain" and thereby facilitated the rapid movement of troops in the southwest. It also shortened Washington–New Orleans mail service to seventeen days.[40]

Once the Choctaws had yielded the land demanded of them, Jackson wrote James Monroe (recently elected President), advising him "that the sooner this country is brought in the market the better." White settlers will flood into the territory, he said, and "give us a population capable of defending that frontier."[41] He further advised that the land be divided into two districts and that his friend, John Coffee, be designated surveyor to do the dividing.[42] In a letter to the acting secretary of war, George Graham, Old Hickory stressed the military importance of selling this land immediately. "Nothing can promote the wellfare of the United States," he argued, "and particularly the southwestern frontier, so much as bringing into market, at an early day, the whole of this fertile country."[43]

It came soon enough. Already thousands of squatters had swarmed into the Creek cession. Speculators. including John Coffee, the new surveyor, and a number of Tennessee cronies, invested heavily in the area. General Coffee subsequently formed the Cypress Land Company, purchased an excellent site at the foot of Muscle Shoals, and laid out the town of Florence, Alabama. At the first auction Jackson himself bought one town lot. No one bid against him. Otherwise the bidding was uncommonly vigorous, shooting prices from the minimum of $2 set by the government to a high of $78 an acre. Although Jackson was keenly interested in stimulating this speculation, his motives had more to do with encouraging settlement in order to protect the frontier and "promote the welfare of the United States" than with personal gain.[44] By 1817 Jackson no longer responded to an internal financial drive.[45] He was beyond that. He appreciated economic motivation, particularly as it affected national growth and development, but he himself no longer needed the satisfaction of personal financial gain.[46]

As the new land fever raged across the south it carried hordes of farmers and adventurers into "this fertile country." The debt that these people—and those who came after them—owed Andrew Jackson was incalculable.

After his great victory at New Orleans, Old Hickory was proudest of his success in defeating the Indians and acquiring their land. The great tribes of the south were broken and their valuable property stripped away. They no longer constituted a menace to the frontier or to the American government. It was only a matter of time until the ravaged remains of a mighty race would be removed from the sight and presence of the white man.

Removal. Already Jackson had formulated in his mind the idea of physically moving the Indians from the east side of the Mississippi River and relocating them on the west side. It was not a novel idea. It went back at least to President Jefferson, who predicted that if the Indians failed to climb the ladder of western civilization and to assimilate with whites, "we shall be obliged to drive them, with the beasts of the forests into the Stony [Rocky] mountains." Most Tennesseans advocated removal. Before Jefferson left office, many of them talked openly of requiring the southern tribes to exchange their present holdings for land beyond the Mississippi. Governor Blount told Jackson in 1809 that such a policy adopted by the United States government would "help us in our foreign policy and gain strength for us" in the south and west. For the Indians themselves, Blount argued, removal meant that they "could longer preserve their national character."[47]

Not until January 1817 did Jackson find himself in a position to undertake the responsibility of initiating the "Principle" of removal. The President authorized him to "extinquish the Indian titles" made in a treaty with the Cherokees in 1806.[48] The instructions were broadened a few months later when Jackson was told to arrange an "exchange" of territory with the Cherokees in accordance with an agreement concluded in 1808. The Cherokees then had agreed to surrender lands on the east side of the Mississippi in return for lands in Arkansas. Over the years, several thousand Indians had accepted new lands on the Arkansas River from the United States without ceding a corresponding amount of land on the east side of the river. Those Cherokees who did *not* migrate were now called upon to provide a compensatory cession, and Andrew Jackson was given the task of making them understand the justice of this demand.

His instructions also authorized Jackson to grant lands to those who would remove to the Arkansas River and the area immediately adjoining the Osage boundary line. In addition he was permitted to grant money for transportation and to provide arms, blankets, and any other article he deemed imperative for the removal. Those heads of families who refused to remove might remain in the east subject to state laws; they would receive 640 acres per family. To assist Jackson in concluding the treaty, General Meriwether and Governor Joseph McMinn of Tennessee were also appointed commissioners.[49]

A summons directed the Indians to meet Jackson and his fellow commissioners at the Cherokee Agency at Hiwassee on June 20, 1817. The General arrived on June 18, but only a few chiefs of the Arkansas Cherokees appeared on time. While waiting, Jackson took advantage of the situation to convince a number of headmen to cede to the United States the remaining Cherokee lands in North Carolina.[50] Ten days later enough of the eastern chiefs and headmen assembled to open the principal negotiations. Jackson acted as the American spokesman. His demands were simple: compensation to the United States for 3,700 Cherokee migrants to the Arkansas and an exchange of land in the west for remaining Cherokee land east of the Mississippi.

Jackson opened his "talk" by explaining his purpose in coming. He had been appointed by their Father, the President, to arrange an exchange of land for the Cherokees now residing on the Arkansas. He assured them of the President's friendship and affection. Then, in detail, he related the events of 1808 that led to this agreement and the necessity now of fulfilling the conditions of the agreement.

Jackson heard grumbling. The chiefs disputed his interpretation of what occurred ten years ago. The deputation that visited President Jefferson, they argued, was not authorized to arrange a division of the Nation. It had gone to Washington only to say goodbye to the President on the eve of his departure from office. Nothing more.[51]

The response infuriated Jackson. Did they think him a fool? They would say anything—even nonsense—to avoid keeping their treaty obligations. But he knew the cause, or thought he did. The "intrigue of base and designing white men . . . and half breeds" had penetrated the councils of the Cherokees and persuaded them to resist his demands.[52] "Their income would be destroyed by the removal of the Indians. These that I have named are like some of our bawling politicians, who loudly exclaim we are the friends of the people, but who . . . care no more for the happiness or wellfare of the people than the Devil does."[53]

Jackson brought forward Tuchelee, a chief of the Cherokee Nation and a member of the deputation from the lower towns who went to Washington in 1808. Tuchelee was a "virtuous and independent man," said Jackson. He also knew better than to cross Sharp Knife. On signal, Tuchelee declared to the other chiefs that he had full powers from the lower towns to treat with President Jefferson and that Jackson spoke the truth about what happened in 1808 leading to the agreement. When he had finished the other chiefs and headmen just stared at him in disbelief, appalled at his treachery. That evening they turned him out of the council, "broke him as chief," and forced him to sign a document disputing Jackson's arguments.[54]

At the next session the Cherokees pleaded with the commissioners. "Friends and brothers," they said to the three men: "We feel assured that our father the President will not compel us into measures so diametrically against the will and interest of a large majority of our nation. . . . We wish to remain on our land, and to hold it fast. We appeal to our father the President of the United States to do us justice. We look to him for protection in the hour of distress."[55]

Unmoved, Jackson, Meriwether, and McMinn said nothing. The Indians persisted. The emigration of a small portion of Cherokees to the Arkansas, they swore, was unauthorized by the chiefs and headmen of the Nation. No exchange was possible; none acceptable. Then they submitted a statement signed by sixty-seven chiefs that refuted Jackson's claims.

Sharp Knife read the document and the names affixed to it, the muscles of his jaw tightening with anger. He looked at the chiefs, fury written all over his face. In measured tones he "called on them to hear and understand it as it was read, that it gave their father the P. the lye, it gave us the lye," and he wanted to know how many of the chiefs were prepared to do this. "Listen well," he thundered, "as we intended taking the voice of every chief one by one." Then he read the document aloud. When he finished he examined the signatures and spotted Tuchelee's name. He called on him to answer first. Tuchelee replied that he did not know what the document contained when he signed it and that he would not give the lie to his father, the President, nor to General Jackson. He repeated that he had full power from his Nation in 1808 to ask President Jefferson for an exchange of land on the Arkansas, that he wished justice, and that everyone should have a free choice to go or to stay. The answer read was not his answer, he declared.[56]

Sharp Knife looked for another friendly name. He called on Chief Old Glass, an ancient warrior. The Chief denied knowing what he signed.

Again, the answer read was not his answer; and he would not give the President the lie. He "wished all a free choic to go over the mississippi or stay as they pleased."[57]

Jackson moved from chief to chief. Again and again the same reply was given, until, said Jackson, "we compleatly exposed this base attempt of fraud and deception."[58] Then he shattered the Indians with a terrifying threat: He told them "to look around and recollect what had happened to our brothers the Creeks."[59] Did they want similar treatment? Were they prepared to face Sharp Knife in combat? That chastened them. That ended their opposition. They agreed to reconsider their position and to admit their Arkansas brothers to their council.

On July 8, 1817, the Cherokees signed the treaty prepared for them.[60]* They ceded two million acres of land in Tennessee, Georgia, and Alabama and received in return "acre for acre" land on the west side of the Mississippi with the understanding that the United States reserved the right to build factories, military posts, and roads within their new domain. Those who removed—6,000 over the next two years—received one rifle and ammunition, one blanket, and one brass kettle or a beaver trap. In addition flat-bottomed boats and provisions would be supplied by the United States for use in the removal. Those who remained on the east side of the river and "who may wish to become citizens of the United States" were granted 640 acres by the government, which heads of families might hold in fee simple. If they later moved, the land reverted to the United States.[61]

It was another handsome cession, though Jackson thought otherwise. "The cession of land obtained is not important, but the Principle Established leads to great importance."[62] The principle was removal. The principle was the termination of the anomaly of tribal government and laws within the territorial limits of the states. It was the termination of conflict over jurisdiction and over sovereignty and domain. It was the final definition of the status of Indians, the assertion of supremacy of the American government, and the pronouncement of the right of Congress to impose its authority and its laws over all people living within the United States. For Jackson, as for most westerners, removal was the only feasible answer to the continuing problem of the Indian presence. Thus the treaty with the Cherokees constituted an excellent beginning to the ultimate application of the principle to every tribe residing east of the Mississippi.[63]

Jackson's success at this convention convinced him of the inevitability, the practicality, and the workability of removal. The "security of all" was guaranteed by this treaty, he said.[64] Those Indians who remained in the east would till the soil, build houses, educate their children, achieve

*See map, page 396.

citizenship, and, for all intents and purposes, become cultural white men. Those who removed would insure their "national existance . . . on the arkansaw."[65] Through removal the Indians would escape certain annihilation and preserve their identity and culture. Removal was in fact the alternative to extinction, and "the only means we have in preserving them as nations, and of protecting them." By 1820 Jackson assured himself that the Indians themselves favored removal "if they had the means."[66]

It is important to note that this treaty mentioned the possibility of citizenship for Indians. It was the first treaty to hold out this hope and it was subsequently repeated in many other treaties. Citizenship was neither demanded nor expected. It would result in the natural course of events for those Indians prepared for "civill life" who remained on the east side of the Mississippi.

Removal was not rape. It was an exchange of land based on the premise that the two races could not live together, that the Indians occupied more land than they needed or would cultivate, and that the Indians, where they were, endangered the frontier and menaced not only settlers but the American nation itself. Removal involved consent, but it was a limited—if not distorted—kind of consent. Individual Indians might choose to go or to stay, but the Indian Nation as Nation must remove. Even so, for legal and moral reasons, the Nation was first asked to agree by treaty to the principle and to the land exchange. Unfortunately, this kind of consensual process invited bribery and fraud. Since the tribe must consent, any hesitation or objection produced "presents" and secret deals to corrupt influential chiefs.

In theory, removal protected everyone: whites, the Indians who stayed, and those who removed. Everyone benefited. Whites obtained the valuable lands relinquished by the departing Indians and thereby strengthened the nation's defenses, particularly near the frontier; the Indians who stayed gave up their wanderings and settled down to civilized life; and the Indians who removed preserved their racial heritage and "national existance."

Still, against their wishes, against their pleas, against what they said was the will and interest of the majority, the Indians were forced to yield their ancestral homes. They were made to do what Andrew Jackson had decided was best for them and best for his country.

It has been asserted that Andrew Jackson hated the Indians and that racial annihilation was his real objective.[67] Nothing could be further from the truth. Jackson neither hated the Indians nor intended genocide. For a slaveowner and Indian fighter he was singularly free of racial bigotry. He killed Indians in battle, but he had no particular appetite for it. He simply performed his duty. Moreover, Jackson befriended many Indians;

dozens of chiefs visited him regularly at the Hermitage. He adopted an Indian orphan (Lyncoya) and raised him as a son. He sanctioned marriages between whites and Indians. He believed citizenship inevitable for the more civilized Indians, and he argued that Indian life and heritage might be preserved (and should be preserved) through removal.[68]

The key to understanding Jackson's attitude toward the Indian is not hatred but paternalism.[69] He always treated the Indians as children who did not know what was good for them. But *he* knew, and he would tell them, and then they must obey. If they refused, they could expect a fearful punishment from a wrathful parent.

But there was nothing extraordinary about this paternalism. It in no way demonstrated bigotry, racism, or any other prejudice against Indians simply because they were Indians. Jackson was just as paternalistic toward his soldiers. As long as they obeyed him, as long as they demonstrated discipline and loyalty, he praised them without stint; but let them falter in their duty and he could exact the supreme penalty.

Nor was this paternalism unique to Jackson. Any number of white men, particularly government officials, practiced the same paternalistic attitude toward the Indians. It was a very common approach and the accepted mode of behavior. The Indians themselves adopted the language of paternalism and frequently spoke of themselves as children of their father, the President.

If Jackson was paternalistic did he decide on removal because it was best for the Indian? Clearly not. He agreed to it because it was best for the American nation. Most important of all, removal meant the elimination of tribal government, tribal organization, tribal sovereignty from white society. It was never the Indians *per se* that bothered Jackson. It was their infernal presence as a tribe, as a unit separate and distinct from the rest of the country, as though the Indians as a Nation had a right to the status of a free, independent and sovereign state. This Jackson could not abide. So he swept it away—beyond the Mississippi. If the Indians wished to exist as tribes, let them go west. If they agree to homestead on a plot of land and obey the laws of the states and the United States, then they may remain in the east. Like the Spanish presence, the existence of Indian nations had to be removed.

One year after signing a treaty with the Cherokees, Jackson stripped the Chickasaws of all their remaining lands in Kentucky and Tennessee.[70] It was another enormous cession. Almost one-third of the entire state of Tennessee and one-tenth of the state of Kentucky were involved. The acquisition constituted all western lands still held by the Indians to the east of the Mississippi River in those states.

Jackson had requested permission from the President to engage in the negotiations because of the economic and military advantages such a cession promised the United States. "Although it may be said that we have sufficient Territory already, and that our settlements ought not to be extended too far, yet every thing should be done to . . . consolidate our settlements." Such action, he told Monroe, would place a wedge between the Northern and Southern tribes, secure commerce on the Ohio and Mississippi, and afford a strong defense within striking distance of the settlements on the Mississippi and Missouri rivers. Jackson then went on to argue his contention that all Indians living within the territorial limits of the United States were subject to its sovereignty and laws and must not exercise separate tribal governmental powers. They were also subject to the states within which they resided. The time had arrived, Jackson insisted, when "their territorial boundary must be curtailed."[71]

The President granted Jackson's request. He and Isaac Shelby were appointed commissioners to arrange a treaty with the Chickasaws. Since this would constitute an extremely important land cession, Jackson invited Shelby to stop at the Hermitage on his way to the treaty grounds for a conference. During the course of one conversation the General asked his guest how high he was willing to go to gain title to the Chickasaw land.

Not more than $300,000 came the reply.[72]

Agreed.

The two men, assisted by Colonel Robert Butler (Jackson's former ward and aide) as secretary and William B. Lewis (Jackson's friend and neighbor) as commissary, arrived at the treaty grounds in Alabama shortly after 9:00 A.M. on October 1, 1818. They found the Indians sulky and ill-humored. For several days the Chickasaws proved to be "very litigious and slow in their decisions," reported the commissioners in their secret journal.[73] There was only one recourse: bribery. The Colbert brothers, mixed bloods, were singled out for special attention; Levi and George exercised great influence over the Chickasaws. Indeed, wrote one future commissioner, "Colbert is to the Chickasaws as the soul is to the body; they move at his bidding."[74] As finally arranged, Levi and George Colbert received $8,500 each; brother James got $1,666.66; Captain Sealey $666.66; and Captain McGilvery $666.66. The sums were to be paid in cash or merchandise, and Jackson, to prove his integrity, posted a bond for the total amount, $20,000.[75] Now the convention could begin.

In his "talk" to the Chickasaws, Jackson asserted that the land he wanted from them had been paid for by white men many years before. The land was granted initially by England to the states of Virginia and North Carolina, he contended, and later conquered from England in the Revolution and confirmed by the Treaty of 1783. Their Father the President had kept the white men away from it so "that his red children might hunt on it; but the game is now gone, and his white children claim it now from him." Whereupon Jackson distributed a map to the Indians to show which land the white men claimed. "It lies in Tennessee and Kentucky," he said, "and they have called on your father the President for it, and he cannot keep it from them any longer."

The talk closed with a warning. "We hear that bad men in your Nation threaten your chiefs with death, if they surrender this land. . . . If this is true we call you all to listen well—if the bad men of your Nation do any act of violence upon your chiefs for treating with your father the President he will put them to death for it. . . . He will not suffer such threats and insolent conduct to pass unpunished." If you refuse to sign the treaty, Jackson concluded, "your father will look on your conduct as acts of ill will and ingratitude."[76]

Levi Colbert spoke first. For his part he would give up the land to prove Chickasaw good will and gratitude. He only hoped their Father the President, by his commissioners, would be liberal in fixing a price.

Jackson rose from the table to answer. He looked around at the chiefs and then said in a loud voice:

"What do you ask for this land?"

"We don't know," replied the chiefs; "what will you give?"

"One hundred and fifty thousand dollars," came the quick reply.

"No!" shouted the chiefs.

"Two hundred thousand," Jackson shot back.

"No!" screamed the Indians, their voices gaining volume. They "loved money well," they told the General, "but they loved their land much better." Two hundred thousand was not acceptable.

"Two hundred and fifty thousand," cried Jackson, his eyes beginning to ignite.

"No!"

"Three hundred thousand."

Suddenly Shelby jumped from the table, outraged—he later said—by the exorbitant price Jackson offered. He would not participate further in the proceedings. The council broke up.

Jackson stormed after Shelby. What treason was this? What villainy? When he caught up with Shelby he could barely contain himself. "G—damn it," he roared, "did you not say you would give $300,000?"

"No sir," Shelby snapped, "I did not authorize you to make any such proposition."[77]

Jackson stared at him, his hands fisted in anger. Shelby looked at those eyes and retreated. Within moments he was preparing to leave for home, but his son spoke to him and prevailed on him to stay. Too much was at stake. After he had calmed down, Shelby agreed to return to the council. He also agreed to the amount offered by Jackson. The $300,000 would be paid to the Indians at the rate of $20,000 a year for the next fifteen years.[78]

The Chickasaws, under the direction of the Colbert brothers, signed the treaty on October 19, 1818, at the Treaty Grounds east of Old Town.*

Jackson's achievement was so notable that he received a special letter of commendation from the new secretary of war, John C. Calhoun. "The notice of the conclusion of the treaty with the Chickasaws is received," wrote Calhoun, "and it affords much satisfaction that so valuable a cession has been obtained, upon terms so favourable."[79] Later there was scandal. Jackson was accused of allowing a salt lick to be leased to his friend, William B. Lewis, "before the ink was fairly dry."[80] In fact Lewis had agreed to post bond in case the government refused the land. The Indians, suspicious of the government, complained that past annuities had not been paid as promised and forced Jackson to send to Nashville for money to appease the chiefs and prove his own good faith.[81] In addition, Colonel Butler, the secretary of the convention, charged such high rates for his services that Calhoun refused to honor his bills.[82] (One request sought to reimburse Butler for the loss of a "very valuable horse" who died from eating green corn.[83]) And of course the arrangement with the Colbert brothers was not included in the treaty—for obvious reasons. Thus certain aspects of the negotiation seemed unfortunate, if not disgraceful. Still they could not diminish the magnitude of the stupendous cession of land.

The frightful blows sustained by the Indians at the hands of Andrew Jackson, supported by the United States government, in the destruction of the Southern tribes have elicited appropriate criticism and indignation from latter-day Americans. But to understand the meaning and significance of Jackson's actions, one must view them in the context of the nineteenth century, not that of the late twentieth century. It cannot be ignored or forgotten that a powerful need existed throughout the country during Jackson's lifetime to subdue the Indians and expel them from territory that was believed to be essential to national expansion and the defense of the country. Jackson was not only a product of that need but the man most responsible for fulfilling it. His military skill and undeviating determination combined to annihilate the Indian tribes and propel thousands of Americans across the south and west. His decree, more than any other, forever separated the white and red races.

The Indians crushed, their land sequestered, and the principle of removal established, the only danger now remaining along the southern frontier was the continued presence of Spain.

*See map, page 396.

CHAPTER 22

To Seize Florida

WHEN THE REPUBLICAN PARTY IN 1816 nominated James Monroe for the presidency over his nearest rival, William H. Crawford, General Jackson was doubly pleased because he detested Crawford and admired Monroe. For a number of years he had supported Monroe's political ambitions, and during the late war he believed he enjoyed the Virginian's favor and assistance. Now he expected even greater deference—in particular, a free hand to deal with military problems in the south.

The easy and amicable relationship between the two men was demonstrated shortly after Monroe's landslide victory in the electoral college over the Federalist party candidate, Rufus King of New York. Jackson did not hesitate to offer advice to the President-elect. And his first suggestion was that Monroe get rid of Crawford. The General urged the appointment of Colonel William Drayton of South Carolina as the new secretary of war, to which advice he received a gracious reply and the later information that Monroe had considered Jackson himself for the post but was concerned about withdrawing him from the southern frontier "where in case of emergency, no one could supply your place." Besides, the new President had heard that Jackson did not want the post.[1]

The General appreciated Monroe's intent but assured him that he looked forward to retirement as soon as the frontier was pacified.[2] And of course he knew, as did the President, that pacification was impossible as long as the Spanish remained in Florida. The two men understood one another quite well; their ambition for Florida was virtually identical.

The War Department was offered to Henry Clay, speaker of the

341

House of Representatives, who rejected it out of hand as beneath his talents. His ambition required the State Department, and when that post went to John Quincy Adams of Massachusetts, Clay developed an instant hostility toward the Monroe administration that frequently flashed into lively debate on the House floor. For a short period the War Department continued in the hands of the acting secretary, George Graham, a hold-over from the Madison administration; then he was replaced by John C. Calhoun of South Carolina. To Jackson's dismay, Crawford was awarded the Treasury Department.[3]

Unfortunately, an unholy row erupted early in the Monroe administration between Jackson and the War Department that showed the General at his egotistical worst. Secretary Graham ordered to New York an engineering officer then under assignment to Jackson without informing the southern commander or gaining his approval. Jackson blew up and, characteristically, went straight to the President with his complaint. Monroe, who was busy inaugurating his administration, failed to notice the storm or to recognize that Jackson's pride and dignity were at stake. Monroe did nothing—which was what Monroe frequently did. Jackson seethed. He ranted and threatened. After forty-nine days—an eternity in Jacksonian time—he issued a division order on April 22, 1817, forbidding his officers to obey War Department instructions unless they came through him "as the proper organ of communication."[4]

The order, a staggering declaration, jolted the country. Several critical newspaper articles appeared, one of which called Jackson's action "mutinous." An anonymous writer sent a copy of this article to the General with the information that the writer of the piece was Brigadier General Winfield Scott. Without seeking corroboration, Jackson demanded an explanation from Scott. Scott replied that he had never seen the article, much less written it, but agreed that the order was indeed mutinous and deserved a presidential reprimand.[5]

That did it. Jackson's fury sent one thunderclap after another rolling over the mountains. To a letter, he scolded Scott, inquiring about a supposed injury, and "clothed in language decorous and unquestionable," he had received an answer "couched in *pompous insolence and bullying expression.*" What kind of soldier would stab a fellow officer in this manner? *"How little of the gentleman and how much of the hectoring bully you have manifested."* And "to the *intermeddling pimps and spies of the War Department,* who are in the garb of gentlemen, I hold myself responsible for any grievance they may labor under on my account, with which you have my permission to number yourself. For what I have said I offer no apology. You have deserved it all and more."[6]

It was wild. The letter even carried the suggestion of a duel, which

Scott gently turned aside on religious grounds. However, he told Jackson, "lest this motive should excite the ridicule of gentlemen of liberal habits of thinking and acting, I beg leave to add, that I decline the honor of *your* invitation from patriotic scruples."[7] A lovely touch.

This regrettable incident, totally unworthy of the national hero, saddened Jackson's friends when it later received widespread publication in the newspapers. Similarly, his feud with the War Department did him no credit. These outrageous displays of pride and self-importance confirmed the fears of some that Andrew Jackson was a very dangerous man. They also should have signaled the administration that they had a high-strung, opinionated, and proud commander to handle, one who readily violated rules and defied superiors when provoked by a prick to his vanity or pride. The secretary of war was placed on notice that Jackson would bypass him or contest his orders without so much as a second thought.

The dispute with the War Department terminated with the appointment of John C. Calhoun as secretary because Calhoun promptly announced that departmental orders in the future would, under normal circumstances, flow through the commanding generals. In a private letter to Jackson he assured the General that he agreed completely with his point of contention. He ended with a statement of personal loyalty. "Permit me to say that to you individually, I participate in those feelings of respect, which any lover of his country has towards you. In any effort to add greater perfection to our military establishment, I must mainly rely for support on your weight of character and information. I cannot therefore conclude, without expressing the wish, that our country may long continue to be benefited by your military services."[8] It is difficult to decide from reading this letter whether Calhoun in fact thought of himself as Jackson's superior. His subsequent letters were all tinged with timorous compliments and invariably sounded deferential. At the bottom of this early letter, Jackson added the words, "adopting the principles I contended for, and on which my famed Genl. order was predicated."[9]

Calhoun no doubt articulated the opinion of many Americans when he expressed the wish that the country might continue to benefit from Jackson's military services. Already an expression was common in Tennessee that whenever Old Hickory left home he never returned without rendering some noble service to the Union and to Tennessee. Americans around the country were saying the same thing, with an emphasis on his national importance. His recent success in negotiating with the Indians was a case in point. Even Monroe acknowledged the nation's debt. "The advantage of the late treaties with the Indians is incalculable," he wrote.[10] Yet that advantage needed to be augmented, as both the President and Jackson knew full well. The southern frontier was unsafe as long as the Spanish occupied Florida and provided a haven for rampaging "savages."

The Spanish position in Florida was totally untenable after the War of 1812. Deserted by the British and incapable of defending—much less administering—the Florida province, the Spanish played a waiting game. They had long since identified the man intent on their expulsion. Andrew Jackson was only the latest in a long series of conspirators who lusted after Spanish possessions. And they were quite convinced—correctly so —that he was prepared to sweep across the Gulf from Florida to Texas and then to Mexico. Other Americans had had such dreams of empire, but Jackson, with his demonstrated military skills, was the man who could realize them.

So the Spanish waited, watched, and wrote hundreds of reports that were copied and recopied but generated nothing in the way of action to protect a crumbling empire. The first move belonged to the Americans. What pretext would trigger that move and incite Jackson and his troops into crashing into Florida the Spanish pondered and wrung their hands over.

One immediate problem was the so-called Negro fort. This outrage stood alongside the Apalachicola River in Florida, some sixty miles from the American border. Fugitive American slaves occupied the fort and— by its very existence—encouraged other slaves to flee their servitude and join them. Every slaveholder along the southern frontier reckoned the fort a threat to his safety and his property. That the Spanish did nothing or were incapable of action intensified southern agitation. Like all slaveholders concerned about the safety of the frontier, Jackson worried over the problem—and in his usual aggressive manner attempted to solve it. In the spring of 1816 he wrote to Mauricio de Zuniga, the commandant of Pensacola, to warn him of the consequence if the situation did not improve. A "negro fort erected during our late war with Britain . . . is now occupied by upwards of two hundred and fifty negros many of whom have been enticed away from the service of their masters—citizens of the United States." Their conduct "will not be tolerated by our government, and if not put down by Spanish Authority will compel us in self Defence to destroy them."[11]

That meant an invasion of Florida. The Spanish were as agitated by the presence of the fort as the Americans and just as anxious to destroy it, but they lacked the military strength to do so. By letter and messenger Zuniga admitted to Jackson his concern over the fort and his willingness to cooperate in its removal. Astoundingly, he added that if the renowned General "Andres" Jackson would care to assist in reducing the fort, he, the Spanish Governor, would be proud to serve under him![12]

Not much later, in the spring of 1816, General Edmund P. Gaines, who constructed Fort Scott near the mouth of the Flint River north of the Florida boundary, sent an expedition across the border that blew up the Negro fort, killing 270 persons.[13] Some of the black leaders were later turned over to the Indians, to be put to a painful death.[14] And that took care of the Negro menace. It was done in the grand American tradition of contemptuously disregarding Spanish sovereignty and territorial integrity.

Another American concern—and a pretext for intervention—was the marauding tactics of the Seminole Indians, who periodically raided Georgia settlements and then retired to the protection of villages inside the Florida border.[15] By 1817 white settlers and speculators in the area were demanding better protection from their government—the kind of protection that eliminated boundaries. Among the interested speculators was a group of Tennesseans headed by Captain John Donelson and Major John H. Eaton, Jackson's biographer, both of whom had been urged by Jackson to invest in Pensacola. It had long been the General's belief that Pensacola was destined for eventual annexation and would then develop into a commercial rival of New Orleans for the Gulf trade. Several members of the Jackson family (but not Jackson himself) ultimately enjoyed a small financial killing on account of their Pensacola speculation.[16]

Another potential pretext for intervention, one that President Monroe seemed to prefer, was the problem of the "banditti" on Amelia Island. The island, situated at the mouth of the St. Mary's River (which formed part of the boundary between Georgia and Florida), was used by smugglers and privateers as a depot for their booty. The "banditti" had an arrangement with the merchants of Savannah and Charleston somewhat similar to the one the Baratarian pirates enjoyed with their customers in New Orleans. The situation seemed to call for the rescue of the island from Spain by American businessmen and then the rescue of the island from the businessmen by the American government. Thus Spain would forfeit another part of her Florida possession.

The cause of American intervention was happily abetted by the actions of the Seminole Indians during 1816 and 1817 in first refusing to acknowledge American claims to lands acquired as a result of the Creek War and then resisting all efforts to force their removal from those lands. This applied particularly to a small party of Seminoles living in Fowltown, just north of the Florida border, on land claimed by the United States under the Treaty of Fort Jackson. Neamathla, chief of the Seminoles in Fowltown, notified General Gaines that he could expect a bloody encounter if any attempt were made to dislodge them. The challenge was irresistible to an American frontier commander. Forthwith, an expedition marched out of Fort Scott, reached Fowltown on November 12, 1817, and burned the town and drove off the warriors and women.[17] Nine days later the Seminoles took revenge by ambushing a large open boat conveying forty soldiers, seven women, and four children as it floated up the Apalachicola River toward Fort Scott. In one swift, horrible bloodbath the men and women were butchered—all but one woman, who was taken captive, and four men, who escaped by jumping overboard and swimming to shore. When the Indians captured the boat they seized the children by their heels and dashed their brains out against the sides of the boat.

Thus began the First Seminole War—with customary barbarism on both sides. Within weeks Gaines was authorized by the secretary of war to pursue the Indians and, if necessary, to cross the Florida line "and attack them within its limits . . . unless they should shelter themselves under a Spanish post. In the last event, you will immediately notify this Department."[18]

The justification for invasion was agreeably strengthened by a filibuster launched against Amelia Island in eastern Florida. This expedition, commanded by Gregor MacGregor and financed by American money, succeeded in seizing the island and proclaiming the independence of Florida. It was also intended as a base of operation against Cuba. When the Spanish failed to oust the invaders from their island, the United States intervened. Gaines was directed "to repair to Amelia Island" and put an end to the filibuster.[19] Thus, from the east and west of the long Florida border, American arms were "provoked" into invading Spanish territory.

But intervention was one thing and seizure another. If seizure were the intention of the administration, the person to command the expedition was Andrew Jackson, whose desire to expel the Spanish from the American continent the administration fully understood. Indeed the administration shared that desire, at least as far as Florida was concerned. It would be preferred that the acquisition be arranged amicably, but Monroe had been involved too long with nibbling away at West Florida to pass up an opportunity to swallow the rest. Thus it came as no surprise that, within ten days of authorizing an invasion of Spanish territory in pursuit of the Indians, the administration ordered Jackson to Fort Scott to take command of the expedition. The action was appropriate in view of the General's overall command of the southern district. But the administration would have to be out of its mind if it expected Jackson to content himself solely with pursuing Indians. Designating him commander of the expedition was certain to embroil the Spanish—as it had before—and the administration had no reason to think otherwise. And in no way was Jackson cautioned about provoking a confrontation with the Spanish or creating a situation that could have international repercussions. Rather, his instructions were very broad. "Adopt the necessary measure," he was told by the secretary of war, "to terminate a conflict which it has ever been the desire of the President, from considerations of humanity, to avoid; but which is now made necessary by their Settled hostilities."[20] A little later, Calhoun wrote to Governor Bibb of Alabama to inform him that Jackson was "authorized to conduct the war as he thought best."[21]

Jackson thought the best way was outright seizure of Florida. But would Monroe authorize it? Would he give permission for the expulsion of the Spanish? Jackson had no problem initiating an invasion. He had done it before without authorization and had gotten away with it. He was dealing with the same man, James Monroe, as before, only now Monroe was President and responsible for the conduct of the government and the actions of his officials in the performance of the duties legitimately assigned to them. Was he prepared to sanction seizure? Was he prepared to accept the consequences of seizure?

Jackson never concerned himself about accepting the responsibility for his own actions. In fact he constantly (and tiresomely) reiterated that he "took responsibility" for whatever was done in his name. But in this instance he may have recalled the Burr conspiracy and the sudden and unexpected cry of treason from the President of the United States at the precise moment the expedition was about to begin. He would have to be insane to allow himself to become another Burr. Inasmuch as he had been accused very recently of "mutinous" behavior toward the War Department he had reason to be doubly cautious. Thus, if Monroe really intended the seizure of Florida, as Jackson believed he did, then the President ought to come right out and say so.

Jackson put the question to him directly. "The Executive Government have ordered . . . Amelia Island to be taken possession of; this order ought to be carried into execution at all hazards, and, simultaneously, the whole of East Florida seized and held as an indemnity for the outrages of Spain upon the property of our Citizens; This done, it puts all opposition down, secures to our Citizens a compleat indemnity, and saves us from a war with Great Britain, or some of the Continental Powers combined with Spain; this can be done without implicating the Government; let it be signified to me through any channel (say Mr. J Rhea [a Congressman from Tennessee]) that the possession of the Floridas would be desirable to the United States, and in sixty days it will be accomplished."[22]

Monroe later claimed that he was ill when the letter reached him and that he never spoke to Rhea. Indeed, as unlikely as it sounds, he claimed he did not read the letter until a full year later. When he did finally examine Jackson's letter—whenever that may have been—he wrote an endorsement on it: "I was sick when I received it, and did not read it, till after rect of letters by Mr Hambly, expld, in my letter to him of Decr 21 [1818]. Hearing afterwards, that an understanding was imputed to me, I asked Mr Rhea, if any thing had ever pass'd between him and me. He declard that he had never heard of the subject before."[23]

Not so, said Jackson. He had a letter from Rhea, received early in 1818, he later claimed, giving him all the assurances he needed. "I expected you would receive the letter you allude to," Rhea wrote Jackson, "and it gives me pleasure to know you have it, for I was certain it would be satisfactory to you. You see by it the sentiments of the President respecting you are the same."[24] The letter seemed to prove Jackson's contention—but it was dated January 12, whereas Jackson's letter to Monroe was dated January 6. Obviously Rhea's letter was written before Monroe received Jackson's; the mail could never have traversed a route from Nashville to Washington and back and left time for Monroe to signal acceptance of the proposal through Rhea. Thus it appears that the President never spoke to Rhea. Moreover, when Jackson's activities in Florida produced an international storm and he was threatened with a reprimand, Rhea wrote to him, "I will for one support your conduct, believing as far as I have read that you have acted for public good."[25] Surely Rhea would not have spoken in this manner had Monroe followed Jackson's suggestion.

In his own mind Jackson always believed he had permission to seize Florida and that the permission came straight from Monroe. For years he vehemently argued his defense and found or invented excuses to close loopholes in that defense wherever they appeared. He even claimed he had burned Rhea's letter at the writer's insistence in order to prevent it from falling into the hands of those who might make improper use of it.[26] This was pure invention, but Jackson did not realize he was fabricating; he simply could not imagine that he was wrong on so important a point.

In fact he was not wrong. He did have Monroe's authorization, only not in the form he remembered. Shortly after writing his letter to Rhea, Jackson received a note from Monroe that stated precisely what he wanted to hear. The letter was actually written before the Rhea letter, but Jackson received it *after* he requested authorization for the seizure. In later months and years Jackson confused the sequence of letters and assumed that the permission he had requested had come through Rhea.

Monroe wrote Jackson on December 28, 1817. The letter was extremely provocative. "This days mail will convey to you an order to repair to the command of the troops now acting against the Seminoles, a tribe which has long violated our rights, & insulted our national character. The mov'ment will bring you, on a theatre, when possibly you may have other services to perform depending on the conduct of the banditti at Amelia Island, and Galvestown."

Since the invasion in pursuit of the Indians had already been approved, what "other services" did Monroe have in mind if not the seizure of Florida? Naturally, the President had to be careful what he put on paper in case his letter should fall into the wrong hands; still, to make his point clear, he added: "This is not a time for you to think of repose. Great interests are at issue, and until our course is carried through triumphantly & every species of danger to which it is exposed is settled on the most solid foundation, you ought not to withdraw your active support from it."[27]

Jackson had always understood Monroe's true position with respect to Florida, just as the President understood his. What then was Jackson to think when his commander-in-chief spoke of "great interests" and settling every species of danger on "the most solid foundation" and not withdrawing his "active support from it" until "our course" triumphed? Was this not the authorization he required, however guardedly written? Surely "great interests" did not mean the "banditti" or the Indians. Great interests meant the Spanish presence in Florida, and the President of the United States was instructing his General not to cease activity until the danger of that presence was settled permanently.

Even without this letter the intentions of the administration were conveyed through its actions. Ordering Andrew Jackson into the area meant that there would be no way to prevent a deliberate and calculated attack upon the Spanish except by explicit instructions. And those instructions would have to come from the President himself, for Jackson had already shown how quickly he could bypass the orders of the secretary of war if he felt so inclined. Such instructions came neither from the President nor the secretary; instead Jackson received orders about "other services" once he arrived at the "theatre" of operation. Monroe knew what Jackson would do in Florida. It would have been an act of supreme folly and irresponsibility to send Jackson on this mission if the administration truly meant to preserve the territorial integrity of Spanish Florida.

Of course the administration could not admit publicly its true intent. The President could not confess complicity in an act of aggression against a foreign power with whom the United States was technically at peace. Jackson should have known this and should have realized that the President would find excuses—such as being sick and not reading his "Rhea Letter" until a year later—to escape the infamy of waging an undeclared war. The extraordinary thing is the number of historians since then who have believed in Monroe's innocence. They ignore his previous conduct toward Florida, how as secretary of state under Madison, for example, he had encouraged General Mathews in 1811 to seize East Florida only "to disavow him when the action became embarrassing."[28]

This is not to excuse Jackson. His protests notwithstanding, he probably had every intention of seizing Florida given any opportunity to do so. He certainly had been threatening such action for some time, and no sooner was he ordered against the Seminoles than he began intimating to his close associates that he might take Florida. "Whether any other service than putting down the seminoles may detain me on the Southern frontier," he wrote his ward and nephew, Andrew Jackson Donelson, "time can only unfold."[29] Moreover, Jackson's subsequent actions toward the Spanish in Florida were illegal and improper—and he was responsible. No authorization, however guarded, justified what he did. But to absolve Monroe from responsibility is unfair, and it was the burden of sole responsibility as a kind of censure that Jackson later resented.[30]

In any event, once ordered to Florida, Jackson gathered his available troops, who numbered some 1,000 men, and on January 22, 1818, departed for Fort Scott. They covered the distance of 450 miles in forty-six days despite heavy rains that turned bad roads into virtually impassable ditches, that greatly slowed the movement of the baggage wagons. Nevertheless he was finally on his way to Florida.

Florida! And he had promised to deliver it in sixty days.

CHAPTER 23

The First Seminole War

KILLING INDIANS WAS EASY ENOUGH, considering the number of men Jackson had on hand to do the job. But taking Florida would require additional troops. So, with characteristic aggressiveness and initiative, Old Hickory authorized some of his old officers to raise additional troops and join him at Fort Scott, presuming (correctly) that the governor of Tennessee would subsequently approve his action.

The appointment of Jackson as executioner threw the Indians into wild alarm. Many of those living on the American side of the boundary within lands claimed by the United States under the Treaty of Fort Jackson fled in terror to Florida when they heard the dreadful news of his appointment. To the Indians General Andrew Jackson had assumed the character and form of an evil spirit: He need only point at them and they perished where they stood. And Jackson encouraged his reputation—not as executioner but as stern father and wise judge who would protect his Indian children (he actually believed he defended Indian rights) provided they obeyed him without question and closed their ears to false friends and prophets like the English and Spanish who encouraged them in their lawlessness. Their susceptibility to evil counsel was precisely the cause of the present trouble, Jackson said. "It is reported to me," he wrote, "that Francis, or Hillis Hago, and Peter McQueen, prophets, who excited the Red Sticks in their late war against the United States, and are now exciting the Seminoles to similar acts of hostility, are at or in the neighborhood of St. Marks. United with them . . . [are] Woodbine, Arbuthnot and other foreigners."[1]

Alexander Arbuthnot! A name that would haunt Jackson's reputation long after the man had been hanged from the yardarm of his own ship. Unlike Woodbine and Nicholls, whose actions were motivated largely by British interests, Arbuthnot genuinely liked the Indians and tried to help them.[2] A Scot by birth, now 70 years of age, he had come to Florida from the Bahamas in 1817 to trade with the Seminoles and the Spanish. He exchanged knives, guns, powder, and blankets for skins, beeswax, and corn. He was so decent in his dealings with the Indians that the Seminoles heeded his counsel and the Creeks conferred on him power of attorney to act on their behalf.[3] He urged them to keep the peace and avoid the provocations that lead to war. Totally committed to the Indians, Arbuthnot believed they had been cynically used and then abandoned by the English as well as robbed and murdered by the Americans. On several occasions he pleaded frantically with the British government to intercede on behalf of the Indians, but his pleas went unheeded.[4] "They have been ill treated by the English," he wrote, "and by the Americans, cheated by those who have dealt with them."[5] Of course Americans misunderstood his concern for Indian welfare. They felt he deserved to be treated with less pity than a "sheep-killing dog."[6]

Soon Arbuthnot was joined by another British subject, the swaggering, roistering braggadocio Robert Ambrister, a former lieutenant of the Royal Marines. Like Arbuthnot (whom he despised as a weak and feckless man), Ambrister championed the Indian cause; unlike Arbuthnot, he counseled the Seminoles to war against the Americans in defense of their rights and property. He strutted before them in his brightly colored uniform, barked orders, and assumed the posture of command—all of which the younger Indians found irresistible. And he encouraged a war to which he one day forfeited his life.

The war moved slowly in the direction of the Seminoles as Jackson steadily drove south. Outside Hartford, in Georgia, he was met by General Gaines, on his way back from Amelia Island, and only recently informed of his replacement by Jackson. On March 9 Old Hickory and his men, now half-starving, reached Fort Scott. And once again he found himself bedeviled by his old problem of supplies. The fort itself was low on provisions and urgent appeals had gone out for help.[7] Several supply ships from New Orleans were expected any moment and it was reported that two supply sloops were lying in the bay at the mouth of the Apalachicola River. Without a moment's hesitation, Jackson determined his course of action. On the morning of March 10, 1818, the day after his arrival at Fort Scott, Jackson ordered the livestock slaughtered and issued to the troops, each man receiving three meat rations and one quart of corn. That exhausted the food supply. Then he wheeled his army out of the fort and headed straight toward Florida and the supply ships. He now commanded nearly 3,000 troops, both regulars and volunteers, and an additional force of 2,000 Indian allies—most of whom, ironically, were Creeks.[8]

Five days later the army reached the location of the Negro fort, which Jackson ordered repaired and fortified. Throughout the campaign the General showed a lively interest in the problem of runaway slaves. This was not simply an Indian war, but a war against defiant blacks. Runaway slaves, he said, needed to be punished, severely.[9]

Happily, the army upon its arrival at the Negro fort met an ascending boatload of food and the troops gorged themselves. But Jackson would not permit a long delay; he soon had the troops back in formation and marching into the heart of Seminole country. Besides, a large flotilla of provisions previously ordered from New Orleans was momentarily expected, and its arrival would solve the food problem once and for all. To safeguard this flotilla, Jackson, with lordly arrogance, notified the Spanish governor at Pensacola of its coming and warned that he wanted no trouble with its passage. The letter was insolent and provocative, brimming with all the spite and nastiness Jackson had accumulated over the years in nurturing his malice against the Spanish. "I wish to be distinctly understood," he wrote, "that any attempt to interrupt the passage of my transports cannot be received in any other light than as a hostile act on your part. I will not permit myself for a moment to believe that you would commit an act so contrary to the interests of the King, your master."[10] He almost seemed to be daring the governor to contradict him. Instead the governor, Colonel José Masot, responded firmly but politely. He would permit passage of the transports this one time, provided the usual duties were paid; for the future Jackson must apply to the proper authority for permission to transit across Spanish territory.[11]

Jackson had reliable information that the Seminoles and their white supporters, along with a motley crew of brigands and slaves who had been enticed from their masters or stolen during the late war with England, were congregating around the town of St. Marks in Spanish Florida, and the General aimed his army straight for this target. St. Marks lay seventy miles to the southeast and approximately ten miles from the coast. "The Spanish government is bound by treaty to keep her Indians at peace with us," Jackson wrote the secretary of war on March 25. "They have acknowledged their incompetency to do this, and are consequently bound, by the law of nations, to yield us all facilities to reduce them."[12]

On April 1 he was joined by additional Creek allies under General William (Chief) McIntosh and a company of Tennessee volunteers under

Colonel Elliott. Together they plunged deeper into Seminole country, further violating Spanish sovereignty and the "law of nations" with respect to the integrity of territorial boundaries. As the army moved it burned and destroyed all hostile villages, seized whatever cattle or foodstuffs were available, and sent hundreds of Indians fleeing to St. Marks. It was a thoroughgoing campaign of terror, more accidental than planned, but effective nonetheless. Whenever possible the hostiles were killed or captured, for Jackson interpreted his orders as a command to pursue the Indians wherever they fled and to make certain they fought no more. To the extent that the Spaniards stayed out of his way their "rights" would be respected.[13] What helped spur Jackson's troops to bloodthirsty revenge was the discovery in the public square in Fowltown of a red pole from which dangled fifty freshly cut scalps "recognized by the hair as torn from the heads" of American settlers.[14]

On April 6, Jackson reached St. Marks and informed the Spanish commandant that he had come to garrison the fortress in order to "chastise" the Indians and the black brigands who were warring against the United States. His action, he said, was totally justifiable on the grounds of self-defense and he anticipated no argument to the contrary from the commandant. He promised to respect Spanish rights and property (whatever that meant in his mind) and to inventory public property and provide a receipt. In short "St Marks was necessary as a depot to ensure the success of my operations." Later, he said, their two governments could work out the problem of his seizure and clear up any difficulties attendant on his action. Once again Jackson expected that his government would support him in everything he did, but he also seemed to understand that his seizure was likely to precipitate diplomatic problems between the United States and Spain. The unfortunate Spanish commandant, who lacked a force with which to contest Jackson's demand, readily capitulated. The Americans occupied the fort; the Spanish flag was unceremoniously lowered, and the Stars and Stripes was run up the flagstaff in its place.[15]

Jackson found St. Marks empty of hostiles, which disappointed him, but he did capture that "noted Scotch villain Arbuthnot who has not only excited but fomented a continuance of the war. I hold him for trial."[16] At the same time Captain Isaac McKeever, a naval commander cooperating with Jackson's expedition, captured Francis the Prophet (sometimes called Josiah Francis or Hillis Hadjo) and Himollemico, two Creek chieftains. McKeever lured them aboard his ship by flying the English flag. The unlucky Indians thought they had discovered allies and expected to find ammunition and powder. The manner of their capture hardly added stature to the reputation of American arms.

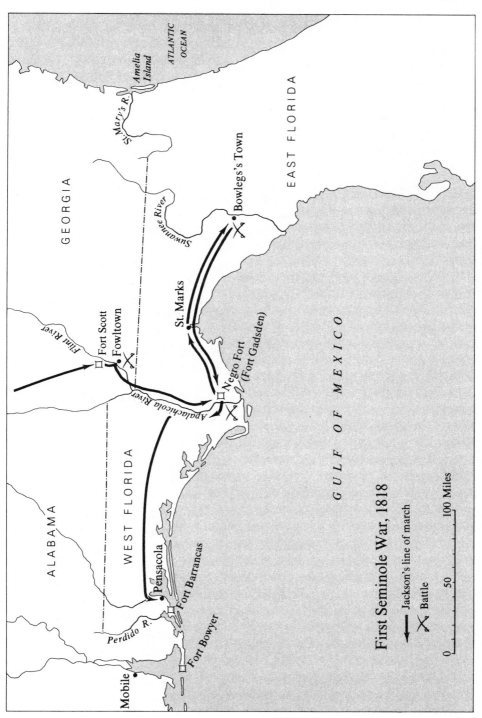

First Seminole War, 1818

"I had Francis the prophet & HoemalleeMecko hung on [April] the 8th," Jackson informed Rachel. They will foment war no more. After the executions the General was asked about the bodies. "Shall they be thrown into the river?" "No," Jackson replied, "they have ceased to be our enemies; let them be buried as decently as our means will admit of. See that it is done!"[17]

Two days after the seizure of St. Marks, Jackson resumed his march. He swung his army toward the town of Chief Billy Bowlegs, on the Suwannee River, a hundred miles to the east. The town was a refuge for runaway slaves, and Jackson believed it also sheltered a strong contingent of Indians. Bowlegs headed the Alachua branch of the Seminoles, one of the more powerful families of the main Seminole tribe. The capture of this town and its inhabitants would speed Jackson's determination to crush all Indian resistance to the American presence in the south.

The route to Bowlegs's town lay through a flat and swampy wilderness, and in many places the army waded through extensive sheets of water. Horses nearly starved for want of forage. On April 16, after two brief skirmishes with some hostiles, Jackson reached the vicinity of Bowlegs's town. Without pausing to catch his breath he formed his lines of attack and sent his men into the Indian town. But the Seminoles had been warned of his approach and had escaped across the Suwannee River. The hostiles suffered the loss of nine blacks and two Indians killed and nine Indians and seven blacks captured.[18]

Another disappointment. Another missed opportunity. Despite the speed with which Jackson had hurried his army across the swamps the Indians had somehow learned of his presence and disappeared into the wilderness. Catching them, killing them, chastising them seemed an impossible task.

A few nights later the swaggering former marine, Robert Ambrister, along with a white attendant, Peter B. Cook, blundered into Bowlegs's town unaware that their Indian friends had decamped and that Jackson and his army now occupied the village. They discovered their mistake soon enough. But something worse followed. On the person of one of the black prisoners a letter was found from Alexander Arbuthnot to his son, John, warning him of Jackson's approach.[19] Now Jackson understood how the Indians had managed to escape him, how they had even contrived to slip away with their families and much of their supplies. "I hope the execution of these two unprincipled villains [Arbuthnot and Ambrister] will prove an awfull example to the world," he wrote to Secretary Calhoun.[20]

After putting more than 300 houses to the torch, Jackson turned around and headed for St. Marks, completing the march in five days. As far as he could tell the war against the Seminoles was over. No appreciable hostile force appeared to do battle. Indians simply vanished into the swamps whenever he appeared. Obviously they could not wage war and probably had never been prepared for one in the first place.

In fact this First Seminole War mauled the Indians rather badly. In addition to everything else, Jackson had destroyed Miccosukee, the largest Seminole town (near Tallahassee), and killed Kinache, its chief; he routed the Negroes on the Suwannee River; and he executed Francis the Prophet and a number of other Red Stick chiefs.[21] Because of his destruction of villages and food supplies, to say nothing of the execution of many important chiefs, he "chastised" the Indians severely enough that they no longer resisted him. So Jackson declared the war at an end. If the Seminoles would not fight, there was little sense to the useless pursuit of them across swampy wastes. With St. Marks in his hands—"the hot bed of the war," he called it[22]—and "foreign" influence on the Indians effectively diminished, he could now address himself to the "great interest" to which Monroe had ordered him to attend: the seizure of Spanish Florida.

First, however, Arbuthnot and Ambrister needed attention. The two "unprincipled villains" required speedy trials and even speedier executions, according to Jackson. Information had been discovered on their persons, he told Calhoun, "pointing out the Instigators of this savage war and in some measure involving the British Government in the Agency."[23] Jackson turned the two prisoners over to a courtmartial, together with the incriminating papers discovered in their possession or in the possession of their associates. The court convened and began hearing evidence late in April in the stone fort at St. Marks. General Gaines presided over a court of twelve officers, most of whom were regulars.

Against Arbuthnot—whom some eastern newspapers thought an alias for Woodbine, "that unfeeling monster"[24]—there were three charges: that he excited the Indians to war, that he acted as a spy for them, and that he incited them to kill William Hambly and Edmund Doyle, two American traders. But the court denied its jurisdiction on the third charge, and it was dropped. In support of the other two, evidence was presented indicating that Arbuthnot had advised the Creek chief, Little Prince, not to comply with the Treaty of Fort Jackson (which was as heinous a criminal offense as Jackson could imagine); that he had supplied the Seminoles with amunition in their war against American settlers; that he had corresponded with British officials as an agent for the Indians; and that his letter to his son had been explained to the Indians at Bowlegs's town, thereby assisting their escape from Jackson's approaching army.[25]

After the evidence was submitted, Arbuthnot spoke in his own defense. He was respectful, calm, and dignified. He dismissed as hearsay the evidence involving him with Little Prince, but he admitted the sale of ten kegs of powder to Bowlegs at Suwannee so that the Indians could hunt. It was meant to help them eat. Not kill Americans. Arbuthnot's defense was generally able and well argued, but it did not convince the sternfaced officers who sat in judgment. "May it please this honorable court," he concluded, "I close my reply to the charges and specifications preferred against me, being fully persuaded that, should there be cause of censure, my judges will, in the language of the law, lean to the side of mercy."[26] But mercy was not to be expected for those who trafficked with Indians, sympathized with them, and tried to aid them. Aiding Indians meant massacring Americans.

After a short deliberation, two-thirds of the court agreed that the 70-year-old Arbuthnot was guilty of both charges and sentenced him to be hanged. Death was the penalty for an imprudent man whose major offense was his affection and regard for the Indian.

Next came Ambrister. He was accused of aiding the enemy and assuming command of the Seminoles to wage war against the United States.[27] The evidence against him was strong; a letter in his own hand acknowledged that he had sent a party of Indians to attack the invading Americans. Against this evidence, Ambrister could offer little defense. He pleaded guilty with justification and threw himself on the mercy of the court. His judges rather liked his soldierly manner and his frank admission of the strength of the evidence against him, but they also understood their duty. They found him guilty of the principal charge and sentenced him to be shot. Then one of the members of the court requested reconsideration of the vote, with the result that the court changed the sentence to fifty lashes on the bare back and confinement with ball and chain to hard labor for twelve months.

The court took only two days to dispose of the "unprincipled villains," reaching their decision on April 28. That evening the commanding general approved the sentence of Arbuthnot and the first sentence of Ambrister, specifically disapproving the reconsideration of the sentence. The evidence was indisputable, Jackson said, that the prisoner had commanded the Indians in war against the United States and therefore had forfeited his allegiance to his country, become an outlaw and pirate, and must be executed. The two men were quickly and legally put to death.

As Arbuthnot swung by the neck at the end of the yardarm of his own ship and Ambrister lay on the ground, his head a mass of wounds, a group of Indians came into the fort to sue for peace and were struck dumb at the sight of their executed friends. They now understood the full fury and fearful vengeance Jackson exacted for warring against him. The executions made a deep and profound impression: General Andrew Jackson was a terrible, vindictive enemy against whom the Indians found only their graves and the confiscation of their property.

Whether the executions of Arbuthnot and Ambrister were necessary or justified may be questioned. The war with the Indians was over and the trials could have been delayed until Jackson had consulted with his superiors in Washington. But Jackson was not a merciful man in these circumstances, nor was it his style to defer to Washington for decisions. He could have delayed the execution of the sentences; he certainly stood on shaky legal ground in decreeing that a person forfeits his nationality and becomes an outlaw by warring against another nation. But this was the early nineteenth century, along a frontier where the Indian menace kept settlers in a perpetual state of alarm and apprehension. Jackson had no patience with those who trifled with this fear. To him, Arbuthnot and Ambrister were guilty of inexcusable crimes and their punishment was obligatory under frontier law and conditions. "The proceedings of the Court martial in this case," he reported to Calhoun, "with the volume of Testimony justifying their condemnation, presents scenes of wickedness, corruption, and barbarity at which the heart sickens and in which in this enlightened age it ought not scarcely to be believed that a christian nation would have participated and yet the British government is involved in the agency." He hoped that the execution of Arbuthnot and Ambrister would "convince the Government of Great Britain as well as her subjects that certain, if slow retribution awaits those unchristian wretches who by false promises delude and excite a Indian tribe to all the horrid deeds of savage war."[28]

The executions took place on April 29. Jackson himself did not witness them; at daybreak he resumed the campaign. He left St. Marks garrisoned by 200 troops and marched to Fort Gadsden—the old Negro fort, now named for the man who had rebuilt it, Jackson's engineer and aide, Captain James Gadsden. After resting a few days at the fort, Jackson wrote Calhoun, giving a full report of his activities and informing the secretary that he intended "to make a movement to the West of the Apalachacola" and to strike at Pensacola. Indians at war with the United States have free access to Pensacola, he said, and from that quarter are kept advised "of all our movements." Moreover, "they are supplied from thence with amunition and munitions of war" and are presently collecting 400 to 500 warriors in that city to continue the war. "Pensacola must be occupied with an American force," Jackson asserted, "The Governor treated according to his deserts or as policy may dictate."[29]

This was an extraordinary assumption of authority. Pensacola was not St. Marks. Pensacola was the center of Spanish rule in Florida—and Jackson was calmly informing the secretary of war of his intention to extinguish that rule. But long ago and with thousands of other Americans, he had decided that the Spanish must leave this continent. Now the opportunity presented itself to accomplish part of this goal and Jackson unhesitatingly seized it. Justification was easy. "So long as Spain has not the power . . . to preserve the Indians within her territory at peace with the U States," he told Calhoun, "no security can be given to our Southern frontier. . . . The moment the American Army retires from Florida, The War hatchet will be again raised, and the same scenes of indiscriminate murder with which our frontier setlers have been visited, will be repeated." So long as the Indians are exposed to the "poison of foreign intrigue," he continued, so long as they receive ammunition and gunpowder from Spanish commandants, "it will be impossible to restrain their outrages." There was only one solution: "The Savages . . . must be made dependant on us. . . . I trust therefore that the measures which have been persued will meet with the approbation of the President of the U States. They have been adopted in pursuance of your instructions."[30]

At the time Jackson wrote this letter it was fully four months since he had invited Monroe's approval of his scheme to seize Florida. Despite his clear intention and his assumption of approval (repeated in several letters), the administration never once cautioned him against violating Spanish rights or sovereignty. Yet later it tried to pretend it was innocent of his purpose in attacking Pensacola. Perhaps if the administration had warned him off, he might have been persuaded to return to Tennessee. In fact, after garrisoning St. Marks and scouring the country west of Apalachicola, he told Calhoun he was inclined to proceed directly to Nashville.[31] If this was his intention, it was short-lived. What probably changed his mind and determined his decision to expel the Spanish was the information he received early in May that hundreds of Indians were assembling at Pensacola and with Spanish assistance were planning to attack American settlements.[32]

When Jackson left St. Marks he commanded 1,200 troops, regulars and volunteers. He had hardly gone more than a half dozen miles when he learned of an outrage visited on Indians by white men. The Indians in question were his allies and under his protection. More than that, they had fed his half-starved troops on their march from Tennessee through Georgia on the way to Fort Scott. Their village was named Chehaw, and most of their young warriors had gone with Jackson to fight beside him or were otherwise enlisted in the service of the United States. Now word came that a Georgia militia under Captain Obed Wright, unaware of the status of Chehaw, had attacked the village, burned the houses, and massacred seven people including a chief named Howard who was an uncle of General William McIntosh. Little Prince wrote immediately to the Indian agent. "The white people came and killed one of the head men," he said, "and five men and a woman, and burnt all their houses. All our young men have gone to war with General Jackson, and there is only a few left to guard the town, and they have come and served us this way. As you are our friend and father, I hope you will try and find out, and get us satisfaction for it. . . . Men do not get up and do this mischief without there is some one at the head of it, and we want you to try and find them out."[33]

Jackson seethed over this outrage. He could kill Indians with the best of them and burn their houses—but not when they were allies, not when they had proved their loyalty by feeding his troops and fighting alongside him. Loyalty was sacred to Jackson. He prized it above all things. Those who returned his loyalty, who trusted him without question, were constantly aware of his abiding friendship. Also, and most particularly, the Indians were under his protection, and in a very real and telling way this outrage cast doubt on his ability to provide that protection. Jackson felt diminished. He felt dishonored. His reaction, then, was violent and passionate. He sent a company of Tennesseans to arrest Captain Wright and convey him in chains to Fort Hawkins, where he was to be kept in close confinement. Then Jackson dashed off a scorching letter to William Rabun, the governor of Georgia.

> I have this moment received by express [a] letter . . . detailing the base, cowardly and inhuman attack, on the old woman and men of the chehaw village, whilst the Warriors of that *village* was with me, fighting the battles of our *country* against the common enemy, and at a time too when undoubted testimony has been obtained and was in my possession . . . of their innocence of the charge of killing Leigh and the other Georgian at cedar Creek.
>
> That a Governor of a state should assume the right to make war against an Indian tribe imperfect peace with and under the protection of the U. States, is assuming a responsibility, that I trust you will be able to excuse to the Government of the U. States, to which you will have to answer, and through which I had so recently passed, promising the aged that remained at home my protection and taking the warriors with me on the campaign is as unwarantable as strange. But it is still more strange that there could exist within the U. States, a cowardly monster in human shape, that could violate the sanctity of a flag, when borne by any person, but more particularly when in the hands of a superanuated Indian chief worn down with age. Such

base cowardice and murderous conduct as this transaction affords, has not its paralel in history and should meet with its merited punishment.

You Sir as Governor of a state within my military Division have no right to give a Military order, whilst I am in the field. . . . Captain Wright must be prosecuted and punished. . . . This act will to the last ages fix a stain upon the character of Georgia.[34]

Cowardly monster in human shape! Murderous conduct! A stain upon the character of Georgia! The letter practically seared the eyeballs of Governor Rabun when he read it. Not only Jackson's "haughty tone" and insulting language offended Rabun but his obvious contempt for civilian authority. "When the liberties of the people of Georgia," the governor fired back, "shall have been prostrated at the feet of military despotism,—then, and not till then, will this imperious doctrine be tamely submitted to."[35] Jackson guffawed. Such nonsense about the people and military despotism "are cant expressions for political purposes." The military have rights just like the civil, he replied, "and in my respect for those of the latter I will never permit those of the former to be outraged with impunity."[36]

Meanwhile Jackson sent a "talk" to the Chehaw Indians to tell them his heart was filled with regret and "my eyes with tears" because of the outrage. He promised punishment for those responsible and an indemnity.[37] At the same time he wrote Calhoun and demanded that the matter be brought to the attention of the President. "All the effects of my campaign may by this one act be destroyed," he said.[38]

In time Captain Wright stood trial and was acquitted by the state of Georgia. The Indians received an indemnity of $8,000 as compensation for the destruction of their homes and property. The Monroe administration, pursuing its usual hands-off policy, steered clear of the Jackson-Rabun dispute, and the controversy eventually faded away. The governor had the satisfaction of seeing Wright go free, and Jackson had the satisfaction of knowing the Indians received "adequate" compensation to acknowledge the white man's guilt in destroying the village.

While the preliminaries of this dispute were in progress, Jackson and his army waded through West Florida on their way to Pensacola. As they neared the town, the Spanish governor, Colonel Masot, roused himself and papered Jackson with a series of warnings protesting the American general's presence in the province and ordering him out if he wished to avoid bloodshed. "If you proceed contrary to my expectations," Masot wrote, "I will repulse you force by force."[39] At long last the Spanish authority in Florida had come alive. Some show of resistance now seemed probable.

Jackson of course disregarded the warnings. Convinced that hostile Indians were massed inside Pensacola (he was wrong), Jackson was determined to seize the town and execute the Seminoles. On May 24, 1818, Jackson and his army arrived at Pensacola. Only a token show of Spanish resistance challenged him, and Jackson easily brushed it aside and captured the town. Just before entering Pensacola he sent a note to the Spanish commanding officer stating that he had been informed of orders to fire upon his troops seeking to obtain supplies from an American ship anchored in the bay. "I wish you to understand distinctly," he wrote, "that if such orders are carried into effect, I will put to death every man found in arms."[40]

Masot had already retreated to Fort Carlos de Barrancas outside Pensacola, where he hoped to make a stand. Jackson went right after him and demanded the surrender of the fort. Governor Masot refused. "Your Excy. has violated the territory of Spain," Masot shrilled, "by taking possession of the post of the Appelachy, and lowering the Spanish colours. . . . I protest before God and man . . . that my ardent wishes are . . . to contribute to the peace and friendship of our respective nations. . . . If your Excelly. will persist in your intentions to occupy this fortrass, I am resolved to defend it to the last extremity, opposing force to force."[41]

Jackson responded to this protest by dragging forward his single nine-pound piece and five eight-inch howitzers and aiming them at the fort. There was a slight puff of resistance that lasted only a few moments and then a white flag broke out over the fort. Masot had demonstrated his loyalty to his king by making at least one small gesture of defiance. Anything more was lunacy in view of the weakness of his position and the size of Jackson's attacking force. So he quickly surrendered and marched his troops out of the fort. "All I regret," Jackson wrote later, "is that I had not stormed the works, captured the Governor, put him on his trial for the murder of Stokes and his family* and hung him for the deed."[42] But that outburst was just so much Jacksonian bombast; in fact he had agreed under the terms of capitulation to allow the Spanish garrison to retire from the fortress with full honors of war, to transport them to Cuba, and to respect Spanish rights and property. The occupation of Florida would continue until such time as Spain could provide a military force of sufficient size to prevent "criminal" acts against the United States or (in more diplomatic language) until Spain could enforce the obligations of existing treaties between the two countries. Jackson said it succinctly: "The articles [of capitulation] with but one condition amount to a complete cession to the u states of that portion of the Floridas hitherto

---

*An American family recently killed in an Indian raid.

under the government of Don Josse Massot."[43]

With little show of military might, Jackson had virtually extinguished the Spanish presence in Florida.[44] In his mind the "complete cession" of Florida had been concluded. In a proclamation issued immediately after taking possession of Pensacola, Jackson justified his actions by invoking the "immutable laws of self defence," as well as the "helpless women [who] have been butchered" on the frontier, and countless babies whose "cradles [were] stained with the blood of innocence."

The proclamation also declared that all Spanish subjects would be respected during the occupation, that Spanish laws would govern in all cases involving property and persons, that religious toleration would be guaranteed and trade with all nations assured. The proclamation then announced the establishment of a provisional government for the Florida province. William King, colonel of the Fourth Infantry, was appointed civil and military governor of Pensacola with authority to enforce the revenue laws of the United States. Captain Gadsden was appointed collector with full powers to nominate subordinate officers to assist him. "He will apply to the Governor of Pensacola for military aid in all cases where it may be necessary to correct attempts at an illicit trade," said Jackson. Moreover, the archives of the province would be taken into American custody and a confidential agent appointed to preserve them. "It is all important," declared Jackson, "that the record of titles and property should be carefully secured."[45]

The arrogance of the proclamation was positively colossal, worthy of the great Napoleon. In one stroke Jackson redirected governmental authority under powers he assumed by virtue of military conquest. It was an appropriate climax to the astounding series of actions that began with the invasion of Spanish Florida without a declaration of war, continued with the executions of Arbuthnot and Ambrister, and culminated in the seizure of Pensacola and the expulsion of the Spanish from Florida. Small wonder the world was shocked and outraged, the Monroe administration shaken and frightened, and Congress driven to an investigation of the entire Seminole War.

On June 2 Jackson notified President Monroe that the Indian War was over now that St. Marks, Fort Gadsden, and the Barrancas were in American hands. "These were the hot beds," he wrote; the "possession of these points" was "essential to the peace and security of our frontier." Now if Monroe would spare him the Fifth Infantry and additional guns, he "would insure Ft St Augustine add another Regt. and one Frigate and I will insure you Cuba in a few days." But, he informed Monroe wearily, the war had crippled him physically. "I am at present worn down with fatigue and by a bad cough with a pain in my left side which produced a spitting of blood, have reduced me to a skelleton. I must have rest, it is uncertain whether my constitution can be restored to stand the fatigues of another campaign, should I find it so I must tender my resignation." He said he was returning to Nashville, where he would write again; in the meantime he wanted Monroe to understand the importance of his conquests in terms of the security of the southern frontier "and *to the growing greatness of our nation.* . . . I have established peace and safety, and hope the government will never yield it."[46]

Fortunately for Spain, Jackson's health necessitated his return to Tennessee—otherwise he was ready to pursue the Spanish to Cuba. He was now a ranting nationalist in full cry, obsessed with the safety of the frontier and the "growing greatness of our nation." If only he had been sent to Canada at the beginning of the war with England, he still complained, he would have settled that frontier too.[47] But his health drove him home. His broken, bleeding body rebelled and he seriously considered resigning his commission.

The First Seminole War demonstrated the ease with which the Spanish could be shoved into the sea. At the first sight of American troops they turned tail. Thus, with Canada gone, it hardly took much imagination to recognize that future American expansion must come at the expense of a crumbling Spanish empire. The seizure of Florida renewed the spirit of American expansion. It also clearly plotted the future direction of that expansion.

Before leaving conquered Florida, Jackson published his usual "Address to His Troops," lavishing praise on them for the difficulties and privations they suffered without complaint and tendering them "an affectionate farewell." He also dispatched two companies of volunteers to "scour the country between the Mobile and Apalachacola rivers, exterminating every hostile party who dare resist, or will not surrender and remove with their families above the 31st Degree of latitude."[48] Again, removal. But that was his proven technique for breaking Indian resistance to the white man's conquest of the southwest. The course of American expansion decreed by Jackson involved both Indian and Spanish submission.

His "Farewell Address" published, Jackson turned over the garrison of troops to Colonel King and departed for Tennessee. But he never fully relinquished command. Even in Nashville he could not resist exercising his military authority in Florida. Learning that hostile Indians had received supplies at St. Augustine from Spanish authorities who retained a token force there, he ordered General Gaines to investigate the complaints and, if he found them substantiated, to attack the Spanish garrison, expel them, and take possession of the town. But before this order could be obeyed and another Jacksonian outrage perpetrated it was countermanded by the secretary of war—which demonstrated that the administration could act to safeguard Spanish rights and property when it wished to do so.

The administration was now faced with a major international crisis. At the outset Monroe had probably thought he could intimidate Spain into yielding Florida by applying a little pressure.[49] Jackson, sent to do the job, had provided more pressure than was needed: He had seized Florida, removed the Spanish government in residence, and executed two British subjects—all of which invited a formal declaration of war from both England and Spain.

Although months had passed since Jackson's Rhea letter was received by the administration, and although Calhoun and Crawford had read the letter even if Monroe had not—which seems unlikely since the President handed it to both Calhoun and Crawford, and at least Calhoun said it required Monroe's attention[50]—no directive instructed Jackson to refrain from provocative or dangerous actions against the Spanish. In late January 1818 Monroe did tell Calhoun to instruct Jackson "not to attack any post occupied by Spanish troops, from the possibility that it might bring the allied powers on us," but these orders were never issued.[51] Calhoun said only that "Genl. Jackson is vested with full powers to conduct the war, in the manner which he may judge best."[52]

In April and May 1818 the newspapers were filled with stories of the capture of St. Marks and the executions of Arbuthnot and Ambrister, which delighted a large segment of the American public. Still no reaction from the administration. No outcry. No indication of concern or displeasure. Nothing. And when Jackson seized Pensacola, the final indignity heaped on the Spanish, Monroe ducked away from the embarrassment by departing for his farm in Loudoun County, a move that the secretary of state, John Quincy Adams, interpreted as procrastination in the face of a "rapidly thickening" storm.[53] Adams was left alone in Washington to face the fury of the Spanish minister, Don Luis de Onís. Adams responded to protests by stating simply that no reply was possible until the President had studied the official documents.[54]

Monroe remained in hiding for over a month, returning to Washington in early July. A week later he summoned his Cabinet, asked for an opinion, and found sharp division. Calhoun, furious because Jackson in his Rhea letter had gone over his head to Monroe for authorization to seize Florida, argued for censure and an official investigation. He contended that the General had commenced a war in violation of the Constitution, that he had determined to seize Pensacola long before he entered Florida, and that he violated his explicit orders. The secretary of the treasury, William H. Crawford, who may have begun to fear Jackson as a potential presidential rival for western and southern votes in 1824, agreed. He also urged the return of Florida to Spain; otherwise the administration would be held responsible for Jackson's actions and for waging an undeclared war against a friendly nation in violation of the Constitution. The attorney general, William Wirt, said little but took the Crawford-Calhoun position. Only the dour, tough-minded, pragmatic Adams defended Jackson, arguing that the military action was defensive and necessitated by circumstances. Jackson had been authorized to invade Spanish Florida in pursuit of Seminoles; the object of the military operation was the submission of the Indians, not the Spanish, and therefore Jackson was perfectly justified in what he did. To prevent further problems with the Indians, Adams argued, St. Marks and Pensacola must be retained.[55]

The Cabinet in effect gave Monroe two alternatives: return Florida and censure Jackson or retain Florida and defend Jackson. Monroe, characteristically, saw a way to slip between the alternatives, a way of taking diplomatic advantage of what the Hero had accomplished while refusing to defend the General or to take responsibility for what had occurred. He drafted a note to the Spanish minister that accused Jackson of exceeding his instructions but insisted that the General had been guided by military necessity in seizing St. Marks and Pensacola. Obviously the President could not censure Jackson because that might encourage Spain to refuse to surrender Florida. (And it might not sit well with the American people.)

Finally, more than six months after receiving the Rhea letter Monroe wrote to Jackson about the seizure of Florida. It was the first statement the General received from the President on that delicate subject. Monroe, who fully appreciated the dimensions of Jackson's temper, pride, and sensitivity to criticism, was extremely cautious in his choice of language. "In transcending the limit prescribed by [your] orders," wrote Monroe, "you acted on your own responsibility, on facts and circumstances, which were unknown to the government, when the orders were given, many of which occurred afterwards, and which you thought imposed on you the measure, as an act of patriotism, essential to the honour and interests of your country."[56] The United States was justified in invading Florida, he continued, by right of the "Law of nations" to pursue an enemy, but an order to attack a Spanish post assumed another character; it assumed the character of a declaration of war, and under the Constitution only Congress can declare war. However, Monroe assured Jackson, he realized how circumstances might occur in which a commanding general may exceed his authority "with essential advantage to his country."[57]

Continuing this theme, Monroe chose words calculated to placate Jackson's vanity and pride. But they hardly became the President of the United States and commander-in-chief in their distortion of events and the reasons motivating them. Worse, he sought Jackson's approval to tamper with the documentary evidence. Some of the General's letters could prove embarrassing and perhaps hinder the administration's negotiations to obtain Florida, so Monroe suggested that Jackson allow them to be doctored. "Your letters to the Department were written in haste, under the pressure of fatigue and infirmity, in a spirit of conscious rectitude, and, in consequence, with less attention to some parts of their contents than would otherwise have been bestowed on them. . . . If you think proper to authorize the secretary or myself to correct those passages it will be done with care."[58] James Monroe, as his enemies said many times, sometimes acted as though he "hasn't got brains enough to hold his hat on."[59]

Jackson dismissed Monroe's crudeness with hardly a notice. What bothered him was the President's comment about "transcending" orders and acting on his own responsibility. He had no problem with responsibility; he stood ready to account for his behavior—and to defend it. "Responsibility is not feared by me if the General good requires its assumption. I never have shrunk from it, and never will." As for transcending orders, Jackson denied it. The order of December 26, 1817, sending him into Florida was comprehensive and gave him the fullest discretion in conducting the campaign; "and for the exercise of a sound discretion, on principles of policy, am I alone responsible."[60]

Jackson came close to a break with the President. After all that had happened during the gradual nibbling away at Spanish Florida, he was appalled that Monroe had not the decency or courage to admit his role in the seizure of the territory. Perhaps unintentionally, Jackson injected a note of sarcasm into his letter when he said, *all the acts* of the inferior [officer] are the acts of the Superior."[61] To a friend he admitted that it was not "my desire to injure" President Monroe "unless impelled in my own defence." He said he was willing to defend his own actions "but when my country is deprived of all the benefits resulting from my acts I will not consent to bear . . . responsibility that ought to be those of another. My situation is . . . delicate. I must for the present be silent."[62]

Having stirred an international tempest, Jackson resumed his former cautious habits of mind and action. Monroe, too, was cautious. He waited two months before replying to Jackson's letter, only to infuriate Jackson the more. He asked the General to write the War Department that a difference of opinion existed between them over the extent of his power and then give his own version of his authority. "This will be answered

. . . in a friendly manner by Mr. Calhoun who has very just and liberal sentiments on the subject."[63] That was a bald-faced lie; far from having liberal sentiments, Calhoun wanted Jackson censured—as Monroe knew full well. No wonder Jackson had a false notion of Calhoun's position over the next ten years. Monroe fed it to him. Of course, Calhoun himself later fostered this impression to the extent that Jackson presumed that the war secretary had defended him before the President and the Cabinet.[64]

Jackson properly refused Monroe's invitation to debate his authority as if it were an open question, and he reasserted his contention that he had not transcended his orders. He shrewdly pointed out that he could hardly refer "to your private and confidential letters" as the basis for an official communication to the secretary of war. On that unpleasant note Jackson dismissed further discussion of his authority, although the President acknowledged its termination with a friendly letter, in the hope of avoiding an open rupture in their relationship.[65]

While Monroe attended the delicate task of appeasing an irate General, John Quincy Adams was busy facing down an irate Spanish minister. Spain demanded the immediate restoration of St. Marks and Pensacola, the disavowal of the military action, and "suitable punishment" for General Andrew Jackson.[66] Adams's reply was a masterful display of diplomatic skill without resort to doctored evidence or contrived interpretation. He blandly informed the Spanish that Jackson occupied Florida not according to orders or as an enemy of Spain but because of military necessity imposed by the war against the Seminoles. Indeed all of the General's actions could be easily and properly explained by his concern over the actions of the Indians and the assistance they received in carrying out attacks upon American settlements. Furthermore, he said, the President "will neither inflict punishment, nor pass a censure upon General Jackson" for his conduct, the motives for which were prompted by the "purest patriotism" and the vindication of which "is written in every page of the law of nations. . . . self defense." Turning the argument around, Adams implied that the Spanish commanders at St. Marks and Pensacola deserved censure for having failed in their responsibility to preserve order within their provinces. And if these officers were indeed powerless to prevent Indian raids, "Spain must immediately make her election, either to place a force in Florida adequate at once to the protection of her territory, and to the fulfilment of her engagements, or cede to the United States a province, of which she retains nothing but the nominal possession, but which is, in fact, a derelict, open to the occupancy of every enemy, civilized or savage, of the United States, and serving no other earthly purpose than as a post of annoyance to them."[67] It was a powerful argument, clearly and succinctly articulated, and it proved persuasive to the ministry in Madrid in view of Spain's recent loss of colonies in Central and South America.

As negotiations for the purchase of Florida commenced, Congress returned to Washington to begin a new session late in 1818. It reconvened in a feisty mood, intending to look carefully into this Florida business in view of the circumvention of its authority in the waging of an undeclared war with Spain. With the submission of the President's annual message, much of which dealt with the Florida expedition, it became apparent that a campaign was building to discredit Jackson—not simply because of his unauthorized behavior against the Spanish (which was bad enough) but because of a growing fear among future presidential contenders that he was emerging as a national leader—and a potential rival for the presidential nomination.

Although Jackson's political intentions were obscure, he commanded enormous popular support. He could easily rival Henry Clay of Kentucky for western votes and William H. Crawford of Georgia for southern votes. Because of this he invited the kind of surgical stroke by master politicians that would cut him down to size. Both Clay and Crawford were skillful knife-wielders, and privately they announced the start of their whittling for the beginning of the new congressional session. Naturally they disguised their intentions and their motives. Not until the Florida question came up for debate in the House did Clay publicly reveal his envy of the "military chieftain." Spite also prompted his actions. In denying Clay the post of secretary of state (the fastest route to the presidency), Monroe fashioned an implacable enemy who would use any excuse to criticize and embarrass the administration. Crawford, on the other hand, acted with more discretion. He operated quietly through friends in Congress and in private discussions in the Cabinet. Jackson disliked and distrusted him but assumed that Crawford's enmity arose over the General's support of Monroe for the presidency in 1816.[68]

Congressmen who supported the move to punish or censure Jackson did so for a wide variety of reasons. Some were genuinely scandalized by the Florida operation and its clear violation of the Constitution. Some worried about Jackson's military prowess and his possible emergence as a "man on horseback"; like Jefferson, they believed him a "dangerous" man—and Jackson sometimes gave them good cause for fear. Others so thoroughly disliked the Monroe administration that they welcomed any opportunity to bludgeon it. And a few congressmen wished to register their dismay at the prevailing spirit of nationalism that gripped the nation. Committed to a states' rights philosophy, they regarded the Florida expedition as a fearful extension of federal—and particularly executive—authority. The implication that the President could conduct a war without

the approval of Congress infuriated them. Their leading organ, the Richmond (Virginia) *Enquirer,* actively encouraged anti-Jackson sentiments
around the country and reprinted articles and editorials critical of the
General. Several articles by Spencer Roane commanded widespread attention because of the virulence of their attack.[69]

As Congress prepared to examine Jackson's actions in Florida, repeated alarms flashed back to Nashville urging the General to hasten to
Washington to assist in his defense. New York and Georgia had joined
forces and there was "much intrigue . . . on foot," he was told.[70] Unless
Jackson wanted his reputation sullied and his achievements demeaned,
he had better bestir himself. Other friends cautioned him about going to
Washington, fearing he might lose his temper and say and do outrageous
things that would prove the charges against him and ruin his cause.[71]
Jackson dismissed the arguments of the nay-sayers. He would confront
his enemies personally—or at least be on hand to provide needed information when necessary. "Major," he said to his friend and neighbor,
William B. Lewis, "there's a combination in Congress to ruin me. I start
for Washington to-morrow morning."[72]

Never a slow traveler, Jackson galloped through the wintery countryside buried inside an overcoat borrowed from Lewis. He arrived in Washington on January 23, 1819, much to the interest of the leading newspapers in the city.[73] He had come, he told his nephew, Andrew Jackson
Donelson, a cadet at West Point, "to explode one of the basest combina-
tions ever formed, the object not to destroy me but the President of the
u states, and to wound my reputation and feelings." These "hellish machinations" were the work of "Mr Wm. H. Crawford and Mr Speaker Clay,"
he added, and "I shall await the 4th of march next when mr Clay has no
congressional privileges to plead."[74]

On January 12 the House Committee on Military Affairs brought out
a report condemning the executions of Ambrister and Arbuthnot, probably the most vulnerable of Jackson's actions in Florida. When the report
reached the floor of the House, Thomas W. Cobb of Georgia, Crawford's
henchman and his leading supporter in the House, moved to amend the
report to disapprove the seizure of St. Marks and Pensacola. He also
recommended the passage of several bills to prohibit the invasion of
a foreign territory without congressional authority (except in pursuit
of a defeated enemy) and to forbid the execution of any captive taken
in time of peace or in an Indian war without the consent of the
President.[75]

So the great debate began. It lasted nearly a month, at that time the
longest debate devoted to a single issue. The galleries overflowed—
crowded to suffocation, according to the newspapers—and the presence

of many ladies encouraged the congressmen to their loftiest flights of oratory.

The high point came with the speech of Speaker Clay. Always a gut fighter, he enjoyed a verbal brawl. Mind and tongue honed to a sharp edge, he cut up opponents with a precision and speed unrivaled in either house. His long, cadaverous body, his lancing eyes, and his wide mouth outlined by thin, bloodless lips added dramatic tension to his appearance. His performances invariably stampeded the gallery and won shouts, whistles, and applause. Now, about to shred the great Hero of New Orleans, he stood in the well of the House and savored every moment of the drama. A slight smile flickered across his face. Then he began. He denied any personal animosity toward Jackson or the administration and insisted he was acting from principle, as he always did. First he attacked the Treaty of Fort Jackson and cited it as the direct cause of the Seminole War. The treaty directly violated the ninth article of the Treaty of Ghent, he said. Then, his voice coated with sarcasm as he halfheartedly tried to keep a straight face, he charged the General with attempting to deny the Indians their religion and forcing them to convert to Christianity. "Spare them their prophets!" he begged in mock appeal. "Spare their delusions! Spare their prejudices and superstitions! Spare them even their religion, such as it is, from open and cruel violence." The audience burst into laughter. It may have been ridiculous, but the gallery loved every word. Also, the structure of repeated phrases excited them with its rhythm as it rose to a climax and then trailed off with an appropriate coda. And Clay hit each line with a smack. Not only what he said but the way he said it enraptured the crowd.

On a more serious note, his countenance grave and troubled, Clay warned his colleagues: "There are two topics which, in Europe, are constantly employed by the friends and minions of legitimacy against our country. The one is an inordinate spirit of aggrandizement—of coveting other people's goods. The other is the treatment which we extend to the Indians." As one of the commissioners who had helped draw up the Treaty of Ghent, he knew what was he was talking about. How can we allay these fears, he asked, "after the unhappy executions on our Southern border"? Clay pilloried Jackson for the execution of Arbuthnot, depicting a cruel tyrant whose only sport was needless killing. Ever so subtly he alluded to Alexander the Great, Caesar, and Napoleon—but quickly and shrewdly denied that the American General had any designs inimical to the liberties of the country. Then he hurried to his conclusion, again employing the rhetorical device of repetition to score his point and bring his listeners roaring to their feet. The representatives, he said, "may bear down all opposition . . . even vote the general the public thanks; they may carry him triumphantly through this House. But, if they do, in my humble judgment, it will be a triumph of the principle of insubordination—a triumph of the military over the civil authority—a triumph over the powers of this house—a triumph over the constitution of the land. And I pray most devoutly to Heaven that it may not prove, in its ultimate effects and consequences, a triumph over the liberties of the people."[76]

Three days later Jackson arrived in Washington. From the moment he read the speech he conceived a full blown, devastating and lasting hatred for Henry Clay. "The hypocracy & baseness of Clay," he told Major Lewis, "in pretending friendship to me, & endeavouring to crush the executive through me, make me despise the Villain." Conscious of the magnitude of his popularity among frontiersmen, Jackson sent copies of Clay's speech to his friends in the west and asked that it be published extensively in the newspapers. "I hope the western people will appreciate his conduct accordingly," he wrote. "You will see him skinned here, & I hope you will roast him in the West."[77] Because John Quincy Adams had defended him so ably in his dealings with the Spanish, Jackson further requested that the newspapers give the secretary a "proper ulogium." Monroe too, whose message to Congress concerning the Florida expedition received the General's total approbation. After some mealy-mouthed letters the previous fall, the President had at last found his backbone. "I knew I could not be mistaken in Mr. Munroe's firmness, he must be supported." The only question mark was Calhoun; but the President has assured Jackson of the secretary's "liberality." Besides, Calhoun "has professed to be my friend," wrote Old Hickory, "approves my conduct and that of the President."[78] So Jackson anointed him a friend who had defended him in the Cabinet—a false impression the secretary assiduously cultivated as the General gained political visibility.

Jackson's presence in the capital, where he was closeted each day with friends and supporters to plan the strategy for defeating the censure motions, immeasurably strengthened the pro-Jackson forces in the House. So complete was his absorption in his defense that the General refused all personal invitations to social affairs.[79] The strategy finally agreed upon called for the Jackson representatives to capture and dominate the debate. Speakers were arranged in precise order to answer Clay and rebut each resolution introduced by Cobb. Richard M. Johnson of Kentucky, Alexander Smyth of Virginia, and George Poindexter of Mississippi among others searched out the weak points in Clay's argument and flung them back at him wrapped in patriotic professions and pious sentiments. "And shall we see him [Jackson] depart from this city in disgrace; censured and dismissed from office by Congress?" asked Smyth. "No; it cannot be. Forbid it, every power that guards the protectors of innocence. Forbid it, policy! Forbid it, gratitude! Forbid it, peace!" Poindexter climaxed the series with a ringing declamation of how Jackson had filled the measure of his country's glory.[80] Such was the tone and temper of the debate.

The defense benefited by the administration's strong support for voting down the motions and by the steady progress toward a treaty with Spain for the purchase of Florida. Further, the attack angered the American people and only increased Jackson's popularity—if that was possible. Senator Rufus King of New York slyly intimated that perhaps the General had deliberately encouraged the investigation to foster his presidential ambitions.[81]

On February 8, 1819, the House meeting as a committee of the whole voted on each of the four resolutions introduced by Cobb. On disapproving the executions of Arbuthnot and Ambrister the count was Yes, 54; No, 90. On prohibiting the execution of captives without executive approval: Yes, 57; No, 98. On condemning the seizure of Pensacola as unconstitutional: Yes, 65; No, 91. On drafting a law to prohibit the invasion of foreign territory without the authorization of Congress except in pursuit of a defeated enemy: Yes, 42; No, 112. This victory for Jackson was followed by three formal votes by the House itself. By a vote of 108 to 62 it refused to condemn the trials and executions of Arbuthnot and Ambrister; by a vote of 107 to 63 it rejected the resolution of censure; and by a vote of 70 to 100 it declined to characterize the seizure of Florida as unconstitutional.[82]

Jackson exulted. He was vindicated, completely vindicated; his laurels, honors and distinctions and his accomplishments remained intact. His spirits soared to such heights that he even deigned to attend a presidential reception. And what a triumph that was! "From the earnestness with which the company pressed round him," wrote the observant Secretary Adams, "the eagerness with which multitudes pushed to obtain personal introductions to him, and the eye of respect and gratitude which from every quarter beamed upon him, it has as much the appearance of being his drawing-room as the President's."[83]

A few days later Clay called at Jackson's hotel to assure the General there had been nothing personal intended in his speech in the House; his commitment to certain basic principles had prompted his remarks. A superb politician, Clay always attempted to divorce personal rancor from public disagreement. It was a characteristic quality of Clay, one that was quite sincere and not at all hypocritical, but Jackson never understood this.

When Clay called Jackson was on his way to New York, intending to visit his godson at West Point. He never reached his destination because everywhere he appeared he was literally mobbed by people who detained him to demonstrate their love and their loyalty. In Philadelphia it became a four-day ovation. The militia, that nascent political engine—no one would realize its potential until a great soldier ran for high office—assumed charge of his schedule. Public addresses and dinners extolled his services and proclaimed him the first man in America. And Jackson instinctively responded with becoming modesty and graciousness, his political skills undergoing a thorough testing. Cheers brought him to his feet, bowing and tipping his hat. Toasts to his greatness brought reminders of past giants. At a public dinner in Philadelphia, hearing himself exorbitantly praised, Jackson raised his glass to "The Memory of Benjamin Franklin"—and the mob roared its delight.[84]

In New York, however, he slipped. At a Tammany banquet in his honor Jackson saluted De Witt Clinton, the builder of the Erie Canal, unaware that Tammany detested Clinton.[85] But it was a natural and honest mistake, one an outsider unacquainted with New York's byzantine politics might make, and the Tammany men just laughed it off. Afterward he was given a reception at City Hall, and the Common Council voted him the freedom of the city—presented in a gold box. New York's festivities lasted five days. "Whenever the General went into the streets it was difficult to find a passage through them, so great was the desire of the people to see him."[86] Jackson left the city escorted by a regiment of artillery and a number of distinguished politicians, including the Vice President of the United States, Daniel D. Tompkins.

Baltimore could barely contain its excitement at Jackson's coming. He had hurried through it two weeks earlier before a proper salute could be organized. Now all was ready. At four o'clock in the morning a salvo of artillery awakened the people and summoned them to greet the approaching Hero. The Regular Blues turned out to escort him to his hotel, where a mob of people waited to welcome him. The Common Council unanimously resolved that his portrait be painted by Charles Peale and hung in the council chamber among the portraits of other distinguished Americans. Jackson graciously consented to sit for the picture. He visited Fort McHenry, where he reviewed the militia and received the honors due his rank. Whenever he entered the room at a reception, an orchestra invariably struck up *See the Conquering Hero Comes.* [87]

The trip was a moment of glory. In the cities he visited the American people seemed anxious to convey to him a message from the entire nation: they loved him, they trusted him, and they were grateful to him. "Among the people," one newspaper said, ". . . his popularity is unbounded—old and young speak of him with rapture."[88] Jackson was deeply affected.

In Baltimore Jackson received the report of the Senate committee investigating the Seminole War presented to the Senate on February 24, 1819. It shot him back to Washington within eight hours. The committee of five, three of whom had concurred in the report, was chaired by Abner Lacock of Pennsylvania, a friend of Crawford. The report was extremely judicious in tone and particularly careful with its facts. Affidavits and other documents supported the text. The fairness and impartiality of the report was so obvious that its unqualified condemnation of the Florida invasion had a devastating impact on Congress and on Jackson. The General was seated at a banquet in his honor in Baltimore when he first learned of the report. It nearly crushed him. Someone then rose and toasted the conquering Hero. Jackson came awake to his surroundings. He struggled to his feet. "What I have done," he responded in a faltering voice, "was for my country."[89]

The report savaged him. "In reviewing the execution of Arbuthnot and Ambrister," it read, "your committee cannot but consider it as an unnecessary act of severity on the part of the commanding general and a departure from that mild and humane system . . . honorable to the national character."[90] Quietly, devastatingly, but without rancor, the report pronounced Jackson's behavior dishonorable. Not only the execution of the two British subjects but his other actions in seizing Florida as well.

The report was released so late in the legislative session that meaningful debate was impossible. Congress planned to adjourn early in March, and it was now late February. Moreover, the Senate understood the mood of the country and the attitude of the people toward those intent on maligning their Hero. Jackson's triumphal tour was one more indication of it. Further, the settlement of the Florida question tended to close out the investigation. On February 22, 1819, Adams and Onís had signed a treaty ceding Florida to the United States and settling the Louisiana boundary in exchange for the assumption by the United States of claims against Spain of up to $5 million. Finally, the case of Arbuthnot and Ambrister faded with the failure of the British government to demand satisfaction. The evidence presented by the American minister, Richard Rush, to Lord Castlereagh was so complete and convincing, and the desire of England to continue its exploitation of the American import market so urgent (to say nothing of the necessity of furthering the goodwill begun with the Rush-Bagot agreement and the Convention of 1818), that the British lodged no protest over Jackson's action.[91]

The Senate decided to kill the report. A vote to table it left the report to expire quietly when Congress adjourned on March 4. This delicate handling was not helped by a rumor (probably manufactured) that Jackson, raging like a madman, threatened "to cut the ears off" Senator John

W. Eppes of Virginia, a member of the investigating committee and a son-in-law of Thomas Jefferson. Jackson was allegedly prevented from entering the Senate chamber to perform the mutilation by Commodore Stephan Decatur, who talked the General into returning to his carriage.[92]

With the report gasping its last on the Senate table, Jackson relaxed. The President extended him every courtesy: a formal reception, a private dinner, and several confidential conversations. The "machinations" of Crawford and Clay properly scotched and Congress in adjournment, the General could afford to return home. Accompanied by a fairly large retinue of hangers-on, he departed Washington on March 9. It was a glorious passage: again the demonstrations, the dinners, the military reviews. Town after town exploded with delight at his presence. But Tennessee outmatched them all. From the border of the state straight through to Nashville, Jackson's homeward trail marked one long, twinkling celebration of the nation's Conquering Hero.

CHAPTER 24

Expansion and Removal

WHEN ANDREW JACKSON HATED, it often became grand passion. He could hate with a Biblical fury and would resort to petty and vindictive acts to nurture his hatred and keep it bright and strong and ferocious. He needed revenge. He always struck back. Thus upon his return to Tennessee following the collapse of the "conspiracy" to censure him, he began immediately to explore means of damaging the reputations of Clay and Crawford. He wrote to John Clark of Georgia, a prominent anti-Crawford politician and later governor of the state, and invited him to share any information that could be used to discredit Crawford. The General wished to have "such facts relative to the Character of Mr Wm H Crawford . . . as may belong to his public Character, or have any connection with his private deportment." He wanted to malign Crawford, to blacken his reputation, to demonstrate his "depravity of heart."[1] Clark happily obliged, but their exchange of letters only revealed two embittered, petty men—men more to be pitied than condemned—quite incapable of doing Crawford serious harm.[2]

At the height of his fame Jackson indulged his mean-spirited streak. In a way he could not help himself. His victories and achievements must not be demeaned or criticized, not by anyone, including the President of the United States. Perhaps some of this display of animus, so unbecoming a man of his unparalleled good fortune, can be excused by Jackson's ill health (which bothered him particularly throughout 1819), combined with the extreme fluctuations of mood that beset him—from rage over the censure "conspiracy" to delirious exultation occasioned by the frenzied receptions the American people repeatedly accorded him. The rapid transitions from dejection to exhiliration may have induced a temporary emotional instability that led him to suspect plots and conspiracies against himself and against the administration. "I thought it a duty I owed to mr munroe," he told his friend and aide, James Gadsden, "to put him on his guard as it respected Crawford. I wrote him that I was informed confidentially, that mr Wm. H Crawford had written a letter to mr Clay the object of which was to form a combination and opposition against mr Munroes reelection."[3]

Jackson's health had cracked under the strain of the military campaigns. He was so worn and debilitated after the Florida adventure that he frequently spoke of his impending death. For the next twenty-five years he felt himself slipping away each time his wounds, the dysentery, or the other infirmities of his body gave him trouble. In the summer of 1819, shortly after his return from Washington, Jackson suffered a major collapse and for a time was not expected to live. At fifty-two his face clearly bore the marks of his discomfort. He grew increasingly emaciated and he barely picked at his food. His chest throbbed constantly, and he brought up blood when he coughed. For a long time he needed a walking stick to steady his faltering steps. Yet this fierce, indomitable man would not yield to the weakness of his body; he fought to stay alive even though he talked of death as something quite imminent. Slowly—very slowly— he recovered.

The General's neighbor, Major Lewis, came over one day to cheer him up, and Jackson offered to show him the site he had selected for a new residence: a level spot in an open field near the old blockhouse. Lewis recommended a different site, one elevated above the general level of the plantation, but Jackson was firm. "No, major. Mrs. Jackson chose this spot, and she shall have her wish. I am going to build this house for *her*. I don't expect to live in it myself."[4]

Jackson's 1,000-acre plantation, of which 400 acres were cleared and cultivated, already had one brick building. This was the Presbyterian church that the General built for his wife when she became a member. Now, in the late summer of 1819, after his health stabilized, he began to build a stately mansion as another gift to her. This was a large two-story brick house, nearly 90 feet across and almost 100 feet in depth. From a small porch, a long hall ran the length of the house with parlors on either side of the main entrance. Behind the left parlor was the dining room, with the kitchen in a small building immediately to the rear of the main house. There was a bedroom (occupied by the General and Rachel) behind the parlor on the right side along with several other sleeping rooms on the second floor. A sweeping staircase at the rear of the main hall connected the two stories; so did a smaller and narrower one tucked away on the far right of the building.

The original Hermitage partially burned in 1831, necessitating extensive remodeling in which Jackson added wings on either side of the house, double porches front and rear, with thick, fluted pillars supporting the upper porch. A false front enlarged the mansion visually and greatly improved its appearance.[5]

In 1819 Jackson engaged William Frost to design a large garden alongside the mansion. The result was a highly stylized and severely tailored arrangement of hedges and flower beds that was all the rage in the nineteenth century. Visible from Rachel's room, the flower beds were traced with pebble paths and edged with red bricks. Immediately in front of the main house an avenue of young cedars was later planted around a guitar-shaped lawn that ran from the entrance of a private road at the turnpike to the mansion itself.

In the beginning the Hermitage was intended as a retreat.. It was never that, although at times Jackson genuinely hoped to retire from public service. But it always rang with the voices of many people, of all ages, visiting friends and relatives and the many children the Jacksons raised as wards.[6] Because he was a national celebrity, visitors from all over the country regularly dropped in to pay their respects. General Coffee occasionally rode up from his home in Alabama and Major Eaton, now a U. S. Senator, and Major Lewis were frequent dinner guests. Eaton and Lewis were brothers-in-law, having married sisters who were also Jackson's wards. Consequently the General looked upon them as sons-in-law as well as friends and advisers. General Carroll, Judge Overton, Henry Lee (the son of the famous revolutionary war general), and Captain John Donelson and his sons were regular visitors; so were Dr. James Bronaugh (the General's military surgeon), Governor Joseph McMinn of Tennessee, and Sam Houston, who was fast becoming the General's favorite protégé despite his frequent problems with higher military authority.[7]

And there were clergymen—hundreds of them. Rachel could not resist inviting clergymen—of whatever denomination—to visit her on their way through Nashville, and together they would sit and converse about Jesus. Many of them left charming remembrances of their stay at the Hermitage; all were struck by the goodness and deep devotion of Mrs. Jackson.[8] Probably no other gift Jackson gave her meant as much as the church he built for her on the plantation grounds.

Soon the Jacksons had another permanent resident. An itinerant portrait painter of middling talent, Ralph E. W. Earl, married Jane Caffery, one of Rachel's nieces. Rachel took a decided fancy to Earl and thought him the most correct young man she had ever met.[9] Jane's premature death a few months after her marriage seemed to settle the matter of Earl's future: Rachel insisted he take up residence in the Hermitage and begin a series of portraits of the General. For the next seventeen years he served as resident artist, general factotum, and traveling companion to Jackson. After Rachel's death in 1828 the General drew very close to Earl and rarely traveled without him. None of Earl's paintings constitute great art, but Jackson appreciated them and paid the artist $50 for each one. The Jackson portraits are not outstanding likenesses, and they betray a primitive quality; but in many respects they capture the General's character, his indomitable strength and imposing will. They invariably show him lean and rawboned, all sharp angles and gritty determination. There is no effort to soften the features, to make the portrait more romantic and the subject more graceful. The Jackson of the paintings always seems rigid, brittle, and unbending. The portraits take getting used to, but after a while, after repeated viewings, they yield a genuine hint of Jackson's spirit and personality.

The quiet of the Hermitage during the period after the Seminole War and the censure "conspiracy" was precisely what Jackson needed. His health responded to the devotion of his wife, though it remained precarious for months and he repeatedly thought of abandoning public life by resigning his army commission. But there was a financial consideration to any decision he might make about resigning; the salary of a major general was not something to turn aside lightly, particularly now that the country was reeling from the shock of a major financial panic.

The immediate cause of the panic was the action of the Second National Bank of the United States to stabilize currency and credit. Because of the many paper notes issued during the War of 1812 and immediately thereafter, the recently chartered Second Bank called in its loans and tried to impose a tight money policy on the entire country. The sudden reversal of policy produced a shock that reverberated in every state. Those banks that had seriously overextended themselves slid into bankruptcy, dragging others down in the process. Specie was demanded everywhere, and paper condemned. Prices collapsed, unemployment rocketed, and by 1819 the country experienced the grip of a severe depression. Like everyone else, Jackson blamed the Second Bank for the catastrophe; but then Jackson never liked banks very much, though he used them all the time and profited from them occasionally.[10]

However, it was neither the panic nor his health that convinced Jackson to stay in the army. Nor was it the national attention he craved, or the invigorating stimulus of involvement in great public questions. It was a matter of duty, plain and simple. He must retain his commission because of the possibility of war with Spain. And nothing would give Andrew Jackson greater pleasure than to lead an American army to victory against the "hated Dons" and "conquer not only the Floridas, but all Spanish North America."

The problem was the Adams-Onís treaty by which the United States was supposed to acquire Florida. The procrastinating Spanish had not ratified it. Perhaps a Jacksonian hammer-blow was needed to hurry them along. This is what happened: When Jackson drove his way into Florida in the spring of 1818, Secretary of State Adams was deadlocked in his negotiations with Luis de Onís, the Spanish minister to the United States, over the western boundary of Louisiana as received from France in 1803. Then came Jackson's outrages against Spanish sovereignty and honor. Once again dispatches crossed the ocean, warning of Jackson's intentions.[11] Only this time it was not Mexico the Spanish saw as his ultimate military objective (as they did in 1814); now they believed his attention focused on Cuba. From the Floridas Jackson would launch an invasion against their island fortress, against their vital military sentry guarding the entire Caribbean area. Worse, he would accomplish it by instigating a mass slave insurrection in Havana to coincide with his invasion.[12]

The Spanish were quite correct. Jackson did in fact hope to seize Cuba if another invasion of Florida became necessary, not only because of its commercial and military significance but to prevent its certain capture in the future by Britain.[13] However, he never for a moment contemplated instigating a slave rebellion—that contradicted every fiber of his being. The Spanish never doubted the identity of their great American enemy or the extent of the danger he represented. They knew his desire for Florida. They had long since divined his passion for Mexico. And somehow they had figured his intentions toward Cuba.

As for Mexico, that province had been seething with rebellion for years. To make matters worse a number of French revolutionaries operating in Louisiana were now seeking to stir up American support for an invasion of Mexico.[14] So Onís revived the negotiations. And in discussing the western boundary of Louisiana with Adams he had specific instructions to keep the Americans as far from Mexico as possible. Texas *must* be preserved, and the empire behind it, even if that meant surrendering the indefensible Floridas. José Garcia de Leon y Pizarro, the Spanish foreign minister, directed Onís to make the best boundary settlement possible.[15]

While Jackson's invasion of Florida heightened her fears for her empire and her need to settle the western boundary of Louisiana as far to the east as possible, the invasion also galvanized Adams and made him bolder. He caught some of Jackson's aggressiveness in dealing with the

Spanish. Although he needed no instruction from the Tennessean on how to pursue an advantage, the shock of Jackson's invasion and its immediate success fired the secretary's enthusiasm for dismantling the Spanish empire in North America. Not even the executions of Arbuthnot and Ambrister and the potential imbroglio with England checked his ardor. He was a perfect complement to Jackson. And between them they created an American empire at Spanish expense.

In mid-July 1818, John Quincy Adams informed Luis de Onís that the western boundary of the United States must be traced by a line from the source of the Colorado River in Texas to the source of the Missouri River and *"thence straight to the Pacific Ocean."*

The man demanded a continent!

Onís blanched. The double-barreled shock of Jackson's seizure of Florida and this demand for a line to the Pacific staggered him.

"So," he said to Adams, catching his breath, "you are trying to dispossess us also of the whole Pacific Coast which belongs to us, and which Juan de Fuca took possession of in the King's name up to 56°!"

"Nonsense," replied Adams. "The English pretend the Columbia River is theirs. The Russians have possessions north of it which you have never disputed, and we have more right than anybody else to the River Columbia. We have establishments on its banks, and we need it to keep open our communications with the interior."

"Here are their views, clear enough," wrote Onís, shortly thereafter.[16] And if Spain did not accede to them, the consequence was inescapable. In effect, Adams had warned Onís to surrender the empire in the Northwest or face the threat of a rampaging American general fully capable and exceedingly desirous of humiliating Spanish military pride still further.[17] What began as a negotiation to save Texas and the territories behind it and, if possible, to win a pledge from the United States not to recognize the independence of the South American colonies in revolt —in return for which Spain would yield the indefensible Floridas—now, suddenly, involved the Pacific Northwest. It was a frightening omen.

Onís came away from the interview badly shaken. He immediately wrote Pizarro an account of the meeting and advised him that if the King could not obtain support from another European power and lacked the resources to declare war on the United States, "then I think it would be best not to delay making the best settlement possible, seeing that things certainly won't be better for a long time." He also warned that United States recognition of the rebel colonies in South America was a real possibility, particularly with respect to the government of Buenos Aires.[18]

Spain's predicament resulted in large measure from fear of Andrew Jackson. The Spanish called him "caudillo" or "the Napoleon of the woods";[19] his latest incursion was known as "the Pensacola outrage."[20] They were terrified of him. He paralyzed their will to resist.[21] In their minds the Spanish created a monster capable of committing every affront they dreaded—including now an invasion of Cuba complete with a slave revolt in Havana.

Adams realized the strength of his bargaining position and the Jackson "magic" that had withered the nerve of Madrid.[22] Andrew Jackson was his unspoken advantage; the slightest hint of bringing him into military operation threw the Spanish into a paroxysm of alarm. Without Jackson and the dreadful fear he generated in the minds of the Spanish, Adams could never hope to negotiate for a continent. And Spanish fears were justified. Jackson stood ready to march into Mexico whenever his country commanded. Sweeping the Spanish out of North America would fulfill a desire he had expressed more than a dozen years before.

But Adams must not be underrated in this reach for empire. He had a stupendous vision. He was a continentalist—and to succeed in this reach would insure the future greatness of the United States.

Onís retired to his summer residence in Bristol, Pennsylvania, to await the restoration of the Florida forts. His negotiations with Adams now continued through the French minister, Hyde de Neuville, who had earlier made available his good offices to prevent a rupture in Spanish-American relations. This gave Adams an opportunity to draw back from his "dangerous suggestion" that the line go as high as the source of the Missouri River. He asked the Frenchman to inform Onís that the boundary should begin at the source of the Trinity River and run due north to the Red River, along the river to its source, across the Rio Grande and along it to its source or the summit of a chain of mountains northward and parallel to it and "there stop, or take a line west to the Pacific."[23] This still harvested much of Texas and Oregon and included the great Columbia River basin.

The territorial greed of the Americans astounded Onís. In an effort to hold the Americans as far east of Texas as possible, he made a counter offer hacking deep into the Louisiana Territory. He proposed the Mermentau and Arroyo Hondo which were approximately fifty miles east of the Sabine River. Monroe was so annoyed that he instructed Adams to intimate to Onís through the French minister that he expected Congress at its next session to empower him to take Florida. Therefore he would reserve American claims to Texas as far as the Rio Grande.[24] But Monroe was actually willing to compromise at the Sabine River, and this was later communicated to Onís in what the secretary called an "ultimatum." This line started with the Sabine and ended at the forty-first parallel on the Pacific.[25]

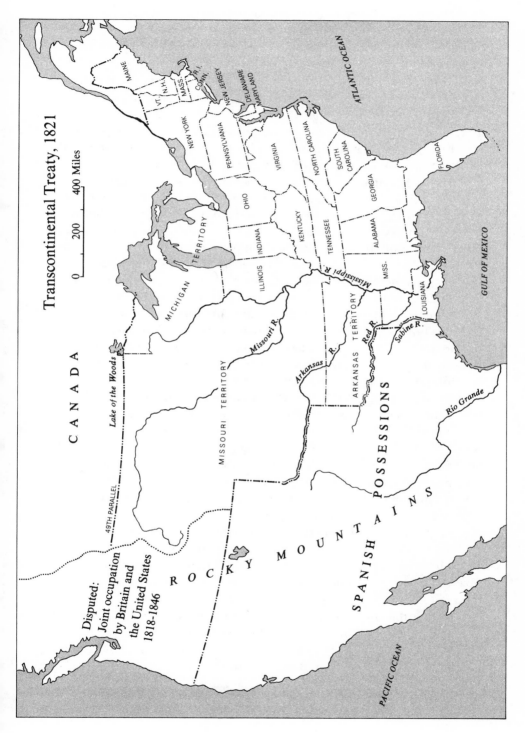

Transcontinental Treaty, 1821

The tempo of negotiations quickened when the Marquis de Yrujo succeeded Pizarro in the Foreign Office. Yrujo was particularly troubled by the possibility of United States recognition of the several provinces of Spanish America in revolt. And he realized that no assistance against the Americans could be expected from other European powers. In a dispatch dated October 10, 1818, he instructed Onís to obtain the Sabine if possible and to settle the rest of the boundary as best he could in order to avoid a break with the United States or an invasion of Mexico. The preferred line, he continued, would follow the Missouri to its source and thence to the Pacific, running as far north as possible.[26]

At last. The Spanish had finally agreed to a transcontinental line. The rest was a matter of time and negotiation. The dispatch reached Onís early in January, and he immediately notified Adams of his readiness to renew their talks with a view to compromise. On February 1, 1819, a new dispatch went off to Onís giving him authority to conclude a treaty without further consultation at home.[27] For the next several weeks the discussions jiggled the boundary back and forth and at the same time took up the purchase of Florida. Monroe directed Adams to consult with Jackson about the terms of the treaty, but in their subsequent talks the only thing Jackson concentrated on was the southern frontier. "With the Floridas in our possession," the General later wrote, ". . . Orleans, the great emporium of the west, is secure."[28] As long as Florida remained under foreign control, he argued, there was no security for the southern states.[29]

On February 22, 1819, the Adams-Onís or Transcontinental Treaty was signed. Spain ceded to the United States all territories east of the Mississippi River known as East and West Florida at a cost to the United States of $5 million in assumed claims against Spain. The western boundary of the United States was fixed at the Sabine, Red, and Arkansas rivers and thence westward to the Pacific Ocean along the forty-second parallel. It was a magnificent achievement. Both sides claimed satisfaction. Spain retained Texas. The Americans gained a continent.

Yet it took several years to ratify the treaty. Spain procrastinated, and there were problems over land grants conferred by King Ferdinand after Jackson had withdrawn his troops and the Floridas had been returned to Spain. The King's action looked like a deliberate effort to scuttle the treaty.

During the spring and summer of 1819, while the treaty remained in limbo, President Monroe toured the western and southern states and visited Jackson at the Hermitage to discuss with him the possibility of his accepting the governorship of the Florida Territory once it was legally acquired. Jackson's initial reaction was negative, but the President continued to press him. Apparently the two men had a lot to talk about—

Monroe had been especially solicitous of Jackson's opinion during the Florida negotiations—because the General not only accompanied the President throughout the tour of Tennessee but joined him in a trip to Lexington, Kentucky. Of course traveling with Jackson guaranteed sizable crowds at every stop, and the President understood the advantage of sporting about the country accompanied by the nation's most popular man.

At Lexington, the home of Henry Clay, they experienced an unpleasant round of journalistic attention. Clay was noticeably absent from the welcoming committee, and the newspapers fussed over this offense to the President and blamed it on the presence of Andrew Jackson in Monroe's entourage.[30] Clay later claimed that private business prevented him from greeting the President, and although it sounds unlikely it is a more plausible reason than that given by the newspapers. Clay was too good a politician to insult the President and the nation's leading hero publicly and then let the newspapers cover it up with a lame excuse. Had he really intended a discourtesy, he could be remarkably inventive.

The tour materially strengthened the relationship between the President and the General. All the old unpleasantness was forgotten—or set aside. When Monroe returned to Washington, Jackson kept reminding him of his "wish to retire to private life." But the willingness was always conditional. "Sir, you know my Services is my countries, as long as I can render any that may be serviceable to her *and your administration of the Government.* But you know my earnest wishes for a retirement, and I am convinced will permit it as early as it would be honourable to myself, and the interests of our common Country, will permit."[31] As long as the Florida situation remained unresolved retirement was out of the question; indeed Jackson was asked by Calhoun to prepare another campaign to attack the Spanish forts in Florida.[32]

Spain continued to delay ratification, making one demand after another, all of which the Monroe administration (prompted by Adams) stoutly resisted. At one point Monroe considered demanding Texas as part of the Louisiana cession—this was the suggestion of Thomas Jefferson—but reluctantly abandoned the idea, again at the insistence of Adams.[33] The haggling for Texas had long since passed. Later Jackson complained bitterly about the abandonment of Texas in the Adams-Onís treaty. At the time, however, he fully approved the boundary lines.[34] His eyes were fixed on Florida. Nothing else. He even offered to help negotiations along by leading another army into Florida—and following that up by seizing Cuba.[35]

But the Spanish could not hold out indefinitely. It was bad enough that the Americans were prepared to break up the Spanish empire in

North America; it was worse that no European power would lift a finger to prevent the dismemberment. England had abandoned Spain and pursued an independent policy, watching with obvious relief as the United States gave its full attention to the south and west. In place of the St. Lawrence River seaway (the loss of which was later overcome with the building of the Erie Canal linking the Great Lakes with the Hudson River), the American people would have to content themselves with the Columbia River basin. Thus Spain was the elected prey, friendless before the vulture. And now if she did not surrender to American demands, she could expect another "Pensacola outrage"—only this time it probably would not stop with Florida.

A further round of hostilities to compel ratification of the Transcontinental Treaty was mercifully avoided when revolutionary forces in Madrid forced King Ferdinand VII to restore parliamentary government, an action that considerably cooled whatever Spanish ardor remained for another encounter with "the Napoleon of the woods." Lord Castlereagh, for his own good and selfish reasons, bluntly advised the new Spanish minister to the United States, Don Francisco Vives, then passing through England on his way to America, that the treaty had better be ratified.[36] Finally, the Spanish Council of State, aware that Spain could expect no support from a European power, urged acceptance of the treaty. The new constitutional Cortes agreed. The King capitulated, signed the document on October 24, 1820, and returned it to Washington. On February 13, 1821, it was resubmitted to the Senate because the original six-month term stipulated for the exchange of ratifications had long since run out. The Senate approved it on February 19 with only four dissenting votes. It was exactly two years after the signing of the treaty that the final exchange of ratifications occurred on February 22, 1821.

A Washington newspaper hailed the acquisition of Florida as "an event among the most important in the annals of our history since 1803."[37] The acquisition of Florida alone increased the size of the United States by 50,000 square miles. It fulfilled a long-cherished desire of many Americans stretching back several decades.[38] Thanks to Andrew Jackson, American expansion continued its steady course. "It is thus we stride, from object to object," commented one newspaper; "and shall eventually light upon the banks of the river Columbia and the shores of the Pacific! What magnificent prospects open upon us!"[39]

More than anything else, John Quincy Adams's diplomatic accomplishment was the triumph of an idea, an idea of continentialism. It was Adams who insisted that the boundary of the United States extend across the plains and mountains and touch the Pacific. But where Adams offered the transcontinental vision, Jackson provided the means by which that vision could be translated into reality. The presence of Andrew Jackson, long schooled in the belief that the foreign presence in the southwest must be expelled and, more important, who encapsulated that belief with demonic determination, provided the essential military conquests to realize the dream. Without Jackson the leap across a continent was unlikely if not impossible.[40]

Which is to take nothing away from John Quincy Adams in negotiating the treaty, or Thomas Jefferson who initiated the purchase of Louisiana in the first place. But more than anyone else, Andrew Jackson determined the course of American expansion. He was, in fact, the greatest expansionist of them all.

Curiously, in spite of his commitment to the destruction of the Spanish presence in the south and his many earlier calls for a march westward into Santa Fe and Mexico, Jackson did not demand the inclusion of Texas in the final boundary settlement of the Adams-Onís treaty. In response to the suggestion of Monroe, Adams called on the General and specifically asked his opinion on the western boundary. Jackson warned Adams away from Texas for two reasons: first, the demand for Texas could jeopardize Florida, and Florida was essential to the safety of the United States; second, expansion into Texas "would bring us again in collision with the Indians," he said, "whom we are removing west of the Mississippi." Jackson further argued that the enemies of the administration would use the inclusion of Texas to attack the entire treaty and that was too great a risk to take. The friends of the administration, on the other hand, would, he thought, "be satisfied" with the existing treaty.[41]

Adams wanted to be absolutely certain the General understood the precise location of the western boundary, and because no other map was available to them they agreed to meet the following day at Adams's house and go over the boundary together with the map used in the negotiations with the Spanish. This was the famous "Map of the United States and the Contiguous British and Spanish Possessions" of John Melish, which was not totally accurate in locating the sources of rivers or the extent of mountains, yet for its day was a miracle of the cartographer's craft. In any event, the following day Jackson appeared at Adams's house and examined the boundary as traced on the Melish map. Again he warned of possible criticism by the enemies of the administration and again he stressed the importance of obtaining the Floridas, which were absolutely essential to the safety of the southern frontier. With that he pointed to the map and explained to Adams the operations of the British army in invading the United States during the late war. As long as the mouths of the Florida rivers were accessible to a foreign naval force, he warned, there could be "no security for the southern part of the United States."[42]

Once landed, an invading force could slice across to the Mississippi above New Orleans and amputate the entire southwest from the rest of the nation.

There may have been yet another reason for Jackson's failure to insist that Texas be included in the treaty. His own censure was then before Congress, and it is possible he was anxious for a speedy conclusion of the negotiations in order to terminate the discussion of his own role in the invasion. Once Spain agreed to the treaty, all debate over his actions should cease. Insisting on Texas might protract the negotiations. As it turned out, the signing of the treaty did indeed help to kill the Senate report that had severely criticized Jackson's behavior and termed it dishonorable.

But once the treaty was ratified and Florida safely nestled within the territorial limits of the United States, and once the threat of his censure passed, Jackson returned to his old demand for Texas. In fact he unfairly attacked Adams for surrendering Texas to the Spanish. He argued that Texas formed part of the Louisiana Purchase and should never have been alienated. So avidly did he hunger for Texas that twenty-five years later, when annexation became an election issue and Adams publicly stated that Jackson had approved the Sabine boundary, the General flew into a rage. "I again declare, that adams statement that I was consulted by him on the boundery of the Florida treaty before it was made and that I agreed to the boundery proposed, the Sabine, is positively *false, false, false, his diary to the contrary notwithstanding.*" The "diary" was not the only evidence; there was a letter to Monroe in Jackson's own hand, dated June 20, 1820, in which the Hero advised the President "to be content with the Floridas."[43] What Jackson forgot in 1844 were all the good reasons that once compelled him to lay aside temporarily his true expansionist sentiments.

When he became President of the United States in 1829, those sentiments promptly reasserted themselves. Almost from the moment he entered the White House as chief executive, Jackson began thinking of ways of "regaining" Texas. "I have long since been aware of the importance of Texas to the United States," he told John Overton, "and of the real necessity of extending our boundery west of the Sabine." Fortunately, nothing had been done to run and mark the boundary following the ratification of the Adams-Onís Treaty. Moreover, Mexico had won its independence from Spain and was struggling to achieve stability and order. "From the deranged state of the finance of Mexico," wrote Jackson, "I hope we may be able to obtain an extension of our Southwestern limits as defined by the late Treaty with Spain, so important to the Safety of Neworleans. How infatuated must have been our councils who gave up the rich country of Texas, for the Floridas, when the latter could have been obtained for the sum we paid for it in mony." And whose fault was that? "It surely must have been with the view to keep the political ascendence in the North, and east," he said, "& cripple the rising greatness of the West." Happily, in 1829 there was now a westerner in the White House. "I shall keep an eye on this object, & the first propitious moment make the attempt to regain the Territory as far South & West, as the great Desert."[44] But this proved easier said than done.

The expansion of the United States, as represented in the Adams-Onís treaty, occurred at almost the same time that another question arose to distress and frighten the nation. Slavery, in the form of an application by Missouri for admission to the Union as a slave state, now demanded the attention of Congress. Jackson's many friends in Washington, particularly southerners, kept him informed of the progress of the debate, repeating all the acrimonious threats about dissolving the Union that ricocheted through Congress each time the extension of slavery was threatened. At length a compromise was arranged by which Missouri entered the Union as a slave state while Maine was detached from Massachusetts and entered the Union as a free state—thereby preserving the balance between slave and free states—and, except for Missouri, slavery was restricted north of the parallel 36°30' within the territory acquired by the Louisiana Purchase. Southerners complained about the compromise "but they ought not," said Senator Eaton, "for it has preserved peace dissipated angry feelings, and dispelled appearances which seemed dark and horrible and threatening to the interest and harmony of the nation."[45]

Jackson too was troubled. And he reacted typically, as southerner and slaveowner. The nationalist in him peered from behind sectional lenses and economic self-interest. But he clearly worried over the nation's future.

The Misouri question so called, has agitated the public mind, and that I sincerely regret and never expected, but that now I see, will be the entering wedge to seperate the union. It is even more wicked, it will excite those who is the subject of discussion to insurrection and masacre. It is a question of political ascendency, and power, and the Eastern interests are determined to succeed regardless of the consequences, the constitution or our national happiness. They will find the southern and western states equally resolved to support their constitutional rights. I hope I may not live to see the evills that must grow out of this wicked design of demagogues, who talk about humanity, but whose sole object is self agrandisement regardless of the happiness of the nation.[46]

As far as Jackson was concerned, "national happiness" included slavery for the south and the west, whether the north liked it or not.

In the early fall of 1820—months before the final ratification of the Florida treaty—Jackson journeyed south into the country of the Choctaw Indians as a representative of the United States to conclude a treaty whereby the Indians would surrender yet another portion of their land. He and General Thomas Hinds of Mississippi were the two commissioners. In arguing with Adams against the inclusion of Texas in the Transcontinental Treaty, Jackson had cited as his second reason the fact that expansion into Texas "would bring us again in collision with the Indians whom we are removing west of the Mississippi."[47]

"Removing west of the Mississippi." Expansion of the United States at Spanish expense was not enough. Removal of the Indian west of the Mississippi was just as vital. Like the Cherokees, the Choctaws must surrender their valuable lands to the white man and then get out. Remove. The present trip to Choctaw country would again demonstrate what he meant.

Jackson met with the chiefs, mingoes, and headmen of the tribe at Doak's Stand on the Natchez Trace in early October 1820. Also there was Colonel Silas Dinsmore, a former Choctaw agent, whose ruling on passports had stirred a short-lived controversy with General Jackson in 1812. The appearance of Dinsmore at Doak's Stand promised trouble. He supposedly had asserted that "the policy of our government towards the Indian tribes was a harsh one," and the remark was subsequently relayed to Jackson.[48] Thus, when Dinsmore arrived at the treaty grounds, Jackson assumed that he had come to use his influence with the Choctaws to oppose the wishes of the commissioners. And the wishes of the commissioners were just as harsh as Dinsmore had said. The commissioners conveyed one message to the Choctaws: surrender your land and remove beyond the Mississippi.

A fearful row between the two white men seemed unavoidable until General Hinds learned at the last moment that Dinsmore was not looking to cause trouble. Rather, it was generally understood among those in attendance that if a cession of land to the United States was signed, a reservation for Dinsmore would be made to indemnify him for the loss of livestock and other property destroyed by "some turbulent young Choctaws" when Dinsmore was away from the agency many years before. Because he had a long-standing pledge from the chiefs to compensate him for his loss, Dinsmore had come to the treaty grounds with the expectation that a tract of land would be granted him in the final treaty. Jackson's "kindling wrath" vanished when Hinds explained the purpose of Dinsmore's presence. A violent and embarrassing scene was narrowly averted.[49]

Jackson paid no attention when Dinsmore appeared. The two men passed each other many times as they walked about the camp, among Indians and whites, exchanging greetings with the Choctaws and conversing about the terms of the treaty. Late one afternoon several men lingered in front of the commissioner's tent, among them Jackson, Dinsmore, and a few Indian chiefs. Dinsmore thought the time had come to break the unnatural silence that existed between himself and the General. Assuming control of the conversation, he turned it deftly to the coming session of Congress and the great debate over Missouri. When he thought the moment propitious, he looked directly at Jackson and in a markedly friendly voice asked whether the Hero would go to Washington to attend the opening session.

The words commanded Jackson's attention. He turned to Dinsmore and then, summoning all the sternness of manner for which he was famous, devastated the unfortunate man with a blast of contempt.

"No, sir," he barked; "I never go where I have no business."

The conversation died. The group dispersed. The chance of Dinsmore's obtaining a tract of land in the treaty totally vanished.[50]

When Jackson arrived at Doak's Stand he found the Indians generally opposed either to ceding or exchanging any land. The few Choctaws who favored a treaty were "compelled to be silent, and every chief threatened with death if he consented to sell or exchange an acre." As expected, the General discovered that "their minds had been poisoned by white men and halfbreeds living among them." Immediately Jackson informed the chiefs that since he had been sent to treat with the entire Nation, not a portion of it, he would send interpreters to summon those absentees who feared to attend the convention because of threats. "This measure had the desired effect," reported Jackson, "as a considerable number arrived at this place in a few days afterward, and in time to give their signatures to the treaty."[51]

To put everyone in a proper mood, Jackson began the convention on October 9 with a "ball-play" among the Indians, followed by a dance in the evening. Indeed, each time the negotiations threatened to break down the General arranged another "ball-play," which tended to restore good feelings and a sense of comradeship.[52] No doubt about it, Jackson had a way with the Indians that was uniquely his own.

The convention opened formally on October 10 with a "talk" by Sharp Knife to more than 500 Choctaw chiefs, headmen, and braves. He told them that the President knew of their depressed condition and that many of them were drunks and beggars and were dying of hunger. "Humanity," he sighed, obliged the President to do something for his Choctaw children. It was the usual beginning—much of it untrue, but the accepted prelude to what followed.

The President had received many demands from white settlers for land in Mississippi, Jackson continued, and the pressure of these demands had prompted the President to initiate this convention before violence ensued. What he proposed, therefore, was the exchange of some of the Choctaw's eastern lands for a larger tract beyond the Mississippi River. For a "slip of land," Jackson cooed, the Indians would get double the amount in the west. But the Indians, as they listened, were not deceived. This "slip" represented more than five million acres, nearly one-third of the remaining Choctaw lands in Mississippi.

"As your game is destroyed, if you all remain here," Jackson continued after a moment's pause, "you must cultivate the earth like your white brothers. You must also, in time, become citizens of the United States, and subject to its laws." As always, he insisted on the destruction of tribal sovereignty east of the Mississippi. Only through removal could tribal identity be preserved.[53]

"To promote the civilization of the [Choctaw] people by the establishment of schools among them," Jackson went on, "and to perpetuate them as a nation was a subject of constant solicitude with the President of the United States. It was an object near to his heart." In fact, said the General, there were "two grand objects" of the treaty proposed by the President: to educate and civilize the Indians and to perpetuate the Nation by removing it west of the Mississippi. Removal guaranteed many blessings. In addition to everything else, Jackson concluded, the Indians would gain in the west "a country of tall trees, many water courses, rich lands and high grass abounding in game of all kinds—buffalo, bear, elk, deer, antelope, beaver, turkeys, honey and fruits of many kinds.

"What say the chiefs and . . . people to this great offer?"[54]

The "talk" concluded, Jackson returned to his place. Pushmataha, Chief of the Six Town District and one of the Choctaws who had fought with the General against the Creeks, the British, and the Spanish, responded. He was a powerful warrior and an impressive speaker. He looked at his former comrade-in-arms for a long moment as a touch of sadness flickered across his face. When he finally spoke, his words were sharp and biting. He accused Jackson of deceiving the Choctaws about the western lands. What the General offered, he said, was wasteland— poor, sterile, useless.

All eyes turned toward Sharp Knife, expecting an explosion. None came. Gravely, Jackson rose from his place and resumed the speaker's stand.

"Brother Push," he said quietly, "you have uttered some hard words.

You have openly accused me of misrepresentation and indirectly of the desire to defraud the red people in behalf of my government. These are heavy charges, charges of a very serious character. You must explain yourself in a manner that will clear them up."

"My great friend, General Jackson," replied Pushmataha, "who familiarly calls me brother, whom my inner soul loveth, and in whose presence I always felt myself a mere boy, has become excited at some of my remarks. . . . He represented the country he wishes to exchange for the 'little slip' as being a very extensive country. . . . I know the country well. . . . The grass is everywhere very short, and for the game it is not plenty, except buffalo and deer. . . . There are but few beavers, and the honey and fruit are rare things."[55]

A long argument ensued. When the chief realized his arguments were unavailing, he switched ground. The land offered by the United States, he said, had many white men living on it. The land was already occupied.

"Moonshine," snapped Sharp Knife.

"I beg your pardon," replied Pushmataha. "There are a great many of them . . . and they will not be ordered off."

"I will send my warriors, and by the eternal I'll drive them into the Mississippi," stormed Jackson.

For three days the Choctaw chiefs debated the exchange of land, counseling privately among themselves. Finally Jackson resorted to threats and a temper tantrum to gain their consent. He warned them of the loss of American friendship; he promised to wage war against them and destroy the Nation; finally he shouted his determination to remove them whether they liked it or not. "Many of your nation are already beyond the Mississippi, and others are every year removing. . . . If you refuse," he warned, ". . . the nation will be destroyed."[56]

The Choctaws cowered at the threats.[57] Even Pushmataha urged his brother chiefs to submit. Better to face the trackless waste beyond the Mississippi than the fearful vengeance of this determined man.

The treaty, signed on October 18, 1820, translated into deed the savage demands of the American general. It spoke of the "grand and humane objects" of the United States government in dispossessing the Choctaws and providing them with land west of the Mississippi between the Arkansas and Red rivers. The land ceded, that "slip of land," was "as fine as any in the United States," said one Mississippi newspaper.[58] It was the heart of the delta. Starting at the Choctaw boundary east of the Pearl River, the cession followed north to the Natchez Road, then to the Black Creek, then on a direct course west to the Mississippi River one mile below the mouth of the Arkansas River and down the Mississippi to the

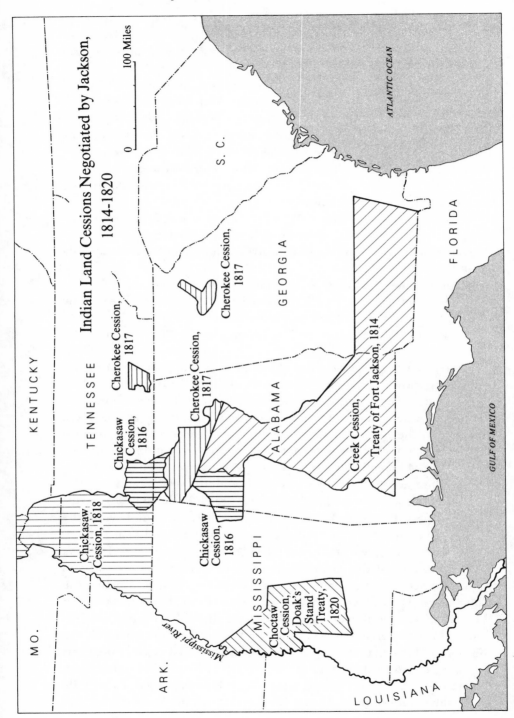

Indian Land Cessions Negotiated by Jackson, 1814-1820

United States border, and then around and back to the Choctaw boundary. For this the Indians were granted "comparable" lands in the west, amounting to nearly thirteen million acres, in what is now the southern half of Oklahoma and part of southwestern Arkansas. In addition, each warrior received a blanket, a kettle, a rifle, bullets, moulds, wipers, and ammunition sufficient for hunting and defense for one year and enough corn to support him and his family for a year. "Presents" also constituted part of the treaty. Some $4,674.50 went for "donations" to twenty-six chiefs, headmen, and "ball-players." Nothing was said of Colonel Silas Dinsmore. As a consequence he got up a petition for an "appropriation of part of Turkeytown for his benefit." But in a letter to the secretary of war the two commissioners disapproved it as "unjust, undeserving and as a bad precedent."[59]

The Treaty of Doak's Stand was a model of Indian removal, a continuation of the policy Jackson had inaugurated with the Cherokees a few years earlier. It provided the government with rich lands in the delta of west central Mississippi and it disposed of an "alien" people with a minimum of difficulty. It even represented a liberal advance in white-red relations. One clause in the treaty reserved some of the land ceded by the Indians for the President to sell in order to provide funds for the support of Choctaw schools in the new territory to which the Indians were migrating. The Reverend Cyrus Kingsbury, superintending missionary to the Choctaws, proposed the establishment of four large and thirty-two small schools, of which the large schools would accommodate from 80 to 100 students each and the small ones from 20 to 40 pupils, at a total cost of $52,000.[60] In one of the first treaties to concern itself with the educational improvement of the Indians, this single provision may have been the only "grand and humane" feature of the entire treaty. However, there was some Indian dissatisfaction with this provision because it constituted a donation, so the commissioners agreed to add $1,000 as an annuity for sixteen years. "This produced all the good effects which were anticipated," said Jackson.[61]

Unfortunately, the United States ceded away Arkansas lands that were especially valuable—Jackson had received specific instructions from Secretary Calhoun as to the lands to be ceded, so the mistake was not his[62]—and the government was later forced to renegotiate the treaty and take back what had been granted, particularly when it was learned that the only salt springs in the territory had been surrendered. A convention was finally signed in Washington in 1825, and the Indians received additional compensation for returning the valuable portion of the Arkansas territory.[63]

The white people of Mississippi were positively ecstatic over the treaty, as were frontiersmen all over the southwest. The governor and the legislature thanked and praised the two generals, as did the President and the secretary of war. Not much later Mississippi named its new capital after Andrew Jackson and the county in which it was located after Thomas Hinds.[64] It was a fitting tribute for their outstanding contribution to the growth and prosperity of Mississippi.

As far as Jackson was concerned the Treaty of Doak's Stand fulfilled all his ideas about how to carry on negotiations with Indians and what to do with tribes that blocked southern and western expansion. It represented the completion of a series of treaties that, over a period of seven years, powerfully influenced and shaped the government's Indian policy. Jackson had accomplished the physical removal of Indian tribes to the west of the Mississippi River. At the same time he had acquired from them millions of acres of fertile land in North Carolina, Florida, Georgia, Alabama, Mississippi, Tennessee, and Kentucky—from the Atlantic to the Mississippi, from the Ohio River to the Gulf of Mexico. If this did not encompass all of the area known as the Cotton Kingdom, it came mighty close.

Andrew Jackson carried the nation far in its course of empire. Now that Florida had been absorbed and the southern frontier secured, the country could turn its attention to Texas and Mexico—and perhaps to Cuba. Starting in 1821, most Americans could begin to contemplate realistically a future in which the United States would sweep along the southern Gulf Coast and "eventually light upon the banks of the river Columbia and the shores of the Pacific," absorbing Texas and California and Oregon.

In terms of acquisition, it is not too farfetched to say that the physical shape of the United States today looks pretty much like it does largely because of the intentions and efforts of Andrew Jackson. And what he personally left undone, other Tennesseans completed. His protégés, Sam Houston and James Knox Polk, fulfilled his dream—the dream of possessing "all Spanish North America."[65]

CHAPTER 25

Governor of Florida

As THE NATION BREATHED A SIGH of relief at having avoided internal conflict over Missouri's admission to the Union as a slave state, confirmation arrived from abroad that Florida at long last belonged to the United States. And no sooner did the President receive this information than he wrote to Jackson and renewed his offer of the governorship of the newly acquired territory. Will you take it, he asked? "The climate will suit you," he purred, "and it will give me pleasure to place you in that trust." Monroe pressed Jackson to make his decision quickly because Congress would adjourn on March 3, and he wanted confirmation before the end of the session.[1]

Monroe's decision to appoint Jackson was another example of his "ficklemindedness," his desire to escape unpleasantness, his inability to cope with potentially nasty situations.[2] Congress had recently reduced the size of the army—much to Jackson's disgust; "the government should be d----d," he wrote, ". . . it should be increased tenfold"[3]—necessitating the demotion of one of its two major generals. And Monroe positively shivered at the thought of "busting" a major general. The two generals were Jackson, who commanded the southern district, and Major General Jacob Brown, who commanded the northern. Both men could be extremely difficult to handle. When Brown, with the aid of his political friends, most notably Crawford, began to apply pressure to retain his rank, Monroe searched desperately for a compromise that would help him out of his predicament. Then he remembered Jackson's letters about retirement. What better place for retirement than the swamps of Florida?

But when Monroe first broached the question of the governorship, a number of Jackson's political friends in Washington, especially Senator John Eaton, warned the President that they would not tolerate anything that might be interpreted as a rebuke to Jackson or that seemed to imply that Brown was a better general. Brown was in fact the senior in service, but, Eaton told the President, the people would resent any act that suggested criticism of their Hero.

Monroe disclaimed any improper motive. Jackson could stay in the army if he preferred, but the President insisted that the governorship was extremely important since it involved the inauguration of a new administration for the territory.[4] It is also possible that in offering Jackson the post, Monroe attempted to make amends to the Hero for all the criticism he had shouldered alone for the Seminole campaign, criticism deserved by Monroe as well as Jackson.[5] John Quincy Adams said the appointment of Jackson would provide "a fortunate occasion to save the nation from the disgrace of even appearing to discard without compunction a man to whom they were so deeply indebted."[6]

Receiving Monroe's assurances regarding the purpose of the appointment, Senator Eaton immediately wrote Jackson and insisted he accept the assignment. He added that the General's friends in Congress were determined to win his appointment. They will force it, said Jackson, "whether I will accept or not, from which I infer there is some strong political reason operating with my friends for their solicitude upon this occasion."[7] But he had already decided to refuse the offer for the very good reason that Rachel considered a stay in Florida "repugnant," and he had so informed Monroe and Calhoun.[8]

Jackson's friends in Nashville, like his friends in Washington, saw the many advantages of his becoming governor. Patronage was one; land was another. His position at the head of the territorial administration could be extremely useful in speculative operations, particularly around Pensacola (which was expected to rival New Orleans), and in securing a number of posts that carried political and economic advantages. His friends urged him to reconsider. He could play a central role in the further development of the southern coastal area. And their arguments scored. As he told one friend, "With a small fund and good recommendations a great spec might be made at Pensacola and Ft St Augustine. . . . I name this to you that you may look and see."[9] But for Jackson personally the encouragement of land speculation was directly connected with larger issues that involved the migration of people to help secure the frontier and thereby "promote the welfare of the United States." Speculation for monetary gain held no interest for him at all. Also, in his mind, the appointment tended to vindicate his entire course of action throughout the Seminole War. That reason, more than any other, operated powerfully upon him. He had taken too much criticism over his invasion (especially in the Senate report), and in some strange and incomprehensible way he needed the vindication. Perhaps if he accepted the post for a short term he could establish the territorial government on a firm basis, take care of his friends, complete the vindication of his Florida performance, and return home.

At length he told his friends he would change his mind if his letters of refusal to the President and Calhoun had not already left the post office. In true post office fashion, they were in fact still sitting there; so they were retrieved and Jackson, with a last-minute shudder of doubt in view of Rachel's reluctance, accepted Monroe's offer.[10] "I sincerely thank you for the friendly manner you have regarded me," he wrote the President, "and the confidence you repose in me by this offer." Although hesitant about "retiring" to Florida, he was willing to accept the appointment provided the President permitted him to resign as soon as the territorial government was organized and in full operation.[11]

Because of his continued doubts, Jackson half hoped that his letter would reach the President after Congress had adjourned, thereby killing the nomination. No such luck. The Congress still sat, and Monroe promptly submitted his name both as commissioner to receive possession of East and West Florida and as governor of the entire territory to be possessed. The salary was $5,000 plus expenses, the same Jackson received as general, and it would commence the moment his military command ceased to exist. That eased somewhat the shock of his separation from the army. As he told Monroe, "My fortune and constitution have already been much impaired in the service of my country . . . yet will I go on, and devote what remains of my strength to its best interests."[12] He did not seem to be aware in quite the same way that his country had also been very good to him in providing fortune, opportunity, and unparalleled honor.

Monroe appointed ten other officers to assist Jackson in administering the territory: two judges, two district attorneys, two secretaries, three collectors, and a marshal. Colonel James Grant Forbes was appointed a marshal and sent to Havana aboard the sloop *Hornet* to receive from the Spanish governor general of Cuba the necessary orders to His Majesty's authorities in Pensacola and St. Augustine for the surrender of Florida and its archives. The Spanish requested that American troops not enter Pensacola until the Spanish forces were completely withdrawn in order to avoid embarrassment and possible trouble between the troops. The garrisons were to be transported to Cuba at the expense of the United States.[13]

Shortly after accepting his commission as territorial governor, Jackson resigned from the army. The date of retirement was fixed at June 1, 1821. On May 31 he issued an address to the troops of the southern division that was a moving testament of his feelings for his life as a soldier and his pride in the men who served under him.

> This day closes my military functions, and having with many of you faced the stormy showers of war, and with many of you Terminated one English and two Indian wars, in which we experienced privations of the severest kind, feeling that friendships thus created, are most durable and my feelings will not permit me to close my military connections with you in silence. Justice to you and to my feelings dictate the propriety of my Testimoney being placed before our common country of my approbation of your military conduct, and of my Individual regard. Many valuable officers who have served with me, must retire under the organization for the reduction of the army under the late act of congress But let this be your consolation, that your country in its Joyfull transports of gratitude hails you as her deliverer in the day of peril . . . your consolation is you have done your duty and . . . bravely supported the american eagle whenever it was endangered.[14]

The last comment applied as well to Jackson himself—perhaps more than anyone.

Then Jackson did something very typical. When he heard that Jacob Brown—who now styled himself Commander-in-Chief (under the President) of the Armies of the United States—had implied that Jackson was too strict with his men, Old Hickory appended a "P.S." (literally) to his farewell address. In it he defended the need for discipline. And it ran twice the length of the main address. But he ended on a pleasant note. "And may you be all happy, and may your country appreciate you her citizen soldiers as you deserve is my Sincere prayer."[15]

Even more typically Jacksonian was his presumption that he still exercised military authority. Although his command [the southern district] ceased as of May 1821, and he himself retired on June 1, he continued to issue orders to the troops. And they were obeyed.[16] Colonel George M. Brooke, the officer in command at Pensacola, asked General Brown whether he was subject to Jackson's military command in Florida and whether he was "safe" in obeying his orders. Certainly not, Brown hotly responded, and the question should never have arisen in the first place. Brown's response to Brooke was channeled through the War Department, intercepted, and shown to the President. The possibility of a fracas with Jackson needed considered thought on the part of the administration. Nothing could fire an explosion quicker than a challenge to

Jackson's authority. So Monroe went to his Cabinet and asked if, in their opinion, soldiers were subject to the military command of Jackson as governor of Florida and safe in obeying his orders. The President, Attorney General Wirt, and Calhoun all thought Jackson lacked command, although Calhoun allowed that in issuing orders the General no doubt "acted upon full deliberation and advisement." But the ever-faithful Adams disagreed with these opinions and defended Jackson's right to military authority. The commission of Jackson's appointment included the powers not only of governor but of captain general of Cuba, Adams argued, which meant military command throughout the province. "The military was the only executive power in the province," said Adams, "and that if the Governor had no military command he had no effective authority, no means of executing his decrees, administrative or judicial."[17] The secretary closed the discussion by asking what necessity required a decision now. "It was, after all," he continued, "a mere question of form."[18] Purely academic.

The appointment won quick confirmation in the Senate, and the secretary of state issued Jackson his several commissions. Immediately upon receiving them, the General, his wife, and the two Andrews took passage down the river to New Orleans. Eight days later, on April 22, they arrived at the great city, but Rachel, almost a fanatic now in her religious commitment, recoiled at what she saw. "Great Babylon is come up before me," she gasped. "Oh, the wickedness, the idolatry of the place! unspeakable the riches and splendor." But at least she had the consolation of her religion. "I know I never was so tried before, tempted, proved in all things. I know that my Redeemer liveth, and that I am his by convenant promised." She wept over the city. "Pray for your sister," she wrote, "in a heathen land, far from my people and church."[19] One of the things that truly upset this godly woman was the idolatry shown her husband. On one occasion he was conducted to the Grand Theater, where at his appearance the audience shouted in unison, "Vive Jackson!" and ladies sang hymns of praise and pressed a crown of laurel on his head. "The Lord has promised his humble followers a crown that fadeth not away," she chided; "the present one is already withered, the leaves are falling off."[20]

While in New Orleans Jackson tried to get an advance of $10,000 or $15,000 from the branch of the Second Bank of the United States on a draft to be drawn upon the Department of State to defray the initial expenses of organizing the Florida government. But the bank refused point blank to negotiate such a draft even though their refusal immeasurably increased the difficulties Jackson would encounter in arriving in Florida without an adequate supply of cash. Nothing could be done. The parent bank in Philadelphia expressly forbade the negotiation of such drafts and tolerated no exception.[21] Jackson told Adams he hoped to obtain the funds at Mobile or Pensacola and asked the government to attend to the matter and see that no further problem arose on account of it.[22]

The Jackson family took passage aboard a ship on Lake Pontchartrain, crossed into the Gulf, and landed at Mobile Bay, where they stayed nine days at a town called Blakely. Then Jackson moved to Montpelier, Alabama, and waited five weeks for the *Hornet* to arrive with the documents ordering the Spanish forces in Pensacola to surrender Florida to him. As the weeks passed the old Jacksonian impatience with the Spanish began to surface. Why was it taking so long for the documents to arrive? What were the Spanish up to? More tricks, no doubt. Convinced of their "treachery"—was it not in their character?—Jackson assured himself that the governor general in Cuba was playing games with him and simply amusing himself at American expense.[23] To hurry things along, therefore, Jackson inaugurated a correspondence with Colonel José Callava, the governor of Pensacola, in the hope that initial arrangements for the transfer of the territory could be begun. But Callava knew his duty and absolutely refused to initiate anything until he had received orders from his chief in Cuba. Being Spanish, Callava did not dare make a move without proper authorization. And authorization meant papers.[24]

Jackson persisted. About the cannons at the forts, these must stay. Wrong, retorted Callava. These remain in Spanish hands as decreed by Article II of the treaty. That article, responded Jackson, clearly assigns the cannons to the United States. And so it went, back and forth, an unproductive wrangle over the fortifications that drove Jackson half mad with anger and frustration.[25] He had not yet arrived in Florida and here he was fuming and arguing and threatening and already beginning to think about getting home as soon as possible. He told John Coffee that one of the reasons for accepting the assignment was the hope that the climate would improve Rachel's health, but he had begun to believe that nothing good would come of this dreadful adventure. "You may therefore rest assured," he added, "after congress meets I am a private citizen."[26]

The cause of the long delay was precisely as Jackson guessed it: Spanish procrastination in Cuba. Colonel Forbes aboard the *Hornet* arrived in Havana on April 22 and waited until May 26 while the necessary documents were slowly dribbled out.[27] Even after a five-week delay he was unable to obtain the land records and archives for West Florida. (East Florida was no problem except for the area around St. Augustine.) When Forbes realized that waiting could be an interminable game, he sailed for

Florida with what he had. Years later Jackson still wanted those documents. He never forgot. As President of the United States he demanded them. The king released them posthaste.[28]

From the very beginning of the negotiations to transfer Florida, the Spanish behaved badly. They invited Jackson's wrath. And they got it. Forbes arrived in Pensacola on June 9 with the transfer orders, and Jackson prepared to enter Florida for the third time in his career. But then came more delay. Again the business of the cannons generated a terrible row as Callava prepared to remove them and ship them off to Cuba. Jackson had explicit instructions from Monroe that said the cannons belonged to the United States, although it seems reasonable that the President would have waived the cannons in the interest of a peaceful, orderly, and swift end to the negotiations. Not Jackson. The cannons were American property, and "by the eternal" he would have them. His patience ended, Jackson acted. Without another word he marched into Florida and took up a position fifteen miles from Pensacola at the home of Manuel Gonzales, a Spanish gentleman. It almost seemed as though he planned to storm the town by force. Instead he waited to see what the Spanish would do.[29] Rachel was much fatigued with the maneuvers and "diplomatic" jockeying, so she, the two Andrews, and their companions proceeded into Pensacola and found suitable quarters.

Jackson sat on his perch, watching eagle-eyed for the next Spanish move. But Callava would not treat with him. He was insulted. Jackson had failed to present his credentials as protocol dictated and the Spaniard regarded the action as another deliberate "outrage." Indeed Jackson should have had the courtesy to present his credentials to Callava as protocol required, but it was against his "principles" to deal with the Spanish when they had purposely stalled the negotiations by refusing to cooperate in the transfer of documents. And Jackson hardly knew how to treat with Spaniards except with the back of his hand. So the negotiations —such as they were—came to a halt.[30] As the delay continued Jackson's health as well as his temper worsened. Rachel begged him to join her in town. His friends also entreated him. "But no. . . . He said that when he came in it should be under his own standard, and that would be the third time he had planted that flag on that wall." Rachel was quite disturbed by his behavior and appearance. "He was very sick," she later wrote.[31]

Eventually they got around the problem of protocol by simply ignoring it. Negotiations were renewed, and Jackson ultimately got his cannons after offering a receipt for them—which satisfied the Spanish need for an honorable compromise. The General even admitted that their major problem all along had been one of language (or communication) since he did not speak Spanish and Callava knew no English. Finally the two men agreed on a date for the delivery of the Floridas: July 17, 1821. On that day Jackson might at long last take possession.[32] Of course the General had sufficient troops to storm his way into Pensacola all along, but he probably acted on administration advice not to introduce troops into the city until after the Spanish had evacuated.[33]

On Tuesday, July 17, at 7:00 A.M., American ceremonial soldiers marched into Pensacola, a band blaring their arrival. The whole town seemed agitated and in motion, excited by what was about to happen. A crowd lined the square in front of Government House, where the ceremony would take place. But there was no shout of joy as the American troops marched in. If anything there was a sense of apprehension. The largely Spanish population had only a vague notion of what life would be like under American rule. That it should begin under General "Andres" Jackson seemed to promise something frightening.

The American troops took their position in front of Government House opposite a small Spanish garrison retained for the ceremony of transition. General Jackson and his staff rode in on horseback. "O how solemn was his pale countenance when he dismounted from his horse," said Rachel, watching from the balcony of her house on Main Street. "Recollection of perils and scenes of war not to be disseevered presented themselves to view."[34]

Callava stepped forward and the two men greeted each other in formal terms. It was now 10:00 A.M. Jackson handed the Spaniard the instruments of his authority to take possession of the territory, and Callava then declared that by virtue of the special mandate dated May 5, 1821, at Havana he herewith surrendered West Florida to the American general. At the same time the keys of the town, the archives, and documents were also surrendered, and Callava, as a final act, released the inhabitants of West Florida from their allegiance to Spain.[35] Then, slowly, solemnly, the Spanish flag was lowered and the American ensign hoisted one hundred feet into the air while the band struck up "the tune of 'long may it wave, o'er the land of the free and the home of the brave.' "[36] The *Hornet,* anchored in the bay, boomed a salute. Spanish Floridians standing in the square "burst into tears to see the last ray of hope departed of their devoted city and country."[37]

The ceremony concluded, the exchange of possession complete, the crowd dispersed and the Spanish garrison departed by ship the following day, escorted by the *Hornet,* the *Anne Marie,* and the *Tom Shields.* "How . . . the city [did] sit solitary and mourn," said Rachel. "Never did my heart feel more for any people. . . . Their manners, laws, and customs, all changed."[38] The transition from Spanish life to American would take time and patience and would not be easy. A northern, Anglo-Saxon,

Protestant culture would replace one that was basically southern, Hispanic, and Catholic. A few Spanish officers and agents, along with Callava, remained in Pensacola to complete the King's business and were expected to depart within six months at their own expense. The following Sunday the Spanish officials dined with the new governor. It was a charming evening, full of bright conversation, and Jackson was courteous and obliging. He seemed determined to climax the transfer with one last gracious act.

And last it was! Thereafter the Spaniards knew nothing but the contempt, fury, and near-manic behavior of the long-suffering, ill, and frustrated Jackson. He was in motion almost immediately, issuing decrees, publishing ordinances, and ordering the lives of a startled and uncomprehending people. The long delay in the surrender of Florida had given Jackson time to prepare all the measures for establishing his rule. On the very day after the ceremonial transfer, the first batch of ordinances and proclamations began flowing from the office of the governor-commander. None of Monroe's appointees to the senior positions had yet arrived, so Jackson assigned their duties to his staff, notably Dr. James C. Bronaugh, H. M. Brackenridge, Captain Richard K. Call, and others, few of whom spoke Spanish. This arrangement satisfied Jackson immensely; it meant he kept total control of the territory in his own hands.

As a matter of fact Jackson was extremely annoyed over the matter of appointments. Not only had the most important officials of the territory been appointed in Washington, but Monroe made his selections without consulting Jackson. "Not one of those I recommended is appointed," he snorted.[39] While the General was given extraordinary authority as governor, his authority was strictly limited. For example, he held all the powers exercised previously by the governor and captain general and intendant of Cuba and by the governors of East and West Florida, but Jackson had no authority to grant or confirm titles or claims to land to any person, nor could he impose or collect any new or additional taxes. These limitations were enough to invalidate some of the reasons Jackson had for accepting the governorship in the first place.

Now, unencumbered by the presence of Monroe's appointees—"intoxicated with the luscious draught of uncontrolled authority," said one inspired critic[40]—the Governor began immediately to establish the new government. One of his first decrees organized Florida into two counties: Escambia, the area between the Perdido and Suwannee rivers, and Saint Johns, the area east of the Suwannee. Three revenue districts were established: Pensacola, St. Marks, and St. Augustine. Jackson created a civil government for each county by appointing mayors and aldermen for the principal towns and justices of the peace.[41] Of the ten justices of the peace for each county, five constituted the county court. Jackson also empowered the mayors and aldermen, acting as the town council, to levy the taxes needed for the support of the town government—an action that critics later argued was a violation of the three commissions Jackson had received authorizing the administration of Florida.[42] In judicial matters the Governor served as the court of highest appeal and no capital punishment was permitted without his express consent. In civil proceedings Spanish laws were to be followed, but in criminal proceedings, common law, "so as to give perfect security to individual rights," said Jackson.[43] Thus trial by jury was assured in all criminal cases. County courts also served as county governments, and for each court the Governor appointed a clerk, a sheriff, and a prosecuting attorney.[44]

The indisputably statesmanlike reform of the governmental system of Florida[45] was accompanied by other decrees touching a wide range of problems.[46] Jackson established a Board of Health under the direction of Dr. James Bronaugh and ordered repaired the several hospital buildings in the Pensacola vicinity. There were ordinances—published in Spanish and English—for the "preservation of health," community protection, establishment of rates of pilotage, and registration of all inhabitants who wished to become American citizens.[47]

Undoubtedly at Rachel's urging, Jackson also cracked down on all ungodly, unchristian, "demonic," and heathen activities she pointed out to him. The gambling, vice, and "sabbath-breaking" had to be stopped if such a godfearing woman as Rachel Jackson were to be expected to stay in Florida. In a letter to a friend she catalogued some of the things that distressed her Presbyterian soul. "The Sabbath profanely kept; a great deal of noise and swearing in the streets; shops kept open; trade going on, I think, more than on any other day. . . . And must I say the worst people here are the cast-out Americans and negroes?"[48] Fortunately, General Jackson knew how to deal with these heathens. Like a clap of thunder, a decree went out against these sabbath-breakers, the worst sinners of all. Violation of the decree meant a $200 fine and the posting of a $500 good-behavior bond.[49] And within a few days of the promulgation of the decree an incredible change settled over the community—or so it seemed to Rachel. "What, what has been done in one week!" she enthused. "Great order was observed; the doors kept shut; the gambling houses demolished; fiddling and dancing not heard any more on the Lord's day; cursing not to be heard."[50] That Jackson! God's anointed! What a Christian soldier!

One of Jackson's immediate problems was the number of speculators and job-seekers who poured into town each day, many of them "cast-out Americans" who thought Pensacola would become a second New Orleans (as Jackson himself had once predicted). They bedeviled the Governor for land claims and patronage. When Monroe's appointees began arriving in Florida, Jackson's limited power in these areas became immediately apparent—which only agitated him the more. He enjoyed rewarding his friends; he also believed it important to the growth of the territory to encourage his old Tennessee cronies to extend their economic interests to the seacoast.

As the administration's appointees appeared in Florida, the wretchedness of Monroe's behavior in the matter became obvious—even to his later biographers.[51] Monroe did not appoint a single person recommended by his Governor; he did not consult Jackson on any of the appointments he did make; and finally, he based all his appointments on individual need for employment rather than proven ability. The President yielded to political pressure and did not screen the candidates carefully.[52] Consequently all his selections were weak. In view of Jackson's disposition and temperament, Monroe had virtually guaranteed a monumental blow-up in the new Florida Territory.

One of the first of the President's appointees to arrive in Florida was Eligius Fromentin, an ex-Jesuit priest who had been expelled from France during the Revolution and had come to America, married a fortune, and after the Revolution abandoned his wife and returned to France to reestablish himself within the Catholic Church. But when his marriage was discovered his ecclesiastical career collapsed. So he returned to the bosom of a forgiving wife and through her family's influence began a new career.[53] Monroe named him federal judge for West Florida. Wily (as all Jesuits were reputed to be, "ex" or not), conspiratorial, suave, urbane, and well educated, though not especially competent as a jurist, he soon took up with Callava, with whom he had much in common. Callava himself was a handsome, dignified, exquisitely mannered Castilian who had won rapid promotion during the peninsula campaign and had been appointed colonel and governor before he reached the age of forty. The two men quickly developed a close relationship and were soon joined by another ambitious entrepreneur, John Innerarity, the Pensacola representative of the trading house of Forbes and Company, which had long enjoyed Spanish privileges as well as extensive connections with the Indians. Indeed, the firm had been associated for many years with Spaniards in New Orleans and Mobile as well as Pensacola.[54]

The federal judge appointed for East Florida was William P. Duval, later territorial governor. Alexander Anderson of Tennessee and John Bird of Georgia were appointed United States attorneys; William G. D. Worthington of Maryland was named secretary for East Florida and George Walton of Georgia for West Florida. The latter appointment particularly annoyed Jackson because he believed it was made at the insistence of William H. Crawford.[55]

The first in a series of explosions that rocked Florida—and involved many of these appointees—occurred in mid-August 1821, when Henry M. Brackenridge, the *alcalde* or mayor of Pensacola, brought to Jackson the plight of one Mercedes Vidal, a free quadroon who was the illegitimate daughter of the late Nicholas Maria Vidal. Vidal, who died in 1806, was a Spanish military auditor who left large landholdings in Louisiana and Pensacola to his several half-caste children. Forbes and Company were designated executors of the will but failed to do anything about arranging a settlement. The surviving Vidals went to court for an accounting, but John Innerarity disregarded the court's orders or the Spanish governor's directives that the papers relevant to the case be delivered.[56] Mercedes Vidal, through sheer perserverance, managed to obtain copies of enough documents to substantiate her claim and raise serious questions about the activities of the company and the reasons for delaying a settlement. She retained Brackenridge and Richard Call as attorneys and urged immediate action because of her suspicion that the records had recently been transferred to the residence of Lieutenant Domingo Sousa, one of Callava's clerks, prior to their intended removal to Havana.[57] The pathetic story of this unfortunate woman, cheated of her inheritance for the past fifteen years, sent Brackenridge scurrying to Jackson rather than Judge Fromentin because the Governor exercised supreme judicial authority. Jackson asked for proof of the charges and the *alcalde* showed him the documents. Immediately a formal demand was drawn up and taken to Sousa, who refused to surrender the documents without an order from Callava. Hauled before the glowering Jackson to answer for his conduct, the terrified Sousa admitted conveying the papers to the house of Colonel Callava. Whereupon the Governor sent Colonel Robert Butler, Brackenridge, and Dr. Bronaugh with Sousa and a guard to Callava's residence to demand the papers. If the request were refused, Sousa was to be jailed immediately.

When the company reached Callava's home they were told that the colonel was dining at the house of Colonel Brooke of the Fourth Infantry, the same Brooke who asked General Brown whether he was subject to Jackson's military commands. The group marched to Brooke's place. Callava was dining with Fromentin, Innerarity, Captain Kearney of the navy, a large number of ladies and gentlemen, and a group of Spanish officers. Informed of the group's presence and purpose, Callava replied spiritedly that he was a royal commissioner and was not subject to such demands. He would neither surrender the papers nor return to his house. "We all left the table," Callava later reported. "Brooke's lady was very much grieved."[58] The group banged their way out of the house, Colonel Brooke at their heels. Brooke was appalled by their behavior and complained that "he had been extremely badly treated in having his company disturbed—that he acknowledged no authority to arrest a man in his House—that he was astonished at our conduct and that it had been extremely indecorous towards him."[59]

Later Callava returned home stricken with indigestion. With him went Innerarity. The group sent by Jackson followed and repeated their demands. Finally Callava yielded and stated that if a list of the documents in question were presented to him in writing, he would surrender them. Half an hour later Brackenridge returned with the list, but Callava supported now by Innerarity, refused to honor his pledge. Whereupon Innerarity said the die was cast. "Yes, he said truly the die was cast," reported Jackson to Secretary Adams, "for he must have clearly seen, that the arts, the influence, the wealth, the power, of no individual, not even of Inerarity himself, could any longer obstruct, the pure channels of justice."[60]

When all this was reported to the Governor, poor Sousa was slapped into prison and a terse "military" order went to Colonel Brooke as the senior military officer in Pensacola. "Sir, you will furnish an officer, sergeant, corporal, and twenty men, and direct the officer to call on me by half past eight o'clock P.M. for orders. They will have their arms and accouterments complete, with twelve rounds of ammunition."[61]

The troops arrived promptly. They were given their orders by Jackson and told that Butler, Brackenridge, and Bronaugh would accompany them. They marched to Callava's house, entered it, and found the Spaniard in bed, fully dressed except for his coat. Again the demand for the papers; again the refusal. So he was commanded to appear before Governor Jackson. Fearful of assassination in the streets (or so he later claimed), Callava swore he would not be removed from his house alive —whereupon Butler ordered the guard to prime and load. Callava jumped from the bed. He knew Butler meant business. He grabbed his coat, surrendered his sword to one of the American officers, "who threw it up the chimney," and without further argument accompanied the arresting party through the streets to face the Governor.[62] A crowd followed.

It was ten o'clock at night when Callava was hauled before General Jackson, sitting now as supreme judge. A number of excited spectators filled the room, so there was a background obbligato of constant babble in Spanish and English. Callava spoke no English and Jackson no Spanish; both men had already worked themselves into towering rages. The scene was set for a boiling, seething, screaming performance.

Jackson waved Callava to a seat at a table in front of him. The *alcalde* took a seat at the other end and acted as interpreter. Immediately Callava poured out a stream of Spanish in loud, excited tones, protesting that as commissioner of Spain he was not answerable as a private individual. Jackson matched him in vocal strength and color, denying his status as a commissioner and demanding the papers.[63] Callava said he wished to write out a protest, whereupon Jackson shouted to Brackenridge, "Why do you not tell him, sir, that I will not permit him to protest?" It was becoming low comedy. When Callava understood Jackson's last remark he refused to say anything at all.[64]

Fullarat, the colonel's steward, was summoned. He admitted that the papers lay hidden in Callava's house, thereby corroborating Sousa's story.[65] These papers, Jackson stormed in a passion so intense that he frightened the spectators into silence, belonged to the archives under Article II of the treaty. "Surrender them!" he bellowed, certain now that Callava was deliberately treating "my authority with contempt."[66] Callava bellowed back, mostly to the spectators, in a long, loud inflammatory flood of Spanish. He repeated "that he could not deliver the papers unless demanded of him as commissioner, or late governor; that they could not be in his hands as a private individual."[67] Jackson reminded Callava of his promise to surrender the papers if he were given a written list. "It is false," cried the colonel. No such promise was ever made.[68]

And so it went for two hours. The shouting, banging, and gesticulating must have been horrendous. At last Jackson could stand it no longer. His nerves shattered, he told the interpreter to inform Callava that he must give up the papers or suffer the consequences. Jackson also appealed to Callava's friends to explain to him his situation. But the Spaniard only stared at the Governor, defiant, proud, and resolute. Jackson produced a commission that had already been prepared and signed it. The order remanded Colonel José Callava to prison, and with him Sousa and Fullarat.[69]

The Spanish officers who witnessed this last scene stood dumbfounded. "The Governor, Don Andrew Jackson," one of them wrote, "with turbulent and violent actions, with disjointed reasonings, blows on the table, his mouth foaming, and possessed with the furies"—it was one of Jackson's greatest performances—ordered the imprisonment of His Catholic Majesty's Royal Commissioner and Governor.[70] It was incredible. It could not happen. It must be a fantasy. But Callava was carted off to the calaboose, a small, dirty, uncomfortable building erected by the Spanish many years before. As he entered the jail, accompanied by a large contingent of Spanish officers, Callava was suddenly struck by the insanity of it all. He reared back and roared with laughter. Soon chairs, cots, and beds were brought in, along with food, cigars, claret, and champagne. There were jokes and uproariously funny imitations of "Don Andrew Jackson, Governor of Florida." The Spaniards made a night of it.

The next morning Jackson issued the necessary writ to have the Vidal papers removed from Callava's house. This was done very expeditiously, without tampering with any other document. Once the papers were in hand the Governor signed an order for the discharge of the prisoners.[71] In fact he cleared out the entire calaboose.

Then events took a portentous and not so funny turn. The friends of Callava, including Innerarity, went to Judge Fromentin and asked for a writ of habeas corpus. With Innerarity standing security, Fromentin issued the writ to be served on the officer of the prison guard.[72] The writ was taken instead to Jackson, who when he read it burst into a furious tirade over this new interference with his determination to administer justice to an unfortunate family. Another judicial meddler! Another Dominick Hall! Worse, an "apostate Priest" long practiced in treachery and deceit.[73] Jackson hastily had a citation drawn up summoning Fromentin to Government House. Using his own judicial authority under his commission, Jackson wanted the judge to "show cause why he has attempted to interfere with my authority as Governor of the Floridas [and] . . . in my judicial capacity as supreme judge over the same."[74]

Fromentin, claiming a rheumatic attack, did not respond immediately to Jackson's summons, but he fully expected a squad of soldiers to burst through his door and drag him before the imperious Governor. Or perhaps that was his hope. But Jackson, who had learned enough from the Hall misadventure to deny the worthy judge additional provocation, fooled him.

Failing in his object, Fromentin appeared before Jackson the following day at four o'clock in the afternoon. At times the conversation was a bit heated. To a large extent Jackson delivered a lecture. More important he knew what he was talking about; he had his facts; he proceeded to administer a verbal tongue-lashing. In measured tones the Governor elaborated on his extensive powers, citing his commissions and expressing the hope that no person would ever again enjoy such extraordinary authority because such power could be dangerous in so concentrated a form. Jackson also remarked in an offhanded way that the poor were fortunate to have a man of his feelings at the head of the government, to protect them against the rapacity of the rich and powerful. He honestly cared for the less fortunate. As Governor he recognized a special obligation toward the weak and underprivileged that probably stemmed from the strong paternalistic sense that was basic to his life as planter, soldier, and commissioner to the Indians. He genuinely believed that he represented the poor despite—or perhaps on account of—his station, rank and wealth. What he said to Fromentin, therefore, was simply a true statement of fact.

It came as a rude shock to Fromentin that Jackson's commissions did indeed give him extensive judicial powers in the territory. The Governor had acted well within his authority. Fromentin could barely respond. He sputtered something in self-defense, but Jackson cut him off. The Governor said that Fromentin's timing of his "interference" was particularly "reprehensible." The Spaniards were anxious to create trouble, and when an American, let alone an American judge appointed by the President, encouraged their mischief-making he deserved the severest punishment.

The "lecture I gave the Judge when he came before me," Jackson later wrote John Quincy Adams, "will, I trust, for the future, cause him to obey the spirit of his commission, aid in the execution of the laws, and administration of the Government, instead of attempting to oppose me, under Spanish influence."[75] But the point he returned to over and over in his letter was the desire of the Spaniards, supported by Fromentin and others, to encourage civil disobedience and insubordination.[76] Then, mindful of the Vidal family and their plight, he expressed to Adams a deeply felt conviction. "I did believe, and ever will believe, that just laws can make no distinction of privilege between the rich and poor, and that when men of high standing attempt to trample upon the rights of the weak, they are the fitest objects for example and punishment. In general, the great can protect themselves, but the poor and humble, require the arm and shield of the law."

This was one of Jackson's abiding principles. Long before he became President of the United States he articulated the fundamental doctrine of Jacksonian Democracy: the obligation of the government to grant no privilege that aids one class over another, to act as honest broker between classes, and to protect the weak and defenseless against the abuses of the rich and powerful. Much of this later appeared in the message accompanying the presidential veto of the Bank bill in 1832, worded by Amos Kendall. But the thought behind it was pure Jackson, the sense totally his. And it explains one element of his greatness as President: he had genuine compassion for the weak and believed himself their defender and guardian.

Perhaps more serious than any of the charges made by Jackson in his lecture to Fromentin was the judge's demonstrated legal incompetence in issuing the writ.[77] In the first place he had no authority to issue it; in the second it was issued without an affidavit. He was obviously trying to create an incident that he might exploit for his own advantage. When the interview closed Fromentin admitted that the writ had been issued hastily, under unusual circumstances, and he promised not to interfere again with Jackson's authority.[78] But both men carried their case to Secretary Adams, complaining bitterly about the improper conduct of the other.

Adams, knowing what awaited him from Florida, hated to face his morning mail. But eventually, on investigation, he supported Jackson as he had done so many times in the past. He reminded Fromentin that his jurisdiction was confined to laws of the United States which Congress had extended to the Floridas, namely those of revenue and the slave trade. "In the different view which you have taken of the subject," Adams wrote, ". . . [the President] deeply regrets the collision of authority and misunderstanding which have arisen between the Governor of the Territory and you."[79] It was the opinion of the attorney general, William Wirt, that Fromentin's writ was illegal in form even if his right to issue it was unquestioned.[80]

With the question of his jurisdiction settled, Jackson proceeded to hear the Vidal case. Not unexpectedly he ruled in favor of the heirs. But there were many appeals before the case was finally adjudicated. A few congressmen who feared or disliked the "dangerous" General considered demanding an investigation into the affair but, reminded of the last such inquiry and the response it elicited from the public, they dropped the idea.[81]

Almost immediately upon his release from prison, Callava bolted to Washington to protest his treatment. There he regaled the Spanish minister with the details of Jackson's conduct. The minister listened in a state of shock, astounded by the impropriety of it all. Dutifully, Callava committed his harrowing account to paper and transmitted it to Secretary Adams.[82] A copy was also slipped to the *National Intelligencer,* a Washington newspaper committed to William Crawford's election to the presidency in 1824. In light of the known rivalry between Jackson and Crawford and their public disdain for one another, and because talk had already begun to circulate around the country that the Hero himself might run for the presidency, the *National Intelligencer* seized the opportunity to discredit the General and published Callava's account.

But not much later the Spanish minister confronted the secretary of state. And, as he had done on several previous occasions—indeed the number of times was almost embarrassing[83]—Adams defended Jackson's conduct. The train of events leading to the unfortunate jailing of Callava, said the secretary, began with Spanish procrastination in Havana over the procurement of papers and documents. That was a deliberate and provocative effort to delay the delivery of Florida to the United States. Furthermore, with respect to the documents demanded for the settlement of the Vidal matter, the shifting of them from person to person to avoid complying with Jackson's order "was a high and aggravated outrage upon his [the Governor's] lawful authority"—and, one might add, his dignity. The imprisonment of Callava was therefore necessary and unavoidable, though deeply regretted. The documents in question were required to settle a legal matter in the courts of the United States, not in Cuba or Spain, and thus the attempts to ferret them away were clearly improper. The Spanish minister's reaction to all this was predictably peppery, but there was little he could do other than to warn Adams that his government was sure to protest.[84]

The blame for the incident belonged in both camps. Jackson could have prevented a diplomatic brouhaha. His official position demanded tact, generosity, and consideration toward a defeated foe, the more so in view of Spanish sensitivity about honor, pride, and outward appearance. No matter how provoked, Jackson need not have imprisoned Callava. It served no purpose except to worsen the situation and make Jackson look ridiculous. Unfortunately, the General gave greater consideration to his own dignity and honor and far less to the possible consequences of humiliating a foreign official. He had in fact acted in the "Spanish way," as both Monroe and Adams recognized.[85] Moreover, Jackson nitpicked with Callava over whether the Spaniard was a commissioner and possessed diplomatic immunity when, in the interest of a speedy and orderly transfer of authority, it behooved Jackson to extend as much courtesy and diplomatic privilege as possible.[86] As long as Callava remained in Florida under the terms of the treaty[87] he deserved the ordinary immunity granted a foreign agent as well as the dignity and respect owed a former official of Florida.[88]

While Callava snorted and fumed in Washington, his officers in Pensacola prepared one last jab at the irascible Governor. They published a protest over Callava's trial and the way Jackson had conducted it. Their purpose, among other things, was aimed at inciting the public against the Governor and continuing the uproar in Washington over the administration of Florida.[89] They tagged Jackson's accusations in court as offensive and not properly translated or interpreted to Callava. No wonder their colonel failed to prove his innocence. Besides, they were all subjected to the shattering effects of the Governor's violence and tyranny and could scarcely be expected to respond to the charges with thoughtful care and logical precision.[90]

The publication of this notice produced a not untypical response from Jackson. He gave the entire staff of Spanish officers four days to get out of the country. After that they risked arrest for contempt and disobedience. Their protest, Jackson said in his responding proclamation, "is calculated to excite resistance to the existing government of the Floridas, and to disturb the harmony, peace, and good order of the same, as well as to weaken the allegiance enjoined by my proclamation, heretofore published."[91] The Spanish officers scooted off as soon as they could gather their belongings, but not before composing a final blast at the Governor, one that reverberated with Spanish bravado and machismo. It was not the terror of Jackson's prisons that hurried them away, they contended, but their desire to imitate the valor and courage of their colonel, who had responded to the Governor's insane behavior with dignified contempt. Unfortunately, no Florida newspaper chose to publish this parting contempt citation, perhaps in order to avoid trouble with the Governor.[92] But the Washington *National Intelligencer* got hold of it and spread it over several columns to document its contention that the country had on its southern frontier a lunatic governor who might easily initiate a war with Spain to satisfy his craving for power. Several years later, in connection with the presidential election of 1828, the newspaper published a full critique under the title, "An Examination of the Civil Administration of Governor Jackson in Florida."[93] But the piece was badly done, its arguments weak and its conclusions unconvincing. Even at the start of this controversy the American people sided with Jackson. All they knew was that the nation had acquired Florida thanks to him. Nothing he did found fault in their eyes.

The Spanish in Florida hardly knew what to make of their wild Governor despite his many efforts to accommodate them. Quite obviously they feared him. Every time they encountered him he seemed to be screaming and gesticulating. One night a fire raged in the business district of Pensacola and the Spanish congregated to watch it. Suddenly, Jackson appeared and immediately began issuing commands and calling for help. But the Spanish, knowing little English, did not understand him. They saw only a wildly excited man waving and yelling at them. In a panic they fled to their homes, leaving the Governor to watch the conflagration alone.[94]

These painful scenes only convinced Jackson that he must leave Florida soon and return home. He hated every moment of his term as Governor, and some of his actions proved it. In a constant state of nervous agitation, he managed to keep going through sheer desperation; only his indomitable will prevented physical collapse. But he had enough sense to realize that if he did not quit this thankless job and return to Tennessee before winter, he might be carried home in a pine box.[95] The governorship had been a mistake from the first. Monroe never trusted him enough to accord him complete freedom. The presidential appointments also rankled. They deprived him of the deep desire to reward his friends. The "one motive for accepting the governorship," wrote, his nephew, Andrew Jackson Donelson, "was the promotion and assistance of his friends."[96] And then to suffer the contempt and defiance of Spanish officials and their American allies was more than duty required. The indignity heaped upon him and his office should have brought swift retaliation.[97] Instead he was reduced to explaining and justifying his actions. A man of his stature forced to answer the complaints of pygmies! It was time to go home.

When Monroe, pursuing his usual careful middle course, tried to wriggle between Jackson and Fromentin in his annual message to Congress by declaring that the collision between the two resulted from a misunderstanding of the act defining their respective powers and that both men had undoubtedly acted in good faith, Jackson sustained the last miserable blow to this entire wretched affair. Monroe's pusillanimous dodge now confirmed Jackson's judgment that the administration barely tolerated his presence in Florida. Many of the General's friends in Washington tried to convince him that the only reason Monroe had appointed him in the first place was to accommodate Crawford and remove him from the presidential race. Although Monroe continued for some time to write the General complimentary letters about his services to the nation, Jackson told him straight out that he felt betrayed, especially by the President's remarks to Congress.[98] The Florida misadventure thus ruptured the relationship between the two and wiped away an uncertain friendship that had more ardor on Jackson's side than on Monroe's.[99] "I [am] still hoping that Mr. Monroe would be able to explain satisfactory to me those things that have tended to my injury," Jackson wrote, "and of the injustice of which, I had a right to complain. I therefore suspend any opinion for the present and await his answer."[100] None ever came.

If Monroe wavered in his loyalty, Adams was a constant and devoted supporter. He was certainly not a friend, and he would have been embarrassed had the term been applied to him. But he believed Jackson's position essentially correct and one the United States was obliged to defend. Thus he backed the General at every turn, particularly in the many Cabinet meetings called by Monroe to respond to the embarrassments constantly occurring in Florida. And Jackson was grateful. "You know my private opinion of Mr. Adams Talents, virtue, and integrity," Jackson told a friend, "and I am free to declare that I have never changed this opinion of Mr. Adams since it was first formed, I think him a man of the first rate mind of any in america as a civilian and scholar, and I have never doubted of his attachment to our republican Government."[101]

Adams's support of Jackson was more than the pragmatic act of a wily secretary of state asserting every available advantage in treating with the Spanish. He understood the General thoroughly and what he was attempting to do. Moreover he honestly felt that Jackson was doing a very commendable job in Florida, however distressing his methods. And indeed Jackson did efficiently organize the government of the Floridas and give it direction and energy. He performed with distinction the essential task of establishing an effective government in accordance with American principles and institutions—as he was sent to do. Furthermore, the "Americanization" of what was fundamentally a foreign country went forward intelligently and with all deliberate haste.

Apart from institutional achievements—government and legal processes, for example—Jackson encouraged many cultural activities to assist the "Americanization" of the territory. On the day the Governor arrived in Pensacola the process began with the opening of the Jacksonian Commonwealth Theatre, which played to capacity audiences. The new Eagle Tavern brought a home away from home to Americans by offering hot and cold baths and a bowling alley. In August a printing press arrived; soon there was a circulating library with a reading room that boasted fifty newspapers and other periodicals. The general use of the English language was introduced with enough intelligent regard for the linguistic limitations of the public to prevent confusion and discord. Jackson hoped to "dispense with all Spanish customs . . . at as early a day as possible," but he realized that this innovation would require time and planning.[102]

One reason for Jackson's success as Governor was the assistance he received from a number of friends. In fact, one of Jackson's real contributions to Florida history was the caliber of men (such as Richard Keith Call and James Gadsden) he brought to the territory.[103] Although Monroe retained for himself an important part of the Florida patronage and dispensed jobs without consulting Jackson, a sizable number of lesser positions remained for the Governor's distribution. And Jackson proved remarkably effective in placing able men in sensitive slots. He appointed reliable associates to a wide range of offices: territorial secretary, surveyor general, registrar of the land office, land sales agents, district judges, district attorneys, sheriffs, postmasters, land commissioners, and clerks.[104] Jackson did not exploit his office for gain, although he was very solicitous in urging men of enterprise to seek financial opportunities in Florida. However arbitrary and authoritarian his rule, he governed according to his honest perception of Florida's needs and interests. He gave the territory a strong beginning.

The Governor was particularly dependent on William G. D. Worthington in handling government affairs in East Florida. Jackson never traveled to that section of the territory and therefore relied on the secretary and on the chief military officer for the area, Captain John R. Bell, to maintain order and to implement faithfully his administrative decrees. Jackson advised Worthington to continue the Spanish form of city government in St. Augustine because of the stability provided by the existing *alcalde, cabildo* (municipal administrative unit composed of councillors and magistrates), and judge. Jackson also instructed Worthington to keep as many native incumbents in office as possible, provided they were of "good character" and they agreed to take an oath of allegiance to the new government.[105]

Jackson's principal problem with East Florida was the brief (and inconsequential) dispute that broke out between the civil and military authorities. Because of the wretched condition of the barracks, Bell wanted to use several public buildings to house his troops, but Worthington insisted the buildings were needed by the government. Although Jackson sympathized with Bell and his predicament, he sided with Worthington and ordered Bell to obey the civil authority.[106] Despite his successful career in the army, Jackson always remained a civilian at heart.

As long as Jackson sat "as the representative of my Government . . . administering [its] laws," he insisted that there was "no distinction between the rich and poor the great and ignoble"—that the government was run for the benefit of all.[107] Indeed, Jackson's views of government were essentially democratic. And to guarantee a democratic process he believed that the franchise must be extended to every freeman. In a letter to Bronaugh, Jackson declared that in Florida "all freemen residents will be bound by your laws, & subject to punishments under them—and of right, ought to be entitled to a voice in making them."[108] Although as Governor he possessed broad powers in Florida, Jackson insisted on democratic procedures. And he repeatedly expressed the hope that no person would ever again enjoy such extraordinary control as his over the operation of government.[109]

Jackson's broad definition of the franchise did not exclude free blacks or, presumably, Indians who remained in the east and became citizens as his treaty with the Cherokees in 1817 suggested. But on the whole Jackson's attitude toward Indians in general lacked understanding and compassion, for it was linked to his expansionist commitment and his determination to terminate the existence of Indian tribes as sovereign agencies within white society. His treatment of them combined paternalism with an absolute resolve to force their eventual removal beyond the Mississippi.

Since the Florida Indians were something of a "hybrid" people that included many Creeks, Jackson was even less sympathetic to their territorial claims.[110] Only through the reduction of their land mass could they be coaxed from savagery; only through removal could they escape the white man's reprisal for their recent warfare against frontier settlers.[111] But Jackson no longer believed in dealing with the Indians by treaty. It was "not only useless but absurd," he said. The bribery and the threats were not worth the effort, and he hoped he would never have to negotiate that way with Indians again. The United States, he said, should simply order the Seminoles to remove. Not ask them. Tell them.[112]

As Governor of Florida, Jackson implemented his removal policy at every possible juncture. As usual, he called the chiefs together for one of his "talks" to instruct them in his policy. When they arrived he put on a theatrical performance. This slab of imperial insolence, surrounded by the trophies and symbols of his power, spoke to them with a sternness mixed with paternal affection. His face permanently creased by pain, his eyes reflecting his mood, his rawboned, sharp-angled body exuding determination and purpose—all deeply affected the Seminoles as they gathered close around him to hear his words.

"I give to you a plain, straight talk," he began, "and do not speak with a forked tongue. It is necessary that you be brought together, either within the bounds of your old Nation, or at some other point, where your Father the President may be enabled to extend to you his fatherly care and assistance. Those who fled from their Nation and joined in the War against us, must return to their country . . . for they cannot be permitted to settle all over the Floridas and on her Sea Coast. Your white brethren must be settled there, to keep from you bad men and bad talks." The chiefs had been told that Jackson would deprive them of their lands, allowing them only 640 acres each to live on. In fact he had a worse fate in mind. He informed the chiefs that the President, their Father, would send an agent who would point out where they would be permitted to settle, "but that he could not nor would not permit them to be scattered over the Floridas as they now are."[113]

Having defeated the Spanish and expelled them from the southern coast, Jackson desired nothing so much as the elimination of the Seminoles from the peninsula. Their removal would complement the Spanish expulsion. Only he did not insist that they migrate west of the Mississippi like the other tribes. He was willing to set up a special reservation for all Florida Indians—who numbered 3,899 in 1822—on the banks of the Apalachicola adjoining the southern border of Alabama and Georgia and running down the river on both sides. He was willing to allow this special reservation because it would permit easy and inexpensive control of the Indians.[114] And this was quite a concession, for he still believed, as he told the secretary of war, that the best policy would be to remove them all to Creek country.[115] Calhoun agreed with Jackson about expelling the Seminoles from Florida and said that the President also agreed, but he pointed out that forcible removal without the sanction of Congress and a special appropriation would be "improper."[116] So Jackson commanded the chiefs to wait for the naming of the President's agent and the instructions he would bring. The "talk" completed, he shook hands with each of the chiefs and ordered provisions granted to them.

Now that the Spanish had departed, the Seminoles did not know what to expect from the new American government. They heard many rumors, each more frightening than the last. Several individual chiefs visited the Governor in his executive chambers to seek reassurance. Jackson always spoke to them, always shook their hands, and they invariably said they were pleased with the talk, as though wishing could make it so.[117] For his part, although he made himself accessible to the Indians, Jackson refused to treat the tribes as a sovereign, independent nation. They were dependents, and their Father, the President, would guide them and protect them. Further, Jackson arrested all white men who treated with the Indians without proper authorization. One thing he would not abide was a "meddlesome" white man undercutting his policy.

On September 28, 1821, Calhoun appointed Captain John Bell as acting agent to the Seminoles and Jean Pénières as subagent. With Jackson as superintendent, the organization for handling the Seminoles was complete and should have begun operating. But Pénières died suddenly, Bell was charged with conduct unbecoming an officer and suspended, and Jackson, ill and disheartened, finally deserted Florida and returned to his home in Tennessee.[118] The final disposition of the Indians had to wait nearly ten years until Jackson became President of the United States.

Jackson served as Governor of the Florida Territory for slightly more than eleven weeks. It was longer than he ever intended. As early as October he had alerted Monroe of his desire to return home; after all, he had accepted the assignment on the clear understanding that once a government for the Floridas was formed he was free to leave.[119] In arguing his need to go home he pleaded the poor health of his wife, never mentioning that his own was far worse. He told Monroe that the government of the Floridas would be left in the capable hands of the two secretaries, and he promised to return immediately if it should prove necessary.[120] His formal letter of resignation, dated November 13, 1821, was hand-delivered to the President by Bronaugh with the wish that it be accepted "at as an early a period as your Convenience will admit."[121] Although Monroe asked weakly that he remain a little longer, he accepted the resignation on December 1, 1821.

On balance, Jackson's tenure as Governor was more successful than either his contemporaries or historians allowed. Of course, it was turbulent and short-lived. At times he acted like a despot, albeit a benevolent despot. But under his direction the history of the peninsula got off to a very responsible start. Some of his ordinances were repealed a year later by Congress in imposing a territorial government according to the pattern set by the Northwest Ordinance.[122] Still he understood the need to unite the two Floridas and provide democratic rule—which had been his goals. More than anything else, he desired and actively sought the immediate integration of the territory into the United States, culturally as well as politically.[123] As he told President Monroe, "Congress ought to provide an energetic code of law for its government, that may as far as possible . . . Americanize the Floridas."[124]

On the night of October 4 a farewell dinner was tendered Andrew and Rachel by the military officers and citizens of Pensacola at Austin's Tavern. In a prepared speech, later reprinted across the country, Jackson told his audience that as Governor he had tried to obtain for the people of Florida "the protection of their persons, property and religion" until such time as they acquired all the privileges of United States citizenship. From the time of his arrival in Florida, that had been the purpose of his tenure.

"I have made no discrimination of persons," Jackson declared. To which his listeners silently agreed. Say what you will, Andrew Jackson treated everyone equally. "My house has been surrounded by no guards, and no one has been kept at a distance by repulsive formalities; all have had free admittance and found a ready ear, when they required my aid for the protection of their rights." Nearly everyone in the room nodded his agreement. Then they began applauding, realizing that despite the noise and the discord of the past two months the people of Florida were extraordinarily fortunate to have had at the head of their government a decent and just man who would listen to their grievances and defend with his life their individual liberties.

The American government is the "freest and strongest in the world," he continued. May it always remain so. As long as its wealth and internal stability are maintained there can be no serious challenge to its preeminence. He then alluded briefly to his quarrel with Callava and defended his actions. With this one exception, he concluded, he had experienced nothing but trust and confidence and support.[125]

The speech was a fitting close to his term as Governor. Defensive and self-congratulatory to be sure, but marked by revealing comments about his approach to government: his openness, his availability, and his determination to protect "persons, property and religion." Three days later a fine carriage drawn by four grey horses departed Government House with the Jacksons aboard. With a sense of relief and anticipation they headed for the peace and rest they knew they could only find at the Hermitage. His official career at long last seemed over. After a leisurely trip they arrived in Nashville on November 7 and were given a "handsome and brilliant reception."[126]

A slightly embarrassed administration in Washington was happy to see him go. Not until December did Monroe get around to accepting his resignation or expressing appreciation for his services.[127] A few hostile newspapers and several apprehensive politicians were also glad to learn of his departure. Once back on his farm in Tennessee, they hoped, he would disappear from public view.

But the American people had a different attitude toward Jackson and his tenure as Governor. They saw his eleven-week term in office as another outstanding accomplishment; in their eyes his struggles reflected once more his democratic commitment, his patriotic purpose. He had defended "the weak against the powerful," they said, the poor against the mighty. He was everything a great man should be, the nation's best image of itself.

Had Jackson's public career closed with his gubernatorial term, the record of his achievements during the previous decade would have earned him his country's everlasting gratitude. Between his victories over the British, the Spanish, and the Indians he had provided the American people with an empire, one in which he hoped there would be "no distinction between the rich and poor the great and ignoble."

But a new phase of his career was about to begin. As the people struggled to find the means to shape their empire into a democracy, as they headed haltingly into the modern industrial age, they looked for leadership from among those whom they could trust. They instinctively turned to Jackson. A man of his accomplishments and democratic principles, they said, did not belong on a farm, rusticating in Tennessee. Such a man was needed in Washington. Such a man belonged in the White House.[128]

Notes

Abbreviations and Short Titles Used in the Notes

Abernethy, *Frontier*	Thomas Abernethy, *From Frontier to Plantation in Tennessee* (Chapel Hill, 1932).
Adams, *Memoirs*	Charles Francis Adams, ed., *Memoirs of John Quincy Adams* (Philadelphia, 1874–1877), 12 volumes.
AGI	Archivo General de Indias, Seville, Spain
AGS	Archivo General de Simancas, Spain
AHA	American Historical Association
AHM	*American Historical Magazine*
AHN	Archivo Historico Nacional, Madrid, Spain
AHR	*American Historical Review*
AJ	Andrew Jackson
Ammon, *Monroe*	Harry Ammon, *James Monroe: The Quest for National Identity* (New York, 1971).
ASPFA	American State Papers, Foreign Affairs
ASPIA	American State Papers, Indian Affairs
ASPM	American State Papers, Miscellaneous
ASPMA	American State Papers, Military Affairs
Bassett, *Jackson*	John Spencer Bassett, *The Life of Andrew Jackson* (New York, 1916).
Bemis, *Adams*	Samuel Flagg Bemis, *John Quincy Adams and the Foundations of American Foreign Policy* (New York, 1950).
Blount Papers	Alice B. Keith and William H. Masterson, eds., *The John Gray Blount Papers* (Raleigh, 1959), 3 volumes.
Brannan, *Official Letters*	John Brannan, ed., *Official Letters of the Military and Naval Officers of the United States During the War with Great Britain in the Years 1812, '13, '14 and '15* (Washington, 1823).

Calhoun Papers	W. Edwin Hamphill, ed., *The Papers of John C. Calhoun* (Columbia, 1963–), 6 volumes.
Carter, *Territorial Papers*	Clarence E. Carter, ed., *The Territorial Papers of the United States* (Washington, 1936–), 22 volumes.
CHS	Chicago Historical Society
Cuba	Papeles de Cuba, AGI
DeGrummond, *Baratarians*	Jane L. DeGrummond, *The Baratarians and the Battle of New Orleans* (Baton Rouge, 1961).
DUL	Duke University Library
ETHSP	*The East Tennessee Historical Society's Publications*
HL	Huntington Library
HUL	Harvard University Library
Jackson, *Correspondence*	John Spencer Bassett, ed., *The Correspondence of Andrew Jackson* (Washington, 1926–1933), 6 volumes.
James, *Jackson*	Marquis James, *The Life of Andrew Jackson* (Indianapolis and New York, 1938).
JPP	Jackson Papers Project, Hermitage, Tennessee
JSH	*Journal of Southern History*
Kendall, *Jackson*	Amos Kendall, *The Life of General Andrew Jackson* (New York, 1844).
Latour, *Historical Memoir*	A. Lacarriere Latour, *Historical Memoir of the War in West Florida and Louisiana* (Philadelphia, 1816).
LC	Library of Congress
leg.	legajos
LHA	Ladies Hermitage Association, Hermitage, Tennessee
ML	Morgan Library
MVHR	*Mississippi Valley Historical Review*
NA	National Archives
NYHS	New York Historical Society
NYPL	New York Public Library
NYSL	New York State Library, Albany
Parton, *Jackson*	James Parton, *Life of Andrew Jackson* (Boston, 1866), 3 volumes.
PRO	Public Record Office, London
PUL	Princeton University Library
Reid and Eaton, *Jackson*	John Reid and John Henry Eaton, *The Life of Andrew Jackson* (University, Alabama, 1974, reprint).
Rogin, *Fathers and Children*	Michael Paul Rogin, *Fathers and Children: Andrew Jackson and the Subjugation of the American Indians* (New York, 1975).
THM	*Tennessee Historical Magazine*
THQ	*Tennessee Historical Quarterly*
THS	Tennessee Historical Society
TSL	Tennessee State Library, Nashville
WSH	State Historical Society of Wisconsin, Madison

CHAPTER 1

1. Parton, *Jackson*, III, 684–685.

2. A document on the early Jackson family is contained in the Jackson Papers, LC, but it is not in Jackson's handwriting. It appears in Jackson, *Correspondence*, I, 1. See also Kendall, *Jackson*, p. 10. This document states that Andrew was the youngest of four brothers. The names of the other brothers are not given. Parton, Kendall, and Reid and Eaton all agree that Andrew was the youngest. However, in a letter to General Jackson dated December 5, 1822, in Jackson, *Correspondence*, III, 180, one Robert Jackson claimed that he was one of the four brothers and named the others: "Andrew Jackson James Hu and Robert myself." He also says that he was 17 years of age when the elder Jackson migrated to America, indicating that he was the youngest. Moreover, he states that young Robert Jackson, Andrew's second son, was born at sea. None of these claims can be verified. Because the Kendall and the Reid and Eaton biographies were prepared under Jackson's supervision I have tended to accept their word in such matters.

3. Jackson, *Correspondence*, I, 1.

4. Bassett, *Jackson*, p. 4, ft. 1, says of the document on the Jackson family that there is no evidence of its reliability.

5. One tradition holds that the Jacksons arrived in Charleston, South Carolina, and proceeded immediately to the Waxhaw region, but all modern biographers reject this tradition. Reid and Eaton, *Jackson*, p. 9, state that the family landed at Charleston. Because the case against the tradition is so convincingly argued by James, *Jackson*, pp. 789–90, ft. 1, I have accepted it and in this particular instance rejected the version by Reid and Eaton. A son of another of the Jackson brothers, Samuel Jackson, later emigrated to Pennsylvania. Kendall, *Jackson*, p. 10.

6. Parton, *Jackson*, I, 49.

7. Mecklenberg County, Deed Book 7, North Carolina, pp. 21–22, North Carolina Department of Archives and History, Raleigh, North Carolina; copy JPP. Andrew Jackson, the future President, sold this land in 1793 after he had moved to Tennessee. Andrew Jackson's Power of Attorney to James Crawford, January 2, 1793, Deed Book B, p. 227, Lancaster County Records, Lancaster, South Carolina; copy JPP.

8. Mecklenberg County, Deed Book 7, pp. 21–22.

9. Jackson's early biographers do not agree about the time of the elder Andrew Jackson's death in 1767. Reid and Eaton, *Jackson*, p. 9, say it occurred shortly after young Andrew's birth; Kendall, *Jackson*, p. 11, puts it "about the time of his birth"; and Parton, *Jackson*, I, 50, claims it was "early in the spring of 1767," just before Andrew's birth. I have chosen to accept Parton's position because it makes sense in explaining the movements of Elizabeth Jackson at the time of Andrew's birth.

10. Parton, *Jackson*, I, 52. Parton is one of the few biographers who accepts this tradition despite Jackson's own repeated testimony; but he did research his biography by visiting the area in the 1850s. Quite extraordinary is the range of disagreement among the early biographers over where the Jacksons landed when they first arrived in America, the time of the father's death, and the location of Andrew's birthplace.

11. AJ to James H. Witherspoon, August 11, 1824, Jackson Papers, LC, reprinted in Jackson, *Correspondence*, III, 265.

12. The controversy over the birthplace can be traced in Elmer Don Herd, Jr., *Andrew Jackson, South Carolinian* (Lancaster, S.C., 1963) for the South Carolina case and Max F. Harris, *The Andrew Jackson Birthplace Problem* (Raleigh, N.C.) for

the North Carolina case. See also James, *Jackson,* pp. 791–797, ft. 17, and Bassett, *Jackson,* p. 6. Reid and Eaton, *Jackson,* p. 9, imply that Jackson was born in South Carolina but do not say so specifically. Kendall, *Jackson,* p. 11, names South Carolina as the birthplace—and it too was written under the General's supervision.

CHAPTER 2

1. Kendall, *Jackson,* p. 12; Reid and Eaton, *Jackson,* p. 10. Arda Walker, "The Educational Training and Views of Andrew Jackson," *ETHSP,* 1944, No. 16, p. 22; J. M. C. Montgomery to AJ, March 20, 1814, in Jackson, *Correspondence,* I, 482.

2. Reid and Eaton, *Jackson,* p. 10.

3. Robert V. Remini, *Andrew Jackson* (New York, 1966), p. 16; Tracy M. Kegley, "James White Stephenson: Teacher of Andrew Jackson," *THS* (March 1948), VII, 38–51.

4. Arda Walker, "The Religious Views of Andrew Jackson," *ETHSP,* 1945, No. 17, p. 64.

5. Parton, *Jackson,* III, 699.

6. AJ to Andrew Jackson Donelson, March 21, 1822, Jackson Papers, LC; Parton, *Jackson,* III, 699. In his letters Jackson frequently quoted Shakespeare: "the Ides of March," "something rotten in the state of Denmark," and "there is a tide in the affairs of men" were favorites (not that these are offered as evidence of outside reading).

7. AJ to Andrew Jackson Donelson, March 21, 1822, Jackson Papers, LC.

8. Parton, *Jackson,* I, 64.

9. Ibid.

10. Ibid., III, 695.

11. Ibid., I, 64.

12. Ibid., I, 65.

13. Psychohistory is a recent development within the historical profession and Andrew Jackson is an inviting case for analysis. This author has been tempted repeatedly to try his hand but lacks the clinical training and knowledge essential to such an undertaking. Historical psychoanalysis demands professional skill; analysis by amateurs, particularly long-distance analysis, is an abomination. One of the better efforts of this genre is Rogin, *Fathers and Children,* although I am frank to admit I disagree with many of the author's conclusions.

For his information on Jackson's early life, Parton often mentions "an old schoolmate" or "persons whose fathers were schoolmates of Andrew Jackson" as his source. In this instance, however, no source is given, perhaps because Parton did not think it important enough.

14. Parton, *Jackson,* I, 64.

15. Rogin, *Fathers and Children,* pp. 42ff.

16. Rogin suggests the similarity to Billy Budd, and I think it is a useful comparison. Ibid., p. 42.

17. See Milton W. Hamilton, "Augustus C. Buell, Fraudulent Historian," *The Pennsylvania Magazine of History and Biography* (1956), LXXX, 478–492. Hamilton concludes that there is "strong probability that what cannot be documented in Buell's *History of Andrew Jackson* from other sources is legendary, garbled or fiction," p. 491. Marquis James in his biography of Jackson is at times suspicious of Buell, but he cites him 32 times nonetheless.

18. Augustus C. Buell, *History of Andrew Jackson* (New York, 1904), II, 410–411.

19. *Taylor Trotwood Magazine* (May 1907), V, 142–143. This "advice" has been reprinted in several versions and a copy is in the Jackson Papers, TSL.

20. "I have nothing to give you but a mother's advice. Never tell a lie, nor take what is not your own, nor sue anybody for slander or assault and battery. *Always settle them cases yourself.*" W. H. Sparks, *The Memories of Fifty Years* (Philadelphia, 1882), pp. 147–148. See also James, *Jackson*, p. 30. For Jackson's own version of his mother's advice—"to indict no man for assault and battery or sue him for slander"—see his letter to Martin Van Buren, December 4, 1838, in Jackson, *Correspondence*, V, 573.

21. Reid and Eaton, *Jackson*, p. 434.

22. Parton, *Jackson*, I, 68.

23. Ibid. This conclusion is strongly contested by Rogin, *Fathers and Children*, p. 46, who argues that Jackson hated his mother for deserting him.

24. Jackson Papers, LC; reprinted in Jackson, *Correspondence*, I, 2. I am told that cockfighting is still common in some parts of the south, including Tennessee. Comparisons to bullfighting are often advanced as an explanation—if not a justification—for it.

25. Dr. Cyrus L. Hunter to James Parton in Parton, *Jackson*, I, 66.

26. This became such a popular cliché that it often appeared in political cartoons in the 1830s. See also Parton, *Jackson*, I, 66.

27. Buell, *Jackson*, I, 37–38. (See note 17 above on Buell's veracity.)

28. Kendall, *Jackson*, p. 14.

29. "Jackson's Reminiscences of His Experiences during the Revolution," extract from notes in Jackson's handwriting made for Amos Kendall in March 1843 for use in Kendall's biography, Jackson Papers, LC.

30. Reid and Eaton, *Jackson*, p. 11.

31. Ibid., p. 10.

32. Kendall, *Jackson*, p. 25.

33. Ibid.

34. Remini, *Jackson*, p. 18; Parton, *Jackson*, I, 72.

35. Parton, *Jackson*, I, 73–74.

36. Ibid., p. 75.

37. Kendall says Elizabeth and sons passed through Charlotte on their way to Mr. M'Culloch's in Guilford Court, North Carolina, in September 1780 and returned in February 1781. Kendall, *Jackson*, pp. 31, 40.

38. Ibid., p. 45.

39. This is the usual story, and Jackson himself remembered the trumpet call. But Jackson believed that the trumpet charge merely hastened the retreat that had begun when two groups of Tories approached the house from different ends of a corn crib and each group, thinking the other to be the enemy, fired at and then fled from the other. "Memorandum and Drawing of the Tory attack on Captain Lands's House," Jackson Papers, LC. The Memorandum is in the handwriting of James A. McLaughlin, nephew of Amos Kendall, who came to the Hermitage in December 1842 to obtain material for the biography of Jackson that Kendall was writing. See also AJ to Kendall, December 12 and 26, 1842, and March 20, 1843, Jackson Papers, LC.

40. These are not, of course, Jackson's actual words but an approximation devised by Parton, *Jackson*, I, 89. The same sense is found in Reid and Eaton, *Jackson*, p. 16.

41. "The sword reached my head, & has left a mark there as durable as the scull, as well as on the fingers." AJ to Kendall, January 9, 1844, Jackson Papers, LC.

42. Reid and Eaton, *Jackson*, p. 12.

43. Kendall, *Jackson*, p. 51.

44. AJ to Sam Houston, July 1824, Jackson Papers, LC.

45. James McLaughlin to Amos Kendall, January 2, 1843, Jackson Papers, LC. This letter contains Jackson's account of his imprisonment and the events which transpired following his exchange.

46. Jackson later remembered that during one threatened attack by the revitalized American army the misery worsened. Because of the possibility of cannonading, the prisoners were taken from the upper rooms and confined in the cells underground. During the day they were permitted to come out of this dungeon and breathe fresh air in the open area in the rear of the prison. AJ to Sam Houston, July 1824, Jackson Papers, LC.

47. AJ to Houston, July 1824, Jackson Papers, LC.

48. "Jackson's Memorandum on his Imprisonment at Camden, April, 1781," Jackson Papers, LC; reprinted in Jackson, *Correspondence*, I, 3.

49. Ibid.

50. Jackson himself does not mention that he came down with smallpox until he was returning home with his mother and brother. But all the earliest biographers, including Reid and Eaton, Kendall, and Parton, state that he contracted the disease in prison even though he suffered the worst of it on his homeward journey.

51. McLaughlin to Kendall, January 2, 1843, Jackson Papers, LC.

52. Kendall, *Jackson*, p. 58.

53. James H. Witherspoon to AJ, April 16, 1825, in Jackson, *Correspondence*, III, 282–283.

54. McLaughlin to Kendall, January 2, 1843, Jackson Papers, LC.

55. Rogin, *Fathers and Children*, p. 46. Rogin makes other conclusions based on this desertion. His assumptions are based on Jackson's actions through life.

56. Parton, *Jackson*, I, 68.

57. AJ to [Willie Blount], January 4, 1813, Jackson Papers, LC.

CHAPTER 3

1. When Elizabeth went to Charleston she left Andrew at the house of Thomas Crawford. Kendall, *Jackson*, pp. 66–67.

2. McLaughlin to Kendall, January 2, 1843, Jackson Papers, LC.

3. Ibid.

4. Ibid.

5. McLaughlin to Kendall, February 14, 1843, Jackson Papers, LC; Kendall, *Jackson*, p. 68; Parton, *Jackson*, I, 98.

6. Reid and Eaton, *Jackson*, p. 14; Arda Walker, "The Educational Training and Views of Andrew Jackson," *ETHSP*, 1944, No. 16, p. 22.

7. Parton, *Jackson*, I, 105.

8. Ibid., pp. 104–105.

9. Ibid., p. 106.

10. Ibid., p. 107.

11. Ibid., p. 109.

12. Apparently Jackson always liked good liquor; he later owned and operated a still. Today, in his study in the Hermitage, there is a handsome carrying case for liquor, which he used when he traveled. Its capacity is considerable. However, Jackson apparently went on the wagon from time to time. In 1806 he and John Verrell pledged not to drink (penalty: a suit of clothes). Coffee Papers, THS; copy JPP.

13. Considering the disease and the length of his illness, it seems miraculous that Jackson was not badly scarred by smallpox; all contemporary accounts and later portraits show him with a clear complexion. Parton, *Jackson*, I, 105.

14. Ibid., p. 111.

15. The source is William B. Lewis, a long and close friend in Tennessee. Parton, *Jackson*, I, 113.

16. Ibid., p. 112.

17. S. G. Heiskell, *Andrew Jackson and Early Tennessee History* (Nashville, 1918), p. 294. For notices of Jackson's license to practice law, see note 19 below. Recognizance Bond, October 28, 1787, private collection, copy JPP.

18. Bassett, *Jackson*, p. 13.

19. William Cupples to AJ, August 19, 1795, in Jackson, *Correspondence*, I, 16, and note 2. In North Carolina, Jackson was admitted to practice law before the Anson County Court in October 1787; the Surry County Court on November 12, 1787; the Guilford County Court on November 20, 1787; the Rockingham County Court on November 26, 1787; and the Randolph County Court on December 11, 1787. County Court Minute Books, North Carolina; copies JPP. In Tennessee, Jackson was licensed to practice law in Washington County on May 12, 1788; Greene County, August 5, 1788; Davidson County, November 3, 1788; and Sumner County, January 12, 1789. County Court Minute Books, Tennessee; copies JPP. On December 15, 1790, Jackson was licensed to practice in the Territory South of the River Ohio, and on July 5, 1796, he received a license to practice in the state of Tennessee from Governor John Sevier.

20. Cupples to AJ, August 19, 1795, in Jackson, *Correspondence*, I, 16.

21. Reid and Eaton, *Jackson*, p. 15.

22. Parton identifies the Searcy who accompanied McNairy and Jackson as "Thomas" Searcy, but he is mistaken. The Blount *Journal* clearly identifies "Bennett" Searcy as the clerk of the court. I am grateful to Mrs. Harriet C. Owsley, associate editor of the Jackson Papers Project, for pointing out this error to me.

23. John Allison, "The Mero District," *AHM* (April 1896), I, 115–127; Ben Allen and Dennis T. Lawson, "The Wataugans and the 'Dangerous Example,'" *THQ* (Summer 1967), XXVI, 137–141.

24. Robert L. Ganyard, "Threat from the West: North Carolina and the Cherokees," *North Carolina Historical Review* (January 1968), XLV, 47–66; Jesse C. Burt, Jr., *Nashville: Its Life and Times* (Nashville, 1959), pp. 5ff.

25. G. H. Alden, "The State of Franklin," *AHR* (January 1903), VIII, 271–289; Carl Driver, *John Sevier: Pioneer of the Old Southwest* (Chapel Hill, 1932), pp. 28ff. Of particular value for early Tennessee history is Abernethy, *Frontier*, pp. 45ff.

26. Abernethy, *Frontier*, p. 96.

27. Reid and Eaton, *Jackson*, p. 19.

CHAPTER 4

1. Jackson took up residence in Jonesborough in the house of William Cables. Kendall, *Jackson*, p. 82.

2. John Allison, *Dropped Stitches in Tennessee History* (Nashville, 1897), p. 10.

3. Abernethy, *Frontier*, p. 124.

4. A bill of sale for November 17, 1788, Washington County Court Minutes, 1788–1793; copy JPP.

5. John Haywood, *The Civil and Political History of the State of Tennessee* (Nashville, 1915), p. 194; Allison, *Dropped Stitches*, pp. 102–107.

6. AJ to Avery, August 12, 1788; copy JPP. This is the earliest known Jackson letter.

7. Parton, *Jackson*, I, 122–123.

8. A. W. Putnam, *History of Middle Tennessee* (Nashville, 1859), pp. 69–79.

9. "Statement of John Overton written to Robert Coleman Foster, May 8, 1827," *United States Telegraph*, June 22, 1827.

10. Parton, *Jackson,* I, 133.

11. Bassett, *Jackson,* p. 18, thinks John Overton had a hand in it.

12. Ibid.

13. "Statement of John Overton," *United States Telegraph,* June 22, 1827; Kendall, *Jackson,* p. 91. Kendall described Robards as "dissolute in habits, morose in temper and jealous in disposition," p. 91.

14. Parton, *Jackson,* I, 168.

15. Ibid.

16. Ibid., p. 169.

17. "Statement of John Overton," *United States Telegraph,* June 22, 1827.

18. Ibid.

19. John Downing to John H. Eaton, December 20, 1826, Dickinson Papers, THS. See also James Breckenridge to ———, April 8, 1827, and Humphrey Marshall to Henry Banker, June 1, 1827, Dickinson Papers, THS.

20. Jackson, *Correspondence,* I, 5.

21. Abernethy, *Frontier,* p. 126. See also Jackson's Memorial to the North Carolina Assembly, November 13, 1789, in Jackson, *Correspondence,* I, 6.

22. The earliest surviving legal document that is signed by Jackson and appears to be in his handwriting is the case *State of North Carolina* v. *Thomas Hendrix,* November term 1788, Miscellaneous Collection, THS.

23. Kendall, *Jackson,* p. 90.

24. Jackson Papers Project has made a thorough search of court records in North Carolina and Tennessee; the judgments given here are based on the Project's findings.

25. McLaughlin to Kendall, March 13, 1843, Jackson Papers, LC.

26. J. G. M. Ramsey, *Annals of Tennessee to the End of the Eighteenth Century* (Charleston, 1953), p. 484; McLaughlin to Kendall, March 13, 1843, Jackson Papers, LC.

27. Putnam, *History of Middle Tennessee,* p. 318.

28. Ibid.

29. Kendall, *Jackson,* pp. 85–86.

30. McLaughlin to Kendall, March 13, 1843, Jackson Papers, LC.

31. Putnam, *History of Middle Tennessee,* p. 318.

32. Ibid.

33. See the letters of General James Robertson to Franco Cruzat, November 4, 1784, and to Thomas Pearson, May 23, 1787, in *AHM* (January 1896), I, 81.

34. Arthur P. Whitaker, *The Spanish American Frontier* (Gloucester, 1962), p. 92. Whitaker makes clear that it was the frontiersmen who initiated the intrigue, deceived the Spanish government and their own, and were "the sole gainers by the intrigue."

35. Robertson to Alexander McGillivray, August 3, 1788, in *AHM* (January 1896), I, 81.

36. Arthur P. Whitaker, "The Muscle Shoals Speculation, 1783–1789," *MVHR* (December 1926), XIII, 365–386; D. C. and Roberta Corbitt, "Papers from the Spanish Archives Relating to Tennessee and the Old Southwest, 1783–1800," ETHSP, No. 18, p. 144; Thomas M. Green, *The Spanish Conspiracy* (Cincinnati, 1891), p. 131.

37. Whitaker, *The Spanish American Frontier,* pp. 102–103.

38. J. W. Caughey, *McGillivray of the Creeks* (Norman, 1938), pp. 178–191.

39. Robertson to McGillivray, 1788, in *AHM* (January 1896), I, 82–84.

40. AJ to Smith, February 13, 1789, in Parton, *Jackson,* I, 141–142. A slightly altered version appears in Jackson, *Correspondence,* I, 7. The original was in the Tennessee Historical Society when John Spencer Bassett made his copy but is now apparently lost.

41. Whitaker, *Spanish American Frontier,* pp. 112–113.

42. Rogin, *Fathers and Children,* pp. 113ff, finds Jackson's relations with the Indians to involve deep psychological problems.

43. James, *Jackson,* p. 57.

44. Smith to Miró, March 11, 1789, Cuba, leg. 196, AGI. See also Miró to Smith, April 20, 1789, and Fagot to Smith, May 4 and 18, 1789, Draper Papers, WSH.

45. Whitaker, *Spanish American Frontier,* p. 113.

46. Blount to John Gray Blount, June 26, 1790, in *Blount Papers,* II, 67.

47. Blount to John Steele, quoted in Alice B. Keith, "The North Carolina Blount Brothers in Business and Politics, 1783–1812," unpublished doctoral dissertation, University of North Carolina, Chapel Hill, 1940, p. 388.

48. Blount to John Gray Blount, June 26, 1790, in *Blount Papers,* II, 68.

49. Blount to John Gray Blount, October 20, 1790, ibid., pp. 126–128.

50. Ibid., p. 127.

51. Keith, "The North Carolina Blount Brothers," p. 392.

52. Blount to Robertson, October 17, 1792, in *AHM* (January 1897), II, 82.

53. Blount to Knox, August 1, 1793, in Carter, *Territorial Papers,* IV, 291.

54. Ibid., p. 299.

55. The appointment notification and license from Blount to practice law are in the Jackson Papers, LC.

56. Blount to Robertson, January 2, 1792, in *AHM* (July 1896), III, 280. See also Blount to Robertson, January 5, 1792, ibid., p. 282, and Blount to Robertson, January 18, 1794, in *AHM* (July 1898), III, 280.

57. Putnam, *History of Middle Tennessee,* p. 351.

58. Blount to Robertson, October 28, 1792, in *AHM* (January 1897), II, 84.

59. Ibid. This was another reason why Jackson decided to stay in Nashville; he was making extraordinary progress with his career, and support from the political powers in the territory was added incentive to remain where he was.

60. AJ to John McKee, January 30, 1793, in Jackson, *Correspondence,* I, 12.

61. See, for example, Thomas Hutchings to AJ, October 2, 1793, Jackson Papers, LC. Hutchings was Jackson's brother-in-law. For a fuller discussion of Jackson's speculations in land see Chapter 7.

62. Miró to Smith, April 20, 1789, Draper Papers, WSH.

63. Despite evidence that Jackson owned property in the Bayou Pierre area, Mississippi, a search of the archives in Madrid, Seville, Washington, Jackson, and Natchez showed no deed of ownership from the Spanish. The Spanish were very careful about keeping records; if Jackson purchased land from the Natchez authorities, there would have been a record. Marquis James assumed that Jackson built a log cabin and a racetrack at Bayou Pierre on the basis of the evidence in W. H. Sparks, *Memories of Fifty Years* (1870), p. 151, but this book suffers many inaccuracies. Thomas Reber, *Proud Old Natchez,* p. 18, claims Jackson had an establishment at Bayou Pierre. It is possible that the property really belonged to Rachel or was acquired from another American without the knowledge of the Spanish, but again no documentary evidence has been found to substantiate these conjectures. If any legal transaction occurred, there should be a surviving record. There is none.

64. See the several account statements in the Jackson Papers, LC, especially those of Melling Woolley of various dates in March, April, and July 1790 and the letter of James Cole Mountflorence to AJ, July 23, 1790, Miscellaneous Collection, THS.

65. George Cochran to AJ, October 21, 1791, Jackson Papers, LC.

66. Ibid. See also Cochran to AJ, April 15, 1797, November 18, 1798, and March 26, 1801, Jackson Papers, LC. It is Harriet Owsley's theory that Cochran was in love with Rachel.

67. "List of Negroes for Jackson" [November 8, 1790], in Jackson, *Correspondence*, I, 9. See Chapter 9 for more detail on the number of slaves held by Jackson during his lifetime.

68. See various bills of sale, Jackson Papers, LC; other bills of sale are located at the Ladies Hermitage Association and the Tennessee State Library; copies JPP.

CHAPTER 5

1. *United States Telegraph*, June 22, 1827.

2. Statement of Thomas Crutcher to Robert C. Foster [May 4, 1827], Dickinson Papers, THS; copy JPP; published in *United States Telegraph*, March 28, 1828.

3. James, *Jackson*, pp. 61, 63.

4. James cites as his source for Jackson's "foray into Kentucky" to rescue Rachel the statement of John Overton in the *United States Telegraph*, June 22, 1827, and then goes on to admit that nothing in that statement remotely suggests a Kentucky trip by Jackson. See James, *Jackson*, p. 803, ft. 6. Nor can it be inferred from the record of the Mercer County Court, which James did not see. James, *Jackson*, pp. 61, 802–803, ft. 45. See Divorce Decree, Mercer County, Kentucky Court of Quarter Sessions Book, 1792–1796, copy JPP. I have been guilty of the same mistake myself; see my *Andrew Jackson*, p. 31. None of the many depositions taken by the Nashville Central Committee in 1827 of the circumstances surrounding the divorce mention a trip by Jackson to Kentucky to rescue Rachel or a reconciliation after Robards left Tennessee. See the Dickinson Papers, THS.

5. *United States Telegraph*, June 22, 1827.

6. Ibid.

7. Ibid.

8. Overton in his statement refers to Stark as simply "Col. Stark." Marquis James calls him "John" Stark but confuses him with someone else and gives no evidence for designating him "John." James, *Jackson*, pp. 64–65. A search of the Spanish archives reveals a "Don Roberto Stark" as an immigrant to Natchez who in 1792 had a wife, four children, one mulatto, seven female and six male negroes, fourteen horses, fourteen cows, forty hogs, 3,000 lbs of tobacco, 300 lbs of cotton, and 300 minots of corn. 1792 Census, Cuba, leg. 2353, AGI. No other "Stark" migrated to Natchez in the 1790s. Since Stark was a colonel the Spanish would automatically refer to him as "Don." I am grateful to G. Douglas Inglis, a graduate student engaged in a demographic study of the Natchez area at the end of the eighteenth century, for this information.

9. *United States Telegraph*, June 22, 1827.

10. John Downing to John H. Eaton, December 20, 1826, Dickinson Papers, THS, is very specific on this point.

11. Previous to his departure for Natchez, Jackson committed all his law business to Overton, assuring him of his intention to return and resume his practice once he delivered his charges safely to their friends in Natchez. Ibid. But Jackson is listed in court appearances in the January, April, and May 1791 terms of the various county courts in Tennessee. Copies of the court records, JPP.

12. There is a tradition that instead of returning to Nashville via the Mississippi and Cumberland rivers (his route going down), Jackson came back via the extremely dangerous Natchez Trace, an overland route swarming with cutthroats and hostile Indians.

13. William W. Hening, *The* [Virginia] *Statutes at Large . . .* (Philadelphia,

1823), XIII, 227. For the information on the committee membership I am grateful to Richard Shenkman of the staff of the Jackson Papers Project.

14. *United States Telegraph,* June 22, 1827.

15. The Jackson Papers Project conducted an extensive search for any record or mention of the marriage in Natchez and Jackson, Mississippi, and Baton Rouge and New Orleans, Louisiana, without success. The Catholic Diocese of Baton Rouge did a thorough inventory of all records held in the parishes founded prior to 1870 and published a *Guide to Archival Materials.* There is no record of a marriage between Jackson and Rachel. Various archives in Georgia and Tennessee as well as archives in Seville, Madrid, and Simancas, Spain, were also searched without success.

16. *United States Telegraph,* June 22, 1827. Italics mine. Overton clearly stated that he did not know this himself. He was made to understand that a marriage took place.

17. Jack D. L. Holmes, *Gayoso, the Life of a Spanish Governor in the Mississippi Valley, 1789–1799* (Baton Rouge, 1965), pp. 77–83; William H. McCardle, *A History of Mississippi* (Hattiesburg, 1973), I, 170–171.

18. James, *Jackson,* pp. 67 and 804, ft. 21.

19. No legal evidence exists that either Rachel or Andrew owned property in the Spanish-held area. However, in a letter to Jackson, George Cochran in Natchez, April 15, 1797, speaks of "your friendly retreat at Bayou Pierre" and Rachel's "quondam neighbours on Bayou Pierre." Jackson Papers, LC. Eron Rowland, "Marking the Natchez Trace," *Publications of the Mississippi Historial Society* (1910), XI, 355–356, claims that Rachel and Andrew owned a double log house with a double hall in the Natchez district. He offers no evidence for this assertion.

20. Divorce Decree, Mercer County, Kentucky Court of Quarter Sessions Book, 1792–1796, copy JPP. In eight issues of the Kentucky *Gazette,* February 4, 11, 18, 25, and March 3, 10, 17, 24, 1792, and in accordance with instructions of the Virginia legislature, Rachel was formally summoned to appear before the court to answer the charge of adultery. Copy JPP. It is inconceivable that Jackson did not know about this summons. It was ignored.

21. Robards to Hays, January 9, 1791, Jackson Papers, LC.

22. Robards to John Coffee, 1803, Coffee Papers, TSL.

23. *United States Telegraph,* June 22, 1827.

24. Ibid.

25. Marriage License, Miscellaneous Jackson Papers, HUL. For a good sketch of Hays see Dan M. Robison, "Robert Hays, Unsung Pioneer of the Cumberland Country," *THQ* (Fall 1967), XXVI, 263–278.

26. Oath of Loyalty before Carlos de Grand-Pre and Antonio Solar, January 12, 1790, Cuba, leg. 2362, AGI. Once again I wish to acknowledge the assistance of G. Douglas Inglis in this research.

27. Cochran to AJ, November 3, 1790, Jackson Papers, LC.

28. Jackson Papers, LC.

29. Davidson County, Wills and Inventories, I, 166–167, 176, 196–201, copy JPP.

30. Cincinnati *Gazette,* April 24, 1827; Davidson County Court of Pleas and Quarter Sessions Records, 1783–1790, pp. 211, 214, 217ff.; Davidson County Court of Pleas and Quarter Sessions Minute Book A, pp. 366, 368–374, copy JPP.

31. This information was made available to me by Dr. Sam B. Smith, editor of the Jackson Papers Project, who has studied Jackson's legal record in Tennessee. I am grateful to him for his invaluable assistance. See also Parton, *Jackson,* Jackson, I, 146.

32. Lewis to Cadwalader, April 1, June 12, 1827, Ford Collection, NYPL.

33. Most of the correspondence between Jackson and Rachel was destroyed in a fire at the Hermitage in 1834. Jackson to Harriet Butler, June 24, 1837, C. Norton Owen Collection, Glencoe, Illinois. (This collection was dispersed shortly before Owen's death and the Jackson letters were sold to an autograph dealer.)

34. Harriette Arnow, *Flowering of the Cumberland* (New York, 1963), p. 14.

35. Parton, *Jackson*, I, 160.

36. Arnow, *Flowering*, p. 49. Any number of letters by Jackson to Rachel show how dependent he was on her for the proper operation of his farm. See especially his letters of 1813, Miscellaneous Jackson Papers, HUL.

37. AJ to Hutchings, April 18, 1833, in Jackson, *Correspondence*, V, 60.

CHAPTER 6

1. Blount to Robertson, February 13, 1793, in *AHM* (July 1897), II, 278.

2. AJ to John McKee, January 30, 1793, in Jackson, *Correspondence*, I, 12. See also Jackson's Memorandum on Indian Depredations, May–November 1793, Jackson Papers, LC.

3. AJ to John McKee, May 16, 1794, in Jackson, *Correspondence*, I, 12–13.

4. This anti-Spanish sentiment is also registered in a circular letter to Jackson from the Kentucky Democratic Society, December 31, 1793, Jackson Papers, LC. See also Arthur P. Whitaker, "Spanish Intrigue in the Old Southwest," *MVHR* (September 1925) XII, 162, 172.

5. Robertson to Blount, October 1, 1794, in *AHM* (October 1898), III, 361. See also his resignation, October 23, 1794, ibid., p. 363.

6. Blount to Robertson, December 4, 1794, ibid., p. 375.

7. Keith, "The North Carolina Blount Brothers," p. 412.

8. Blount to John Gray Blount, October 26, 1794, in *Blount Papers*, II, 449.

9. Blount to Robertson, November 22, 1794, quoted in Keith, "The North Carolina Blount Brothers," p. 412. See also Blount to John Gray Blount, July 1, 1794, in *Blount Papers*, II, 413.

10. Blount to John Gray Blount, March 28, 1795, ibid., p. 523.

11. A. V. Goodpasture, "William Blount and the Old Southwest Territory," *AHM* (1903), VIII, 210.

12. Ramsey, *Annals of Tennessee*, p. 648.

13. Ibid.

14. Ibid.

15. Anderson to AJ, December 3, 1795, Jackson Papers, LC.

16. Blount to Robertson, October 3, 1795, in *AHM* (January 1899), IV, 74.

17. A search of Blount materials and letters has turned up no direct evidence of his assistance in Jackson's candidacy. In fact there is very little documentary evidence at all about the election of delegates or the proceedings of the convention.

18. See *Journal of the Proceedings of the Tennessee Constitutional Convention . . .* (Knoxville, 1852).

19. Ramsey, *Annals of Tennessee*, p. 653.

20. *Journal . . . of the Tennessee Constitutional Convention, passim;* AJ to James Bronaugh, August 27, 1822, quoted in Herbert J. Doherty, Jr., "Andrew Jackson's Cronies in Florida's Territorial Politics," *Florida Historical Quarterly* (July 1955), XXXIV, 23.

21. John D. Barnhart, "The Tennessee Constitution of 1796," *JSH* (November 1943), IX, 532–548.

22. Ibid., p. 654.

23. Mark Mitchell to AJ, [October?] 12th 1795, Hurja Collection, THS. Mitchell wrote: "Your Sise is against you I never knew a man of a Hundred and

forty in Congress if you would get you a pre [pair] of Cloth Over hols, and Ware your Big Coat you might pass you have loud Speach, I dont Know how the Districts may be Divided if this Country is taken in With Comberland I can do Somthing and Will do all I can for you if you Offer and I hop you Will. how the Matter Stands betwixt us I will be Damd if I know when I see you We can Settle With Out fighting. My Boy gros Fineley Mrs. Mitchell joins me in Comps. to you tell Mrs. Jackson Howday and bleave Me to be your friend."

24. AJ to Macon, October 4, 1795, in Jackson, *Correspondence*, I, 17–18.

25. Jackson reported to Blount that the "people Generally approve of the Constitution; and I shall only add that the Conduct of the members during Convention has reached this County; the Conduct of Some have verry much detracted from their popularity." AJ to William Blount, February 29, 1796, Blount Collection, LC.

26. Charlotte Williams, "Congressional Action on the Admission of Tennessee into the Union," *THQ* (December 1943), II, 291–315.

27. Ibid.; Samuel C. Williams, "The Admission of Tennessee into the Union," *THQ* (December 1945), IV, 291–319.

28. *Annals of Congress*, 4th Congress, 1st Session, pp. 1311–1315, 1474.

29. Ramsey, *Annals of Tennessee*, p. 674.

30. Blount and Cocke to Sevier, June 2, 1796, quoted in Keith, "The North Carolina Blount Brothers," p. 426.

31. Abernethy, *Frontier*, pp. 165–166. See also Blount's very friendly letter to AJ, April 24, 1796, Jackson Papers, LC.

32. Overton to AJ, March 10, 1795, Jackson Papers, LC.

33. James Parton, an early Jackson biographer, thinks he was chosen to run for the House of Representatives because of his warm espousal of the claims of the state and the fact that he was expected to support those claims in Congress.

34. Anderson to AJ, August 4, 1796, Jackson Papers, LC.

35. From Mero and Hamilton counties Jackson received 795 votes; from Washington County he received 318 votes and James Rody 12 votes. "Voting Certifications," Election Returns of U. S. Congressmen, TSL; copy JPP.

36. Overton to AJ, March 10, 1796, Jackson Papers, LC. See also James Grant to AJ, November 16, 1795, Jackson Papers, LC.

37. Remonstrance to the Assembly of Tennessee, April 1796, Jackson Papers, LC.

CHAPTER 7

1. For much of the information dealing with Jackson's land speculations I am indebted to Dr. Sam B. Smith, editor of the Jackson Papers Project, who provided me with a typescript copy (prior to publication) of his article, "Andrew Jackson and Land Speculation." Pages 1–3 give the background of the western land grab.

2. Ibid., p. 6.

3. Articles of Agreement, May 12, 1794, Jackson Papers, LC.

4. Smith, "Andrew Jackson and Land Speculation," pp. 6–7.

5. This suggestion has been advanced by Richard Lackey, who did a master's essay on land acquisition in Mississippi. I am indebted for this information to Dr. John D. W. Guice of the University of Southern Mississippi, who was Lackey's mentor.

6. The Jackson Papers Project instituted a thorough search for deeds, land warrants, transfers, and the like in several states, including Tennessee, Mississippi, Georgia, and Alabama, as well as Washington, D. C., involving Jackson's land operations. A considerable amount of information was obtained, but there are still many gaps in the record.

7. "Memorandum for A Jackson in Phila" from John Overton, March 8, 1795, Jackson Papers, LC.

8. AJ to Overton, June 9, 1795, Claybrooke and Overton Papers, THS.

9. "Memorandum for A Jackson" from Overton, March 8, 1795; Power of Attorney Joel Rice to AJ, April 5, 1795; AJ to Overton, January 9, 1795, Jackson Papers, LC.

10. Account book of the partnership is located at the Hermitage, LHA.

11. The Allison Transaction, no date, Jackson Papers, LC.

12. Ibid.

13. AJ to Overton, June 9, 1795, Claybrooke and Overton Papers, THS.

14. Ibid.

15. Meeker, Cochran and Co. to AJ, August 22, 1795, Jackson Papers, LC. A slightly different version with a different date (August 11) is given in Jackson, *Correspondence*, I, 16.

16. John B. Evans and Co. to AJ, January 14, 1796, Jackson Papers, LC.

17. See Jackson's settlement of accounts with Samuel Donelson in AJ to Donelson, no date but filed under 1796, Jackson Papers, LC. He probably sold the store in September or October 1795.

18. Blount to Stuart, April 5, 6, 1796; Stuart to Blount, April 5, 1796; Stuart to AJ, April 17, 1796; Jackson Memorandum, Allison Affair, July 15, 1801; Jackson Papers, LC. There were also debts due to John Overton, William Purnell, George Neville, and Daniel Smith. See AJ to James Jackson, August 25, 1819; Stockley Donelson to AJ, June 16, 1796; AJ to George Neville, March 17, 1796, Jackson Papers, LC.

19. Davidson County Wills and Inventories, II, 40. Frances Clinton, "John Overton as Andrew Jackson's Friend," *THQ* (March 1952), XI, 23–40. Overton's embarrassment on account of the Allison business was more extensive than Jackson's. See Overton to James King, May 23, 1797, and Overton to Samuel Meeker, June 6, 1797, Claybrooke and Overton Papers, THS. Smith, "Andrew Jackson and Land Speculation," p. 11.

20. Smith, "Andrew Jackson and Land Speculation," p. 11.

21. John Shannon to AJ, March 10, 1796, Jackson Papers, LC. John Shannon had purchased the land from Robards. Deed, Davidson County, Tennessee, Deed Book C, p. 495.

22. Davidson County and Knox County Deed Books C and D, pp. 492–496, 454–456 and North Carolina Land Grant Book, vol. 88, p. 328; copies JPP.

23. The Allison Transaction, no date, Jackson Papers, LC.

24. AJ to James Jackson, August 25, 1819, in Jackson, *Correspondence*, II, 427.

25. Allison to AJ, June 8, 11, 1796; Blount to AJ, June 11, 1796, Jackson Papers, LC.

26. See Blount's note, June 11, 1796, Jackson Papers, LC.

27. Allison to AJ, May 13, 1795 in *Jackson* v. *Andrew Erwin et al.*, Case Record; copy JPP.

28. Goods transported from Philadelphia to Tennessee were first shipped by wagon to Pittsburgh, then reloaded on keelboats and floated down the Ohio River to Louisville. There they were loaded on wagons for transportation around the falls and then reloaded on boats and floated the rest of the way by river. To traverse the route in 1795 took Jackson five weeks: three weeks from Philadelphia to Pittsburgh, one week to Louisville, and one week to Nashville.

29. Donelson to AJ, June 16, 1796, Jackson Papers, LC.

30. AJ to Rachel Jackson, May 9, 1796, Provine Papers, TSL. This is a copy; the original could not be found. Clearly Jackson's punctuation, spelling, and sentence structure have been edited here.

31. Parton, *Jackson*, I, 196.

32. See Jackson's account with Watson, December 3, 1796, Jackson Papers, LC.

33. Parton, *Jackson*, I, 196.

34. James Thomas Flexner, *George Washington: Anguish and Farewell, 1793–1799* (Boston, 1972), IV, 292–307.

35. *Annals of Congress*, 4th Congress, 2nd Session, p. 1668.

36. AJ to Hays, December 16, 1796, Jackson Papers, LC.

37. AJ to John Donelson, January 18, 1797, in the *Kentucky Yeoman*, November 5, 1847; copy JPP.

38. AJ to Overton, February 24, 1797, Hurja Collection, THS.

39. See letters of Tazewell, Macon, and Stevens Mason of Virginia (for example), Jackson Papers, LC.

40. AJ to Hays, January 8, 1797, in Jackson, *Correspondence*, I, 24.

41. *Annals of Congress*, 4th Congress, 2nd Session, p. 1737.

42. See, for example, AJ to Sevier, January 18, 1797, Jackson Papers, LC. Sevier prodded Jackson about this claim at the beginning of the session. Sevier to AJ, December 12, 1796, Sevier Papers, TSL.

43. *Annals of Congress*, 4th Congress, 2nd Session, p. 1738.

44. Ibid.

45. Ibid.

46. Ibid., p. 1739

47. Kasper Mansker was one of the earliest settlers of the Cumberland Valley. The Chickasaw Indians lived peaceably with whites but were attacked by Creeks. In 1795 Mansker led a group of volunteers and drove off the Creeks. Jackson's petition to reimburse the Chickasaws ultimately failed. Walter T. Durham, "Kasper Mansker: Cumberland Frontiersman," *THQ* (Summer 1971), XXX, 169–170.

48. *Annals of Congress*, 4th Congress, 2nd Session, p. 1741.

49. AJ to Robert Hays, January 8, 1797, in Jackson, *Correspondence*, I, 24.

50. *Annals of Congress*, 4th Congress, 2nd Session, p. 1742.

51. Ibid.

52. Ibid.

53. Ibid.

54. Ibid., p. 2155.

55. "The payment of Seviers expedition," William C. C. Claiborne wrote to Jackson, July 20, 1797, "has heightened the esteem of the people for the General Government and secured to yourself a permanent interest." Jackson Papers, LC.

56. See, for example, AJ to Daniel Smith, December 18, 1796, Jackson Papers, LC.

57. AJ to Sevier, January 18, 1797, Jackson Papers, LC.

58. AJ to Hays, January 8, 1797, in Jackson, *Correspondence*, I, 27.

59. AJ to Sevier, January 18, 1797, Jackson Papers, LC.

60. Ibid.

61. Ibid.

62. *Annals of Congress*, 4th Congress, 2nd Session, pp. 1705ff.

63. Ibid., pp. 1942–1943.

64. Ibid., p. 1986.

65. John Caffery to AJ, April 1797, Jackson Papers, LC.

66. A. V. Goodpasture, "Genesis of the Jackson-Sevier Feud," *AHM* (January 1900), V, 117.

67. Sevier to AJ, May 8, 1797, and AJ to Sevier, May 8, 1797, in Jackson, *Correspondence*, I, 31–33.

68. Such is implied in John Caffery to AJ, April 1797, Jackson Papers, LC.

69. Sevier to AJ, May 11, 1797, in Jackson, *Correspondence*, I, 36.

70. AJ to Sevier, May 10, 1797, ibid., I, 35.

71. McNairy to AJ, May 4, 1797, and AJ to McNairy, May 9, 1797, ibid., I, 30–31, 34.

72. Ramsey, *Annals of Tennessee*, p. 677.

73. Blount to Robertson, October 28, 1792, in *AHM* (July 1897), II, 84.

74. William H. Masterson, *William Blount* (Baton Rouge, 1954), p. 311.

75. AJ to Robert Hays, January 8, 1797, in Jackson, *Correspondence*, I, 24. Benjamin Hawkins, the Indian agent to the Creek Nation, told Zachariah Cox that "the french are now in, and are about to take possession of the floridas." Cox to AJ, April 27, 1797, Jackson Papers, LC.

76. Blount's plans, like Burr's, were not exactly clear; at one point he seemed to be planning the removal of the Indians west of the Mississippi. Keith, "The North Carolina Blount Brothers," p. 436. On the Blount Conspiracy see especially Thomas P. Abernethy, *The South in the New Nation, 1789–1819* (Baton Rouge, 1961), pp. 169–191.

77. *ASPFA*, II, 72–74. *Annals of Congress*, 5th Congress, 1st Session, I, 72–74.

78. Sevier wrote Jackson, November 26, 1797, "A great number of people are determined to discend the Mississippi, and if the measures are pursued, that now so impertinently Stare us in the face; I fear one half of our Citizens will flock over into another government [Spain]; indeed, they are now doing it daily." Sevier Papers, TSL. Archibald Henderson, "The Spanish Conspiracy in Tennessee," *THM* (1917), No. 3, pp. 229–249.

79. Put another way, Blount's mistake was to conspire in favor of Great Britain, Burr's to conspire for himself. Jackson's success was shaped because he was more concerned about the expansion of the United States.

80. *Annals of Congress*, 5th Congress, 1st Session, I, 947.

81. Arthur P. Whitaker, *The Mississippi Question, 1795–1803* (Gloucester, 1962), pp. 104–115, gives an excellent account of the Blount conspiracy. So does Masterson, *Blount.*

82. Quoted in Masterson, *Blount*, pp. 320–321.

83. See, for example, AJ to Willie Blount, February 21, 1798, and December 15, 1797, particularly the "P.S." Blount Collection, LC.

84. Blount to John Gray Blount, November 7, 1797, in *Blount Papers*, III, 175.

85. The background of the quasi war with France is much more complicated and involves additional events such as the XYZ Affair. For a detailed discussion see Alexander DeConde, *The Quasi War* (New York, 1966).

86. Blount to John Gray Blount, November 7, 1797, in *Blount Papers*, III, 175.

87. Blount to Robertson, April 24, 1797, in *AHM* (October 1899), IV, 342.

88. Blount to John Gray Blount, November 7, 1797, *Blount Papers*, III, 175.

89. Ibid.

90. Ibid., pp. 174–175.

91. Ibid., pp. 175–176.

92. AJ to William Cocke, November 9, 1797, Jackson Papers, LC.

93. AJ to Cocke, June 25, 1798, Jackson Papers, LC.

94. Ibid.

95. AJ to Robert Hays, November 2, 1797, Jackson Papers, LC.

96. Parton, *Jackson*, I, 219.

97. AJ to Overton, February 3, 23, 1798, Murdock Collection, THS.

98. AJ to James Jackson, August 25, 1819, in Jackson, *Correspondence*, II, 427.

99. Blount to Robertson, April 24, 1797, in *AHM* (October 1899), IV, 343.

100. For the statistical information on Jackson's congressional career, both as representative and senator, I am indebted to Richard Shenkman, a staff member of the Jackson Papers Project.

101. AJ to Robertson, January 11, 1798, in Jackson, *Correspondence,* I, 42.

102. AJ to Overton, January 22, 1798, ibid., I, 43.

103. Anderson, AJ, and Claiborne to Adams [March, 1798], Governors' Papers, TSL.

104. Anderson, AJ, and Claiborne to Adams, March 5, 1798, ibid.

105. Kendall, *Jackson,* p. 101.

106. AJ to Robertson, January 11, 1798, in Jackson, *Correspondence,* I, 42; AJ to Hays, March 2, 1798, Jackson Papers, LC.

107. AJ to Hays, March 2, 1798, Jackson Papers, LC.

108. Sevier to AJ, April 5, 1798, Sevier Papers, THS; Anderson, AJ, and Claiborne to James McHenry, February 12, 1798, Governors' Papers, TSL.

109. Parton, *Jackson,* I, 242.

110. Kendall, who prepared his biography of Jackson with the subject's assistance, wrote: "Unambitious of political distinction, disgusted with the administration of the government, and believing that another [Daniel Smith] would better serve the people of Tennessee in the capacity of senator, he [Jackson] resigned." Kendall, *Jackson,* p. 101.

CHAPTER 8

1. Blount to Sevier, July 6, 1798, in *AHM* (January 1900), V, 121–122.

2. Blount to Sevier, August 12, 1798, ibid., p. 123.

3. Sevier to AJ, August 29, 1798, John Sevier Papers, TSL.

4. His commission, signed by Sevier, was dated September 20, 1798, Jackson Papers, TSL. The notice of election by the legislature, undated, is in the William Blount Papers, TSL. A notice of his election by joint ballot of both houses of the legislature states that the election occurred on December 20, 1798, LHA.

5. AJ to Blount, February 29, 1796, Blount Collection, LC.

6. Parton, *Jackson,* I, 227. Parton took this from Kendall, who said, "his opinions were always clear, short, and to the point, aiming at justice without the affectation of eloquence or of superior learning." Kendall, *Jackson,* p. 107.

7. The five include *Richard Woods* v. *Batt Wood, Thomas Wood, and Benjamin Gist* (Washington County, 1799–1803); *William Gardner* v. *Mary Looney and Heirs of Benjamin Looney* (Washington County, 1799–1800); *Ruth Brown* v. *William Whitson, Exr. of John McDowell* (Washington County, 1799–1802); *Mary Parker* v. *Nathaniel Parker* (Davidson County, 1800–1802); and *Leonard Henry Bullock and others* v. *Henderson and Company* (Washington County, 1802). For this information I am grateful to William Theodore Brown, Jr., a law student and member of the Jackson Papers Project staff.

8. Parton, *Jackson,* I, 228–229. A slightly different account is contained in James A. McLaughlin to Amos Kendall, January 3, 1843, Jackson Papers, LC. See also Kendall, *Jackson,* pp. 102–103.

9. Affidavit of Michel Gleave, June 15, 1800, in Jackson, *Correspondence,* I, 57.

10. AJ to Hays, September 9, 1801, Jackson Papers, LC.

11. Ibid.

12. See, for example, Mark Armstrong to AJ, August 19, 1803, and the petition to AJ signed by various individuals, October 7, 1803, Jackson Papers, LC.

13. "Early Connection with Masonry," in Jackson, *Correspondence,* I, 59.

14. See Jackson's Statement regarding the land frauds, December 6, 1797, along with Alexander Martin's accompanying letter to Governor Samuel Ashe of North Carolina, December 7, 1797, Miscellaneous Jackson Papers, North Carolina Department of Archives and History, Raleigh, North Carolina. Later Jackson

became confused and referred to John Love as "Charles" Love, a close friend.

15. AJ to Overton, January 22, 1798, in Jackson, *Correspondence*, I, 42.

16. Abernethy, *Frontier*, p. 173.

17. Bassett, *Jackson*, p. 58; AJ to Overton, January 8, 1798, Jackson Papers, LC; Report—Glasgow Land Frauds—Basil Gaither and Samuel D. Purviance to William R. Davie, June 28, 1799, North Carolina Secretary of State Papers, Box 753, Raleigh, N.C.; copy JPP.

18. Abernethy, *Frontier*, pp. 174–175.

19. Ibid., p. 176.

20. Sevier to AJ, March 27, 1799, Jackson Papers, LC. Abernethy, *Frontier*, p. 173, claims Jackson had the information against Sevier for three years.

21. Major General Conway had died in 1801, and the new election was scheduled for February 5, 1802.

22. AJ to Sevier, March 27, 1802, Jackson Papers, LC. David Campbell wrote Jackson on January 25, 1802: "Since the reception of your letter I have reflected on the subject of your being held up 'as a candidate for Major General I must confess at first I had my doubt whether your holding such an appointment would be consistent with the constitution or not but on examining the constitution and consulting with Governor Roane Judge Cambell and Col McClung my doubts are nearly removed. Should you be held up as a candidate I shall use my influence as far as proper on your behalf. I expect some will object to the propriety of your holding the appointment." Jackson Papers, LC. These doubts stemmed from the fact that Jackson served on Superior Court.

23. Carl S. Driver, *John Sevier, Pioneer of the Old Southwest* (Chapel Hill, 1932), p. 146; W. R. Garrett and A. V. Goodpasture, *History of Tennessee* (Nashville, 1900), p. 147. Jackson's commission as major general, signed by Governor Roane, was dated April 1, 1803. Commission of Andrew Jackson as Major General of Tennessee, Jackson Papers, LHA.

24. Carl S. Driver, *John Sevier, Pioneer of the Old Southwest* (Chapel Hill, 1932), pp. 145–146.

25. Copy in *AHM* (January 1899), IV, 374–381.

26. Kendall, *Jackson*, pp. 105–106.

27. Jackson himself claims he had a sword cane and Sevier a cutlass. AJ to Sevier, October 3, 1803, in Jackson, *Correspondence*, I, 71.

28. Parton, *Jackson*, I, 164.

29. AJ to Sevier, October 2, 1803, in Jackson, *Correspondence*, I, 71.

30. Sevier to AJ, October 3, 1803, Miscellaneous Papers, THS.

31. AJ to Sevier, October 3, 1803, in Jackson, *Correspondence*, I, 71.

32. AJ to Sevier, October 9, 1803, Jackson Papers, LC. With all this dallying it is possible that neither man really wanted to risk his life and career on a duel but that both wished to stigmatize the other with a refusal to fight. Perhaps it should be pointed out that Sevier had eighteen children.

33. Sevier to AJ, October 10, 1803, John Sevier Papers, THS.

34. Many of the details of the fight are taken from the affidavit of Andrew Greer, October 23, 1803, in *AHM*, V, 208. Parton, *Jackson*, I, 234–235, gives a slightly different version of the fight. Kendall, *Jackson*, p. 107, says that Jackson advanced on horseback toward Sevier and when he came to within 100 yards of his target leveled his cane sword like a knight of the Middle Ages and put spur to horse. Sevier dismounted to avoid the shock.

35. Driver, *Sevier*, p. 168.

36. Ibid., p. 148.

37. Sevier to Robertson, in *AHM* (October 1899), IV, 374.

38. AJ to McNairy, May 9, 1797; McNairy to AJ, May 12, 1797; and AJ to

McNairy, May 9, 1797, in Jackson, *Correspondence,* I, 34–37.
    39. Driver, *Sevier,* p. 98.

CHAPTER 9

1. Arthur P. Whitaker, "Spanish Intrigue in the Old Southwest," *MVHR* (September 1925), XII, 162.
    2. Jefferson to Livingston, April 18, 1802, in P. L. Ford, ed., *Writings of Thomas Jefferson* (Washington, 1935), VIII, 143–147.
    3. Jefferson to John B. Colvin, September 20, 1810, ibid., IX, 279.
    4. Jackson's General Order to the Militia as to Spanish Threats, August 7, 1803, in Jackson, *Correspondence,* I, 68. The secretary of war ordered him to procure enough boats to convey 1,500 men from Tennessee by December 20, 1803, at the latest. Henry Dearborn to AJ, October 31, 1802, War Department, NA.
    5. AJ to Jefferson, August 7, 1804, in Jackson, *Correspondence,* I, 68.
    6. AJ to Coffee, April 28, 1804, Coffee Papers, THS.
    7. This is the reason given by his biographer. Kendall, *Jackson,* p. 103.
    8. If such cases came before Jackson he would obviously have to disqualify himself; in any event the state needed another judge.
    9. Smith, "Andrew Jackson and Land Speculation," p. 16; James Jackson to AJ, September 21, 1805, Jackson Papers, LC.
    10. Joseph Anderson, congressman from Tennessee, was assisting Pryor in the sale; he employed Jackson to arrange the foreclosure and sale. Thus the sale of 40,000 acres was for Pryor, the sale of 35,000 acres for Anderson, and the sale of 10,000 acres for Jackson. Smith, "Andrew Jackson and Land Speculation," pp. 16–17, 19.
    11. Ibid., p. 19.
    12. AJ to James Jackson, August 25, 1819, in Jackson, *Correspondence,* II, 428.
    13. Ibid.
    14. Smith, "Andrew Jackson and Land Speculation," p. 19.
    15. AJ to James Jackson, August 25, 1819, in Jackson, *Correspondence,* II, 428.
    16. It is possible that John Strother, who shared an office in Nashville with William B. Lewis (Jackson's friend and neighbor), traveled with Jackson to Georgia. Strother represented the interests of the Blounts. Since the land had originally been obtained by Allison from the Blounts the purpose of Strother's journey would have been to make some arrangement about Allison's indebtedness to the Blounts.
    17. AJ to James Jackson, August 25, 1819, in Jackson, *Correspondence,* II, 428.
    18. Deed, Allison Heirs to AJ, Middle Tennessee Superior Court Records, Box 25; copy JPP.
    19. AJ to James Jackson, August 25, 1819, in Jackson, *Correspondence,* II, 428.
    20. Deed, AJ to Overton, July 21, 1813, Bedford County Deed Book E, pp. 95–96; copy JPP.
    21. Smith, "Andrew Jackson and Land Speculation," p. 29.
    22. The meeting between Jackson and Mrs. Erwin took place near the Old Stone Fort in Bedford County. Bedford County Deed Book AAA, pp. 362–365; copy JPP.
    23. Parton, *Jackson,* I, 249.
    24. The Hunter's Hill property was sold of "necessity (as Security for Thomas Watson & John Hutchings) . . ." The Hermitage property was, over the years, steadily expanded until it extended over 1,200 acres. The first 420 acres was purchased from Nathaniel Hays, the rest from William Donelson and Frank Sanders. AJ to Andrew Jr., December 1, 1844, Private Collection, LC. The origi-

nal purchase from Hays on August 4, 1804, cost Jackson $3,400. A copy of the deed is held by the Jackson Papers Project.

25. AJ to Watson, January 25, 1804, Jackson Papers, LC.

26. See articles of agreement and dissolution, Jackson Papers, LC.

27. Gordon Chappell, "The Life and Activities of General John Coffee," *THQ* (March 1942), I, 128. On the Clover Bottom store see Coffee Papers, THS.

28. W. C. C. Claiborne to AJ, January 9, 1802, Jackson Papers, LC.

29. Parton, *Jackson*, I, 249.

30. See John Campbell (who ran the Cantonment) to AJ, June 2, 1805, Jackson Papers, LC.

31. Jackson Papers, LC.

32. Farm Journal, 1829, LHA.

33. The highest number of slaves Jackson owned, according to Arda Walker, "approximated" 200; by 1842 the number had been reduced to something over 150. Walker, "Andrew Jackson; Planter," *ETHSP* (1943), No. 15, p. 30.

34. AJ to Andrew Jr., July 4, 1829, in Jackson, *Correspondence*, IV, 49–50.

35. AJ to Andrew Hutchings, June 2, 1833, ibid., V, 105.

36. AJ to Andrew Jackson Donelson, July 3, 1821, ibid., III, 87. It is possible that Jackson only threatened the whipping; the letter is not altogether clear.

37. AJ to Andrew Jackson Donelson, July 28, 1822, ibid., p. 166.

38. Jackson's affidavit concerning the destruction of his distillery, January 3, 1801, in Jackson, *Correspondence*, I, 57.

39. Jackson's Agreement with John Verell for purchasing Truxton, May 11, 1805, ibid., I, 113–114.

40. Parton, *Jackson*, I, 253.

41. Chappell, "The Life and Activities of General John Coffee," *THQ* (March 1942), I, 129.

42. Parton, *Jackson*, I, 250–251.

43. Abernethy, *Frontier*, p. 269; Shelby County Deed Book 1, pp. 260–263; copy JPP.

44. Abernethy, *Frontier*, pp. 271–272

45. Ibid.

46. Smith, "Andrew Jackson and Land Speculation," p. 26.

47. The best examination of this highly complex and confusing subject is Sam B. Smith's article (cited above), on which much of the evidence of Jackson's land speculation described in this chapter is based. I have also been aided by an appendix to the first volume of the Jackson Papers, soon to be published, prepared by William Theodore Brown, Jr., which catalogues all Jackson's legal and business transactions.

48. Kendall, *Jackson*, p. 115.

49. Bassett, *Jackson*, p. 61.

50. Statement of Swann, February 1, 1806, in Jackson, *Correspondence*, I, 123.

51. Swann to AJ, January 3, 1806, ibid.

52. AJ to Swann, January 7, 1806, ibid., p. 124.

53. Swann's statement, quoted in Parton, *Jackson*, I, 272.

54. John Coffee's statement, in Jackson, *Correspondence*, I, 130.

55. Dickinson to AJ, January 10, 1806, quoted in Parton, *Jackson*, I, 274.

56. Ibid., p. 275.

57. Letters and Statements relative to the duel with Charles Dickinson, in Jackson, *Correspondence*, I, 138.

58. Parton, *Jackson*, I, 286.

59. Ibid., p. 288.

60. Ibid., p. 291.

61. The Duel with Dickinson: The Card that Provoked the Challenge, in Jackson, *Correspondence*, I, 142–143.

62. AJ to Dickinson, May 23, 1806, in Jackson, *Correspondence*, I, 143–144.

63. Parton, *Jackson*, I, 295.

64. Ibid., p. 296.

65. Ibid., p. 298.

66. Ibid., p. 299.

67. Kendall, *Jackson*, p. 117.

68. Parton, *Jackson*, pp. 299–300.

69. Ibid., p. 303.

70. Ibid.

71. AJ to Thomas Eastin, no date, Jackson Papers, TSL.

CHAPTER 10

1. The Republican party ran Jefferson and Burr in 1800, intending Jefferson for President and Burr for Vice President. But both men received the same number of electoral votes, so the election went to the House of Representatives where, in 1801, after 36 ballots, Jefferson was chosen President and Burr Vice President. Republicans had expected Burr to decline the presidency and were appalled when he did not.

2. Joe Gray Taylor, "Andrew Jackson and the Aaron Burr Conspiracy," *The West Tennessee Historical Society Papers* (1947), No. 1, 81–90.

3. On the Burr Conspiracy see Thomas P. Abernethy, *The Burr Conspiracy* (New York, 1954); Walter McCaleb, *The Aaron Burr Conspiracy* (New York, 1936); Francis S. Philbrick, *The Rise of the New West, 1754–1830* (New York, 1965); Nathan Schachner, *Aaron Burr* (New York, 1937); Thomas P. Abernethy, *The South in the New Nation, 1789–1819* (Baton Rouge, 1961); Dumas Malone, *Jefferson the President: Second Term 1805–1809* (Boston, 1974); Marshall Smelser, *The Democratic Republic, 1801–1815* (New York, 1968).

4. Isaac J. Cox, *The West Florida Controversy, 1798–1813* (Baltimore, 1918), p. 190.

5. Wilkinson's treason can be easily documented. The Archives of Seville contain many legajos filled with his letters to Spanish officials. See particularly leg. 2373, 2374, 2375. Each of these legajos contains 150 to 200 letters.

6. Abernethy, *Burr Conspiracy*, p. 4.

7. Ibid., p. 20.

8. Parton, *Jackson*, I, 311.

9. Abernethy, *Burr Conspiracy*, p. 28.

10. AJ to ———, September 25, 1806, in Jackson, *Correspondence*, I, 149.

11. Parton, *Jackson*, I, 316.

12. Ibid.

13. Ibid., 312–317; Burr to AJ, April 5, 1806, Mississippi Department of History and Archives, Jackson, Mississippi.

14. See AJ to Claiborne, November 12, 1806, in Jackson, *Correspondence*, I, 153. See also James B. Ranck, "Andrew Jackson and the Burr Conspiracy," *THM* (October 1930), 2nd series, I, 17–28.

15. To the Generals Commanding Within the Second Division of Tennessee Militia, October 4, 1806, in Jackson, *Correspondence*, I, 150.

16. See Jackson's General Order to the Militia as to Spanish Threats, August 7, 1803, ibid., p. 68. Order to the Militia, October 4, 1806, ibid., p. 150.

17. AJ to James Winchester, October 4, 1806, Jackson Papers, LC.

18. *Impartial Review*, October 4, 8, November 22, 29, 1806.

19. Ibid.

20. AJ to Claiborne, November 12, 1806, in Jackson, *Correspondence*, I, 153.

21. AJ to Daniel Smith, November 12, 1806, Jackson Papers, LC.

22. AJ to George W. Campbell, January 15, 1807, in Jackson, *Correspondence*, I, 168–169.

23. AJ to Jefferson, August 7, 1803, Jackson Papers, LC.

24. Jefferson to AJ, September 19, 1803, cited in Bassett, *Jackson*, p. 50. See also Butler to AJ, April 17, 1805, and AJ to Jefferson, September 23, 1805, Jackson Papers, LC.

25. AJ to Campbell, January 15, 1807, in Jackson, *Correspondence*, I, 169.

26. AJ to Smith, November 12, 1806, Jackson Papers, LC; Henry Dearborn to AJ, December 19, 1806, NA.

27. AJ to Claiborne, November 12, 1806, in Jackson, *Correspondence*, I, 153.

28. AJ to Jefferson, November 12, 1806, ibid., 156. As governor, Sevier did not consult Jackson on military appointments, so Jackson's sensitivity about "my command" is understandable. Driver, *Sevier*, p. 192. When a call for volunteers came from the federal government in November 1803 (to thwart a possible Spanish refusal to relinquish Louisiana) Sevier ignored Jackson in raising the force. Jackson's friends retaliated by discouraging enlistments in West Tennessee. Arthur P. Whitaker, *The Mississippi Question*, p. 241.

29. Jefferson to AJ, December 3, 1806, Jefferson Papers, LC; McCaleb, *Burr Conspiracy*, p. 75.

30. AJ to Daniel Smith, November 17, 1806, in Jackson, *Correspondence*, I, 156.

31. AJ and Hutchings to Clay, October 27, 1806, Coffee Papers, THS.

32. Quoted in Abernethy, *Burr Conspiracy*, p. 99.

33. Ibid.

34. AJ to Campbell, January 15, 1807, in Jackson, *Correspondence*, I, 169.

35. Ibid.

36. Ibid.

37. Dumas Malone, *Jefferson the President: Second Term, 1805–1809*, p. 247.

38. AJ to Dearborn, January 4, 1807, Jackson Papers, LC.

39. Ibid.

40. AJ to Patten Anderson, January 4, 1807, in Jackson, *Correspondence*, I, 160.

41. Captain Bissell to AJ, January 5, 1807, quoted in Parton, *Jackson*, I, 324.

42. Parton, *Jackson*, I, 326.

43. Ibid.

44. AJ to Dearborn, January 8, 1807, Jackson Papers, LC. See also W. C. C. Claiborne to Wilkinson, December 16, 1806, Dunbar Rowland ed., *Official Letters of W. C. C. Clairborne* (Jackson, Miss., 1917), IV, 61.

45. Bassett, *Jackson*, p. 52.

46. AJ to Dearborn, March 17, 1807, Jackson Papers, LC.

47. Ibid.

48. AJ to Jenkins Whiteside, February 10, 1810; AJ to John Randolph, February 20, 1810, Jackson Papers, LC.

49. A superb discussion of Jefferson's behavior during the conspiracy can be found in Dumas Malone, *Jefferson the President: Second Term*, pp. 215–371.

50. Abernethy, *Burr Conspiracy*, p. 240; David Robertson, *Report of the Trials of Colonel Aaron Burr* (New York, 1875), I, 312. Jackson was summoned to testify. He describes the trial in a letter to Thomas Bayly, June 27, 1807, Jackson Papers, HL.

51. AJ to W. P. Anderson, June 16, 1807, in Jackson, *Correspondence*, I, 181.

52. AJ to Daniel Smith, November 28, 1807, Jackson Papers, LC.

53. Benton, *Thirty Years View* (New York, 1854), I, 736.

54. Benton to AJ, January 30, 1812, Jackson Papers, LC.

55. AJ to Daniel Smith, November 28, 1807, Jackson Papers, LC.

56. AJ to Jenkins Whiteside, February 10, 1810; Wade Hampton to AJ,

December 9, 1810; Donelson Caffery to AJ, December 5, 1810, Jackson Papers, LC. Although Jackson considered a move to Mississippi over a period of several months and indeed authorized Jenkins Whiteside to accept a judgeship in the territory in his name if it were offered, I do not think he was completely serious about the removal. He gave as one condition: "if permanent residence is not required."

57. For the information on Jackson's wards and the genealogy chart in this book I am grateful to Harriet C. Owsley, associate editor of the Jackson Papers Project. On Jackson's wards see Thomas Butler to AJ, March 4, 1805, Jackson Papers, LC; John H. De Witt, "Andrew Jackson and His Ward, Andrew Jackson Hutchings," *THM* (January 1931), 2nd series, I, 83–106; and Pauline Wilcox Burke, *Emily Donelson of Tennessee* (Richmond, 1941), I, 29.

58. When Jackson begged forgiveness for the daughter and a parental blessing, Daniel Smith supposedly replied: "Tell her to forget that she has a father and a mother, and we shall forget that we ever had a daughter. Tell Sam Donelson to keep out of my way, and as for you, Andrew Jackson, keep out of my way also." Father and daughter were reconciled with the birth of her first child. Smith also appreciated Jackson's willingness to become the guardian of his daughter's children after the death of Samuel Donelson. Burke, *Emily Donelson*, I, 25–30.

59. This is as Jackson remembered it. AJ to Andrew Jr., December 1, 1844, copy JPP.

60. Parton, *Jackson*, I, 340.

61. Ibid., p. 344.

62. James, *Jackson*, p. 134.

63. Grundy to AJ, February 12, 1812, Jackson Papers, LC.

64. AJ to Campbell, September 1812, quoted in Parton, *Jackson*, I, 357.

65. Ibid., p. 358.

66. Ibid., p. 342.

CHAPTER 11

1. List of Jackson's taxable property, January 1, 1812, Jackson Papers, LC.

2. For a discussion of the causes of the War of 1812 see Reginald Horsman, *The Causes of the War of 1812* (Philadelphia, 1962), and Roger H. Brown, *The Republic in Peril: 1812* (New York, 1964).

3. Quoted in George Dangerfield, *The Era of Good Feelings* (New York, 1952), p. 39.

4. Ibid., p. 127.

5. The expansionist argument as a cause of the War of 1812 is set forth in Julius Pratt, *Expansionists of 1812* (New York, 1925). Modern historians are less inclined toward expansionist reasons as a cause of the war. See Bradford Perkins, *Prologue to War: England and the United States, 1805–1812* (Berkeley, 1963); Norman Risjord, *The Old Republicans: Southern Conservatism in the Age of Jefferson* (New York, 1965); and A. L. Burt, *The United States, Great Britain and British North America* (New Haven, 1940). On western aims see Julius W. Pratt, "Western Aims in the War of 1812," *MVHR* (June 1925), XII, 37–50, and Reginald Horsman, "Western War Aims, 1811–1812," *Indiana Magazine of History* (January 1957), LIII, 1–18.

6. Pratt, *Expansionists of 1812*, pp. 145, 148.

7. *Annals of Congress,* 12th Congress, 1st Session, I, 533.

8. Quoted in Rogin, *Fathers and Children*, p. 352, note 97.

9. Grundy to AJ, November 28, December 4, 1811, Jackson Papers, LC.

10. AJ to Harrison, November 30, 1811, Jackson Papers, LC.

11. George W. Campbell to AJ, December 24, 1811, Jackson Papers, LC.

12. Blount to Eustis, January 25, 1812, Jackson Papers, LC.

13. Division Orders, March 7, 1812, Jackson Papers, LC.

14. These threats were nothing new; only the language was more intense. See AJ to George Colbert, June 5, 1812, Jackson Papers, LC.

15. Jackson's Address to his Troops, July 31, 1812, Jackson Papers, LC.

16. Eustis to Blount, October 21, 1812, in Jackson, *Correspondence,* I, 240, note 5.

17. AJ to Blount, November 11, 1812, ibid., pp. 238–239.

18. Ibid.

19. Blount to AJ, November 11, 1812, ibid., pp. 239–241.

20. Jackson's Announcement to his Soldiers, November 14, 1812, ibid., p. 241.

21. Jackson's General Orders, November 23, 1812, Jackson Papers, LC.

22. Parton, *Jackson,* I, 368.

23. Aaron M. Brown, "John Coffee, Citizen Soldier," *THQ* (September 1963), XXII, 227.

24. Blount to AJ, December 31, 1812, AJ to [Blount], January 4, 1813, Jackson Papers, LC.

25. AJ to Eustis, January 7, 1812, quoted in Parton, *Jackson,* I, 372.

26. Rachel to AJ, January 1813, in Jackson, *Correspondence,* I, 272.

27. AJ to Rachel [January 18, 1813], ibid., pp. 271–272. This letter has been obviously edited. See also AJ to Rachel, February 15, 1813, Jackson Papers, HL.

28. Rachel to AJ [January 1813], in Jackson, *Correspondence,* I, 272–273. This letter, too, has been edited to improve style and grammar.

29. Wilkinson to AJ, January 22, 25, February 22, March 1, 8, 1813; AJ to Wilkinson, February 16, 20, March 1, 8, 15, 1813, Jackson Papers, LC.

30. AJ to Wilkinson, February 16, 1813, Jackson Papers, LC.

31. AJ to Rachel, February 22, 1813, in Jackson, *Correspondence,* I, 280.

32. John Armstrong to AJ, February 5, 1813, ibid., pp. 275–276.

33. Wilkinson to AJ, March 8, 16, 1813, Jackson Papers, LC; Parton, *Jackson,* I, 380; Bassett, *Jackson,* pp. 84–85.

34. Actually Jackson was not disobeying a direct order. All he had been ordered to do was to dismiss the army and deliver all public property to Wilkinson.

35. A speech by Thomas Hart Benton, quoted in Parton, *Jackson,* I, 378.

36. AJ to Armstrong, March 13, 15, 1813, Jackson Papers, LC.

37. AJ to Madison, March 15, 1813, in Jackson, *Correspondence,* I, 292–293.

38. AJ to W. B. Lewis, April 9, 1813, ibid., p. 304.

39. AJ to Rachel, March 15, 1813, Jackson Papers, LC.

CHAPTER 12

1. AJ to Rachel, March 15, 1813, Jackson Papers, LC.

2. Parton, *Jackson,* I, 382; Kendall, *Jackson,* p. 149.

3. Parton, *Jackson,* I, 384, 486.

4. Ibid.

5. Even before returning to Nashville from Natchez, Jackson had begun speaking of himself as a father to his men. See AJ to Rachel, March 15, 1813, Jackson Papers, LC.

6. William Carroll to Andrew J. Donelson, October 4, 1824, in Jackson, *Correspondence,* I, 311, note 1.

7. Parton, *Jackson,* I, 387.

8. Ibid., p. 388.

9. Statement of AJ and Armstrong, August 23, 1813, Jackson Papers, LC; letter of William Carroll dated October 24, 1824, printed in the *Knoxville Register,* copy JPP.

10. Parton, *Jackson,* I, 388.

11. Benton to AJ, June 15, 1813, Jackson Papers, LC.

12. AJ to Benton, July 19, 1813, Jackson Papers, LC.

13. Benton to AJ, July 25, 1813, in Jackson, *Correspondence,* I, 312–313.

14. Ibid., p. 314.

15. Parton, *Jackson,* I, 392.

16. Certificate of James Sitler, September 5, 1813, in Jackson, *Correspondence,* I, 317.

17. Benton's Account of the Duel with Jackson, September 10, 1813, ibid., p. 318.

18. Quoted in Parton, *Jackson,* I, 395.

19. Benton held a commission as lieutenant colonel but Jackson became supreme military chief in the southwest and under him Benton could expect no advancement. While other Tennesseans won fame in the Creek War Benton saw little action and no promotion. So at war's end he resigned his commission and went to Missouri.

CHAPTER 13

1. The problem of these roads in generating hostility between Indians and whites is excellently described in Reginald Horsman, *Expansion and American Indian Policy* (East Lansing, Mich., 1967), pp. 160–164. Frank Lawrence Owsley, Jr., emphasizes resentment to white culture as the principal cause of Indian hostility in his *Struggle for the Gulf: The Role of the Gulf States in the War of 1812* (Gainesville, 1977). I am grateful to Owsley for sharing many of his findings with me about the Creek War.

2. There is some question whether or not Red Eagle chose to live with the Indians of his own free will. He had lived as a white man and may have been forced to join the Red Sticks when his wife and children were seized as hostages. After the Fort Mims massacre it made little difference. See Thomas S. Woodward, *Woodward's Reminiscences of the Creek . . . Indians . . .* (Tuscaloosa, 1939).

3. The Cherokee Indians, living mostly in western Georgia and eastern Tennessee, sided pretty much with the United States during the war. Chickasaws and Choctaws, living on the eastern bank of the Mississippi from Ohio to the Gulf, took little part in the war. Harry Coles, *The War of 1812* (Chicago, 1965), p. 192.

4. Reginald Horsman, "British Indian Policy in the Northwest, 1807–1812," *MVHR* (April 1958), XLV, 51–67.

5. Owsley, *Struggle for the Gulf,* Chapter 2.

6. J. F. H. Claiborne, *Mississippi as a Province, Territory and State* (Jackson, 1880), p. 317.

7. H. S. Halbert and T. H. Hall, *The Creek War of 1813 and 1814* (University, Alabama, 1969), pp. 79–80.

8. Hawkins attempted a policy of assimilation that many Indians clearly disliked. John K. Mahon, *War of 1812* (Gainesville, 1972), p. 232, states that this policy was itself an important cause of hostilities.

9. Halbert and Hall, *Creek War,* pp. 125–142; Francis P. Prucha, *The Sword of the Republic* (New York, 1969), p. 114.

10. Negro slavery among Indians, particularly among the Cherokees, is examined in Michael D. Roethler's doctoral dissertation, "Negro Slavery among the Cherokee Indians," Fordham University, 1964. See also Owsley, *Struggle for the Gulf,* Chapter 3.

11. Albert J. Pickett, *History of Alabama* . . . (Charleston, 1851), II, 275; Halbert and Hall, *Creek War,* pp. 151–164. Many women and children were burned alive in the buildings in which they were hiding.

12. AJ to Coffee, September 29, 1813, de Coppet Collection, PUL; AJ to Blount, July 13, 1813, in *ASPIA,* I, 850.

13. AJ to Blount, July 13, 1813, ibid.

14. General Order, September 10, 1813, Jackson Papers, LC.

15. Reid and Eaton, *Jackson,* p. 33.

16. Blount to AJ, September 24, 1813, in Brannon, *Official Letters,* p. 215; Blount to AJ, September 25, 1813, Jackson Papers, LC.

17. AJ to Leroy Pope, October 31, 1813, in Jackson, *Correspondence,* I, 339; J. Lyon to AJ, October 27, 1813, Jackson Papers, LC.

18. Jackson's letters at this time are full of statements that the Spanish and British influence in the southwest must be terminated. See especially AJ to Coffee, September 29, 1813, de Coppet Collection, PUL; and AJ to Leroy Pope, October 31, 1813, in Jackson, *Correspondence,* I, 339.

19. Owsley, *Struggle for the Gulf,* Chapter 4, has an excellent discussion of the overall strategy.

20. Jackson wanted it rumored "so that it may reach the Creeks" that he was about to march to Mobile. AJ to Coffee, September 25, 1813, Jackson Papers, LC. The letters of John Reid to members of his family, located in the Library of Congress, constitute one of the best sources on the Creek War, particularly with respect to Jackson's involvement; they have been used extensively in this chapter and the next. I am grateful to John McDonough of the staff of the manuscripts division of the Library of Congress for his assistance in using these papers.

21. AJ to Lewis, October 24, 1813, Jackson Papers, LC; James F. Doster, *The Creek Indians and Their Florida Lands, 1740–1823* (New York and London, 1974), II, 87.

22. Message to the Troops, October 24, 1813; AJ to Chief Chennabee, October 19, 1813; Chief Pathkiller to AJ, October 22, 1813; AJ to Chief Pathkiller, October 23, November 2, 1813, Jackson Papers, LC. The list of friendly Creek towns is in the Jackson Papers, LC.

23. AJ to Rachel, November 4, 1813, Jackson Papers, LC; Davy Crockett, *Life of Davy Crockett* (New York, 1854), p. 75.

24. Call's "Journal," quoted in Herbert J. Doherty, Jr., *Richard Keith Call: Southern Unionist* (Gainesville, 1961), p. 6.

25. Coffee to AJ, November 4, 1813, in Palmer, ed., *Historical Register,* I, 333–335; John Reid to Nathan Reid, November 21, 1813, Reid Papers, LC.

26. AJ to Blount, November 4, 1813; AJ to Leroy Pope, November 4, 1813, in Jackson, *Correspondence,* I, 341; AJ to Rachel, November 4, 1814, Miscellaneous Jackson Papers, HUL.

27. Parton, *Jackson,* I, 439. "I send on a little Indian boy for Andrew to Huntsville. . . . all his family is destroyed. he is about the age of *Theodore.*" AJ to Rachel, November 4, 1814, Miscellaneous Jackson Papers, HUL.

28. AJ to Rachel, December 29, 1813, Jackson Papers, HL.

29. Kendall, *Jackson,* p. 200. Andrew Jr. to AJ, April 8 [no year], Jackson Papers, LC.

30. Kendall, *Jackson,* p. 201. The obituary notice in the *United States Telegraph* attributed death to "a pulmonary complaint." Kendall specifies tuberculosis.

31. AJ to Blount, November 11, 1813, in Brannan, *Official Letters,* p. 265; AJ to Rachel, November 12, 1813, Jackson Papers, Thomas Gilcrease Institute, Tulsa, Oklahoma; AJ to Blount, November 15, 1813, Jackson Papers, LC.

32. Reid and Eaton, *Jackson,* p. 56.

33. AJ to Blount, November 11, 1813, in Brannan, *Official Letters,* p. 265; Coffee to John Donelson, November 12, 1813, in *AHM* (April 1901), VI, 176; John Reid to Nathan Reid, December 24, 1813, John Reid Papers, LC.

34. AJ to Blount, November 15, 1813; AJ to Thomas Pinckney, December 3, 1813, Jackson Papers, LC.

35. Reid and Eaton, *Jackson,* p. 60.

36. Parton, *Jackson,* I, 446; Kendall, *Jackson,* p. 207.

37. Address of Officers [November 1813], Jackson Papers, LC.

38. Reid and Eaton, *Jackson,* p. 63; AJ to Rachel, December 9, 1813, Jackson Papers, LC.

39. Reid and Eaton, *Jackson,* pp. 65–66. At one point the soldiers just laughed at him. Reid to Elizabeth Reid, December 9, 1813, Reid Papers, LC.

40. Reid and Eaton, *Jackson,* p. 68.

41. Ibid.

42. Ibid., p. 69.

43. Ibid., pp. 69–71; Kendall, *Jackson,* pp. 216–217.

44. AJ to Blount, November 29, 1813, Jackson Papers, LC.

45. Coffee to John Donelson, December 22, 1813, in *AHM* (April 1901), VI, 178.

46. AJ to Coffee, December 9, 1813, Jackson Papers, LC.

47. Reid and Eaton, *Jackson,* p. 84.

48. Ibid.

49. AJ to Rachel, December 14, 1813, in Jackson, *Correspondence,* I, 391–392.

50. Reid and Eaton, *Jackson,* p. 85; Kendall, *Jackson,* pp. 219–220; AJ to Rachel, December 29, 1813, Jackson Papers, HL.

51. Doherty, *Richard Keith Call,* p. 7; Reid to Nathan Reid, October 1813, Reid Papers, LC.

52. Parton, *Jackson,* I, Appendix III, 629ff.

53. AJ to Armstrong, December 16, 30, 1813, in *ASPMA,* III, 787.

54. Coffee to AJ, December 20, 1813, Jackson Papers, LC.

55. Blount to AJ, December 7, 1813; Armstrong to Blount, January 3, 1814, Jackson Papers, LC.

56. Blount to AJ, December 22, 1813, in *ASPMA,* III, 698.

57. AJ to Blount, December 29, 1813, in Jackson, *Correspondence,* I, 416–420. A different and more subdued version can be found in Reid and Eaton, *Jackson,* pp. 101–106, which is reprinted in Parton, *Jackson,* I, 480–484, and excerpted in Bassett, *Jackson,* pp. 109–110.

58. AJ to Coffee, December 31, 1813, in Jackson, *Correspondence,* I, 431.

59. AJ to Pinckney, January 29, 1814, ibid., p. 448.

CHAPTER 14

1. Floyd to Pinckney, December 4, 1813; Ferdinand L. Claiborne to John Armstrong, January 1, 1814, in Brannan, *Official Letters,* pp. 283–285, 294–296.

2. AJ to Pinckney, January 29, 1814, in Jackson, *Correspondence,* I, 448.

3. Blount to Armstrong, January 5, 1814, in *ASPMA,* III, 698.

4. Reid and Eaton, *Jackson,* p. 128. In a tender letter to Rachel, Jackson informed her of young Alexander Donelson's death. "It was the fate of our brave Nephew Alexander Donelson to *fall,*" he said, "but he fell like a hero. . . . He fell roman like." February 21, 1814, Jackson Papers, Missouri Historical Society.

5. Reid and Eaton, *Jackson,* p. 129.

6. AJ to Pinckney, January 29, 1814, in Jackson, *Correspondence,* I, 448–450.

7. Jackson put a good face on his retreat in his letter to Pinckney, ibid., p. 451.

8. Ibid.

9. Ibid., p. 452.

10. Reid and Eaton, *Jackson*, p. 136; John Reid to Nathan Reid, October 17, 1813, Reid Papers, LC.

11. Bassett, *Jackson*, p. 114.

12. Pinckney to Armstrong, February 6, 1814, quoted in Parton, *Jackson*, I, 498.

13. Rachel to AJ, February 10, 1814, Jackson Papers, LC.

14. AJ to Pinckney, February 12, 1814, Jackson Papers, LC.

15. John Reid to Nathan Reid, October 17, November 6, 1813, Reid Papers, LC.

16. Parton, *Jackson*, I, 508.

17. General Order, March 12, 1814, in Jackson, *Correspondence*, I, 479.

18. Reid and Eaton, *Jackson*, pp. 142–143. In a letter to his wife, John Reid said he sympathized with Woods's family. Reid to Elizabeth Reid, March 14, 1814, Reid Papers, LC.

19. AJ to Pinckney, March 14, 1814, Jackson Papers, LC; Halbert and Hall, *Creek War*, pp. 246–247.

20. Reid and Eaton, *Jackson*, p. 149.

21. Ibid., pp. 148–149; AJ to Blount, March 31, 1814, in Jackson, *Correspondence*, I, 490; AJ to John Armstrong, April 2, 1814, NA.

22. Reid and Eaton, *Jackson*, p. 148.

23. AJ to Pinckney, March 28, 1814, in Jackson, *Correspondence*, I, 488–489.

24. AJ to Blount, March 31, 1814, ibid., p. 491; AJ to Blount, April 1, 1814, Jackson Papers, LC; Reid to Elizabeth Reid, April 1, 1814; Reid to Nathan Reid, April 5, 1814, Reid Papers, LC.

25. Coffee says Montgomery reached the wall, fired through a porthole, and killed an Indian, "and in an instant afterward was shot through the same hole and fell dead—never spoke." Coffee to John Donelson, April 1, 1814, in *AHM* (April 1901), VI, 183. For Coffee's operation see his report to Jackson, April 1, 1814, Jackson Papers, LC.

26. AJ to Rachel, April 1, 1814, in Jackson, *Correspondence*, I, 493.

27. Halbert and Hall, *Creek War*, pp. 276–277.

28. Kendall, *Jackson*, p. 282.

29. AJ to Blount, March 31, 1814, in Jackson, *Correspondence*, I, 491–492.

30. Ibid. Coffee said 500 squaws and children were captured. Coffee to John Donelson, April 1, 1814, in *AHM* (April 1901), VI, 183.

31. AJ to Blount, March 31, 1814, in Jackson, *Correspondence*, I, 491–492; Coffee to Mary Coffee, April 1, 1814, Coffee Papers, THS.

32. AJ to Rachel, April 1, 1814, in Jackson, *Correspondence*, I, 493.

33. AJ to Rachel, April 14, 1814, Jackson Papers, LC. The significance of Horseshoe Bend is well presented in Owsley, *Struggle for the Gulf.*

34. Reid and Eaton, *Jackson*, pp. 156–157. AJ to Rachel, April 6, 1814, Miscellaneous Jackson Papers, HUL.

35. Reid and Eaton, *Jackson*, pp. 164–165. At about this time the blacks taken at Fort Mims were surrendered. Reid to Elizabeth Reid, April 18, 1814, Reid Papers, LC.

36. Reid and Eaton, *Jackson*, p. 165. Another version of this interview, written three years after the Battle of Horseshoe Bend, in Anne Royall, *Letters from Alabama* (Tuscaloosa, 1969), pp. 91–92, is fairly close to the version given here.

37. Reid and Eaton, *Jackson*, p. 166. A partial transcript of this interview is in the Reid Papers, LC.

38. Reid and Eaton, *Jackson*, pp. 166–167; Coffee to Mary Coffee, April 18, 1814, Coffee Papers, THS.

39. Pinckney to AJ, April 14, 1814, Jackson Papers, LC. Angie Debo, *The Road to Disappearance* (Norman, Oklahoma, 1967), p. 82.

40. Reid and Eaton, *Jackson*, p. 168.

41. AJ to Pinckney, April 18, 1814, in Jackson, *Correspondence*, I, 504.

42. AJ to Blount, April 18, 1814, ibid., p. 503.

43. Owsley, *Struggle for the Gulf*, Chapter 7.

44. In fact these commissioners were appointed before the Battle of Horseshoe Bend; but Jackson's strength and obvious command of the situation encouraged the secretary to commence the process of establishing peace.

45. AJ to Pinckney, May 18, 1814, in Jackson, *Correspondence*, II, 1–2.

46. As expected and ordered, Jackson took care to leave a sufficient force at each of the posts that had been established to maintain peace in the area. AJ to Armstrong, April 25, 1814, ibid., I, 508.

47. Reid and Eaton, *Jackson*, pp. 173–174.

48. Parton, *Jackson*, I, 542–543; John Reid to Nathan Reid, June 15, 1814, Reid Papers, LC.

49. Overton to AJ, May 8, 1814, Jackson Papers, LC.

50. Armstrong to AJ, May 22, 1814, Jackson Papers, LC.

51. Armstrong to AJ, May 22, 28, 1814; AJ to Armstrong, June 8, 1814; G. W. Campbell to AJ, May 29, 1814, Jackson Papers, LC.

52. AJ to Rachel, September 22, 1814, Jackson Papers, HL.

53. Armstrong to AJ, May 24, 1814, in *ASPMA*, III, 785.

54. Armstrong to Pinckney, March 17, 20, 1814, in *ASPIA*, I, 836–837.

55. Merritt B. Pound, *Benjamin Hawkins, Indian Agent* (Athens, 1951), pp. 234–235.

56. AJ to Armstrong, June 27, 1814, Jackson Papers, LC.

57. Armstrong states that President Madison delayed the sending of the letter but does not explain why. Probably Madison delayed it in an effort to keep his options open, for he was not averse to a Florida invasion per se; should he need to break off relations for diplomatic reasons the letter could not embarrass him. John Armstrong, *Notices of the War of 1812* (New York, 1840), I, 16, note 1.

58. Armstrong to AJ, July 18, 1814, quoted in Reid and Eaton, *Jackson*, pp. 196–197.

59. Ibid., p. 197.

60. AJ to Hawkins, July 11, 1814, Jackson Papers, LC; Merritt P. Pound, *Benjamin Hawkins*, p. 236.

61. AJ to Coffee, July 17, 1814, Jackson Papers, LC.

62. Reid and Eaton, *Jackson*, p. 186.

63. Rogin, *Fathers and Children*, gives a much more psychoanalytical explanation for Jackson's motives and behavior toward the Indians; while I feel there are many excellent insights into Jackson's character in this book, I do not accept its fundamental analysis of Jackson's motivation.

64. At the time Jackson said he asked for the whole of Alabama. AJ to Blount, August 9, 1814, Jackson Papers, LC.

65. Treaty of Fort Jackson, in *ASPIA*, I, 826–827.

66. Ibid.

67. Reid and Eaton, *Jackson*, p. 191. One historian called the treaty the "Robbery of Fort Jackson," Doster, *Creek Indians*, II, 113–114.

68. Kendall, *Jackson*, p. 89.

69. Reid and Eaton, *Jackson*, pp. 187–188.

70. Ibid., pp. 189–190. Talk of Tustunnuggee Thlucco, August 8, 1814, in *ASPIA*, I, 838.

71. Reid and Eaton, *Jackson,* p. 173.

72. Quoted in Owsley, *Struggle for the Gulf* Chapter 8.

73. Reid and Eaton, *Jackson,* pp. 190–191.

74. Pinckney to Hawkins, April 23, 1814, in *ASPIA,* I, 858.

75. AJ to Blount, August 9, 1814, Jackson Papers, LC.

76. Ibid.; AJ to Armstrong, August 10, 1814, in *ASPMA,* III, 783.

77. Reid and Eaton, *Jackson,* p. 191. As far as the Red Sticks in Florida were concerned Jackson told the chiefs not to interfere. He said to the assembled Indians, "if you kill them I will kill you, let them alone the war is ended with the Indians." Big Warrior to AJ, April 16, 1816, Jackson Papers, LC.

78. AJ to Armstrong, August 10, 1814, in *ASPMA,* III, 792. Jackson acknowledged aid from Benjamin Hawkins in getting the Indians to sign the treaty. Pound, *Benjamin Hawkins,* p. 237.

79. Parton, *Jackson,* I, 557.

80. Ibid. The full terms of the treaty are contained in Charles Kappler, *Indian Affairs: Laws and Treaties* (Washington, 1904), II, 107–109. See also Charles C. Royce, *Indian Land Cessions in the United States* (Washington, 1900), pp. 678–679, and plates 1, 15.

81. AJ to Rachel, August 10, 1814, private collection; copy JPP.

82. AJ to Overton, August 20, 1814, Claybrooke Collection, TSL. The federal government realized approximately $12 million in the sale of this land. Debo, *Road to Disappearance,* p. 83.

83. AJ to Armstrong, August 10, 1814, in *ASPMA,* III, 792.

84. AJ to Rachel, August 5, 1814, Jackson Papers, HL.

85. Armstrong to AJ, July 18, 1814, quoted in Reid and Eaton, *Jackson,* pp. 196–197.

86. Ibid.

87. AJ to González Manrique, August 24, 1814, Jackson Papers, LC.

CHAPTER 15

1. Robin Reilly, *The British at the Gates* (New York, 1974), pp. 130–131. This is an excellent book in many respects, although I have not always agreed with the author's interpretations or conclusions.

2. Reginald Horsman, *The War of 1812* (New York, 1969), p. 227; Frank L. Owsley, Jr., "Role of the South in the British Grand Strategy in the War of 1812," *THQ* (Spring 1972), XXXI, 29–30; DeGrummond, *Baratarians,* p. 31.

3. Pigot to Cochrane, June 8, 1814, PRO Admirality 1/506. Cochrane had replaced Admiral Sir John Borlase Warren in April 1814. Warren had earlier proposed an invasion of New Orleans as a diversion to remove the pressure on the Canadian frontier. Reilly, *British at the Gates,* p. 170. John K. Mahon, "British Command Decisions Relative to the Battle of New Orleans," *Louisiana History* (Winter 1965), VI, 53. Lord Bathurst recognized the monetary difficulty of holding Louisiana. See Perkins, *Castlereagh and Adams,* p. 141.

4. For a negative view of the plan see Sir John Fortescue, *History of the British Army* (London, 1899–1930), X, 151.

5. If not Warren, then Charles Cameron, governor of Nassau, may have originally conceived the plan to capture New Orleans.

6. AJ to Armstrong, August 5, 1814, Jackson Papers, LC.

7. Claiborne to AJ, August 24, 1814; AJ to Armstrong, August 25, 1814; AJ to Claiborne, August 30, 1814, Jackson Papers, LC.

8. Lt. Col. William MacRea to AJ, September 9, 1814, in Jackson, *Correspondence,* II, 46–47.

9. AJ to Colonel Robert Butler, August 27, 1814; AJ to Claiborne, August

30, 1814; AJ to Blount, August 27, 1814, Jackson Papers, LC.

10. González Manrique to Ruiz Apodaca, December 6, 1814, Cuba, leg. 1795, AGI.

11. AJ to González Manrique, August 30, 1814; González Manrique to Ruiz Apodaca, September 10, December 6, 1814, Cuba, leg. 1795, AGI.

12. Frank L. Owsley, Jr., "British and Indian Activities in Spanish West Florida During the War of 1812," *Florida Historical Quarterly* (October 1967), XLVI, 122. "The citizens exclaimed that the choctaws were more civilized than the British," Jackson wrote Rachel, November 15, 1814, Miscellaneous Jackson Papers, HUL.

13. AJ to Butler, September 17, 1814, Jackson Papers, LC.

14. William Lawrence to AJ, September 15, 1814, in Brannan, *Official Letters*, pp. 424–425; Reid and Eaton, *Jackson*, pp. 214–215; Parton, *Jackson*, I, 608; Horsman, *War of 1812*, pp. 232–233.

15. Jackson's Proclamation to the People of Louisiana, September 21, 1814, in Jackson, *Correspondence*, II, 57–59.

16. Wilbert S. Brown, *The Amphibious Campaign for West Florida and Louisiana* (University, Alabama, 1969), p. 49, does not think that Jackson should be criticized for delaying at Mobile since all indications pointed to an invasion at that place.

17. Monroe to AJ, October 10, 1814, in Jackson, *Correspondence*, II, 71.

18. AJ to Rachel, October 21, 1814, ibid., p. 79.

19. Monroe to AJ, October 21, 1814, ibid.

20. Armstrong to AJ, July 18, 1815, quoted in Reid and Eaton, *Jackson*, pp. 196–197.

21. "You will receive all the support in the power of the government, relating to the Spaniards," Jackson was told by Charles Cassiday of the War Department, "if it should be necessary to notice them in a hostile manner. Colonel Monroe spoke in *strong* terms on the subject, as well as on subjects relating to extensive national policy." Cassiday to AJ, September 13, 1814, Jackson Papers, LC.

22. AJ to Monroe, October 26, 1814, in Jackson, *Correspondence*, II, 82–83.

23. Cassiday to AJ, September 13, 1814, Jackson Papers, LC.

24. The record is clear that the British intended to use Spanish Florida as a base of operations with or without a Spanish invitation. They also expected the Spanish to cooperate with them in the invasion by participating in it. See Frank L. Owsley, Jr., "Jackson's Capture of Pensacola," *Alabama Review* (July 1966), XIX, 175–179.

25. AJ to González Manrique, November 6, 1814, Cuba, leg. 1795, AGI.

26. Parton, *Jackson*, I, 620.

27. A second letter was dispatched to the governor and delivered; the terms were rejected by the governor's council.

28. AJ to Monroe, November 14, 1814, in Jackson, *Correspondence*, II, 97; Coffee to Mary Coffee, November 15, 1814, Coffee Papers, THS. Jackson had a great deal of information about Pensacola supplied by his superior intelligence operation. Owsley, "Jackson's Capture of Pensacola," pp. 182–183.

29. AJ to Rachel, November 15, 1814, Miscellaneous Jackson Papers, HUL. The British claimed that the loss of Pensacola was due to Spanish jealousy of the British and their failure to cooperate in the attack. Ruth Anna Fisher, "The Surrender of Pensacola as Told by the British," *AHR* (January 1949), LIV, 327.

30. AJ to Blount, November 14, 1814, in Brannan, *Official Letters*, p. 452. Jackson described the battle in a letter to Rachel, November 15, 1814, Miscellaneous Jackson Papers, HUL.

31. AJ to Monroe, November 14, 1814, in Jackson, *Correspondence*, II, 99. The

British rolled into the water and blew up 300 double barrels of gunpowder, destroyed a large magazine of every sort of ordnance stores, two stores of provisions for 500 men, and the carriages of the guns in the upper and lower fort, spiked the guns, and blew up the blockhouse. Fisher, "Surrender of Pensacola," p. 328.

32. AJ to Monroe, November 14, 1814, in Jackson, *Correspondence*, II, 99.
33. Ibid.
34. Reid and Eaton, *Jackson*, p. 235.
35. AJ to Blount, November 14, 1814, Jackson Papers, LC.
36. Claiborne to AJ, November 19, 1814, ibid.
37. AJ to González Manrique, November 9, 1814, Cuba, leg. 1795, AGI.
38. González Manrique to AJ, November 9, 1814, ibid.
39. AJ to Winchester, November 22, 1814, Miscellaneous Jackson Papers, NYHS.
40. AJ to Monroe, November 20, 1814, in Jackson, *Correspondence*, II, 102.
41. AJ to Rachel, November 15, 1814, Miscellaneous Jackson Papers, HUL; AJ to Rachel, November 17, 1814, Jackson Papers, Missouri Historical Society.

CHAPTER 16

1. Howell Tatum, "Major Howell Tatum's Journal," in John S. Bassett, ed., *Smith College Studies in History* (1912–1922), VII, 100–101. Coles, *War of 1812*, pp. 210–212; Horsman, *War of 1812*, p. 237.
2. Monroe to AJ, December 10, 1814, in Jackson, *Correspondence*, II, 110.
3. Alexander Walker, *Jackson and New Orleans* (New York, 1856), p. 93; Bernard Marigny, "Reflections on the Campaign of Gen. Andrew Jackson in Louisiana in 1814 and '15," *The Louisiana Historical Quarterly* (January 1923), VI, 68; Horsman, *War of 1812*, p. 236. A letter of Wellington states flatly that the entire campaign was planned with booty in mind, but this is an exaggeration. "Letter of the Duke of Wellington on the Battle of New Orleans," *The Louisiana Historical Quarterly* (January 1926), IX, 247–266.
4. Several accounts written later, including Parton, *Jackson*, II, 25, state that Jackson arrived in New Orleans on December 2, but Jackson himself gives December 1 as his date of arrival. See AJ to Coffee, December 11, 1814, in Jackson, *Correspondence*, II, 112; and AJ to Winchester, December 11, 1814, Jackson Papers, LC.
5. Louise Livingston Hunt, *Memoir of Mrs. Edward Livingston with Letters Hitherto Unpublished* (New York, 1886), pp. 53–54.
6. Walker, *Jackson and New Orleans*, p. 17. Jackson's predecessor, General Thomas Flournoy, made no secret of his contempt for the citizens of New Orleans. Livingston, like Jackson, served in Congress in 1796 and voted against the tribute to George Washington. He and Jackson had much in common.
7. The best description of Jackson's entrance to New Orleans is Walker, *Jackson and New Orleans*, pp. 17–18, but an excellent modern secondary account of the arrival is Reilly, *British at the Gates*, pp. 209–210. See also Marigny, "Reflections on the Campaign of Gen. Andrew Jackson," p. 64.
8. Walker, *Jackson and New Orleans*, pp. 17–18.
9. Parton, *Jackson*, II, 31.
10. Tatum, "Journal," pp. 96–97.
11. Ibid., p. 102; AJ to Villeré, December 22, 1814, NA.
12. Vincent Nolte, *Fifty Years in Both Hemispheres* (New York, 1854), p. 207; AJ to Winchester, December 11, 1814, Jackson Papers, LC.
13. See, for example, González Manrique to AJ, July 26, 1814, Jackson Papers, LC.

14. AJ to Claiborne, September 30, 1814, Jackson Papers, LC.

15. Jackson's Proclamation to the People of Louisiana, in Jackson, *Correspondence*, II, 58.

16. For excellent background material on Lafitte and the pirates see De-Grummond, *Baratarians*, pp. 7–9.

17. Lafitte himself was offered the rank of captain in the British navy.

18. Lafitte to Lockyer, September 4, 1814, and Lafitte to Claiborne, no date, in Latour, *Historical Memoir*, pp. xi–xii, xiii–xiv; Charles B. Brooks, *The Seige of New Orleans* (Seattle, 1961), pp. 40–47; Brown, *Amphibious Campaign*, p. 42.

19. DeGrummond, *Baratarians*, pp. 37–48, 58–70.

20. Marigny, "Reflections on the Campaign of Gen. Andrew Jackson," p. 65.

21. Resolutions of the Louisiana Legislature Concerning the Baratarians, December 14, 1814, in Jackson, *Correspondence*, II, 114.

22. Latour, *Historical Memoir*, p. 71. See also Tatum, "Journal," p. 106. According to DeGrummond, *Baratarians*, p. 81, Lafitte offered cannons and ammunition to Jackson immediately after Judge Hall's action.

23. Latour, *Historical Memoir*, p. 72.

24. Captain Lockyer kept his appointment with Lafitte, returning two weeks later as requested. When he found Grand Terre deserted he sent back a report that his mission had failed. DeGrummond, *Baratarians*, pp. 65–71.

25. AJ to Claiborne, September 21, 1814, Jackson Papers, LC.

26. To the Free Coloured Inhabitants of Louisiana, in Jackson, *Correspondence*, II, 59.

27. AJ to W. Allen, December 23, 1814, Jackson Papers, LC.

28. AJ to Coffee, December 11, 1814, Jackson Papers, LC.

CHAPTER 17

1. Latour, *Historical Memoirs*, pp. xxxiii–xxxv.

2. Ibid.; Brooks, *Seige of New Orleans*, pp. 92–96; Horsman, *War of 1812*, pp. 238–239.

3. For all intents and purposes it also terminated sea access to Mobile, a potentially serious setback. See AJ to Winchester, December 16, 1814, and AJ to Coffee, December 17, 1814, Jackson Papers, LC.

4. The exact number of American troops in the New Orleans vicinity was probably unknown to anyone, including Jackson. Perhaps 3,500 to 4,000 Americans is the best approximation of Jackson's strength.

5. The ferrying operation started on December 17 and continued until December 22. For Americans the great advantage of this long ferrying process was that it allowed additional time to bring more American troops into New Orleans.

6. AJ to Carroll, December 16, 1814; Coffee to AJ, December 17, 1814; John Hynes to Coffee, December 16, 1814, Jackson Papers, LC.

7. Charles Gayarré, *History of Louisiana* (New York, 1866), IV, 419.

8. Jackson's Address to the Troops in New Orleans, in Jackson, *Correspondence*, II, 118–119; Parton, *Jackson*, II, 63; Gayarré, *History of Louisiana*, IV, 419. According to Parton the manuscript of this Address was in Livingston's handwriting.

9. Walker, *Jackson and New Orleans*, pp. 143–144; AJ to Coffee, December 19, 1814, Jackson Papers, LC.

10. Reid and Eaton, *Jackson*, p. 306.

11. Gayarré, *History of Louisiana*, IV, 419.

12. Ibid., p. 421; Horsman, *War of 1812*, p. 240.

13. Walker, *Jackson and New Orleans*, p. 126; Brooks, *Seige of New Orleans*, pp. 133–134.

14. DeGrummond, *Baratarians*, pp. 75–76, 85–86.

15. Walker, *Jackson and New Orleans,* p. 150.

16. Ibid., p. 151; Latour, *Historical Memoir,* p. 88.

17. Nolte, *Fifty Years,* pp. 209-210.

18. When Jackson was informed of the arrival of the British by Villeré and friends is not absolutely certain. Jackson reported to Monroe that he received news of the British arrival about noon on December 23, but he does not mention the source. It is possible that he himself was indirectly responsible for generating the information. Having heard rumors of the British arrival, he sent his engineers, Tatum and Latour, to investigate. On the road south they met several refugees fleeing before the enemy. Tatum immediately returned to the city to notify Jackson while Latour continued to Villeré's plantation to discover the strength and disposition of the invading troops. See Latour, *Historical Memoir,* p. 88. Some historians prefer this story (to the one presented in this text) since it is more sober and less dramatic and sounds more likely. See Brown, *Amphibious Campaign,* pp. 96 and 201, note 22. Robin Reilly, the most recent scholar of this campaign, neatly combines both stories in *British at the Gates,* p. 240. In a letter to a friend, dated January 28, 1815, Elegius Fromentin, U.S. senator from Louisiana, said that Villeré was the first to bring the news of the British arrival. *Niles Weekly Register,* February 4, 1815.

19. Nolte, *Fifty Years,* p. 209; Reid to Elizabeth Reid, December 20, 1814, Reid Papers, LC.

20. AJ to Monroe, December 27, 1814, in Jackson, *Correspondence,* II, 127.

21. Ibid.; Robert V. Remini, ed., "Andrew Jackson's Account of the Battle of New Orleans," *THS* (Spring 1967), XXVI, 26-31.

22. Latour, *Historical Memoir,* pp. 102-103; Report of Killed, Wounded and Missing . . . December 23 and 25, 1814 . . . , Jackson Papers, LC.

23. Latour, *Historical Memoir,* p. 112. See also Reid to Abram Maury, December 25, 1814, and Reid to Nathan Reid, December 30, 1814, Reid Papers, LC.

24. And it probably aided the British by filling the canals and facilitating the movement of heavy equipment by the British. DeGrummond, *Baratarians,* p. 101.

25. Reid to Nathan Reid, December 30, 1814, Reid Papers, LC; Remini, ed., "Andrew Jackson's Account of the Battle of New Orleans," pp. 31-33.

26. Fortescue, *History of the British Army,* X, 161.

27. Brown, *Amphibious Campaign,* p. 112; DeGrummond, *Baratarians,* pp. 97-103.

28. AJ to Monroe, December 29, 1814, in Brannan, *Official Letters,* p. 455; Remini, ed., "Andrew Jackson's Account of the Battle of New Orleans," p. 33.

29. Latour, *Historical Memoir,* p. 128.

30. Walker, *Jackson and New Orleans,* p. 227.

31. DeGrummond, *Baratarians,* pp. 106-107. In this engagement American casualties included 9 killed and 8 wounded. Latour, *Historical Memoir,* p. lix; Remini, ed., "Andrew Jackson's Account of the Battle of New Orleans," pp. 33-35.

32. Nolte, *Fifty Years,* p. 214.

33. Reid and Eaton, *Jackson,* pp. 320-321.

34. Parton, *Jackson,* II, 143.

35. Ibid.

36. Marigny, "Reflections on the Campaign of Gen. Andrew Jackson," pp. 66-68.

37. Latour, *Historical Memoir,* pp. 147-148, 126-127; Marigny, "Reflections on the Campaign of Gen. Andrew Jackson," p. 67.

38. Robin Reilly is the only historian who doubts that a review took place and dismisses George R. Gleig, *The Campaigns of the British Army at Washington and New*

Orleans . . . (London, 1836), a contemporary source, on the ground that he could not see over the rampart to what was going on behind it. Reilly, *British at the Gates,* p. 355, note 24.

39. DeGrummond, *Baratarians,* pp. 115–116; Gleig, *Campaigns of the British Army,* p. 173.

40. Nolte, *Fifty Years,* p. 217; Brooks, *Siege of New Orleans,* p. 202.

41. Tatum, "Journal," p. 121.

42. Walker, *Jackson and New Orleans,* p. 256.

43. Ibid; Reid to Elizabeth Reid, February 10, 1815, Reid Papers, LC.

44. AJ to Monroe, January 2, 1815, Jackson Papers, LC.

45. Coles, *War of 1812,* p. 224.

46. Brown, *Amphibious Campaign,* p. 124.

47. Latour, *Historical Memoir,* p. lix.

48. DeGrummond, *Baratarians,* p. 115.

49. AJ to Monroe, January 3, 1815, Jackson Papers, LC.

50. Unknown to Jackson, those unarmed returned to camp. DeGrummond, *Baratarians,* pp. 128–130.

51. Brown, *Amphibious Campaign,* p. 139; Latour, *Historical Memoir,* pp. 165–166.

52. Patterson to AJ, January 7, 1815, Jackson Papers, LC.

53. Walker, *Jackson and New Orleans,* pp. 318–319.

54. In a letter to Monroe, Jackson said he had no more than 3,000 men on the left bank, of whom 600 were regulars. AJ to Monroe, February 13, 1815, Jackson Papers, LC.

55. Lambert to Lord Bathurst, January 10, 1815, in Latour, *Historical Memoir,* p. cl; Horsman, *War of 1812,* pp. 245–246.

CHAPTER 18

1. Reilly, *British at the Gates,* p. 295.

2. It does not seem possible that Mullens could have forgotten what Pakenham had expressly ordered him to do. When the Forty-fourth returned to the forward position after picking up the ladders and fascines, Mullens was not with them. Reilly, *British at the Gates,* p. 296. Mullens believed his regiment had been ordered to its execution and that the bodies of his men were intended to fill the ditch. DeGrummond, *Baratarians,* p. 131.

3. Reid and Eaton, *Jackson,* p. 338.

4. Ibid., p. 339.

5. Walker, *Jackson and New Orleans,* p. 327; Tatum, "Journal," pp. 122–124.

6. *Niles Weekly Register,* February 11, 1815; Walker, *Jackson and New Orleans,* p. 327. The artillery smoke became so thick that General Adair asked batteries 7 and 8 to cease fire temporarily. Parton, *Jackson,* II, 207.

7. Sir Harry Smith, *The Autobiography of Lieutenant General Sir Harry Smith* (London, 1902), I, 236; see also Claiborne to Monroe, January 9, 1815, in Dunbar Rowland, ed., *Official Letter Books of W. C. C. Claiborne* (Jackson, 1917), VI, 332.

8. "A Contemporary Account of the Battle of New Orleans by a Soldier in the Ranks," *The Louisiana Historical Quarterly* (January 1926), IX, 11.

9. Walker, *Jackson and New Orleans,* p. 329; Parton, *Jackson,* II, 196; DeGrummond, *Baratarians,* p. 135. Mullens was not hanged but courtmartialed in June 1815 and cashiered for shamefully neglecting and disobeying orders, which led to the disorder and disaster that ensued. "General Court Martial . . . for the Trial of Brevet Lieutenant Colonel Hon. Thomas Mullins [*sic*]," reprinted in *The Louisiana Historical Quarterly* (January 1926), IX, 109. Reilly, *British at the Gates,* p. 338, is mistaken when he says that Mullens was convicted of "scandalous and infamous

misbehaviour"; he was specifically found not guilty of that charge.

10. Reid and Eaton, *Jackson*, p. 339.

11. Parton, *Jackson*, II, 197; Brown, *Amphibious Campaign*, p. 150.

12. Parton, *Jackson*, II, 197. For a British account of this action see John Henry Cooke, *A Narrative . . . of the Attack on New Orleans in 1814 and 1815* (London, 1835), pp. 234–235. See also John Buchan, *The History of the Royal Scots Fusiliers, 1678–1918* (London, 1925); John S. Cooper, *Rough Notes of Seven Campaigns in Portugal, Spain, France and America During the Years 1809–15* (Carlisle, 1914); Benson E. Hill, *Recollections of an Artillery Officer . . .* (London, 1836); and William Surtees, *Twenty Five Years in the Rifle Brigade* (London, 1833).

13. Parton, *Jackson*, II, 197; Brooks, *Seige of New Orleans*, p. 239.

14. Walker, *Jackson and New Orleans*, p. 330; Reid to Abram Maury, January 9, 1815, Reid Papers, LC; Reilly, *British at the Gates*, p. 299.

15. Lambert to Lord Bathurst, January 10, 1815, in Latour, *Historical Memoir*, p. cli.

16. Ibid.

17. Reid to Abram Maury, January 9, 1815, Reid Papers, LC. A number of British soldiers actually made it to the rampart. Major Thomas Wilkinson, followed by Lieutenant John Lavack, reached the ditch and got across. Wilkinson clambered up the breastwork and raised his head and shoulders over the top only to be riddled with bullets. Other men floundered in the ditch or skidded down the slippery parapet as they attempted to climb it. Lavack managed to reach the summit unharmed just as Wilkinson called out, "Now, why don't the troops come on? The day is our own." As Wilkinson fell before the hail of bullets, Lavack demanded the swords of two American officers standing close to him. "Oh, no," one of them replied, "you are alone, and, therefore, ought to consider yourself *our* prisoner." And looking around and seeing he was indeed all alone, Lavack allowed himself to be taken prisoner without offering resistance. Parton, *Jackson*, II, 199.

18. Coffee to John Donelson, January 25, 1815, in *AHM* (April 1901), VI, 186.

19. Lambert to Lord Bathurst, January 10, 1815, in Latour, *Historical Memoir*, p. cli; Parton, *Jackson*, II, 207.

20. Walker, *Jackson and New Orleans*, p. 332.

21. Tatum, "Journal," p. 126.

22. Brown, *Amphibious Campaign*, p. 148.

23. Walker, *Jackson and New Orleans*, p. 337.

24. Parton, *Jackson*, II, 212. Had Pakenham decided to transport his entire army to the opposite side of the river and then march on New Orleans, Jackson would have been forced to retreat to the city. Under those circumstances it is probable the city would have been destroyed. Alternatively, if Thornton had captured Patterson's guns in time, he could have "completely enfiladed" Jackson's line and "rendered it altogether untenable." Reid and Eaton, *Jackson*, p. 349.

25. Ibid., p. 345.

26. Patterson to the secretary of the navy, January 13, 1815, in Latour, *Historical Memoir*, pp. lx–lxiv.

27. Ibid., p. 167.

28. Ibid., pp. 167–168; Patterson to the secretary of the navy, January 13, 1815, ibid., pp. lx–lxiv.

29. Walker, *Jackson and New Orleans*, p. 353; Robert V. Remini, ed., "Andrew Jackson's Account of the Battle of New Orleans," *THQ* (Spring 1967), XXVI, 35.

30. See "Genl. David B. Morgan's Defense of the Conduct of the Louisiana Militia in the Battle on the Left Side of the River," *The Louisiana Historical Quarterly*

(January 1926), IX, 16–29; Reid to Abram Maury, January 9, 1815, Reid Papers, LC.

31. Walker, *Jackson and New Orleans*, p. 354; Parton, *Jackson*, II, 216; Brooks, *Seige of New Orleans*, pp. 242–243.

32. Lambert to Lord Bathurst, January 10, 1815, in Latour, *Historical Memoir*, p. clii.

33. Raleigh (North Carolina) *Star*, February 10, 1815; *Niles Weekly Register*, February 25, 1815.

34. Walker, *Jackson and New Orleans*, p. 341.

35. "A Contemporary Account of the Battle of New Orleans by a Soldier in the Ranks," p. 14.

36. Parton, *Jackson*, II, 208–209.

37. Walker, *Jackson and New Orleans*, p. 343.

38. Ibid.

39. AJ to Monroe, January 13, 1815, Jackson Papers, LC; Latour, *Historical Memoir*, p. lx.

40. A. P. Hayne to AJ, January 13, 1815, in Brannan, *Official Letters*, p. 459. The casualty reports in the Jackson Papers, LC, state that the action on December 23, 1814, saw 26 killed, 115 wounded, and 72 missing; on December 28, 7 killed and 8 wounded; on January 1, 11 killed and 23 wounded. The total for the four actions on both sides of the river totaled 55 killed, 185 wounded, and 93 missing.

41. Lambert to Bathurst, January 10, 1815, in Latour, *Historical Memoir*, p. clii; Lambert to Bathurst, January 28, 1815, PRO War Office 1/141.

42. AJ to Monroe, January 13, 1815, Jackson Papers, LC.

43. Walker, *Jackson and New Orleans*, p. 369.

44. Tatum, "Journal," p. 125.

45. The British landed between 11,000 and 14,550 men at New Orleans. The size of Lambert's army was therefore considerable. See Return of Casualties . . . 8th of January, 1815, PRO, War Office 1/141; and Latour, *Historical Memoir*, p. lx.

46. Brown, *Amphibious Campaign*, p. 159.

47. Remini, ed., "Andrew Jackson's Account of the Battle of New Orleans," pp. 36–37.

48. See the many letters between Lambert and Jackson, January 8, 9, 11, 12, 16, 1815, Jackson Papers, LC, and in the National Archives, several of which are reprinted in Jackson, *Correspondence*, II, 133–144.

49. AJ to Hays, January 26, 1815, Jackson Papers, LC.

50. AJ to Monroe, February 17, 1815, Jackson Papers, LC.

51. Jackson's Address to his troops on the Right Bank, January 8, 1815, in Latour, *Historical Memoir*, pp. lxiv–lxvi.

52. Extract of proceedings of a court of inquiry into the retreat on the right bank of the Mississippi on 8 January 1815, ibid., p. lxxxii; Brown, *Amphibious Campaign*, pp. 157, 181.

53. Carroll to AJ, September 11, 1817, Jackson Papers, LC; Parton, *Jackson*, II, 383ff. When Congress voted its appreciation to Patterson, only Samuel McKee of Kentucky voted no. *Annals of Congress*, 13th Congress, 3rd Session, p. 1167.

54. W. H. Overton to AJ, January 19, 1815, in Brannan, *Official Letters*, p. 464; Tatum, "Journal," p. 132; Latour, *Historical Memoir*, pp. 187–197.

55. Nolte, *Fifty Years*, p. 224; Remini, ed., "Andrew Jackson's Account of the Battle of New Orleans," p. 39.

56. AJ to Monroe, January 19, 1815, Jackson Papers, LC. "Brave as he is, there is not a man in the world of more caution & prudence than Genl. Jackson. One reason is he would dread a defeat, a thousand times worse than death," John

Reid said. Reid to ———— [March 1814], Reid Papers, LC.

57. The situation was in fact hopeless because of the shortage of provisions and supplies and the near impossibility of getting help; he was surrounded by thousands and commanded only a few hundred men. Lawrence to AJ, February 12, 1815, *Niles Weekly Register*, March 25, 1815.

58. AJ to Monroe, January 19, 1815, Jackson Papers, LC; see also Parton, *Jackson*, II, 270.

59. Abbé Dubourg to AJ, no date, in Jackson, *Correspondence*, II, 150, note 1.

60. Latour, *Historical Memoir*, pp. 197–198.

61. Ibid., pp. 199–200; Reid to Elizabeth Reid, February 10, 1815, Reid Papers, LC. Reid says the girls carried roses and garlands.

62. Latour, *Historical Memoir*, p. 199; Parton, *Jackson*, II, 273.

63. AJ to Robert Hays, February 9, 1815, Jackson Papers, LC.

64. Reid and Eaton, *Jackson*, p. 369.

65. Reid to Elizabeth Reid, February 10, 1815, Reid Papers, LC; Address of Abbé Dubourg to AJ, January 23, 1815, in Brannan, *Official Letters*, pp. 467ff.

66. Parton, *Jackson*, II, 274.

67. Jackson's reply to the Abbé Dubourg, in Brannan, *Official Letters*, p. 468.

68. Latour, *Historical Memoir*, pp. 199–200; Parton, *Jackson*, II, 274.

69. On January 26 the Washington *National Intelligencer* reported that a rumor from Baltimore claimed that the British had been driven from New Orleans. The newspaper doubted the rumor; it could not believe that the British could be driven from their objective so readily.

70. Washington *National Intelligencer*, February 7, 1815.

71. *Niles Weekly Register*, February 14, 1815.

72. John Binns, *Autobiography*, quoted in Parton, *Jackson*, II, 248.

73. Niles *Weekly Register*, February 18, March 4, 1815.

74. William Graham Sumner, *Andrew Jackson* (Boston, 1882), p. 51.

75. *Annals of Congress*, 13th Congress, 3rd Session, pp. 1124–1125, 1167. When Jackson's opinion was solicited for a motto for the medal, he proposed *Dei Voluntas*, "The Will of God." *Calhoun Papers*, II, 29.

76. *Annals of Congress*, 13th Congress, 3rd Session, p. 1155.

77. Ibid., p. 1161.

78. Washington *National Intelligencer*, March 18, 1815.

79. Monroe to AJ, February 5, 1815, Jackson Papers, LC.

80. Copy in Jackson Papers, LC.

81. Indeed many Americans would have agreed with Jackson; for some time many believed that January 8 would be remembered like July 4. After the Civil War, however, the date lost all meaning for Americans—by then the War of 1812 seemed insignificant compared to what the nation had just experienced. Even today the War of 1812 is a vague event in the minds of most Americans. It is one of the least remembered wars in American history. Jackson's opinion of the significance of the date is given in his letter to Robert Hays, February 9, 1815, Jackson Papers, LC.

CHAPTER 19

1. My views on the War of 1812 underwent considerable revision following a research trip to Spain in 1975 and an investigation of Spanish archives in Seville, Madrid, and Simancas. These views were reinforced by a review of notes taken on a research trip to London in 1968. I have been greatly aided by Owsley's *Struggle for the Gulf,* and I am grateful to him for sharing his research and his insights with me.

2. Reilly, *British at the Gates*, p. 343; Brown, *Amphibious Campaign*, pp. 166–167;

Frank L. Owsley, Jr., "Role of the South in the British Grand Strategy in the War of 1812," *THQ* (Spring 1972), XXXI, 36; DeGrummond, *Baratarians*, p. 32. The fourth British memorandum delivered on October 8, 1814, to the American peace commissioners in Ghent contained unmistakable innuendos about the legality of the Louisiana Purchase.

3. The United States seized West Florida in two actions: the first, in 1810, took the far western portion to the Pearl River; the second, in 1812, amputated a further portion extending as far east as the Perdido River. See Isaac J. Cox, *The West Florida Controversy, 1798–1813* (Baltimore, 1918), pp. 487–529.

4. "It is their [the British] wish to recover Louisiana, & to render the Floridas secure," John Reid wrote. Unquestionably this attitude reflected Jackson's view. Reid to Elizabeth Reid, 1814, Reid Papers, LC. See also Owsley, "Role of the South," p. 37.

5. Onís to Duque de San Carolos, March 11, 1815, Estado, leg. 5557, AHN; Cevallos (Spain's foreign minister) to Fernán Núñez (Spain's minister to London), December 8, 1814, Estado, leg. 2675, Simancas AGS.

6. Cevallos to Núñez, April 21, 1815, Estado, leg. 2675, Simancas, AGS.

7. Monroe to Madison, May 3, 1815, Monroe Papers, LC. Loss of the Battle of New Orleans opens up many possibilities, but the argument here concerns Britain's intentions before the battle, not "what if" questions. See J. Leitch Wright, Jr., *Britain and the American Frontier, 1783–1815* (Athens, Ga., 1975), pp. 172–174, and Abernethy, *The South in the New Nation*, p. 401.

8. Although the Treaty of Ghent specifically called for the mutual restoration of all territory, places, and possessions whatsoever "taken by either party from the other" during the war or after the signing of the treaty, the invasion instructions to Admiral Cochrane and General Pakenham clearly described Britain's intention to keep as an option the retention of conquests in Louisiana after the war. The evidence and arguments for this statement are forcefully and, to my mind, convincingly advanced by Brown, *Amphibious Campaign*, pp. 166–167, and Reilly, *British at the Gates*, p. 343. It is Brown's contention that the British intended to reopen negotiations for a new treaty after Jackson was defeated. It should be remembered that the treaty stipulated that hostilities would not cease until an exchange of ratifications had been completed. This did not take place until February 16, 1815, at which time the war officially ended. See Wright, *Britain and the American Frontier*, p. 179.

9. Winchester to AJ, February 20, 1815, Jackson Papers, LC.

10. Reilly, *British at the Gates*, p. 343.

11. Mahon, *War of 1812*, p. 341.

12. Horsman, *War of 1812*, pp. 226–227; Mahon, *War of 1812*, pp. 341–343.

13. Owsley, "Role of the South," p. 33.

14. J. Leitch Wright, Jr., "A Note on the First Seminole War as Seen by the Indians, Negroes and the British Advisers," *Journal of Southern History* (November 1968), XXXIV, 569.

15. Owsley, *Struggle for the Gulf*, Chapter 17; Bradford Perkins, *Castlereagh and Adams: England and the United States, 1812–1823* (Berkeley and Los Angeles, 1964), pp. 71–72, 78, 82.

16. Fred Israel, ed., *Major Peace Treaties of Modern History, 1648–1967* (New York, 1967), I, 704. Since the Treaty of Fort Jackson was signed by only one Red Stick chief, who could hardly speak for the entire hostile faction of the Creek Nation, the United States was still technically at war with the Creeks. Consequently neither the Red Sticks nor the British ever recognized the validity of the Treaty of Fort Jackson. Owsley, *Struggle for the Gulf*, Chapter 8. Henry Clay, one of the commissioners at Ghent, claimed that the Treaty of Fort Jackson violated the ninth article of the Treaty of Ghent. Moreover, he contended that "if the

treaty [of Fort Jackson] really were made by a minority of the nation, it was not obligatory upon the whole nation." *Annals of Congress,* 15th Congress, 2nd Session, pp. 633–635.

17. Cochrane to Nicholls, February 14, 1815, PRO Admiralty 1/508.

18. Cochrane to Malcolm, February 17, 1815; Cochrane to Lambert, February 3, 1815, PRO War Office 1/143.

19. Nicholls to Hawkins, May 12, 1815, in *Niles Weekly Register,* June 24, 1815; A. J. Dallas to AJ, June 12, 1815, in Carter, *Territorial Papers,* XV, 62.

20. It should be remembered that the invasion of the Gulf was in part an attempt to distract the United States from invading Canada. By 1815, however, Lord Castlereagh had already inaugurated a policy of conciliation toward the United States. An excellent account of diplomatic relations between the United States and Britain after the war is Perkins, *Castlereagh and Adams.* On Canada as hostage to Anglo-American peace see ibid., p. 198. Also excellent on the diplomacy of this period (and a work I have relied on heavily) is Bemis, *Adams,* pp. 196ff.

21. The negotiations leading to the Anglo-American Convention can be traced in Bemis, *Adams,* pp. 278–299. Perkins, *Castlereagh and Adams,* is excellent on both the Convention and the Rush-Bagot agreement.

22. Bathurst to Charles Cameron, June 8, 1816, PRO Foreign Office 5/127.

23. Wright, "A Note on the First Seminole War," p. 572; John K. Mahon, "British Strategy and Southern Indians: War of 1812," *Florida Historical Quarterly* (April 1966), XLIV, 300.

24. Owsley, *Struggle for the Gulf,* Chapter 16. Nicholls was so intent on his objective that he signed a treaty of alliance with the Creeks on his own initiative and informed Hawkins of his action, implying official approval. Nicholls to Hawkins, May 12, 1815, in *Niles Weekly Register,* June 24, 1815. When word of Nicholls's action reached London it was immediately disavowed. Perkins, *Castlereagh and Adams,* p. 285. However, the disavowal was not made in a public manner and various distinctions were later bestowed on him. Bemis, *Adams,* p. 303.

25. Nicholls to Bathurst, August 24, 1815, PRO War Office 1/143.

26. Coles, *War of 1812,* p. 188; Owsley, *Struggle for the Gulf,* Chapter 17.

27. See, for example, the letters of John Reid, particularly Reid to Nathan Reid, October 17, 1813, Reid Papers, LC.

28. Rogin, *Fathers and Children,* p. 165.

29. It was in researching the archives of Seville and reading American history from a Spanish perspective that I got a totally different impression of American activities and motivations in the southwest—particularly the activities of General Jackson. The Spanish recognized what he was about, and they saw him as their greatest and most dangerous enemy. See González Manrique to Juan Ruiz de Apodaca, January 10, 27, February 15, July 23, 1814, Cuba, leg. 1795, AGI. Like the Indians, the Spanish struggled valiantly to retain their land against determined Americans committed to dispossessing them.

CHAPTER 20

1. See, for example, Lambert to AJ, January 20, February 8, 27, March 18, 1815; Cochrane to AJ, February 20, 1815, in Jackson, *Correspondence,* II, 151, 161–162, 175–176, 181, 191.

2. AJ to Claiborne, February 3, 1815, Jackson Papers, LC.

3. Claiborne to AJ, February 24, 1815, Jackson Papers, LC.

4. Extract from a General Order, February 28, 1815, in Jackson, *Correspondence,* II, 181.

5. The Creoles were so flabbergasted by this latest outrage that they sup-

posedly began calling Jackson a "tyrant." Gayarré, *History of Louisiana*, IV, 585.

6. Parton, *Jackson*, II, 311.

7. AJ to Arbuckle, March 5, 1815, Jackson Papers, LC.

8. Reid and Eaton, *Jackson*, p. 381; an account of the incident can also be found in Claiborne to Monroe, February 10, 1815, in Dunbar Rowland, ed., *Official Letter Books of W. C. C. Claiborne*, VI, 344.

9. Nolte, *Fifty Years*, p. 599.

10. AJ to Lambert, March 6, 1815, in Jackson, *Correspondence*, II, 184.

11. Jackson's Order to D. A. Hall, March 11, 1815, ibid., p. 189.

12. Latour, *Historical Memoir*, pp. ciii, cv; other variations can be found in Parton, *Jackson*, II, 316–317, and Jackson, *Correspondence*, II, 195–196.

13. Latour, *Historical Memoir*, pp. cxvi–cxvii.

14. Reid and Eaton, *Jackson*, p. 384.

15. Parton, *Jackson*, II, 318–319; Gayarré, *History of Louisiana*, IV, 620. Messrs. Dick, Robinson, and Henning argued the case for the prosecution. See *Niles Weekly Register*, June 3, 10, 1815, for the trial proceedings. A number of papers relating to the trial are contained in the Jackson Papers, LC.

16. Reid and Eaton, *Jackson*, pp. 386–387.

17. Statement in Reid's hand in Jackson Papers, LC. A slightly different version is given in Reid and Eaton, *Jackson*, p. 387.

18. A Louisiana investigation committee later called the fine "extravagant" in view of the depressed state of monetary affairs in the country. "Andrew Jackson and Judge D. A. Hall," *The Louisiana Historical Quarterly* (October 1922), V, 511.

19. Statement in Jackson Papers, LC; Bassett, *Jackson*, p. 229. Hall's position was ably defended in the Louisiana *Gazette*, April 15, 1815, reprinted in *Niles Weekly Register*, June 17, 1815.

20. Reid and Eaton, *Jackson*, p. 387.

21. Gayarré, *History of Louisiana*, IV, 625.

22. Dallas to AJ, April 12, 1815, in Jackson, *Correspondence*, II, 204.

23. AJ to Rachel, August 10, 1814, copy JPP. Rachel to Robert Hays, March 5, 1815, Jackson Papers, LC. For Rachel's later views of New Orleans see her letter to Mrs. Eliza Kingsley, April 27, 1821, quoted in Parton, *Jackson*, II, 595.

24. Parton, Jackson, II, 323–324.

25. Nolte, *Fifty Years*, p. 238; Rachel to Robert Hays, March 5, 1815, Jackson Papers, LC; Reid to Elizabeth Reid, February 22, 1815, Reid Papers, LC.

26. Parton, *Jackson*, II, 324–325.

27. AJ to Coffee, April 24, 1815, Jackson Papers, LC.

28. Reid to John Williams, April 1815, Reid Papers, LC; AJ to Coffee, April 28, 1815, Jackson Papers, LC.

29. Reid to Sophia Reid, April 20, 1815, Reid Papers. LC.

30. Parton, *Jackson*, II, 329.

31. Ibid.

32. Livingston to AJ, January 4, 1816, in Jackson, *Correspondence*, II, 224.

33. Reid to Sophia Reid, October 25, 1815, Reid Papers, LC.

34. See Reid's letters to his mother, November and December, 1815, Reid Papers LC.

35. Describing his trip to Virginia, Jackson said he had "the pleasure of seeing all the great men at the city, was friendly greeted by all, and was obliged to flee the profered hospitality of the surrounding cities to restore my health and preserve life." AJ to Robert Butler, December 31, 1815, Jackson Papers, LC; Parton, *Jackson*, II, 334.

36. Dallas to AJ, July 1, 1815, in Jackson, *Correspondence*, II, 212.

37. Andrew Hynes to AJ, October 24, 1815, Jackson Papers, LC. See also William Carroll to AJ, October 4, 1815, Jackson Papers, LC.

CHAPTER 21

1. Doherty, *Richard Keith Call,* p. 14.

2. Parton, *Jackson,* II, 333.

3. Governor of Georgia to General Gaines, February 5, 1817, in *ASPMA,* I, 681.

4. Rogin, *Fathers and Children,* p. 169.

5. Ibid., p. 170.

6. Jackson's Talk to the Creeks, September 4, 1815, in Jackson, *Correspondence,* II, 216–217, and his Talk on August 5, 1815, Jackson Papers, LC. See also AJ to George Colbert, February 13, 1816, Jackson Papers, LC.

7. Reid had accompanied Jackson and Rachel to Washington late in 1815 because of the apparent attempt of some members of Congress to punish, impeach, or reprimand Jackson for his treatment of Judge Hall. Jackson of course was far too popular for anything to come of this effort, and the administration strongly supported him. They left Washington on December 31, 1815, and Reid went for a visit with his family in Virginia, where he died.

8. The biography was reissued in 1974 by the University of Alabama Press in an excellent edition edited by Frank Lawrence Owsley, Jr. For information on Reid and the early editions of the book see the editor's introduction, particularly pp. vii–xii. Reid's Papers, in three volumes, are located in the Library of Congress.

9. AJ to James Brown, September 6, 1816, in Jackson, *Correspondence,* II, 259.

10. Ibid.

11. Coffee undertook an unwarranted, independent survey of the cession in January 1816, which Jackson approved. This, too, the Cherokees reported to Washington as part of their complaint. The fact that Coffee did it alone, without the attendance of the other commissioners assigned to the task, caused the War Department to question the legality of the survey. Annie Heloise Abel, "The History of Events Resulting in Indian Consolidation West of the Mississippi River," AHA, *Annual Report,* 1906, p. 279; Gordon T. Chappell, "John Coffee: Surveyor and Land Agent," *Alabama Review* (July 1961), XIV, 189–190.

12. *ASPIA,* II, 89–91. Tennesseans in Davidson County were particularly vociferous and expressed their outrage directly to the President. See their Remonstrance against the Treaty, ibid.

13. AJ to Crawford, June 10, 1816, in *ASPIA,* II, 110; AJ to Crawford, June 4, 1816, Jackson Papers, DUL; Chase C. Mooney, *William H. Crawford* (Lexington, 1974), p. 84; Crawford to AJ, March 8, 1816; AJ to Crawford, February 13, 1816, in Jackson, *Correspondence,* II, 235, 231–232.

14. Instructions of the secretary of war to the commissioners can be found in *ASPIA,* II, 100–123.

15. AJ to Coffee, September 19, 1816, Coffee Papers, THS.

16. Abel, "Indian Consolidation," p. 280.

17. AJ to Monroe, March 4, 1817, Monroe Papers, NYPL.

18. Ibid.

19. AJ to Coffee, September 19, 1816, Coffee Papers, THS; AJ to Monroe, March 4, 1817, Monroe Papers, NYPL.

20. AJ to Henry Atkinson, May 15, 1819, in *Calhoun Papers,* IV, 63.

21. AJ to Crawford, July 20, 1816, in *ASPIA,* II, 103.

22. Thomas L. McKenney to Christopher Vandeventer, October 24, 1818, in *Calhoun Papers,* III, 231.

23. AJ, Meriwether, and Franklin to Crawford, September 20, 1816, in *ASPIA,* II, 105.

24. AJ to Calhoun, August 24, 1819, in *Calhoun Papers,* IV, 271–272. The

same sentiment was expressed the following year. "And it is now discovered that nothing can be done without corrupting their Chiefs. This is so inconsistent with the principles of our Government that it is high time the Legislature should exercise its function and pass all laws for the regulation of the Indians. If they have too much land circumscribe them. Furnish them with the means of agriculture, and you will thereby lay the foundation of their civilization by making them husbandmen. Treat them humanely and Liberally but put an end to treating with them, and obtaining their Country by corrupting their Chiefs which is the only *way* by which a Treaty can be obtained." AJ to Calhoun, August 25, 1820, Jackson Papers, LC.

25. AJ to Crawford, July 20, 1816, in *ASPIA,* II, 103.

26. AJ to Crawford, 1816, Jackson, in *Correspondence,* II, 248.

27. AJ, Meriwether, and Franklin to Crawford, September 20, 1816, in *ASPIA,* II, 104–105.

28. AJ's "Talk," September 8, 1816, Jackson Papers, LC.

29. AJ to Monroe, October 23, 1816, in Jackson, *Correspondence,* II, 261; AJ to Governor McMinn, September 15, 1816, in "McMinn Correspondence," *AHM,* VIII, 386–387; Treaty with the Cherokees, in *ASPIA,* II, 92; Kappler, *Indian Affairs,* II, 133–134; see also Charles C. Royce, *Indian Land Cessions in the United States* (Washington, 1900), pp. 682–683, plate 1.

30. AJ, Meriwether, and Franklin to Crawford, September 20, 1816, in *ASPIA,* II, 105; Grace S. Woodward, *The Cherokees* (Norman, 1963), p. 135; R. S. Cotterill, *The Southern Tribes* (Norman, 1954), p. 200.

31. AJ, Meriwether, and Franklin to Crawford, September 20, 1816, in *ASPIA,* II, 105.

32. AJ to Rachel, September 18, 1816, Thomas Gilcrease Institute, Tulsa, Oklahoma.

33. Arrell M. Gibson, *The Chickasaws* (Norman, 1971), p. 105.

34. Treaty with the Chickasaws, in *ASPIA,* II, 92; Kappler, *Indian Affairs,* II, 135–137; Royce, *Land Cessions,* pp. 682–683, plates 1, 38, 56, 57, 58.

35. AJ to Monroe, October 23, 1816, in Jackson, *Correspondence,* II, 261; AJ, Meriwether, and Franklin to Crawford, September 20, 1816, in *ASPIA,* II, 105.

36. Terms of the treaty are given in *ASPIA,* II, 92; Instructions to the Commissioners, ibid., pp. 100–123. See also Gibson, *Chickasaws,* pp. 100–101.

37. Treaty with the Choctaws, in *ASPIA,* II, 95; Arthur H. De Rosier, Jr., *The Removal of the Choctaw Indians* (Knoxville, 1970), p. 37; Kappler, *Indian Affairs,* II, 137.

38. AJ to Crawford, November 12, 1816, in *ASPIA,* II, 117.

39. Ibid.

40. Chappell, "John Coffee: Surveyor and Land Agent," *Alabama Review* (October 1961), XIV, 243; AJ to Calhoun, July 8, 1820, Jackson Papers, LC; William A. Love, "General Jackson's Military Road," *Publications of the Mississippi Historical Society* (1910), XI, 402–417.

41. AJ to Monroe, October 23, 1816, in Jackson, *Correspondence,* II, 261.

42. Ibid.

43. AJ to Graham, December 21, 1816, in *ASPIA,* II, 123.

44. AJ to Monroe, November 12, October 23, 1816, in Jackson, *Correspondence,* II, 261, 263–264; AJ to Monroe, March 4, 1817, Monroe Papers, NYPL; Gordon Chappell, "The Life and Activities of General John Coffee," *THQ* (March 1942), I, 137–138.

45. AJ to John Hutchins, April 22, 1816, Coffee Papers, THS.

46. Chappell, "John Coffee: Surveyor and Land Agent," p. 246; AJ to Coffee, January 27, 1818, Coffee Papers, THS; Rogin, *Fathers and Children,* pp. 174–178. According to Rogin, Coffee, Overton, and John Donelson made fortunes but

Jackson did not. Jackson's desire to fill up this land was not limited to friends and relatives, as his many letters to Monroe and Crawford attest.

47. Reginald Horsman, "American Indian Policy and the Origins of Manifest Destiny," in Francis Paul Prucha, ed., *The Indian in American History* (New York, 1971), p. 23; Wilber R. Jacobs, *Dispossessing the American Indian* (New York, 1972), p. 158. See also Bernard Sheehan, *Seeds of Extinction* (Chapel Hill, 1973), pp. 243–275; Abel, "Indian Consolidation," pp. 250–259. Blount to AJ, December 28, 1809, Jackson Papers, LC.

48. George Graham to AJ, January 13, 1817, in *ASPIA,* II, 140. Reginald Horsman, *The Origins of Indian Removal* (East Lansing, 1970), pp. 8–9.

49. George Graham to AJ, May 16, 1817, in *ASPIA,* p. 143. Jackson probably allowed the Cherokees to resist his earlier demand for their land on the north side of the Tennessee River so that they would have "sufficient area left to obtain by barter a sufficient country west of the Mississippi for their whole nation." AJ to Joseph McMinn, October 16, 1816, in *AHM,* VIII, 387–388.

50. Woodward, *Cherokees,* pp. 136–137.

51. Jackson's Talk with the Cherokees, June 28, 1817, Jackson Papers, LC; Chiefs and Headmen to Commissioners, July 2, 1817, in *ASPIA,* II, 143; Rachel C. Eaton, *John Ross and the Cherokee Indians* (Chicago, 1921), p. 26.

52. Commissioners to George Graham, July 8, 1817, Jackson Papers, LC.

53. AJ to Robert Butler, June 21, 1817, Jackson Papers, LC.

54. Commissioners to Graham, July 8, 1817, Jackson Papers, LC.

55. Chiefs and Headmen to Commissioners, July 2, 1817, in *ASPIA,* II, 143.

56. Commissioners to Graham, July 8, 1817, Jackson Papers, LC.

57. Ibid.

58. Ibid.

59. "Instructions of a Deputation of our Warriors . . . for the Affairs of the Cherokee Nation," September 19, 1817, in *ASPIA,* II, 145.

60. Jackson was not always successful in his first negotiations with Indians. He failed with the Choctaws in 1819 but succeeded the following year. De Rosier, *Removal of the Choctaw Indians,* pp. 50–51; AJ to Calhoun, August 24, 1819, in *Calhoun Papers,* IV, 271–272. After his initial failure with the Choctaws Jackson was reluctant to take on other negotiations with the Indians—but he soon relented.

61. Treaty with Cherokees, July 8, 1817, in *ASPIA,* II, 130; Royce, *Land Cessions,* pp. 684–685, plate 15; Gideon Morgan, Jr., to Calhoun, February 12, 1819, in *Calhoun Papers,* III, 571–572.

62. Commissioners to Graham, July 8, 1817, Jackson Papers, LC.

63. On the problems encountered in implementing this treaty and arranging for removal see Mary E. Young, *Redskins, Ruffleshirts and Rednecks* (Norman, 1961), p. 12. The treaty had to be renegotiated, and removal of the entire tribe had to await Jackson's election to the presidency. Lawrence F. Schmeckebier, *The Office of Indian Affairs* (Baltimore, 1927), p. 30.

64. Commissioners to Graham, July 8, 1817, Jackson Papers, LC.

65. Ibid.

66. AJ to Calhoun, September 2, 1820, Jackson Papers, LC; AJ to Overton, June 8, 1829, Dickinson Papers, TSL.

67. The most recent examination of this question is Richard H. Faust, "Another Look at General Jackson and the Indians of the Mississippi Territory," *The Alabama Review* (July 1975), XXVIII, 202ff. See also Roy H. Pearce, *The Savages of America* (Baltimore, 1953), p. 70.

68. The best defense of Jackson's removal policy as policy is Francis P. Prucha, "Andrew Jackson's Indian Policy: A Reassessment," *Journal of American History* (December 1969), LVI, 527–539. See also Ronald N. Satz, *American Indian Policy in the Jacksonian Era* (Lincoln, 1975), pp. 9–12.

69. This idea is developed at length with all of its psychological overtones and undertones in Rogin, *Fathers and Children.*

70. Treaty signed October 19, 1818, in Kappler, *Indian Affairs,* II, 135–137; see also Royce, *Land Cessions,* pp. 694–695, plates 56, 57, 58; AJ to George W. Campbell, October 5, 1815, in Jackson, *Correspondence,* II, 395; and Gibson, *Chickasaws,* p. 105. On early removal see Horsman, *Origins of Indian Removal, passim.*

71. AJ to Monroe, March 4, 1817, Monroe Papers, NYPL.

72. Samuel C. Williams, *Beginnings of West Tennessee in the Land of the Chickasaws, 1541–1841* (Johnson City, Tennessee, 1930), pp. 86–89. Shelby pretty much left the arrangements for the convention to Jackson. Ibid., p. 86.

73. Ibid., p. 87.

74. Quoted in Young, *Redskins, Ruffleshirts and Rednecks,* p. 40. See also William Vans to Calhoun, June 23, 1820, in *Calhoun Papers,* V, 214; Levi Colbert and Samuel Seeley to Calhoun, February 11, 1819, ibid., III, 566. Calhoun had authorized $4,500 in cash for gifts and expenses and an additional $6,500 worth of goods. Calhoun to Isaac Shelby and AJ, May 2, 1818, ibid., II, 277.

75. AJ to Thomas Kirkman, October 20, 1818, and AJ to Washington Jackson, December 28, 1818, in *AHM* (April 1899), V, 99–101; Abel, "Indian Consolidation," p. 284, ft. g; AJ to Calhoun, July 31, 1818, in *Calhoun Papers,* II, 446–447; Williams, *Beginnings of West Tennessee,* p. 296.

76. AJ's Talk to the Chickasaws, October 1818, Jackson Papers, LC. Details of the negotiations with the Chickasaws can be found in the Journal of the Convention, Jackson Papers, LC, reprinted in Williams, *Beginnings of West Tennessee,* pp. 283–300, and Robert Butler to Calhoun, October 2, 1818, in *Calhoun Papers,* III, 182–184.

77. Journal of the Convention, Jackson Papers, LC; Williams, *Beginnings of West Tennessee,* pp. 89, 297. During the presidential election of 1828, when this incident received some attention in the newspapers, Shelby admitted he had cited the $300,000 figure when queried by Jackson, but he also insisted that his meaning had been misunderstood.

78. Kappler, *Indian Affairs,* II, 135–137, 174–177.

79. Calhoun to AJ, November 13, 1818, in Carter, *Territorial Papers,* XVIII, 466.

80. Abel, "Indian Consolidation," p. 284, ft. g.

81. Williams, *Beginnings of West Tennessee,* pp. 87–92.

82. Abel, "Indian Consolidation," p. 284, ft. g.

83. Isaac Shelby to Calhoun, October 29, 20, 1818, in *Calhoun Papers,* III, 242, 245.

CHAPTER 22

1. AJ to Monroe, October 23, 1816, in Jackson, *Correspondence,* II, 262; Monroe to AJ, March 1, 1817, Jackson Papers, LC.

2. AJ to Monroe, March 18, 1817, Jackson Papers, LC.

3. Actually Crawford had been appointed secretary of the treasury by President Madison and took office on October 22, 1816. He was reappointed to the post by Monroe. When Crawford resigned as war secretary his chief clerk, George Graham, served as acting secretary until the appointment of Calhoun.

4. Division Order, April 22, 1817, Jackson Papers, LC, reprinted in Parton, *Jackson,* II, 373, and in Jackson, *Correspondence,* II, 291–292; Charles Wiltse, *John C. Calhoun, Nationalist* (New York and Indianapolis, 1944), pp. 150–151.

5. AJ to Scott, September 8, 1817; Scott to AJ, October 4, 1817, Jackson Papers, LC. In his initial letter Jackson said he did not believe Scott guilty of the

charges but that "candor" required him to ask "how far they may be incorrectly stated." Scott's replies to Jackson do him no credit either.

6. AJ to Scott, December 3, 1817, in Jackson, *Correspondence*, II, 338–339.

7. Scott to AJ, January 2, 1818, Jackson Papers, LC. See also Scott's exchange of letters with the secretary of war on this subject, in *Calhoun Papers*, III, 604–605, 632, 641–643, 654–655.

8. Calhoun to AJ, December 29, 1817, Jackson Papers, LC.

9. Ibid.; Wiltse, *Calhoun*, p. 155.

10. Monroe to AJ, December 14, 1816, in Jackson, *Correspondence*, II, 266.

11. AJ to Zuniga, April 23, 1816, ibid., 241.

12. Zuniga to AJ, May 26, 1816, Jackson Papers, LC; Captain Ferdinand Amelung to AJ, June 4, 1816, in Jackson, *Correspondence*, II, 242–243.

13. The cannons had little effect on the walls of the fort, but when the balls were heated and lobbed inside the fortress, one of them landed in a magazine in which Nicholls had stored more than 700 barrels of powder. The explosion was devastating. Edwin C. McReynolds, *The Seminoles* (Norman, 1957), p. 77.

14. General Edmund P. Gaines to D. C. Clinch, May 23, 1816, in *ASPFA*, IV, 558; Prucha, *Sword of the Republic*, p. 130; James W. Silver, *Edmund Pendleton Gaines, Frontier General* (Baton Rouge, 1949), p. 63.

15. On the Seminole raids see W. W. Bibb to AJ, May 19, 1818, in Carter, *Territorial Papers*, XVIII, 331–333.

16. Abernethy, *Frontier*, p. 272. See also statement of John H. Eaton attesting to Jackson's lack of connection with the Pensacola enterprise, in *ASPMA*, I, 751.

17. Gaines to AJ, November 21, 1817, in *ASPMA*, I, 686; Silver, *Gaines*, p. 69.

18. Calhoun to Gaines, December 16, 1817, in *ASPMA*, I, 689.

19. Ibid.

20. Calhoun to AJ, December 26, 1817, ibid.

21. Benton, *Thirty Years View*, I, 170.

22. AJ to Monroe, January 6, 1818, Monroe Papers, NYPL; copy in Jackson, *Correspondence*, II, 345–346.

23. Monroe to Adams, March 11, 1830; Monroe to Calhoun, May 19, 1830, in Stanislaus Murray Hamilton, ed., *Writings of James Monroe* (New York, 1903), VII, 209, 217; Wiltse, *Calhoun*, pp. 156–157.

24. Rhea to AJ, January 12, 1818, in Jackson, *Correspondence*, II, 348.

25. Rhea to AJ, December 18, 1818, ibid., p. 404. On the floor of Congress during the House investigation of the Seminole War, Rhea said Jackson informed the secretary of war on January 20, 1818, of his intended actions and received a reply on February 6 "acquainting him of the entire approbation of the President of all the measures he had adopted to terminate the war." *Annals of Congress*, 15th Congress, 2nd Session, p. 863.

26. Benton, *Thirty Years View*, I, 179.

27. Monroe to AJ, December 28, 1817, Monroe Papers, NYPL.

28. Bemis, *Adams*, p. 314.

29. AJ to Donelson, February 5, 1818, in Jackson, *Correspondence*, II, 353.

30. Historians have gone round and round on this controversy because they miss the central point. They argue over responsibility on an either/or basis: either they defend Monroe or they defend Jackson. It seems to me both Jackson and the administration share the responsibility for the seizure, one being just about as guilty as the other. For the various viewpoints see Bassett, *Jackson*, pp. 247ff.; James, *Jackson*, pp. 827ff; Richard R. Stenberg, "Jackson's Rhea Letter Hoax," *JSH* (1936), II, 480–496; Ammon, *Monroe*, pp. 415–417; Bemis, *Adams*, p. 314; Remini, *Jackson*, pp. 79–81; George Dangerfield, *The Era of Good Feelings* (New York, 1952), pp. 126, 138–140.

CHAPTER 23

1. AJ to Captain McKeever, March 1818, in Parton, *Jackson,* II, 447.

2. *ASPMA,* I, 682, 726.

3. Hubert B. Fuller, *The Purchase of Florida* (Gainesville, 1964), p. 247. McReynolds, *Seminoles,* p. 78.

4. J. Leitch Wright, Jr., "A Note on the First Seminole War," p. 575.

5. Arbuthnot's Journal, in *ASPFA,* IV, 610.

6. *Niles Weekly Register,* May 31, 1817.

7. AJ to Calhoun, February 10, 26, March 25, 1818, in *ASPMA,* I, 697, 698–699.

8. Ibid., p. 690. "We have experienced bad roads, high waters, & constant rain, with the dreary prospects of great scarcity of provisions," Jackson told Rachel after he arrived at the Negro fort. AJ to Rachel, March 26, 1818, Miscellaneous Jackson Papers, HUL.

9. AJ to Calhoun, February 14, 1818; AJ to Gaines, April 8, 1816, Jackson Papers, LC; AJ to Rachel, March 26, April 10, 1818, Miscellaneous Jackson Papers, HUL.

10. AJ to Masot, March 25, 1818, in *ASPFA,* IV, 562.

11. Masot to AJ, April 15, 1818, Jackson Papers, LC; in Jackson, *Correspondence,* II, 359–360.

12. *ASPMA,* I, 698.

13. Fuller, *Purchase of Florida,* p. 246; McReynolds, *Seminoles,* p. 84.

14. AJ to Calhoun, April 8, 1818, in Jackson, *Correspondence,* II, 358.

15. Ibid., pp. 358–359.

16. AJ to Rachel, April 8, 1818, ibid., p. 358; AJ to Calhoun, May 5, 1818, in *ASPMA,* I, 702.

17. AJ to Calhoun, May 5, 1818, in *ASPMA,* I, p. 700; AJ to Rachel, April 10, 1818, Miscellaneous Jackson Papers, HUL; *Niles Weekly Register,* August 21, 1819.

18. AJ to Calhoun, April 20, 1818, in *ASPMA,* I, 700–701.

19. Arbuthnot to John Arbuthnot, April 2, 1818, ibid., p. 722. Peter Cook disliked Arbuthnot and assisted in incriminating him. Cook to Elizabeth Carney, January 19, 1818, in *ASPFA,* IV, 605.

20. AJ to Calhoun, May 5, 1818, in *ASPMA,* I, 702.

21. Wright, "A Note on the First Seminole War," p. 574.

22. AJ to Rachel, April 8, 1818, in Jackson, *Correspondence,* II, 357.

23. AJ to Calhoun, April 26, 1818, ibid., p. 363.

24. *Niles Weekly Register,* June 6, 1818.

25. *ASPMA,* I, 734.

26. Ibid.

27. *ASPFA,* IV, 595.

28. AJ to Calhoun, May 5, 1818, in Jackson, *Correspondence,* II, 367.

29. AJ to Calhoun, May 5, 1818, in *ASPFA,* IV, 601–602; AJ to Calhoun, May 19, 1818, in *Calhoun Papers,* III, 547.

30. AJ to Calhoun, May 5, 1818, in *ASPFA,* IV, 601–602.

31. AJ to Calhoun, April 26, 1818, in Jackson, *Correspondence,* II, 363–364.

32. AJ to Calhoun, May 5, 1818, ibid., p. 367.

33. Several letters and documents respecting the Chehaw affair can be found in *ASPMA,* I, 774–778. See also Parton, *Jackson,* II, 491.

34. AJ to Rabun, May 7, 1818, in *ASPMA,* I, 777.

35. Rabun to AJ, June 1, 1818, Jackson Papers, LC.

36. AJ to Rabun, August 1, 1818, in Parton, *Jackson,* II, 495.

37. Parton, *Jackson*, II, 492–493; AJ to General William McIntosh, July 8, 1818, in *Calhoun Papers*, II, 367.

38. AJ to Calhoun, May 7, 1818, ibid., p. 371.

39. Masot to AJ, May 22, 1818, ibid.

40. AJ to the Commanding Officer of Pensacola, May 24, 1818, ibid.

41. Masot to AJ, May 24, 1818, ibid., pp. 372–373; also in *ASPFA*, IV, 569, and *ASPMA*, I, 713.

42. Parton, *Jackson*, II, 492–493.

43. AJ to Calhoun, June 2, 1818, in *ASPFA*, IV, 602–603; Caroline Mays Brevard, *A History of Florida*, James Alexander Robertson, ed., (De Land, Florida, 1924), I, 55.

44. Small pockets of Spanish soldiers remained in certain towns like St. Augustine, but they were weak and virtually insignificant; for all practical purposes Jackson had destroyed Spanish rule in Florida by his campaign.

45. Proclamation, May 29, 1818, in Jackson, *Correspondence*, II, 374–375; State Papers, 15th Congress, 2nd Session, No. 14, 100.

46. AJ to Monroe, June 2, 1818, Monroe Papers, NYPL. Italics mine.

47. AJ to Calhoun, January 4, 1821, Jackson Papers, LC. In fact Jackson always believed he could have taken Canada if he had been assigned to the northern frontier. See his letters to the secretary of war, March 1, 15, 1813, in Jackson, *Correspondence*, I, 285–286, 291–292.

48. AJ to Calhoun, June 2, 1818, ibid., II, 380.

49. Ammon, *Monroe*, pp. 417–425.

50. Ibid., p. 416; Margaret L. Coit, *John C. Calhoun, American Portrait* (Boston, 1950), p. 123.

51. Monroe to Calhoun, January 30, 1818, in *Calhoun Papers*, II, 104; Ammon, *Monroe*, pp. 416–417.

52. Calhoun to W. W. Bibb, May 13, 1818, in *Calhoun Papers*, II, 291.

53. Adams, *Memoirs*, IV, 103–107; Ammon, *Monroe*, p. 421.

54. Adams, *Memoirs*, IV, 103–107; Ammon, *Monroe*, p. 421.

55. Adams, *Memoirs*, IV, 108–114; Mooney, *Crawford*, p. 178.

56. Monroe to AJ, July 19, 1818, in Monroe, *Writings*, VI, 54–61.

57. Ibid. A portion of this letter is reprinted in Jackson, *Correspondence*, II, 382–383.

58. Monroe, *Writings*, VI, 54–61.

59. Coit, *Calhoun*, p. 124.

60. AJ to Monroe, August 19, 1818, in Jackson, *Correspondence*, II, 389–391.

61. Ibid., p. 389.

62. AJ to Thomas Cooper, August 24, 1818, Jackson Papers, LC; James, *Jackson*, p. 294.

63. Monroe to AJ, October 20, 1818, in Jackson, *Correspondence*, II, 398. See also Calhoun to Monroe, September 12, 1818, in *Calhoun Papers*, III, 121.

64. Calhoun to AJ, September 8, 1818, ibid., p. 393. This misunderstanding and deception produced a full-scale controversy during Jackson's first administration as President, when Calhoun's true position was revealed. Calhoun defended himself by publishing many letters that discussed both the authorization for the Florida seizure and Calhoun's recommendation to the President on the question of Jackson's censure. For the entire correspondence see the *United States Telegraph*, February 17, 21, 23, 26, 1831; Washington *Globe*, February 25, 1831; *Niles Weekly Register*, April 2, 1831. Portions of this correspondence can be found in Remini, ed., *The Age of Jackson* (New York, 1972), pp. 33–43. A good defense of Calhoun's position is Wiltse, *Calhoun*, pp. 155–163. Margaret Coit, *Calhoun*, pp. 122–127, is very balanced in her appraisal of Calhoun's mental state at the time.

65. AJ to Monroe, December 7, 1818; Monroe to AJ, December 21, 1818, in Jackson, *Correspondence*, II, 402–405.

66. Onís to Adams, July 8, 1818, in *ASPFA*, IV, 496–497; Adams, *Memoirs*, IV, 102–107.

67. Adams to Onís, July 23, 1818, in *ASPFA*, IV, 497–499. Adams's defense of Jackson was truly heroic. His most convincing statement was a letter of instruction to George W. Erving, minister to Spain, on November 28, 1818, which Erving was to communicate to the Spanish government and copies of which were distributed to the Washington press. Adams's biographer calls it the "greatest state paper" of Adams's "diplomatic career." Bemis, *Adams*, p. 326. In it Adams forcefully argued Spain's responsibility to police Florida or cede it to the United States; demonstrated British involvement in Florida affairs; defended the executions of Arbuthnot and Ambrister; and accompanied all this with massive documentation. For a full discussion of this state paper see Bemis, *Adams*, pp. 326–329.

68. Adams, *Memoirs*, IV, 239.

69. Ibid., p. 109; Ammon, *Monroe*, p. 430.

70. Robert Butler to AJ, December 15, 1818, in Jackson, *Correspondence*, II, 403; Poindexter to AJ, December 12, 1818, Jackson Papers, LC.

71. Eaton to AJ, December 14, 1818, in Jackson, *Correspondence*, II, 403.

72. Parton, *Jackson*, II, 533.

73. AJ to Donelson, January 31, 1819, in Jackson, *Correspondence*, II, 408.

74. Ibid.

75. Chase Mooney, *Crawford*, p. 180, thinks Cobb's actions were neither influenced nor determined by anyone but himself. This is an assumption on Mooney's part; he offers no evidence for his conclusion. He does admit that Cobb was Crawford's supporter. The report of the House Committee on Military Affairs is in *ASPMA*, I, 735, followed by a minority report by Richard M. Johnson, pp. 736–739.

76. *Annals of Congress*, 15th Congress, 2nd Session, pp. 631–655. Clay was surprisingly easy on the Monroe administration in this speech. Glyndon G. Van Deusen, *The Life of Henry Clay* (Boston, 1937), pp. 125–126.

77. AJ to Lewis, January 25, 30, 1819, Jackson-Lewis Papers, NYPL. Apparently Clay did get a roasting. "Your late speech on the Seminole war," he was told, "in which you condemn the conduct of Genl. Jackson is disapproved of by some—and some of your friends are apprehensive that you can lose friends as a consequence." James Morrison to Clay, February 17, 1819, in James F. Hopkins, *The Papers of Henry Clay* (Lexington, Kentucky, 1961), II, 671.

78. AJ to Lewis, January 25, 30, 1819, Jackson-Lewis Papers, NYPL.

79. Adams, *Memoirs*, IV, 232.

80. *Annals of Congress*, 15th Congress, 2nd Session, pp. 518–527, 655–703, 936–986.

81. Rufus King to Jeremiah Mason, February 7, 1819, quoted in Charles King, *Life of Rufus King* (New York, 1898), VI, 205; Ammon, *Monroe*, p. 431.

82. *Annals of Congress*, 15th Congress, 2nd Session, pp. 1136–1138; pp. 515–530, 583–1138 carries the full debate.

83. Adams, *Memoirs*, IV, 243.

84. Parton, *Jackson*, II, 557–558.

85. It is also possible that Jackson knew precisely what he was doing and was honoring Clinton because he was the leader of the anti-Crawford faction in New York.

86. Parton, *Jackson*, II, 565.

87. Ibid., p. 566.

88. Franklin (Tennessee) *Gazette*, July 17, 1818.

89. Parton, *Jackson*, II, 568.

90. *ASPMA*, I, 743. See also "Strictures on Mr. Lacock's Report on the Seminole War" and "Mr. Lacock's Reply to the Foregoing Strictures," *National*

Intelligencer, March 8, 20, 1819; reprinted in *Annals of Congress*, 15th Congress, 2nd Session, appendix, pp. 2350-2378.

91. There was considerable public excitement in London over the executions. See Richard Rush, *Memoranda of a Residence at the Court of London* (Philadelphia, 1845), p. 140; George Dangerfield, *The Awakening of American Nationalism* (New York, 1965), p. 63. For British reaction to the executions see Perkins, *Castlereagh and Adams*, pp. 289-294.

92. *Truth's Advocate and Monthly Anti-Jackson Expositor for 1828*, quoted in Parton, *Jackson*, II, 570.

CHAPTER 24

1. AJ to Clark, April 20, 1819, Jackson Papers, LC.

2. Clark to AJ, May 24, 1819; AJ to Clark, July 13, 1819; Clark to AJ, August 18, 1819; AJ to Clark, November 23, 1819, Jackson Papers, LC.

3. AJ to Gadsden, August 1, 1819, Jackson Papers, LC.

4. Parton, *Jackson*, II, 644. There are many stories in Parton's biography of Jackson in which Lewis is the obvious author. Parton is an excellent source, but much of what he researched in Nashville was filtered through Lewis.

5. In 1974 the Ladies Hermitage Association carried on an extensive restoration program of the Hermitage mansion. In exposing many interior parts of the house to reinforce the structure, it became obvious that the workmanship and skill of construction were extraordinarily high. The materials, especially the wood, were in excellent condition. The care and precision with which wooden sections had been joined was remarkable. The false front of the house is not obvious to the layman; it in no way detracts from the overall beauty and symmetry of the house.

6. The list of Jackson's wards is almost endless, and no careful count of them has ever been made. New names turn up with fresh examination. Additional names include Andrew, Campbell, Charles, and Hugh Hays, the children of Samuel Hays, for whom Jackson was legal guardian. See Settlement of Estate of Samuel Hays, Wills and Inventories, Davidson County Court of Pleas and Quarter Sessions Minutes. For the information on Jackson's wards I am indebted to Harriet C. Owsley.

7. Houston got into trouble because he frequently appeared in Washington dressed in loincloth and blanket. On one occasion he visited the secretary of war with a delegation of Indians and was tongue-lashed by Calhoun for daring to appear before the secretary "dressed as a savage." James, *The Raven*, p. 44.

8. Many of these reminiscences are preserved in the Jackson Papers, TSL.

9. Rachel to Ralph E. W. Earl, February 22, 1819, Jackson Papers, LC.

10. See Murray N. Rothbard, *The Panic of 1819* (New York, 1962). Jackson's view of banks was stated directly to Nicholas Biddle, president of the Second National Bank, many years later. "I do not dislike your bank any more than all banks," Jackson said. "But ever since I read the history of the South Sea Bubble I have been afraid of banks." Biddle Memorandum, no date, Biddle Papers, LC.

11. Cirilio de Morant to Francisco Caso y Luengo, June, 1818, Cuba, leg. 1877, AGI.

12. Ibid. See also Cirilio Lasasier to Caso y Luengo, June 26, 1818, and Luengo to Cienfuegos, July 10, 1818, Cuba, leg. 1877, AGI.

13. Calhoun to AJ, January 23, 1820, in Jackson, *Correspondence*, III, 12; Perkins, *Castlereagh and Adams*, p. 296.

14. Philip C. Brooks, *Diplomacy and the Borderlands* (New York, 1970), p. 100; Arthur P. Whitaker, *The United States and Latin America, 1800-1830* (Baltimore, 1941), pp. 43-44, 370-371.

15. Pizarro to Onís, August 30, 1818, Estado, leg. 5643, AHN. See also Onís to José de Cienfuegos, August 31, 1818, Cuba, leg. 1898, AGI, and Perkins, *Castlereagh and Adams,* p. 294.

16. This translation appears in Bemis, *Adams,* pp. 318–319, from a letter of Onís to Pizarro, July 18, 1818.

17. Ibid. Jackson's incursion "did have an electric effect on the negotiations," Charles C. Griffin, *The United States and the Disruption of the Spanish Empire* (New York, 1968), p. 176.

18. Bemis, *Adams,* pp. 318–319.

19. Brooks, *Diplomacy and the Borderlands,* pp. 100, 142.

20. Griffin, *Disruption of the Spanish Empire,* p. 169.

21. Dangerfield, *Era of Good Feelings,* p. 146.

22. Ibid.; Brooks, *Diplomacy and the Borderlands,* p. 137.

23. Bemis, *Adams,* p. 321; Adams, *Memoirs,* IV, 110.

24. Bemis, *Adams,* p. 322.

25. Adams to Onís, October 31, 1818, in *ASPFA,* IV, 530–531.

26. Yrujo to Onís, October 10, 1818, Estado, leg. 5643, AHN.

27. Brooks, *Diplomacy and the Borderlands,* pp. 157–158.

28. AJ to Monroe, June 20, 1820, Monroe Papers, NYPL.

29. Adams, *Memoirs,* IV, 239.

30. Ammon, *Monroe,* p. 438.

31. AJ to Monroe, November 16, 1819, Monroe Papers, NYPL.

32. Calhoun to AJ, December 10, 1819, in "Correspondence of John C. Calhoun," American Historical Association, *Annual Report* (1899), II, 165.

33. Ammon, *Monroe,* p. 444.

34. See especially AJ to Monroe, June 20, 1820, Monroe Papers, NYPL.

35. AJ to Monroe, December 10, 1819; AJ to Calhoun, January 10, 1820, in Jackson, *Correspondence,* II, 446; III, 2.

36. Dangerfield, *Awakening of American Nationalism,* p. 70.

37. *National Intelligencer,* April 7, 1821.

38. Adams, *Memoirs,* IV, 274.

39. *The National Register,* quoted in Brooks, *Diplomacy and the Borderlands,* p. 171.

40. Jackson also kept insisting that he could have taken Canada too. Under his leadership "we would not have met disaster, disgrace and defeat." AJ to Calhoun, January 4, 1821, Jackson Papers, LC. The quotation is taken out of context but the sentiment was genuinely his.

41. Adams, *Memoirs,* IV, 238.

42. Ibid., p. 239.

43. AJ to Francies P. Blair, October 24, 1844, in Jackson, *Correspondence,* VI, 326. In 1836 Jackson was told that Adams's diary contradicted his claim about the Texas boundary. "His Diary!" Jackson retorted, "don't tell me any thing more about his diary. Sir, that diary comes up on all occasions—one would think that its pages were as immutable as the laws of the Medes and Persians! Sir, that diary will be the death of me. I wonder if James Monroe kept a *diary!* If he did, it is to be hoped that it will be looked to, to see if it contains any thing about this Adams and De Onis treaty. Sir, I did not see it; I was *not* consulted about it." Parton, *Jackson,* II, 587. AJ to Monroe, June 20, 1820, Monroe Papers, NYPL.

44. AJ to Overton, June 8, 1829, Dickinson Papers, THS.

45. Eaton to AJ, March 11, 1820, Jackson Papers, LC.

46. AJ to Donelson, no date, Jackson Papers, LC. See also Calhoun to AJ, May 24, 1820, and AJ to Calhoun, June 19, 1820, Jackson Papers, LC.

47. Adams, *Memoirs,* IV, 238. Jackson had been reluctant to undertake the

assignment but felt he owed it to the people of Mississippi for their support in the War of 1812 as well as to Monroe. AJ to Calhoun, June 19, 1820, in *Calhoun Papers*, V, 196.

48. Parton, *Jackson*, II, 578. Details of this convention can be found in DeRosier, *Removal of the Choctaw Indians*, pp. 53–69.

49. Parton, *Jackson*, II, 578.

50. Ibid., p. 581.

51. Journal of the Convention, 1820, Jackson Papers, LC.

52. Ibid.

53. Ibid.; DeRosier, *Removal*, p. 64; *ASPIA*, II, 236–237. Jackson actually gave the Indians three "talks": the first on October 9; the second after sending out runners to round up friendly Choctaws; and the third on October 17. His intentions in dealing with the Indians are outlined in his letter to Calhoun, June 19, 1820, in *Calhoun Papers*, V, 196.

54. Gideon Lincecum, "Life of Apushimataha," *Publications of the Mississippi Historical Society* (1906), IX, 466–467; *ASPIA*, II, 239.

55. Lincecum, "Life of Apushimataha," pp. 469–470.

56. Ibid., pp. 471–472; *ASPIA*, II, 236. Jackson was mistaken about the presence of white men on the land offered by the United States.

57. DeRosier, *Removal*, p. 67. Choctaw opposition to the treaty seems to have been led by Chief Puckshenubbee (who received a $500 gift in the treaty) although there is some evidence that only the whites and half-breeds living with the Nation objected to the exchange of land. Silas McBee to AJ, May 1, 1820, in *Calhoun Papers*, V, 87–88, and AJ to Calhoun, August 10, 1820, Jackson Papers, LC.

58. Quoted in DeRosier, *Removal*, p. 67.

59. Doak's Stand Treaty, in *ASPIA*, II, 225; see also Kappler, *Indian Affairs*, II, 191–195, and Royce, *Land Cessions*, pp. 700–701, plate 36; Calhoun to AJ and Hinds, July 12, 1820, Jackson Papers, LC; AJ and Hinds to Calhoun, October 19, 21, 1820, in *ASPIA*, II, 241–244; Angie Debo, *The Rise and Fall of the Choctaw Republic* (Norman, 1961), p. 49.

60. Some of the problems created by this provision are narrated in Cyrus Kingsbury to Calhoun, January 5, 1821, in *Calhoun Papers*, V, 532. Kingsbury suggested that one large and five small schools be built each year until the total number was reached. He also suggested building three large and twenty-four small schools on the east side of the Mississippi and one large and eight small schools on the west side. See Kingsbury to AJ and Hinds, October 18, 1820, in *ASPIA*, II, 232.

61. Journal of the Convention, 1820, Jackson Papers, LC.

62. Calhoun to AJ, May 24, July 20, 1820, and Calhoun to Hinds and AJ, July 12, 1820, Jackson Papers, LC. See also the protest of James W. Bates to Calhoun, November 28, 1820, in *Calhoun Papers*, V, 456.

63. *ASPIA*, II, 225; Francis P. Prucha, *American Indian Policy in the Formative Years* (Lincoln, 1970), pp. 171–173, 224.

64. DeRosier, *Removal*, p. 68.

65. In the fall of 1819, Colonel Sam Houston, adjutant general of the state of Tennessee and formerly of the Thirty-ninth Infantry Regiment, was recommended by Jackson for appointment as Indian agent. "I know," Jackson said in his recommendation, "that in the capacity of Agent, he can draw to the Arkansas in a few years the whole strength of the Cherokee Nation, now on the East of the Mississippi River. This, as I conceive, would be greatly to the interests of the States of Georgia, and Tennessee, as well as a great saving to the U States. I have no hesitation in saying that Col. Sam Houston is better qualified for this station than any man of his age I am acquainted with; he is honourable, honest and brave.

. . . I well know Col. Houston both as a Soldier and a Citizen, and can vouch for him as an honourable man, and a brave Soldier and well calculated to wield the Indians beneficially for their own happiness, and the interests of the U States, and as such I recommend him to you for the Agency of the Cherokees on the Arkansas." AJ to Calhoun, September 30, 1819, in *Calhoun Papers*, IV, 354–355. Houston, however, declined the post. AJ to Calhoun, January 17, 1819, ibid., p. 581.

CHAPTER 25

1. Monroe to AJ, January 24, 1821, Jackson Papers, LC.
2. Benjamin F. Butler to Harriet Butler, May 7, 1823, Butler Papers, NYSL.
3. Parton, *Jackson*, II, 589.
4. Eaton to AJ, March 9, 1821, Jackson Papers, LC.
5. Monroe's biographer suggests that the appointment reflected Monroe's gratitude for Jackson's resignation and Jackson's "past services." Ammon, *Monroe*, p. 502.
6. Adams, *Memoirs*, V, 322.
7. AJ to John Coffee, March 1, 1821, Coffee Papers, THS.
8. AJ to Bronaugh, February 11, 1821, Jackson Papers, LC.
9. Ibid.
10. AJ to Coffee, March 1, 1821, Coffee Papers, THS.
11. AJ to Monroe, February 11, 1821, Monroe Papers, NYPL.
12. Ibid.
13. Adams to AJ, March 12, April 24, 1821, in *ASPFA*, IV, 750–751, 756.
14. Jackson's Address to his Army on Giving Up Command, May 31, 1821, in Jackson, *Correspondence*, III, 62–63.
15. Ibid., p. 65. The Address, and particularly the "P.S.," underwent considerable revision before it was published.
16. Adams, *Memoirs*, V, 366.
17. Ibid., p. 367.
18. Ibid.
19. Rachel to Mrs. Eliza Kingsley, April 27, 1821, in Parton, *Jackson*, II, 595–596.
20. Ibid.
21. AJ to Adams, April 24, 1821, in *ASPFA*, IV, 756.
22. Ibid.
23. AJ to Colonel James Gadsden, May 21, 1821, Jackson Papers, LC.
24. AJ to Callava, April 30, May 11, June 12, 17, 20, 23, 1821; Callava to AJ, June 10, 19, 22, 25, 1821, in Jackson, *Correspondence*, III, 50–81.
25. See particularly the exchanges in June 1821, ibid., pp. 66–81. Jackson narrates his problems at length in AJ to Adams, July 30, 1821, in Carter, *Territorial Papers*, XXII, 139–142.
26. AJ to Coffee, May 11, 1821, Coffee Papers, THS.
27. Forbes to AJ, May 7, 1821, in *ASPFA*, IV, 744. Sidney W. Martin, *Florida During the Territorial Days* (Athens, 1944), p. 19.
28. Jackson's Fourth Annual Message to Congress, in Richardson, *Messages and Papers of the Presidents*, II, 1156.
29. Jackson probably delayed because of the presidential order not to introduce troops into the city until the Spanish had evacuated theirs. Adams cautioned him to avoid friction. Adams to AJ, May 21, 1821, Jackson Papers, LC.
30. On the Jackson-Callava standoff see AJ to Adams, July 30, 1821, in Carter, *Territorial Papers*, XXII, 143–144.
31. Rachel to Mrs. Eliza Kingsley, July 23, 1821, in Parton, *Jackson*, II, 605.
32. Callava to AJ, July 10, 11, 13, 16, 1821; AJ to Callava, July 12, 13, 15,

16, 1821, in *ASPFA*, IV, 759–761; Martin, *Florida During Territorial Days*, p. 22.

33. Herbert J. Doherty, Jr., "The Governorship of Andrew Jackson," *Florida Historical Quarterly* (July 1954), XXXIII, 8.

34. Rachel to Mrs. Eliza Kingsley, July 23, 1821, in Parton, *Jackson*, II, 605.

35. AJ to Adams, July 18, 1821, in *ASPFA*, IV, 764–765. Jackson and Richard K. Call acted for the United States and Callava and José Cruzat for Spain in signing the transfer agreement.

36. AJ to W. G. D. Worthington, July 26, 1821, Jackson Papers, LC.

37. Rachel to Mrs. Eliza Kingsley, July 23, 1821, in Parton, *Jackson*, II, 604. On June 6, a similar ceremony at St. Augustine transferred East Florida to the United States. Colonel Robert Butler, adjutant general for the southern district, acted for Jackson in the transfer. He received East Florida from Don José Coppinger.

38. Rachel to Eliza Kingsley, July 23, 1821, in Parton, *Jackson*, II, 604.

39. AJ to Bronaugh, June 9, 1821, in Jackson, *Correspondence*, III, 65. For a full list of Monroe's appointees see Adams to AJ, May 22, 1821, in Carter, *Territorial Papers*, XXII, 51.

40. *National Intelligencer*, September 23, 1828.

41. According to the Spanish scheme of municipal administration, Jackson said, there should be an Alcalde (mayor), a Judge de Partido, a Fiscal, a Cabillo or Corporation, and Alguazils or sheriffs and constables. AJ to Adams, July 30, 1821, in Carter, *Territorial Papers*, XXII, 150.

42. The Proclamations of various dates are in the Jackson Papers, LC.

43. AJ to Calhoun, July 29, 1821, in *Calhoun Papers*, VI, 291.

44. Ordinance on County Courts, July 26, 1821, in *ASPM*, II, 900, 907; Herbert J. Doherty, Jr., "The Governorship of Andrew Jackson," p. 12.

45. The most recent historian to study Jackson's tenure as governor concluded that his reform of the existing government was "much to its betterment." Ibid., p. 25.

46. The Ordinances issued by Jackson include:
Ordinance for Preservation of Good Order and Health at Pensacola, July 18, 1821
Ordinance for Preservation of Health in Pensacola, July 19, 1821
Ordinance for Prescribing Mode of Carrying 6th Article of Treaty into Effect, July 21, 1821
Ordinance for Dividing Florida into Counties and Establishing Courts, July 21, 1821
Ordinance for Explaining Mode of Proceedings in Courts, July 26, 1821
Ordinance for Regulating Fees for Justice of the Peace, August 21, 1821
Ordinance for Explaining Ordinance for the Preservation of Health, September 6, 1821 Carter, *Territorial Papers*, XXII, 156–157, ft. 4.

47. *ASPM*, II, 905–907; Doherty, "Governorship of Andrew Jackson," p. 12.

48. Rachel to Mrs. Eliza Kingsley, July 23, 1821, in Parton, *Jackson*, II, 604. It is interesting that Rachel seemed more concerned about sabbath-breaking than gambling, immorality, or criminal violence. She was forever muttering words like "Jerusalem" and "Babylon." Doherty, *Richard Keith Call*, p. 19.

49. Proclamation, July 17, 1821, Jackson Papers, LC.

50. Rachel to Eliza Kingsley, July 23, 1821, in Parton, *Jackson*, II, 604.

51. Even as friendly and recent a biographer as Harry Ammon admits the appointments were weak. Ammon, *Monroe*, p. 502.

52. Ibid.

53. Jackson described his career in most unfriendly terms. AJ to Calhoun, July 29, 1821, in *Calhoun Papers*, VI, 293.

54. Doherty, "Governorship of Andrew Jackson," p. 15; Isaac J. Cox, *The West Florida Controversy*, p. 180.

55. AJ to Calhoun, July 29, 1821, Jackson Papers, LC.

56. *ASPM*, II, 849–875.

57. Brackenridge to AJ, August 24, 1821, in *ASPM*, II, 811–812. Call later criticized Brackenridge for not seizing the papers when he had a chance. Because of Brackenridge's weakness, Call contended, Jackson was dragged into the Vidal affair. Doherty, *Richard Keith Call,* p. 21.

58. Callava's Protest, October 3, 1821, in *ASPFA*, IV, 769.

59. Bronaugh to AJ, August 23, 1821, in Jackson, *Correspondence*, III, 112.

60. AJ to Adams, August 26, 1821, in *ASPM*, II, 801.

61. Affidavit of H. M. Brackenridge, in *ASPM*, II, 829.

62. Ibid.

63. Minutes of the examination of Callava, August 22, 1821, in *ASPFA*, IV, 783.

64. Affidavit of Brackenridge, in *ASPM*, II, 830–831.

65. Interrogation of Fullarat, in *ASPFA*, IV, 784.

66. AJ to Adams, August 26, 1821, in *ASPM*, II, 801.

67. Affidavit of Brackenridge, in *ASPM*, II, 830–831.

68. Ibid.

69. Ibid.

70. *ASPFA*, IV, 770; Parton, *Jackson*, II, 631.

71. *ASPM*, II, 809.

72. Ibid., p. 822.

73. AJ to Call, November 15, 1821, Jackson Papers, LC.

74. Parton, *Jackson*, II, 634.

75. AJ to Adams, August 26, 1821, in *ASPM*, II, 801.

76. Ibid.

77. Members of the Pensacola Bar sent President Monroe a memorial protesting the appointment of Fromentin as unworthy. Carter, *Territorial Papers*, XXII, 183.

78. Fromentin to AJ, September 3, 1821, in *ASPM*, II, 821.

79. Adams to Fromentin, October 26, 1821, in *ASPM*, II, 848; see also Fromentin to Adams, August 26, September 6, 1821, in *ASPM*, II, 834–836, 838–841.

80. Adams, *Memoirs*, V, 359. See also Adams to AJ, October 26, 1821, in *ASPM*, II, 818. Wirt wrote: "I am myself perfectly persuaded that Governor Jackson's intentions have been correct throughout the whole of the affair. His judgment too has been essentially right; for both Callava and Fromentin had done wrong; and the Governor's error, I think, consists of his having taken their punishment into his own hands." Wirt to Monroe, October 11, 1821, in Carter, *Territorial Papers*, XXII, 257.

81. Bronaugh to AJ, February 8, 16, 23, 1822, in Jackson, *Correspondence*, III, 145–148, 151–153.

82. Callava's Protest, October 3, 1821, in *ASPFA*, IV, 768–771; see also appendix to the Protest, ibid., p. 7719.

83. Jackson and Adams engaged in a long and important correspondence during this period. Adams understood Jackson and what he was trying to do, and Jackson never had a better advocate or defender than Adams. Adams's letter to Erving over the seizure of Florida and his defense of Jackson's treatment of Callava to the Spanish minister were masterful; see especially *ASPFA*, IV, 802–807.

84. Adams to deAnduaga, April 15, 1822, in *ASPFA*, IV, 802–807; Bassett, *Jackson*, p. 314.

85. Monroe to Wirt, October 7, 1821, in Carter, *Territorial Papers*, XXII, 242.

86. Callava had refused to show Jackson his credentials as commissioner of transfer and insisted he would surrender the province as governor and not by special authority. Thus Jackson argued—probably correctly—that Callava by his own act was debarred from immunity and became a private citizen once the transfer was finalized. Jackson in several letters contended that Callava had no diplomatic powers at all from the Spanish government. AJ to Adams, November 22, 1821, in Jackson, *Correspondence,* III, 134, 137. Monroe said Callava was entitled to rights as a commissioner. Adams to AJ, October 26, 1821, in Carter, *Territorial Papers,* XXII, 261.

87. Jackson simply regarded Callava as a military agent of Spain appointed by the captain general of Cuba to deliver the province. Once that task was completed he had no diplomatic status.

88. Jackson gives a full account of his controversy with Callava in AJ to Adams, November 22, 1821, in Jackson, *Correspondence,* III, 133–139.

89. Jackson believed Fromentin incited them. See AJ to Adams, September 30, 1821, in *ASPM,* II, 814.

90. Ibid., p. 813.

91. Ibid.; Parton, *Jackson,* II, 638. The Proclamation, dated September 29, 1821, can be found in *ASPM,* II, 813–814.

92. It was not altogether a fear of Jackson that stilled their pens. Some thought the controversy too silly for notice. The final statement of the Spanish officers is carried in *Niles Weekly Register,* November 10, 1821.

93. *National Intelligencer,* June 21, 26, 28, July 3, 17, August 2, 7, September 4, 23, 1828.

94. Martin, *Florida During the Territorial Days,* p. 31.

95. "I will be with you in all the month of October next," Jackson wrote John Coffee, "if health and life permits." AJ to Coffee, August 26, 1821, Coffee Papers, THS.

96. Quoted in Doherty, "Governorship of Andrew Jackson," p. 9.

97. AJ to Adams, September 30, 1821, in *ASPM,* II, 813.

98. AJ to Monroe, March 19, 1822, Jackson Papers, LC. On the Fromentin affair Monroe was not sympathetic to Jackson. Adams, *Memoirs,* V, 373.

99. In Monroe's defense it should be remembered that Jackson's loyalty was accompanied by much embarrassment to the administration whenever the Spanish were involved. Monroe tried to avoid a public quarrel with Jackson, but his patience was stretched at times to the breaking point.

100. AJ to Gadsden, May 2, 1822, Jackson Papers, LC.

101. AJ to Gadsden, December 6, 1821, Jackson Papers, LC.

102. Doherty, *Richard Keith Call,* p. 20; AJ to Monroe, October 5, 1821 in Jackson, *Correspondence,* III, 123.

103. Charlton W. Tebeau, *A History of Florida* (Coral Gables, 1971), p. 121; Arthur W. Thompson, *Jacksonian Democracy on the Florida Frontier* (Gainesville, 1961), p. 2.

104. For Jackson's appointments see Carter, *Territorial Papers,* XXII, *passim.*

105. Doherty, "Governorship of Andrew Jackson," pp. 13–14.

106. Ibid., p. 14.

107. AJ to Adams, November 22, 1821, in Jackson, *Correspondence,* III, 139.

108. AJ to Bronaugh, August 27, 1822, quoted in Herbert J. Doherty, Jr., "Andrew Jackson's Cronies in Florida Territorial Politics," *Florida Historical Quarterly* (July 1955), XXXIV, 23.

109. See, for example, AJ to Adams, August 26, 1821, in *ASPM,* II, 801.

110. Doherty, "Governorship of Andrew Jackson," p. 19.

111. AJ to Adams, April 24, 1821, in *ASPFA,* IV, 755.

112. AJ to Calhoun, September 17, 1821, Jackson Papers, LC. More general

justice can be done the Indians, Jackson said, by the legislative provisions of Congress than by treaties. AJ to Adams, October 6, 1821, in Carter, *Territorial Papers*, XXII, 233.

113. Jackson's Talk with Indian Chieftains, September 20, 1821, in Jackson, *Correspondence*, III, 118, 120.

114. Martin, *Florida During the Territorial Days*, p. 66; AJ to Calhoun, September 2, 1821, in *Calhoun Papers*, VI, 363.

115. AJ to Calhoun, September 20, 1821, Jackson Papers, LC.

116. Calhoun to AJ, November 16, 1821, Jackson Papers, LC.

117. Jackson's Talk, in Jackson, *Correspondence*, III, 120.

118. AJ to Calhoun, September 17, 1821, in *ASPM*, II, 911–912; John K. Mahon, *History of the Second Seminole War* (Gainesville, 1967), p. 34.

119. AJ to Monroe, November 13, 1821, in Carter, *Territorial Papers*, XXII, 275.

120. AJ to Monroe, October 5, 1821, in Jackson, *Correspondence*, III, 122–124.

121. AJ to Monroe, November 14, 1821, ibid., p. 129.

122. See U.S. Statutes, 17th Congress, 1st Session, p. 65, and House Report, No. 450, 27th Congress, 2nd Session.

123. AJ to Adams, October 6, 1821, in *ASPM*, II, 909–910.

124. AJ to Monroe, October 5, 1821, in Jackson, *Correspondence*, III, 123.

125. (Pensacola) *Floridian*, October 8, 1821; reprinted in *Niles Weekly Register*, November 10, 1821.

126. George Walton to AJ, December 17, 1821, in Carter, *Territorial Papers*, XXII, 298.

127. Monroe to AJ, December 31, 1821, ibid., p. 316. The letter is brief and not overly complimentary.

128. George Walton, acting governor of West Florida, told Jackson: "Let it be Known that you are a Candidate for the Presidency of the United States, and the descendents of those men, who, by their acts, emancipated us from the yoke of George Third, will rally around you." Walton to AJ, December 10, 1821, ibid., p. 298. See also Samuel R. Overton to AJ, August 1, 1821, Jackson Papers, LC.

Index